To the Patrons of the Library
with my best wishes,
Ramm Dugg

Dallas
Aug. 20, 1984

On Reagan

Other books by Ronnie Dugger:

The Politician: The Life and Times of Lyndon Johnson, From the Frontier to Master of the Senate. New York: W. W. Norton, 1982.

Our Invaded Universities: Form, Reform, and New Starts. New York: W. W. Norton, 1974.

Dark Star: Hiroshima Reconsidered in the Life of Claude Eatherly. New York: World, 1967. London: Gollancz, 1967.

Three Men in Texas, Bedichek, Webb, and Dobie. Essays by Their Friends in the Texas Observer (ed.). Austin: University of Texas Press, 1967.

ON REAGAN

The Man & His Presidency

Ronnie Dugger

McGraw-Hill Book Company

New York   St. Louis   Toronto   Mexico   Hamburg
San Francisco   London   Sydney

1 2 3 4 5 6 7 8 9 DOCDOC 8 7 6 5 4 3

ISBN 0-07-017974-3

LIBRARY OF CONGRESS CATALOGING IN PUBLICATION DATA

Dugger, Ronnie.
On Reagan: the man and his presidency.
1. Reagan, Ronald.   2. United States—Politics and government—1981-   .   3. Presidents—United States—
Biography.   I. Title.
E877.D83 1983   973.927'092'4   83-9833
ISBN 0-07-017974-3

Book design by Elisabeth Brandfass

For Patricia

As Socrates said many years ago
Socrates all of us to live, thoughout.
function of whom? C.P.B 1/14/ 1974

Contents

Introduction

This book is an attempt to understand Ronald Reagan and his administration.

I am concerned here not with Reagan's personality, but with his policies. This is not a personal biography, but a policy biography, an analysis and discussion of what Reagan is doing as President against the background of his career and his ideas.

In 1980 the Reagan campaign staff deliberately and successfully withheld from the national press the complete sets of the transcripts of his revelatory radio broadcasts between 1975 and 1979. He was presenting himself to the country as a moderate, but these transcripts showed beyond a doubt that deep down he was a hard-line right-wing ideologue with fully formed and recently expressed prejudices on all of the outstanding issues of the times.

Not long before the campaign ended I obtained sets of the 1978 and 1979 transcripts from Reagan's political action committee in California; later I obtained some of the 1975 broadcasts from the Democratic National Committee. I have made full use of these transcripts, which apparently no other journalist has obtained. On every major issue one's understanding of Reaganism is deepened by what Reagan said on the radio.

Despite the extremism of many of Reagan's views, there is some wisdom in them. His Great Reaction against the New Deal could not have triumphed on the strength of selfishness and negativism alone, although that was part of it. His ascent to the White House in 1981 also expressed justified grievances, valid criticisms, and second and third thoughts.

It is true, for example, that welfare can create cycles of dependency and reduced self-regard. It is true there are welfare cheaters. There has been unconscionable fraud in some government programs. The bureaucracy is top-heavy and rule-entangled, there is too much paperwork and gobbledygook, and regulations that were intended to advance the public interest can unfairly handicap small business. Some bureaucrats are petty tyrants. Local self-government is important. The rights of victims should have standing in the same theater of values as the rights of the accused. And however much the pacific sides of our natures may dislike the fact, without an adequate police force crime or anarchy would reign in society and without an adequate military defense system the United States might well be attacked.

One morning in San Antonio a few days after Reagan had been elected, I joined a group in a Mexican restaurant to have breakfast with Senator Howard Metzenbaum, the liberal Democrat from Ohio who has been fighting the special interests for many years. "There *is* too much government," he said to us suddenly. "The bureaucracy is a problem. Heads of agencies can't control the people under them."

The director of the city's Community Services Organization, Juan Patlan, who was sitting across from the senator, agreed with him. Patlan's group had been offered an additional federal grant, but on the condition that he would not appeal any of the decisions of the granting agency. "I called up," Patlan said, "and I asked them, 'What country is this? What country am I living in?' . . . Congress passes a law in response to local conditions. Then the bureaucrats, who don't know anything about local conditions, try to enforce it uniformly. It doesn't work."

So Reagan's reaction is having its full sway, and we have a right to expect whatever benefits it will bring us, less waste of the taxpayers' money, fewer haughty bureaucrats, a more efficient provision of government services, and especially the reconsideration of everything that has been more or less taken for granted since the New Deal.

But what else is the reaction bringing? What explains this war on Social Security? On the environment? Why are the rich suddenly paying much lower taxes—what is Reagan up to on the income tax? What about minorities and women? Civil liberties? Have government programs that help the middle classes and the poor been badly damaged? Has Reagan unleashed a new Mc-Carthyism? Why are we finding ourselves back in bed with right-wing dictators? Have the poor been cut to the quick to help the government buy more nuclear bombs, planes, and ships? Is a nuclear war coming?

We are awash these days in so much information that sorting out the salient facts and connecting them into patterns which mean something is one kind of heavy work for which few people have the time and fewer the inclination. In composing the story of the Reagan administration's actual deeds in consistent service to its leader's ideology, I have drawn on many thousands of articles in newspapers and periodicals and on the various other books about Reagan. I want to emphasize particularly my debt to three of the great national dailies, the *New York Times*, the *Washington Post*, and the *Wall Street Journal*. In the notes I specify and thereby acknowledge my sources, and while I could not reasonably name all the reporters whose bylines appeared on stories that contributed to my knowledge, I have named the writers of stories that seemed to reflect unusual professional initiative.

As I close this book in the summer of 1983, the economy has turned upward and most of the signs in Reagan's and his men's political conduct seem to mean that he will seek re-election. On the other hand, he could use an improving economy as an excuse to go home to California on the ground that he had accomplished his mission. In any event the issue in 1984 will be Reaganism and responsibility for it. If a senator declares to us that we should make Ronald Reagan our President, and if we then do that, the senator is answerable to us for how President

Reagan turns out: the credit for the good, the blame for the bad. The Republicans and many Democrats have heavy moral responsibility for what has happened and for what is to come.

George Bush, when he was running against Reagan, not only called his foe's nostrums "voodoo economics," he declared: "It is impossible for Governor Reagan to balance the budget . . . if he is to reduce taxes by more than $220 billion over the next three years." Yet as Reagan's vice president, Bush has passionately defended Reaganomics. "I believe strongly in the Reagan economic program," he said in February 1982.

In 1976 Gerald Ford, defending his own presidency against Reagan's drive to seize the GOP nomination from him, charged that the Californian had "favorably called attention to a voluntary plan that would ruin" Social Security. Did Ford repeat that warning in 1980 as he campaigned hard for Reagan's election? He did not.

What are the responsibilities of the congressional Democrats who defected in large numbers in 1981 to support Reagan's fiscally irrational budget and tax cuts? What is the self-designated burden of Republican Representative Marc Lincoln Marks of Pennsylvania, who fervently backed Reagan's programs all the way until suddenly he resigned with a shamed admission that he had acted out of political cowardice, fearing to breast the tide? Reagan's new general chairman of the Republican Party, Senator Paul Laxalt of Nevada, reportedly said without contradiction during a large White House meeting which Reagan also attended that "if there had been a secret ballot in the Senate (in 1981), there wouldn't have been more than twelve votes for the (Reagan) tax cut." Yet it had passed, and overwhelmingly. Vice presidents and ex-presidents, senators and congressmen, the politicians seem to practice public virtue after their fashion, as if the citizens should always amiably forgive them for doing mainly what will advance their own careers.

Senator Howard Baker, the Republican majority leader, a loyal Reagan team player until things went badly awry and still "carrying his flag" in 1983; Senator Bob Dole, the Republicans' Senate Finance Committee chairman, boldly leading the 1982 revolt against Reagan on taxes and calling a halt to his slashes in food stamps and aid to dependent children; Representative Jack Kemp, another presidential aspirant, pressuring Reagan to defy Dole on taxes and even to return to the gold standard—all these actors will be judged, will stand or fall in 1984, as Reagan himself will if he is running again, on the sums and the substances of Reaganism.

No ordinary person could have achieved what Reagan has. When it counted he was underestimated by his natural adversaries the liberals, initially in California during his first run for the governorship, then in 1980 throughout the country. They thought he was just an actor, and not too bright. In fact he is a serious right-wing ideologue, he is a mesmerizing speaker, he is tactically resilient and opportunistic, and he is smart. Fun-loving and friendly, "a quick study" and often wrong on the facts, he is nevertheless a serious man.

His style is free of self-doubt; his substance, considered across the last two decades, is militaristic and anti-Communist abroad and at home antigovernment and probusiness. When he can't win he bides his time and perseveres, accepting less than he wants if less is all he can get. From time to time, when it is expedient, he projects an image of moderation. He is always willing to subscribe to the liberal verities, the general ideals, values, and purposes (treating everyone equally, the rights of the accused, helping the poor, the separation of church and state, protecting the environment, reducing nuclear arms), but he enters into battle against almost every practical attempt to make them real, plucking from his quiver whichever of his ample supply of conservative principles comes to hand and dispatching it on a high arc into the heart of the liberal enemy. Most remarkably, across the years he is a dogged right-wing ideologue at the same time that he is a compromiser and a politician with many faces. He acquired his facility in donning disguises for the engagement of the day as he acted for first one, then another, then another, and yet another tribe in the political forest, the pro-Soviet left, the liberals, the conservatives, the fundamentalist right. He knows what is what because he has been there.

The best advice for evaluating national administrations since Vietnam and Watergate was given by President Nixon's attorney general, John Mitchell, when he said that we should watch what they do and not what they say. It is my thesis here that Reagan and his administration, in what they are actually doing, offend and violate what Archibald Cox has called "the basic idealism of the American people." During the late 1950s and the 1960s, in the course of becoming the foremost leader of the nation's most successful right-wing movement of the modern era, Reagan adapted his hostility toward home-bred Communists into an all-out assault on most of the activities of the government of the United States. Now he is using his presidency in an attempt to convert the public's opposition to Communist systems into hostility against their own government. In this undertaking, which characterizes his career more than anything else, he has caused a critical confusion. Even if we must shake our heads in wonder at having to reaffirm something so obvious, the United States is not a dictatorship, the United States is a democracy. If, like Reagan, one sees government as inherently oppressive and evil while private autonomy (especially whatever corporations want to do) is always best, then the idea of public service and the government as the instrument of democracy is lost.

After a biographical sketch and a discussion of Reagan's people in Washington, each chapter in this book is given over to one issue or a group of related controversies, with a closing chapter of commentaries and an appendix drawn from Reagan's radio broadcasts. However, the subject of the penultimate chapter, Reagan's fateful acceleration of the nuclear arms race, is immeasurably more important than all the other issues combined.

During his first two and a half years President Reagan has brought the world significantly closer to a nuclear war. He has long been allied with the most bellicose elements in the American military establishment; now he is using the power and glory the White House gives him to bring about a little-understood but mortally dangerous shift in U.S. nuclear strategy. He is insisting that the United States deploy accurate Pershing 2 nuclear missiles five minutes from Soviet borders and build two accurate new nuclear weapons systems, the MX missile and the Trident 2 submarine with the D-5 missile. Although the administration denies it, these weapons, when they are considered in relationship to other new weapons systems, would give the United States what nuclear strategists call a first-strike capability, which they define as the ability to destroy the Soviet Union without receiving "unacceptable damage" in retaliation. Reagan says that all this apocalyptic new firepower will convince the Soviets to negotiate seriously concerning the deep arms reductions that he desires. On the basis of the U.S.–Soviet nuclear arms race since Hiroshima, it is far likelier to cause them to seek a first-strike capability of their own; they may already be doing so. We stand on the threshold of a first-strike world in which either one of the superpowers may decide to launch its missiles against the other at the first warning of an attack or to strike first from fear of being struck first itself. Rather than increasing our national security, Reagan's reckless first-strike buildup jeopardizes the survival of the United States and human civilization.

Responding to the Reagan presidency, the Democrats were at first so demoralized and supine and then so confused amidst the welterings of their would-be leaders, they may not be able to offer the country a credible or persuasive alternative. Nothing matters more, then, than that the people understand what is happening while it is happening; to control the American present they must first understand Reagan himself, his ideas, and what he is actually doing and then hold strictly accountable all the congressmen, governors, mayors, Republicans, Democrats, editors, columnists, intellectuals, and business tycoons who accepted his leadership and told us all to stay his course.

Committing this book to the publisher as the events of Reagan's first term continue to rush past—and before the crisis breaks over the installation of U.S. missiles in Europe in December—I believe that in addition to Reagan's decision about 1984, there are two principal uncertainties, the economy and the arms race. The likelihood, as it appears to me now, is that the economy will continue to recover unless interest rates rise sharply again or the debtor nations default, but that the nuclear arms race, while appearing to lessen, will enter a destabilized and very possibly terminal stage. We are all now trapped in a general human emergency that may well end in a nuclear holocaust. Each of us carries on in the midst of this emergency as if we still assume, as we used to, that there will be a human future, but if there ever was a time for active civic virtue, if there ever was a place for active civic labor, it is here and now that every American must be a citizen above all. To neglect our country now is to neglect, for all time, our kind.

R. D.

Washington Square North, New York City
July 1, 1983

A Note to the Reader

Readers wanting more information on a point other than the sources can avoid wasting time by turning to a reference note only if its number in the text is printed in italic (for example: [3]). Numbers set in roman type designate notes that contain only sources (for example: [3]).

1

Swerving from Left to Right

There is a mystery about Ronald Reagan's life. How and why did he change from what he was, a shining liberal who memorized parts of Roosevelt's inaugural address and campaigned for Truman and Humphrey in 1948, into the nation's most right-wing President since McKinley? To the extent we can understand why he undertook his resolute crusade against what had been his own ardent convictions, we will penetrate not only the personal but also the historical mystery of his career and his presidency.

Delving into Reagan's origins, British genealogists ascertained that his family line probably runs back to a nephew of an Irish national hero, Brian Boru, who was the high king of Ireland from 1002 to 1014. Reagan's Catholic great-grandfather, Michael O'Regan, left his poor, landless life in County Tipperary during the potato famine of the 1840s. Michael Reagan, Ronald's grandfather, may have slipped into the U.S. from Canada without immigration papers.

Ronald Wilson Reagan himself was born on February 6, 1911, in a second-story apartment above a store in the tiny town of Tampico, Ill. He was called "Dutch" throughout his youth, most of which he spent in Dixon, Ill., a town of 8,000. His father, Jack Reagan, was a merchant, a Catholic, a liberal Democrat, and an alcoholic. His mother Nelle was a doer of good who visited prisoners in the local jails and tuberculosis patients who were confined in a sanitarium for the poor. They had been married in a Catholic church, but Nelle raised Dutch as a Presbyterian.

"We were damned poor," Reagan has said. He always wore the hand-me-downs of his brother Moon, who was two years older. At the dinner table one of Dutch's favorites was "oatmeal meat," hamburger stretched out with oatmeal. Some Christmases Jack spent the little money they had on booze. Reagan remembers going outside the house early in the morning in the snow, just a boy, to pull his drunken dad inside.

Dutch absorbed the small-town values of Dixon, patriotism, hard work, Godliness, and he read his family's collection of Horatio Alger and Tom Swift books and the Bible, but life as he lived it meant football, which he has said was no mere game to him but "a matter of life and death." His hero, the high school fullback, went on to Eureka College about 20 miles from Peoria, so Dutch decided to do that, too.

Eureka College, located in the town of Eureka, had about 250 students then. It had been supported financially by the Christian Church (Disciples of Christ) since its founding in 1855, and attendance at chapel was required. Dutch joined a fraternity, played football, acted in the school plays, and participated in a successful student strike against a proposal by the college administration to cut back academic programs. To make some money he washed dishes in his frat house and a girls' dorm, and he was a lifeguard.

He majored in economics and sociology. Eureka's one professor for both of those fields was an advocate of social reform who might hold forth to his students on, for example, the monotony of the work on Henry Ford's assembly line. Dutch could have been a star student because he had a photographic memory, but he focused it on his school books just long enough to get him through the quizzes. "Most of my high school and college career," he told Barbara Walters on ABC, "a C average was eligibility for sports and I figured that that was the standard to shoot at to remain eligible. . . . See, I never knew anything above C's."

He graduated in 1932, in the midst of the Depression. During the New Deal his father distributed government food and worked for the WPA, and Dutch was a staunch liberal—"I was an enthusiastic New Deal Democrat," he wrote in his autobiography. They were a close family, and after his father's first heart attack Dutch sent his parents a monthly check. He gave them, too, before they died, a small home of their own.

Ronald Reagan seems to have lived two lives passing from the first into the second one across an eight-year span that connected them.

His first career, in show business, was fairly successful, but then tailed off. Building on his love of sports, he started out as a radio sportscaster in the midwest. In 1937 he was given a screen test by Warner Brothers, and during the next quarter of a century he made fifty-two or fifty-three films, first mostly B movies, but then some better ones.

He joined the Screen Actors Guild (SAG) in 1938. When his fellow actors berated Roosevelt, he defended the President and criticized the American economic system. He told his biographer Lou Cannon, a reporter from California who now works for the *Washington Post*, that in the aftermath of World War I "I became a pacifist and thought the whole thing was a frame-up." He joined the United World Federalists, an organization which wants one federal world government to replace the existing system of warring nationalisms.

In college he had been so nearsighted, he said, that his vision on the football field had been limited to the square yard of turf occupied by the other team's right guard. Corneal lenses had corrected this, but during World War II the Army Air Force assigned him to a motion picture unit in Hollywood, where he spent the war narrating training films and playing the lead in a musical comedy about the Army. He was promoted to captain, but when he was put up for major he asked that the recommendation be canceled, since "who was I to be a major for serving in California, without ever hearing a shot fired in anger?"

After the war he found that his movie career had almost stalled out, and in 1954 he took a job as host on General Electric's TV theater. When that ended in 1962 he was an actor in the TV horse opera, *Death Valley Days,* and a TV pitchman for Borateem soap.[1] This would have been the beginning of the end for an ordinary person, but for Reagan it was just the end of his second beginning.

His second career flowed easily out of his first one because in its pretense politics is like show business and the politician is an actor. Far less obvious, though, is the metamorphosis of his sunny New Deal liberalism into the thoroughly right-wing faith of his second life, a faith that propelled him into the political campaign of a John Birch Society candidate and onto a platform in front of the zealots of the Christian Anti-Communist Crusade.

"What I've always wanted to know about you," Tom Hayden asked him, "is exactly why you shifted politically from the left to the right." The New Left leader and Reagan had run into each other one night in 1979 on the late shuttle from San Francisco to Los Angeles. In his book *The American Future,* Hayden related:

"The Hollywood Left of the 1940s, Reagan said with feeling, was manipulative, tightly organized from the top down, and operated through secret caucuses within larger, legitimate organizations. Feeling himself used, Reagan drifted toward the center. It was not until he began hosting General Electric's television theater series, he said, that his shift to conservatism became complete."

Reagan's liberalism had led him into fouled waters. For those who were not blinded by ideological faith or hope that was too fierce, there was plentiful evidence in the thirties that the Soviet Union under Stalin was a criminal system of mass terror. Evidently Reagan was one of the many American idealists of that period who either did not believe or did not pay attention to the gathering evidence that Stalin had murdered millions of Soviet citizens in the name of communism. Reagan's later awareness of his folly about the Soviet Union was one, but only one reason for his turn against himself.

When read carefully, his confessions on the point (in his autobiography *Where's the Rest of Me?*) explain some things, but seem to conceal others. "I knew little and cared less about the rumors about Communists," he wrote. "I was truly so naive I thought the nearest Communists were fighting in Stalingrad. . . . I was a near-hopeless hemophiliac liberal. I bled for 'causes.' . . . I was blindly and busily joining every organization I could find that would guarantee to save the world."

He was, he continued, "an active (though unconscious) partisan in what now and then turned out to be Communist causes. . . . There were some of our associates, I'm sure, who believed I was red as Moscow."

He made a lot of speeches without realizing, he wrote, that his material and audiences were hand-picked, "or at least I was being spoon-fed and steered more than a little bit." One evening in the spring of 1946, though, when he was thirty-five years old, he denounced communism and sensed "ghastly" disapproval.

His involvement with alleged Communist fronts was used against him two decades later in his contest with George Christopher, then the mayor of San Francisco, for the Republican nomination for governor of California. Christopher asked publicly about Reagan: "Did he jointly sponsor protests on United States atomic policies with the chairman of the Communist party in Los Angeles and how long did this association last? . . . Did Mr. Reagan appear in broadcasts sponsored by the Mobilization for Democracy during and after the House Un-American Activities Committee [HUAC] had reported this as 'one of the most potentially potent front organizations created by the Communists since 1945'?"

It is one of the petty ironies of postwar American history that the late liberal columnist Drew Pearson joined in roughing up Ronald Reagan—McCarthyizing him, as we say now—for his involvement with the pro-Soviet left. Just before the voting that made Reagan governor for the first time, Pearson laid out facts which the Republican researchers on Reagan had turned up.

On February 26, 1946, the *Communist Peoples World* reported that Reagan was a sponsor of the "Los Angeles Committee for a Democratic Far Eastern Policy," a group which charged that

"U.S. foreign policy in Asia is sowing the seeds of a third world war" and urged "the removal of troops from China." On September 7, 1946 (some months after his denunciation of communism which he relates in his autobiography), Reagan was listed by *Peoples World,* the organ of the Communist party on the west coast, as the star in "Operation Terror," identified as a series of thirteen weekly broadcasts sponsored by "Mobilization for Democracy" and produced with the cooperation of the "Hollywood Writers Mobilization."

Pearson continued pouring the research into the record: according to HUAC in a 1961 report, the Mobilization for Democracy was "created by California Communists since 1945. It is a Communist-inspired and dominated organization . . . engaged in inciting riots, racial hatred, and disrespect for law and order. It is one of the 'key' Communist fronts in California." The Hollywood Writers Mobilization, according to a 1958 report of the California State Senate Un-American Activities Committee, was a direct successor of the Pacific Coast branch of the League of American Writers, said to be a "Communist front for literary Communist and Communist fellow travelers. . . . The record proves," Pearson said, "that the 'patriotism' indicated on the part of the leaders of this Communist front organization was dependent upon their secret loyalty to the Soviet Union." In 1947 and 1948, the group was cited as "subversive and Communist" by U.S. Attorney General Tom Clark.

Pearson wrote that some Republicans had "their fingers crossed." Since Reagan, "once teamed up with extreme leftists, was now backed by extreme rightists," the Republican skeptics "wonder whether, if elected, he would prove to be a 'revolving door' governor, given to sudden policy reversals."

Reagan explained to Bill Moyers in 1980: "I happened to be on the board of directors of two groups that subsequently turned out to be Communist front groups." He said one of them was the Hollywood Independent Citizens Committee of the Arts, Sciences, and Professions (HICCASP), which the California legislature's red-hunting committee soon thereafter called one of "two key Communist fronts in California." A group of liberals in HICCASP, including Reagan, Jimmy Roosevelt, and

Olivia de Havilland, became suspicious of their fellow board members. "We very carefully wrote a resolution that we knew that no one who was a Communist or a Communist sympathizer could adopt," Reagan said, "and we introduced it to see what would happen. We were the only votes on our side. . . . We evidently were the front behind which they were operating. . . . I was their boy!"

During this meeting, according to Reagan's autobiography, Dore Schary, then head of MGM Studios, invited Reagan to join him afterwards at de Havilland's apartment. It was there Reagan learned that the anti-Communist resolution had been a plot to smoke out the reds. Reagan remembers that he kept grinning at de Havilland until she asked what was so funny. "Nothing, except that I thought you were one," he said. "I thought *you* were one. Until tonight, that is," she replied. Reagan's group resigned.

Beginning in March 1945 and continuing into 1947, there were a half-dozen strikes in the film industry in Hollywood which according to Reagan cost workers $28 million and moviemakers about $150 million. Returning from the service to his job with Warner Brothers, Reagan had also returned to the board of the Screen Actors Guild, which played a mediating role between the studios and the strikers, who were led by Herb Sorrell's Conference of Studio Unions (CSU). In the course of rancorous negotiations in this essentially jurisdictional dispute, Reagan says, Bill Hutcheson, president of the carpenters' union, told him and his group that if things went his way on an issue in dispute, he, Hutcheson, would run a certain union and "the Commies" out of Hollywood in five minutes. Reagan later concluded that the strikes were tangled up in a Communist plot to take over Hollywood. The plan of "the class warfare boys," he says, was "to line up big-name dupes" (like himself for a while) to infiltrate the talent guilds and craft unions and turn movies into propaganda.

The American Veterans Committee (AVC), a liberal veterans' organization to which Reagan belonged, was convulsed by the issue of ousting Communists. Reagan, who later concluded AVC had become "a hotbed of Communists in Hollywood," said that someone in the organization told him to picket a studio in his Air Force uniform, but that when he discovered that the proposal to picket had been approved by only 73 of 1,300 AVC members, he said he would denounce the action instead, and it was canceled. In 1947 he quit AVC.

During some of the labor strife, fighting broke out—cars were overturned, homes bombed, workers slugged. Reagan says he was warned by an anonymous caller that some people were going to "fix you so you won't ever act again." Police guarded his home, and from morning to night he wore a loaded .32 Smith and Wesson pistol in a shoulder holster. "I learned how much a person gets to lean on hardware like that," he said. Later actor Sterling Hayden testified that Reagan had been "a one-man battalion" against the CSU strikers.

J. Edgar Hoover, the FBI director, passed some information to actor George Murphy, who passed it on to Reagan, and sometime during this immediate postwar period Reagan was visited by three men who were evidently FBI agents (he says only that they came from "a well-known government agency"). "We got to talking," Reagan wrote. "I came to admire these men: they never accused anyone of being a Communist unless they had every last bit of evidence which would stand up against the most vicious court assault. They were extremely careful never to smear anyone or guess even on good but less than complete evidence. . . . We exchanged information for a few hours."

HUAC held hearings on Communists in Hollywood (Richard Nixon was one of the investigating congressmen). Reagan was a friendly witness, but whatever he had told the government agents in private, in public he refused to name names. During the questioning of him before HUAC about disruptive members of SAG, HUAC counsel Robert Stripling asked him, "You have no knowledge yourself as to whether or not any of them are members of the Communist party?" "No, sir," Reagan replied; "I have no investigative force, or anything, and I do not know." He went further: "I hope we are never prompted by fear of communism into compromising any of our democratic principles," and he indicated that he would not like to see any political party, including the Communist one, outlawed on the basis of ideology.

On the other hand, he supported barring Communists from SAG. The guild, of which he became president, identified Communists as enemies of the U.S., barred them from membership, and said it would not try to force any employer to hire any actor who had so offended American public opinion as to make himself "unsalable at the box office."

It was the standard procedure of the Motion Picture Industry Council, of which Reagan was chairman in 1949, to require Hollywood figures who were challenged by HUAC to go before the committee and "name names," as Reagan said, and then to issue a statement of repentance. Reagan apparently approved of this: he wrote that the Communists reacted by "claiming they were victims of a 'blacklist'—when they were actually working members of a conspiracy directed by Soviet Russia."

Actress Anne Revere related that when she had been called to testify at the HUAC hearings, Reagan had told her, "It's so simple. All you've got to do is just name a couple of names that have already been named." She did not do this. Ten witnesses who refused to answer HUAC's questions were blacklisted, and Reagan agreed with the policy announced by the Motion Picture Association of America that it would not hire any of "the Hollywood Ten" until they were acquitted of charges or purged of contempt and declared that they were not Communists.

Reagan's first marriage broke up in the midst of all this turmoil. Actress Jane Wyman and he had married in 1940. They had had one child, Maureen, and had adopted a second one, Michael. "I arrived home from the Washington [HUAC] hearing to be told I was leaving," Reagan wrote.

Research by John Sherwood of the *Los Angeles Times* into the movie fan magazines of the period yielded some information about the breakup. A *Photoplay* reporter quoted Wyman, "We're finished, and it's all my fault." His career was waning and hers was on the rise. "Jane takes her work too seriously," Reagan told Louella Parsons. Discussing with Hedda Hopper his wife's intention to divorce him, Reagan said, "I hope to live with her the rest of my life."

Wyman had reacted against her husband's immersion in politics. In December 1946 a movie magazine quoted her as having told him tongue-in-cheek, "Go away, you bother me. Go get the world straightened out and then maybe I'll talk to you." At the court hearing she said he spent too much time at politics, which she found "uninteresting." In a book cited by Cannon, a friend of hers quoted her saying that it was exasperating to get up early to get to work "and have someone at the breakfast table, newspaper in hand, expounding on the far right, far left, the conservative right, the conservative left, the middle of the road." Nor was this just her observation. Ginger Rogers told Barbara Walters that when she had lunch with Reagan while they were costarring in a picture, "He talked politics during the whole hour of every lunchtime."

The key period for understanding the evolution of Reagan's political orientation is 1948–1950, the three years between the end of the HUAC hearings in Hollywood and "that pleasant California evening," probably during the spring of 1951, when he met the actress Nancy Davis. During the HUAC inquiry and its aftermath Reagan had behaved equivocally, refusing to name names in public himself but apparently advising Revere to name some who had already been named, expressing concern about protecting innocent people but implicitly going along with the blacklisting of the Hollywood Ten. Once released from the theater of treason, though, he continued for the next three years to advocate compassionate social change. Like many American liberals who had become or were becoming anti-Communist, he continued to support Democratic candidates and liberal programs for domestic reform. Anticommunism had not driven him into the right wing; he had simply made anticommunism a part of his liberalism. The mystery about his metamorphosis is not his postwar turn against Stalinism, but his subsequent switch from liberalism to extreme reaction on domestic issues.

Joe Ball of Minnesota was just the kind of U.S. senator Reagan would later admire, a conservative Republican. In 1948, during a radio talk on behalf of the election of the young mayor of Minneapolis, Hubert Humphrey, who was on his way to defeating Senator Ball, Reagan said: "While Ball is the banner carrier for Wall Street, Mayor Humphrey is fighting for all the principles advocated by President Truman, for adequate low-cost housing, for civil rights, for prices people can afford to pay

and for a labor movement free of the Taft-Hartley Law."
Reagan also headed up the Labor League of Hollywood Voters
for Truman. Supporting Humphrey, Truman, and that basket
of issues in 1948, he was still a liberal. Two years later he supported the whole Democratic ticket in California, including
Helen Gahagan Douglas, one of the more high-minded liberals
in the country, who was opposing Richard Nixon for the Senate.
Nixon won after conducting a notoriously vicious campaign. As
actress Patricia Neal said, "When I knew (Reagan) he was very
liberal. And I think he was liberal until he met his present wife."[2]

Reagan has written that during his "second bachelorhood,"
from 1948 to 1951, he had a comfortable apartment and a collection of telephone numbers—he ran up nightclub bills of $750
a month. This came to an end shortly after he helped the young
actress, Nancy Davis, a Smith College graduate, to clear herself
of a suspicion of Communist affiliation that had arisen because
she was being confused with someone else. At the SAG office,
Reagan said, "We did a little quick checking and could discover
nothing detrimental to her." He gave her the news at dinner,
and in time they fell in love. They married on March 4, 1952,
about a year after they met. They were to have two children, first
Patti, then Ron.

Nancy Reagan regards her stepfather who made her his
adopted daughter, the late Chicago neurosurgeon Dr. Loyal
Davis, as her real father. Cannon reports that Davis was "intolerant of minorities." As Cannon perceived Mrs. Reagan in the
Governor's Mansion, she "did not enjoy the company of ordinary people," and her interests were "fashion and money and
the gossip of the wealthy, socialite circle" in southern California.
In her memoir she touched here and there upon the issues that
matter to her: law and order, capital punishment, prayer in the
schools, and self-censorship by moviemakers (all of which she
favors), and marijuana, abortions, premarital sex, and permis-
sive child-raising (all of which she's against). About the protests
of the sixties she wrote, "The students were demonstrating on
campuses, rioting against authority, burning property." This
was the strongminded, prudish, conservative beauty whom
the amiable, love-happy Ronald Reagan now married. Cannon

believes she is the most important and influential person in his
life.

The Reagans take pains to dispute speculation that either she
or Loyal Davis affected Reagan much politically. "When I married Nancy," Reagan has been quoted, "she hadn't given a
thought to politics," and as for Dr. Davis, he "was most tactful—
we didn't talk politics." Mrs. Reagan says she does not involve
herself "in matters of public policy." She concedes: "That
doesn't mean that we don't talk politics all the time, because we
do. And it doesn't mean we don't influence each other." But
"he's the one who makes the decisions."

In 1952 Reagan voted for Eisenhower. The next year he
persisted in supporting a candidate for mayor of Los Angeles
whom the liberals liked. Meanwhile, though, his professional
prospects were faltering, and the new couple found themselves
deep in debt. "Returning from the Army Air Force," Nancy
wrote, "he found himself all but forgotten. . . . He was offered
a lot of films but few good ones." His $3,500-a-week contract
with Warner Brothers had not been renewed, and he was just a
freelance actor. They agreed he would turn down the second-
rate roles he was being offered until something good came
along. "Waiting it out without working was hard on the budget,
but we got by," according to Nancy. "We were coming to the end
of the line," Reagan has written, "when General Electric made
their offer. I took it."

In 1954 Reagan's agent sold his services to GE for $125,000 a
year, which was soon increased to $150,000. He would introduce
the "General Electric Theater" on TV and star in a few of the
plays each year, and for a number of weeks each year he would
make personal appearance tours of GE plants, visiting the company's employees. During his eight-year run with the GE Theater (the eight years that were the bridge across to his second
career), Reagan visited all 135 GE plants and met, more or less,
the company's 250,000 employees. Making as many as fourteen
speeches a day, he calculates he was on his feet in front of a
microphone for about 40,000 hours. An accomplished actor was
becoming an accomplished public speaker.

Gradually his talks to luncheon meetings became the central

events of his tours. At first he spoke a lot about Hollywood and its labor troubles, but "as the years went on," he wrote, "my speeches underwent a kind of evolution." GE was known as a conservative and Republican company, and Reagan was blending in. In 1956 he voted for Eisenhower again, but still as a Democrat. One day, Mrs. Reagan says, he came home from a speaking tour and told her he was realizing that the Democrats were responsible for the things he was speaking out against. Cannon argues that since Reagan was speaking to service clubs and corporate audiences, he just changed as he responded to their conservative postures—by 1957 he was frequently addressing such groups as the National Association of Manufacturers. Still, he did not change parties. Once he did that, he would not be able to turn back. One total reversal of direction could be plausible—but not two. In 1960 he was a "Democrat for Nixon," and his speeches had become, as texts of them show, harsh, rapid-fire assaults on communism, domestic programs that the Democrats were advancing, and similarities and connections that he now perceived between these two phenomena. In 1962 he switched his party registration to Republican.

Reporter Patrick Owens, inquiring into Reagan's GE period, learned that his pay came from the public and employee relations budget that was supervised by Lemuel Boulware, a GE vice president. Boulware inundated GE's workers with messages about the evils of big government and big unions. His bargaining strategy in labor disputes was to have the company present a single tempting offer and then refuse to bargain further.

Boulware denied to Owens that he had been involved with Reagan except for a ten-minute chat when he first arrived, but it does not stand to reason that Reagan was oblivious to the policy positions of his paymasters. His transformation may have taken place in a passive way—the gifted actor who had simply gone along with his conservative new wife and his conservative new employers and friends.

In one case Reagan tells about, he dropped one of the points in his speech to please the boss. It happened that one of his targets, the Tennessee Valley Authority, which he was attacking as "a government power octopus," was a GE customer for $50 million worth of equipment; TVA's business at that point had provided a total of $187 million in revenues to the company. Protest developed, GE denied responsibility for Reagan's views, and the director of Reagan's tour for GE told him a government bureaucrat was on the warpath. "It was made pretty plain that I was to be fired, and there was pointed reference to $50 million worth of government business that could be taken elsewhere," Reagan said.

By Reagan's account Ralph Cordiner, the chairman of GE, did not say anything to him about TVA, but Reagan on his own initiative phoned him and said, "Mr. Cordiner, what would you say if I said I could make my speech just as effectively without mentioning TVA?" After a long pause, Cordiner said, "Well, it would make my job easier." Reagan dropped TVA from his speech.

Reagan's later skepticism toward the antitrust laws may have had its genesis in his identification with GE. While he was speaking under its sponsorship, the company was convicted and fined and three of its executives were jailed for fixing prices and rigging bids in league with other firms.

In 1961 Reagan moved further to the right. At that time in many parts of the country large crowds were being whipped into frenzies of fear and hate by Dr. Fred Schwarz's Christian Anti-Communist Crusade. Reagan appeared on the platform at one of the rallies. The next year he spoke at a $50-a-plate fundraiser for the re-election to Congress of John Rousselot, a national public relations director of the extreme-right John Birch Society. These rash steps carry us to the quick of the mystery. When he now depicted liberalism as a mere waystation on the road to communism, was Reagan sincerely convinced that what he was saying was true and fair, or was he intellectually dishonest, using a handy but slanderous argument to make his own strange evolution more dramatic and more attractive to his conservative audiences? As he savaged all of the liberal domestic reforms he had championed until his fortieth year, was he applying his new wisdom about totalitarianism, or was he making his new living among businessmen by telling them what they wanted to hear? Bouncing off the far-left wall all the way back across to the far-right wall, was he returning to the patriotic and religious verities of his youth, or was he acting out with a different script the same attraction to extremes that had earlier involved him with the pro-Soviet left?

This riddle of motivation can be found mildly described and still unsolved in an account of Reagan's conversion that the first millionaire backer who approached him to run for governor, Holmes Tuttle, gave to Ray J. Harris, Jr., of the *Wall Street Journal.* Tuttle attributed Reagan's about-face to his bitter experiences with Communists *and* to his job with GE. The experiences in Hollywood "in a large measure" changed him, Tuttle said, and the work for GE brought him into close relationship with the business world "and he saw what the free-enterprise, capitalistic system was like" at the same time that executives were beginning to know him as an articulate spokesman for industry.

Evidently, however, Reagan had careened too far to the right for corporate comfort. An executive of an advertising agency that was involved in his work for GE phoned him in 1962 and asked how he would feel about limiting his speaking to commercial pitches about GE products. Reagan responded that if his speeches were an issue, he could see no solution but ending the relationship. "Twenty-four hours later," Reagan said, "the GE Theater was canceled."

A year after GE dropped him, Reagan complained in a speech that even though the electrification of farms had been accomplished, the Rural Electrification Agency "does not go into retirement." This enraged the rural co-op people, and GE felt it necessary to tell them that he did not work for them any more. "The REAs are valued customers of the General Electric Co.," the company added.[3]

It was during this period that Reagan was reduced to TV's *Death Valley Days* and Borateem. Was he too far out politically and too far gone professionally to return to the movies? Perhaps. In any case he was ready to plunge into national politics, and his chance came quickly. Long after the cause of Barry Goldwater for President had become hopeless, Reagan appeared on national television and delivered an electrifying oration on behalf of Goldwater's election. This historic, forensically masterful

speech, which raised $8 million in small contributions, vitally
refreshed the right-wing movement on the eve of its electoral
calamity and established Ronald Reagan as that calamity's pre-
eminent survivor. From then on he was a politician, glib, elo-
quent, hyperconservative, ambitious, and evasive when necessary.

The 1964 landslide for Lyndon Johnson convinced Reagan
that the rightists had to stand their ground but change their
tactics. A week after the election he declaimed to Young Republicans, "We don't intend to turn the Republican Party over to the
traitors in the battle just ended. . . . Turning the party over to
the so-called moderates wouldn't make any sense at all." Writing
in the right-wing journal, *National Review,* he said, "There are no
plans for retreating from our present positions, but we can't
advance without reinforcements." The winners had portrayed
the Goldwaterites, he said, "as advancing a kind of radical departure from the status quo. . . . In short—time now for the soft
sell to prove our radicalism was an optical illusion."

He had come to oppose the progressive income tax as Marxist, a viewpoint that was also being advanced by the John Birch
Society. Rousselot favored making Social Security voluntary,
which Reagan thought was a persuasive idea. As he was preparing to run for governor, Reagan exclaimed that "Johnny Rousselot is a terrific fellow" and had said "he would do anything
from calling me names in public to endorsement—whatever we
want."

But as the campaign neared he grew cagier. When first asked
about accepting support from Birchers, he said he wouldn't issue a questionnaire to his supporters, though he was in "great
disagreement" with Robert Welch, the Birchers' guru. Late in
1965 he said the society had been infiltrated by "a kind of lunatic
fringe" and he would not solicit Birch support. In the Reagan
camp the problem of how to handle this was called "the Birch
issue." He would accept their support if they accepted his philosophy, he said during his first campaign. But would he follow
Nixon's example of refusing to appear with any candidate who
was also a Bircher? "No, this is not my position," Reagan replied.

He wrote letters soliciting funds for Young Americans for

Freedom (the board of which he joined) and for *National Review* and another right-wing periodical, *Human Events*. Republicans had raised questions about his early left-wing scrapes; now the Democrats, seeking to re-elect Governor Pat Brown, charged that Reagan was a right-wing extremist. The state Democratic chairman issued a 29-page report entitled, "Ronald Reagan, Extremist Collaborator, An Exposé," and charged that he had worked on a committee including 17 top figures in the Birch Society to raise funds for *Human Events*. Brown called Reagan "the crown prince of the extreme right" whose election would give "the extremist movement in America" a new lease on life. Columnist Joseph Alsop warmed to the theme: Reagan was "nothing but Goldwater mutton dressed as middle-of-the-road lamb."

Clenching himself into the fist of public indignation against demonstrations and disorders on college campuses during the Vietnam war, Reagan was swept into the governorship. As he jested, "I am part of government now (a funny thing happened to me on the way to Death Valley) . . ." A funny thing happened to Lyndon Johnson's war on poverty on the way to Death Valley, too: Governor Reagan appointed a former member of the Birch Society as his director of the California Office of Economic Opportunity, the agency charged with administering the federal effort in California.[4]

Reagan labored in Sacramento to carry out his antiwelfare state conservatism, but he could not overcome the basically liberal California legislature. The central trends in his eight-year record contradicted his purposes and convictions: yearly state spending went from $4.6 billion to $10.2 billion and taxes increased from $6.64 to $7.62 per $100 of personal income. This left some of his far-right backers feeling had. Pragmatism, opportunism, and a dislike of continuing conflict all were factors in his willingness to abandon some of his positions and sign legislation which, by the record, he disapproved. Signing a fat spending program, he would ask where people proposed to start cutting.

In 1976 President Gerald Ford's campaign committee called Reagan "the biggest taxer and spender" in California's history.

Lou Cannon has delivered a most affirmative judgment: "He left office with a moderate and generally satisfactory record." Another *Washington Post* reporter, Leroy F. Aarons, wrote as Reagan's governorship ended, "the doomsayers are admitting with grudging disbelief that the state still exists."

"He did very little good and very little harm," according to the editor of the *Los Angeles Times* editorial page, Anthony Day. "He was a perfectly average governor." A. Alan Post, the broadly respected California legislative analyst during Reagan's time, said much the same thing with a different emphasis: "He inherited a good state with a good tax base, but my feeling is that he really had very little impact on California. His mission in life was to keep the lid on the expenses of government, and he kept as tight a lid as anyone could have expected. But he didn't change the pot any. He just held down the lid."

Midway in his first term as governor, Reagan had made an implausible try for the Republican presidential nomination in 1968 against Nixon, even stating to the California delegation that he was a candidate and waiting out the convention roll call through to the end. There can be little if any doubt that when he left Sacramento in 1975 he hoped he was bound for the White House. Ford twice tried to head him off with offers of Cabinet posts, which he rejected. He wrote a column for 174 newspapers, he made scores of speeches, and he began his pithy five-minute radio broadcasts on hundreds of stations. Announcing against Ford in the fall of 1975, Reagan conducted an aggressive campaign from the right against what he characterized as the unacceptable moderation of the seated President and the Secretary of State, Henry Kissinger. Ford carried the GOP convention by only 117 delegates, 1,187 to Reagan's 1,070. Jimmy Carter's election then, Ford believed, was Reagan's fault.[5]

Defeated, Reagan resumed his radio broadcasts. Throughout the second half of the 1970s he expressed himself in these short talks on most of the foreign and domestic issues of our period. According to an aide of his at that time, Peter Hannaford, Reagan usually wrote these five-minute, five-day-a-week broadcasts himself. He probably suspected that his radio audience included many of his right-wing followers. Almost nothing he was saying into the microphone got into the newspapers at the time. Perhaps these circumstances explain why he was so candid and politically unguarded on the radio in sharp contrast to the much more politic newspaper columns he signed before his presidential campaigns of 1976 and 1980. His headlong and frequently heedless expressions of his opinions glitter forth from the pages of the radio transcripts like uncut diamonds. As he signed off the series he said of the programs, "writing them has been a lot of fun. I've scratched them out on a yellow tablet in airplanes, riding in cars, and at the ranch when the sun went down." His parting line was: "Sometime later today if you happen to catch me on television you'll understand why I can no longer bring you these commentaries." On the television of that day, November 20, 1979, he announced for President again.

A basically successful attempt by Reagan's campaign press staff to conceal the transcripts of his radio broadcasts was the decisive tactic in an orchestrated strategy to present him to the voters in 1980 as a moderate. A few reporters had been working hesitantly with some of the transcripts, a few of which had been doled out by the Reagan camp, but a complete set of them was nowhere to be found.

In October 1980 press officers for the National Reagan–Bush Committee in Arlington, Virginia, refused my direct request to see their set of the transcripts, as they had refused others who had inquired earlier. "The access to that file will be impossible," Robin Gray, one of the Reagan press people, told me. Pressed why, he replied, "We have them in a small area that's hard to get to." He offered to show me "three or four" of the transcripts if I would specify the subjects I was interested in. No, I wanted to see the whole set, I told him.

Gray referred me, as he said the Reagan people had referred others, cross-country to O'Connor Creative Services in Los Angeles. This was the agency that had transcribed the broadcasts. Its vice president referred me to Santa Monica to the Citizens for the Republic (CFR), the organization that Reagan had established with $1.5 million in campaign funds left over from his 1976 campaign. A political action committee, it was used to raise

more campaign money and to administer Reagan's political activities until he ran again in 1980. Reagan was its founder and
chairman; its September 1980 newsletter listed him as chairman
emeritus. Ed Meese, a campaign consultant to Reagan in 1980,
was also CFR's paid legal counsel that year.

Bill Stetson, the editor of CFR's newsletter, confirmed that
he possessed a set of the transcripts, but said he thought I should
get them from the national Reagan committee. Informed that the
committee would not provide them, he said spontaneously, "I'll
tell them if they won't give them to you, I will. Maybe after that
they'll give them to you. We're not trying to hide anything.
Whatever Governor Reagan's said is public record."

Before telephoning the Reagan committee about it, Stetson
later told me, he and his superior at CFR decided that whatever
the decision was in Virginia, Stetson would keep his word with
me (and, he added, with National Public Radio) to provide sets
of the transcripts if the Reagan committee would not. Stetson
then telephoned Ken Towery, another Reagan press aide at the
headquarters in Virginia, and reported back to me that Towery
had said the policy was that journalists could be given three or
four of the transcripts if they asked for them by specific subjects,
"but they are less accommodating when people have wanted
every transcript." Stetson told Towery of CFR's decision that, if
the Reagan committee's answer was no, CFR would give me and
NPR sets, but no one else. Towery, who used to be a reporter,
replied, " 'That's fine with us,' " Stetson said. Stetson then provided me with copies of the 472 transcripts for 1978 and 1979.
Evidently NPR never claimed its set. (As noted earlier, subsequently I obtained a goodly number of the 1975 broadcasts,
also.)[6]

Unless they happened to have listened to the radio when
Reagan was on, the voters went to the polls in 1980 knowing
almost nothing about the contents of his opinion-spiked radio
broadcasts in 1975 and during the years immediately preceding
his successful campaign for the most powerful position on earth.
That is what the Reagan staffers wanted to happen and that is
what happened. The Reagan of those broadcasts is a very different Reagan from the Reagan who was sold to the voters.

The strategy of the winning Reagan campaign was based on the obvious fact that anyone who is perceived as far-right cannot be elected President of the United States. Rousselot, Reagan's friend from the early sixties (and by then a former Bircher), said that it was important for Reagan to convince the voters that he was "not going to be a wild President."

Complaining of their inability to learn from Reagan or his advisers the meaning of his "headline-making rhetoric," *Washington Post* reporters Don Oberdorfer and George C. Wilson wrote, "This lack of information is characteristic of a campaign that has provided little in the way of details to undergird the words of the candidate, who has been insulated and protected in extraordinary fashion from questioners and questions." In addition to withholding the radio transcripts, the strategy entailed keeping reporters away from the candidate, trying to refuse to comment on specific questions of military intervention, projecting moderation, and revising or reversing some of Reagan's positions.

A reporter complained to John Sears, II, when he was Reagan's campaign manager in 1979, that the candidate hadn't said anything new in months. Sears smiled and said, "I certainly hope he hasn't." Reagan's press aide Lyn Nofziger said, when (because of a split with Sears) he was on the outside looking in, that Reagan wanted so much to be President, he was not saying what he believed: "They have him so intimidated, so convinced he shouldn't speak out for what he believes, that he's not Ronald Reagan." But with Sears out and Nofziger back in, the press secretary cheerfully joined in the work of keeping reporters away from the candidate. A journalist reported asking Nofziger whether there would be time to see Reagan, and Nofziger replied, "Not if I can help it." Elizabeth Drew, the *New Yorker* reporter, saw Reagan's staff keeping reporters away from the candidate as he talked to people in a crowd. "They are not simply protecting Reagan from the press; they are trying to protect him from himself," she wrote.

"I'm not changing, I have not changed," Reagan had protested in September 1979. "It's not very flattering to think someone would modify his beliefs to get a few votes. It wouldn't be

worth going through this if I didn't have very firmly held convictions." He had them, all right, but he changed some of them to
win. Late in the campaign *Business Week* predicted he would
"soft-pedal the conservative positions on labor issues" and "ditch
or modify some of his previous antilabor rhetoric," and in October he did so. A Reagan planner was quoted, "The question is
how much do we gain and how much do we lose by softening his
position." He switched from opposition to support of farm subsidies, federal aid for New York and Chrysler, and the Davis-
Bacon prevailing wages act, and he talked tirelessly about peace.
(Was this easier for him because he had once been a Truman
Democrat and a world federalist?) But he denied the opportunism of his switches even though it was totally obvious. "Look," he
said, "I've been on the mashed potato circuit so long, I was on
radio so many years with those five-day-a-week commentaries, I
had a twice-a-week column in more than 100 newspapers
throughout the country, how could I change my positions?" The
radio commentaries were squirreled away from the press even as
he spoke.[7]

For American democracy and the nuclear-menaced human
race, the 1980 election was a perfect trap. Justified disappointment and disgust with the incumbent President were widespread. People had generally thought Reagan was a radical, but
the leading journalists' dislike of Carter was so strong, the press
as a whole let Reagan get away with a disguise. In the last four or
five days before the voting several elements coalesced in
Reagan's favor—Reagan's victory with the help of Carter's briefing book in the candidates' TV debate, Reagan's telling questions about whether people were better off than four years earlier, the dramatic return of Iran's American hostages to the news
but not yet to the country—and Reagan won the White House,
with a conservative Congress to go with it.

Although Reagan led Carter by 10 percentage points and
won in the electoral college eleven to one, and although many of
the serious humanists in Congress were defeated in the Republican sweep, the election was not the transformation that the right
wished it to be. Asked their main one or two reasons for voting
for Reagan, only 11 percent of his voters said, "He's a real con-

servative," while 38 percent preferred the much milder statement, "It's time for a change." Reagan seemed to be the lesser of
two evils—said comedian Mark Russell, the evil of two lessers. In
a poll taken the week after the election 72 percent of the voters
disapproved of the job Carter had done, compared to only 28
percent who approved. George Gallup wrote after the election
that both candidates "rated lower on personal appeal than any
other presidential candidates whose appeal we have measured
during the last three decades." Fewer eligible voters went to the
polls than in any national election in the preceding thirty-two
years. The 43 million Americans who voted for Reagan were
only 27 percent of the voting-age population; 75 million adult
Americans did not vote. Furthermore, 27 percent of the voters
who called themselves liberals voted for either Reagan or John
Anderson. The people were sad, angry, and confused, and most
of them were silent.

Even if they had been given a truer picture of the man they
elected their fortieth President, they might not have been able to
understand him. The mysteries in his motivations do not yield
themselves readily into the light of day. It can be said, as Mayor
Christopher of San Francisco did say, that "Mr. Reagan can
swing from the radical left and Communist fronts to the radical
right with remarkable facility." But his reaction against the Sta-
linists in the Hollywood organizations did not cause him to abandon his liberalism; he continued to be a fighting liberal until he
met his second wife. As a participant in pro-Communist causes
and then an anti-Communist liberal cleansing himself of the
potential consequences of those actions, certainly he was scarred
by the early stages of what became the McCarthy era. But what is
the explanation of the behavior of a man who, while continu-
ously presenting himself as a man of highest principle, went on
to immerse himself in the antiunion politics of GE and became,
by 1960, a fervent enemy of his former associates—the liberal
Democrats and all their causes? He says he saw that he had been
wrong and changed his mind. It is possible that it was as simple
as that, but it is also possible that it was not, and now what was in
itself an enigma that concerned only one man's life has had
momentous effects in the national life. When Ronald Reagan

and his wife Nancy moved into the White House, the picture of
Harry Truman was taken down off the wall in the Cabinet
Room, and Calvin Coolidge was put up in his place.[8] That
change signified the new American President's repudiation of
everything the American people had learned about government
in the preceding fifty years.

2

The Board of Directors of the United States

"The Cabinet," Reagan said during his campaign in 1980, "would be my inner circle of advisers . . . almost like the board of directors." When the members of his Cabinet did in fact assemble with him in the White House in the early days of 1981, he told them with emphasis that they would operate as such a board. A simile in his mind had become the dominant characteristic of his administration, for his Cabinet is like nothing so much as the board of directors of a federal government transformed into a giant conglomerate corporation. Although one of the directors runs the Labor Department, no one from labor sits at the table.

This could not surprise informed voters. Reagan's forty-seven-member, all-male "executive advisory committee" for his 1980 campaign was headed by William E. Simon, the former treasury secretary and a financial consultant in New York City, and included W. Clement Stone, the insurance millionaire from Chicago, Clifton C. Garvin, Jr., the board chairman and chief executive officer of Exxon, and former Treasury Secretary John Connally, who was practicing lucrative corporate law in Houston and Washington. Reagan also announced a forty-person "business advisory committee" composed of top executives of Bendix, Sperry, Morgan Stanley & Company, the New York Stock Exchange, Prudential, Metropolitan Life, Goodyear, Pfizer, Merrill Lynch, Allied Stores, Fluor, Monsanto, Weyerhauser, Procter & Gamble, the Continental group, Estée Lauder, and other companies.[1]

When Reagan was governor he said, "My administration makes no bones about being business-oriented." Democrats naturally put the matter differently; Assembly Leader Jess Unruh said the shots in Sacramento were called by a "handful of half-hidden millionaires." Reagan's second career cannot be accurately understood if one omits the decisive role of millionaires.

Holmes Tuttle, who is a Ford dealer in Los Angeles, has told several reporters how he, Henry Salvatori, the founder of Western Geophysical Company, and A. C. Rubel, the chairman of Union Oil, met in 1965 to discuss where the conservative movement should go after the Goldwater disaster. To Robert Lindsey of the *New York Times*, Tuttle recalled: "'Gentlemen,' I said, 'I think we've got a candidate right here. How about Ron?'" They agreed; Cannon quotes Rubel as saying at the time, "Reagan is the man who can enunciate our principles to the people." Tuttle said he went to Reagan and "told him if he'd run for the governorship, we'd see that he got the money." These three men, Cannon has written, were "the millionaire triumvirate that put him forward." When "The Friends of Ronald Reagan" organized to promote him for governor, its first headquarters was Rubel's office at Union Oil. A letter they sent out concerning the forthcoming campaign, which closed with the note "corporate checks are acceptable," raised $135,000. For Reagan's 1968 presidential campaign the expanding group of millionaire advisers raised at least $367,000.

Members of this inmost clique, passing on all Reagan's top appointments, met regularly in private clubs in Los Angeles or at the governor's home on weekends. Reagan told Cannon during this period that his hope in making his appointments was to attract "some of the big names in business—men who make $100,000 a year." The kitchen cabinet's intimate influence continued straight through to Reagan's selection of the top 200 or 300 people for his administration in Washington. In 1980 the chairman of the kitchen cabinet was Los Angeles attorney William French Smith, and the members included Tuttle (who was by then owner of six Ford dealerships); Salvatori; Earle M. Jorgenson, the chairman of a steel company; Jack Wrather, the chairman of an oil, entertainment, and real estate company; Alfred Bloomingdale, who for many years had run the Diners Club; William Wilson, an investor and an executive of Lockheed; Joseph Coors, the right-wing Colorado brewer; and Daniel Terra, a Chicago businessman and Reagan's finance chairman. They personally winnowed through lists of possible appointees and came up with their recommendations. "I took the names that they had given me," Reagan told PBS. "Some of them are names that had been unknown to me. . . . I take them on home, and from then on it's my problem."[2]

Who, then, are the members of the board of directors of the United States, and what are their connections, backgrounds, and financial situations?

The chairman of the board, Reagan himself, reports his net worth at $1.1 million for 1981, but the *New York Times* estimates the figure at $4 million to $5 million. Reagan reported his income for the two years before his major runs for President as $282,000 in 1975 and $516,000 in 1979. In the latter year his profits as he sold off his stocks were $234,000 and he grossed $318,000 from speaking, $58,000 from his radio broadcasts, and $27,000 for newspaper columns. During the Reagans' first year in the White House they had an income of $741,000, of which roughly a quarter of a million dollars was interest and another quarter million was a capital gain from their sale of a home they had in California for $1 million.

The transaction that originally made Reagan a millionaire

occurred less than a month after he was elected governor. In 1951 he had bought 236-acre and 54-acre parcels of land in Malibu Canyon for about $85,000. Twentieth Century-Fox Film Corporation owned 2,500 acres surrounding the two tracts. After the election returns were in, Reagan sold the 236 acres to Twentieth Century-Fox for $8,178 an acre, or a total of $1,930,000, which on a per-acre basis was more than 25 times what he had paid for the land 15 years earlier.

There were questions and some charges. Jim Drinkhall has reported in the *Wall Street Journal* that in 1968 a Los Angeles County assessment appeals board, acting on the judgment of appraisers for the county and for Fox and Reagan, agreed that the 236 acres Governor Reagan had sold were worth $944,000, or $4,000 an acre, less than half what he had received for them. One county appraiser concluded that the 1966 transaction was "not a fair-market sale." This led Unruh, the Democrat who ran for governor against Reagan in 1970, to charge that his opponent had gotten "an incredible deal." Fox called Unruh's statements preposterous. By 1972 reappraisals had lifted the value of the 236 acres to $1,459,000, but that was still $471,000 less than the governor had received.

In 1974, before Reagan left Sacramento, the California state parks and recreation board bought Fox's 2,500 acres along with the 236 acres that had been the governor's. Because large ranches sell for much less per acre than smaller tracts, a simple comparison of the 1966 and 1974 per-acre prices would be unfair to Reagan. But the fact was noted that Fox received from the state only $1,800 per acre, less than a fourth of the $8,178 an acre that Reagan had received for the same land eight years earlier.

Reagan profited handsomely again in a subsequent ranch deal. For $526,000 he bought the 688-acre Rancho del Cielo in the Santa Barbara mountains, to which he and Mrs. Reagan return from the White House for rest and respite.[3]

The secretary of defense in the Reagan administration, Casper Weinberger, was magna cum laude at Harvard, where he later graduated in law. In California politics he favored moderate Nelson Rockefeller over Goldwater in 1964 and liberal

George Christopher over Reagan in 1966, but he became Reagan's finance director in Sacramento. Under Presidents Nixon and Ford he ran the Federal Trade Commission, the budget office, and the Department of Health, Education and Welfare. From Washington he returned to California to become vice president and general counsel of the Bechtel Group, Inc., of San Francisco. With 120,000 employees, this is one of the nation's three largest engineering and construction companies. In 1980, for example, Bechtel obtained contracts worth $11 billion.

The first secretary of state, Alexander Haig, came into the government directly from his job as president of the third largest U.S. defense contractor, United Technologies, a manufacturer of jet engines and other products which made $393 million profit on $12 billion in sales in 1980. Haig, a brigade commander in Vietnam, had been Nixon's chief of staff during Watergate and then NATO commander. When he left the administration in 1982, Haig returned to United Technologies part-time as a consultant on "global business politics." His successor at State, George Shultz, had been Nixon's secretary of labor and then of the treasury. In private life Shultz had taught economics for 22 years, but after his service in Washington he became president of Bechtel Group.

The chairman and chief of Merrill Lynch, the largest brokerage firm in the United States (600 officers with 8,000 account executives), became secretary of the treasury. Donald T. Regan was also a member of the Business Roundtable, which consists of the chief executive officers of many of the nation's largest companies. A Harvard graduate in English, he was a Marine in World War II.

The attorney general, the same William French Smith who was a member of Reagan's kitchen cabinet of millionaires, is the President's close friend. He was one of the three trustees of the Ronald Reagan trust, which handled Reagan's investments. Summa cum laude in his undergraduate studies, Smith graduated from Harvard law. He has been a specialist in labor law on behalf of management: "he was the management man keeping Los Angeles nonunion," Fred Dutton, who served with Smith on the University of California board of regents, told the *Washington Post*. "I've spent thirty years dealing with the teamsters union and the construction workers union and a few others," Smith added. He was a director of Crocker National Bank, Pullman, Inc., Pacific Lighting, Pacific Telephone and Telegraph, and other companies.

A Yale-educated Westerner who favored former CIA Director George Bush over Reagan in 1980, Commerce Secretary Malcolm Baldridge had been chairman of Scovill, Inc., a consumer products manufacturer (Hamilton Beach appliances, Yale locks) that has sales of $1 billion a year. He was a director of Bendix, Uniroyal, and AMF.

The hubbub about alleged wrongdoing by Reagan's choice for labor secretary, Raymond Donovan, almost obscured the fact that he was executive vice president of a construction company that did $150 million worth of business annually, primarily building tunnels and highways. Donovan had bargained with unions on behalf of his Schiavone Construction Company of Secaucus, N.J., which is a union-shop company, and he said after his nomination that "unions add an awful lot" to the country. Still, Schiavone had had trouble in the past with prevailing wage, health and safety, and sex discrimination laws and regulations. Donovan was Reagan's campaign manager in New Jersey in 1980, and it was his special tie to the President that he had raised $680,000 in contributions before the primaries.

The only black in the Cabinet is a Park Avenue lawyer who was a director of Prudential Insurance Company and U.S. Industries. Samuel Pierce, Jr., was Phi Beta Kappa at Cornell, where he graduated in law. A Rockefeller Republican, he held federal posts under Eisenhower and Nixon. Becoming Reagan's secretary of housing and urban development, he had no experience in housing matters, but he relieved the composition of the original all-male Cabinet by being, anyway, black. Unfortunately, the story got out that Reagan ran into him at a reception and mistook him for a visiting mayor ("How are you, Mr. Mayor?" he said. "How are things in your city?").

The U.S. trade representative, William Brock, III, was heir to a candy fortune, the vice president of the Brock Candy

Company. A former senator, he was Ford's chairman of the Republican National Committee.

A Harvard business graduate who specialized in strengthening weak companies, Drew Lewis, Reagan's first secretary of transportation, had his own consulting firm, and he had run a venture capital company with the Greek shipping tycoon Aristotle Onassis. After two years Lewis resigned from the Cabinet to become chairman of Warner Amex, a cable television company that operates more than forty cable TV systems.

To replace Lewis, Reagan turned to a woman. Elizabeth Dole had been serving quietly as his White House assistant for public liaison. A Phi Beta Kappa graduate of Duke in political science and of Harvard law school, she had represented poor people as a lawyer and then had served in Democratic and Republican administrations in Washington. In 1973 Nixon appointed her to the Federal Trade Commission, and in 1975 she married Bob Dole, the senator from Kansas who, as chairman of the Senate Finance Committee now, has deadly power over Reagan's budgets. At the FTC Elizabeth Dole had a reputation as a tough regulator of business.

For secretary of the interior Reagan chose, not a businessman, but an anti-environmentalist lawyer who had been at one point the U.S. Chamber of Commerce spokesman on public lands, energy, and water pollution. An honor graduate of the University of Wyoming, James Watt served as an official at Interior and a member of the Federal Power Commission under Nixon and Ford. When called into the Reagan administration he was president of the Mountain States Legal Foundation, which had been established by Coors, the beer maker, and was further financed and directed by businessmen associated with such companies as Phillips, Amoco, Exxon, Shell, Boise Cascade, Kennecott, and Union Pacific. During Watt's three years with the foundation, it had filed lawsuits, mostly against the department he was taking over, seeking to bar the government from preventing overgrazing, to challenge federal land-use principles and water management policies, and, as *Time* summarized some of the other cases, "to fight against discount utility rates for elderly and disabled people in Colorado, federal strip-mining regulations, a plan to designate part of a Wyoming oilfield a protected wilderness area and a National Park Service ban on motorized rafts in the Grand Canyon." Watt assured doubters that he would pursue a policy balancing economic development with conservation, but environmentalists were appalled. "To put him in charge of the Interior Department," said the president of the Audubon Society, "is a crime."

For secretary of agriculture, Reagan chose a West Point–educated former paratrooper, John Block, whose family owns a 3,000-acre hog and grain farm that grosses more than $1 million a year and may have a value of more than $10 million.

Richard Schweiker, Reagan's first secretary of health and human services, is a Phi Beta Kappa graduate of Pennsylvania State. He worked in his family's business but entered politics in 1960. In the U.S. Senate he had a liberal record for a Republican—resisting Nixon on Vietnam and opposing the development of antiballistic missiles, for example—until 1976, when Reagan chose him as his vice presidential running mate. After that Schweiker moved rightward. He left the government early in 1983 to become president of the American Council of Life Insurance, the trade association for 572 life insurance companies which have combined assets of half a trillion dollars. As the *New York Times* pointed out, in 1981 life insurance companies received about 30 percent of their receipts from health insurance. Schweiker's new employers are therefore in direct competition with medicare, the federal health insurance program that Schweiker administered before joining them.

Schweiker's successor, Margaret Heckler, a graduate of Boston College law school, had served 16 years in Congress, where she had supported the equal rights amendment and other women's rights, but had opposed federal funding of abortions. She had been defeated for reelection in 1982 by a liberal Democrat.

Reagan elevated the post of CIA director into a Cabinet position and gave the job to his 1980 campaign chairman, William J. Casey, who has been a Republican strategist since 1940. A graduate of St. John's law school, Casey is a tax lawyer and has published "desk books" for other tax and estate lawyers. During World War II he was chief of intelligence for the European theater; under Nixon and Ford he became chairman of the Securities and Exchange Commission and president of the Export-Import Bank.

It was a little awkward, choosing Cabinet members for the two departments Reagan proposed to abolish (subsidiaries, one might say, that were doomed to be liquidated). The job of secretary of energy devolved upon a dental surgeon who had been the first Republican governor of South Carolina in a century, James Edwards. He said he'd like to shut down the department and work himself out of a job, but two years later, the department still open, he went back home to run a medical college. He was succeeded by Donald Hodel, a former public power administrator who had been head of an industry organization, the National Electric Reliability Council. By the time Hodel took over at Energy he had already earned the enmity of environmental groups as Watt's under secretary.

To run the other agency marked for extinction, Education, Reagan settled on a leader of the educational bureaucracy in Utah, T. H. Bell, who had also been the U.S. commissioner of education under Nixon and Ford. Bell agreed in advance to support whatever Reagan's policy turned out to be on the future of the department.

The Cabinet-level position of U.S. representative to the United Nations went to a hawkish Democrat, Jeane J. Kirkpatrick, who is liberal on domestic issues. A graduate of Barnard who received her doctorate from Columbia, she was a political science professor at Georgetown University and a resident scholar at the conservative American Enterprise Institute. Kirkpatrick argues the thesis that while totalitarian Communist states have never evolved into democracies, authoritarian right-wing states have, and on this foundation she upholds U.S. alliances with right-wing dictatorships.

Just below Cabinet rank there stood a young official whose work was to be more important than that of any of perhaps half the members of the Cabinet. David Stockman had been an antiwar activist during the Vietnam era. A history major at Michigan State, he was chairman of a group that advocated the recognition of the National Liberation Front. He and thirty-two other young men signed an ad paid for by Students for a Democratic Society in which they said they would refuse to be drafted. The Michigan State Police kept an illegal file on an anti-war group, "Vietnam Summer," of which young Stockman was the only paid staff member. But advancing in his career as a congressional aide, Stockman was struck either by ambition or the light and became a conservative, as which he was elected to Congress in 1976. Playing the part of President Carter during Reagan's rehearsals for the 1980 TV debate, Stockman was so convincing, he told the *New York Times,* "They even began to doubt my loyalty." This was the young man, still only in his mid-thirties, whom Reagan selected to do the real dirty work, the cutting and slashing of the domestic budget as the director of the Office of Management and Budget.

Another sub-cabinet appointment of importance went to Anne Burford (then named Gorsuch), a Colorado-educated lawyer and former state legislator who had a reputation for opposing stiff controls over hazardous wastes. She had also been a lawyer for Mountain Bell Telephone. She became the director of the Environmental Protection Agency (EPA), but after a scandalous uproar was replaced by EPA's original director, William Ruckelshaus. (For this saga see Chapter 4.)

To the consternation of the far right, Reagan's chief of staff is a George Bush man, James A. Baker III. Grandson of the founder of the large Houston law firm, Baker, Botts, a Marine, and now himself a millionaire lawyer, Baker was the campaign manager in Houston when Bush ran for the Senate (but lost) in 1970. Then Baker became a Commerce Department official under Ford and in 1976 Ford's delegate hunter for the Republican national convention. A former Democrat, Baker ran for state office in Texas as a Republican in 1978 and lost with 46 percent of the vote. In 1980 he managed Bush's campaign against Reagan. With this background Baker naturally attracted the suspicions of right-wingers, especially when he went public for military spending cuts that his boss later ruled against.

Ed Meese, a law-and-order conservative, is the most ideological of the top staff trio of Baker, Meese, and Mike Deaver. Meese prosecuted some students who occupied Sproul Hall at Berkeley during the free speech movement, and he helped organize plans to control demonstrations. A Yale graduate, he was a deputy district attorney when Reagan brought him into the government in California. His position on the presidential staff is counselor to the President with Cabinet rank; his special purview is domestic policy. He was supposed to have lost his preeminence to Baker, but he and Reagan are close in their views and his daily influence depends on Reagan.

The third man in the staff triumvirate, the President's trusted aide Deaver, also came to Washington in Reagan's California group. He occupies the office next to the President's and controls appointments. He and Peter Hannaford, with whom he had formed a public relations firm, were Reagan's managers in the 1970s, marketing his columns and radio broadcasts. Reagan has not carried money for ten years, and it's Deaver who has seen to paying the bills.

Deaver has said that the fourth most powerful staffer in the White House is presidential assistant Richard Darman, a Harvard-educated business graduate who has generally been associated in government with Eliot Richardson, the moderate Republican. Darman selects Reagan's night reading, and he has been an important ally of Baker and Stockman in trying to change the President's mind about the budgetary realities.

Reagan's first national security adviser, Richard Allen, was a government in-and-outer who had a history of questionable deals when Reagan appointed him his top policy adviser for the 1980 campaign. Five days before the election, a story by Jonathan Kwitny in the *Wall Street Journal* charged that Allen had used his connections in the Nixon administration to advance his own financial interests. Denying any improprieties, Allen left the campaign. A week later—two days after the election—Reagan said the charges were not substantial and made Allen the top man on national security in the White House. Then came an unpleasant and seemingly interminable uproar about $1,000 which Allen had accepted and put in a safe (forgetting about it there, he said)—a gift allegedly intended for Nancy Reagan in appreciation of her having agreed to give an interview to a Japanese magazine. Because of this mess, Allen finally left the President's staff for good. A year later he turned up with a $300,000-a-year contract to lobby for Japanese companies that want to persuade the U.S. government to let them build a new Panama canal.

Reagan had made a right-wing crony of his, William P. Clark, a deputy secretary of state. An attorney, Clark had been Reagan's cabinet secretary and chief of staff in Sacramento, and then Reagan had put him on the state supreme court. To succeed Allen as his national security adviser, President Reagan now brought Clark over from State. Clark's lofty new role and his friendship with and direct access to Reagan placed him at once within the small circle of the four or five most powerful men on the White House staff, giving Meese a formidable new ally against the moderates Baker and Darman.[4]

Except for Watt and Bell, all of the members of Reagan's original Cabinet are millionaires or approaching that status. Little wonder, then, that officials in Reagan's White House and Justice Department have indicated they may (possibly in the first year of his second term) seek repeal of the law requiring top federal officials to disclose their finances. The reports filed by the members of Reagan's original Cabinet showed approximate net assets for Weinberger of between $2.2 million and $3.5 million; Haig, $0.7–$2.1 million; Smith and his wife, $2.9–$5.8 million; Baldridge and his wife, $1.2–$1.7 million; Pierce, $1 to $2 million; Donovan and his immediate family, $1.5–$2.3 million; Casey, $3.3–$5.6 million; Brock and his immediate family, $4.8–$9.2 million. The Reagans reported assets of $1.2–$2.4 million and liabilities of $0.6–$1.1 million. Edwards had a total net worth of about $1 million. The wife and children of multimillionaire Lewis were beneficiaries of trusts worth almost $5 million. Block showed assets of $3.3–$4.1 million against liabilities with business associates of $5.1–$6.7 million. Schweiker and his immediate family showed combined worth of more than $690,000. (None of the top White House staffers had wealth in these ranges except Baker, who estimated the value of his immediate family's assets, including those of his mother, at about $7 million, including extensive oil stock holdings.) In 1980 Reagan was paid $954,986 by Merrill Lynch, Baldridge $369,000 by Scovill. The firms of the three practicing lawyers, Pierce, Smith, and Casey, paid them $280,000, $325,000, and $100,000, respectively, in 1980. Haig received $415,519 from United Technologies in 1980 and a bonus of $390,000 payable in 1981. United Technologies makes the engines for AWACs aircraft, the sale of which to Saudi Arabia provoked national controversy in 1981. That year the total income received by Secretary of State Haig from United Technologies, including his profit from a stock option which he exercised, was at least $895,000.

Assets went into blind trusts when government service began in most cases; a New York investment official is the trustee of the Reagans' trust. But Weinberger did not form a blind trust, and Casey defiantly retained control of his stocks, which meant that he was running the CIA around the world and tucking away in his mind valuable top-secret information while he was also personally controlling his stocks in such companies as Dome Petroleum, Kerr McGee, Superior Oil, and Schlumberger, Ltd., the international oil-servicing firm.[5]

Never before has one American corporation been as publicly and dramatically identified with a national administration as Bechtel is with Reagan's. For comparison one may think of Lyndon Johnson's career-long liaison with Brown & Root of Houston, another construction company, which became worldwide economically as Johnson became worldwide politically. But President Johnson did not make Brown & Root executives his secretaries of defense and state, as President Reagan has Bechtel men. Moreover, Reagan placed at the pinnacle of operational federal policy on nuclear power, as deputy secretary of energy, Bechtel Power Corporation's vice president for nuclear development, W. Kenneth Davis. Before going to Bechtel, Davis had been head of reactor development at the Atomic Energy Commission. By putting him over U.S. policy on nuclear power the President specifically correlated a major Bechtel specialization, nuclear power, with federal policymaking, leaving the two separated only by the invisible electrical field that cuts off, or does not cut off, public from private interests. Davis, who reported assets worth at least $4.5 million, sold his Bechtel stock (worth more than $750,000) upon taking office (which he left in 1983).

A secretive, privately held company, Bechtel historically has been closely and profitably allied with John McCone, who in his time became a director of the CIA, and at the outset of the Reagan administration had Richard Helms, another former CIA director, on retainer, but denies that it has a CIA connection.

In 1981, when Shultz was still Bechtel's president, the company bought controlling interest in Dillon Read & Company, the Wall Street investment firm, whose managing director remarked to the *Wall Street Journal* on the occasion of the transaction, "the private handling of private matters by private people makes sense." The *Journal* then quoted a San Francisco source about Bechtel itself, "They're a very, very private and silent company."

Even so, much is known and the facts raise questions. The day before the Pentagon awarded a Bechtel unit a $19 million contract for development work on a basing mode for the MX missile, Weinberger felt it necessary to sign a memorandum disqualifying himself from "any official acts involving the interests" of Bechtel. Reagan has been championing nuclear power for years; Bechtel built nearly 40 percent of the nuclear power plants in the United States. In 1979 about half of all its business was derived from nuclear power activity, and it is actively helping to build new plants all over the world. As will be seen, the Reagan administration has a dubious record in combating nuclear proliferation; Bechtel has profited from involvement with the nuclear breeder reactor (which produces plutonium that can be recycled into nuclear weapons) and profits from the spread of nuclear power plants abroad. The secretaries of state and defense must be evenhanded in dealing with the Israelis and the Arabs in the Middle East; Bechtel is involved in many important construction projects in the Arab states. For instance, Bechtel is building in Saudi Arabia, at a cost which may reach an almost unbelievable $135 billion, the new city of Jubail on the Persian Gulf, which will have refineries, a steel mill, petrochemical plants, and a population as large as that of Minneapolis. The administration fought hard and successfully for the AWACs sale to Saudi Arabia; Bechtel (as well as United Technologies) openly lobbied for it. Reagan's envoy to the Middle East, Philip C. Habib, was suddenly revealed, in mid-1982, to have been on Bechtel's payroll as a consultant at the same time that he was conducting, on behalf of the United States, delicate negotiations in the volatile Lebanese crisis. Senator Larry Pressler (R.–S. Dak.) called for his resignation, but a White House spokesman said that "any implication of any conflict is absurd."

As in every question of conflict of interest, the Bechtel problem in the Reagan administration is not dissolved by recourse to the undoubtedly high characters of the persons involved. The concern is whether high officials find themselves serving, or trying to avoid appearing to serve, two masters. In the case of Bechtel the predicament is hardly limited to a few realms of domestic and foreign policy. Bechtel is building or helping to build (among much else) an airport in Saudi Arabia, an offshore oil production platform in the North Sea, a coal-fueled power project in Utah, a hydropower complex in Quebec, an oil refinery in Indonesia, a $500 million tourist resort in Malaysia, a copper and gold mine in Papua, New Guinea, and a $250 million palace for the Sultan of Brunei.[6]

Thus the barriers against conflicts of interest have dropped perilously low in Reagan's Washington. The enterprising daily newspapers, especially the *Washington Post* and the *New York Times,* have turned up other cases of such conflicts in various forms. Perhaps the first question is: by their own example what kind of conduct do the Reagans encourage? The answer: not fastidious.

In Sacramento the Reagans (Mrs. Reagan especially) regarded the official Governor's Mansion as a firetrap, so they moved into a private mansion, for which they paid rent of $15,000 a year. In his 1969 book on Reagan, Lou Cannon reported that a GOP financier, Lee Kaiser, sent letters to the lobbyists in Sacramento asking each of them for a $1,000 gift toward a fund to build a $500,000 private mansion for the governor. When this came out, Reagan passed it off by jesting, "You never look a gift house in the mouth." Kaiser's initiative having foundered, a group of seventeen businessmen bought the mansion the Reagans were renting and leased it back to them for the same rent they had been paying. The furnishings, Mrs. Reagan has written, were "donated," and accepted on behalf of the state. In the White House, Mrs. Reagan raised at least $822,000 in "private donations" for redecorations. In both instances the Reagans were accepting contributions mostly from rich people to pay for public property which enhanced their personal comfort. The expenses of a 60-member orchestra which performed on the South Lawn of the White House in honor of Indian Prime Minister Indira Gandhi were paid by Citibank. Mrs. Reagan accepted on behalf of the United States, from a Fifth Avenue diamond merchant, a diamond necklace and diamond earrings worth several hundred thousand dollars. Ultimately she returned them because of a feeling, an official said, that "there shouldn't be state jewels." She also accepted as personal gifts a dozen expensive designer outfits, which she gave to museums after wearing them; she discontinued the practice when she was criticized for it. Reagan's 1976 financial statement mentioned a "gift exceeding $1,000" he had received from his rich friend, retail tycoon Justin Dart (whom he appointed a director of the Communications Satellite Corp. in 1982); in accordance with law Reagan reported that in 1981 he and his wife accepted personal gifts in 1981 valued at more than $31,000, including a sculpture of an American eagle, valued at $2,500, that had been given by Henry Salvatori, one of the three millionaires who first pushed Reagan forward in 1965. (Vice President George Bush and his wife recorded, as required by law, that in 1981 they accepted more than $17,000 worth of gifts.) The press reported that Dennis E. LeBlanc, who was a security man for Reagan in Sacramento and worked for him on his ranch, is paid $58,500 as a telecommunications bureaucrat in the Commerce Department, but frequently spends his official time chopping wood and doing other ranch-hand's chores at Rancho del Cielo.[7]

Eleven days before taking office, Attorney General Smith had accepted a $50,000 severance payment from the Jorgensen steel company, of which he was a director; he returned the money when the payment was challenged by the Office of Government Ethics. He also had invested in a $3 for $1 tax shelter; questioned, he backed away from it. The Justice Department, of which he is the head, and the President, who is his friend, cleared him of any improprieties in these two matters.

According to *Common Cause* magazine, Thomas Reed, a special assistant to the President who was on William Clark's staff, received highly unusual treatment from the Securities and Exchange Commission (SEC). A veteran of Reagan's California staff, Reed had helped organize a political action committee which had spent $1.27 million for Reagan's election in 1980. In 1981 the SEC charged that Reed had engaged in prohibited insider trading that had turned his $3,000 investment in call options into $427,000 in 48 hours. He denied any insider trading. *Common Cause* said his file showed that he had backdated brokerage forms and signed other people's names to them, yet in the settlement of the charges the SEC had allowed him to maintain his innocence while requiring him to put the $427,000 in escrow. Despite this case, Clark had brought him onto the White House staff to work on strategic weapons policy. Faced with a widening scandal over the matter—including the announcement by a U.S. attorney of an inquiry to see whether criminal charges should be brought—Reed left the government.

Before becoming Reagan's secretary of the navy, John F. Lehman was president of a consulting company whose clients included defense contractors Northrup, Boeing, and TRW. A British peer to whom Lehman sold the rights to use the name of his consulting business overseas told the *New York Times* that Lehman had kept an option to get back the overseas business when he left the government. At first Lehman did not deny to the *Times* that there was any such agreement or understanding, but after the story appeared he did deny it. Lehman sits on a board that controls all Pentagon weapons projects.

Perhaps the most pervasive problem in Reagan's government is the pattern of assigning people to government jobs to regulate or supervise official relationships with the industries they have just left. Here are some examples cited in Arthur E. Rowse's book, *One Sweet Guy.* An attorney for broadcasting companies, Mark S. Fowler, heads the Federal Communications Commission. The vice chairman of E. F. Hutton, John S. R. Shad, heads the Securities and Exchange Commission. The former president of Piper Aircraft, J. Lynn Helms, heads the Federal Aviation Administration. A former lobbyist for the National Cattleman's Association, C. W. McMillan, is put in charge of meat labeling and other regulations enforced by the Department of Agriculture. The chief legal adviser to the Chicago Board of Trade, Philip Johnson, headed the government agency that regulates futures trading (but has now resigned).

Nowhere is this pattern more pronounced than in posts that are concerned with protection of the environment. The nominations of Watt and Burford to the two uppermost such positions set the pattern. John B. Crowell, Jr., who runs the Forest Service, was general counsel to the timber company, Louisiana-Pacific. Rita Lavelle, EPA's assistant administrator for solid waste and emergency response, whom Reagan eventually fired, had come to the government from the Aerojet-General Corporation of California, which was accused of causing problems of toxic waste disposal. EPA's chief of staff, John E. Daniel, formerly lobbied for Johns-Mansville Corporation and the American Paper Institute.

Andy Pasztor reported in the *Wall Street Journal* that Reagan's choice to be the director of Interior's office of surface mining, which enforces strip-mining laws, had recently bought nearly 1,500 acres of valuable land at bargain prices from two of the nation's largest coal producers and had an option to buy another 1,030 acres from one of the companies at similarly low prices.

Upon Reagan's election to the presidency, a North Carolina apparel manufacturer, G. Erwin Dixon, was quoted as saying, "We've finally got a man who thinks like a businessman."[8] He was right. Deliberately and thoroughly, Reagan and his business advisers put into place a new team of public officials who think like businessmen or will please those who do.

3

The War on Social Security

The man in the White House is a dedicated foe of Social Security. He regards it as welfare, which he detests. In 1964 he agreed with Goldwater that Social Security should be made voluntary. In 1975 Reagan in effect proposed to abolish the whole system, and in 1978 he declared that Social Security "is in effect, bankrupt." From the White House he has led a war on the Social Security system.

Despite his statements in his 1980 campaign that he would save and strengthen Social Security, four months into his presidency he formally proposed to the Congress, through his secretary of health and human services, to decimate the system and decimate it again, cutting it 22 percent over the long run.

An alarmed Congress gave him some cuts, but foiled him on the basic proposal, which he then abandoned. In 1982 he returned to the offensive by endorsing a plan of Senate Republicans to cut Social Security $40 billion in the next three years. That couldn't pass, either, so the senators dropped it.

The Social Security system was not in danger of bankruptcy. Its short-term cash-flow problem, caused by wages not having kept up with prices, was about 4 percent short of the money required to keep the checks going out, according to Wilbur J. Cohen, one of the architects of the original system. By Reagan's outcries that the system was in danger of bankruptcy, he and his agents did profound damage: polls showed that people were afraid that they would not get their benefits when their turn came. Having proved that he could make shreds of welfare programs, Reagan also sought to limit Social Security benefits only to the poor, which would put the system in the same vulnerable political position as food stamps and Aid to Families with Dependent Children.

Going into the 1982 elections, Reagan strenuously denied that he had proposed the Social Security cuts he had proposed. One had to wonder if the mass-media techniques of big-money American politics have handed Presidents electronic erasers that are almost as effective as state control of the media for the instantaneous obliteration of the immediate past in the memories of the people. In 1983 Congress, yielding to Reagan's demands for more cuts, unnecessarily damaged the interests of working people and beneficiaries as it revised the system, and in the White House Reagan told his men that in his next battle he will go all-out to make the system voluntary—that is, to abolish it.

Social Security is the most successful and widely valued program of the New Deal. Today more than 30 million older or disabled Americans receive benefits from the system, and another 100 million workers are expecting benefits when they retire. Workers and the self-employed have to pay in a percentage of their earnings, and in return, if they are disabled or when they retire they receive benefits set by the Congress. Employers must match their workers' pay-in. There is nothing radical about Social Security; it was one of the devices with which the New Deal saved American capitalism.

There is a general attitude that people earn their Social Security benefits. The government's contract with working people is also, as John Myles specifies, "an intergenerational transfer system in which the working population supports the retired population." According to a Harris poll in mid-1981, three-fourths of the elderly knew that when they made their contributions, the money was used immediately to meet current obligations—only 9 percent thought their payments had been earmarked for their own personal retirement.[1] People who would object to receiving welfare as charity receive their Social Security benefits as their earned retirement. For instance, my father worked every weekday of his life that he wasn't sick (and many Saturday mornings) running the office of his company, which then retired him with no pension. My mother worked forty years in retail trade, but received no pension. Although my father was a conservative Democrat, my parents relied on their Social Security and their savings with perfect equanimity. Such equanimity has now been upset by Reagan's campaign against Social Security.

Despite a blizzard of obfuscation, the issue is still the same one that led to the establishment of the system in the first place: Shall society provide older citizens with an assured minimum income when they retire in return for required contributions during their earning years? Shall the old be guaranteed that, after working during their best years, they shall not be abandoned by society in their last years? And shall working adults be relatively free of the crushing costs of supporting their aging parents?

Reagan's original interest in making Social Security voluntary came from his friend Representative Rousselot, the former member of the Birch Society. In one of Reagan's basic speeches in the early sixties he said, "In a proposal to make Social Security voluntary, Congressman Rousselot had pointed out that the young man twenty or twenty-one . . . must, with his employer, contribute at least $1.69 for every dollar he'll receive in benefits."

In that period Reagan often returned to Rousselot's theme. In San Antonio, speaking of Social Security, Reagan said, "You and I are unfunded in this program . . . and who pays for this—our sons." Two decades ago he was voicing the same kind of alarmism about the bankruptcy of the system that became a kind of scandal in the first year of his presidency. "One generation of senior citizens in the near future," he said in 1962, "is going to approach the cupboard and find that it's bare."

Established and controlled by the people's elected representatives in Congress, Social Security is not a conventional private insurance system, it is a retirement compact between workers and the government. It has been one of the themes of the right-wing critics that Social Security must be placed on the same "sound actuarial basis" that is characteristic of the private insurance companies which, seen as a system, have failed to provide more than 50 percent of the people with private occupational retirement insurance. In 1978 Social Security paid the elderly almost five times as much income as private pensions did; some of the company plans are seriously underfunded. The private system's actuarial standards are then to be the model for the public system? Yet this argument was present in Reagan's mind in 1962 as he advocated, in his own voice, that participation in the Social Security system should be made "more voluntary."

"Is it being an extremist," he asked, "to suggest that the program be reorganized and put on a sound actuarial basis? . . . I think the system could be more voluntary. If a citizen wants to contribute more of his own earnings, he should be able to and know that he has increased the benefits he is going to get."

In Amarillo, Texas, in this same period, Reagan said: "The flagship of the liberal cause is Social Security. It is offered as the proven vehicle for the medical insurance program. . . . I am not against the basic principles of Social Security . . . there should be provisions made for the old age of citizens who cannot provide for themselves."

It is the basic principle of the Social Security system that it is not limited to the elderly poor, but includes everyone. Knowingly or unknowingly, Reagan misrepresented that principle to express his own, that Social Security should be limited to welfare for the poor.

Reciting testimony he said officials of Social Security had given in a court case, Reagan stated: "They said Social Security wasn't actually insurance—but they used that term to sell it to the people. Social Security dues are a tax for the general use of the government and payment of that tax does not automatically entitle anyone to the receipt of the benefits. The benefits are a welfare program which can be canceled or curtailed by Congress at any time."

Reagan was referring to a 1960 Supreme Court case, *Fleming v. Nestor,* in which it was held that Social Security is not a legal contract since Congress retained the right to amend or repeal the law establishing it. "So when Reagan says the benefits can be curtailed at any time, that is technically correct," according to Wilbur Cohen (who was Johnson's Secretary of Health, Education, and Welfare). On the other hand, Title 2 of the Social Security Act "does give the person the automatic entitlement to it and you can go to court and sue for the benefit due you as long as the law has not been repealed," Cohen continued. As technical adviser to the chairman of the Social Security Board in the thirties, Cohen said, "I was the one who said let's undermine the attack on welfare by having the Congress call it insurance," and the Congress did this in the Federal Insurance Contributions Act—"That's what FICA means."

In his famous television speech for Goldwater, Reagan said that Social Security "is not insurance but a welfare program and Social Security dues are a tax for the general use of government," and he asked, "can't we introduce voluntary features that would permit a citizen to do better on his own?"

Johnson's triumph over Goldwater taught Reagan something about the people and Social Security. In 1968, waiting on a runway for a private plane that was being repaired, Reagan was idling away some time with reporters by making various suggestions for changing Social Security. One of them asked him if he planned to discuss these ideas in future campaigns. Reagan looked at him incredulously and said, "You can't run against Social Security. Barry proved that."[2]

Despite this knowledge, eight years ago, in a series of three radio broadcasts that received no news coverage that has come to my attention, Reagan harshly attacked Social Security and advanced as "a better solution" the conversion of the entire system into a mixture of private pension funds and government retirement bonds.

"There was a basic flaw in the design of Social Security," he said in these 1975 broadcasts. "Congress decided to let a government agency collect the workers' contributions, pay out the retirement benefits, and manage the trust fund."

In Reagan's ideology the participation of the government was the mistake. In consequence of this "fatal flaw," he continued, contributions became taxes, which had gone much higher. "Tomorrow," he said, "I'll tell you how Social Security reduces your chances of ever being able to enjoy a comfortable retirement income."

On the second day he said the federal workers who have kept themselves out of the Social Security system had been "betting our money on a sure loser, at no risk to themselves." (Social Security was now "a sure loser.") Reagan then began quoting "a noted Harvard economist," whom he did not name but who was Martin Feldstein, now the powerful chairman of his Council of Economic Advisers.

"He found," Reagan said, "that Social Security has cut private savings by 38 percent, reducing the ability of our people to invest in and reap the rewards of national growth. He found that the lost savings are reflected in an annual reduction in the gross national product of $120 billion, a loss of almost $600 for every man, woman, and child. If there were no Social Security, he found, wages would be 15 percent higher and interest would be 28 percent lower."

In 1974 Feldstein had completed a study that concluded Social Security had reduced personal saving by 50 percent. Six years later, however, two economists with the Social Security Administration discovered that the computer program for the study had mistakenly repeated a calculation over and over, producing a result that greatly overestimated the value that consumers place on Social Security. The two economists challenging Feldstein said their work showed that on balance Social Security had "no effect" on savings. Feldstein replied tortuously that when the error was corrected and 1972 benefit increases, which had changed the situation, were taken account of, his original conclusion was sustained. Other economists disagreed. "It is simply not true that saving, however measured, has tended to drop off as Social Security has grown in importance," according to

Henry Aaron, an economist at the Brookings Institution, whose data show that total savings since World War II have been virtually constant at 16 percent of the gross national product. Feldstein's former student Alicia Munnell, a vice president of the Federal Reserve Bank in Boston, said there is "no evidence" to support Feldstein's contention.

After citing Feldstein's work in his 1975 broadcast, Reagan then said in his own name: "The apologists for Social Security claim that these drawbacks are insignificant compared to what the program does for 'the little guy.' That's a cruel joke. Let me tell you what Social Security does, not for, but *to* the little guy and his family." The emphasis is in Reagan's original.

"The biggest losers in the present Social Security scheme," he went on, "are middle- and low-income workers and their families. Their money makes up virtually all of that 38 percent loss in personal savings. What little money they could be putting aside . . . is taken up by Social Security taxes. And all they get . . . is a government promise that, if there's any money left in the trust fund when they retire, they might get enough of a handout to scrape by on. . . .

"There's a better solution: one that will preserve the retirement income of retired workers, now and in the future. Tomorrow I'll tell you about it."

On day three, Reagan proposed in effect to kill off the Social Security system. The first step in the scheme he advanced as "a better solution" was the abolition of both employer and employee contributions into the system. With no income there could be no Social Security system.

"Social Security can be reformed," he said, "by simply restoring government to its proper role as the protector of individual choice.

"Here's one proposal, published recently, which demonstrates what I mean. It starts by removing the monopoly over basic retirement funds now exercised by the Social Security Administration. Social Security taxes would be eliminated, and both the employees' and the employers' shares added to the workers' wages.

"Each worker would then choose between investing in a gov-

ernment-insured private pension plan or a new series of U.S.
Retirement Bonds with annuity payoff. . . . The bonds would
be convertible . . . into private pension funds at the option of
the worker. Thus, the government and the private pension plans
would compete. . . .

"With these reforms," Reagan concluded, "the traditional
American principles of preventing monopoly and expanding
individual choice would slowly but surely work the program out
of its present debt."

Closing, Reagan suggested his listeners urge Congress to give
the proposal "serious consideration."[3] But having called that
proposal "a better solution" and then saying it would achieve the
corrections he desired, Reagan here advocated, in the stead of
the abolished Social Security system, a new annuity system—
whether voluntary or mandatory he did not say—based on government bonds and government-insured private insurance.

The payroll tax under the present system is highly regressive
(that is, costs proportionally more the less you have), but the
benefits are progressive (that is, are skewed in favor of lower-
wage families). Reagan did not mention any progressive factor
in the benefits under his proposed alternative, and from everything else that is known about his and Feldstein's views, one can
presume that they would want none.

In 1976, running for President, Reagan hinted that he favored some interruption in Social Security payments down the
road (what he said was that he would permit no interruption for
those already getting benefits or planning to retire "in the next
decade or so"). He suggested Social Security funds might be
invested in the stock market or industrial bonds. President Ford,
his fellow Republican, jumped him for that and for suggesting
or advocating that the system be made voluntary. In a booming
warning shot, Ford said Reagan had "favorably called attention
to a voluntary plan that would ruin" Social Security.

Listening with innocent ears to Reagan's 1980 promises on
the subject (and most voters, not having been told the full background, did have innocent ears), one could conclude that he had
become Social Security's champion and protector. He promised
to reform Social Security and not to make it voluntary. "No

changes should be made to make the . . . system voluntary," said his campaign handout. The GOP platform promised to "first save and then strengthen" Social Security.

Reagan seemed to promise no cutbacks. "The strategy for growth," he said, "does not require altering or taking back necessary entitlements already granted to the American people." In June he said benefits would not be lowered for people who had worked hard all their lives: ". . . we will make certain," he said, "that no senior citizen will ever miss a Social Security payment." Furthermore, "I will make sure," he said, "that benefits are adjusted to reflect the cost of living."

Most people, listening to him on their televisions, had to think he was saying he would not cut their retirement benefits, but Reagan's words had been carefully woven into a garment designed to deceive. In his vow not to alter or take back entitlements there was the word "necessary," concealing his radical opinion that Social Security should be limited to the poor, and there were the words "already granted," barely suggesting—and only to the well-informed—that if you are not already receiving benefits your future benefits can be cut. His promise that no senior citizen will ever miss a Social Security payment did not promise that the payments would not be *reduced*. His promise to index benefits (breached by his subsequent proposals to delay the effect of such indexing) concealed his meaning that he wanted to index *reduced* benefits.

Once in 1980 he did suggest, but only obliquely, that he might want some cuts. "Let's take the disability program under Social Security, for instance," he said. "Son of Sam, the murderer, is getting $300 a month because he is too mentally incapacitated to hold a job." Most voters hearing that probably thought he just wanted to cut off the mass murderer's benefits. Surely he would not treat them like Son of Sam; certainly people did not conclude that when elected he would immediately ask Congress to slash the entire Social Security disability benefits program by one-third, which he did.

The calculatedness of all this deception was apparent in the assertion of a campaign staff spokesman to me just before the election that Reagan had repeatedly said no changes should be

made in the system "at present." The 1980 campaign tended to
focus on such questions as whether Reagan's proposal to remove
the earnings limitation for beneficiaries would cost as much as $7
billion, and 55 percent of Americans sixty-five or older voted for
him. But even as they were deciding to do so, behind the closed
doors of the Reaganists' policy meetings plans were being made
that were directly contrary to what their candidate seemed to be
saying to the people. Brooks Jackson of the *Wall Street Journal*
found the candidate's planners huddled together considering
raising the age at which benefits begin and saying that the consumer price index might be revised to produce lower inflation
figures and, therefore, lower benefit increases.[4]

The Reaganists abandoned the President's soothing rhetoric
as they moved into Washington. "Social Security—Don't Count
On It," warned a headline in the business magazine *Forbes*. A
member of Reagan's task force publicized his estimate of a
"long-run" deficit of $1 trillion in the main trust fund, advocated
raising the retirement age to sixty-eight (that is, sharply cutting
benefits), and then lamented, "Young workers today wonder
whether they will receive retirement benefits."

In his first economic message as President, Reagan promised
that "the social safety net" would continue to protect "the full
retirement benefits of the more than 31 million Social Security
recipients . . . along with an annual cost of living increase."
Why just 31 million? He quickly proposed to eliminate the minimum Social Security benefit, which averaged $150 a month for
three million people, and Congress obligingly abolished it. He
also proposed cutting off all benefits for college-age students
who are children of retired workers and cutting by 25 percent
the benefits then being paid to 772,000 such students (an average $228 a month for help on tuition and living expenses). Con-
gress gave him that, too, and further obliged him by cutting off
death benefits where there is neither a spouse nor a minor child
to receive them. Merely by "round[ing] benefits to next lower
dime at each intermediate step and to next lower dollar at final
step," in the words of one committee report, the "savers" of
Social Security reduced benefits by $1.5 billion in five years.
Representative Jake Pickle of Texas, chairman of the House

subcommittee on Social Security, whose staffers are specialists on the subject, said the 1981 budget ultimately cut $4 billion from Social Security in 1982 and $90 billion by 1990.[5]

On May 12, 1981, Reagan had HHS Secretary Schweiker ask Congress for deep and immediate cuts in basic Social Security benefits. (Reagan "believed it was the right thing to do," budget director Stockman told William Greider, who reported the remark in the *Atlantic*. Chief of staff Baker later said Reagan deserved an "A+" for political courage in making the proposal.) For the 18 million Americans who would reach retirement age in the ensuing five years, Reagan asked Congress to cut the permanent, basic Social Security benefits by one-eighth. Under Reagan's plan (as Pickle's staffer Janice Gregory explained), after 1987 the new lower basis of benefits would be frozen at 88 percent of present levels and would never be restored. Reagan wanted to sharply penalize workers for retiring before sixty-five by cutting their scheduled benefits (at sixty-two, for instance, from 80 percent of full benefits down to 55 percent). And he proposed then to terminate one-third of the insurance program for disabled workers by harshly changing the rules of eligibility.

Speaking of all Social Security except medicare (speaking, that is, of "OASDI"), the Library of Congress Congressional Research Service calculated that "the administration's package would reduce the overall cost of the OASDI program in the long run by 22 percent." In one pass, in the first of his four years, Reagan was proposing to lop off more than one-fifth of the entire Social Security retirement and disability programs. "It's an attempt," said Robert M. Ball, Social Security commissioner from 1962 to 1973, "to shrink the Social Security rolls by a quarter and to reduce people's rights to Social Security by about 25 percent."

Each year about a million and a half workers begin receiving retirement benefits, and 70 percent of them choose reduced early-retirement payment schedules. This is what they want to do, and their early retirement reduces unemployment by reducing the size of the workforce. Under the Reagan proposal benefits would be one-third lower for workers retiring at sixty-two—

an average earner retiring in 1987 at sixty-two would get $232 a month instead of $348.

These cuts were to become effective immediately in 1982. An average-earning sixty-one-year-old man in 1981, banking and planning on retiring the next year, would have had his benefits cut from $248 to $164 a month—with no time to try to make up the difference from somewhere.

"My wife and I have been paying into Social Security since 1937, for forty-four years," Mr. and Mrs. William Borg of Fort Worth wrote Representative Martin Frost (D.–Tex.). "Now that we are sixty-one and considering retirement, they want to change the rules, make us wait until we are sixty-five, then possibly in the interim, change the rules again to sixty-eight. . . . We feel as if the government had betrayed us. It is having a devastating effect on us, our lifelong dreams are shattered."

Reagan's disability cuts were to be brought about mostly by two changes. To get benefits, a worker has to have worked five of the ten years before his disability; Reagan wanted that increased to seven and a half of the ten years. And he wanted to limit the basis for disability benefits to medical factors only, disallowing experience, skills, and age. About one in four workers' awards has been based on the vocational considerations Reagan wanted to strike out. In the dry language of the Congressional Research Service, "The person's age, experience, and skills would no longer be considered in determining if, in conjunction with the impairment, he or she can no longer work." What this means to real people (as a later example will show) is that if, say, a construction worker loses his leg on the job but can still work as, say, a parking lot attendant, he is not entitled to disability benefits.

Reagan's "savings" were so much in excess of any reasonably predictable need for funds in the system, they would have created surpluses. Schweiker therefore proposed to cut the tax rate, too. Far from "strengthening" the system by raising the tax rate or putting in new funds if necessary, Reagan was proposing to cut benefits so deeply the payroll tax could be cut.

Listening to Schweiker on May 12, one would have thought Reagan was a dedicated reformer. "I am today announcing Social Security reform proposals," Schweiker said, "which will keep the system from going broke, protect the basic benefit structure, and reduce the tax burden on American workers." The proposals would stop discouraging "senior citizens from remaining in the workforce." They would "turn the system away from bankruptcy." They would "reduce the welfare-oriented elements" in Social Security. They would "end this inequity" of college benefits for children of early retirees.

Yet Chairman Pickle (who was so worried about the damage being caused by the attacks on Social Security that the Democratic leaders of the House had to slap him down on his "bipartisan" bill to reduce benefits almost as much as Reagan wanted) announced that Reagan's cuts in the budget combined with the May 12 proposals came to total cuts of $280 billion by 1990. This from the candidate who had promised the voters six months earlier to "strengthen and protect" the system.

A mere two months after he proposed his devastating cuts in 1981, Reagan on national television promised current beneficiaries they would receive their benefits "in full." In the pose of the champion of the elderly, he said, "I will not stand by and see those of you who are dependent on Social Security deprived of your benefits." The dishonesty of this posture was so conscious it was stupefying. Had honesty been the President's purpose he would have added, "And I will not stand by either and see those of you who will become dependent on Social Security next year get your full benefits. Two months ago I proposed to cut your retirement and disability benefits for the long term about 22 percent."[6]

Despite Reagan's beguiling assurances, the facts were the facts: the Republicans were attacking Social Security as welfare and on the lip of bankruptcy, and Reagan had proposed deep cuts. Many people became alarmed and frightened. Some became angry. Sen. Patrick Moynihan (D.–N.Y.) exclaimed: "They come in shouting, 'Crisis! Crisis! Bankrupt! Bankrupt!' " Moynihan accused the Reagan administration of actions that "terrorized older people into thinking that they won't get their Social Security." What had impelled even the moderate Moynihan to make such a fierce accusation?

The system was "teetering on the verge of bankruptcy," Pres-

ident Reagan had said nine days after he proposed to cut the
system by 22 percent. "Unless we . . . act, a sword of Damocles
will soon hang over the welfare of millions of our citizens." By
"act," of course, he meant cut benefits, not increase the system's
income.

It was "the stark, ominous, and unavoidable fact," said
budget director Stockman at a public hearing two weeks after
Schweiker's proposals, that unless Congress passed a bill Reagan
could sign in the next fifteen months, "the most devastating
bankruptcy in history will occur on or about November 3, 1982."

By law three of Reagan's Cabinet members, Schweiker, Regan, and Donovan, automatically serve now as the trustees of the
Social Security system. In July 1981 their report inspired press
stories that the retirement fund could "go broke" by 1982 and
the medicare program could "topple within the decade."
Reagan's first Social Security administrator, John A. Svahn, said
the main retirement fund would be "effectively bankrupt" by
Thanksgiving 1982.

In the Republican-controlled Senate, as the subcommittee on
Social Security opened its hearings that first summer of the
Reagan administration, an aide to the panel's chairman (Senator William Armstrong, R.–Colo.) told the *Wall Street Journal*
about a deliberate plan to fill the air with the word "crisis." "It
will be well orchestrated—lots of horror stories," the aide said.
"We've got to show just how close the system is to going bankrupt."

As former Social Security Commissioner William Driver has
indicated, "scare stories in the press" have been one cause of the
anxiety about the system. National reporters have written that
Social Security would "run out of cash" and its trust fund "will be
depleted" in a year or several. In May 1982, a *Time* cover de-
picted a Social Security card as a billboard peeling off in a storm,
and the story inside stated that the trust fund "will be nearly
empty by July 1, 1982" The *New York Times* stated in an editorial
late in 1982, "Social Security is broke."

But who created the confusion that led to these outcries of
alarm? Reagan and the Reaganists. It is a wonder of rhetoric that
on the record he had himself made, Reagan told the White

House Conference on Aging in December 1981 that on Social Security, "There has been political demagoguery and outright falsehood, and as a result many who rely on Social Security for their livelihood have been needlessly and cruelly frightened. Those that did that frightening either didn't know what they were talking about or they were deliberately lying"[7] That was quite true, but those who did the frightening were Reagan and his men.

In common sense, "bankruptcy" means kaput. A company ceases to do business. If you are broke, you have no money. The short-term problem for Social Security was the fact that for every $10 paid in benefits the system was collecting only about $9.50 in taxes. Mickey Levy, an associate of the conservative American Enterprise Institute, has pointed out that the system's trust funds—the ones the Reaganists keep saying were going bankrupt—are not trust funds in the ordinary sense, they are contingency funds for short-term shortages. "Even if the trust funds went completely dry," Levy told a reporter, "you'd still have payroll taxes coming in which would be enough to cover 95 percent of all benefits." A member of Reagan's preinaugural task force on Social Security, Colin D. Campbell, said, "The term bankruptcy is inappropriate." A. Haeworth Robinson, the chief actuary for Social Security from 1975 to 1978, said before the 1982 legislation passed, "The system is only spending $3 billion or $4 billion a year more than it is taking in, and it is taking in $150 billion a year, so we are talking about relatively small shortages." Social Security would not "run out of cash"; the trust fund, if misconceived as the system's bank, would not be "nearly empty." Even the conservative *U.S. News & World Report* stated in the summer of 1982, "there's no chance that monthly checks will be halted very long. At worst, checks might be delayed until enough is in the till to pay full benefits." The National Commission on Social Security Reform, the study group formed by Reagan to put off the issue until after the 1982 elections, agreed that the system needed, on fairly pessimistic assumptions about the economy, $150 to $200 billion in the next seven years.

Furthermore, these relatively small shortages were a short-run problem only. Beginning in 1990, as the ranks of contributors are swelled by the baby boom population, the funds will take in more than they pay out. Not until 2025—more than forty years hence—will that cohort of workers retire. This creates a problem for Congress about a generation from now, but Robert A. Beck, chairman of the Prudential Insurance Company of America, was quoted in June 1982: "I don't know of any reasonable study that didn't conclude that the system is basically sound." Even Feldstein, Reagan's mistaken tutor on Social Security in the mid-seventies, wrote in 1977 that as *long as the voters support the Social Security system it will be able to pay the benefits that it promises*" (emphasis in the original). Former Commissioner Ball said "there's no great big disaster hovering over this system" and contending that short-term problems have to be solved by long-term cuts is "absolutely nonsense and 100 percent poppycock." According to the National Commission, the system could be kept in balance for the next seventy-five years by adjustments totaling less than 2 percent of the nation's wages.[8]

There was no crisis; the whole outcry would have been ludicrous if these facts had been made clear. Instead of following the facts, Reagan deliberately created the panic. One is impelled to conclude that he is using his presidency to undermine Social Security with specious alarms and arguments that conceal his ideological purpose. He is against government, he is against welfare, and Social Security, being in his mind government welfare, has to go. He wants Social Security reduced to welfare so it can then be attacked as welfare. But he cannot say this—Goldwater's debacle taught him that—so he is hitting and running to return and hit again.

Reagan's "sword of Damocles" and Stockman's "most devastating bankruptcy in history . . . on or about Nov. 3, 1982" were child's play to avert—the Congress approved a simple fix, an interfund transfer inside the system. Instead of advocating this obvious and available step, the Reaganists had blown up the problem to justify cutting benefits a fifth.

To deal with predicted subsequent shortfalls in the contingency funds, many methods were available. House Ways and Means Chairman Dan Rostenkowski, Pickle, Democratic economist Charles L. Schultze, and others were open to putting in money from general revenue. Representative Millicent Fenwick

(R.–N.J.) suggested raising the payroll tax and making it deductible on the income tax. Scheduled increases in the payroll tax could come sooner. As both the *New York Times* and the *Washington Post* advocated, benefits could be taxed and the revenues dedicated to the system. If Congress was liberal (which it is not) the payroll tax, which is flat-rate and therefore falls heaviest on the poorest, could be graduated; or, as Representative Eugene Atkinson (D.–Pa.) proposed, the limit on covered wages could be lifted to $60,000 (it was $35,700 in 1983), putting the short-term burden on higher-paid workers. The 1.9 million federal employees and the members of Congress could be required to come into the system like everybody else.

The ease of making up the shortfall, given a will to do it, was dramatized by Wilbur Cohen. Speaking of Reagan's income tax cut of 10 percent a year, Cohen said, "I'd reduce the taxes only 9 percent and put the other 1 percent in Social Security." Reagan's elaborately camouflaged position was exposed in the statement of his commissioner, Svahn: "It's our policy that we not raise taxes and that we not use general revenues to bail out Social Security." Social Security was "bankrupt" only if Reagan and his men convinced Congress not to fund it. The most serious problem of the system was not financial, but political, and the source of that problem was Reagan in the White House.

In the fall of 1981 Reagan openly advanced his theme that Social Security should be only for the poor. He told the nation, "There is . . . a sizable percentage of recipients who are adequately provided for by pensions or other income *and should not be adding to the burden of Social Security.*" (Emphasis supplied.) AP-NBC polled citizens on the question, and 72 percent favored continued benefits on the basis of payroll contributions—just 24 percent agreed with Reagan that the benefits should be paid only on the basis of need.

Although Chairman Pickle was the man in the middle on all this, he would not stand still there for Reagan's desire to turn Social Security into welfare. "The biggest problem," he said, "is that many people have hit upon a phrase that the way to save Social Security is 'to take the welfare out of it.' The truth is that no—and I mean *no*—welfare programs are funded out of Social Security. SSI [Supplemental Security Income], AFDC [Aid to

Families with Dependent Children], aid to refugees, food
stamps—all these and others come out of the general treasury,
not out of Social Security taxes. The special security payroll tax
funds only the Social Security retirement, survivors, disability
and Medicare/hospital insurance programs. . . .

"The fact is that Social Security is a social insurance program.
Social Security pays benefits not only to the worker who has paid
the payroll tax, but to his or her family as well. While it is based
on an insurance principle, it is not a straight annuity, and was
not intended to be. If it were, it could not offer the full base of
national protection that one finds in the current program. . . .
All Social Security benefits are earned, and I am fundamentally
opposed to imposing any form of needs test in the Social Security program."

Social Security and SSI, the program for the needy aged,
blind, and disabled, pay benefits to about seven million disabled
citizens. Reagan's preelection hint that he would go after disability benefits materialized in a nightmare of meanness.

In 1980 Congress had scheduled an eligibility review program to begin in January 1982. Feldstein wrote before he became Reagan's chief economist that the political cost would be
minimal for cutting excessively generous payments for disabled
workers, which he contended had "made disability status a more
attractive option than working for many who could otherwise
find only low-wage jobs. A return to the old eligibility rules
would probably eliminate one-half to two-thirds of current beneficiaries. . . . Moreover, many of these individuals would find
productive employment and become taxpayers."

Under Reagan, then, the Social Security headquarters in Baltimore started the scheduled review ten months early (two
months after Reagan took office) and began sending out about
30,000 cases a month for review. In the first thirteen months,
175,000 people receiving disability benefits were cut off—40
percent of the cases reviewed. Law required people thrown off
disability rolls to prove they had been wronged, so people who
were too ill or too poor to get a lawyer or gather the evidence
themselves just lost out. Representative Claude Pepper (D.–Fla.)
said that there was "a wholesale purge of the disability rolls." In

federal court an association of more than 500 of the government's administrative law judges eventually charged that the administration had required judges to hear a quota of disability cases each month and had actually prohibited the judges from finding against the government in more than two-thirds of the cases. Commissioner Svahn denied that there was any such quota system.

Apparently the bureaucrats concentrated on knocking the mentally ill off the rolls. The American Psychiatric Association found that "large numbers of schizophrenics and other chronically mentally ill persons" were losing their benefits. According to one state director of the disability reviews, the new federal standards took a "minimal ability to function" as the same thing as the ability to work in a competitive environment. After studying forty cases in which mentally ill persons had been cut off, the General Accounting Office concluded that twenty-seven of them could not work in a competitive environment and more information was needed about the other thirteen before a good judgment could be made. "Many" people had been terminated, said the agency, "despite having severe impairments and, in our opinion, having little or no capability to function in a competitive work environment." Noting that in 1981 and 1982 in New York State the rejection rate for disability applicants who had been encouraged to apply by local officials had jumped from 31 percent to 73 percent, the *New York Times* declared editorially that the need to control spending "does not grant a license for meanness."

According to the staff of Senator Carl Levin (D.–Mich.), by mid-1982 at least nine people had committed suicide leaving messages about their loss of disability benefits. A man shot himself to death in front of the Social Security office in Lansing, Mich. In Troy, N.Y., a depressed woman and a man with mental illness both killed themselves after losing benefits. A Dallas lawyer who has been defending psychotic people who have lost their benefits, Carl Weisbrod, told the *Dallas Times-Herald*, "It's like picking on children."

A Pennsylvania man who had to have his leg amputated at the hip joint was cut off by the government, as well, after nine years of benefits. Explaining how such a thing can happen, Svahn said, "a person who has lost a leg can easily work, for example, as a parking lot attendant." One man testified to congressmen that he had certificates from doctors attesting that he had one kidney, was blind in one eye, had reduced hearing in one ear, and had received psychotherapy for depression, but his benefits were cut off anyway.

In New York State, about 30 percent of the people dropped were turning up on state or local relief. As for new applicants, in Reagan's first year, 1981, fewer of them were granted disability benefits than in any year since 1969, even though there had been a 34 percent increase since then in the number of people covered by Social Security. But new applicants who employed lawyers to appeal negative decisions had three times the chance of getting benefits as those who did not, a fact which gave some indication of how harshly the bureaucrats under Reagan were dealing with untutored disabled applicants. Late in 1982 a shamefaced Congress approved a law to let disabled people stay on the rolls while their cases are being processed and have face-to-face interviews with their examiners.[9]

The people Reagan has given administrative power over Social Security, following Reagan's "Son of Sam" example, have been doing what they can to smear the system. Finding two (repeat, two) cases of murderers of their parents who were being paid survivors' benefits, Schweiker himself made an indignant public statement ("I'm not going to stand by and let a juvenile delinquent get money out of the Social Security fund because he killed his parent") and ordered the 1,300 district offices to comb their files for any other such cases. Predictably, the headlines ranged from "U.S. Chokes Off Benefits to Murderers of Parents" in the *Washington Post* to the *New York Post*'s screamer, "KIDS WHO KILL FOR SS BENEFITS." Svahn announced "Project Specter," complete with carefully chosen horror stories for the Associated Press and the *Saturday Evening Post*: in 8,518 cases (which works out to one out of about every 4,200 beneficiaries, or one-fiftieth of one percent) benefits had been sent to dead people. "Social Security pays millions to dead people," bannered the *San Antonio Evening News*.

The system's antiquated computers and other problems (which need attending to) became, in a *Wall Street Journal* headline, " 'Breakdown' . . . Fraud, Human Error, Sabotage, and Confusion." With the approval of Stockman's shop, Svahn (saying that he was trying to avert "a disaster of epic proportions") began modernizing the system by taking about half a billion dollars out of the benefits money rather than asking Congress for an appropriation.

At forty-four "debt collection" centers, bureaucrats dun aged Social Security recipients for overpayments to them which the government says total $2 billion. At the Dallas center, the *Journal* reported, such bureaucrats were bringing in $130,000 a month. Columnist Jack Anderson revealed that Social Security under Reagan was threatening poor pensioners who get SSI benefits with an illegal cutoff of benefits unless they opened their income tax records to Social Security. A federal judge in New York State ruled that the program to recoup overpayments made seven and eight years ago "comes entirely too late, for any reduction in these benefits may cause a real and imminent loss of food, shelter, and other basic necessities."

In paying benefits, too, the Reagan-era Social Security Administration could be memorably niggardly. A widow in Nebraska received a demand for the return of her late husband's check for May 1982 because he had died thirty-seven minutes before that month ended. She had spent it and angrily refused. In such a poisoned atmosphere even the administration's quite proper crackdown on payments to the dead and another one against fraudulent Social Security cards had the effect of depreciating the system rather than merely reforming it.[10]

From the first Reagan had frightened and angered elements in Congress on Social Security. His May 12 recommendations, said House Speaker Tip O'Neill, were "a rotten thing to do . . . a despicable breach of faith." The Senate rejected the immediate scaling down of early retirement by a 96-0 vote, and the Senate Republicans for once joined with the Democrats to slap Reagan down. The House voted 404-20 to preserve the minimum benefit for those then receiving it. It became clear that the repeal of the minimum benefit would deny an average of about $70 a month to about 400,000 of the elderly poor, mostly women, whom the administration admittedly was expecting to be too proud to apply for welfare. "We are absolutely opposed to the deep cuts. . . . We're going to fight," declared House Majority Leader Jim Wright of Texas. When the Democrats renewed the proposal of interfund borrowing—GOP opposition to it collapsed—Reagan's May 12 plan was dead, and everyone knew it. Nevertheless, the minimum benefit and benefits for college students were killed for newly eligible recipients beginning in 1982.[11]

Why had Reagan's own Republicans deserted him on his May proposals? The polls told. Pollster Peter Hart said Democrats had a 60 to 16 percent advantage on the Social Security issue. In a Harris poll in the fall of 1981, 85 percent of all those polled opposed reducing benefits for future retirees, 73 percent opposed cutting the cost of living adjustments, 64 percent opposed a means test, 62 percent opposed cutting the benefits of children of retired workers, and 59 percent opposed raising the retirement age to sixty-eight. A 56 percent majority favored basing the cost of living on the lower of price or wage increases. But 76 percent wanted federal workers brought in, 62 percent favored using general revenue when needed, and 51 percent favored raising payroll taxes (with only 39 percent opposed to that).

Real damage to confidence in the system also turned up in the polls, though: in one, 66 percent of people under 45 no longer believed the system would exist to pay them their benefits in their old age. This damage is showing up also as more public employees and nonprofit groups withdraw from the system— possibly then only to provide their employees with less protection under private retirement plans.[12]

The decennial White House Conference on the Aging in December 1981 was a problem for the sponsor. The delegates had been chosen by governors and congressmen usually from among people who worked with the elderly. What if the White House Conference embarrassed the White House by condemning Social Security cuts? To prevent this the White House took extraordinary measures that turned the conference into a meaningless farce.

First, the GOP polled the 1,800 original delegates on what they thought of Reagan and his performance. (An aide to Texas GOP Governor Bill Clements, in a memo to the cochair of the Republican National Committee which was leaked to the press, identified delegates "who would put loyalty to the President ahead of their commitment to the elderly.") Next the White House added 400 delegates of its own, apparently chosen, Burt Schorr reported in the *Wall Street Journal*, "mainly on the basis of loyalty to President Reagan." Many of these sinkers were assigned to the strategic committees.

Then, wipeout: Schweiker ruled for the administration, much as someone in the Kremlin might for the Politburo, that the delegates would be prohibited from voting separately on resolutions from the fourteen committees. All they would be permitted to do was vote once yes or no on *all* the resolutions considered together. This guaranteed there would be no way to tell what the White House conferees believed about Social Security cuts. Reagan, speaking to his conference, said, "I look forward to receiving the results of your work," but delegates who tried to challenge the one-vote-only rule were not recognized from the chair, and so all 600 resolutions were adopted, among shouts of protest, by the one voice vote. In the administration's published conference report six months later, the wealth and well-being of the aged were celebrated and the resolutions against benefit cuts were nowhere to be found.[13]

Continuing to strive for his purpose as he always does, Reagan in the spring of 1982 agreed with his congressional leaders on a package that included cuts in Social Security by $40 billion over the ensuing three years, but no details were given. Two weeks later Senate GOP leaders dropped the plan, deciding to wait until after the fall elections. With Democratic acquiescence, Reagan charged his "bipartisan" panel to recommend what to do after the elections (its members, oddly for a bipartisan panel, ten chosen by the Reagan side and five by the Democratic side).[14]

In a nationwide TV ad campaign that summer, the GOP had a friendly postman, while delivering Social Security checks that reflected a scheduled 7.4 percent cost-of-living increase, declare that President Reagan "promised that raise and he has kept his promise." On the surface this presented as a friend of Social Security recipients the President who one year before had proposed cutting the system 22 percent. Reagan's 1981 proposals, had they been adopted, would have delayed the 7.4 percent increase three months in 1982, thus reducing it by a fourth. Representative Pepper, who is the chairman of the House committee on aging, said the ad "lowers the art of deception to depths not explored since the Nixon administration." Considering the depths explored by the Nixon administration this went too far, but O'Neill was surely justified when he said, "The President knows the ad is not true." The Speaker added the detail that Reagan officials had renewed their proposed delay in the increase in 1982 and had raised the possibility of "capping" the increase at 4 percent—only Congress' refusal to go along had forestalled these cuts.

That summer Reagan appointed Feldstein to preside over his Council of Economic Advisers—the same Feldstein who had said about Social Security the year before, "We must find ways to get the level of benefits down," and had proposed annual reductions in the cost-of-living index to accomplish an overall cut of about 17 percent in the level of benefits. Yet, campaigning in the closing days before the 1982 voting, Reagan accused the Democrats of spreading "one of the most dishonest canards" that the Reagan administration was "on our way to changing or reducing or doing away with Social Security."[15]

The National Commission on Social Security Reform demonstrated how easy it would be, given the will, to correct the short-term cash-flow problem. The members agreed new federal and nonprofit employees should be brought into the system. They considered a variety of ways to improve the cash-flow. As financial writer Sylvia Porter said, "the solutions are so obvious, even easy; the reasons for [the system's] troubles so simple to explain." Jim Wright suggested a 50-cent increase in the tax for a gallon of distilled spirits, or a tax on offshore oil production, dedicated to Social Security.

But that would be spending general revenue on pensions for the nation's old people, which was almost unthinkable in the Reaganized environment. The commission decided against such a step even as proof of the continuing war on the system appeared in many quarters. A two-part attack on Social Security, written by Nixon's Secretary of Commerce Peter G. Peterson (now chairman of the board of Lehman Brothers Kuhn Loeb), was published—after the November elections—in the *New York Review of Books*. Peterson emphasized that Social Security, "the biggest government social program in world history . . . now spends each year more than the combined net investment . . . of all the private companies in the United States." He argued that "Social Security . . . threatens the entire economy." His solution? Very deep cuts; raise the age of retirement "by at least three years" (earlier he had suggested a retirement age of seventy). The National Republican Congressional Committee had slipped in sending out a fund-raising letter asking for people to vote on whether to make Social Security voluntary. Then the pro-Reagan think tank, the Heritage Foundation, proposed phasing out Social Security, and going into the climactic 1983 fight, Representative Barber Conable (R.–N.Y.) said there were still people in the White House "who talk about making it voluntary." There were indeed: a senior policy adviser at the White House, Peter J. Ferrara, floated a proposal remarkably similar to Reagan's in 1975. Workers and employers would stop paying taxes into Social Security and would start paying into private investment accounts instead. In short, after the program was phased in: no more Social Security system.

The commission's five liberals were under intense pressures. Members of Congress wanted a compromise they could hide behind as they voted for it. The Republicans wanted a compromise the Democrats agreed to so that (as Dole said) Reagan's fingerprints would not be on the final solution. Public opinion was clear: a late-1982 *Los Angeles Times* poll showed opinion supporting using general revenues for Social Security, 59 to 28 percent, and a Harris poll showed 70 to 24 percent support for "keeping Social Security benefits as they are now, even if it means having to raise Social Security taxes." But Reagan insisted on tens of billions in benefit cuts by the end of the decade: the liberal bloc on the commission had to decide whether to give him that or go to the mat on the issue, if necessary into the 1984 presidential election. In the end they caved in and agreed to a

$40 billion cut in benefits by 1990 in the form of a recurring six-month delay in cost-of-living adjustments (which in effect cuts these adjustments in half). In return, Reagan agreed to increasing payroll and self-employment taxes.

Reagan and O'Neill endorsed the program while Senate Majority Leader Robert Byrd (D.–W. Va.) held his counsel. The commission's plan did not solve the long-run problem, and to that end Reagan endorsed gradually raising the retirement age to sixty-six, which is of course a cut in benefits.

Stockman had explained to Greider with blinding candor that the Reaganists' real purpose was to help cut spending by cutting Social Security in the context of the system's problems. "It will permit the politicians," he said, "to make it look like they're doing something *for* the beneficiary population when they are doing something *to* it which they normally wouldn't have the courage to undertake," Stockman said. And despite the good features of the great Social Security compromise of 1983, this is just about how things turned out.

Benefits were cut in several ways. Cost-of-living increases were cut in half for the rest of this decade. Benefits on retirement at sixty-two were cut from 80 to 70 percent. The age of full-eligibility retirement will increase to sixty-six by the year 2009 and to sixty-seven by 2027. Benefits will be taxed if half of Social Security benefits plus other income exceeds $25,000 for an individual or $32,000 on a joint return. This indirectly introduces a kind of means test for the first time, but also directly uses general revenues for the system for the first time since the proceeds of the tax will be dedicated to the system.

The payroll tax will be increased from 6.7 to 7.65 percent by 1990 as scheduled, but in quicker stages, and the self-employment tax goes up, too. The combination of lower benefits and higher taxes produces $164 billion more money in the system during the rest of this decade. Newly hired federal workers, including members of Congress, are required to join the system, as are employees of nonprofit organizations, and employees of state and local governments are denied the right to withdraw.

"A dark cloud has been lifted," said President Reagan. "I am gratified that great, good sense did prevail over partisan concerns."[16] But he also told a group of students, "I don't think there would be anything if we had some solid studies made as to whether we could improve the (Social Security) program for all of you so that it would be more fair for you and for the younger workers. . . ." To his aides, Reagan continued to advocate making the system voluntary.

He would not be able to do much more damage to Social Security in the election year of 1984, but if he is reelected he can be expected to continue to carve away on it. He favors a new system; he wants Social Security cut down to the poor and then, no doubt, the remnant transferred to the states or anyplace else where it will disappear. He has been hostile toward the Social Security system since the early 1960s, and despite his many recent statements to the contrary, he would like to see it destroyed.

4

"A Wholesale
Giveaway to
Private Interests"

As the Reagan administration was getting organized, leaders of environmental organizations met with Interior Secretary James Watt several times. Michael McCloskey, the executive director of the Sierra Club, told writer Ron Hollander that during McCloskey's last such meeting, over lunch at the Department of Interior, Watt said to him, "We're going to get things fixed here"—Watt smiled then—"and you guys are never going to get it unfixed when you get in." That's exactly what the nation's environmentalists have concluded that the Reagan administration is up to.

The Sierra Club, which has almost doubled its membership since Reagan was elected, collected 1.1 million signatures calling for Watt's dismissal and decided to begin endorsing proenvironment candidates for Congress. After a year of making Watt the target, the environmental movement turned away from him and confronted the President himself. "Mr. Reagan is the real James Watt," charged Friends of the Earth in a full-page advertisement in the *New York Times.* "Our President is taking apart nearly every institution that protects planetary and human life. His actions and his rhetoric are consistent: Destructive, disdainful and uncomprehending of environmental values."[1]

For anyone who was listening and watching carefully, Reagan gave plenty of warning about his attitudes before the people elected him President. He regards conservationists who resist industry's exploitation of natural resources as extremists and elitists. He believes the states should have control of the hundreds of millions of acres of federal land ("Is the federal government a better custodian . . . than the states would be?" he asked). When President Ford vetoed a bill regulating strip mining, Reagan approved the veto. National wilderness areas, Reagan said, limit access to "those robust enough to go back-packing."

The Alaskan lands bill, Reagan charged in the fall of 1979, "will disrupt the lives of Alaskans and the development of the state's major industries." Just in time, late in 1980, Congress passed the bill, placing 104 million acres, an area larger than California, into protected categories. Signing the act during his last full month in office, President Carter said:

"By designating more than 97 million acres for new parks and refuges, we are doubling the size of our National Park and Wildlife Refuge System. By protecting 25 free-flowing Alaskan rivers in their natural state, we are almost doubling the size of our Wild and Scenic Rivers System. By classifying 56 million acres of some of the most magnificent land in our Federal estate as wilderness, we are tripling the size of our Wilderness System."

Carter added that 100 percent of the offshore areas and 95 percent of the potentially productive oil and mineral areas of Alaska would be available for exploration or drilling. But had Congress failed to act before Reagan came to power the law would have been dead.

The prepresidential Reagan was put off idiosyncratically by various trends in the environmental movement. The Delaney

Amendment of 1958 provided that no food additive could be deemed safe if it was found to cause cancer in humans or animals. Condemning "the precipitous reactions of the FDA (Food and Drug Administration) to sketchy scientific evidence about saccharin and nitrates," Reagan, on the radio in 1979, called for "serious changes" in the Delaney Amendment (although it had already been watered down). In a bizarre broadcast, he declared that insect plagues have returned to the world because of the outlawing of pesticides, especially DDT. He favored more use of coal and the removal of "unnecessarily restrictive" federal rules that inhibit its use (Bechtel owns part of Peabody Coal Company). Extemporaneously he passed along an old wives' tale that prevailing winds which blow over permanent oil slicks in the Santa Barbara channel off California are good for people's health.

As on many other subjects, Reagan has been given to misstatements of fact about conservation. He got his figures about auto emissions bollixed up. He said 93 percent of nitrogen oxide pollutants come from plants and trees, confusing nitrous oxide, which is harmless, with the pollutant nitrogen dioxide. Late in his 1980 campaign he said air pollution had been "substantially controlled" in the U.S. just as Los Angeles was having its worst smog alert in history.[2]

Nevertheless, his environmental record as governor was pretty good. He could claim credit for adding 145,000 acres, including 41 miles of ocean frontage, to California's state park system. He blocked a trans-Sierra highway and a high dam, both of which environmentalists opposed. Two underwater park preserves were created. Bike trails, boat harbors, and urban parks were improved. Reagan signed strict auto emission and water pollution control measures, even though he was accused of capitulating to industrial and transportation interests on air pollution enforcement.

One of his peeves in California was the Coastal Planning Commission, which regulates the use of the state's ocean beaches. The commission "can practically imprison a child for building a sand castle on the beach," he said in the late 1970s—it had assumed "dictatorial powers," showed "hostility to any private ownership of ocean frontage," and engaged in "blackmail." When Reaganist George Deukmejian was elected governor of California in 1982 he made it a first order of business to deprive the commission of its authority over the planning of offshore oil drilling.[3]

Environmental concerns, broadly speaking, have two kinds of objectives: first, the protection of the natural heritage by conservation and by establishing parks, river and trail systems, and national forest and wilderness areas, and second, the prevention of pollution. In recent years the negative task of stemming pollution has become a high priority in public opinion, but on the national level Reagan takes the position that environmentalists are putting the protection of nature ahead of jobs and industrial growth, and as a practical matter he sides with business against the environmentalists. In his first two years as President he tried to hobble antipollution efforts in various ways, and he curbed the long-run national trend of expanding the protected natural heritage. His administration is still bound by the laws protecting the environment, but how assiduously his people are enforcing those laws has become a political issue of the first magnitude.

The administration's response to the rising alarm about poisonous wastes (the "toxic substances" problem) illuminates its overall conduct as the advocate of business against environmentalists.

Roughly 1 metric ton of hazardous waste is being generated every year in the United States for every citizen—225 million to 275 million metric tons—and there are as many as 14,000 dangerous dumps for these wastes in the U.S. (Love Canal is merely the most famous of them, so far.) Congress in 1976 ordered the Environmental Protection Agency (EPA) to classify and regulate commercial and industrial chemicals. In 1980, again just a step ahead of Reagan's arrival in Washington, Carter signed a law taxing chemical companies $1.4 billion across a five-year period to create the "superfund" to pay for cleaning up the most dangerous dumps.

Toxic is toxic, but then, too, among the Reaganists, regulation is regulation—and business is business. EPA had classified 58,000 chemicals that are used in the U.S.; by 1980, 38 were spotlighted as suspicious. The 1976 law required companies to notify EPA before putting new chemicals into the environment. EPA under Reagan's first administrator, Anne Burford, exempted about 60 percent of all new chemicals from that requirement, suggested that industry itself should be the chief monitor of PCBs (which are suspected of causing cancer), and decided that formaldehyde and DEHP, suspected carcinogens that are in many products (toothpaste, toys), will not be either banned or restricted.[4]

In October 1981 new standards prohibited the burying of drums containing liquid chemicals at the waste dumps. The ensuing spring EPA proposed to let a fourth of the capacity of the dumps be filled with liquid wastes in drums (and gave everyone a month during which they could dump such wastes even though the new rule wasn't adopted yet). "A giant step backward," said a lawyer for the Environmental Defense Fund. "Those things leak. That's why they were banned in the first place." Revising the rule, EPA required that absorbent material be put into the drums to soak up the liquid chemicals, but a maverick EPA official said: "It will still leak out. It may just take an extra six months." Finally, the EPA prohibited liquid in the drums.

The Reaganists' first ploy on the superfund, turning the cleanup job over to the states, did not pass muster with environmentalist Republicans like Senator Robert Stafford (R.–Vt.), who is chairman of the Environment and Public Works Committee. EPA put out a list of 115 of the most dangerous dumps, then named another 45, but the House Interior Committee, suspecting footdragging, demanded to see the agency's enforcement records. Burford declined to produce them and the House voted to cite her for contempt of Congress, an unprecedented event. Soon after, the total of dangerous dumps on EPA's list jumped to 418.

EPA had to admit that after two years it had actually cleaned up only five of the dumps. At a 14-acre dump for 60,000 barrels of toxic wastes in Seymour, Ind., the agency hoped it had created its model for industry compliance. The cleanup cost at Seymour was initially estimated at $30 million. EPA obtained $7.7 million from 24 companies (including IBM, GE, GM, Ford, Du

Pont, and United Technologies); another 170 firms would have to pay part of the cost or be sued. Some cited this settlement as proof that EPA was seeking "real-world" solutions to problems, but another interpretation was possible. Some of the documents Burford was withholding from Congress pertained to the Seymour settlement. Allegedly "on order from higher up," EPA settled for $25,000 with a company responsible for a dump in Bridgeport, N.J. that will cost at least $10 million to clean up; Burford withheld documents in this case, too.

EPA opposed amending the superfund law to end present exemptions for small-scale waste generators, heating oil wastes, and toxic materials that are recycled as useful products, despite the estimate of a House leader in this area that these exemptions leave as much toxic waste unregulated as the law now regulates. And Burford said the superfund probably would not need to be renewed in 1985 despite a judgment by the Conservation Foundation that the fund contains enough money to deal with only 300 of more than 2,000 existing hazardous dumps.

EPA's director of the cleanup of the dumps, William M. Hedeman, Jr., later told Congress that the agency had an "implicit policy" to curtail the superfund program and that Rita Lavelle, the assistant administrator for waste programs, pushed him to finish a survey of the 15,000 or so hazardous sites while "expressing concern" that they might provide a basis for expanding the superfund.

In an evaluation of federal rules to protect the public from toxic wastes, Congress' Office of Technology Assessment said "many loopholes" let waste escape proper control and that dioxin, one of the most toxic chemicals, is not even classified as hazardous. EPA's inspector general, trying to evaluate the agency's expenditure of $180 million of superfund money, reported that he could not show that $54 million of it had been spent for the fund's intended purposes. TRW, a potential defendant at a leaking dump in Riverside, Calif., was hired by EPA to study the causes of pollution at fifteen sites, including Riverside, until a House committee exposed the situation.[5]

Pesticides used by farmers kill crop pests, but also get into the food chain and wash into rivers, lakes and underground water tables. In Montana in the summer of 1982, for example, state officials learned that waterfowl there contained in their bodies as many as nineteen toxic pesticides. Some of the birds had levels of endrin, which causes birth defects, nearly ten times higher than are permitted for domestic poultry, and pregnant mothers were cautioned not to eat any wild birds.

That same summer, after receiving potent if neutral inquiries from aides to Vice President Bush and James Baker, EPA approved for use on rice crops a pesticide that some studies indicate damages human immune and reproductive systems. Reporter Stephen Barlas had also learned that EPA-granted statewide exemptions for banned pesticides (including strychnine and heptaclor) had about tripled in 1982 compared to 1978. The basis for such exemptions is an agricultural emergency. For instance, EPA authorized the use of a pesticide suspected of causing sterility in males, DBCP, to save 20,000 acres of peach orchards in South Carolina from tiny roundworms (the exemption was blocked by a court order).

According to a House subcommittee staff investigation, EPA under Burford increased by 10 to 100 times the levels of the government's definition of acceptable cancer risk from pesticides. Going along with a request from nine pesticide makers for protection from foreign competitors, EPA told scientists and others that they may not publish its health and science data about pesticides and herbicides except in brief excerpts or summaries. Some saw this as an attempt to handicap serious scientific criticism of government studies and standards.[6]

Before his election Reagan had called for a moratorium on regulation of the auto industry, and his administration proposed a two-year delay on rules that require the reduction of emissions from diesel trucks and cars. On the subject of lead in gasoline, though, his administration quickly crashed into the facts.

Lead in gasoline is one of the two principal causes (the other, lead-based paint) of dangerous levels of lead in people's blood. Low-level exposure to lead is associated with reduced intelligence in children, and high lead levels affect children's nervous systems, kidneys, and brains. The National Center for Health Statistics calculated that about one out of every twenty-five U.S.

children between six months and five years of age has high levels of lead in his or her blood, and almost one in five urban minority children is thus endangered.

Refiners put lead in gasoline because it is a cheap way to increase octane ratings and prevent knocking in motors, but one tankful of leaded gasoline can put as much as 2 ounces of lead into the environment. Largely as a result of federal regulations, the total lead used by U.S. cars annually had declined from 359 million pounds in 1975 to 118 million in 1981. During Reagan's first summer in the White House his regulatory task force instructed EPA to lower the government's barriers against putting lead in gasoline, and early in 1982 EPA announced that it would consider relaxing or repealing its limits on the practice, but the ferocity of the negative reaction led eventually to an EPA decision on behalf of the public health.

"If the Reagan administration has its way," said Clarence M. Ditlow, the director of the Center for Auto Safety, "an old environmental hazard that caused brain damage, retardation, and learning disabilities in young children will reappear." By EPA estimates, repealing the limit on lead would save refiners one-tenth of a cent per gallon, leading the *New York Times* to ask editorially, "What civilized government would want to take the risk of deadening its children's minds" even for a far greater saving than that? The Center for Auto Safety revealed that EPA on its own had already increased the lead content of regular gasoline by nearly 10 percent above the formal limit. The U.S. Center for Disease Control estimates that 675,000 American children already have blood lead levels higher than the designated safe maximum; an internal EPA report estimated that abolishing the lead limit would cause lead poisoning in another 200,000 children.

On July 30, 1982, environmental groups and three children who had lead poisoning sued EPA seeking to require it to reduce lead pollution in the air. The next day, EPA gave out the news that it was reversing its course on the issue. The prospect of many more retarded children could not be satisfactorily translated into numbers for the government's cost-benefit formulas. Under new EPA rules, the total amount of lead permitted in gasoline by 1990 will be 31 percent less than would otherwise have been permitted.[7]

According to the National Clean Air Coalition, 312 U.S. industrial plants release three billion pounds of toxic substances into the air every year. The Office of Technology Assessment estimates that sulfur-related air pollution causes 51,000 premature deaths annually in the U.S. and Canada. Emissions from power plants and vehicles are leading causes of the acid rains that are damaging lakes and rivers in North America and eastern Canada. In the Adirondacks many lakes have become too acidic and the fish in them are dying—in some of the lakes all the fish are gone. A study of 27 states by a scientist at the Institute of Ecology in Indianapolis determined that about 9,400 of a total of 17,000 lakes and about 51,000 out of 117,000 miles of streams had become more acidic; about 3,000 lakes and 25,000 miles of streams in the northeast were found to be acidic. According to the Conservation Foundation, 140 acidified lakes in Canada have lost fish populations, nine acidified rivers in Nova Scotia are barren, and "thousands of lakes are threatened and could become devoid of fish by the end of the decade."

Critics who regard the government as bubble-headed on pollution got support of a kind in 1979 when the Carter administration's EPA, using the strategem of imagining that a plant has a huge bubble over it, ruled that pollution from some sources at the plant could increase as long as the total pollution rising to the top of the imaginary bubble decreased.

Reagan's EPA then made it far easier for plants to use the bubble rule even if they were located in areas that had not complied with federal air-pollution standards. Pollution would be permitted to increase within a plant's bubble, the EPA now said, by up to 100 tons a year. At a press conference Burford revealed other changes which enhanced what *New York Times* environmental writer Philip Shabecoff described as "the ability of companies to buy and sell, or trade, rights to pollute the air." Plants which reduced emissions to below applicable limits, Burford announced, could sell or trade the "surplus" reductions to other companies which could then produce that much pollution above their own limits. (But the scheme ran somewhat afoul of the law:

a federal appeals court struck down the expanded bubble rule for areas that had not yet complied with federal air-pollution standards.)[8]

Though the Reaganists usually played a complicated game on air pollution, they simply showed their hand on the Clean Air Act. Reagan wants to materially weaken that act's requirements, but he and his industrial and union allies on the issue were rebuffed in the relevant Senate committee and lost out even in the House committee where they thought they had the votes.

The administration first realized it had a problem when its draft revision of the act was publicized. Enforcement lawsuits were to become optional instead of mandatory. States were to make the judgments whether enough progress against pollution had been made and whether cleanup deadlines should be extended. The requirement that polluted areas make progress toward national standards was gone. So was the law's prohibition against deterioration in still-clean areas. And the draft said nothing about acid rain, industrial plant emissions, and threats to the high atmosphere. "A blueprint for destruction of our clean air laws," a key congressman, Henry Waxman (D.–Calif.), exclaimed. From this moment the administration had lost the initiative on the Clean Air Act.

On the Senate side, Stafford's committee ignored the administration's proposals to add risk assessment and scientific peer review to the law. A proposal from industrial interests to eliminate the law's required "margin of safety" for the elderly, children, and pollution-sensitive individuals was passed over, too. Instead, Stafford's panel proposed to require utilities and other industries in a thirty-one-state area to reduce their pollution 8 million tons a year by 1995 (this was aimed at the acid rain problem), to require the EPA to move faster in evaluating thirty-seven suspect airborne chemicals, and to prohibit "significant deterioration" of air quality in parks and other clean-air areas.

This not being what Reagan had in mind at all, the administration endorsed instead a House bill that was supported by industry and the unions of the building trades and autoworkers (but was opposed by the steel and the oil, chemical, and atomic workers' unions). Under its terms, auto pollutants would have been permitted to double. States and cities whose air is polluted would get an extra six years to comply with minimum standards. The federal government could no longer withhold highway and sewer money from states that failed to comply. Current strict limits on air pollution in clean-air regions would have been repealed. In national parks and wilderness areas, where pollution standards can be violated only once a year now, five violations a year would have been permitted. On a test vote in the House Energy and Commerce Committee Reagan's side lost, and despite the President's request for action in the lame-duck session, both the House and Senate bills were dead.

While environmentalists had thus successfully protected earlier gains in the long-run campaign against air pollution, the Senate committee's proposed new curb on acid rain, approved by a 15 to 1 vote, had been lost in the stalemate. Not only that: Reagan's budgeteers had slashed funding for acid rain studies. Despite this the National Academy of Sciences reported in 1983 that there is a direct causal connection between sulfur dioxide emissions from factories and acid rain, increasing pressure on the administration to yield. There was less reason to expect the Reaganists to move to regulate the production and use of chlorofluorocarbon gases, which some scientists believe are causing chemical changes in the high air which reduce the protective ultraviolet radiation that reaches the earth and thereby increase skin cancer.[9]

As for the Clean Water Act, the Reagan administration asked Congress to increase penalties for violating it, but also to abandon some required national standards for treating industrial wastes that are discharged into municipal sewers, to extend deadlines for water cleanups by four years, and to double from five to ten years the duration of industry water pollution permits. Environmentalists were pleased about the higher penalties and relieved that Reagan's people did not advocate less stringent protection of wetlands from development and exploitation, but a lawyer for the Natural Resources Defense Council called the other requested changes "a collection of special-interest loopholes and back-door fixes." Industry was seeking waivers in the legislation from requirements that "best available technology" be used against water pollution, and Burford told Congress she would be "more than happy" to work on that idea. Then, in 1983, Watt was more than happy, himself, to propose wetlands legislation which an environmental leader said would continue 90 percent of federal subsidies to developments that encroach on them.

Reagan's budget cuts indicated a 60 percent reduction in funding for sewage treatment plants. Burford's EPA prepared new rules about water pollution that would let states decide that lakes and rivers are too far gone to meet present federal goals for waters that people can drink or swim and fish in. For instance, states could give up an "existing stream use for economic growth and development." EPA officials told the *Wall Street Journal* (as the newspaper summarized what they said) that the package of proposed changes "goes as far as the current law allows in giving states additional authority to weaken pollution-control requirements on industry and to delay cleanup of heavily polluted rivers and lakes." The U.S. Corps of Engineers promulgated (despite dissent from the Interior Department) new regulations to exempt millions of acres of wetlands from a requirement that permits must be obtained for any dredging and filling that would affect them. And there were signs that EPA was preparing to grant more municipalities and industries permission to dump wastes in the ocean.[10]

Despite a warning from Senator Stafford that excessive economies at EPA "could amount to a de facto repeal of some environmental laws," EPA's overall budget has been cut by a third, and its research budget for 1983 was only 60 percent of the pre-Reagan level. Such cuts, as EPA acknowledged to the President's budget office, were bound to hurt research and monitoring on air pollution, water quality, and toxic substances. Even more telltale was Reagan's veto of a bill that would have required EPA to conduct environmental research on acid rain, offshore oil, and indoor air pollution. (He stated as his reason for the veto a requirement in the bill that EPA's science advisory committee had to be broadly representative of different constituencies.)

Inevitably EPA became the focus of charges that the Reagan administration was selling out pollution control. After the first round of cuts, Russell E. Train, who was the administrator of EPA under Nixon and Ford and who voted for Reagan, wrote, "The Environmental Protection Agency is rapidly being destroyed as an effective institution in the federal government. Current and planned budget and personnel cuts, if continued, will inevitably reduce the agency to a state of ineffectualness and demoralization from which it is unlikely to recover for at least ten years, if ever."

In a summary after nearly two years, ten environmental groups said that a 90 percent cut in funds had virtually closed the EPA's research lab on the Great Lakes, and cuts of up to 50 percent in grants to the states for antipollution programs had come just when the states were too strapped to take up the slack. Testimony from the states bore this out, but Reagan asked for another 25 percent cut for 1984.

"Enforcement has ground practically to a halt," Train charged. Before the first year was out EPA had asked the Justice Department to drop fifty enforcement lawsuits. Burford abolished her own office of enforcement, promising to emphasize voluntary compliance. EPA's enforcement chief was stripped of his independent authority and resigned. In mid-1982 a staff report prepared for Senator Patrick J. Leahy (D.–Vt.) concluded that EPA enforcement efforts had dropped by 70 to 80 percent in a year. A House committee study said that EPA had projected 723 inspections of chemical plants in fiscal 1982, but had conducted only three. An EPA spokesman explained that while the emphasis had changed, overall inspections had doubled in that year.

Hugh Kaufman, the senior waste adviser at EPA, went public in 1981 as a whistleblower against both the Carter and Reagan administrations, saying, for example, "What is going on in Washington vis-à-vis hazardous waste is almost criminal." He was promptly investigated by EPA, allegedly because of suspicion that he had used government phones for personal calls and improperly requested sick leave. Independent Labor Department investigators ruled instead that EPA was improperly engaged in "an apparent attempt to discredit" and "silence" Kaufman.

A special assistant to Burford admitted to a House panel that during negotiations in which EPA was seeking the payment of $850,000 from a paint manufacturer for the cleanup of a dump in California, he told the company that EPA would actually accept $700,000. "Highly improper," concluded Representative Albert Gore, Jr. (D.–Tenn.).

Burford herself went pretty far in the same direction, judging from a report prepared by EPA's inspector general at the request of a Democratic congressman. Six persons attested that they were present at a meeting during which the EPA administrator promised that a small oil refinery would not be penalized if it violated federal lead standards—"that they had her word on nonenforcement." Witnesses said that a lawyer representing the company asked Burford to put this in writing, but she refused to do that. In her version of what she said, she had promised, not that the company could break the law with impunity, but that she would mitigate any penalty that was likely to drive it out of business.

In her and her agency's defense, Burford wrote that there had been no mass firings or wholesale abandonments of key programs, more than 90 percent of industry was "on schedule" to meet clean air and water goals, the superfund program was under way, and new regulations had been issued on safe management at active toxic dumps. A 99.99 percent level of destruction had been required in high-temperature incineration. Progress was being made, she said, on testing toxic chemicals, limiting toxic discharges into waterways, and making air pollution control at industrial plants more cost-effective. "The sky is not falling at the EPA, as some critics keep crying," she said. "The sky isn't even getting dirtier."[11]

Putting pollution to one side for the time being, what about the protection and enlargement of the national heritage of parks and wilderness? Republicans stand forward among the heroes of the conservation movement, but Reagan is not the Teddy Roosevelt kind of Republican. With a few exceptions, he has concentrated on accelerating the exploitation of the natural heritage for private profit.

The National Park System is now used by the people ten

times as much as it was in 1950, and the population is still growing, but Secretary Watt has tried to call a halt to the acquisition
of new U.S. parklands. He prefers to spend the land-purchase
money instead on improving the facilities of existing parks. Environmentalists charged that Watt's (and Reagan's) approach
would mean abandoning plans to buy lands for sixty-five parks
and recreation areas in thirty-two states, and Congress went
ahead and authorized some new parkland despite the opposition
of the administration. Reagan did assent to a law that established
the important 35,000-acre Cranberry Wilderness in West Virginia. But he vetoed a bill, supported by every member of Congress from Florida, to create a 50,000-acre wilderness forest in
Florida. It was his stated reason that the government would have
had to pay four companies for their phosphate deposits in the
forest, but Watt had already ruled that the ecology was too delicate for them to mine there.

Some of the national parks, Watts has said, "are probably too
big." He has hinted that parks near the great population centers
should be cut loose by the federal government, apparently to be
run by a combination of local and commercial elements. "I do
not believe the National Park System should run urban parks,"
he told a meeting of concessionaires. "We will use the budget
system to be the excuse to make major policy decisions," he
added. One result, an example given by Audubon president
Russell Peterson: a proposed national park in the Santa Monica
mountains, "an extraordinary near-wilderness region within a
day's drive of 10 million urban dwellers . . . is about to be lost to
subdividers."

Watt turned over to the state of Texas the management of
19,000 acres of a federal wildlife refuge on the Gulf of Mexico
side of the 27-mile Matagorda Island, one of the last unspoiled
barrier islands on the Texas coast. The state land commissioner,
an environmentalist, obtained restrictions against development,
but the Sierra Club and Defenders of Wildlife sued to stop the
transfer anyway. The organizations fear that the state, which
historically has promoted recreational development, will favor
that at the expense of the wildlife; the sanctuary lies along an
important bird-migration flyway. Even more, they are thinking

about the precedent for other sanctuaries in other states. They contend that the transfer violates U.S. law which requires the secretary of the interior to administer all parts of the wildlife refuge system.

At this writing Interior was favorably considering returning 50 acres within the 42,000-acre Apostle Islands National Lakeshore in Wisconsin to the family that originally owned the small tract and gave it up only under pressure. Once again environmentalists feared the precedent this would create.

The Reaganists' ideological opposition to federal intervention in the private sector provided the rationale for their support of one conservation measure that was signed into law by Reagan. Watt's agency worked up a list of 188 barrier beaches along 750 miles of the Atlantic and Gulf coasts which (minus about 50 miles of the beaches that Congress exempted over Watt's opposition) became the areas affected by the new law. Under its provisions, the federal government can no longer help to pay for a public infrastructure (roads, bridges, and so forth) or for most erosion control projects in these areas. Development can proceed, but at commercial investors' risk, not the taxpayers'. The next step, according to environmentalist Laurence Rockefeller, should be federal purchase of these undeveloped, but still unprotected coastal areas. The administration's opposition to acquiring new parklands probably rules that out.[12]

Watt has announced policy changes to permit motorboats on the Colorado River in the Grand Canyon, off-road vehicles on beaches and in wilderness areas, and more snowmobiles and motorbicycles in national parks. When a congressman proposed legislation to give the interior secretary power to prohibit such developments as nuclear waste dumps and fertilizer plants near national parks, Watt sent word that he didn't want the power. Of course he didn't; he himself has been trying to permit the strip mining of coal near Bryce Canyon National Park in Utah.

Both Reagan and his secretary of the interior see the nation's public resources as a blessed plenitude that should be made available promptly for exploitation by private interests. Perhaps the most vivid example of this concerns the 410 U.S. wildlife refuges, which cover about 89 million acres. Jane Perlez of the

New York Times reported that in 1982 the deputy director of the U.S. Fish and Wildlife Service, complying with Watt's philosophy, sent out a memorandum telling the managers of the refuges: "We believe that there is potential to expand economic uses in such areas as grazing, haying, farming, timber harvest, trapping, oil and gas extraction, small hydroelectric generation, concessions, commercial hunting and fishing guides, guided interpretive tours and commercial fishing." The Reagan-era memorandum added: "We place a high priority on this."

Reagan's allegiance to business interests that yearn to exploit the wilderness is what really lies behind his disdain for "extreme environmentalists" and his opposition to the Alaskan lands law of 1980. "We will mine more, drill more, cut more timber," Watt said on arriving in Washington. One of the first stated goals of Watt's Department of Interior was, literally: "Open the wilderness."

Probably the main issue between the oil industry and government as Reagan came into office, according to Gulf Oil chairman Jerry McAfee, was the industry's desire for much more access to federally owned lands. Michel Halbouty, a Houston oilman who ran Reagan's energy advisory panel for the transition, told the *Wall Street Journal:* "We want more production. More, more, more." Two years later the federal onshore acreage that was leased for oil and gas exploration had more than quadrupled, from 11.3 million to 50 million acres. In the one year 1982 Watt leased more onshore acreage for oil and gas than Carter's administration did in his entire four years. And Watt proposed to make available for oil and gas leasing more than one billion acres offshore, nearly all the acreage under U.S. coastal waters—the Atlantic coast, the Gulf of Mexico, all of the west coast, and offshore Alaska. This was twenty-five times as much acreage as had been offered to oil and gas drillers since federal offshore leasing began in the early 1950s. Every year for five years, Watt said, 200 million acres offshore would be available to the oil companies. That should solve the oil industry's main problem with the government.

Did it not stand to reason that pushing the offshore leasing so avidly, the United States would reduce competition for the tracts and therefore get far less for them? Under Carter, no offshore leases were authorized for less than 16.67 percent royalty, but Watt had dropped that to 12.5 percent on some leases. A spokesman for the Citizen-Labor Energy Coalition, pointing out that U.S. royalty rates are lower than those in other countries, charged: "We are seeing a wholesale giveaway of the offshore oil lands."

At such an accelerated pace of leasing, could a budget-cut Interior Department protect the environment adequately? The director of the Office of Planning and Research for then Governor Jerry Brown in California, Deni Greene, wrote that the damage to commercial fisheries, marine mammals, endangered species, recreation, and tourism could be irreparable. "Coastal splendors could be ruined by oil spills, tanker and barge traffic, busy harbors and air pollution," she said. "The subsistence economies of native Alaskans would be destroyed forever." All 1,100 miles of the California coast from Mexico to Oregon would be leased, she said, "without regard for environmental risk or the nature of the local economies."

As finally submitted, Watt's proposal still made almost a billion acres available for industry's consideration, but only specific tracts were to be leased. He dropped proposed sales of some environmentally sensitive areas off Alaska, northern California, and North Carolina, but basically he bulled ahead, contending that the environmental risks could be studied further as the drilling proceeded.

By the end of 1982 offshore acreage under lease had increased immensely. Deep drilling began 200 miles off the Atlantic shore in the teeming fishing grounds of the Georges bank. The discovery of a large new offshore oilfield 60 miles from Santa Barbara renewed memories of the calamitous 1969 oil spill in that area. Emboldened by the new federal policies, a group of oil companies sued to try to discontinue the existence of one of the six marine sanctuaries where oil drilling is prohibited.[13]

Under a conservation law passed in 1964, the 80 million acres of protected wilderness areas are permanently closed to new drilling or mining leases after 1983. Watt, with Reagan's backing, proposed to allow wilderness leasing to continue through 2003 (another twenty years). Reagan announced that the government would solicit proposals concerning which parts of the nation's 734 million acres of public land should be opened for exploration and development. (Those lands, a White House paper said, "represent a vast, largely undeveloped storehouse of resources that are important to this nation's welfare.") Watt proposed to open five national recreation areas in the West, totaling 403,000 acres, to mineral leasing.

As the Reaganists became more embattled on environmental issues, Watt seemed to back off some on exploiting the wilderness. Close the wilderness areas until the year 2000, he then said, except that the President should be able to grant exemptions without congressional approval in cases of "urgent national need." Then, starting in 2000, parts of the wilderness would be opened for mining and drilling. In effect Watt had simply restated the Reagan proposal to repeal the permanent protection of the wilderness areas. The plan would "gut the nation's wilderness system," charged Representative James. R. Sieberling (D.– Ohio), the chairman of the House Subcommittee on Public Lands and National Parks.

Watt's bureaucrats granted five oil and gas leases in the middle of the two watersheds that serve the cities of Seattle and Tacoma until the resulting local uproar changed their minds. Oil leases were issued permitting drilling in the Capitan Wilderness in New Mexico, the first ever granted in a protected wilderness area. Watt tried to permit natural gas exploration in the Bob Marshall Wilderness in Montana. Congress intervened, first by forestalling these two exploitations of wilderness, then by more general prohibitions. In August 1982 the House by an angry 340–58 margin voted to prohibit oil and certain mineral development in 30 million acres of wilderness. The Senate appropriations committee followed suit concerning oil and gas leasing. The House-voted prohibition died in a Senate committee, but Congress as a whole prohibited Watt from oil leasing in the wilderness until the last three months of 1983 (after which it would be prohibited again). The conservationist Republicans had joined the Democrats to hogtie Watt and his boss. The Democrats' gains in the offyear elections made it even plainer that

Congress was not going to permit the administration to gut the conservation laws.

As soon as the lame-duck Congress of 1982 left town, Watt announced that 173 areas covering about 670,000 acres that were under study for possible dedication as wilderness areas were liable to be removed from consideration. The stated reason was a legal opinion generated within Watt's agency that certain areas should be barred from wilderness status. Perhaps as much as 2 million acres could be dropped, although the areas affected might still be protected under other public lands programs.

That done, Watt and Reagan appeared to give up the fight on oil and gas leasing in the wilderness areas. "I gave my best shot at it. Congress' wisdom will prevail," Watt said. Never again, he said, would he issue such leases, either in protected wilderness areas or the areas still under study as potential wilderness. "Gratifying, if true," Sieberling remarked. But Watt did not say he would protect the wilderness areas from *mineral* leasing.[14]

Strip mining is regulated by the Federal Surface Mining Act. Watt first tried to dismantle the Office of Surface Mining and pass the regulatory authority to the states. Stymied there by Congress, Interior's bureaucrats apparently went to work to accomplish the desired changes piecemeal. In the autumn of 1982 Norman L. Dean, a staff lawyer of the National Wildlife Federation, made revelatory charges.

"Buried in more than 450 pages of notices issued by [Watt's] department," Dean wrote on the op-ed page of the *New York Times*, "are hundreds of proposals to weaken the existing surface-mining rules." By changing the definition of existing rights, Dean said, Watt had proposed to open up about 1.2 million acres of national forest and wildlife refuges to strip mining. The attorney continued:

"The secretary is proposing other changes in definitions that would allow mining next to many vacation homes, on certain privately owned lands that have been given the status of public parks and on privately owned lands that are listed in the National Register of Historic Places. . . .

"He would delete specific requirements to protect the migratory routes of wildlife, to protect eagles and other birds from electrocution on power lines and to protect wildlife from toxic-waste ponds. Major loopholes would be provided in the requirement that coal miners restore the land to its approximate original contour after mining. Existing restrictions on the use of persistent pesticides by miners would be lifted. . . . Hunters, fishermen, hikers and others who use but don't own environmentally sensitive lands would lose their existing right to petition to have them declared unsuitable for strip mining."

As the comedian Mark Russell said, Reagan had appointed officials "whose idea of communing with nature is a cookout in a strip mine." Under one of the pending proposals, Dean wrote, design criteria for mine equipment or facilities would be replaced by weaker performance standards, and "Responsibility for compliance with many of the new standards would be assigned to certified professional engineers selected and paid by mining companies."

Watt has delegated to a majority of the coal-producing states "primacy" in administering the control of strip mining, and the goal is to pass the authority to all of them. Early in 1983 Interior also proposed to give states the authority to decide whether companies may mine coal which the companies own in national parks, national forests, wilderness areas, wildlife refuges, and other protected lands. A federal ban on mining family burial grounds would be dropped under another Watt proposal. Toxic waste ponds near coal mines would no longer have to be fenced to protect wildlife unless states required it. Reagan canceled President Nixon's order which had prohibited killing predators on public lands with poisons that persist in the environment. Confronted by environmentalists on this, Ed Meese explained that the administration had decided to side with sheep ranchers.

The acreage leased to coal companies by the United States had quintupled by Reagan's nineteenth month in power. Despite the "new federalism" rhetoric, fourteen western governors charged that in granting coal leases Watt was reducing real participation by the states. In 1981, for example, despite a recommendation from the regional state-federal coal team that 800 billion tons of coal in the Powder River Basin of Montana and Wyoming be put under lease to companies, Interior made 1.2

billion tons available. The royalties paid to the government in the ensuing giant sale of 1.6 billion tons of coal were alleged to be pittances because Interior had reduced the minimum bids and made most of the sales without competitive bidding. After the 1982 elections Watt gave in to the governors on a set of changes they demanded to restore the power of the states.[15]

On the question of how much timber to let companies cut how fast in the national forests, Reagan's prepresidential views again help to explain what his administration is doing. He has long favored letting the lumber companies greatly increase their take of wood. He argues that this will reduce the costs of lumber and thus of home construction while increasing employment. One of his interests is more cutting of "overmature" trees, old, big ones with lots of wood in them.

As governor of California he seemed opposed to the 90,000-acre national redwoods park that had been proposed by the Sierra Club, saying at a Cabinet meeting that he had never been given a good reason why the park was needed. Once he told a group of wood producers "a tree is a tree, how many more do you need to look at?" As Cannon has explained, Norman Livermore, the director of resources in Reagan's Sacramento administration, led the governor to accept the 53,000-acre redwoods park which Congress did establish. But in 1978, on radio, Reagan scoffed at the enactment of a bill authorizing federal purchase of 48,000 acres of forest as a buffer zone for the same park—the zone, he said, was "a run-of-the-mill mix of redwoods and fir trees."

Pristine forest bears no resemblance to the managed commercial forest of the lumber companies, criss-crossed with roads and sites for the burning of slash (the waste branches). There are several different ways to log. A forest can be selectively logged again and again. Under the shelterwood method, which also involves cuttings at intervals of several years, saplings are planted under the overwood, which is then cut when the saplings bid to become the overwood themselves. Then there is clearcutting, taking down all the commercial trees in strips or patches and relying for new growth on seeds from the uncut adjacent areas or scattered in the course of the logging. To restore a forest, direct seeding or the planting of young nursery-grown trees may become necessary.

In another of his little-publicized broadcasts in 1975, Reagan celebrated clearcutting forests. Clearcutting, he said, is "usually the best [method] for insuring maximum regeneration of some of our most valuable commercial tree species. . . . Nature was the original 'clearcutter.' Overgrown, overmature forests were cleared out by fire, landslides, wind, and insect invasions. Today, man does a better job through systematic rotation of his harvests and by cleaning up his logging debris and replanting the forest for a new harvest later on."

Like the lumber companies themselves, Reagan sees the forests as places of business. Citing a column by John Chamberlain, he said on another broadcast, "the industry only owns 16 percent of the nation's standing softwood . . . the federal government owns 52 percent. So . . . the U.S. Department of Agriculture could be the key to lower housing costs. . . . Uncle Sam's 52 percent offers the best chance of increased supply.

"Now I'm sure," Reagan continued in 1978, "all of us want conservation of trees in our national forests. No one would suggest wholesale cutting to meet commercial demand. But . . . trees . . . grow old and die. This apparently is not recognized by some environmental extremists who confuse conservation with preservation." Reagan said Lassen National Forest in California could produce a cut of 268 million board-feet a year, up from 150 million, "if the timber cutters were allowed to harvest only the overmature and dying trees. . . . So what's the federal government waiting for?"

The answer, under President Reagan, is damn little. As the administration has stated, in its budgeting "priority was placed on programs which could help improve the nation's economic conditions while maintaining a minimum level of protection for the nation's natural resource base." As the Conservation Foundation says, "Commercial resource extraction has become the dominant use of the national forest system."

To run the national forests, which cover 191 million acres of the United States, Reagan appointed, as already noted, the general counsel for Louisiana-Pacific, one of the largest cutters of federal timber. John Crowell's language, now in his role as assistant secretary of agriculture for national resources and environment, tells how he sees the national forests: ". . . old-growth forest that has a large inventory. . . . These forests have been underharvested. . . . We can make the national forest more productive than it's ever been."

Crowell has increased the target cut in the federal forests 50 percent overall, has proposed to let the supervisors of each forest decide if the cut in each one is to be increased, and has accelerated plans to build logging roads into virgin timber. Laying a road through a forest automatically renders it ineligible for wilderness-area status. "They are going out of their way to sell timber in these areas," Representative Jim Weaver (D.–Oreg.), chairman of the House forestry subcommittee, told Ward Sinclair of the *Washington Post*. "They want to liquidate the national forests. . . ." "Utter nonsense," Crowell responded. But then, in February 1983, Crowell in effect canceled earlier recommendations that more than 7 million acres of forest be designated as wilderness areas, and he authorized logging and other development in about 26 million acres of roadless forest that had not been recommended for wilderness status.

The administration's stated hope is that the total cut from federal lands, which was 11 billion board feet in 1982, can be increased to 20 billion board feet a year, admittedly at a cost to the wildlife habitat. Even as the administration put on pressure to increase the cut, timber companies angled in Congress for a bailout. They sought to be released from previous contracts to buy federal timber because they already had a three-year backlog of standing federal trees and the price of wood had dropped since they had signed the contracts.[16]

"I want to open as much land as I can," Watt said. In his announcement that the government would sell about 35 million acres of U.S. public land—up to 5 percent of the total—in the next five years, he promised, "We will protect the parks, the refuges, the wilderness, the wild and scenic rivers, the Indian trust lands, the recreational privileges and other important values so important to the people." Notably absent from this reassuring list were the national forests, and a few months later

Agriculture Secretary Block announced that 60,000 acres of Forest Service lands would be sold immediately and 140 million acres, including lands in national forests and grasslands, would be studied for possible sale. Block indicated that the target acreage to be sold by the Forest Service is 15 to 18 million acres. Peter Kirby of the Wilderness Society said this was just another step in the administration's "campaign to turn over the wealth of the public lands to corporate interests at giveaway prices." Another 307 tracts covering 60,000 acres of federal land have been put on the market, and the signs point toward a huge government land sale.

Land without water is lifeless, and in 1979 the Carter administration ruled that the United States can use water that runs through federal property (as 60 percent of the west's water does) provided it is not already reserved for state or private interests. The Reagan administration has prohibited all federal agencies from claiming water under these circumstances, which means that more of the west's most necessary substance will go to private, state, and municipal users.

Initial company response to the newly wide-open oil leasing offshore and the coal leasing in the Powder Basin was slack, and bids were comparatively low. Pointing to these facts and to the increased timber cut in spite of the three-year backlog of unsold timber, the principled conservative columnist George Will commented, "The administration is nothing if not reverent about the law of supply and demand, but it seems careless about increasing supply in a period of slack demand."

The Conservation Foundation, which before Reagan had strictly avoided anything that might be called political, has been driven from its idyllic glen by the lightning storm of events. "The regulated industries, rather than the environmental groups, have become the primary constituency of EPA and the other resource and environmental agencies," the foundation now charges. "New regulatory initiatives have almost ceased, except for some proposals to ease the burden on regulated industries. Research on environmental problems has been sharply reduced. Efforts to encourage public participation and to disseminate information have been abandoned. . . . The administration has taken major steps to pass on to the states, or to leave to the private sector, responsibilities that the federal government had assumed during the 1970s."

And there has begun to form, among critics of Reagan's policies on the environment, the most serious accusation of all: giveaway. Environmentalists are condemning all the policy changes—the pressure for oil, coal, and other mineral lease sales and the land sales in the midst of the worst recession since the Depression—as one coordinated program to hand over public property to private interests. A coalition of ten of the largest environmental organizations (including Sierra, Wilderness, and Audubon) said in a joint report, "The President and his officials are engaging in a wholesale giveaway to private interests of our most precious natural resources." Representative Sieberling charged that the administration was making a systematic effort to dispose of the nation's birthright at "fire sale prices." And Representative Morris Udall (D.–Ariz.) said Watt and Burford "have done for the environment what Bonnie and Clyde did for banks."[17]

Quite to the contrary, Watt calls himself the nation's "number one environmentalist." He presents the growth of leasing under his management as an achievement, but there are also some gains by environmentalists' standards. The administration supported an international ban on commercial whaling, to begin in 1985. Federal spending was stopped on a dam that would have flooded forest areas in Maine. After initially threatening to discontinue making additions to the endangered species list, in 1982 the administration swung in behind the renewal of the Endangered Species Act, and early in 1983 it announced that sixty-two vertebrates will probably be added to the list of protected species. Moreover, Watt can assert that his department in 1982 added 245 miles to the Wild and Scenic Rivers System, designated 192 trails totaling 7,182 miles in length, and established eighteen new national historic landmarks and six new national natural landmarks.

While he cannot imagine that this list will overwhelm his critics, he gets high marks from the one auditor of his performance who most matters. "I am convinced that Jim Watt is doing exactly what the President wants him to," said the GOP national chairman in mid-1982, Richard Richards.

Reagan and his people have argued—as the House Republican Study Committee put it—that environmentalists are selfish members of the "affluent wine and cheese set" who "garner the benefits of extremist environmental protection" because "only they have the money and time" to frequent scenic refuges, while their very environmentalism is threatening "natural resource development and economic growth." Environmentalism has been pitted against the need for jobs.

But studies show no such clear conflict. EPA said in 1982 that employers reported that cumulatively 32,611 workers have lost their jobs because of environmental laws. Yet a 1981 EPA study showed that 200,000 people work in water pollution control, and Interior estimates that another 120,000 work in air pollution control. EPA also said that if present environmental standards were maintained, 524,000 jobs would be created by 1987 in connection with pollution control systems. Instead of this, the pollution control business, until Reagan a growth industry, had become demoralized and was cutting back.

The Reaganists realized during the first half of 1982 that they had so far lost the argument about the environment. Polls showed that Watt was phenomenally unpopular and he was told to lower his voice. EPA reversed itself on a plan to let toxic waste dumps expand 50 percent without first obtaining permits; attempts to weaken incineration and landfill standards were dropped.

August was the month of the turnaround. A Harris poll showed that the public favored, 85 to 10 percent, "strict enforcement of air and water pollution controls as now required by the clean air and clean water acts." Suddenly, the House banned the oil drilling in the wilderness and extended the strong pesticide control law, and a House committee approved tough standards against airborne pollutants.

In addition to the Sierra Club's membership surge during Reagan's presidency, the Wilderness Society's 1981 appeal for funds raised ten times more than the year before. Environmental organizations, which altogether have about 14 million members, reportedly provided 15,000 volunteers who worked for 70 or so congressional candidates in 1982. The Sierra Club and four other environmental groups that have political action committees spent more than $1.5 million for 48 candidates, 34 of whom won.[18]

In the winter of 1982–83, Anne Burford's EPA exploded into "Sewergate." The demand of a House committee for EPA's records on the superfund, denied by the White House on the basis of executive privilege, had placed Burford under threat of prosecution. The Justice Department would not proceed with the case before a grand jury; the White House would not really budge on releasing the records, and more and more House committees clambered onto the stage, demanding records and holding hearings. Suddenly, in February, the press went wild with the story, which lacked for almost nothing. Critical documents had been shredded at EPA—or just extra copies of them. Some agency officials, called before committees to testify, talked out of school; others were accused of lying under oath. It came out that EPA apparently had been timing grants from the superfund to help elect favored Republican candidates, and "pro and con" lists had been kept in the agency showing which bureaucrats were for and against the administration. Evidence emerged that certain EPA officials had allegedly dealt with cases affecting their former employers. The settlement in the Seymour dump case was condemned as a "sweetheart deal"; what had been meant to be a model for toxic dump settlements became a hot potato, instead. On March 1, Representative John Dingell (D.– Mich.), chairman of one of the House panels, said he had "specific information of criminal conduct and other wrongdoing" at EPA, a statement that left the President almost no ground to stand on if he continued to withhold the records Congress was demanding. Even more decisively, perhaps, a public opinion poll that appeared March 5 showed that by a 2 to 1 margin, those having an opinion said Reagan cared more "about protecting the firms that are violating" antipollution laws than he cared about enforcing the laws.

Although Reagan said he was proud of Burford's work and she could stay on as long as she wished (she had been doing what he wanted her to, after all), she resigned, and the great boxes of EPA records were hauled over to the Hill. Burford's first replacement, Assistant Administrator John W. Hernandez, Jr., immediately became caught up in serious charges that he had ordered subordinates to show a report on extensive dioxin contamination to the company accused of responsibility in the matter, Dow Chemical, after which a statement implicating the company had been stricken from the report. Reagan had personally fired Rita Lavelle, and now other resignations ravaged the agency.

While all this was going on, the bureaucrats at EPA began to do some strange things, like miscreants suddenly on good behavior. The agency offered to buy out the homes and businesses of the town of Times Beach, Mo., which is contaminated by dioxin, for a total of $33 million. Plans were announced to regulate 46 of the more than 100 chemical substances that are dumped into rivers and lakes by the chemical industry. The agency asked for a ban on the disposal of dioxin wastes in boilers and landfills. New standards were proposed to control airborne radioactivity. EPA announced plans, not to settle with, but to sue accused companies for help in cleaning up toxic waste dumps near Riverside, Calif., and Hamilton, Ohio. A new environmental crimes unit at the Justice Department brought five criminal cases alleging illegal dumping of hazardous substances. All this happened between January and April.

The gravity of the scandal was signified by Reagan's decision to bring in, as EPA's new administrator, William Ruckelshaus. During his first tour of duty as Nixon's chief of the agency, Ruckelshaus had championed auto emission controls, had banned certain herbicides (including DDT), and had required industries to install pollution control equipment. Leaving the government then, he had become an attorney and lobbyist for companies opposing EPA regulation, and in 1975 he became senior vice president of the Weyerhaeuser Company, the large timber and wood products company that has been cited and fined for violating water pollution laws. In 1979, Ruckelshaus had said in a speech that "EPA must abandon or at least modify its traditional role as an advocate for a cleaner environment and instead adopt the role of educator." The fact also emerged that in January 1981 he had written Vice President Bush attacking the Clean Air Act and saying that as EPA's first administrator, "I am largely to blame for most of the bad things done to business by environmental regulations over the last decade."

But in his new situation in 1983, Ruckelshaus promised Congress to remove himself from EPA matters in which Weyerhaeuser and other companies he once worked for had a direct interest. And he went further: he said that EPA should assume that even minute amounts of cancer-causing chemicals should be kept out of the environment; he said coal-burning plants in the east and midwest may have to cut their total sulfur emissions by more than 50 percent and that even this may not be enough to reduce acid rain; he indicated an intention to reverse rules EPA had adopted to weaken water pollution control and extend compliance deadlines for industry; and he won administration support for a 20 percent increase in EPA's 1984 budget for day-to-day operations and the cleanup of chemical dumps.

All things considered, the "extreme environmentalists" had fought the extreme commercialists of the Reagan administration to a standstill at both Interior and EPA; but they could take little comfort in it. EPA's whistleblower, Hugh Kaufman, had told a House committee, "People's air and water is being poisoned and the government continues to lie to them about how they are being protected." How much would Ruckelshaus do— how much would Reagan let him do—with the EPA? As James Watt had said with a smile when he started out, "We're going to get things fixed here, and you guys are never going to get it unfixed when you get in." Two years later he told Shabecoff of the *Times* that he would be concentrating during the rest of his tenure, not on legislation, but on recruiting and promoting employees and moving around career civil servants to accomplish his goals. His policies were being codified, he said, by the rewriting of not only the regulations, but also Interior's operating manuals and directives. "I will build," he vowed, "an institutional memory that will be here for decades."[19]

5

Riding Down the Marxist Income Tax

The 1981 tax cut, by which in effect abolished a fourth of the personal income tax and slashed corporate taxation, was the major domestic event of Reagan's first two years, and it may turn out to be the most disastrous act of Congress since the Gulf of Tonkin resolution. That the rich would get richer was a foregone conclusion. That spending cuts could not nearly match the income lost, that $200-billion-a-year deficits would open up, and that this would create a rolling crisis of pressure to continue eviscerating the government—all this was the deeper point. The 1981 raid on the Treasury was, as former Cabinet member James Schlesinger said, "the most irresponsible fiscal action of modern times," but it was what the President wanted, and once he had it he fought every attempt to delay it or rescind part of it.

This historic tax cut was passed, not because of "Reaganomics" and not because Congress was converted to supply-side economics, but because of the President's ideology, the starting point of which is his belief that the income tax is Marxist. There are always pressures to cut taxes, but behind Reagan's drive against the federal income tax there lay opinions so extreme, most Americans did not immediately understand what was involved.

The progressive income tax is based, as Senator Russell Long of Louisiana says, "on the principle that those with large incomes should pay a higher percentage than those with low incomes." Reagan is opposed to the progressive income tax precisely *because* it is based on the ability to pay—*because* the percentage of taxable income that a person pays is lowest for poor people and, through graduations upward, highest for rich people. His position is hard to take in, but there is no question about it. In place of what he calls "this evil day of progressive taxation," Reagan would establish, if he could, a flat-rate system whereby everyone, no matter how rich or poor, would pay the same percentage rate. If a person earning $5,000 paid at a rate of 10 percent, a person who had $5 million income would pay at the same 10 percent rate.

All the tax proposals Reagan cherishes reduce taxes on rich people, and the same objective lies at the root of his hostility toward government: he is opposed to the redistribution of wealth by taxation. In the actual national situation this means he uses his political power to redistribute money away from the poor and the middle classes into the bank accounts of wealthier Americans, both by cutting taxes for rich people and by doing away with government programs that benefit the poor and the middle class. In California his record did not match his rhetoric on taxes, but he is stubborn, and setbacks do not deter him. He keeps on.

He ridicules taxes on corporations, which he says are all passed on to the buyers of the companies' products. The idea of corporate tax loopholes has no meaning for him because he doesn't believe in taxing corporations at all. In March 1980 he said he would like to eliminate business taxes altogether, "but I know you can't campaign on this." Two years into his presidency he said "there isn't really a justification" for the corporate tax and asked why it isn't "simply passed on to the stockholder" to be taxed as individual income. He opposes the oil windfall profits tax on the same basis: "Only people pay taxes."

People, not corporations, pay the capital gains and inheritance taxes, but on these matters, too, Reagan simply follows out his pattern: lower taxes on the rich. He wishes labor leaders would demand "that the capital gains tax be reduced if not eliminated," he said on radio in 1978. He wants the inheritance tax stopped altogether, canceled.

In Reagan's mind social programs funded through progressive taxation constitute socialism, and stricter meanings for the word be damned. According to "the big spenders," he said in his GE days, "government should take it from us through taxation and buy for us the welfare programs we are too stupid to buy for ourselves. . . . It is dishonest to see social legislation under the guise of taxation. If we are to adopt socialism, then let it be presented to the people as socialism."

He argued frequently in the early 1960s that the U.S. tax system was Marx's idea. "We have received this progressive tax direct from Karl Marx, who designed it," he said. Again he said, "The originator of this system of taxation, Karl Marx, said you should use progressive taxation to tax the middle class out of existence, because you can't have socialism where you have a strong middle class."

Reagan explained that the U.S. has adopted the Marxist tax "because of our willingness to accept the idea that those best able to pay should lighten the burden of those with lesser earnings," but "nothing in the Constitution permits taxation as a means to direct the economy or redistribute earnings. . . . To secure social legislation under the guise of taxation . . . cannot be excused on the grounds of humanitarian goals." At the time the top rate was 91 percent. "There is no moral right," Reagan said, "in a government taking anywhere from one-half to nine-tenths of the dollar a man can earn by his own ability. . . . The government cannot justify such confiscation on the basis of real need."

Not all of Reagan's early thoughts on taxes were so abstract. Former California Assembly Speaker Bob Moretti has been quoted: "One time Reagan told me he personally favored a flat percentage to be applied universally, whether the individual's income was $100,000 or $5,000. He brushed aside my remarks that such a tax would be manifestly unfair and regressive in the extreme." Moretti said Reagan went on to tell about actor Bill Holden moving to Switzerland to avoid U.S. taxes, saying, "Bill sat down with the Swiss people and negotiated how much he would pay. . . . Now that's a great system."

In July 1980 Howell Raines of the *New York Times* asked Reagan incredulously: Had he really once said the progressive income tax was spawned by Karl Marx? "Well, it was," Reagan replied. "He was the first one who thought of it." The Republican candidate for President was galloping down, lance raised and braced, on the Marxist income tax.

Although he certainly did not want the people to know about it in 1980 (and the press did not hold him to it then), in a radio broadcast late in 1978 Reagan made clear his determination to lower tax rates on the rich. He said: "Andrew Mellon, who was secretary of the treasury under Presidents Harding, Coolidge and Hoover, in his book . . . explains why the progressive tax idea is really a rip-off, not of the rich but of the worker. He says, 'The history of taxation shows that taxes which are inherently excessive are not paid. . . . The high tax rates inevitably put pressure upon the taxpayer to withdraw his capital from productive business and . . . find . . . lawful methods of avoiding the realization of taxable income. . . .'" Reagan continued: "Mellon succeeded in getting Congress to cut the highest bracket from the World War I high of 66 to 25 percent. There were no screams of protest about benefiting the rich and very soon there was such an expansion of the economy and such prosperity for all. . . ."

On radio in 1979—just a year before his race for President—Reagan repeated his long-held belief that proportionate, flat-rate 10 percent tithing is "part of our Judeo-Christian tradition. . . . The Lord's share is considered to be one-tenth. And, we are told that if the Lord prospers us ten times as much, we must give back to Him ten times as much." But this is "unacceptable to government," for under the present income tax, if you prosper ten times, you are taxed 50 times as much. "This is the philosophy of 'soak the rich,' which theoretically lightens the burden for the less affluent—those with lower earnings," Reagan said.

(While Reagan uses the tithing concept as an argument for a

flat-rate system, the Reagans do not tithe 10 percent themselves. On their 1981 return, for example, they reported adjusted gross income of $412,730 and deductible contributions of $11,895, less than 3 percent; on their 1982 return their reported contributions came to 2 percent of their income.)

"To suggest exchanging the progressive tax for a proportionate system," Reagan said three years before he took office, "would be political suicide for any office holder. Even the Kemp-Roth bill . . . would have retained the progressive feature." Kemp-Roth proposed a 30 percent "across-the-board" reduction in income tax rates. Reagan endorsed, instead, "lowering the steeply progressive rates on the upper brackets," which he contended would increase taxes on the wealthy. He did not say how, but presumably he meant that taxing the rich less will reduce their efforts to avoid paying taxes.

In California, Reagan was a client of a cattle management firm which provided tax benefits for the wealthy. He admitted that in 1970, because of investment losses, he paid no state income tax on income of $73,000. In 1979–1980, when Rancho del Cielo was worth between $1 million and $2 million, he paid property taxes on it of about $900 a year on a valuation of about $20,000 because he qualifies it as an "agricultural preserve" under California law. In 1982 it was publicized that the Reagans had paid more than $20,000 in back taxes and interest to the federal government and California because IRS had disallowed certain business losses they had claimed on the operation of the ranch.

How would one holding Reagan's views about taxation respond to the traditional liberal Democratic rhetoric about tax loopholes that benefit the rich? Just the way Reagan did in the fall of 1972 against George McGovern: "The entire loophole story is a fairy tale . . . a campaign gimmick." "The White House wants to increase the progressivity of the income tax," he said on radio in 1978. "This is known as getting the most feathers possible from the fewest geese in order to minimize the quacking." To Reagan it is part of the liberals' fairy tale, too, that they "continue to insist that the sales tax is unfair and that average citizens believe in the present graduated income tax." He answered Carter directly: "No we don't need 'a more progressive system of taxation.'" He referred to those who believe "that taxation is a method of redistributing the earnings from the most productive to the least productive."

He picked up and buckled on the Kemp-Roth income tax cut of 10 percent a year for three years, but Kemp-Roth was simply the handy, already-loaded belt of grenades with which to begin blowing up the Marxist income tax. Jimmy Carter's campaign manager, Robert Strauss, certainly no liberal, wrote indignantly that the Republicans' proposed tax cut would "reduce taxes on lower-income Americans—those earning $6,700 to $10,000 annually—by $75 to $120 while reducing taxes on an individual earning $200,000 a year by $12,000. In other words, a person earning 30 times as much money would get a tax break 160 times as large." What Strauss and the country did not realize—probably could not really believe—was that this was only the beginning of what Reagan intended.

The candidate was smart enough to put it another way. "Why," Reagan was asked, "did you design your program [to provide] more benefits to taxpayers whose income falls in the upper brackets?" "The program doesn't," he replied, because, in an example he gave, a person paying $270 was saving $27, while a person paying $130,000 was saving $13,000, so "they are each getting an equal share—10 percent of their tax burden lifted."[1]

But the truth was told by Reagan's key man on domestic policy, David Stockman, to William Greider. "The hard part of the supply-side tax cut is dropping the top rate from 70 to 50 percent—the rest of it is a secondary matter," Stockman explained. "The original argument was that the top bracket was too high, and that's having the most devastating effect on the economy. Then, the general argument was that, in order to make this palatable as a political matter, you had to bring down all the brackets. But, I mean, Kemp-Roth was always a Trojan horse to bring down the top rate."

A second strategy to make the tax cuts for the rich palatable was Stockman's proposal for ten cuts in tax benefits for business and the rich—eliminating the oil depletion allowance, a "mansion cap" on home mortgage deductions, an attack on tax-exempt industrial-development bonds, and other such changes. But Reagan simply rejected these reforms. They never made the short trip from the White House to the Hill.

The bill that required all this camouflage cut down the size of the progressive income tax by a fourth. As Reagan wished, Congress gave him a cut "across the board in the personal income tax rates," and this reduced its progressivity to the advantage of the rich. He had to settle for a 25 instead of 30 percent cut, but a long step had been taken toward his goal of flat-rate taxation.

Under Reagan's kind of reform, investment income is taxed at a maximum rate of 50 instead of 70 percent. The top rate for investment income exceeding $215,400 on a joint return, for instance, dropped that entire 20 points—the biggest tax break in the 1981 tax cut. It was initiated by some House Democrats, but Reagan welcomed it before it was enacted.

In advance of the showdown in Congress, the Treasury said that Reagan's three-year 25 percent cut would give those earning less than $15,000, who file more than half the returns, only 9 percent of the tax relief. Families earning $30,000 or more, who file 19 percent of the returns, would get 62 percent of the benefits. The 5 percent of the taxpayers with incomes of $50,000 or more were to receive 36 percent of the benefits.

When Democrats tried to redress this situation, Reaganists argued back that those paying the most taxes naturally get the biggest cuts. The logic prevailing was Reagan's. Republican Congressman Henson Moore of Louisiana related to the press that when he told Reagan that Democrats were planning to try to reduce the benefits for the well-off to give more relief to poorer taxpayers, Reagan replied that he'd have to consider vetoing it if they did. The result of Reagan's obstinacy, as figures for the July 1, 1982 cut from the Joint Committee on Taxation showed, was that the 31,700,000 filers earning $15,000 or less a year received $2.9 billion in cuts, compared to the $3.6 billion received by the 162,000 filers with incomes of $200,000 or more.

The "equal-to-everyone" rhetoric about the across-the-board tax cut was a sham. "People in these top brackets are really getting the biggest tax break," James E. Power, a tax partner at Deloitte Haskins & Sells, told Karen W. Arenson of the *New York Times*, because the three-year cut works out to 23 percent for everyone except the highest-bracket taxpayers, who get 29 percent. (The effective maximum rate for earned income, 50 percent, continued unchanged. For taxpayers who were in the 65 percent or higher brackets because of unearned income such as dividends, interest, or rents, the tax cut from 70 to 50 percent on unearned income was a 29 percent reduction. The maximum tax on capital gains was also cut this much, from 28 to 20 percent.)

Secondly, in absolute terms the cuts helped the well-off far more than the average person. The application of Reagan's flat-rate theory in the real world means that the couple with taxable income of $15,000 gets a $474 cut by 1984, the $35,000 couple gets $1,870, the $50,000 couple gets $3,410, the $100,000 couple gets $9,598, and the $200,000 couple gets $25,632.

But there is a third, even more fundamental reason the "across-the-board" rhetoric was misleading. With the exception of the highest-bracket taxpayers, the Reagan tax cut gives all taxpayers a 23 percent cut by 1984. That sounds fair only for as long as one doesn't think about it. A fourth of a 20 percent tax rate is 5 percentage points; a fourth of a 40 percent tax rate is ten. "Across-the-board" actually works out to bigger percentage-point cuts as you go up the board.

By 1984 under the Reagan cut, the $15,000 couple's rate drops 5 percentage points (from 21 to 16 percent), the $35,000 couple's drops 9 (37 to 28), the $50,000 couple's 11 (49 to 38), the $100,000 couple's 14 (59 to 45), and the $200,000 couple's rate drops 18 points (68 to 50). In sum, the $15,000 couple gets a break of 5 points, the $200,000 couple a break of 18—three and a half times more.[2] Reagan's "across-the-board" cut has made the income tax sharply less progressive.

Reagan also carried to and through the Congress what his treasury secretary called "the largest tax cut in the history of American business." A plan for accelerated depreciation, the business bonanza was projected to cost the Treasury $158 billion across 5 years. The 10-5-3 plan, as it was called (after the new shorter write-off terms for different investments), helped profitable companies by definition since you had to be making money for faster write-offs to matter. According to government studies, the bill as passed actually gave corporations a negative tax rate on income from some machinery. Just one industry, telecommunications, got tax breaks worth about $46 billion over ten years. The *Wall Street Journal* reported that one obscure clause, giving the Treasury authority to alter rules retroactively, can mean $14 billion to AT&T, alone, in that time.[3]

This much Reagan and his men planned and intended. On the 10-5-3 plan they knew they could count on help from powerful Democrats like Senator Lloyd Bentsen of Texas, who had been urging programs like it for several years. What no one could have foretold was the rush for the cornucopia of tax cuts by other corporate interests and the trading and bidding among Democrats and Republicans that then broke out—special interests gone wild.

The oilstate Democrats extracted $12 billion in benefits: special write-offs for oil drillers and a limited exemption for royalty owners from the windfall profits tax. There were lucrative breaks for truckers and for developers on old buildings. Bargaining for votes, Reagan reversed course and endorsed income tax indexing in 1985. *Time* reported that the new depreciation rules turned out to be so liberal, many economists thought many or even most corporations would pay no taxes over the next few years. About five out of six people who otherwise would pay estate or gift taxes were relieved of liability. The estate tax was effectively abolished by 1987 for all but the very largest estates (those of $600,000 or more) and the top rate for those was dropped from 70 to 50 percent. As even Stockman told Greider, "Do you realize the greed that came to the forefront? The hogs were really feeding. The greed level, the level of opportunism, just got out of control. . . . The basic strategy was to match or exceed the Democrats, and we did." And everyone knew—at one point Representative Dan Rostenkowski (D.–Ill.), the chairman of House Ways and Means, declared, "The auction is over."[4]

One almost unnoticed change expanded the practice of "tax leasing"—letting troubled corporations in effect sell tax benefits they could not use to profitable corporations that could use them to reduce their taxes. As the deficit ballooned out of control, however, the consequences of this provision attracted attention in the press. Money-losing Ford sold its unusable benefits to

IBM, which made a net gain on them of between $100 and $200 million. GE, although highly profitable, turned its tax liability into a $100 million refund with its bought tax breaks. Weakened companies did benefit: a bankrupt railroad made $50 million in two years selling its credits, Chrysler made $26 million, Ohio Edison $36 million, Asarco $32 million. But highly profitable companies also sold benefits they could not use. Occidental Petroleum, qualifying because most of its $711 million profit in 1981 was earned abroad, made about $25 million selling benefits to another firm. Amoco, with pretax income of $3.5 billion, reduced its tax liability by $159 million under the provision. The value of property involved in this one lulu was estimated at $22 billion—by 1987 the sale of benefits was to cost the Treasury $27 billion. Economist Alan Greenspan (who was to become the head of Reagan's Social Security study commission) approvingly called the program "the equivalent of food stamps for undernourished corporations." But finally Senator Dole, the chairman of the Senate Finance Committee, brought the play to an end ("indefensible," he said, "in a year in which the federal deficit will reach nearly $100 billion") with an announcement that he would seek the provision's repeal retroactively to a certain date. By the time they were stopped the special deals had financed almost $40 billion worth of assets.[5]

With all these plums heaped up in the basket, the Republicans spent half a million dollars on a radio campaign to bear it through the Congress into law. Reagan phoned members for aye votes. Most of the Senate's Democrats having paled at the challenge of explaining voting no to their home folks, the omnibus 1981 tax bonanza passed there 89–11 and then cleared the House 238–195. Despite all their bidding and compromises, the House Democrats had lost their proposed alternative bill (while also neatly storing away some claims on future campaign contributions from business interests). The bill that passed, Treasury Secretary Regan said, "includes 95 percent of what the President wanted."

It was also, as Dole said, "the largest tax cut in U.S. history." In the next five years the U.S. Treasury would lose $750 billion. In 1983 the administration admitted in its budget that the 1981 tax cut had reduced government revenues "by more than $1 trillion over 1984–1988." Led by the President, the Congress had gone on a wild binge—Rostenkowski called it "Mardi Gras." There was no good reason to believe that the budget could be cut enough to prevent chronic annual deficits. There was no assurance that the promised magical effects on business—a spurt in new capital formation and a prompt economic recovery from the already-deep recession—would occur. Evidently there was little calculation whether, in the light of Reagan's obdurate determination to increase military spending, total government spending could be cut at all. He had turned the politicians' perennial rhetoric against taxes into an uncontrollable stampede to actually cut taxes in every direction with no thought for the morrow.

When the tax cut passed Reagan had already won the first-stage vote in the year's budget cutting, but the actual cutting remained to be done. Paul Volcker, chairman of the Federal Reserve Board, had warned Congress early that tax cuts should be linked with definite spending cuts. "If you cut spending by 10 percent then we'd have room for tax cuts," but cutting taxes before spending would be "an extremely high-risk course" for the economy, Volcker said. In retort, Reagan's man Regan told Congress the tax cuts "can't wait until budget outlays are reduced." Of making the tax cuts dependent on spending cuts Regan said, "You're holding business up there," and the individual should be able "to plan taxes and not have it 'if' and 'maybe.' " Trying to calm the tax cutters, House Democrats called what was happening "the equivalent of faith in a free lunch," but when Rostenkowski proposed a 1-year cut, Regan called it "less than half a loaf."

"Reagan not only rides along with the public's antitax attitude, he accelerates it," former California Governor Pat Brown had concluded after years of watching his nemesis. In 1981 Reagan addressed the question of responsibility on June 12, while the tax outcome was still in doubt, with these words spoken in the East Room of the White House:

"Now there are those who are insisting that we settle for less (than the 25 percent cut). They demand proof in advance that what we propose will work. . . . Our opponents want more money from your family budget so they can spend it on the federal budget and make it remain high. . . . It's your money, not theirs. You earned it, they didn't. . . . *And when they insist we can't reduce taxes and spending and balance the budget too, one six-word answer will do: 'Yes we can, and yes we will.'*" (Emphasis supplied.)

The Great Treasury Heist of 1981 left the federal deficit for 1982 at $110 billion, an all-time record, and by the second winter of Reagan's term the 1983 deficit was expected to approach $200 billion—this despite two years of fierce cuts in social spending and despite Dole's second-year achievement of a restoration of $98 billion of the lost $435 billion in tax revenues over the first three years. James Schlesinger, who is a certified hawk on military spending, nevertheless told the *New York Times* in October 1982 that Congress had to cut back Reagan's military budget. "That is the inevitable outcome of the destruction of the tax base," he said.[6]

The witty, maverick Republican chairman of Senate Finance had come to a similar conclusion, and Bob Dole was also worried about "a perception that we've been too hard on poor people." He knew somebody had to stop Reagan and the Democrats couldn't, so he would.

For months the President resisted raising taxes immediately after axing away so much of the tax base. "There certainly will be no change in taxes in 1982, I guarantee you," he said just before Christmas of 1981. But by the end of January the guarantee had become just another New Year's resolution. With unemployment rising, a secret terror of a second Great Depression had seized some members of the government in the Congress and the White House. While Reagan vacillated, Dole prepared to raise taxes, arguing that there was a danger of "$600 billion in federal red ink over the next three years." In May the Senate thwarted Democratic attempts to delay or cancel the third-year cut, but meanwhile Dole was judging, item by item, what Reagan would stand still for.

Dole in control, the Senate Republicans wrote and passed over Democratic opposition a bill that raised $98 billion in three years from business and consumers, partly with taxes, partly by stiffened collection procedures. As finally passed, Dole's best

effort against the gaping deficit levied a tax on federal employees to pay for Medicare, lowered the threshold one-third (to
$12,000 a year for single workers) above which unemployment
compensation benefits are taxable, increased the employer tax
for unemployment compensation, increased the depreciation
and certain other business tax breaks, broadened the minimum
tax, severely restricted the sale of corporate tax benefits, reduced the tax value of industrial development bonds, curbed
defense contractors from deferring taxes on their longer-term
contracts, doubled the cigarette tax, tripled the telephone use
tax, increased the tax on airline tickets 60 percent, levied a new
tax on small fishing boats, materially reduced income tax deductions permitted for medical bills, required 10 percent withholding on dividends and interest, and tightened up the taxing of
tips. "The Reagan Revolution" was already lurching back on
itself.

The Senate Democrats tried but failed to limit the income tax
reductions to taxpayers who earn less than $79,000 a year and to
strike the taxes on cigarettes and telephones, but the House
Democrats did nothing at all. Seeing very well the case for Dole's
bill and fearing to be blamed for increasing taxes in an election
year, Rostenkowski's Ways and Means Democrats abdicated
their constitutional duty to originate tax bills and accepted the
bill the Senate had sent over. This was the lowest point in the
Democrats' cowardice and opportunism during Reagan's first
two years.

While Reagan's right wing, led by Representative Jack
Kemp (R.–N.Y.), objected that their President was selling out
the prosperity just around the corner, Reagan himself "swallowed hard" and took to TV to uphold the bill as best he could.
Leading Democrats—O'Neill, Rostenkowski, Senator Edward
Kennedy—grinned and sided with Dole and the President, but
the 1982 tax increases exposed an alarming incoherence in the
government.[7]

Next to the flat tax, a sales tax would most nearly carry out
Reagan's theories. To the extent that a sales tax is collected on
products that everyone buys, it is a regressive flat tax that hits
the poor and middle classes the hardest. Reagan often advocates

"user fees"—higher campground fees, waterways use fees, and the like—because they are similar to sales taxes.

Late in 1982 the Democrats, in league with congressional Republicans, endorsed an almost perfect flat tax. Transportation Secretary Lewis had originated the idea of more than doubling the federal gasoline tax (from 4 to 9 cents a gallon) and using the proceeds to finance construction and repair of highways and bridges and to assist urban mass transit systems. Threatened again by a Congress that was going ahead without him, Reagan endorsed the plan; but of course, as a way of raising taxes, he would. The enactment of the gasoline tax in the lame duck session was another defeat for Reagan—it was another tax increase, and it would fund a hated "make-work" program. But it was also another proof that his flat-tax approach was prevailing, even among the Democrats, during his first two years.[8]

Secure in his knowledge that the American people did not know what he advocated on radio in the late seventies, Reagan in mid-1982 called the flat tax "a very tempting thing" that should be considered. This was a pose; his key men already knew the program. Meese said "the progressive income tax is immoral" and he's for a one-rate flat tax. The treasury secretary said "a straight, across-the-board" tax would be fairest. Stockman informed the public that Reagan was "very sympathetic" to the flat tax.

Congressmen of both parties began toying with the idea. Senator Jesse Helms (R.–N.C.) had a 12 percent flat-tax bill that the Congressional Budget Office said would increase taxes 147 percent on those with $5,000 to $10,000 a year and reduce taxes 47 percent on those with between $100,000 and $200,000. Senator Dennis DeConcini (D.–Ariz.) proposed a flat tax that protected the poor but socked the middle class. Senator Bill Bradley (D.–N.J.) and Representative Richard A. Gephardt (D.–Mo.) suggested a flat-tax base with a graduated surcharge.

Making their case in surprise that they were being taken seriously, the flat taxers emphasized the need to simplify the tax system (granted, Senator Long says, but a separate issue). One also heard statements that the income tax is not progressive, which were untrue. (As sociologist Maurice Zeitlin pointed out, in 1979 taxpayers with annual incomes of $1 million or more paid 34 percent income tax on the average, those with $50,000 to $100,000 paid 23 percent, those with $20,000 to $25,000 paid 13 percent, and those with $5,000 to $10,000 paid 4 percent.) Some flat taxers, following Reagan and Meese, argued outright that the principle of ability to pay is wrong. A *Wall Street Journal* editorialist said that the present system is "based on the notion that those who can afford to pay more, should. This is, of course, only one notion of equity. . . . The question of who would pay more under a flat-rate system is trivial next to the question of who loses now under the current system." (And who loses? The nation's economy, this argument concluded.)

"The people who are pushing the flat-rate tax are trying to reduce the tax burden on the rich. It's as simple as that," said Joseph Pechman, a Brookings Institution economist. "There's no question that the effect is to raise taxes for low- and middle-income people," according to Jerome Kurtz, the IRS commissioner under Carter. "The trouble with the true flat tax," commented *Fortune Magazine,* is that "it punishes the poor." A Congressional Budget Office paper by Joseph J. Minarik concluded that four flat-tax schemes would reduce the liability of taxpayers earning more than $50,000 a year by a fourth to more than a half. Senator Dole himself said, "The people in the middle would have to pick up the tab."

But rather unexpectedly, it was the son of the great populist Huey Long who planted himself directly in the path that Reagan was pursuing toward the flat tax. "Justice and fairness require," said the ranking Democrat on the Senate Finance Committee, Russell Long, "that those who make large amounts of money should pay a higher rate of tax on income than middle- and low-income families. It seems totally unfair to have a person earning $15,000 a year paying the same rate as someone making $1 million."

When the President made Martin Feldstein the chairman of his Council of Economic Advisers, the underlying purposes of the administration could no longer be gainsaid. One year before he was appointed Feldstein had written: "The best way to avoid the tax problems caused by inflation and to encourage savings and investment is to *eliminate the current corporate income tax and personal income tax and to replace them with a tax on consumer spending.*" (Italics supplied.) The man Reagan had chosen to supervise economic policy was perfectly attuned to the President's own determination to abolish the personal and corporate income taxes and increase taxes on what the masses of the people buy.

Under Feldstein's draft consumer tax, a citizen would calculate total income, including borrowed money as income, and then deduct interest and principal paid on loans and money spent on savings, stocks, bonds, mutual funds, other investments, and pension accounts. The balance, which would be presumed spent, would be taxed.

Economist Pechman said the consumption tax "does not meet the test of taxation according to the ability to pay" and "it would lead to an excessive concentration of wealth. . . . A tax that omits savings from the tax base can be shown to be the same as a tax applying only to labor income and exempting all property income."

The Democratic House voted in 1983 to "cap" a taxpayer's gain from the third-year tax cut at $720. But Dole was back in line, Reagan condemned "the politics of envy" and promised a veto, and the Senate Republicans killed the cap.

Given Reagan's ideology and purposes, he has already done remarkably well on taxes. According to the Treasury itself, 4.4 percent of the taxpayers, those with $50,000 or more a year, are receiving a third of the benefits from thirty-three changes made in the IRS code during the past two years. Stockman's hint that the flat taxers would make their move to kill the progressive income tax before 1984 seemed exotic. As Kurtz said, "While economists and social philosophers may debate whether a progressive tax system is fair, the fact is that most people think it is," and neither Reagan nor a successor-nominee was likely to go to the country asking approval for trying to convince them otherwise. But everything we know underscores the likelihood that if Reagan wins a second term he will summon forth all the Republicans' resources and all his own rhetorical powers to abolish the progressive income tax.[9]

6

Big Money and Big Business in the White House

Ⅰt is a rule among smart politicians that if you have to take a position that is likely to cost you support, do it quickly, briefly, and if possible only once. "I don't believe in government funding of elections," we should "not have government in it," and there should be no restrictions on the amount of money a presidential candidate raises, Ronald Reagan said on December 13, 1979. Then he dropped the subject. Although his own 1980 campaign accepted $37 million from the presidential election campaign fund, he and Mrs. Reagan regularly refuse to specify on their tax return that $1 should go to that fund for each of them.

Reagan knows—he could not fail to know—that the rich and the highly placed have funded his political career.

During his 1966 campaign, according to an insider's estimate, about $3 million of the $4 million raised for him was received in sums of $5,000 or more. To get reelected four years later he spent $3.6 million, $1.05 for each vote compared to his Democratic opponent's 42 cents.

With unspent money from his 1976 presidential campaign he organized the political action committee Citizens for the Republic, of which he is still president emeritus. (Even though he is now in the White House, he has permitted this group to present its contributors the "Distinguished Presidential Support Certificate," which thanks them for "supporting President Ronald Reagan through the political action committee he founded. . . .")

In 1978 Senator Paul Laxalt (R.–Nev.), whom Reagan later made general chairman of the Republican Party, said, "We found that our 'friends,' the *Fortune* 500, were playing both sides. When you push water for them as long as we have, that's a little hard to swallow." Reagan agreed: he told a conference of corporate public affairs officers the same year, "I don't think the Republican party has received the kind of financial support from corporate PACs [political action committees] that its record deserves. Why does half the business PAC money go to candidates who may not be friends of business?" Lest there be any question whether he was a "friend of business," he and his wife were hosts to the "Eagles," those who give the Republican Party $10,000 a year or more, during a dinner cruise on the Potomac that year. Elizabeth Drew reported in the *New Yorker*, in a penetrating study about political money, that the Reagans gave two fund-raising parties in a house in rural Virginia, one in September 1979 for the Eagles and another in October 1980 for contributors of "soft money" (which can come directly from corporate treasuries and yet be worked into political campaigns) in sums ranging between $10,000 and $50,000 from each donor. Reagan himself then was directly and actively involved in soliciting millions of dollars from big business.

In 1980, Drew calculates, much more private than public money went into Reagan's campaign—$10 million from "independent committees," at least $9 million in soft money, $4.6 million spent through the national GOP, a total of $26 million, plus what the state parties dispensed. Reagan had a $15 million media budget, of which a third was spent in the campaign's final week (Carter received less than a fifth of what Reagan did from private donors). One wealthy Texan, Cecil R. Haden, quite legally spent $413,221 on behalf of Reagan.

Reagan insiders specialize in directing these steamy flows of cash. Lyn Nofziger, the in-and-out Reagan aide, has been quoted: "In a state where it's allowed, you get corporate money and spend it for damn near anything. And if I give $50,000 in corporate funds in California, that frees the campaign to spend $50,000 for whatever it wants." To keep the White House informed about public opinion, the Republican National Committee paid chief Reagan pollster Richard Wirthlin's firm $900,000 in 1981 alone. The deputy chairman of the Republican National Committee in 1982, Rich Bond, boasted that he had in effect bought votes for Reagan's budget cuts by promising to give two members of Congress the maximum permissible contributions for their campaigns (to "max out" for them) if they voted right on the cuts. The same Rich Bond told Drew: "If Mobil Oil wanted to give you twenty million bucks I think they could give you twenty million bucks, and you don't have to show it."

Democrats won back twenty-six seats in the House in 1982, but Democratic National Chairman Charles Manatt said that "money alone can buy ten or twelve seats," and the executive director of the National Republican Congressional Committee, Nancy Sinnott, confirmed as "plausible" the estimate that the Republicans' money advantage did in fact cost the Democrats ten or twelve—which is to say, itself averted a Democratic landslide. In 1982 "the assets-and-priorities group" met once a week in the White House to direct the flow of campaign money to chosen candidates and against chosen targets, Drew learned. Lee Atwater, the deputy assistant to President Reagan for political affairs, told her: "I've got to think that the money and all the other resources combined will be worth about two percentage points for about thirty candidates. I think the story of this off year election is that we've marshalled our resources and bought one or two Senate seats and fifteen to twenty House seats, and that's really good."

Money pouring into elections has become a bipartisan national scandal. *Congressional Quarterly* estimated that campaign expenditures in 1980 totaled $900 million, and candidates for the presidency alone spent a fourth of a billion dollars; the congressional campaigns of 1982 cost a third of a billion. "I honestly believe," said Representative Fenwick after losing a Senate race to a multimillionaire Democrat who spent $2.6 million of his own money, "we're going to have to take a new look at our whole electoral process. I think it's being corrupted by money." In the *Wall Street Journal* Norman C. Miller wrote, "PACs virtually own some members of Congess." Representative Leon Panetta (D.–Calif.) said, "Congress is literally being bought and sold by PAC contributions." Elizabeth Drew concluded her study: "We have allowed the basic idea of our democratic process—representative government—to slip away."[1] Yet in the summer of 1983, as a reluctant and deeply compromised Congress turned again to the subject of campaign finance reform, there was still no concern or leadership on the issue coming from the White House—none whatsoever.

As he had approached the presidency, Reagan with bold candor had repeatedly signaled big business that he would serve it from the White House. He had "faith in the marketplace," he said. "Let's quit tinkering with the free enterprise system." The federal government was "at war with its own business community," and "I would like to make government a friend of the American industrial community, not an enemy." Cannon says that Reagan's campaign planners John Sears and Nofziger "tried without success for years to get (him) to say something unkind about big business." A former aide of Reagan's told the *Wall Street Journal,* "Reagan's support is populist, but he's not. All of his instincts are pro–big business."

Although the connections between campaign finance reform and national economic issues are not simple or confined to one party, the connections between Reagan's opposition to such reform and his allegiances to big business are self-evident. Special interests can now contribute unlimited amounts to presidential campaigns and buy votes in Congress for their special bills. Reagan's election to the White House as the beneficiary of unlimited private spending sealed with much more than a kiss his intimate alliance with the various business interests. While his acquiescence in the commercialization of the presidency and Congress is its most important single expression, his liaison with business has many incarnations from industry to industry and many rendezvous as the occasions of the hour and their settings change.

In his politico-economic cosmology, government alone causes inflation, so companies can hardly be blamed for raising their prices, and government's attempts to control prices and wages with voluntary guidelines or mandatory controls are precluded by faith in "the magic of the marketplace."

In California Reagan created a department of consumer affairs, but the consensus was that it was dominated by business. He appointed businessmen to the Public Utility Commission, which then allowed telephone rates to skyrocket. In national politics he opposed the creation of a federal consumer protection agency, and on radio he rejoiced in the defeat of congressmen identified as "friends of consumers." And he went further: He specifically defended higher prices that were imposed by various lines of business. He warned in advance that he favored lifting all price controls on oil and gas, and he said that OPEC could not be faulted for raising oil prices since such prices were figured in dollars and the dollar had been losing strength against foreign currencies. He opposed government-set limits on hospital costs. He defended rising utility bills.

"Now before you scream and say look at my last month's bill, hear me out," he said in 1978. "We actually pay less per kilowatt hour of electricity than we did 20, 30, or 50 years ago. Our bills are up because we use electricity for more things. . . . We aren't being ripped off by the producers of that electricity."

He blasted Carter's "cheap food policy" and promised to give the heave-ho to consumer-oriented officials at the Department of Agriculture. What was needed, he said, was a change of the policy "which is based on cheap food, appealing to the consumer, to a policy that recognizes the necessity of . . . agriculture—and you don't do that by having a deputy secretary of agriculture whose whole interest is consumers." In 1979 he declared: "Free enterprise is becoming far less free in the name of something called consumerism."[2]

Why, then, one might ask, did President Reagan appoint Virginia Knauer to run his White House Office of Consumer Affairs? For show, apparently. In 1982 consumer advocate Ralph Nader proposed its abolition as a fraud and a waste of money. After five years' study, the FTC had ruled in 1981 that used car dealers would be required, on pain of a $10,000 fine, to tell prospective buyers (on car window stickers) about any known defects in cars on their lots. Knauer wrote a letter endorsing the rule, but she spoke too soon: Reagan's budget office said her endorsement was just her personal opinion, and the requirement would be an onerous burden on the dealers. Congress, saturated with shrewdly distributed contributions from the used car dealers, vetoed the rule by wide margins in both chambers. Reagan's chairman of the Federal Trade Commission, James C. Miller, III, took no part in the promulgation of the rule or the fight in Congress, but when the FTC subsequently voted to require funeral directors to itemize prices and services, he voted no.[3]

Never has a successful presidential candidate proclaimed his alliance with big oil more openly than Reagan. In 1976 he called for the restoration of the oil depletion allowance on grounds that the way to solve energy shortages is to funnel more money to the oil companies so they can find and produce more oil. Again and again he said he would free oil from government restraints: "Get the government out of the way and turn the industry loose." "Turn them loose to solve their own problems." "Get government out of the energy industry." "Get the government out of the oil industry and turn it loose in the marketplace." As his energy adviser, oilman Michel Halbouty, said, "The goal is to keep the government out of the field of energy production. Turn the whole ball of wax over to private industry."[4]

To help finance their prepresidential planning, the Reagan group collected $450,000 in private contributions from donors whose names were not made public. For Reagan's gaudy inaugural the Reaganists made more than $8 million in interest-free loans from corporations and others. Atlantic Richfield, for an example, lent the inaugural committee $50,000 and bought half a million dollars worth of commercials to benefit the effort, and a spokesman for Arco said this reflected "the company's interest in maintaining good relations with the incoming administration. Obviously, we are terribly interested in legislation that is coming."

Carter had already created a deregulatory trend for Reagan in oil and gas prices; oil price controls, first imposed by Nixon in 1971, were to expire in October 1981. With Stockman and Energy Secretary Edwards predicting that the result would be gasoline prices 3 to 5 cents more a gallon in several months' time, Reagan, acting by executive order after one week in office, abolished the remaining price and allocation controls on domestic oil. Exxon raised its gasoline price twice in less than a week, by a total of 8 cents; Gulf announced three price hikes in nine days, totaling 6 cents a gallon, and every other major oil company increased gasoline and heating oil prices 2 to 5 cents within six days of Reagan's act. Each penny added to the average price of a gallon of gas at the pump costs American consumers $1 billion a year; Reagan's Department of Energy (DOE) estimated the industry's gain at $2 billion.[5]

A month after Reagan decontrolled the price of domestic oil, Mrs. Reagan solicited private contributions to decorate the White House, and the information subsequently was extracted from the White House that $270,000 of the money came from oilmen. The government had offered Mrs. Reagan $50,000 for the job, but she had returned it. "Fifty thousand dollars wouldn't even buy throw rugs in my house," said Oklahoma oilman Jack L. Hodges as he gave Mrs. Reagan's fund $50,000 all by himself. Holmes Tuttle of Reagan's kitchen cabinet had solicited contributions from oilmen in Houston and Oklahoma City, and his secretary was quoted that "the response was phenomenal at $10,000 a shot." Armand Hammer of Occidental Petroleum gave $20,000, a number of other oilmen $10,000 apiece. According to Senator William Proxmire (D.–Wisc.), "There is no way to escape the clear connection between the pro-oil policies of the administration, worth so much to the industry, and the payoff in contributions to the White House"—it was "as blatant a presidential conflict of interest as I can recall in the more than twenty years I've been in Congress."[6]

During the 1973 oil embargo the government had set oil prices on a schedule designed to encourage new drilling that resulted in prices for the oldest oil that were almost $30 a barrel below the world price. The government, which was keeping the companies under some financial surveillance, charged that widespread price gouging occurred as old oil was falsely certified to be new oil, for which much more could be charged. Ultimately the Carter administration filed civil claims against major firms, including Exxon, Mobil, and Texaco, for $11 billion in alleged overcharge violations.

Despite the fact that the enforcement office of the DOE, by pursuing these claims, was bringing in more money for the government than it spent, the Reagan administration early in 1981 proposed to cut its funding 80 percent. Barton R. House, the acting administrator of the agency's Economic Regulation Administration, wrote his superiors memos warning that such cuts would "signal DOE's reluctance to follow through on existing identified violations and will seriously weaken DOE's position in negotiating settlements," as well as causing the oil industry "to opt for waiting us out rather than settling," but his objections were ignored; in two years the enforcement staff was cut by nearly 50 percent, the number of field offices assigned to recover the overcharges declined from more than forty to eight, and by further cuts the administration sought to shrink the program to one-fifth of what it had been under Carter. Accused of preparing to forgive billions of dollars in rebates that were due to customers, Reagan officials vowed to prosecute the cases. But in 1982 Raymond Hanzlik, the head of DOE's overcharge enforcement office, said to reporters that he expected major oil companies to reimburse customers or the government at between 10 cents and 30 cents for each dollar of overcharges they were accused of, and then, late in the winter of 1983, DOE proposed settling for $27 million its charge that Mobil had claimed excessive costs totaling $920 million. This gave rise to a charge, which DOE and Mobil disputed, that this was a pilot settlement for the big companies at 3 cents on the dollar.[7]

Federal control of the price of natural gas at the wellhead has been an inflammatory issue in Congress for a third of a century. In 1956 President Eisenhower vetoed a decontrol bill after a Republican senator revealed what was widely construed as the offer of a bribe to get him to vote for it. In 1978, on grounds that there was a natural gas shortage and drilling for new supplies had to be encouraged, Carter led Congress into decontrolling the price of all new gas on a phased schedule completely freeing it from control in 1985. The prices of "old gas," that which was first tapped before 1978, continued under federal price control, but were allowed to rise with inflation. Early in 1979, on radio, Reagan declared himself for total decontrol. "The magic word," he said, "is 'decontrol' of the wellhead price. . . . What are we waiting for?"

Natural gas supplies about a fourth of the nation's energy and is used by 55 percent of all homes and businesses. The price for it began rising rapidly, as intended, after Carter's and the Congress' phased decontrol in 1978. In Reagan's term the price rose 17 percent in 1981 and as much as 60 percent in 1982; increases of 25 percent were expected in 1983. A widespread customers' rebellion stiffened resistance among state utility regulators, and Reagan found his congressional leaders unwilling to fight for total decontrol unless it was linked with an excess profits tax on natural gas profits. Several major oil company chiefs were amenable to such a tax—the chairmen of Mobil and Conoco, for example—but Reagan was opposed to it (would in fact veto it "with pleasure"), and decontrol was put off for two years. In February 1983—saying nary a word about a windfall profits tax—Reagan asked Congress to completely decontrol gas prices by 1986.

The second month after Reagan had lifted oil price controls, heating oil prices had increased 9 percent and gasoline 7.5 percent. In due time, however, as is well known, a worldwide oil glut developed and OPEC lost its control over its member nations' oil production, sending worldwide oil prices much lower. Arguing in 1983 for gas price decontrol, Reagan said disingenuously that gas prices would go down just as those for oil had. Under his proposal, gas and pipeline companies could negotiate new contracts immediately without price controls. Pipelines' pass-along increases would be restrained until 1986, but not after that. In 1985 there would be a cap on gas prices under old contracts, consisting of the average national price, but that, too, would end in 1986.

DOE said gas prices would go up slightly under the plan, but then might come down. In the Democrats' response, Representative W. G. Hefner of North Carolina said prices would go up 67 percent in four years; Democratic Governor Mario Cuomo of New York said the plan would add $450 to $600 a year to residential heating bills, and the Citizen-Labor Energy Coalition said consumers would have to pay, under the plan, $50 billion more in the next four years.

Fuel is of course a necessity, and the natural gas business is not competitive in any ordinary sense. Most of the major oil companies rank among the top twenty domestic gas producers; the top five gas producers are Mobil, Exxon, Texaco, Shell, and Gulf. The producers of gas usually can sell to only one pipeline, and consumers of it usually can buy from only one company. Some gas companies have come under criticism for buying high-cost gas from their own subsidiaries rather than lower-cost gas that is just as available to them. Pipelines sign long-term contracts with their suppliers at prices fixed for the duration of the contracts. As Representative Silvio Conte (R.—Mass.) explains, this distribution system "does not allow the consumer a variety of choices for a purchase; therefore the sellers have little incentive to keep their prices as low as possible."

By 1983, according to the National Consumer Law Center, the price of natural gas had become the dominant factor in the budgets of low-income families. Representative George Crockett, Jr. (D.–Mich.) said that in February 1983 10,000 households in the Detroit area had no heat because people could not pay their gas bills. In the Kansas City area, according to Representative Ike Skelton (D.–Mo.), 6,000 people were without heat for the same reason, and only the mildness of the winter of 1982–1983 averted the prospect that a third of a million Americans would lose their heat. The law center study found that in forty-three states and the District of Columbia, the elderly poor who receive the maximum Supplemental Security Income benefit have less than $50 a week for all other expenses (housing, food, and so on) after paying their energy bills, but before receiving low-income home-energy assistance. Reagan's budget for 1984 proposed a 34 percent cut in that assistance.[8]

Apart from raising oil and gas prices and subsidizing nuclear power, the administration has no coherent energy policy, despite the lessons supposedly learned from the two foreign-induced energy crises of the 1970s.

The Strategic Petroleum Reserve, which contained 110 million barrels when Reagan took office, has been increased beyond 300 million barrels, but Reagan ignored legislation directing that more be deposited than the administration permitted. At the same time, Reagan allowed the Navy oil reserves to be pumped down at the rate of 62 million barrels a year, almost as fast as the buildup. Federal appropriations for energy conservation, solar power, and synfuel alternatives to fossil fuels have plummeted. One might attribute this to Reagan's expressed commitment to the free market if it were not for the case of the nuclear power industry. The administration's energy policy is faithful, not to the free market, but to the oil and nuclear industries at the expense of their rivals.

Reagan's determination to abolish the Department of Energy exemplifies his policy. He wanted energy turned over to private industry completely, so what was the need for a government department on the subject? He was not interested in continuing the department's programs to promote solar power, synfuels, and conservation because his energy policy is oil and nuclear. Congress foiled him about DOE, in no small part because half the department's functions are concerned with the manufacture and distribution of nuclear weapons, which Congress is not about to abolish. But the fact that the first secretary of energy, the South Carolina dental surgeon, knew nothing about energy qualified him well for what Reagan wanted him to do.

Since 1973 Congress has granted the President emergency powers during severe oil shortages to allocate fuel supplies and control their prices. When the law giving him these powers expired in 1981, Reagan opposed its reenactment on grounds that the market would do the job better than bureaucrats. In defiance of his position, Congress passed a bill anyway (86–7 in the Senate, 246–144 in the House) giving him the emergency authority, but he vetoed it, saying, "What I do not have, do not want and do not need is general power to reimpose on all Americans another web of price controls and mandatory allocations." If there is another grave oil shortage during Reagan's presidency, therefore, the oil companies and the states will do the allocating and the price setting.

Reagan's ambivalence concerning the U.S. Synthetic Fuels Corporation likewise proceeds from his opposition to government action on energy. The government-owned company, which Congress provided $20 billion to use to aid private companies' ventures in the production of synthetic fuels, did nothing with its money during Reagan's first two years, but then in 1983 suddenly announced new plans to provide loan guarantees and price supports at 200 percent of market prices for oil shale and coal gasification projects.

If the government's program for energy independence was, as Carter said, the "moral equivalent of war," the Reagan administration's position was the war's Maginot Line. Two of Carter's men spoke out angrily. Stuart E. Eizenstat, Carter's chief domestic policy adviser, said "the crumbling of our infant alternative-energy industry" was "a national tragedy." Carter's press secretary, Jody Powell, wrote: "Plans for obtaining 20 percent of our energy from solar and other renewable resources by the end of this century have been totally abandoned. Federal support for gasohol, solar energy, and other alternatives to oil has gone from $648 million to less than $100 million. The synfuels effort and the corporation established to oversee it are a hollow shell." Reagan's preparations for another energy crisis, Powell concluded, are "worse than nothing" and "willfully negligent."[9]

Reagan's antagonism toward governmentally encouraged conservation programs is the feature of his energy policy that is most difficult to fathom. He said, campaigning in 1980, that conservation is "no answer" to the country's energy problem. Asked why he would not seek greater conservation, he replied, "Conservation means we'll all be too hot in the summer and too cold in the winter." His administration killed requirements, just before they were to go into effect, for energy efficiency in appliances. Energy performance standards for new buildings were dropped. So were Carter's programs to help low-income people insulate their residences, support research and demonstration projects to reduce the use of energy in industry, teach drivers of fleets of cars to use less fuel, and require electric and gas utilities to perform energy audits at homes, which the Carter people had estimated would save Americans $34 billion. It is the Reagan administration's position that higher energy prices cause people to conserve fuel more effectively than government programs. As Secretary Edwards told Congress, "the very nature of conservation implies that it be undertaken voluntarily out of the self-interest of individuals and businesses" and there is "little need for federal participation." When Reagan fired DOE's top conservation official, Deputy Assistant Secretary of Energy for Conservation Maxine Savitz, the reason given was her refusal to accept a transfer to Colorado, but she said her dismissal was part of the administration's program to "do away with all federal conservation programs."[10]

Reagan has no real interest in solar energy; he expresses the same position that is generally taken in oil company advertisements, that solar power will help, but only a little and not soon. "In years to come," he says, "solar energy may provide an answer, but for the next two or three decades we need to do such things as master the chemistry of coal." He calls the anti-nuclear-power movement irrational in advocating solar power as a substitute for nuclear power (and accuses it of being Communist-inspired [see Appendix]). "Solar won't amount to much," Ed Meese told environmentalist leaders. "What can a few windmills provide?" In 1981 Reagan converted these attitudes into figures, proposing to cut the federal solar power budget from $559 million to $193 million, and the slashing continued into 1983. Edwards fired a third of the solar energy staff at DOE. The administration refused to carry out the law creating a solar bank to finance energy conservation by homeowners. Consumer groups and others went to court, and Reagan was compelled to "faithfully execute the laws" by establishing the bank whether he wanted to or not, but the prospects for a nascent federal enterprise the President opposed were hardly bright. Federal research into such basic technologies of the future as photovoltaic cells was aborted; federally supported solar firms faced sudden cutoffs from Washington.[11]

As the budding solar industry could expect no help from Reagan in its competition with oil and nuclear, neither could small businesses in general expect much help from Reagan's Washington in their struggles for survival in dominated markets. "The role of government should remain neutral between large and small business," Reagan's transition task force on small business advised him. "Your administration's small business policy should *not* consist of more small-business subsidies, loan programs, selective tax exemptions, and government contract favors."

Keyed to this policy, the Reaganized Small Business Administration (SBA) sought to abolish its direct lender program, and the agency's guaranteed loans to small business were marked for cuts in the 1983 budget to only slightly more than half pre-Reagan levels. The White House budget office in effect abolished SBA's guaranteed tax-exempt bond program that had enabled more than 200 small businesses to finance pollution control equipment. In 1981 a new law required the government to pay the legal costs of small businesses that proved they had been maltreated by federal bureaucrats, but the administration sought to restrict who could recover in such actions and how much. When Congress moved to guarantee small business a tiny percentage of certain federal research budgets, the administration opposed a 3 percent guaranteed level in favor of the 1 percent level that prevailed in the legislative consensus.[12]

Plainly, there was to be no "welfare" for small business. But what about big business? Businessmen "have got to believe in the marketplace, too," Reagan had said. On the subject of the Chrysler bailout he snapped "What's wrong with bankruptcy?" and the Reaganists stood fast when Braniff failed, just letting it go on under. But the administration exempted the banking and savings and loan industries from "the magic of the marketplace," propping them up with taxpayers' money.

In 1982, with the strong support of the administration, Congress—acting under the cover of deregulation—pledged the credit of the United States to an open-ended bailout of the bank and savings and loan industries. While most press attention was centered on the new law's deregulation of interest rates that depository institutions pay, Congress committed the taxpayers' Treasury to guarantee the net worth of banks and savings and loan associations—that is, their solvency.

The thrift industry started the debate with a laugh by asking Congress for $10 billion in immediate financial aid while calling on Reagan to cut the federal deficit. He would not support an outright appropriation for them, so the House approved an $8.5 billion fund to finance "net worth guarantees" for institutions whose net worth dropped dangerously low. The Senate, led on this issue by Senator Jake Garn (R.–Utah), added new provisions to the bill and passed it, but then both versions disappeared into the conference committee of the two chambers.

In the preceding two years 437 thrifts had been "merged" out of existence, and *Fortune* reported that another 1,000 of them with $200 billion of assets were headed for zero net worth by the end of 1983. Their depositors were already insured; what the thrifts wanted now was new capital from the federal government. U.S. policy would shift away from merging weak institutions out of existence toward the entirely new policy of putting up federal capital to perpetuate them.

In the closing weeks of the regular 1982 session of the Ninety-seventh Congress, the conferees sprang forth with the most radical law on banks and thrifts in fifty years. It was pushed through the House in the session's closing hours under a "closed rule" that prohibited members from proposing amendments to propositions they have never considered before. Representative Jim Mattox (D.–Tex.) objected to restructuring the whole financial industry "in the closing hours . . . under a closed rule," and Representative Dingell of Michigan saw no reason why they should write the legislation "with a bag on our heads tonight," but they did: they passed the Net Worth Certificate Act of 1982, and without making a record that would show how each member had voted.

Under this new law, which Reagan (as he signed it) called

"the most important legislation for financial institutions in the last fifty years," the taxpayers, in return for nothing, contribute capital to private banks and savings associations and pay their debts if they go under.

The contrivance at the center of the act is the "net worth certificate." The Federal Deposit Insurance Corporation (FDIC), for the banks, and the Federal Savings and Loan Insurance Corporation (FSLIC), for the savings and loan associations and savings banks, give net worth certificates, which are promissory notes guaranteed by the U.S. Treasury, to troubled depository institutions to shore up their net worth to 3 percent of their assets. The certificates are considered capital and therefore increase the net worth of the assisted institutions. The humbug to one side, in reality the federal government is giving capital to the private institutions. If an assisted institution becomes sound again, it returns its certificate to the government. If it goes under, the "guaranteed" net worth having vanished, the government pays the firm's creditors. Not, mind, the depositors: they are already insured up to $100,000 for each account. *The creditors.* "The bailout," William J. Quirk wrote in *Fortune,* "will benefit only a small group: the executives and shareholders of the thrifts, the thrifts' employees, holders of accounts over $100,000, subordinated debt holders, and general creditors." The taxpayers invest, but receive neither stock nor property in return; they become liable for debts they did not incur and losses they did not cause; the public credit is given away as private losses are socialized. Under the new law mergers of failed S&Ls would continue, but about 2,100 S&Ls were expected to receive more than $1 billion in net worth certificates by the end of 1983.

The act, commented the business weekly *Barron's,* "grants a veritable blank check on the Treasury to bolster ailing thrifts and . . . mortgage-heavy commercial banks" and thereby "commits the taxpayers, as a matter of national policy, to underwriting the survival of mutual and stockholder-owned institutions alike . . . guaranteeing the survival, at regulators' discretion, of the worst-managed institutions. . . . It's not so much 'the public be damned' as 'the public be soaked.' "[13]

In the White House repainted green, the Reagan administra-

tion's thorough allegiance to big business even extended to the
defense of corporate bribery of the officials of other nations. A
certain restraint was maintained: Bribing foreign officials was
not advocated. But the Reaganists' cynical acceptance of the
practice was not concealed.

In the 1970s more than 450 American companies were
caught bribing—or, as the euphemism went, making "questionable payments"—to promote sales abroad. The allegations included payments to five heads of government, one vice president or deputy premier, two aides to heads of governments, and
twenty-two cabinet members or heads of agencies. Governments
were destabilized by the scandals in Japan, South Korea, the
Netherlands; corporations paid huge fines; two Japanese politicians were convicted of taking bribes from Lockheed (which
admitted making a total of $220 million in questionable pay-
ments). In 1977 a shamed Congress passed the Foreign Corrupt
Practices Act, which prohibits such overseas payments where
there is "reason to know" they are bribes, requires companies to
keep records to prove they are not paying them, and gives the
Securities and Exchange Commission (SEC) enforcement responsibilities.

By 1980 Reagan had joined a general outcry from big business against the law. Asked by *Business Week* if he would relax
restrictions against foreign payments, he replied with the ambig-
uous cynicism which would come to characterize his administration on the point. "We don't want to give up our protection
against monopoly at home," he said, "but why can't we make it
possible for American concerns to compete on the world market
and not have it called collusion or restraint of trade? Bribery
disclosures are always treated here as if they were an evil on the
part of American business. Yet, to the rest of the world, using
agents, or 'fixers' is their way of doing business." Could a presidential candidate let that stand as his position? No. Reagan
added: "Enlightened exporting nations should get together and
agree they will not hold still for it."

The administration's actual argument, stripped of rhetorical
obfuscations, is that bribes are expected abroad and if American
companies cannot pay them they are placed at a competitive

disadvantage. Reagan's transition task force for the SEC recommended dropping the 1977 law's criminal penalties. The administration enforced the law (for instance filing criminal charges against a California company and its president alleging that they helped bribe officials of Mexico's government oil company), but all the while tried to change the law. Its position was that Congress should remove all the law's requirements for record keeping and strip the SEC of its enforcement role. Speaking for Reagan, Trade Representative Brock alluded to "the so-called Foreign Corrupt Practices Act" and asked for the removal of the "reason to know" test of guilt. Brock also called the 1977 law a trade barrier that was costing "American jobs." The Justice Department, making no announcement of the fact, abolished its multinational fraud branch; the Republican Senate passed a bill which struck the "reason to know" test, removed the SEC from its enforcement role, and renamed the 1977 law the "Business Records and Practices Act." That was stopped by Representative Timothy Wirth (D.–Colo.) in the House, but in the Ninety-Eighth Congress Senator John Heinz (R.–Pa.) was back with a bill to legalize "any expenditures . . . associated with the selling and purchasing of goods or services" overseas. Difficult to accept though the fact might be, the Reagan administration was conducting a crusade to make it easier for American corporations to get away with bribing foreign officials.[14]

7

Uranium, Plutonium, and Bechtel

T he nuclear power industry is government-subsidized; nuclear power plants might not exist but for the $25 billion the government has invested in them in the last quarter of a century. Despite Reagan's commitment to the free market, the industry correctly perceived him as its reliable ally in its efforts to preserve these federal subsidies. Reagan's election, said the president of the Atomic Industrial Forum, "produced mixed emotions in our industry: ecstasy, joy, pleasure, and euphoria." The nuclear power people were confident that he would try to give them more money and less regulation, and they were right.

In his first budget, while cutting solar, conservation, and all other energy programs, Reagan raised spending for nuclear power 36 percent, to $1.6 billion. In his second one, nuclear-fission energy was booked for $1.02 billion, compared to $83 million for all renewable energy programs. When the governor of Pennsylvania proposed that the federal government pay $190 million to help clean up the crippled reactor at the Three Mile

Island plant in Pennsylvania, budget director Stockman said the administration accepted the "framework" of the plan and favored spending "in excess of $100 million" on the cleanup.

Representative Richard Ottinger (D.–N.Y.), who is chairman of the House Energy Conservation and Power Subcommittee, exposed the existence of a memorandum written by DOE's director of planning and policy recommending that federal bureaucrats campaign for nuclear power by making public appearances with the help of hired flacks; arranging interviews of themselves by supposedly favorable columnists Hugh Sidey, George Will, William Buckley, James Reston, and Carl Rowan; hiring writers to prepare articles to be signed by DOE officials, extolling nuclear power; and distributing pronuclear power materials from the industry. DOE was to sponsor a $200,000 study by a pronuclear organization. The U.S. surgeon-general was to be asked to "certify the negligible effects of nuclear power reactors." Ottinger called the proposals "a blatant propaganda campaign for the nuclear power industry that will cost the American taxpayers millions of dollars."

The enrichment of uranium to make it usable in nuclear power reactors, as well as in nuclear weapons, has been conducted by the government in the United States. In 1982 the DOE began spending $300 million to develop a laser process of enrichment, which is expected to greatly reduce costs. At the same time, however, the administration asked Congress to agree to spend about $9 billion to complete construction of the government's plant in Ohio to enrich uranium by a gas centrifuge process. The General Accounting Office (an arm of Congress) said the laser process and declining demand for uranium made the Ohio plant unnecessary, but the Reaganists were hell-bent to get the plant even as they continued ripping and slashing most domestic spending.

Early in 1982, sources told United Press International about a secret meeting of top industry officials and Vice President Bush, arranged by Secretary Edwards and White House science adviser George Keyworth. At this meeting, the chairman of the Tennessee Valley Authority proposed that the United States put up $50 billion to buy some unfinished atomic reactors, to complete their construction, and to make capital available to utilities to complete other atomic plants that they have started building—a bailout to take the breath away.[1]

As an unfazable champion of nuclear power, Reagan scoffs at the problem of disposing of radioactive wastes. "The waste from one nuclear plant in a year would take less storage space than a dining room table," he said on the radio in 1979. "The truth is, all the nuclear waste now on hand and yet to be accumulated between now and the year 2000 could be stacked on a single football field and the stack would be only 6 feet high." He favored leaving the disposal of nuclear waste "in the hands of the private power companies, with the strictest of rules as to safety"—a position that Bush, as a candidate against him, called "irresponsible and, in fact, dangerous."

At present most nuclear power wastes are stored at sites near the plants; Reagan's officials supported temporary storage away from the plants, which would entail trucking the wastes on the public highways. Reagan signed a bill into law setting July 1983 as the deadline for federal recommendations concerning permanent burial sites, and the administration supported a federal grant to experiment in waste disposal technology using Three Mile Island's highly radioactive wastes.

No matter how blithely the President dismisses the problem of radioactive waste, it is enormous. The production of this generation's nuclear energy and weapons has already created problems for the next 300 generations. Late in 1982 the Nuclear Regulatory Commission (NRC) approved the first federal regulations for disposing of low-level radioactive wastes, in three classes depending on how many years must elapse before they become relatively harmless: liquid wastes to be stored in containers protected for 100 years, or solidified or packaged wastes to be kept secure for 300 years, or solidified wastes to be buried at least 15 meters underground and kept secure for 500 years. For the highly radioactive waste—7,500 metric tons of it from commercial reactors and 76 million gallons of military-related waste—the federal government is considering storage in seven geological formations in Washington State, Nevada, Utah, Texas, Louisiana, and Mississippi for "at least 10,000 years with no

prediction of significant decreases in isolation beyond that time."
After a study of how to mark a site in order to keep it undis-
turbed for at least 10,000 years, an archaeologist recommended
the erection of 29 to 30 stones, each 20 feet high and each
bearing the warning "Do not dig deeply here" in English,
French, Arabic, Spanish, Russian and Chinese. In case those
who came upon the site did not speak any of those languages,
each monolith would also display a drawing in a circle of a human form digging a hole, with a black line slashed diagonally
across the scene.[2]

In nuclear "breeder" reactors, used nuclear fuel is reprocessed to produce more freshly usable nuclear fuel than the
reprocessing consumes. However, since one of the fuels produced is plutonium, which can be used to make nuclear weapons, the construction of breeder reactors increases the likelihood
of the spread of nuclear weapons around the world. Between
1966 and 1972, in a plant at West Valley, N.Y., used nuclear
power plant fuel was reprocessed into uranium and plutonium,
but Ford and Carter successively banned the use of the process;
both Presidents wished to be able to argue plausibly against the
construction of breeder reactors abroad. Construction of a reprocessing plant at Barnwell, S.C., was halted in the mid-1970s,
and Carter vetoed an appropriation for a breeder reactor plant
on a peninsula that juts into the Clinch River in Tennessee, near
Oak Ridge.

The next year, Reagan commented on radio: "If we processed [nuclear] waste we'd recover additional fuel, but Uncle
Sam says 'no.' Our government is afraid this would lead to the
proliferation of nuclear weapons in the world. Frankly that is
foolish. Much of the reclaimed fuel could be used in our own
power plants. The rest . . . can be . . . buried deep in rock or
salt formations."

Congress kept paying for research for the Clinch River plant,
and when he attained the White House Reagan not only lifted
the ban on fuel reprocessing, he asked Congress to put up
money to encourage private companies to start producing uranium and plutonium at both Barnwell and Clinch River. DOE
ordered ten steam generator units for Clinch River from West-

inghouse, and late in 1982 workmen began clearing the site on
the peninsula. In 1983 Congress seemed bent on slaying "this
nuclear Dracula" (as Representative Dingell calls it), but if
Reagan has his way the United States will join the four other
nations which now have plants that "breed" plutonium.[3]

The President's partisanship for nuclear power is so un-
qualified, he joins the industry in belittling the safety dangers of
the plants. "Smoke from a coal-burning plant releases more radioactivity into the air than comes from a nuclear plant," he said
in 1980.

Before the 1979 near disaster at the Three Mile Island plant
Reagan apparently relied extensively on "the Rasmussen report," which was a slanted proindustry study paid for by the
pronuclear U.S. Atomic Energy Commission (AEC). Moreover,
as Daniel Ford, executive director of the Union of Concerned
Scientists, revealed in an investigation based on AEC records,
the government twisted and misrepresented the report to falsely
minimize the dangers of the plants. For instance: meltdowns,
which could cause thousands of deaths, might occur once every
five years, according to one technical review of the report for the
AEC, but this judgment did not reach the public; the technical
appendix of the draft report was written by an engineer employed by Westinghouse, a leading maker of nuclear reactors;
the summary in the final report, on which the press relied, discussed prospective fatalities from accidents without stating that
they were only the "early fatalities" and did not include later
deaths caused by cancer; a physicist calculated that for every ten
deaths mentioned in the summary, by the study's own detailed
analysis there would also be 7,000 cancer deaths.

In 1978, on radio, Reagan said that the odds against a fatal
nuclear power accident were 300 million to one. "You have
75,000 times the danger of dying in an auto accident," he said.
The odds on a plant meltdown were such, he said, that there
would be at most one in three million years. How serious, then,
was the need for government regulations to make the plants
safe? Not very. For a laugh Reagan told his fans that "paper, not
nuclear waste, is our real storage problem. The legal work for
the Seabrook plant in New Hampshire alone has generated a 5-

foot shelf of state hearing transcripts; twenty 3-inch-thick volumes of applications . . . 12,522 pages of transcripts . . . another 5-foot shelf of papers. . . . Anybody got a match?"[4]

At Three Mile Island (TMI), a valve at the top of a pressurizer for a reactor stuck open, letting radioactive steam escape. The shift superviser, William Zewe, said his crew started injecting water into the reactor, but stopped because they had no idea what was happening inside the thing. For two hours and twenty minutes the open valve was not detected, and the temperature inside the reactor reached 4,000 degrees; another 30 minutes or an hour and it could have reached 6,000 degrees and a meltdown, releasing radioactivity upon an area that contained a million people. The crew realized what was happening in time and stopped the process. Tens of thousands of people fled the area, but no one had been hurt.

This was the worst accident in the history of commercial nuclear power, but Reagan assured his radio listeners: "The fuel used in nuclear power plants has been reduced to where it simply cannot explode. . . .

"Some catastrophe! No one was killed, no one was injured, and there will probably not be a single additional death from cancer among the 2 million people living within a 50-mile radius. . . . The total radioactivity . . . in the immediate vicinity of the plant was less than the difference between living in Dallas or living in the higher altitude of Denver."

Reagan's source for his statement that the TMI accident would cause no cancer deaths, Joseph Califano, the secretary of health, education, and welfare, subsequently modified his information: there had been more fallout than was thought, and one person might die. "No one can take this lightly," Reagan acknowledged, "but the question arises—will we ever know?"

The owner of TMI, General Public Utilities (GPU), sued the manufacturer of the reactor for $4 billion and the NRC for a like amount. GPU charged that the manufacturer, Babcock and Wilson (B&W), had failed to pass along to the many companies using its reactors a memo warning that safety procedures should be changed because of the very problem that had caused the TMI accident. From the government the company wanted $4 billion on grounds that if the commission "had acted with due care . . . the TMI accident would not have occurred."

In the trial of the suit against B&W, the manufacturer countered with evidence that operators at TMI had falsified reports about steam leakage in the system for several weeks before the accident, that GPU itself had found a year before the accident that "the quality of operator personnel is on a continuous downward trend due to lack of training," and that the GPU official in charge of training the new operators had obtained an operator's license himself only by having someone else take half his examination. The disclosures were so damaging, GPU settled out of court for $37 million, which B&W was to pay in the form of services in the TMI cleanup. According to the *New York Times,* "The companies were reported eager to bring the trial to an end because further disclosures could damage the future of the nuclear power industry in which both parties had a large stake."[5]

After TMI, Reagan's question, "Anybody got a match?" found a different application. Utility officials in charge of planning new plants had plenty of matches, and they used them to set fire to every proposal they received to buy a new nuclear power reactor. Not one such reactor has been ordered since 1978. Since 1972 a total of 102 orders for reactors have been canceled—18 of them in 1982 alone. "The Nuclear Industry Begins to Die," *Life* entitled a story in May 1982. Costs of the plants were increasing sixfold, tenfold, even as the accident at TMI ended the plausibility of the safety statistics which Reagan and industry officials were citing. Gradually the knowledge sank in that the dangers of reactor breakdown increase as the reactors get older. More and more plants were having to shut down for mandatory repairs. Two reactors were scrapped in Washington State at a loss of $2.5 billion to investors; two more were then abandoned in Oklahoma; between 1978 and 1982, the TVA halted work on eight of them.[6]

Late in 1981 President Reagan ordered DOE to speed up the licensing and regulatory process for nuclear plants, and a week later DOE obligingly proclaimed that if a new "significant" risk was found at a plant, no correction would be required as long as the risk was not "unacceptable." Regulatory hearings were to be narrowed and restricted; utilities would be able to get both their construction and operating licenses at the same time.

Just five months later, a reactor safety engineer with the NRC, Demetrios L. Basdekas, acting in apparent defiance of his wand-waving superiors, wrote:

"There is a high, increasing likelihood that someday soon, during a seemingly minor malfunction at any of a dozen or more nuclear plants around the United States, the steel vessel that houses the radioactive core is going to crack like a piece of glass. The result will be a core meltdown . . . which will injure many people, destroy the plant, and probably destroy the nuclear industry with it. . . .

"Another serious accident is very likely because the wrong metal was used in the reactor vessels, and with each day of operation, neutron radiation is making the metal more brittle and more prone to crack in case of sudden temperature change under pressure.

"One manufacturer of nuclear reactors has reported to the NRC that in three to five more years, the vessels in some plants will be too brittle to operate safely. . . . Some plants are already too dangerous to operate without corrective measures."

According to the government's risk assessment in the 1975 Rasmussen study, there would be one major accident in 20,000 years of reactor operation. In 1982, in a study conducted for NRC by the Oak Ridge National Laboratory, the likelihood was found to be one in 1,000 reactor years, twenty times higher than the estimate of the Rasmussen study. Since there are seventy-four operating plants in the U.S., the government's latest study in effect predicts a major nuclear accident every thirteen and a half years.

Attorneys for the industry continued to put the chance at one in 12 million years of reactor operation. A lawyer for Con Edison told Matthew L. Wald of the *New York Times* that such a major accident is "less probable than you or I being struck by lightning." Yet Wald calculated that on the basis of the Oak

Ridge study and with more than sixty additional reactors under construction, by the end of the century there is likely to be about one major nuclear plant accident in the U.S. each decade.

According to the government's 1975 reassurances to the public, in the worst-case accident (melting of the uranium fuel, failure of all safety systems, a large release of radioactivity into the atmosphere, and facilitating weather conditions) there would be 3,300 early deaths and $14 billion in property damage. Late in 1982 other scientists dealt the Rasmussen report the conclusive blow. A study for NRC by Sandia National Laboratories concluded that a worst-case accident could cause more than 100,000 "early deaths" and more than $300 billion in property damage. Under the Price-Anderson Act of 1957 as amended, the nuclear industry's liability in the event of an extraordinary nuclear accident is limited to $560 million. If the NRC staff is correct that the probability of a worst-case accident is 1 in 100,000 reactor years, there is about 1 chance in 50 that such a nuclear-power disaster will happen in the U.S. before the end of the century.

In late February 1983 an automatic "scram" system that is supposed to shut off the nuclear reaction in a nuclear power plant failed at the Salem plant in South Jersey. The operator shut off the reaction manually twenty-four seconds after the failure, barely averting core damage. The NRC had predicted, according to the *New York Times*, that such a failure would happen once in 33,000 reactor years.[7]

Despite the trendiness of deregulation and the President's known bias, the five members of the NRC, who would themselves be personally responsible should there be a core meltdown and thousands of deaths, increased pressures on the industry for more safety. Reagan's chairman, Nunzio J. Palladino, had designed nuclear reactor cores for Westinghouse for many years, but five months of running the NRC threw him in a state of shock about the atomic power industry.

Only a few days after Reagan's order to the government to speed up licensings of new plants, the NRC under Palladino suspended the license for the Diablo Canyon plant in California because of the discovery that blueprints for one of its reactors had been switched and used in the construction of a different reactor, thus invalidating the stress computations for five systems at the plant. Speaking soon thereafter to the Atomic Industrial Forum of which he had recently been a director, Palladino said the deficiencies in quality assurance at some nuclear power plants were "inexcusable." According to the NRC chairman: "There have been lapses of many kinds—in design analysis, resulting in built-in design errors; in poor construction practices; in falsified documents; in harassment of quality control personnel; and in inadequate training of reactor operators." Not only Diablo, but also plants in Texas, Ohio, Indiana, and Michigan had major problems, Palladino said.

Trying to restore public confidence in nuclear power, the NRC was riding a wounded dragon. The agency issued a proposed policy statement on safety goals, but Commissioner Peter Bradford, a holdover from the Carter administration, pointed out that one statistically stated objective implicitly meant the acceptance of 13,000 deaths during the life of the 150 plants operating or awaiting licensing. An NRC official told the commission that up to half the nuclear plants were "generally deficient" in one or more areas in their ability to respond to accidents. Six months after NRC engineer Basdekas' warning concerning brittle reactor walls, the NRC staff announced that at least eleven plants would require "modifications in the near future" to prevent the rupturing of their reactor walls, but that nothing had to be done right away. The commission set a limit of spending for repairs at nuclear plants at $1,000 for each rem* of radiation exposure presumably foreclosed by a repair. Commissioner James Asseltine objected, saying this was not enough money to pay for the necessary repairs at existing plants. Belatedly, the NRC discovered that hundreds or thousands of fraudulently represented steel parts, which could withstand much less pressure than required, had been used in some nuclear power plants, including the reprocessing plant at Barnwell, and there seemed to be no way to find all the weak pipes and tubes.

---

* A rem is the quantity of ionizing radiation the effect of which is equal to the biological effect of 1 roentgen of x-ray dosage.

The NRC's safety watch over the individual nuclear plants was wild, too. GPU, the owner of the damaged TMI plant, was fined $100,000 for allowing five operators to cheat on NRC licensing exams. Although the Zimmer plant 28 miles from Cincinnati was 97 percent complete, the NRC halted construction because of many alleged problems: missing and doctored records, thousands of deficient welds, harassment of safety inspectors. The NRC let the Indian Point plant 35 miles north of midtown Manhattan reopen without an approved emergency preparedness plan, but then the Federal Emergency Management Agency said in a report that the area around the plant was not prepared for a possible accident at the reactors and the safety of the 288,000 people living within 10 miles of the plant could not be assured. After local officials rejected an emergency evacuation plan for the Shoreham plant on Long Island and the head official in the county at risk expressed his opinion that an acceptable evacuation plan could never be devised, Governor Cuomo ordered the state not to approve an emergency plan for the plant.[8]

The marketplace was making its cruel judgment on nuclear power. Why, in defiance of "the magic of the marketplace" that he professed to revere, did Reagan continue the government's subsidy and favoritism for the industry? Considering the fact that $150 billion has been invested in it, his general alliance with big business might be a sufficient explanation. There is, however, a likelier one: his specific alliance with Bechtel.

Having won more than fifty contracts at nuclear power plants, Bechtel may have been the busiest nuclear power company in the world. The company whose former officials now head Reagan's departments of Defense and State built two-fifths of the nation's nuclear plants and more than thirty of the eighty or so that exist in the rest of the world. What hurts nuclear power hurts Bechtel. "The state of the nuclear industry is tragic," said the vice president of Bechtel Power Corporation, Howard W. Wahl, in the fall of 1981. "No one is building new plants."

Bechtel built the plant that produced the first nuclear source of electric power in the United States, the experimental breeder reactor in Arco, Idaho. The company went on to build the first commercial nuclear power plant in the country, at Dresden, Illinois, and the first nuclear power station in Canada. Bechtel has management responsibility for the recently closed Diablo Canyon nuclear plant; it is helping to build the Palo Verde nuclear plant near Phoenix, which, when finished, will be the largest one in the country. To help defeat a nuclear-power safeguards initiative in California, Bechtel spent almost $400,000.

Willy-nilly, events are dramatizing the Reagan-Bechtel connection on nuclear power. Bechtel has the billion-dollar cleanup contract at TMI. As safety problems have developed throughout the industry Bechtel has specialized in safety fixes, opening an office in Oak Ridge to manage its work in the decontamination and restoration of nuclear (as well as chemical) facilities in the east.

The company has had its problems on its own projects. Consumers Power Company alleged that Bechtel and other companies were at fault when tubes in the Palisades nuclear plant corroded and radioactive water leaked into the steam generating system; admitting no fault, Bechtel settled for $14 million. In Bechtel's Midland, Mich., nuclear power station, reinforcing bar joints were found to be defective. A faulty control room wall, alleged to be insufficiently reinforced against earthquakes, put the Trojan nuclear power plant at Rainier, Oregon, out of operation for nine months during 1979, and the presiding utility, Portland General Electric, charged Bechtel with design negligence; that charge and Bechtel's countersuit were settled out of court, the settlement not announced.

When Brown and Root, Inc., the Lyndon Johnson–connected construction company, was removed as architect and engineer of the embattled South Texas Nuclear Project construction job, Bechtel was hired as project engineer and construction management firm. The day before the NRC shut down safety related work at the Zimmer plant in Ohio, the Cincinnati Gas and Electric Company hired Bechtel as "joint manager" for a plant review at Zimmer, provoking a private investigator who had found evidence of false records at the plant to tell the press, "Bechtel is politically untouchable. So anybody who gets Bechtel on its side is assured of protection."

In 1975 Bechtel helped write a Ford administration proposal

to give private companies as much as $8 billion in guarantees to encourage them to enter the business of uranium enrichment, the government monopoly; Congress narrowly defeated the proposal. Bechtel has expressed interest in buying the government's incomplete Barnwell nuclear fuel reprocessing plant, provided the government gives it "assurances against expropriation of investor capital," and, according to Senator Metzenbaum of Ohio, Bechtel has also expressed interest in running the government's uranium enrichment facility at Oak Ridge. The close correlation between the Reagan administration and Bechtel's interest is manifest, therefore, in Reagan's 1981 request for a government study of the feasibility of obtaining plutonium through competitive procurement from private industry instead of relying solely on government production. DOE has been considering whether the government might guarantee to buy the plutonium produced at Barnwell and promise to buy out future investors if the plant was later closed.

Furthermore, the administration has been encouraging the export of nuclear technology by private U.S. companies. The Export-Import Bank has continued to finance such export, and Reagan's DOE has formally offered to supply Mexico with nuclear fuel at favorable prices if Mexico will let U.S. companies build at least two light-water nuclear reactors at a total cost of about $3 billion. "Guess who built the atomic plant at Tarapur?" Secretary of State Shultz reportedly asked an aide concerning the facility near Bombay, in northwestern India. "Who?" the aide responded. "Bechtel," Shultz replied. Bechtel has also been involved in or is now working on nuclear power plants in Korea, Italy, Spain, and Taiwan. In 1982 Bechtel asked Reagan's DOE for permission to explore constructing a large nuclear reprocessing plant in Japan that would be capable of extracting 1,200 tons of plutonium a year, which would give Japan its own source of weapons-grade plutonium.[9]

With Secretary Edwards back home in South Carolina, what would be the likely position of Reagan's new secretary of energy, Donald Hodel, on nuclear power? As head of the Bonneville Power Administration, Hodel had been an influential and insistent advocate of the construction of three of the nuclear power reactors that were planned by the Washington Public Power Supply System. After $24 billion in cost overruns, this project became widely known as "Whoops." Two of the five units were canceled, causing investors to lose $2.5 billion and still further increasing the costs of the three remaining reactors.[10] Would Hodel be any more influenced by the downfall of Whoops than Reagan himself had been by the stallout of the entire nuclear power industry? Considering the circumstances, it did not seem likely. The secretary of state and the secretary of defense were not presently working for Bechtel, but they knew who built the atomic power plant at Tarapur, and so did Ronald Reagan.

8

Unleashing Free Enterprise

Government regulation of business developed out of the necessity at the turn of the century to curb rapacious business practices. Reformers and some business leaders supported regulation as a way to avert more radical government control or ownership. In time, then, the regulated industries penetrated and overwhelmed the government agencies that supposedly were regulating them; the agencies became pet hounds of the regulated industries. In general, the government fixed prices for the companies, divided up markets among them, and barred new companies from competing with the old ones. The very cartels which the federal antitrust laws prohibited were created and sanctioned by the government for the regulated industries.

The Carter administration and its leading free enterprise theorist Alfred Kahn provided Reagan with a trend against regulation that was already well under way. Under Carter many regulatory restrictions had been lifted on airlines, railroads, trucking, communications, and financial institutions. In principle, the deregulation to which Reagan subscribed was grounded, like Carter's, in the theory of competitive free enterprise. In the mid-1970s, for example, Reagan proposed an end to federal price fixing and all federal restrictions against new entrants in nonmonopoly industries. In practice, however, Reagan uses deregulation as a pretext for new privileges for business and the abandonment or weakening of federal rules to protect the public health and safety.

Coming into power, Reagan froze last-minute Carter administration regulations and issued an executive order instructing all agencies whose heads the President appoints to take no new regulatory action of any kind "unless the potential benefits to society . . . outweigh the potential costs to society." He gave his budget office the power to rewrite or block regulations. Vice President Bush was made chairman of the Presidential Task Force on Regulatory Relief, which listed more than 100 regulations that were targeted for revision or extinction.[1]

Under Reagan-era "deregulation" of radio and television, existing stations are to be protected from challenge by new competitors, and people are going to have to watch more and more commercials as the price for seeing and hearing the programs they like. Reagan's chairman of the Federal Communications Commission (FCC) is proposing to give present TV station owners permanent title to their licensed access to the publicly owned airways, immune from competitive challenge, and to remove the limits on how many radio and TV stations one company can own. On the other hand, the Reaganized FCC is opening some new communications technologies to free competition.

The Carter administration promulgated a rule which, by narrowing the spacing between radio signals, would have made room for from 400 to as many as 1,000 new radio stations. Acting in accord with the trade association of the existing stations, which protested against possible interference with their signals, the FCC killed the rule and thus the potential new competition.

Citizens who find radio jingles stimulating were well served when the FCC discontinued the long-standing guidelines which had limited the time a radio station could devote to commercials and had established minimum requirements for radio air time devoted to news and public service. Predictably (although with a court challenge pending), some stations dropped newscasts and added commercials. The quality of the national life thus enriched, Mark Fowler, the FCC chairman, indicated that he wanted to abolish existing limits on TV commercials and the minimums for time that must be devoted to TV news and public affairs, too. Thirty years ago the broadcasting industry agreed to a voluntary code that supposedly limited stations to five consecutive commercials and advertising to eight and one-half minutes an hour. Under Carter, acting in the name of antitrust, the government sued the broadcasters for agreeing to restrict advertising; under Reagan, the Justice Department and the broadcasters agreed that the broadcasters would drop all restraints on TV commercials.

James Miller, Reagan's chairman of the Federal Trade Commission (FTC), said he could well recommend eliminating the present requirement that advertisers substantiate their claims in advance of making them. He might even favor repeal of the government's authority to regulate "unfair" advertising practices, he said. The government should challenge an ad, in his view, only if it injures buyers and "reasonable consumers" cannot see that it is false or exaggerated. The director of the FTC's consumer protection bureau recommended discarding a rule that set minimum standards for ads which proclaim that a food is natural, low in cholesterol or fatty acids, or "high-energy." A three-year study on the advisability of regulating children's advertising was simply dropped.

Fowler, the FCC chairman, wants the government to scrap the rule that requires stations to give political candidates equal time. He would also abandon "the fairness doctrine," the requirement that broadcasters present all sides of controversial issues, the abolition of which would give rich persons and corporations the unchallengeable power to saturate the public airways with propagandistic advertising.

In fostering competition in new technologies—low-power TV stations that send their signals out only five to fifteen miles, TV stations broadcasting from orbiting satellites, and radio telephones—Fowler has conformed to the free-enterprise model for deregulation. The FCC was pursuing the same principle in recent moves to deregulate the U.S. end of international telecommunications, although competition in this field is confounded to some extent by the European pattern of state monopolies.

But Fowler also invoked the panacea of deregulation to justify the termination of governmental authority to renew the licenses of radio and TV stations on the basis of their performance as measured against standards of the public interest. "No renewal filings," Fowler said; "no brownie points for doing this right, no finger-wagging for doing that wrong." Since public ownership of the airways has been accepted as a fact for half a century, Fowler was proposing to tell the broadcasters to do as they please and to present them with titles to public property on the grounds that they already have access to it, much as one might give a camper a national park because he is bivouacked there. In exchange for paying the government a proposed "user fee," Fowler informed broadcasters, "you'd achieve a guaranteed renewal from the government—in short you'd get a property interest in your station."

As one can see from what is happening in communications alone, deregulation has all kinds of possibilities. In the same spirit as Fowler's, Senator Goldwater, who is generally thought to be a paragon of highmindedness on free enterprise, proposed in 1983 to protect radio and television stations from challengers at license-renewal time by (in Goldwater's own words) "barring competing applications." His bill provided that the FCC "shall not have authority to consider the application of any other person for the facilities for which renewal is sought," and the Senate passed it without a recorded vote. The three giant TV networks decided that deregulation was a fine basis for seeking the repeal of an FCC rule that prohibits them from demanding shares of production profits and distribution rights in exchange for airing independent productions. Fowler not only wants to end the antitrust limits on station ownership, he also wants to permit networks and other broadcasters to buy cable systems.[2]

"I challenge anyone to prove," Reagan told the board of the American Trucking Association in 1974, "there is a need to con-

tinue the ICC or that it serves any useful purpose." Under the
1980 truck deregulation act, the Interstate Commerce Commission was ordered to let companies vary rates within a range and
relax rules that barred new competitors from the business. Price
wars did break out, and rates generally declined; nonunion carriers gained ground against the Teamsters, who had to yield on
new wage demands; truckers' profits headed downward, and
there were bankruptcies. An FTC study showed that trucking
service to small towns was not deteriorating, and thousands of
new companies entered the business.

The Teamsters were the only major union that supported
Reagan, and the man he appointed chairman of the ICC, Reese
Taylor, Jr., opposed opening routes to new operators and condemned some price cutting as "predatory," which sounded like
the old government cartel-as-usual; he was accused of, but denied, trying to "reregulate" the industry. Another of Reagan's
ICC appointees, Frederic Andre, was quoted in a transcript of a
closed meeting that was obtained by the *Washington Post* defending bribes paid in the trucking business as "the free market at
work" and monopoly pricing as perfectly acceptable. The White
House and some of Andre's colleagues repudiated his views, but
Reagan disregarded calls from Congress that he fire him.[3]

Deregulated in 1978, airlines suffered three straight years of
heavy losses—perhaps half a billion dollars among the major
carriers in 1982 alone. The Reagan administration stoutly rejecting a bailout, Braniff went belly-up. However, lost in the exercises of free-enterprise theory is the mainstay of public utilities
law, "the public convenience and necessity," under which regulators and courts had protected, for example, the right of small
towns to transportation service. Under airline deregulation
some small airlines have been very successful, but there is a
dispute whether small communities have air service as good as
they had before. Fare wars, which have attracted public interest and approval, can also threaten smaller companies with destruction.

In this shifting situation the Reagan administration has taken
three steps concerning airline deregulation, each odd in its own
way. First, at Reagan's instance the administration appears to be

continuing antitrust immunity for U.S. airlines that operate overseas when they make price-fixing agreements with other airlines on international routes. Second, the Federal Aviation Administration has proposed to let the airlines themselves decide how to meet federal safety standards. And third, the Civil Aeronautics Board, by approving a new rule concerning travel agents, in effect authorized the mighty American and United airlines to hold on to a float of as much as $2.4 billion a year in cash for tickets they sell for other airlines, quite possibly (as *Forbes* reports) further weakening already shaky competitors.[4]

Buses were deregulated by a law Reagan signed in 1982, and now small towns are losing bus service. Discussing earlier deregulation in Florida, a vice president of Greyhound said, apparently with pleasure, "We were able to cut out 90 to 95 percent of our small towns." With deregulation national, Greyhound announced plans to drop 1,300 little towns around the country, and Trailways was expected to follow the same course. Obviously this hits the elderly and poor who cannot drive or don't have cars. But some mom-and-pop companies began entering the field, and optimists predicted lower fares.[5]

The federal government's alliance with business under Reagan is perhaps most visible at the Securities and Exchange Commission (SEC), which regulates corporate securities and disclosure to stockholders and watches out for various forms of corporate fraud.

More than 1,300 large corporations have been permitted to experiment with greatly simplified "shelf registration" statements concerning securities they issue. Heretofore corporations have been required to disclose any extra work performed for them by their auditors to help assure the auditor's independence; this has been dropped. The agency invited comments on a proposal to let corporations' shareholders adopt by majority vote rules that govern whether stockholder proposals will be given a hearing, a change which, if adopted, predictably (albeit cleverly) would stultify the "corporate democracy" movement. At present, different companies which have common directors must disclose the amount of business the companies do with each other if it exceeds 1 percent of their gross revenues; the

SEC proposed to raise this threshold to 5 percent. Vice presidents and other corporate officers who do not set company policy would be excused from compensation and conflict-of-interest reporting, in another SEC proposal. Stockholders now must be informed in annual reports about the compensation of top management in a unified table. In 1983 the SEC proposed to permit noncash benefits to be listed elsewhere in the annual report and the value of stock options to be reported only when they are granted, not annually, as was required before.

In its boldest reversal of past policy, Reagan's SEC has rejected its staff recommendation that Citicorp, the nation's second largest bank holding company, be prosecuted in a civil action for failing to disclose to its shareholders that $46 million of its earnings in the 1970s had come from allegedly sham foreign currency transactions which the SEC staff said were illegal under foreign laws and were authorized by the men who were running the company.

David Edwards, an assistant vice president at the bank, had blown the whistle inside Citicorp on allegedly contrived shifts of profits from Europe, where taxes are high, to the Bahamas, where they are low. For his trouble Citicorp fired him. The SEC staff investigation, which Edwards then provoked, concluded that top Citicorp management, including chairman Walter Wriston, had authorized the deliberate evasion of European nations' banking requirements. While the bank maintained that its practices were "basically proper," the SEC staff concluded that Citicorp used "thousands of false documents" in thousands of "artificial" transactions that usually involved artificial prices. Citicorp had kept two sets of books, one for foreign banking authorities, another for top management, the staff said.

Citicorp paid France, Switzerland, and Germany $10.5 million in fines and back taxes related to foreign currency transactions, but the new SEC decided to let it go. As Jeff Gerth reported in an investigative story in the *New York Times,* the new SEC enforcement chief, John Fedders, arguing against prosecution, said the illegal conduct did not appear to have hurt Citicorp economically, and he added, "I do not subscribe to the theory that a company that violates tax and exchange control regulations is a bad corporation." The agency's Office of the General Counsel and Division of Corporation Finance contended that bringing charges of disclosure violations concerning illegal or improper conduct by a company's executives would be inappropriate unless the company had made "affirmative representations as to management's honesty and integrity in some document." To this, the two divisions added the argument to end the argument: that Citicorp's management, by taking the "most profitable course" despite knowing it was probably illegal, "made a reasonable and standard business judgment."

Richard L. Hudson, who covers the SEC for the *Wall Street Journal,* reported a remarkable speech by John Fedders. "Some shareholders," the SEC enforcement chief told a lawyers' conference, "not only wish to maximize their investment, but also have a desire that the corporation in which they invest comply with certain ethical and legal standards. The preference is laudable, and one I share. But the securities laws cannot address the specific concerns of all. The common interest among all investors is the expectation of a return on investment," and "the commission's law enforcement program must reflect the interests of investors and the marketplace."

In recent court decisions, Fedders contended, he had perceived that "illegal management conduct undertaken solely to advance corporate interests may not have to be disclosed." Fedders' tough predecessor as SEC's enforcement chief, Stanley Sporkin, retorted that this was like the director of the FBI "telling companies if you engage in drug dealing, then it's all right so long as it furthers the aims of the corporation."

The SEC has continued to file lawsuits against business interests for insider trading and stock manipulation. Readers will recall, however, the charges concerning SEC's leniency in permitting Thomas Reed, a member of Reagan's national security staff, to renounce profits from alleged insider trading while admitting to no wrongdoing. At Fedders' urging the SEC has asked Congress to provide stiffer civil and criminal penalties for insider trading, but in yet another case the agency has continued its practices that were questioned in the Reed case.

Just before Kuwait announced that it would buy the U.S. oil

company Santa Fe International, there was unusual trading activity in options on the company's stock. The SEC accused a group of investors, including one Santa Fe director, of earning illegal trading profits totaling $8.5 million and sued to require them to pay back their gains, but again without admitting or denying guilt. At a court hearing on these matters, federal judge William Orrick, Jr., said, "These are thieves we're talking about. The government is prosecuting people for stealing Social Security checks out of the mail, welfare frauds, and here these people come down and get a slap on the wrist."[6]

Deregulation of financial institutions was a top priority of Treasury Secretary Regan's. He proposed to let savings and loan associations and savings banks (the thrifts) expand into consumer loans and equipment leasing and to permit banks to have money market funds and underwrite municipal revenue bonds. All depository institutions, he said, "should be free to compete for the financial consumer's dollar."

Although its boldest provisions created the open-ended federal bailout of banks and thrifts already discussed, the radical 1982 bank deregulation law did a lot more than end government ceilings on interest rates that banks and thrifts can pay on some accounts. For potential homebuyers, the law's most important feature, which was specifically endorsed by the administration, overruled state law so that banks and thrifts can "call in" home loans to prevent homeowners from transferring their low-interest mortgages to new buyers of their homes. Thrifts have tried to call in old, low-rate mortgages when homeowners have tried to transfer them to new buyers, but state laws have restricted this "due on sale" maneuver. The new federal law weakens the likelihood that a homebuyer can assume a low-rate mortgage.

Traditionally the thrifts have been the specialized source of mortgage loans. In recent years, however, they have just about gone out of this line of lending: in 1976 they provided 56 percent of mortgage funds, but in the last quarter of 1981 the face value of the mortgages they sold exceeded that of those they provided. At the administration's behest, the Net Worth Guarantee Act of 1982 (the deregulation law) permits thrifts to expand nonresidential real estate lending to up to 40 percent of their assets, consumer loans to 30 percent, and commercial and agricultural lending to 10 percent by 1984. Representative Henry Gonzalez (D.–Tex.), the chairman of the housing subcommittee of the House Banking Committee, warned that this change "might well mean the end of homebuilding as a national enterprise" because buyers will "have to compete for general loans with General Motors, and I think you know who will win." Under the 1982 law, he continued, "Savings institutions will no longer exist just to provide mortgage money. . . . No one can really say where mortgage money will come from." Six months after the law passed an official of the National Association of Realtors said "housing has been seriously hurt" as a result of it. Although only one in eleven Americans can now afford to buy a home, Washington is still moving, not toward the facilitation of home ownership, but away from it.

The act allows banks and thrifts to offer $2,500-minimum-deposit accounts at market interest rates with no withdrawal penalties. This "deregulation of interest rates" not only enabled the insured depository institutions to compete with uninsured money market funds, it also ended federal control of financial institutions' interest rates on checking accounts of at least $2,500, a change which the *Wall Street Journal* reported "will put banks and S&Ls back in the 1920s, in a gloves-off competition for the consumer's dollar." A former research director of the Federal Deposit Insurance Corp. said the effect of the 1982 deregulation "will be the greatest of anything since 1933." The chief economist of Bank of America in San Francisco called the new money-market deposit accounts the most significant change in the financial markets "in half a century," that is, since the early 1930s.

When one recalls what happened half a century ago, misgivings arise. The former chairman of the Federal Home Loan Bank Board, Thomas Bomar, was quoted: "I think it is an exceedingly dangerous experiment. A very large portion of the financial industry is incapable of meeting an additional rapid increase in cost" (which of course is what having to pay higher interest is). Oppenheimer & Company's bank analyst, Mark Biderman, told *Forbes* that if the institutions put their new money-market billions into mortgage loans, "they could wind up killing themselves a couple of years from now, if interest rates climb back up."

Another Reagan-backed provision in the deregulation law expands federal authority to arrange "interstate and cross-industry acquisitions" of troubled banks and thrifts. Representative Wright, the House Democratic majority leader, charged that it is a monopolistic law that "invites big banks to do branch banking across state lines" and "swallows up small independent banks at an ever-accelerating pace." The new law, Gonzalez agreed, "lays the ground for a vast acceleration of the growing concentration of this nation's financial powers." Another Texan, Representative Martin Frost, believes that enlarging the thrifts' functions enhances the possibility that "big out-of-state bankers will come in and buy S&L chains."

Interstate banking has long been regarded as a nemesis of the 12,000 hometown, or community, banks, but Attorney General Smith declared on April 6, 1982, that "there is nothing inherent in the notion of interstate banking that runs counter to antitrust policy. To the contrary, the present system of geographic limitations constitutes a regulatory intrusion upon the free workings of the marketplace." If community banks lose business, he said fatalistically, "it would likely be because consumers in the community choose to take their deposits elsewhere."

One day after the attorney general's speech, on April 7, 1982, a consortium of twenty-six banks, including Bank of America, Chase Manhattan, and Continental Illinois National, announced their formation of a nationwide automated teller machine system for their customers' withdrawals and interaccount transfers. Interstate deposits, still illegal, were not permitted in the new system, but under Smith's new doctrine that could not be long in coming.

As the former assistant managing editor of *Business Week* Gordon Williams has pointed out, financial giants that are not called banks have become far more important than most banks. Sears, Roebuck has an insurance complex, a money-market fund, a thrift, the nation's largest real estate brokering firm, the fifth-largest stockbroker firm, Dean Witter Reynolds, and 20 million credit customers. Prudential bought Bache, the sixth-largest brokerage firm, and a small bank in Georgia. American Express has the second-largest stockbroker, Shearson Loeb Rhoades, and an insurance complex. Merrill Lynch operates in many ways like a bank.

On the other hand, banks and S&Ls are beginning to operate more like financial conglomerates. Interstate mergers of thrifts have been approved. The Federal Reserve Board authorized Citicorp, the nation's second largest bank holding company, to acquire the troubled $2.9 billion Fidelity Savings and Loan of San Francisco, probably the tenth largest S&L in California. This was the first time a bank holding company was permitted to buy an S&L in another state. The president-elect of the California Bankers Association said it gave Citicorp an interstate banking franchise and an interindustry franchise that were both "denied to other bank holding companies." The head of the California Savings and Loan Commission, Linda Tsao Yang, was quoted: "This approval is really a de facto rewriting of the national banking law. What's to keep Citicorp from gobbling up another institution across state lines on the guise of its being a 'sick' institution? In effect, this is creating a national system of banking."

As 1983 opened almost 600 banks and thrifts had announced plans to enter the discount stock brokerage business, and BankAmerica Corporation, the owner of the largest bank in the country, became the nation's largest discount broker when the Federal Reserve Board allowed it to buy Charles A. Schwab & Company. Fed chairman Paul Volcker has said that the movement of banks into the securities business "raises questions of risk, self-dealing, and conflict-of-interest," but in the Reaganized climate the trend continued anyway. Deregulation of financial institutions has gone much farther on its own than Congress has authorized. As Gordon Williams wrote: "We're now in the age of the giants—widely diversified, loosely regulated financial conglomerates—operating in a dozen different businesses in which the only common thread is money."[7]

No one was seriously proposing an end to FDIC examination

of banks, but even under examination more than two dozen U.S. banks went under in 1982, and not altogether because of the recession.

The failure of the $500 million Penn Square Bank of Oklahoma City posed the central questions. A "go-go" bank that had vigorously pushed loans to oil and gas drillers, Penn Square had been warned by the comptroller of the currency that it was "flirting with disaster," but the comptroller never rated it lower than a 3 on a danger scale of 1 to 5, meaning that the chance of its failure was remote. How effective, then, was the system of federal bank examination? Federal officials called Penn Square an "aberration." One could only hope they were correct, because late in 1982 nearly 300 banks were rated 3 or worse.

Penn Square had lent several hundred million dollars to its own officers or insider companies. Jeff Gerth reported in the *Times* that Michigan National Corporation, a $6.2 billion bank holding company, has lent more than $100 million to insider companies, more than half of them in trouble. Yet in 1983 the SEC excused bank holding companies from disclosing details about loans to their officers unless the loans are "nonperforming."

There was also the question how major banks were "conned" (to quote the chairman of the House Banking Committee, Representative Fernand J. St. Germain [D.–R.I.]) by Penn Square. Continental Illinois of Chicago had bought $1 billion worth of Penn Square's loans, Seattle First National had $400 million, Chase Manhattan $200 million.

The only unregulated financial market in the U.S., the buying and selling of government securities, was jolted in 1982 when three firms in the business went under—one of them, Drysdale, accumulating losses of more than $300 million before the end. Chase Manhattan absorbed a loss of $135 million from its dealings with Drysdale. For a time it seemed that dubious practices in trading government securities had come to an end, but an official in the comptroller's office warned during the ensuing winter that some banks and securities firms had fallen back into the same dangerous ways.

In recent years "offshore banking" has flourished, especially on Caribbean islands, to deal in the $1.3 trillion in "Eurodollars," U.S. dollars that now belong to interests abroad. An offshore bank may be nothing but an office, a clerk, and piles of banking forms—a shell operation created entirely to avoid U.S. and other national tax, currency, and banking laws. Early in 1981 the Federal Reserve for the first time supported the creation of "free banking zones" in the United States. Banks will be permitted to create "International Banking Facilities" (IBFs) to engage in international and offshore banking. Money they set aside in their IBFs does not have to be protected by non-interest-bearing reserves.

All these problems could pale next to the third world debt. OPEC nations deposited their 1970s oil-profit surpluses in U.S. and western European banks. Wanting to make money on these funds, the banks loaned billions to third world nations at very high interest rates. The worldwide recession has in effect put some of these nations into bankruptcy: they cannot repay their loans. The international debt of third world and eastern European nations has reached the potentially catastrophic level of $700 billion. Federal Reserve Board figures showed that as of June 30, 1982, the nine largest U.S. banks had an amount equal to 112.5 percent of their combined capital, $30.5 billion, lent to just three countries, Mexico, Brazil, and Argentina.

The response of the Reagan administration has been two-fold. The SEC joined the Federal Reserve Board in recommending new regulatory controls on U.S. banks' lending abroad. It appeared that Congress would go along if only because many American banks have put themselves at the mercy of foreign governments that in a sense control them by owing them so much money. Senator Heinz of Pennsylvania said some banks in effect "bet the bank" on one country.

In addition the administration has asked Congress to increase by $8.5 billion the U.S. share of emergency funds for the International Monetary Fund (IMF). This is the agency that provides money on loan to the indebted third world countries in exchange for such "austerity" measures as an end to wage increases and cutbacks in government help to the poor. In effect then the Reaganists are recommending that U.S. taxpayers pro-

vide additional billions in credit to indebted third world countries which those countries will use to repay bad loans made to
them by U.S. banks.

U.S. banks have been enabled by the Reagan administration
to compete with the uninsured money-market funds. More gen-
uine competition is occurring in financial services, but the hometown banks may find the going much tougher. Because of higher
interest costs, all banks are becoming more vulnerable to sharp
shifts in interest rates. They have also been weakened by the
recession, and the breakdown or shakeout in international banking menaces not only U.S. banks, but the entire world economy. Perhaps events would in due time confirm that the early
1980s were not the time to begin the deregulation of financial
institutions.[8]

Deregulation of nonmonopoly industries has had, so far,
mixed results. The government's cartelization of such industries
in the course of regulating them, a historical corruption of the
competitive free enterprise system, had to be cauterized. But
deregulation, in dismantling sanctioned monopolies, releases
anew the same anticompetitive tendencies, the big dogs eating up
the little ones, that brought forth the antitrust laws in the first
place. Moreover, regulation is still as necessary as it has always
been for natural monopolies (those lines of business in which
competition would be economically inefficient and irrational);
yet some free marketeers are seriously proposing the deregulation of electric power generation.

Deregulation under Reagan has also become a disguise for
objectionable policies, just as regulation disguised monopoly. Do
the citizens really want radio and TV station owners freed to
cram down their throats an unlimited number of high-pressure
commercials? In what way would giving public property to private interests, as the FCC chairman proposes to give the public
airways to present station owners, deregulate private business?
If, as first Reagan and more recently a House Republican research committee recommended, the ICC is now completely
abolished, who is going to see to it that small towns get necessary
bus, rail, and air service?[9] Should deregulation mean relieving
corporations of their present legal duty to inform their stock-

holders about illegal conduct? With the savings and loan associations permitted to move into commercial and consumer loans, where will home loans come from? And does not the very idea of deregulating banks throw us back toward the high-rolling practices of the 1920s that ended in the collapse of the entire banking system?

9

Trusting Business with Health and Safety

In Reagan's ideology it is presumed that anything emanating from government that limits what business can do should probably be choked off as "costly and unnecessary." Joan B. Claybrook, who was head of the National Highway Safety Administration under Carter, writes, "It is not widely understood that health and safety regulation is a modern form of preventive medicine." It certainly is not widely understood in the Reagan administration.

Since 1970 there has been pressure in the public discourse to make businesses and executives criminally liable for actions that endanger people's lives or safety. In 1979, in response to support in the Carter administration for such a change, the Business Roundtable agreed to legislation that would make it a felony, punishable by up to seven years in prison, for a business executive to "engage in conduct that he knows places another person in imminent danger of death or serious bodily injury" or that "manifests an unjustified disregard for human life while violating federal regulations governing air and water quality, mine safety, or food purity." The Reagan administration, backed by the U.S. Chamber of Commerce, opposed writing this into the law, and the Senate judiciary committee tossed the proposal aside.[1]

His first spring in office Reagan announced a one-year delay in the requirement that cars have automatic restraint systems, a reduction in pollution controls on trucks and on cars with diesel engines, elimination of a requirement that cars have devices which warn of low tire pressure, and rejection of a proposed requirement that drivers have minimum fields of direct view through car and truck windshields. The auto industry was in serious trouble, the President said, and government must not "unnecessarily hamper its efforts through excessive regulation and interference."

Automobile bumpers had been required to be strong enough to prevent damage in a collision with a fixed object at 5 mph; Reagan lowered the speed to half that. Some automakers maintained the stronger bumpers, but in 1983 models, weaker 2.5-mph bumpers were installed on many models. In 1983 the National Highway Traffic Safety Administration (NHTSA) suspended as misleading a grading standard which had provided consumers with information concerning the comparative durability of tires.

Each year automobile accidents cause about 50,000 deaths. Ralph Nader's original contribution to the consumer movement was his work that persuaded the federal government to regulate auto safety. Federal rules had required automatic passive restraints (in effect, either airbags or automatically locking seat belts) in new full-size cars in 1981, mid-size cars in 1982, and compacts in 1983. Following Reagan's announcement of the year's delay in these requirements, GM and Ford dropped plans to install airbags in their cars. Then Raymond Peck, director of NHTSA, altogether rescinded the passive restraint requirements despite government and independent estimates that such restraints would prevent 9,000 deaths and 65,000 serious injuries annually.

In 1982, however, a three-judge federal appeals court ruled that Peck's bureaucratic act was "arbitrary and unlawful" and that the agency had acted "arbitrarily and capriciously" and "without any legal justification." The court said that the passive restraint system may be, "from an economic point of view, as important as any environmental, health, or safety rule now on the books. . . . At present rates, one in every sixty children born today is expected to die in an automobile accident and two out of every three will suffer injuries in a crash." Peck's defense that the requirement "no longer met the statutory criteria" of being reasonable, practical, and appropriate was swept aside as the court ordered that all cars sold after September 1983 be equipped with airbags or automatic seat belts. In a heavy blow to the administration, the Supreme Court unanimously upheld the appeals court, setting aside the deadline, but ordering the government to reconsider its position.

Late in 1979 federal officials began an investigation into reports that 1980 GM X cars had a tendency to lock their rear brakes. In mid-1981 the government told GM the brakes had a safety-related defect, but the previous practice of making a public announcement in such circumstances was not followed. GM recalled 47,000 cars for repairs. Stories by David Burnham in the *New York Times* subsequently revealed that a far wider recall was needed. Representative Timothy Wirth, who is chairman of the House Committee on Energy and Commerce, said he had reports that NHTSA "may be covering up the existence of very serious defects," and he asked: "If NHTSA has known about the possibility of a defect since 1979, why has the agency taken so long to order a recall of the X car?" Ten days later NHTSA admitted, in a preliminary finding, that the brakes on 320,000 1980 X model GM cars were defective, that these 320,000 cars "are subject to failures in performance which can result in accidents, injuries, death or property damage," and that GM's repairs on the 47,000 cars recalled had "not corrected" the defective brakes. As of early 1983 the government was aware of 1,200 complaints and fourteen deaths that had been associated with brake failures in the cars. The agency scheduled a hearing on its findings, but five days beforehand GM recalled 240,000 X cars and the agency canceled the hearing. The head of the Center for Auto Safety said this still left more than 80,000 1980 X cars with defective brakes on the road, but a spokesman for the government said GM had modified the defective brakes earlier than it had originally thought. On the Hill, Wirth told Peck, "You were delinquent in fulfilling your responsibilities." "That's unmitigated rubbish," Peck replied.

The job of the Transportation Department, said Clarence Ditlow, III, of the Center for Auto Safety, "is to save lives, not deregulate the auto industry." Nader called the federal safety agency the National Highway Traffic Fatality Administration.[2]

According to the United Auto Workers, job hazards kill 114,000 American workers every year—one every five minutes. A Labor Department study in 1981 said that although nearly 2 million Americans were severely or partially disabled from an occupational disease (with lost income estimated at $11 billion), only 5 percent of the severely disabled workers received workers' compensation. Manville Corporation has entered bankruptcy rather than pay up in connection with 17,000 lawsuits filed against it by workers suffering from cancer and lung diseases allegedly because of their exposure to asbestos. Such widespread patterns of injury and illness may elude the imagination, but an example given by *Business Week* is less likely to do so: twenty workers at a California chemical company were found to have been made sterile by a chemical that had been known for sixteen years to cause sterility in animals.

"We're here to do what the President was elected to do—provide regulatory relief," said Thorne Auchter, Reagan's chief of the Occupational Safety and Health Administration (OSHA), which is charged to enforce safe conditions at the workplace. "One of the most pernicious of the watchdog agencies," Reagan called OSHA two years before he became President. In the spring of 1979, on radio, Reagan quoted a report which said that "OSHA should be abolished. Safety and health in the workplace would not suffer measurably. . . . An agency perceived primar-

ily as a tool of government harassment would be eliminated."
Reagan's comment on this was "Amen!"

Backing off from abolition of the agency as he courted labor
votes during the ensuing campaign, Reagan proposed that
OSHA become "kind of a helpful research organization that
would ask businesses what their safety problems were and then
devise a plan for helping them solve those problems." Instead of
a police dog, he wanted a pussy cat. OSHA, he said, "would do
research and study how things could be improved," and industry
"could go to it" and ask for advice.

Both Auchter and his superior, Labor Secretary Donovan,
had been nipped by OSHA when it was a police dog. Auchter's
Florida construction company was cited by OSHA forty-nine
times and fined a total of $1,200 for safety violations in the
1970s. The Schiavone Construction Co. of which Donovan was
executive vice president was cited for 135 health and safety violations by OSHA from 1974 to 1978 as a result of forty-nine
inspections—almost three violations per inspection.

Auchter's central principle of enforcement is to exempt most
workplaces from inspection and concentrate on job sites with a
background of bad reports. Under his voluntary compliance
programs, the job sites of 13 million workers and more than
three-fourths of all manufacturing firms are no longer inspected
regularly. He is especially enthusiastic about "self-inspection"
as this is exemplified in a system developed by the Bechtel
Group for a nuclear plant site in California. A committee of
the unions on the job and management inspect the workplace once a month, and routine governmental inspections are
dropped.

Under Auchter OSHA has proposed to reduce the records
which employers are required to keep of workers' exposure to
dangerous substances: the number of covered substances would
drop from 40,000 to 4,000, and employers would be permitted
to claim a need to protect trade secrets as a basis for exceptions.
Auchter also proposed to eliminate the requirement that
474,000 companies keep health and safety records concerning
their 18 million workers. The exempted firms would be those in
retail trade, finance, insurance, real estate, and service industries

wherein statistics show that 94 percent of the employers have fewer than two injuries per establishment a year.

In 1981 OSHA inspections declined 21 percent and followup inspections dropped 72 percent. Evidently finding these figures difficult to defend, the administration restored the agency's budget, and the number of inspections reported then returned to pre-Reagan totals. Nonetheless, AFL-CIO President Lane Kirkland pointed out that under Auchter's targeting system, "inspectors first visit the workplace to check its records. If the records show no evidence of hazard, the inspector simply departs, without inspecting the plant. Yet [Auchter] insists that these are real inspections."

Auchter is proud that the number of lawsuits filed against OSHA have declined—proof of new OSHA-industry cooperation, he says; but an AFL-CIO expert attributes the falloff to failure to enforce the standards. Auchter now requires inspectors to report to headquarters any citations that entail more than $10,000 in penalties against employers. On the ground that 194 OSHA health and safety standards are formulated in terms of what employers "should" do rather than what they must do, Auchter has proposed simply to revoke them all.

In 1978 a federal standard was set to limit cotton dust in the workplace. When OSHA sought to subject this standard to cost-benefit analysis, the Supreme Court ruled that the law permitted only the consideration of workers' safety. Auchter withdrew from distribution an OSHA booklet that contained photographs and quotations from textile workers who had been made seriously ill by exposure to cotton dust. An aide was quoted as saying that Auchter threw the booklet down on a coffee table and exclaimed, "Get rid of it!"

Plans at OSHA to regulate workers' exposure to chromium and nickel, which are carcinogens, have been shelved. All three of OSHA's staff physicians resigned in one week, refusing to say why. OSHA rejected requests that it establish emergency standards controlling exposure to a gasoline additive and a pesticide. A federal judge concluded that he had to order the agency to issue such a standard on a carcinogenic gas, ethylene oxide. Action on formaldehyde, which has been shown to cause cancer in animals, has been delayed at OSHA until there is data about its effects on people. The agency has substantially weakened regulations to require employers to protect their workers' hearing.[3]

American miners, 216,000 of them, work in about 2,100 deep mines and 2,800 surface ones. Before 1952, between 500 and 2,000 U.S. mineworkers died in mine accidents every year. Federal inspections and sanctions began that year and annual deaths dropped to about 100 a year. Reagan reduced the number of inspectors 10 percent, there were 5,000 fewer inspections in 1981 than the year before, minimum fines for safety violations by mine operators were decreased, and deaths increased to 155, the most since 1972. Shaken, the administration restored the budget of the Mine Safety and Health Administration. Still, its new administrator, Ford B. Ford, soon proposed that required inspections be halved and that mine operators be trusted to correct violations, rather than being reinspected. Federal safety inspections at sand, gravel, and stone pits have been stopped altogether by budget cuts.

Each year, it is estimated, about 4,000 miners die gasping from black lung disease, which is caused by breathing in coal dust. A benefit program for black-lung miners and their families is partially funded by the government, and Reagan proposed to cut the government's participation by 78 percent. The administration contended that the program was approaching "an automatic pension." The miners got so angry, the administration backed down.[4]

About 1.3 million elderly adults live in 18,000 nursing homes which receive medicare and medicaid funds. Behind the scenes, Reagan's Department of Health and Human Services began planning to do away with federal requirements that these homes have a physician as medical director, make arrangements for the patients' social well-being, and train their staffs in such matters as the control of infections, fire and accident prevention, and respect for the patients. Secretary Schweiker killed outright this attempt to "deregulate" the health and safety of the helpless old. But then he announced new proposals that would dispense with mandatory annual inspections of the nursing homes and with the requirement that when inspectors find violations they must return to check up ninety days later. Instead, the administration proposed inspections every three years for hospitals and every two for all other facilities (except homes for the mentally retarded, which would still be inspected annually). If states wished under the new rules, nursing homes' accreditation for medicare and medicaid could be granted by a private group (the Joint Commission on Accreditation of Hospitals) rather than by public authorities.[5]

Just before he left the Cabinet, Schweiker proposed the relaxation of federal standards for about 1,500 small and rural hospitals which participate in medicare and medicaid. While tightening standards concerning surgery, anesthesia, and infection control, the new rules would also dispense with a requirement that these hospitals have medical libraries; end federal standards for the social work departments of the hospitals that have them; replace many specific standards with one general requirement for "quality care"; dispense with rules that all tissue removed by surgery must be examined; and cease prohibiting doctors from splitting fees.[6]

Reagan's chairwoman of the Consumer Product Safety Commission (CPSC) provides sharp contrast in the administration's record. Nancy Harvey Steorts, who had served as a consumer adviser under Nixon and Ford, states forthrightly: "About 36 million adults and children are injured and 30,000 are killed each year in product-related accidents in the U.S." After receiving reports of about 25,000 injuries caused by baby walkers that tipped over, her CPSC put out a warning and called in the manufacturers to discuss the situation. Steorts participated affirmatively as CPSC fined Sears, Roebuck and an affiliate $1 million for failing to inform the agency about a defective garden tiller and for not correcting the defect quickly; prohibited urea formaldehyde foam insulation on grounds of public health (concerning which a federal court overruled her); adopted a mandatory safety standard governing the manufacture of unvented gas space heaters; and refused to delay a standard requiring an automatic motor shut-off on electric lawnmowers (which are involved in 100,000 injuries a year). On the latter problem Con-

gress overruled the agency, approving a weaker standard. But
Steorts' toughness as a protector of consumers makes her seem
like a wild card in Reagan's deck—proof that the administration's personnel screeners could not foretell how all their appointees would turn out.[7]

The Department of Agriculture dropped a requirement that
labels on cans of mechanically deboned meat state that such
meat contains powdered bone, stopped publishing the names of
meat companies that chronically violate meatpacking requirements, reduced the frequency and duration of meat company
inspections and the number of inspectors, and increased the rate
at which carcasses pass by inspectors on conveyors. In its defense, the department said in 1983 that its program had become
more efficient while continuing to be just as effective, since the
rate of condemnation of meats had continued steady, generally,
since 1975.[8]

Originally   the   administration   endorsed   legislation   to
toughen health warnings on cigarette packages by specifying the
dangers of emphysema, lung cancer and heart disease, and damage to the unborn children of mothers who smoke, but the tobacco industry protested and the administration backed down.
The White House budget office refused to allow the FTC to
distribute a survey intended to determine how large the warnings on the packages should be. The Civil Aeronautics Board
canceled regulations that required the segregation of cigar and
pipe smokers on airplanes and that prohibited smoking when a
plane's ventilation system was not fully working. Ordering these
rules restored, a federal appeals court ruling said the agency had
given "no reasoning" in support of its turning these matters back
to the companies.

More generally, a group working under the President's Office of Science and Technology has been considering an entirely
new standard for regulating cancer-causing substances. For two
decades, any level of exposure to such substances has engen-
dered regulation. Administration officials, in concord with industry scientists, contend that with scientific measurement much
more precise now, thresholds of "significant risk" should be established, instead. A spokesman for the Chemical Manufactur-

ers Association said that "the concept of zero exposure is not realistic any more." Taking over at EPA, Ruckelshaus seemed to differ; the outcome remained to be seen.[9]

Reagan's personal attack on the Delaney amendment, which bans food additives shown to cause cancer in animals, probably expressed the same industry displeasure that has churned up the Congress on the issue since 1981. Measures were introduced to scale down a requirement of reasonable certainty that a substance is not harmful to "the absence of significant risk." This language was approved in substance by a working group of the Reagan administration.

The Carter administration had proposed to require that the ingredients of alcoholic beverages be listed on their labels or advertised there as available. Booze can contain red dye, urea, ox blood, sugar, egg albumen, or any of hundreds of other preservatives, artificial flavors, stabilizers, and foam enhancers, and of course the buyer knows nothing about it. Reagan's Treasury Department threw out the regulation. A federal judge called Treasury's action "arbitrary and capricious" and ordered the rules put into effect.

The Reagan-era Food and Drug Administration (FDA) had refused to require that salt content be disclosed on packages, relying instead on voluntary labeling by manufacturers. Because deficient infant formula can injure children, Congress ordered FDA to establish testing procedures for it; Reagan's FDA has deferred to voluntary industry procedures. According to Nader-connected public interest lawyers, FDA has also turned over the problem of toxic shock syndrome to an industry group.

FDA acted firmly against defective x-ray scanners and against starch-blocking diet aids that were causing intestinal illness. But the agency suspended regulations—one month before they were to take effect—that were to provide buyers of ten widely prescribed drugs (including Valium, Darvon, and Librium) with information about how to use them and about their potential hazards. Speeding up its procedures for approving new drugs for the market, FDA stumbled badly over Oraflex, an antiarthritis preparation. Although "important adverse findings" about Oraflex were pointed out by FDA's staff nine

months before it was approved for the market and although
three months before the approval eight Oraflex-related deaths
had been reported by the manufacturer to British health authorities, it was marketed in the U.S. for three months. When the
death toll reached sixty-one in Britain and it was banned there,
the manufacturer withdrew it worldwide.

In what is grotesquely called the "orphan drug" problem,
pharmaceutical companies fail to develop drugs required to
treat about 2,000 rare diseases because there is not enough
profit in the drugs and, in many cases, because they are not
patentable. Congress unanimously passed a bill to subsidize the
companies (about $75 million over five years) to induce them to
develop and market these drugs, but some of Reagan's advisers
wanted him to veto the measure as governmental intrusion into
private business. Facing a rising outcry about the threatened
veto, Reagan signed.[10]

The Reaganists take as a gauge of their regulatory success the
decline in the bulk of the Federal Register, in which federal
regulations are printed, by about a third in two years. Reagan
said his deregulation was saving business, and therefore indirectly consumers, $7 billion a year. The director of the Bush
deregulatory task force, Christopher DeMuth, asserted that the
flow of new regulatory proposals was down to 15,000 a year
from 21,000 in 1980, and most of the new ones soften existing
rules.

There was a flaw in these claims of progress: the "benefit"
had been dropped out of the administration's "cost-benefit analysis" of regulations. Everybody dislikes paperwork, and some of
the government's regulations no doubt went too far. But the
need for reform had degenerated into a pell-mell rush for relief.
Cost-benefit analysis was handy in tearing down the case for a
given regulation, but when claiming general progress the
Reaganists just recited the costs they said they had saved business. Wrote Walter Guzzardi, Jr., in *Fortune*: "The charge that
the administration is merely probusiness rather than proreform
is not easy to dismiss." Nader, noting the administration's claim
that weakening the car bumper standard saved $300 million a
year and that not requiring a device to warn drivers of low air in

their tires saved $130 million, observed: "There's no mention of the lives lost." Mark Green, head of a public policy research institute, ticked off a few of the benefits that are threatened by the administration: Reduced water pollution could save $12 billion by 1985, and the net benefit of requiring airbags in 1982–1985 model cars has been estimated at $10 billion. Saving people's health and their very lives must certainly count as a benefit of, say, the regulation of asbestos: the National Cancer Institute has estimated that workers' inhalation of asbestos fibers will result in 2.5 million premature cancer deaths over the next thirty-five years. The federal standard for cribs has reduced by half the number of infant deaths from strangulation; studies show that between 1973 and 1979, child-resistant bottle caps saved the lives of 200 to 300 children under the age of five.[11]

Cost-benefit analysis is a tool for the rational analysis of alternative programs, but Reagan has used it like a sledgehammer against all government regulation. The President seeks to gravely weaken the modern-day exercise of the federal authority to regulate commerce among the states and to provide for the general welfare. He is saying, trust business to protect people from business practices and products that jeopardize the public health and safety, and look how much money this will save business! But even if one agrees to convert health and life into dollars, one can hardly claim the reduced costs of business as gains while leaving out of the equation the reduced health and safety of the people.

10

The Turn Against Antitrust

Reagan's hostility to government regulation of business extends to the enforcement of the antitrust laws. In his administration, three of the government's four major pending antitrust suits have been dropped and the fourth one settled under puzzling and controversial terms. The Justice Department has continued to prosecute bid-rigging, but approves of manufacturers' price fixing at the retail level even though such activity is quite illegal. Combinations among exporting companies now have the government's approval. "Bigness" is in and corporate mergers long opposed by U.S. antitrust authorities because of their anticompetitive implications now have government approval.

The President's earlier experiences with the antitrust laws—through his personal identification with the movie industry and GE—were not pleasant.

He blamed the government for requiring movie studios to divest themselves of their chains of movie houses, even though he conceded the studios had a "virtual monopoly." He wrote in his autobiography:

"The studios—seven majors—were the boss of the place [Hollywood]. They controlled, within the limits of active competition, every major aspect of the industry. They accounted for more than 90 percent of the pictures shown around the world. . . . They controlled the theaters that showed their movies and, generally, could regulate the business as efficiently as De Beers today keeps up the artificial price of diamonds." De Beers was (and to an extent still is) the international diamond cartel. Yet Reagan argued that when the government in 1948 invoked the antitrust law against the studios, they were left in the position where they could spend millions making a movie "with an excellent chance of no return," presumably because they could not control the theaters like De Beers controlled diamonds.

He likened film production companies to candy stores. In a letter he said that "what Hollywood needs is to eliminate the court decree that separated production and exhibition. Hollywood should be allowed, like a candy store, to make the pictures in the backroom and sell them in the front." But of course a candy store does not have the "virtual monopoly" which Reagan conceded the movie producers did.

As mentioned earlier, GE, the corporation that was Reagan's benefactor for eight years, was punished for price fixing under the antitrust laws. In 1966 Reagan criticized "the harassing powers of the antitrust laws and Bureau of Internal Revenue," which he said had been "used" against business. His interest in antitrust subsided as he became immersed in California affairs, but in a 1979 radio broadcast, as he prepared his final push for the presidency, he argued against antitrust prosecutions that are based on the domination of markets.

The Justice Department and the Federal Trade Commission, he said, had a plan "to attack as monopolists firms that, by operating efficiently and making consumer goods available at a fair price, have won a large share of the market." He opposed as "a perversion of the antitrust laws" a suit pending against Du Pont that was based on facts involving the company's capture of 40 percent of the market for titanium oxide pigments. Du Pont had

40 percent of sales, Reagan said, because it had developed a low-cost production method and had passed the savings along to consumers.[1]

The first signal that there would be a historic reversal of antitrust policy under Reagan came a month before he entered the White House. For decades the antitrust subcommittee of the Senate Judiciary Committee had been a focus of antitrust activity and theory; its hearings, in conjunction with those held in the House, provided responsible and, what was more, public evidence on the anticompetitive behavior of U.S. corporations. With the election of a Republican majority in the Senate in 1980, however, Senator Strom Thurmond (R.–S.C.) became the judiciary chairman, and he simply abolished the subcommittee by announcing that "antitrust . . . will be kept in full committee."

The second signal was a thunderous return to the basic argument against antitrust, that bigness is not badness. Attorney General Smith announced exactly that: "Bigness in business does not necessarily mean badness. . . . The disappearance of some should not be taken as indisputable proof that something is amiss in an industry."

The decisive event, however, was the designation of a self-described "harsh critic" of the antitrust laws, William Baxter, as the assistant attorney general in charge of the Justice Department's antitrust division. Baxter has testified that "the thesis that large corporate size yields overweening political power" is not even "remotely true." To the contrary, in fact. "No one in his right mind could possibly suppose," according to the nation's chief antitrust enforcer, that "there was a connection between the concentration of economic markets and political power." Responsibility for enforcing the antitrust laws has been divided between the Justice Department and the FTC; Baxter would strip the FTC of "all its antitrust jurisdiction" because of the "deplorable job" it has done over the years. "It is true, in a sense, we are going to turn back the clock on antitrust," he said, "because there is an awful lot of rubbish that has been passed around under the name of antitrust." At his confirmation hearing he declared, "I am not sympathetic to the view that concentrated industries as a rule should be broken up." According to

Baxter, "The antitrust laws interfere with a lot of efficient business practices." His job, he told a reporter, could be described as deregulating big business. Reagan had his man.

A professor of law at Stanford for twenty years, Baxter had consulted for such private clients as AT&T, Exxon, Levi Strauss, Northrup, and the American Petroleum Institute. He designed antitrust seminars for Exxon; before Congress, for the API, he testified against legislation designed to restrain oil companies from buying other companies with profits from the decontrol of oil prices. Now, as the federal antitrust chief, he said he would follow a strategy of refusing to file cases that might lead to court precedents of which he would disapprove, easing up guidelines on mergers, and intervening in private antitrust suits on the side of the defendants.[2]

In 1973 the FTC had filed an antitrust complaint against the eight largest U.S. oil companies seeking to break them up into separate production, pipeline, refining, and distributing companies. They began a pattern of delaying tactics in the courts, and five years later Reagan came to their defense, on radio. Oil, he said, is accused of "being a monopoly," but "there are more than 10,000 companies competing with each other in oil and gas exploration and production; 133 companies operate 264 refineries and more than 100 pipeline companies transport crude oil, liquefied natural gas and refined products. In the wholesale side of the industry there are 15,000 companies selling petroleum products to over 300,000 retailers. . . . There are more than 1,500 different brands of gasoline. . . . That's not much of a monopoly." This approach ignored the patterns of market domination by the majors. In the autumn of Reagan's first year as President the FTC dismissed the case against the eight biggest companies on grounds that the litigation could drag on another decade. A year later, when the FTC was considering whether the awarding of more than $2 billion in oil drilling leases off Alaska would have anticompetitive effects, Baxter gave the Interior Department a go-ahead on the leases without waiting for the FTC's conclusions.[3]

On the last day of the Johnson administration in 1969, the Justice Department had charged IBM with intentionally using predatory pricing and other illegal tactics to monopolize the general-purpose computer market. The government wanted to break IBM up into smaller companies. The lawyer who directed the case for the government from 1972 to 1977, Raymond Carlson, told the *Washington Post* that in 1972 the Nixon administration's Council of Economic Advisers ratified the suit by deciding that it should go to trial. The proceedings dragged on, but early in 1982 Baxter, acting for the United States, told the presiding judge that the case was "without merit" and should be dismissed.

Baxter had not reckoned on the fury of the judge, who had supervised the suit for a decade and was only a few months away from writing his decree. In an extraordinary showing of judicial ire, Judge David N. Edelstein of Manhattan entered into the record letters showing that in the mid-1970s, for a fee, Baxter had helped line up witnesses for IBM in its defense in a private antitrust lawsuit. The judge scheduled a hearing on whether Baxter, in dismissing the government's suit against IBM, had had a conflict of interest. At Baxter's confirmation hearing Senator Metzenbaum had asked him to list all his past consulting work, and in a written answer, knowing that the IBM lawsuit was pending, he had not mentioned his work for IBM. His explanation was that he had left behind his records for years before 1978 at Stanford, so he had just listed his clients from 1978 on.

It was subsequently publicized that IBM had paid Baxter's professorial salary in 1968–1969 while he took a year off to study and to write a paper for IBM on how to sell computers to lawyers; that in 1976 he had written the incoming Carter administration that the IBM antitrust suit should never have been filed; and that two months after dismissing the IBM suit in 1982 he intervened as assistant attorney general on behalf of IBM in an antitrust suit that had been brought against it by the European Economic Commission on a charge of dominating the European computer market.

IBM fought Edelstein up to the next highest judicial level, a three-member appeals court, and on June 17, 1982, a Justice Department official told the higher court that the department's inquiry concerning its assistant attorney general for antitrust had concluded that "there was no conflict of interest" that barred him from dismissing the suit. To reporters the Justice Department acknowledged that the investigation had concluded that Baxter's failure to disclose his past connections with IBM had caused "the appearance of a conflict of interest." The appeals court concluded that Edelstein had "abused his power by continuing a lawsuit which the parties have sought eagerly to dismiss" and ordered him to "conduct no further proceedings of any kind whatsoever" concerning it. So that was that.

In 1969, when the suit was brought, IBM had roughly 70 percent of the mainframe computer market; as the case was dismissed thirteen years later it still had about the same share. According to industry sources, its share of computer systems in the thousand largest computer installations in the U.S. was up from 69 percent in 1978 to 77 percent in 1982. Carlson, who had prosecuted the case against IBM under Nixon, Ford, and Carter, called Baxter's dismissal of it a public disservice. "If I am a company the size of IBM and run it well and put people out of business by predatory pricing," Carlson said, "the decision seems to say one can do what the law forbids."[4]

"The FTC is prosecuting Kellogg, General Foods, and General Mills," Ronald Reagan informed his radio audience in 1979. The suit had been filed during the Nixon administration in 1972. The three firms, with about 80 percent of the market for ready-to-eat cereals, were charged with acting as a "shared monopoly" by setting prices among themselves, producing scores of brands, and refusing to sell "private label" brands to major retail chains.

"They are charged with 'brand proliferation,'" Reagan continued on the radio. "In other words, because these companies offer us a variety of breakfast cereals they are guilty of 'a shared monopoly.' . . . They'd be all right in the eyes of the government had they just stuck to corn flakes.

"When the Sherman antitrust bill was passed in 1890, Senator Sherman said it was intended to outlaw arrangements which tended to raise the cost to the consumer. Indeed, when the Senate Judiciary Committee explained the bill to the senator, they declared that a man who 'got the whole business because nobody

could do it as well as he could' would not be in violation. . . .
The Federal Trade Commission is embarked on a witchhunt
which could very conceivably result in increased prices for all of
us."

The witchhunt, if it was that, ended in 1982 when the FTC
voted 3–1 to uphold a hearing officer's ruling in favor of the
companies. Reagan's chairman, James Miller, voted to close the
case, saying that restructuring the industry would hurt consumers more than help them. The liberal holdover commissioner, Michael Pertschuk, voting that the lawsuit be pursued,
spoke of its implications for other "concentrated industries that
do not operate competitively."[5]

In its sheer scope, the agreement which Baxter negotiated to
sever the $137 billion American Telegraph and Telegraph Com-
pany (AT&T) from its twenty-two operating companies was historic, justifying the comparisons that were made with the
breakup of Standard Oil in 1911. But these comparisons obscured a momentous billion-dollar shell game that will leave
Americans staring at higher phone bills. Local phone service was
still a regulated natural monopoly which in its nature could not be
competitive, and although competition had broken in on
AT&T's long-distance service, AT&T still held the great bulk of
the long-distance business. In the agreement, AT&T lost the
local phone business, but kept all its interstate and about half its
intrastate long-distance, and both local and long-distance service
are still regulated by state and federal agencies. AT&T's twenty-
two operating companies are to be replaced by seven regional
companies that will run the local telephone companies. As a practical matter, then, the agreement merely replaced one regulated
national telephone monopoly with seven regulated regional monopolies for local phone service and an AT&T freed to use its
guaranteed profits from its regulated long-distance business to
subsidize its competition with its unsubsidized rivals in other
lines of business. The settlement reflected the competition which
is emerging in long-distance telecommunications, but the seven
regional monopolies are permitted to maintain one nationwide
"Central Staff Organization," which could eventually raise the
question of whether, concerning local phone service, the central-
ized monopoly has been extinguished or simply reorganized.

In the original lawsuit, which was filed by the Justice Department in 1974 under Ford, the government charged AT&T with serious anticompetitive violations on the theory that even a regulated natural monopoly cannot violate the antitrust laws in the parts of its business that can be made subject to competition. According to the government in 1974, AT&T had imposed unfair requirements on companies trying to compete with it in equipment sales, had bought its equipment from its own Western Electric subsidiary when better and cheaper products could be bought from other manufacturers, had refused to cooperate in providing connections for new long-distance competitors, and had used its regulated monopoly business to subsidize low prices in the competitive parts of its business.

Nevertheless, in the telephone monopoly, according to Almarin Phillips, a professor of public management, economics, and law at the University of Pennsylvania, "There were significant economies of scale as well as scope. Competition, in the literal sense of competition, is not possible in that market."

What, then, did the divestiture accomplish? The presiding judge in the case, Harold Greene, ruled that AT&T's giving up its operating companies was "clearly in the public interest." Obviously the one national monopoly had more concentrated marketing power than would the shorn AT&T or any of the seven regional monopolies, if operating separately.

From AT&T's point of view, the government's seven-year-old lawsuit had made the company much more vulnerable to private antitrust actions. In 1980 AT&T had been hit with a $1.8 billion judgment in favor of one of its long-distance competitors, MCI. The settlement of the federal suit without findings of guilt ended this open-ended danger for the company.

Legislation had been working its way through Congress which might have kept AT&T heavily regulated in return for letting it go into new areas of telecommunications competition. AT&T was faced with the possibility that Congress would prohibit it from using its long-distance revenues in its competitive activities.

In his first press conference, Baxter made it clear that he would insist that AT&T divest itself of its regulated companies in exchange for the cancellation of a 1956 consent decree that barred it from competing in unrelated lines of business. The administration made a decision that it preferred to settle the matter by legislation and sought to persuade Greene to delay the case until Congress acted, but the judge refused. Despite other pressures from Commerce and Defense to dismiss the case, Baxter then went forward with it in the courts. AT&T itself moved to persuade the judge to dismiss it, and the hammer fell: refusing, Greene said the government's case had demonstrated "that the Bell System has violated the antitrust laws in a number of ways over a lengthy period of time," and the burden was on Bell to prove the contrary.

AT&T then had to accept the possibility that either Greene or Congress might well order it to divest itself of its most profitable lines of business—long distance, Western Electric, Bell Labs. Baxter told reporters he had been suggesting divestiture of the regulated lines of business—both local and long-distance telephones—informally. In December 1981 at its monthly board meeting, AT&T authorized its chairman to consent to divestiture of the local phone service, provided the company kept long distance, Western Electric, and the labs. This was what Baxter agreed to and announced on January 8, 1982, the same day on which he had dismissed the IBM suit.

Although regulatory analysts dispute the underlying facts, it is generally believed that about 20 percent of AT&T's long-distance profits had been used to subsidize local telephone rates. Under the agreement, this stops. Well-placed officials predicted that local phone rates would increase sharply. A spokesman for AT&T said the day the settlement was announced: "The long-distance subsidy will be gone, and obviously the local companies will be under a lot of pressure to raise prices." The president of AT&T and local officials of the New York Telephone and Southern Bell predicted doubled local rates in five years; the chairman of AT&T from 1972 to 1979, John D. deButts, said "the local customer is going to have to pay more." Representative Wirth exclaimed: "Staggering increases appear to be in store, especially in rural areas."

This cast the settlement in a highly questionable light: evidently AT&T had put one over on consumers in the very act of divesting itself of two-thirds of its assets. The company sent out a memo ordering its officials to correct "this misunderstanding." Baxter pointed out cogently that regulators would still be able to permit local companies to charge long-distance companies connection fees high enough to make up for the lost subsidies. And in his final divestiture order, Judge Greene decreed that the local companies would keep the lucrative Yellow Pages business (which Baxter had proposed to let AT&T keep) and could market (although not manufacture) telephone equipment and office switchboards.

But meanwhile, Reagan's FCC ruled that local phone companies must increase household phone bills $2 a month in 1983, rising to $7 a month in 1986, to offset the loss of the long-distance subsidies. The FCC also authorized depreciation of telephone equipment four to six times faster than before, a change which will further increase household rates. A member of the Florida Public Service Commission estimated to the *New York Times* that the average monthly cost of household phone service may go to $20 or $30 in a few years, plus inflation (it was $8.61 in 1980). Local phone bills are generally expected to double in 1984.

The divestiture agreement was at one and the same time a historic defeat and a brilliant coup for what had been the nation's largest monopoly. No longer is AT&T "Ma Bell" (although Ma could have a reincarnation). But the company kept for itself its high-profit lines of business while getting rid of the tightly regulated, low-profit local phone business, and it won the right to compete in unregulated markets with its long-distance profits and its retained accumulated capital of perhaps $40 billion. By marshaling its stockholders in 1982 into a lobbying campaign, the company blocked Wirth's bill to prevent it from using profits from long-distance in its other ventures.

Protest against the Reagan administration's puzzling advocacy of divestiture in the lawsuit against AT&T came from a professor of economics at Yale, Paul W. MacAvoy, who was a member of Ford's Council of Economic Advisers. MacAvoy declared that separate operating and long-distance phone companies cannot maintain the service reliability and universality of service that are central to public utilities. And he asked the difficult question, "Why should [the government] want to break up a regulated company?" As he saw it, ending the long-distance cross-subsidy to local phone rates would cause local monthly charges to increase by $6 billion or more. "The question has to be raised," he said, "as to why this AT&T settlement should lead the experts to predict higher rates on local service and stock market gains for the new Bell Long Lines. Since when do landmark [antitrust] decisions raise prices, and leave the divested company more profitable? This is not landmark but rather cloakroom antitrust."[6]

Bid rigging is one activity prohibited by the antitrust laws with which William Baxter has no sympathy, and the Reagan administration has continued vigorous prosecution of contractors in fourteen southern states for price fixing and bid rigging on asphalt and concrete paving contracts. In 1981, according to the Justice Department, the average corporate fine in these cases was $211,000 and the average jail sentence five and one-half months. Hundreds of individuals and corporations have been charged; sentences have run as high as three years, and one corporate fine reached $7.5 million. According to Baxter, the administration put more businessmen in jail for price fixing during its first eighteen months than have been imprisoned for this offense since the Sherman Act was passed in 1890. In 1982 six New York bakeries were indicted on charges of fixing prices for pastry.

The government was provided a tape recording of American Airlines president Robert L. Crandall saying on the phone to the president of Braniff, Howard Putnam, a few months before Braniff's bankruptcy, "Raise your goddam fares 20 percent, I'll raise mine the next morning. . . . You'll make more money and I will too." Putnam declined to discuss the proposal with him. Baxter filed a civil antitrust suit against Crandall charging him with attempting to fix prices and asking that he be barred from top airline jobs for two years. The assistant attorney general even floated a proposal (promptly disavowed by his superiors) that chief executive officers should be prohibited from talking to each other on the telephone unless they tape their conversations.

At the FTC, too, chairman Miller drew the line when the tide of deregulation threatened to end federal prosecution of anti-competitive and deceptive practices in the medical professions. As Miller pointed out, the FTC's rule preventing states and professional organizations from prohibiting the advertising of eyeglasses and contact lenses had dropped the average prices for those products sharply. The FTC had acted against doctors and dentists conspiring to undermine cost-containment programs, against medical codes that prevented doctors from working for low-cost group medical plans, and against a medical association rule that stopped a group of doctors who wanted to offer a house-call service from advertising the fact.

The political action committees (PACs) of the trade associations of doctors, dentists, and optometrists greased the Congress by giving $1 million in contributions to cosponsors of their "deregulatory" legislation and to members of the key committees that would handle it. The House voted 245–155 to prevent the FTC from bringing complaints against any individual professional or professional group that was regulated in any way by state laws.

Miller snapped: "This exemption would place professionals above the laws which apply to all other Americans, laws which protect consumers from deceptive practices, price fixing, boycotts, and other anticompetitive conduct." He knew, Miller said, what deregulation was, and "this ain't the animal." The bill was killed.[7]

One could make a case, although a somewhat uncertain one, that antitrust is alive and well at the FTC, compared to the Justice Department. With Miller vigorously dissenting, the FTC voted 3–1 to test a new conception of anticompetitive pricing among price leaders in an industry: "signaling" by such devices as advance announcements. The agency ruled that Du Pont and Ethyl Corporation had illegally restrained trade by setting prices together through simple but definite signals.

At the Justice Department Baxter had declared that he intended to "undo some of this bad old law," and one way he undid it was to disregard its existence. A statute prohibits manufacturers from fixing the prices at which retailers must sell their products, but Baxter disapproves of the law and publicly gave his approval to most of these practices.

In 1975, with President Ford contending that "legalized price fixing" was costing consumers $2 billion annually, Congress made it illegal for manufacturers to dictate prices to stores. Subsequent Supreme Court decisions have confirmed the law. In two interviews in 1982, Baxter conceded that such price fixing was illegal but said it usually did not suppress competition and he would not prosecute instances of it except in unusual circumstances.

Senator Leahy of Vermont said Baxter was using the prosecutor's discretion to "effectively amend statutes," to which Baxter replied: "It's perfectly true that I am disregarding some of the things that the Supreme Court and other courts have from time to time said about the antitrust laws."

Baxter conceded that manufacturers' price fixing may result in higher costs to consumers. Nevertheless, he said, makers of technologically complex products should be allowed to fix their retail prices to prevent consumers from using expensive retail sales services and then walking to a discount store to buy the products. Such price fixing is OK, Baxter argues, as long as it does not facilitate "horizontal collusion" (for example, price fixing among retailers).

The antitrust division has stopped bringing "these silly cases" against manufacturer-fixed retail prices, Baxter said. He dropped a suit filed in 1979 charging Mercedes-Benz of North America with illegally tying in dealers' car purchases to their purchases of replacement parts. (That didn't hurt competition, he explained.) A jury and a federal court of appeals held that Monsanto, in a conspiracy with distributors to fix prices, had cut off one of its distributors which had been discounting. At Baxter's instance the Justice Department entered the case on Monsanto's side and asked the Supreme Court to consider overturning its rule against such price fixing. He and the FTC were on the winning side in 1983 when the high court made it easier for companies to defend setting different prices in different areas.[8]

As a presidential candidate in 1980, Reagan made it clear that he wanted to stop antitrust prosecutions against U.S. companies operating abroad. As mentioned before, he told *Business*

Week: "We don't want to give up our protection against monopoly at home, but why can't we make it possible for American concerns to compete on the world market and not have it called collusion or restraint of trade?" Accordingly, Baxter advocated early on that in industries that have a number of small companies, "The solution would be for them to get together in groups of ten or fifteen or twenty such companies and form a joint venture which would give them the necessary scale" to function as "joint export groups."

In 1982 Reagan suddenly endorsed the pending Export Trading Company Act, which had first been proposed by Carter. The bill would create "several hundred thousand new jobs," Reagan said. As passed overwhelmingly two weeks later, the law allows competing American companies to obtain certificates authorizing them to act together to sell their goods and services abroad; it reduces the penalties for these export groups' antitrust activities in the U.S. from treble to single damages; and it lets bank holding companies invest their own money in these ventures, breaching for the first time the rule that banks cannot engage in commercial enterprises. In substantial effect, the export groups are exempted in their operations abroad from U.S. antitrust laws. The law is "a major departure from the scheme of the antitrust laws that have been in effect now since 1890," warned Representative Sieberling of Ohio. Said freshman Representative Bob Shamansky (D.–Ohio), "you have a prescription for getting around the antitrust laws—get one of these certificates. And what you do internally, within the United States, is down to single damages instead of treble damages."[9]

Urged on by Reagan, Congress would probably pass in 1983 a law granting antitrust immunity to U.S. ocean shipping companies that take part in organizations which pool revenues and divide up routes. The companies had been subject to antitrust regulation by the Federal Maritime Commission, but the law would end that. Senator Metzenbaum, a dedicated antitruster, cried out on the Senate floor: "How can an administration ostensibly dedicated to the free enterprise system have the audacity to bring this bill before the Congress of the United States? This is not free enterprise. This is fixed enterprise—fixed enterprise against the American consumer. . . . Reaganomics supports the cartel. Beautiful." The Senate passed the bill 64–33; the House had passed it once before.[10]

No single nation can now contain or regulate big business. International cartels flourish beyond the reach of national antitrust laws, and national boundaries are mere abstractions to be obviated. No effective international antitrust structure has been devised, so each nation must decide for itself how to respond to international anticompetitive activity committed by its native companies. Under the Reagan administration, U.S. policy is not to fight the international cartels, but to submit to them. National businesses are not to be encouraged to do battle with multinational conspiracies in restraint of trade; the idea is, join them. The implications of this policy for competitive free enterprise in the western world are profound.

Kuwait's state-owned petroleum company bought the California-based drilling contractor, Santa Fe International, for $2.5 billion; the Justice Department terminated its antitrust inquiry into the purchase. The Justice Department having closed down the Carter-era inquiry into the auto industry, GM and Toyota— international competitors—announced a joint venture to produce cars together in the U.S., confident that the Justice Department would approve. Corporations from five nations (United Technologies of the U.S., Fiat of Italy, Rolls-Royce of Great Britain, a West German company, and a Japanese consortium including Mitsubishi and Kawasaki) planned to jointly manufacture a jet engine for a new passenger plane, provided antitrust authorities approved.[11] Sanctioning such joint ventures by international consortiums, the Reaganists were moving quietly but steadily toward the acceptance of an evolving new international order dominated by privately held transnational monopolies.

In keeping with their bias for bigness, leading Reagan officials gave conglomerate mergers within the U.S. a powerful forward thrust. As long as these mergers did not blend two major companies in the same business, they were all right with the administration. "There is no such thing as a vertical problem," according to William Baxter—that is, it is perfectly all right for a company at the top of a vertical chain of production and distribution to buy up businesses further down the chain. In an interview that was widely perceived as a high-sign to the merger mills on Wall Street, Baxter said in a *Wall Street Journal* interview that during the 1960s, "the Supreme Court cooked up a variety of esoteric and totally baseless theories about the harm caused by conglomerate mergers" and "simply made up wacko economic propositions to justify their predilections." (One may only imagine the high justices' mutterings as they read in the *Journal* that the chief antitrust officer regarded one of their antitrust propositions as "ludicrous on its face" and many of their decisions as "rubbish.") Nor was Baxter out of tune with Reagan's other men concerning mergers. According to FTC chairman Miller, conglomerate mergers "tend to generate efficiencies." SEC chairman Shad, who helped plan billions of dollars worth of mergers and corporate financings when he was with E. F. Hutton, said mergers generally result in "net economic gain."

Under the prevailing measures of market concentration, an industry was regarded as concentrated, and mergers in it subject to challenge, if four companies together had 75 percent or more of the market or if the merging companies each had a market share of 5 percent or more. Baxter replaced this standard with a set of rules which in effect told corporate planners that there were some mergers the government definitely would not challenge. The new rules are based on the Herfindahl index, which numerically assays the intensity of concentration in an industry according to the total of the squares of each company's market share in it. In general, Baxter acknowledged, the new standards are "more lenient."[12]

In practice, the administration still regards some horizontal mergers as anticompetitive, but not others.

Baxter blocked the bids of Heileman Brewing Company to acquire Schlitz and Pabst and let Stroh Brewery acquire Schlitz only after Stroh agreed to sell off one Schlitz plant in the southeast. He sued to force the Chicago Tribune Company to sell five Florida weeklies, charging that competition for local advertising had been lessened or eliminated. The FTC sued the oil-field services company, Schlumberger, Ltd., to reverse its acquisition of a company that ranked seventh in U.S. production of a certain kind of equipment for which Schlumberger was the U.S. leader.

Mobil is one of the "seven sisters," the big seven international oil companies. In addition Mobil is the second largest oil company and the second largest industrial company in the United States. When this giant moved to buy Conoco, the ninth largest U.S. oil company, Baxter indicated skepticism by asking for more information, and Du Pont stepped in and—with the government's blessing—bought Conoco for $7.8 billion in the largest corporate merger in the history of the country.

Not to be thwarted, Mobil then moved to acquire, for $6.5 billion, the sixteenth largest oil company, Marathon. Preferring to be wed, instead, to U.S. Steel, the nation's leading steel company, Marathon sued to deter Mobil, and a federal judge ruled that the merger of the two oil companies would substantially lessen competition in gasoline sales in six states. Two weeks later the FTC helpfully filed an antitrust suit to prevent Mobil's takeover of Marathon—unless Mobil agreed to divest certain specified assets of Marathon's. Representative Gore of Tennessee charged that the FTC had written "a blueprint" for takeovers and given "the green light," saying to middle-tier oil companies, "it's OK to buy up reserves as long as you sell off other assets." But U.S. Steel and Marathon were already too attached to each other; Mobil tried to block the marriage at the Supreme Court level, but it went through. U.S. Steel's acquisition of Marathon for $6.2 billion became the *second* largest merger in U.S. history.

A charge of cynical manipulation of the FTC was made by Cities Service, a takeover target company which believed that Gulf Oil, another of the seven sisters, used the agency in a scheme to back out of a buy-out bid which it had quickly come to regret. Gulf, the nation's sixth largest oil company, had sought to buy Cities Service, the nineteenth largest one, for $5.1 billion; the ensuing merger would have made Gulf the fifth largest. The FTC unanimously challenged the merger, saying that it would violate antitrust laws by increasing concentration in gasoline marketing, kerosene jet fuel, and the shipping of petroleum by pipeline. After first vowing that it would contest the FTC lawsuit, Gulf dropped its bid. Cities Service then sued Gulf for $3 billion, alleging that it had engaged in an illegal scheme to induce the FTC to bar the acquisition. Why? Because, Cities Service alleged, Congress was considering changes in tax law that would have foreclosed tax gains Gulf had been counting on in the merger, and there had been widespread skepticism on Wall Street about the wisdom of Gulf's offer.

Occidental Petroleum, taking all this in, had an idea: Would Cities Service sell itself to Occidental for a billion dollars less than Gulf had offered? Done: with government assent, of course. Occidental had accomplished the *third* largest merger in American history.

Thus the three largest mergers in U.S. history, all involving oil companies, occurred in the first two years of the Reagan administration. *Fortune*'s lists of the 50 biggest deals for each of these two years (total value, almost $100 billion) also showed Standard Oil of Ohio buying Kennecott Copper and the coal properties of U.S. Steel (oil companies now produce a third of the nation's copper, a fourth of the coal, and a fourth of the uranium), American Express buying Shearson Loeb Rhoades, Sears buying Dean Witter Reynolds, General Foods buying Oscar Mayer, Tenneco buying Houston Oil & Minerals, Union Pacific buying Missouri Pacific, Coca Cola buying Columbia Pictures. Phillips Petroleum bought a Texas oil company; Dreyfus, which runs money funds, bought a small bank; Xerox bought a leading property and casualty insurer. The professionals of hostile takeovers developed a special lingo for the game: "the bear hug," "the white knight," "shark repellant," "the golden parachute." The business world was agog as Bendix bid to buy Martin Marietta, which turned around and tried to buy Bendix, only to have United Technologies bid for Bendix too and offer to split half of the target company's assets with Martin Marietta— then all of these suitors were suddenly left at the gate when Allied Corporation rushed in and swooped Bendix off her feet for $1.9 billion. What the country had as a result of this dizzy game was an oil, gas, chemical, fibers, plastics, electrical, electronics, automotive, aerospace, and industrial company that didn't exist before, in just that form.

Under the Sherman Antitrust Act and the Clayton Act, the basic antitrust laws, private parties who are victims of anticompetitive behavior can sue and collect triple their money damages. As a practical matter this has been one of the most effective and important remedies in the law. In the spring of 1983 Reagan signaled his intention to ask Congress to abolish treble damages in private antitrust actions except for offenses such as bid rigging that the courts regard as illegal "per se." If formally proposed and enacted, this change would manifestly weaken the nation's laws against monopoly.[13]

One's opinion about all this may depend on whether one finds ever-bigger corporations more beguiling than competitive free enterprise. As Robert Sherrill points out, between 1948 and 1979 the 200 largest companies increased their share of manufacturing assets from 48 to 59 percent. Under Reagan this trend continues apace. Michael Pertschuk says that "the question is, will antitrust enforcement be confined to catching people in hotel rooms fixing prices?" The economist Milton Friedman believes, "mergers promote efficiency by enabling managements that are not using their resources effectively to be replaced." But in a study of "the bottom line" on the major mergers of 1971 ten years later, *Fortune* concluded that "investing in unfamiliar businesses is unduly perilous" and that most of the acquiring companies turned out to be bad investments from the stockholder's point of view. By William Baxter's doctrine, if a few big companies have attained dominance in an industry, that fact in itself means they are more efficient than their competitors and cracking down on them for anticompetitive practices would only punish efficiency. By Ralph Nader's, the Reagan administration wishes to replace a free market with "a regime characterized by concentrated markets, giant conglomerates, and private agreements not to compete." Baxter says he is not concerned that the biggest companies may get bigger and the economy more concentrated—if Congress wants to deconcentrate industries, he says, it should use tax disincentives instead of the antitrust laws. But Howard Metzenbaum points out that Congress had already passed laws to control economic size and power, not once but at least four times: the Sherman Antitrust Act of 1890, the Federal Trade Commission Act of 1914, and the Clayton Acts of 1914 and 1950. "Mr. Baxter may think this is rubbish," says the senator from Ohio, "but it's the law."[14] The trouble is that the President thinks it's rubbish, too.

11

"All These Beautiful White People"

On civil rights, here is the paradox. Reagan was raised by parents who, ahead of their time, saw the evils of racial and ethnic prejudice, and Reagan himself professes passionately that he has no prejudice. "I am heart and soul in favor of the things that have been done in the name of civil rights and desegregation and so forth," he told the nation in 1980. Yet he has opposed every major civil rights law of this period, whether it protects citizens' access to hotels, restaurants, and restrooms, to the voting booth, or to housing. As President he has abandoned court-ordered busing as a remedy to achieve school desegregation, he has jettisoned affirmative action programs that were designed to equalize job opportunities, he has slowed or stopped federal enforcement of other civil rights laws, and he has fought to grant valuable federal tax exemptions to colleges that exclude blacks. He seeks to wave away the problem in this record by applying some of his racism-free conservative principles to each case at hand. A few critics have sought to dissolve the paradox instead by suggesting that there must be some racism lurking somewhere in such a record. Others have argued more to the point that whether or not Reagan is personally racist, the seated President of the United States is marshaling all his persuasion and powers of office to reverse the historic civil rights revolution that the blacks and Lyndon Johnson started two decades ago.

Reagan's father Jack disliked the Ku Klux Klan and would not let his children see the movie *Birth of a Nation*, believing the Klan was glorified in it. Reagan tells a story in which his father, welcomed to a hotel with the clerk's statement that he'd like it there because they didn't let Jews in, raged at the clerk that next they'd be turning away Catholics, too, and spent a cold night in his car rather than sleep in the place. Reagan's mother, too, taught her children to judge people as individuals, not by their creed or color, the President has recalled.

Reagan tells stories from his younger days to demonstrate his commitment to racial justice. The Eureka College football team had two black players, and when a hotel refused them rooms during an out-of-town trip for a game, Reagan took them all the way back to his home in Dixon to spend the night. And as a sports announcer, Reagan says, he fought baseball's official description of itself as a game for Caucasian gentlemen (blacks were not permitted to play in the regular leagues).

Twice in his 1965 autobiography, Reagan referred to the black players on the Eureka team as "colored boys." In one of the games, he said, a player on the other side baited one of Reagan's black teammates with racial epithets and was trying to smash the black's already-hurt knee. Instead, though, the black youth bore down and knocked the offending player out of the game. The white player, in tears, but respecting his adversary, shook the black's hand, and Reagan finishes the story: "He, who had used the term 'black bastard' on almost every play, now said, 'You're the whitest man I ever knew.'" If Reagan realized that this compliment called for a double-take he didn't say so.

These details in Reagan's storytelling are only mildly disconcerting, though, compared to a joke he permitted himself in the book. He was discussing labor strife during the conflict about Communists in Hollywood. Concerning some confusing phraseology that had been put forward by a carpenters' union, he commented "there was a carpenter in the woodpile."

In 1968, the riots and disorders in black ghettoes fresh in his mind, Reagan told a reporter on an airplane a different kind of story about his early days: there had once been a race riot in Dixon. It began, he said, during a card game, when "a Negro bum slashed a white bum," and then "all of a sudden there were no names, only color." Whites charged blacks' homes and terrorized them; whites tossed screaming black children onto freight train boxcars, and they were carried away hundreds of miles in fright and panic. No one was killed. In the context of the disorders in the cities, Reagan said to the reporter: "The greatest proof of how far we've advanced in race relations is that the white community today hasn't lifted a finger against the Negroes."

The first lady was not raised in a prejudice-free home as her husband was. Cannon reports that the man she regarded as her father, the neurosurgeon Loyal Davis, "was not fond of blacks, and the interns avenged themselves by naming various black children after the surgeon" until he prohibited them from doing it.[1]

In 1948, four years before Reagan married a second time, he apparently favored civil rights as liberal Democrats of that time conceived of them. Just in campaigning for Truman's election Reagan was in effect assenting to the President's then-revolutionary programs for protecting the rights of blacks, which included a federal fair-employment practices commission.

The Democrats' civil rights laws of the late fifties were toothless and escaped Reagan's recorded public comment, but he opposed the 1964, 1965, and 1968 civil rights laws of the Johnson administration. It was now Reagan's underlying rationale that, as he said, "You can't guarantee someone's freedom by imposing on someone else's."

Although in California he had supported the Unruh Act, a public accommodations law, he opposed the national law on the same subject. In an arresting example of how rapidly he could about-face on civil rights when it suited him, he declared in the autumn of 1965, "I favor the civil rights act of 1964, and it must be enforced at gunpoint, if necessary." But eight months later he said, "I would have voted against the civil rights act of 1964," which he called "a bad piece of legislation."

The 1964 law opened hotels, motels, restaurants, and public restrooms to blacks and anyone else who had been kept out of them because of race; the 1965 Voting Rights Act removed barriers that blocked blacks and Hispanics from the voting booth. Opposing the 1965 law, Reagan contended that "The Constitution very specifically relegates control of voter registration to local government." True, he said, it is the job of the federal government to see that voter registration procedures apply to everyone equally, but "additional legislation is unnecessary." David Broder reported: "He said he was 'in complete sympathy with the goals and purposes' of the 1964 and 1965 civil rights acts, but opposed their enactment because they had 'legislative flaws and faults and parts of them were, in my view, unconstitutional.'" President Reagan told Laurence Barrett that the 1965 Voting Rights Act was "humiliating to the south."

Fair housing laws, Reagan had consistently resisted. California's Rumford Act, which covered about a third of the state's dwellings, prohibited an owner from offering property for sale or rent on the open market and then withdrawing it solely because of racial or religious factors. Reagan favored the repeal of this law. A group of black legislators reported that he told them he regarded the fair housing law as a form of fascism and asked them, "You wouldn't want to sell your house to a red-headed Kiwanian if you didn't want to, would you?"

In 1967, when fair housing legislation was still unfinished business in the Johnson administration and the Congress, Reagan said, "I am opposed to telling the people what they can or can't do with their property." Foiling suspicions of racism with conservative principle, he added, "This has nothing to do with discrimination. It has to do with our freedom. . . ."

Carl Greenberg of the *Los Angeles Times* asked the governor what he would say to a black who declared that he had a right to buy or rent wherever he could afford to. "I agree with him," Reagan replied. But, he added, "the people who are infected with the sickness of prejudice and discrimination . . . have certain constitutional rights" that should not be violated. At the same time, he said, he opposed restrictive covenants (which seek to exclude minorities as buyers of a property) because the majority has no right to govern "the individual's right to the disposition of his property." In 1968, shocked into action by the assassination of Martin Luther King, Congress passed a national fair housing law. A decade passed before President Carter proposed regulations to carry out the law; Reagan withdrew them. Now, though, Reagan wants to let the Justice Department sue on behalf of individuals who allege housing discrimination.

In just a few words while campaigning in 1980, Reagan signified his acceptance of the public accommodations law. "I recognize now," he said, "that it is institutionalized and it has, let's say, hastened the solution of a lot of problems."[2]

Since racism, the attribution of personal characteristics to a person on the basis of his or her membership in a racial or ethnic group, is subtle and can be unconscious, a political figure must expect to be watched carefully on such matters. Before Reagan made his way into the White House, his public life had been ruffled from time to time by dubious or at least curious incidents—racial *faux pas* or remarks or positions taken that had a racial implication of some kind.

In 1965, when he was being groomed to run for governor, he paid a well-publicized visit to Edward Brooke, a black who was then the attorney general of Massachusetts. On this occasion Reagan, while speaking of the emergent African nations, joked, "When they have a man for lunch, they really have him for lunch." One found again, in Reagan's radio broadcasts in the late seventies, a tendency to stress features of African life which might make people laugh on the basis of stereotypes of blacks (see Appendix).

Reporter Joseph Lewis believed, correctly or not, that he perceived a racial purpose in radio spots for Reagan in 1966. "Every day," Reagan had declared in one such commercial, "the jungle draws a little closer. . . . Our city streets are jungle paths after dark, with more crimes of violence." "A jungle?" Lewis mused. "In the backlash context of 1966, it touched a nerve, especially among low-income whites who lived near the ghettoes."

A person can express a liberal position in an unconsciously racist way. This may have been what was happening when, in the spring of 1968, in the course of advocating that conservatives help blacks and other minorities achieve what they are entitled to, Reagan said: "Our education system had failed them . . . they are just passed on from grade to grade without being able to read or write. . . . They have reached the end of the road and their only answer is the last, hopeless gesture of the club and the torch."

After the Detroit riot in 1967 Reagan had said the rioters were "mad dogs against the people." On the day of Martin Luther King's funeral, Reagan said that King's death "was a great tragedy that began when we began compromising with law and order and people started choosing which laws they'd break," a statement that associated King's death with his historic campaign of civil disobedience against segregation laws.

Making a southern swing in pursuance of his initial presidential bid that year, Reagan refused to express disagreement publicly with the segregationist views of Governor George Wallace of Alabama. Asked what opinions of Wallace's he disagreed with, he responded, "Well, now, lately on the basis of his speeches that would be kind of hard to pin down because he's been speaking a lot of things that I think the people of America are in agreement with." Wallace did not have his philosophy, Reagan said, because Wallace as the governor of Alabama had not fought federal aid and spending. Nevertheless, Reagan said, "Right at the moment he's dwelling mainly on law and order, patriotism, and so forth . . . and I'm sure there are very few people in disagreement." Reagan told reporters that he didn't want the racist vote, but that openly disavowing Wallace's racism would hurt his own ability to sell southerners Republicanism.

Preparing for his 1976 challenge to Ford, Reagan again turned for bedrock support to white southern conservatives. The Mississippi GOP chairman said to him at a rally in that state,

"We've loved you for a long time. Nowhere else in this country are you better understood and respected." Reagan told the rally, "If there's a southern strategy, I'm a part of it." Governor Wallace, introducing Reagan during a chamber of commerce banquet at Cullman, Alabama, said to him, "You're among friends." Musing later on what he regarded as the impracticability of his teaming up with Wallace in a presidential campaign, Reagan said, "We're completely different on a lot of issues, especially economics."

In Fort Lauderdale, speaking to an overflow rally during his attempt to wrest the nomination from Ford, Reagan went considerably further than refusing to condemn Wallace's racism. Working people were outraged, Reagan told the Floridians, when they waited in lines at grocery store checkout counters while a "strapping young buck" ahead of them bought T-bone steaks with food stamps. Suddenly there it was out in the open under the wide blue Florida sky: the welfare cheat was black. Reagan thought better of the formulation. Before a luncheon group at Fort Walton Beach, conjuring up the same scene, he referred instead to "some young fellow."

Just as the questions of statehood for Alaska and Hawaii concealed many racial issues until statehood was granted, so now do the questions of statehood for Puerto Rico and the District of Columbia. Reagan has always been receptive to statehood for Puerto Rico: he says he will support it as soon as the Puerto Ricans vote for it in an election. He is opposed to statehood for the District of Columbia.

To the argument that the District is entitled to statehood because it is bigger than seven of the states, Reagan replies that the federal government is bigger than it should be. In four discussions of the topic on the radio in the late seventies, he argued that low voter turnout in the District shows that its residents are not "panting" to have a voice in the government; that the District is represented by the whole Congress; that if the people of the District only want representation they can cede the residential part of the city back to Maryland; and that since most of the District's residents are government employees, there is no way their representatives in Congress "would free themselves from a built-in conflict of interest. They would undoubtedly vote for higher taxes and expansion of the government payroll." Reagan did not, however, discuss one politically relevant fact: the people who live in the District are mostly black (according to the 1980 census, 448,229 blacks compared to 171,796 whites).

A New Hampshire snowstorm grounded Reagan as he campaigned early in 1980, and in these circumstances it was arranged that Mrs. Reagan, who was attending a campaign fundraiser in Chicago, would talk to her husband on an amplified telephone hookup. Thus it was that with 200 or so supporters and the press listening, Mrs. Reagan said to her husband that she wished he could be there to "see all these beautiful white people."

According to UPI, she hesitated, paled slightly, and corrected herself: "Beautiful black and white people."

She was quoted later, "I'm so sorry, I didn't mean it." The manager of Reagan's Illinois campaign said she had gotten mixed up talking to her husband about the white snow in New Hampshire.

If Mrs. Reagan had jeopardized her husband's already slight claim on blacks' votes, the candidate hurt his own chances with Poles and Italians by telling a joke that asked for laughter at Poles as stupid and Italians as associated with the Mafia. ("How do you tell who the Polish fellow is at a cock fight?" Reagan asked. "He's the one with the duck. How do you tell who the Italian is at the cock fight? He's the one who bets on the duck. How do you know the Mafia was there? The duck wins.")

Even as he condemned busing and quotas to achieve racial balance, Reagan sought to come through in 1980 as a man without prejudice, a fair man. In May, during an interview on board an airplane, he said, "The federal government's responsibility is to protect the constitutional rights of every individual, at the point of a bayonet if necessary," and, "Incidentally . . . the first man who resorted to those bayonets was Dwight Eisenhower, the Republican President." Endorsed by the Ku Klux Klan, he rejected the endorsement and asked blacks not to consider him "antipoor, antiblack, and antidisadvantaged." He was, he said, "committed to the protection of the civil rights of black Americans." Just a few weeks before the voting he told the people he

had been hurt by doubts raised about his freedom from prejudice. "I could never personally tolerate," he said, "any kind of
discrimination."[3]

One practical approach that arose out of the civil rights
movement was compensatory discrimination. The underlying
idea was that blacks and Hispanics have a right to transitional
favoritism in order to offset their historically imposed handicaps
and the residual discriminations they suffer. This concept was
kept tacit, though, because of its vulnerability to attack as reverse
discrimination. It has been the essential work of the Reagan
counterrevolution in civil rights to isolate this idea that underlies
affirmative action and contrast it to the ideal of dealing with
everyone only on the basis of individual merit.

Reagan has held forth at length against the injustice done to
Allan Bakke, the white student who was excluded from medical
school because of affirmative action policies that admitted a certain number of blacks even though they were scoring lower than
white applicants on tests. The key official in Reagan's counterrevolution, William Bradford Reynolds, who is the assistant attorney general for civil rights, likewise proclaims "the right of
every person to pursue his or her goals in an environment of
racial and sexual neutrality." No more, Reynolds said, will the
government "in any respect support the use of quotas or any
other numerical or statistical formulas" designed to achieve racial balance. In even more seductive formulations of these ideals,
Reynolds said "our goal must always be genuinely color-blind
state action," "the color-blind ideal of equal opportunity for all."
What Reagan has really done, as civil rights leader Harold C.
Fleming has perceived, is try "to reduce the whole area of civil
rights to a question of individuals." *Patterns* of discrimination
become irrelevant. "We believe," says Attorney General Smith,
"that the civil rights laws were intended to guarantee individual
rights, not group results."[4]

Bilingual education, which is both an educational and a civil
rights issue, was the first victim of the new neutralism. The
Carter administration had proposed regulations to require bilingual education for about a million students whose comprehen-
sion of English was so poor that they were likely to fall behind

quickly unless they were taught in their native language as well as in English. Education Secretary Bell immediately junked the Carter proposals as "unworkable and incredibly costly." Hispanic organizations reacted with indignation, but the deed was done. While bilingual education programs continue to evolve slowly, they cannot advance at the rapid rate envisioned by the Carter Democrats. In 1982 Bell announced that school districts would no longer be held to civil rights agreements to provide bilingual education. At its high point in fiscal 1980 the federal bilingual program had helped about 324,000 students, but for 1983 the Reagan administration asked for enough money to provide the service to only about 125,000 children. An Education Department study showed that there is a need for 56,000 more teachers who are qualified to teach bilingually—only about 2,000 a year are produced now—but the Reagan administration is cutting back.

The federal bureaucrats are carrying forward their President's wishes. Bilingual education as a transition to English is all right, Reagan says, but he does not like the part of the program intended to help students maintain their proficiency in their mother tongue (which is Spanish in about two-thirds of the cases). "It's absolutely wrongheaded to encourage and preserve native languages" instead of teaching English, in Reagan's opinion. He asserts that in helping students continue to be bilingual, the schools forsake the melting pot tradition in favor of teaching the foreign-born "how to be different and remain apart from the mainstream of American living." (He also opposes bilingual ballots—"When we vote, we vote as Americans who share our political language, English," he says—but he did not fight the extension of bilingual voting in the voting rights legislation of 1982.)[5]

As with bilingual education, Reagan's rhetoric against court-ordered busing was transformed by his election into federal executive policy. The busing issue is often oversimplified. The operative question is not, do people like forced busing; the question is, when federal courts rule that busing is necessary to achieve a constitutionally required level of school desegregation, shall that court-ordered busing be prohibited anyway? Reagan answers yes.

Busing has advocates and critics among minorities as well as segregationists; like bilingual education, this is a complicated subject. Even so, some liberals believe that the persistent campaign to prohibit court-ordered busing by an act of Congress is actually an effort to stop school integration, or at least slow it to a crawl. Reagan's top civil rights lawyer, Bradford Reynolds, lends credence to this belief by his frank declarations. "We aren't going to compel children who don't want to have an integrated education to have one," Reynolds has said. "Every kid in America has a right to an integrated education where he wants it. But I don't think that means the government can compel an integrated education," he says. The Reaganists' ideals, "an environment of racial . . . neutrality," "genuinely color-blind state action," and "the color-blind ideal of equal opportunity for all," turn out to require the reversal of *Brown v. Board of Education,* the 1954 school desegregation order in which the Supreme Court required in effect that whether children want an integrated education or not, the state may not discriminate against minority students on the basis of color.

Early in 1970 Reagan condemned as "ridiculous" a Los Angeles judge's order, issued after an extended study, that required school integration in Los Angeles on constitutional grounds. Reagan then signed a bill making it illegal to bus school children without their parents' consent. Forced busing "is so wrong," he said in 1976. He favored, as an alternative to it, a voucher system whereby, instead of aid to schools, the federal government would give parents vouchers which they could use to enroll students in schools of their choice. His budget for 1984 proposed such a system.

If the only way to eliminate busing is a constitutional amendment, he favors that, Reagan has said. In the fall of 1979 he discussed favorably the constitutional amendment proposed by Representative Ron Mottl, a conservative Democrat from Ohio, which would provide that "no student shall be compelled to attend public school other than the one nearest his residence." (The House narrowly defeated the amendment that year. Mottl persisted with it, but in 1982 he was defeated at the polls and pronounced his amendment dead. See Appendix.)

Going into his 1980 campaign Reagan asserted, "I do believe

that no public school should discriminate on account of race, ethnic origin, sex, or creed." In the light of his subsequent actions favoring racist private colleges, the word "public" in that statement acquired retrospective significance. Another meaningful qualification occurred in a statement he made the month before the 1980 election: he would vigorously support federal action against "intentional discrimination." Certain Supreme Court rulings had seemed to prohibit patterns of discrimination only if they were proved to have been intentional, a much more difficult test than the requirement of proof only that the results of state action were discriminatory.[6] As he achieved the presidency it was already manifest that if Reagan would not tolerate any discrimination personally he would tolerate plenty of it as a public official.

In the Senate, southerners took the lead in the busing fight, and despite an eight-month filibuster led by Senator Lowell Weicker (R.–Conn.), the Senate approved two antibusing riders to the Justice Department appropriation. One, sponsored by J. Bennett Johnston (D.–La.), would tell federal courts they cannot issue orders to transport children to school more than five miles or fifteen minutes away from home. The other, by Jesse Helms, would prohibit the Justice Department from using any money to litigate school busing cases (beside the point for the time being, since Reagan's Justice Department had announced it would not pursue busing remedies).

The Senate debate was predictable, opponents of busing saying it had failed, opponents of the riders saying Congress cannot constitutionally order the courts not to enforce the Constitution by certain means. "The overwhelming social science evidence is that busing has failed across America and increased racial isolation," said Johnston. The riders, said Senate Dale Bumpers (D.– Ark.), were an attempt to change the Constitution by a statute and part of a "continuing, sinister, devious attack" on the Constitution.

As the debate moved to the House, three former attorneys general warned against the measure. The Carter administration's Benjamin Civiletti said it would deprive the courts of "the only effective remedy in many school desegregation cases." A

Reagan spokesman told a House panel that the bill was constitutional, but that its terms did not reach the powers of the Supreme Court. The U.S. Civil Rights Commission, which Reagan had been vainly seeking to cleanse of its liberalism, issued a report charging: "If a school desegregation plan requires the transportation of students for effectiveness, then busing is required. To speak against busing in these circumstances is to speak against school desegregation."

This was the tortured congressional situation as the administration decided to go ahead with some Carter-era school desegregation cases without seeking busing remedies and to stress voluntary student transfers in three major cases, those in St. Louis, Chicago, and East Baton Rouge Parish, Louisiana. In the St. Louis plan, students voluntarily transferring into integrated schools would receive free tuition credit at state colleges. In the Chicago plan, which a federal judge upheld as constitutional, the busing of students is not required.

The Justice Department went forward to a federal judge in Louisiana asking that he in effect reverse his earlier order requiring school busing in East Baton Rouge Parish. "Voluntary incentives . . . can more effectively dismantle this dual system of long standing," the department argued. The plan proposed that students be invited to transfer voluntarily into "magnet schools." In black neighborhoods the magnet for whites would be "innovative" schools; in white neighborhoods, blacks would be attracted by vocational-emphasis schools. Busing would continue only for two isolated rural schools. The government conceded that the plan would reduce desegregation at first, but maintained that white flight from the system would be lessened. An NAACP spokesman said, "I don't see how this could possibly work. This district has resisted desegregation for a quarter of a century. . . . This isn't a desegregation plan. This is a plan to keep whites in the school system." The local school board voted against the Reaganists' plan, 10 to 2, and Reynolds dropped out of the situation.

If not by busing, how shall schools be desegregated? As Charles Babcock reported in the *Washington Post*, Reaganists have been advising school officials to use other methods. But the administration has so severely reduced funds for emergency school aid to be used on desegregation problems, the schools don't have the money to pay for other methods.[7]

The same gap between the rhetoric and the reality has opened up in the government's efforts, under Reagan, to achieve equal job opportunity.

In 1965 President Johnson issued Executive Order 11246 committing the government to affirmative action "to ensure that applicants are employed, and that employees are treated during employment, without regard to their race, color, religion, sex, or national origin." Under Nixon and his Labor Secretary Shultz (later of course Reagan's secretary of state) federal contractors were for the first time required to establish goals and timetables for achieving adequate employment of blacks and other minorities (women were included later). But this bipartisan movement toward affirmative action displeased Reagan.

"Government orders what is in effect a quota system—but they don't call it a quota system," he said in 1976. "It is an 'affirmative' action program—with 'goals and timetables' for the hiring of particular groups. If you happen to belong to an ethnic group not recognized by the federal government as entitled to special treatment, you are a victim of reverse discrimination. I'd like an opportunity to put an end to this federal distortion of the principle of equal rights." In October 1980 he said again, "I see affirmative action becoming a kind of quota system . . . a kind of reverse discrimination."

As President, Reagan had the opportunity he wanted. His transition team on the Equal Employment Opportunities Commission (EEOC) set the scene with a charge that the agency, by pursuing affirmative action quotas, had "created a new racism in America." Reagan proposed to modify Johnson's executive order in order to relieve federal contractors who were responsible for 7.5 million jobs of affirmative action pressures to hire minorities and women. He also wished to discontinue back-pay awards as penalties for failure to make satisfactory progress against job discrimination. Furious reaction from civil rights organizations moderated the changes, and a maximum penalty of two years' back pay continued in effect.

Quotas, according to Attorney General Smith, invariably limit "opportunities afforded to one race in an effort to remedy past discrimination against another." Says Bradford Reynolds: society cannot transcend racism "by borrowing the tools of the racist"; the electorate has rejected "race-conscious affirmative action"; not only quotas, but also goals and timetables are "offensive to the law and the Constitution."

Reagan announced his view that the Weber case had been wrongly decided. The Supreme Court in that case had upheld the legality of an affirmative action plan that had been negotiated by the Kaiser Aluminum and Chemical Corporation and the United Steelworkers of America. Under the terms of their collective bargaining agreement, 50 percent of the openings in the company's on-the-job training program were reserved for black employees until the percentage of black workers in the plant matched the percentage of blacks in the local workforce. "The President and the Department of Justice," said Reagan's spokesman, "find this racial quota unacceptable."

Once again the U.S. Civil Rights Commission protested the Reagan counterrevolution. The main reason blacks and Hispanics suffer higher unemployment rates than those of whites, the commission said, was racial discrimination. A member of the commission added: "The administration, in backing down from a commitment to affirmative action, backs down from the crucial antidiscrimination order. . . ." But the most penetrating criticism came from the disenchanted Arthur Flemming, the moderate Republican whom Reagan had summarily fired as chairman of the commission. Flemming said, "the strategy of the opposition is to either eliminate or weaken the methods that you have got to employ in order to implement the laws and the court decisions."

Early in 1983 the Reaganists aggressively challenged compensatory discrimination as a method of correcting old wrongs. The Justice Department intervened to set aside two federal court decisions that had sanctioned affirmative action solutions for patterns of employment discrimination.

In Boston, a court had ordered the city to hire black and Hispanic police officers and firefighters until their numbers approximated their percentages of the local population. In New Orleans, black plaintiffs and the city had agreed that the city would promote one black officer for each white officer promoted until 50 percent of the supervisors were black (the city is 55 percent black).

When layoffs of police and firefighters became necessary in Boston, a federal court ordered that they be carried out in a way that would not adversely affect the minority employees. The Reagan administration, charging that this order unconstitutionally created a new class of victims who had not themselves committed discriminatory acts, sued to set it aside. "White firefighters and police officers—some with more than ten years of service—were furloughed while black and Hispanic employees with as little as two years' seniority were retained. This was not . . . permissible," said the U.S. solicitor general, Rex E. Lee. Reagan himself said the issue in the case was "quotas for minority groups." Similarly in the New Orleans case the government contended that the one-for-one promotion agreement violated the interests of "innocent nonblack employees."[8]

The strategy Flemming had espied, eliminating or weakening the methods necessary to enforce the civil rights laws, was most apparent in the Reaganists' duck-and-weave attempts to weaken the 1965 Voting Rights Act, which came up for extension in 1982. This law was unquestionably a historic one. Blacks who were registered to vote in the south increased from 29 to 57 percent between 1965 and 1980; blacks holding office in all the southern states increased from fewer than 300 to more than 2,400 and the blacks in Congress from five to eighteen. Hispanics have made similar gains.

While the administration slowly conducted a study concerning the extension of the act, the House extended it by a vote of 389 to 24. The Supreme Court having indicated that voting discrimination could be proved only by showing it was intentional, the House provided to the contrary that proof of discriminatory *effects* would suffice. This "intent vs. effects" issue was central: Benjamin Hooks, executive director of the NAACP, said, "There is usually little or no evidence of the purpose of the [discriminatory] schemes, many of which are decades old." It is far easier to prove discriminatory effects than discriminatory intent.

The act requires that areas with a history of discrimination clear proposed election changes in advance with the Justice Department. The House bill provided that in order to get out from under this "preclearance" requirement, an election district had to show it had been discrimination-free for ten years and had made "constructive efforts" to facilitate minority voting.

Their concealed hand forced when the House shoved in its stack, the Reaganists then advocated a simple extension of the unmodified law and initiated a maneuver to require proof of intent to discriminate. Once again they were pursuing the strategy of professing their fidelity to civil rights while weakening the methods available to protect and achieve them.

The House "has been pretty extreme in what it's done," Reagan himself said. "I believe the act should retain the 'intent' test under existing law, rather than changing to a new and untested 'effects' standard," he argued. He indicated he did not like the requirement of proof of "constructive efforts"—his attorney general remarked, "Nobody knows what 'constructive efforts' means." Robert Pear reported in the *New York Times* that Smith had written Reagan a confidential twenty-one-page report saying that the objective of the "results" standard was "to facilitate challenges to the at-large method of election and other practices that dilute the voting rights of minority groups" and that "we are opposed" to the provision. The civil rights organizations accused Reagan of proposing "an empty shell" and trying to make the act meaningless with his objections to the House bill.

Shoving in *their* stack now, Reagan's men advanced on the Senate giving in on everything but the effects test, charging that its application would produce a quota system in democracy, itself. Bradford Reynolds said the effects standard of proof would all but require the "proportional representation" of minorities in federal, state, and local elections. Attorney General Smith took to the op-ed pages, arguing that the effects test "could gradually lead to a system of proportional representation . . . essentially a quota system for electoral politics," and Reagan said the same thing. Yet the House bill plainly provided, "The fact that members of a minority group have not been elected in numbers equal to the group's proportion of the population shall not, in and of itself, constitute a violation."

In the Senate as in the House there was next to no support for the Reaganists' position. As the senators joined the game at this democratic poker table, Senator Dole moved into the controlling position and produced a "compromise" that wasn't a compromise. The effects test was retained, but the "totality of circumstances" had to be considered. The intents test was not required. Proportional representation as a right of minorities was specifically repudiated.

Reagan at once endorsed the compromise. In effect Dole had called his hand and found him with a pair of deuces. By an astounding 85–8 vote the Voting Rights Act was approved in the Senate substantially as it had passed the House.

Hispanic activists sued under the new law to challenge the discriminatory effects of at-large (that is, citywide or countywide) elections in south Texas, but the Justice Department asked the Supreme Court to construe the new law to permit Lockhart, Texas, to keep its at-large system, which allegedly had worked to keep members of minorities out of office.[9] Although he had lost the pot to Congress on voting rights, true to form Reagan wasn't quitting the game; he was dealing another hand.

Nothing put the Reaganists' posture as civil rights advocates more at risk than the administration's sudden announcement on January 8, 1982, that racially discriminatory schools would henceforth be granted federal tax exemptions. For eleven years, as a result of a ruling affirmed by the Supreme Court, the government had denied such schools these valuable exemptions. The Justice Department now moved in court to assure Bob Jones University, which expels students for interracial dating or marriage, and the Goldsboro Christian Schools, which bar blacks on the ground that God separated the races, that they were tax-exempt.

This meant more than 100 such schools and other organizations would be exempt from paying unemployment, Social Security, or federal income taxes and their benefactors could deduct their contributions on their own income taxes. As was later argued before the Supreme Court, such an exemption is in effect a matching grant from the Treasury. Stimulated by the federal help, other racist schools might be encouraged to organize.

Although Senator Thurmond of South Carolina, who is a trustee of Bob Jones, welcomed the announcement as an end to "trampling on religious and private civil rights," the general reaction was anything but approving. The Democrats' national chairman said the decision made every taxpayer "a forced contributor to segregationist schools." NAACP's Hooks exclaimed: "The President is pandering to the worst racist attitudes in this nation"—while he had not yet called the administration racist, Hooks said, this "puts them mighty close." Senator Kennedy referred to "these racist tax subsidies." And columnists in two leading eastern newspapers almost raised their voices. "If this isn't actively promoting racial discrimination, what is?" asked Tom Wicker in the *Times*. Wrote Haynes Johnson in the *Washington Post*, "There can be no clearer case of the United States endorsing racial discrimination in education, with the cost to be borne by every American taxpayer."

Among Reagan's men, Meese and Deputy Treasury Secretary R. T. McNamara were associated with the new policy; Baker and Deaver evidently moved, after it was announced, to temper it. But through all the tricks and dodges that then flashed past the public's flickering attention, the policy itself held fast.

Four days after the announcement, the President abruptly shifted his stance, advocating that Congress pass a law prohibiting the exemptions. "I am unalterably opposed to discrimination in any form," he said. "I would not knowingly contribute to any organization that supports racial discrimination." But the exemptions would be granted, his spokesmen made clear, unless Congress acted. The sole basis for the new policy to grant the exemptions, Reagan said, was the need to prevent agencies like the Internal Revenue Service (IRS) from governing by "administrative fiat." The *Times* editorialized angrily that "the President clings to the new racist policy" of "tax-exempt hate."

Reagan switched a second time: the exemptions would be withheld *until* Congress acted, except for the two schools that had been promised them in court action. But as Reagan proposed his bill to outlaw what he had just authorized, it became apparent that both sides in Congress would say no, one on principle, the other on the ground that such exemptions were already void.

A canny attempt was made to show that Reagan had not made the decision that he had made. Meese told a reporter that he had briefed Reagan on the new policy about the exemptions "for information only" and did not recall that Reagan had said anything back. The President's men were trying to shield him from the import of the action he had taken. But then CBS learned that well beforehand Representative Trent Lott (R.– Miss.) had written Reagan asking the White House to intervene to grant the exemptions, Reagan had written in response, "I think we should," and Lott had sent copies of Reagan's comment to high Treasury and Justice Department officials. The truth out, Reagan now told the press, "No one put anything over on me . . . I'm the originator of the whole thing."

Some time before, in fact. In 1976 Reagan had told an Alabama audience that he did not believe the federal government should sue all-white private schools that receive federal or state aid in order to try to force them to integrate. He believed in "an open society," he said at that time, but "people have a right to disagree." The 1980 GOP platform had called for an end to tax rules "against independent schools." As the candidate that year Reagan had accused Carter of letting the IRS prepare an "unconstitutional regulatory vendetta" to impose affirmative action rules on private church schools.

Finally admitting that the new policy was his, Reagan argued that "there was no basis in the law for what they were doing" (that is, the IRS denying the exemptions to racist schools). This was not so. As Stuart Taylor, Jr., reviewed the matter in the *New York Times*, a three-judge federal court had ruled against such an exemption, the Supreme Court had affirmed the ruling without comment, and four federal appeals courts had followed the reasoning in later cases. More than 100 of the 176 lawyers in the civil rights division wrote Reynolds that such an exemption "violates existing federal civil rights law" (only to be told by a Justice Department spokesman that they were "welcome to leave").

With Reagan's bill lying dead in the Congress, were the racist schools tax-exempt or not? Reynolds said maybe they would be; then an appeals court temporarily barred the government from granting the exemptions and held a hearing at which the Reagan administration switched a third time—back to granting the exemptions whether Congress acted or not. Reynolds, acting for Reagan, argued in tandem with the Bob Jones and Goldsboro schools that there was "no evidence" to support the IRS policy against the exemptions. In an 8-to-1 decision that humiliated the administration, the Supreme Court ruled in May 1983 that such exemptions are clearly illegal. IRS policy on the question, said the highest court, was "wholly consistent with what Congress, the executive, and the courts have repeatedly declared," and Congress has repeatedly refused to overturn the policy.[10]

It is no doubt too early to assess the overall civil rights enforcement pattern of Reagan's government—cases are complicated and records take time to come to light—but a reading can be taken now.

The U.S. Commission on Civil Rights reported that under Reagan's 1983 budget proposals the government would be spending nearly a fourth less on civil rights enforcement than three years before. As we know, the Justice Department will not seek or enforce court orders for busing, and goals and timetables for federally associated hiring are abandoned. Justice will no longer seek districtwide desegregation where segregation is shown in only part of a district.

Without public announcement the administration exempted from civil rights laws—at first from those on sex discrimination, eventually from all the antidiscrimination laws—colleges where guaranteed student loans are the only federal aid that is received. Education Secretary Bell, in an astonishing letter to a senator which reached the *Wall Street Journal,* said: "The courts may soon be after us for not enforcing civil rights laws and regulations. It seems that we have some laws that we shouldn't have, and my obligation to enforce them is against my own philosophy."

There are allegations that the enforcement of job discrimination suits at the EEOC has become lax and proemployer and that the Justice Department is less than interested in enforcing the fair housing law. "For the first time in fifty years," charges Father Robert Drinan, the head of Americans for Democratic Action, "we have a President who is opposed to the enforcement of civil rights."

On the other hand, Justice maintains that it has been more rigorous than previous administrations in pressing criminal prosecutions for racial violence and police brutality and in rejecting as discriminatory redistricting plans from southern states and New York City. Reynolds has said the department is more concerned to prevent discrimination in the quality of education provided students in all-black schools than in getting blacks into integrated schools, and he plans to sue school districts that provide inferior education to students in black and Hispanic schools. Through mid-September 1982 the administration said it filed sixty-two new criminal civil rights cases, fifty-two cases have been conducted, and it had been involved in thirty-two voting rights cases.[11]

The administration's reputation for tolerance has hardly been helped by a few notable slips by Reagan nominees. J. Peter Grace, the chairman of Reagan's Private Sector Survey on Cost Control, said in a speech in Dallas that the food stamp program is "basically a Puerto Rican program," and Grace illustrated his point with a statistical chart entitled "Puerto Rican Food Stamps." He was wrong factually. He denied being a racist, and the Reagan administration did not ask for his resignation.

One of Reagan's nominees to the board of the Legal Services Corporation, George E. Paras, had written a Hispanic judge calling him "a professional Mexican," and to clarify his meaning Paras had later said, "There are such things as professional blacks, professional Greeks, professional Dagos, professional Jews, people who put their ethnic origin ahead of everything else." Senator Thomas Eagleton (D.–Mo.) told Paras, "I think your quotation about professional Dagos has caught you as you really are. . . . You are a 14-karat bigot."

In a memorandum to Bradford Reynolds, his assistant Robert D'Agostino stated: "Blacks, because of their family, cultural, and economic background, are more disruptive in the classroom on the average. It appears they would benefit from programs for the emotionally disturbed." About 120 of the civil rights division's lawyers protested this memo, and all this was publicized, but Reynolds responded by cracking down on his lawyers' relationships with the press.

A bill introduced by two Republican senators, Orrin Hatch of Utah and John East of North Carolina, demonstrated that conceivably the legislative pendulum could swing all the way back to racism writ bold on the face of the law. The Hatch-East bill would prohibit considering race as a factor in assigning students to schools in order to correct illegal segregation. In its "congressional findings" the bill says desegregation orders have failed to demonstrate benefits commensurate with the disruption they have caused.[12]

All these events, the substantial and the circumstantial, have locked the Republicans back into their traditional modern-era stereotype as the white man's party. Senator Kennedy says the administration has tried to encourage "those committed to the concept of segregated schools." Hooks accuses the Justice Department of leading "a sustained, orchestrated attack" on the rights of minorities. "If racial justice were sex, the Reagan administration would have a perpetual headache," writes columnist Richard Cohen. Not so, says Attorney General Smith: "There has been no retreat on the overall question of discrimination." Except for busing and affirmative action, he says, "we've enforced the civil rights law the same as ever."

In the spring of 1983 the usually muted chairman of the Civil Rights Commission, Clarence Pendleton, joined in as the commission warned the White House and federal agencies that it would use its subpoena powers if necessary to get from them documents bearing on civil rights compliance. The White House stepped up its cooperation, but the commission voted to issue subpoenas to the Labor and Education departments.

Donovan's Labor Department headed off the subpoena by sending the documents, but had some explaining to do. Information had come to light that the department's bureaucrats had been telling federal contractors that they would violate federal rules if their yearly goals for hiring minorities exceeded the proportion of the minorities in the work force who were able to

b. The director of equal employment affairs for Merck & ld the *Wall Street Journal*: "Basically, they're discouraging us from taking affirmative action." But a conflicting signal came from the Transportation Department, where Secretary Dole, responsive to a new provision of law, threatened to cut off highway and mass transit aid to states that fail to award a tenth of their contract funds to minority-owned businesses.

Politically Reagan is in a tight spot. Pollster Peter Hart said in the fall of 1982, "Blacks hate Reagan with a vengeance. There is nothing of comparable intensity in survey data." One of the many causes must be the fact that his budget cuts were, as Urban League President John Jacob said, "concentrated in programs in which blacks were a third to a half of all beneficiaries." Perhaps some blacks see this somewhat in the way the late Senator Hubert Humphrey did. Humphrey believed that Reagan, Ford, and "about anybody who uses the word 'Washington' as a code word for an attack" on social programs were using "a disguise for a new form of racism." The attacks, Humphrey reasoned, "are not so much aimed at the programs as they are at the people who need the programs," and "the effect of ending these programs will add up to a total lack of concern for the poor, the elderly, the minorities—the least fortunate in our society."

The chairman of the black caucus of the Democratic National Committee, Representative Mickey Leland (D.–Tex.), said of Reagan: "Black people in this country believe, whether he denies the allegation or not, that he is racist." "Reagan is no bigot," writes Lou Cannon, who knows him. "I don't consider Mr. Reagan personally a racist," Benjamin Hooks said. "But around him there may be some people who are racists."

Within a few days of each other, two of the *Washington Post*'s black columnists came pretty close to calling Reagan a name. "The impression here," wrote William Raspberry, "is that Reagan is not a racist in the manner of some of his antiblack . . . supporters, but that he simply doesn't give much of a damn one way or the other. In practical effect it amounts to the same thing." Carl T. Rowan wrote that "his administration encourages, subsidizes, and defends racism" and is "brutally hostile to the nonwhite people of America." The day after Rowan's column, Reagan telephoned Raspberry to say again that he is opposed to racial discrimination, and as the year progressed the White House political planners scheduled him into "photo opportunities" with blacks: Reagan calling on a couple who had had a Klan cross burned in their yard, Reagan visiting a black school, Reagan going to a black college to announce government grants to ten such institutions. The Justice Department sued a suburb of Chicago, the town of Cicero, alleging that its officials had "verbally and physically harassed blacks" trying to move there to live.[13]

The problem for the administration lay not in appearances but in policies. If Reagan had had his way, minorities would still be excluded from hotels, restaurants, and restrooms at the whim of proprietors. The Voting Rights Act of 1965 would have been defeated and many states would still be getting away with devices to keep blacks and Hispanics from voting. People could still refuse to sell or rent to blacks or Hispanics without legal concern, because the Fair Housing Act of 1968 would not have been enacted. Now, if Reagan has his way as President, the courts will be prohibited from using busing to achieve school desegregation, Hispanic children will not be encouraged to stay proficient in their mother tongue, public- and private-sector goals and timetables for achieving equal job opportunities will be junked, the 70 percent black District of Columbia will continue to be denied statehood, and but for an aroused Supreme Court, racist private schools would receive a large infusion of money from the U.S. taxpayers. Let us concede that President Reagan describes himself as he sees himself when he says, "I am opposed with every fiber of my being to discrimination."[14] But what he does with every fiber of his public power is strengthen it.

12

Sneering at the Women's Movement

The momentously successful women's movement of the 1970s proposed, roughly speaking, to double the productive and civic potential of the American population by granting women full, equal access to work and political life. To each of the principal demands of this movement, the right to an abortion, the Equal Rights Amendment, and affirmative action for fair pay and treatment in jobs, Reagan says no.

During the 1980 election the polltakers came upon "the gender gap": more women opposed Reagan than supported him, while more men supported him than opposed him. Conceiving of this gap as the difference in the spreads of opinion for men and women, it was eight and a half points in 1980 and about the same again in the 1982 congressional voting.

Carter won over Reagan among women blue-collar workers by seven points; Reagan won 47 percent of the male unionists, but only 39 percent of the women unionists. In 1982 women supported Democratic candidates for Congress 57–40, while men supported the Democrats 53–44. Other 1982 preelection polls showed that while 49 percent of men wanted Reagan to run again, only 39 percent of women did and that while 50 percent of men approved of Reagan's handling of the presidency only 41 percent of women did.

The gender gap is too new to draw conclusions about, and it was complicated in 1982 by the "marriage gap," the evidence in the polls that significantly fewer unmarried men and women supported Reagan than married people because of the higher economic insecurity among singles of both sexes. Nevertheless, polls showed that in the 1982 voting women gave the Democrats between 4 and 6 percentage points more support than men did.

The gender gap may be temporary or it may have long-run historical significance. Social scientists Frances Fox Piven and Richard A. Cloward comment upon the 1980 evidence that "Female political values tip to the side of peace, greater equality, and economic security . . . with women showing greater opposition to Reagan on matters of foreign policy, militarization, equality, and the social programs." In 1982, when the CBS–*New York Times* poll asked voters whether they were "afraid that Reagan will get us into war," men said *no* 57 to 36 percent, but women said *yes* 56 to 36—an astounding divergence. The *Wall Street Journal* assembled a panel of twelve mostly middle-class women, most of whom had voted for Reagan in 1980, to discuss him and national issues. On the basis of their opinions the *Journal* concluded that "the women's attitudes appear more clearly anti-Reagan on issues of war and peace in general and on nuclear weapons in particular" and that "probably more than most male voters, these women are bothered by what they believe is the human suffering caused by Reaganomics."

The White House people could read these signs: the administration would have to try to regain lost ground among women voters. A "senior presidential adviser" told the *New York Times*: "Reagan is going to have to develop a compassion issue."[1] If the tendencies in the early studies hold up, women are taking positions different from men on a set of recognizable considerations that are by no means confined to the major issues in the women's movement. And if it should turn out (as in an evolutionary adaptation) that women have become more independent of men in the voting booth and are therefore giving more political strength to compassion and to concerns about peace, the implications could become worldwide as women's movements sweep through nation after nation.

Against the causes and the portents of the women's movement, Reagan advances essentially legalistic objections in an equivocally but unmistakably chauvinist style. In no other policy area is he so dated by his advanced age. His wife of three decades does not challenge him on women's issues, but supports and perhaps reinforces his position in many ways. She is, for him, the old-fashioned kind of wife who is the female ideal in the patriarchal family.

Reagan exposed his visceral reaction to "women's liberation" in his response to a letter that W. E. Bolton of Castro Valley, California, wrote to him when he was governor. The exchange is reported in a book written by Reagan's long-time assistant, Helene von Damm, whom he appointed ambassador to Austria in 1983.

"I've been listening to some women on television hold forth on this new fad called women's liberation and I developed a great feeling of emptiness in my chest," Bolton wrote him. "Women need to be liberated like a humming bird needs a flight manual.

"What I am saying isn't against women. Not in the least. I love women. They are good conversational companions; they bring light into a man's life.

"But I sneer at their current drive for liberation—whatever the hell that means.

"I know where women come from. God made the first one, Eve, from one of Adam's ribs . . . and I think that was where all the trouble started. It all boils down to simple jealousy!

"Women are jealous of men!"

Bolton continued for another nine paragraphs in the same vein. Reagan replied: "I have read your letter anent ribs and women with great interest. I am pleased to tell you I share your views about women's liberation." The governor added some jocular remarks about man's missing rib and then thanked Bolton "from the bottom of my heart" for his letter.

In language feminists discovered the presumption of male precedence exposed in the common usage. By men's reactions to this discovery (adaptive, evasive, or derisive) they took up their new positions under challenge. Reagan was displeased in the spring of 1979 because the Department of Defense had barred from correct military discourse usages which presume that females are silently included in male terms. In a radio broadcast Reagan said:

"I want to be very careful with the next one. . . . I don't want to offend anyone with this item.

"The genders have been used in general terms for centuries in ways that actually have no reference to sex identity. For example, we use the term 'man' or 'mankind' when we speak of all humanity. We call a battleship a 'man-of-war' yet we always refer to a ship as 'she.'

"Now having said that, I'll give you the news item and run for cover," he continued. "The Department of Defense has recommended that gender-designating words be removed from military vocabularies. Graduates of the Naval Academy at Annapolis will become midshippeople. The Navy will now have ordnance persons, torpedo persons mates and ablebodied seamen will be called sailors. A captain of the *U.S.S. Detroit* says, 'I thought there were more important things to worry about.' He's right, there are, but silliness has triumphed again."

Reagan himself uses "the term 'man' or 'mankind' when we speak of all humanity." Consider the implications for women (not to mention democracy) of Reagan's dictum in his autobiography: "The conservatives believe the collective responsibility of the qualified men in a community should decide its course." He told Barbara Walters, "There's a great conflict going on in the world for the souls and minds of men." He does not seem to understand that this ancient usage is evidence of the ancient presumption of male precedence, passed from man to man in language.

The president, the vice president, the attorney general, and the secretary of defense in this administration belong to the all-male Bohemian Club, which is so sexist that women are not even permitted to work at the club's 2,700-acre retreat in California. The late Herbert Hoover, another member, once called it "the greatest men's party on earth." Both Reagan and Smith have explicitly refused to resign. The attorney general argues that belonging to a one-gender private organization does not violate equality under the law (he also refuses to give up his membership in the all-male California Club that has not admitted blacks, either).

"I'm like a woman. I changed my mind," jested Reagan's man Lyn Nofziger, to pass off a flipflop for which he was being criticized. And one of those "senior presidential advisers" of Reagan's was quoted, "Women don't understand interest rates as well as men."

Laughing off questions of equal treatment for women can have substantial consequences. As a private citizen in 1978, Ronald Reagan made light of a court ruling that women students must be permitted to play football. That might lead, he thought, to an "amazon-type" woman winning the Heisman trophy or to "rejects" from the male varsity team taking over the "girls' team." In 1982 a federal judge ruled that since a Virginia college's athletic department did not receive "direct federal financial assistance," the Department of Education could not investigate it concerning discrimination. Reagan's chief civil rights enforcer (Bradford Reynolds) said the decision, being "pretty sound as a matter of law," would not be appealed.[2]

Nancy Reagan uses nonsexist forms like "his or her" in her autobiography, and she expresses her belief in equal pay for equal work. Her ideal of marriage, romantic and idealistic, is based on woman's service to man.

"I expected to marry, have children, and lead an 'ordinary' life," she said in her memoir. Although she continued her career as an actress four years into her marriage and her husband had never asked her to quit acting, she had no wish, she said, to have both a career and a marriage.

Nancy Reynolds, an aide to Governor Reagan in California, has been quoted as saying that Nancy Reagan "has made life wonderful for him. When he comes through that door, Nancy Reagan is waiting for him. She looks like a million bucks. There's a terrific dinner on. She's the best listener you ever saw."

"My family comes first," Nancy Reagan told *Newsweek* early

on in Washington. "I have to get Ronnie settled and know that he's comfortable." A close friend of hers, Deedie Wrigley Chaucey, has said, "She had a good upbringing with the old-fashioned head-of-the-family situation. . . . Now she defers to Ronnie like she did to her dad."

"My parents' marriage is an ideal one," Mrs. Reagan said in her memoir. "My father always said my mother made it possible for him to have a life beyond his professional commitments, a social life with family and friends. . . . She probably helped enhance his professional standing by improving his social contacts. . . . Mother became the ideal doctor's wife. He was a prominent doctor, and she hosted his social affairs. She even organized and developed the gift shop at Passavant Hospital."

"What I really wanted out of life was to be a wife to the man I loved and mother to our children," she wrote. "I always wanted someone to take care of me, someone I could take care of. That doesn't mean that I don't believe in an independence of mind and spirit because I do. . . . I have my own interests and causes."

Despite her adoption of gender-free pronouns, the President's wife displays some attitudes that appear to accept male precedence. "Today," she wrote, "we tear down our heroes. Instead of what makes a man more than other men, we look for those shortcomings . . . I prefer to judge a man by his accomplishments."

When their first child was born Mrs. Reagan thought her husband might be disappointed that it was not a son. "For some reason," she wrote, "I had been sure I was going to have a boy." Her husband reassured her, but when the second baby turned out to be a boy, she wanted to cry out "whoopee."

"I'm sorry politics is such a dirty word these days. We need good men, badly—especially now," she wrote. From the perspective of the women's movement we need more good women in politics, too, and the achievement has been limited (14,225 female elected officials in 1979 compared to 5,765 in 1975, more than 900 state legislators in 1983 compared to 301 in 1969, but still only 12 percent women in the state legislatures, only two of 100 U.S. senators, only 21 of 435 House members).[3]

Women criticize Reagan more than men do, for one reason,

because women are more vulnerable than men economically. More and more, poverty has become a woman's problem. According to census figures about half the families living in poverty in 1980 were headed by women who did not have a husband living in the home. Half of all families run by women who have related children under eighteen are living in poverty.

According to the vice chairwoman of the New York Commission on the Status of Women, Lynn Hecht Schafran, women have borne the brunt of Reagan's social-spending cuts. When he killed the minimum Social Security benefit 86 percent of the people who lost money were women. When he hacked down the size of the new social-service block grant he hurt elderly women, working women who need government child-care programs, battered women who need protection from domestic violence. When he cut food stamps 69 percent of the households from which he was removing income were headed by women. Seven out of ten clients of the Legal Services Corporation that Reagan wants to close are poor women who need help on Social Security, divorce, food stamps, and AFDC. In cutting AFDC Reagan is pinching households that are almost all headed by women. Cutting public housing construction and raising the rents for the lower-income people living in the existing units, he hurts families more than two-thirds of which are run by women. "The poverty rate of families headed by women," according to Schafran, "is triple that of other families."

What accounts for this? True, welfare rules have made it harder for poor families to get benefits if the man continues to live with his family. Another factor is persisting attitudes among some men that women don't need to work as much as men do, aren't as good at it as men, shouldn't get paid as much as men, and ought to stay home. But also, the men who gather at the Bohemian Club know very well that one major source of cheap labor in the United States is women.

Big business is of course run almost entirely by men (in the uppermost fifty American companies only one executive in twenty is a woman). The Bechtel business empire which has provided the Reagan administration with its secretaries of defense and state had to pay $1.34 million in back pay to women as the result of a sex discrimination suit filed by "9 to 5," the National Association of Working Women. The longtime leader of the National Organization of Women, Eleanor Smeal, sees a connection between two facts: business makes money from sex discrimination, and the supporters of ERA did not include the National Association of Manufacturers or a single trade association, businessman's alliance, or chamber of commerce. Self-evidently there is also a connection between the subordination of women at home and in the workplace. A woman obedient at home is less likely to help organize a union at work. The pliancy of women as women assures their pliancy as workers.

Part of the unemployment problem, President Reagan said at a press conference, "is the great increase in the people going into the job market, and ladies, I'm not picking on anyone, but [unemployment goes up] because of the increase in women who are working today and two-worker families and so forth." Molly Ivins, a columnist for the *Dallas Times-Herald*, thought Reagan meant "that half these people don't count because, after all, they're only women."

"The reality of the two-paycheck family in this country," according to the director of the Women's Legal Defense Fund, "is that two paychecks bring home one and a half incomes." This is no small matter in the lives of tens of millions of Americans. For the first time in U.S. history, more children have mothers who work than who don't. Twenty years ago only a third of married women worked—now half of them do. Thirty million men are married to women who are underpaid in the persistent patterns of job sexism.

A working woman in the United States makes about two-thirds of what a working man does—as of 1981, 59 cents for every dollar a man makes. Women classroom teachers make $3,000 a year less than men classroom teachers. Women managers and administrators make $13,000, men, $24,000. Per week, women sales workers make $190, men $366; waitresses $144, waiters $200 (though 90 percent of people who wait tables are women); women engineers, $371, men $547; women lawyers $407, men $574. Jobs held predominantly by men are high-paying and by women, low: physicians make about four times as much as nurses do.

Reagan may have indicated his real attitude toward sex discrimination on the job in a radio broadcast in 1978. A woman reporter who worked for *Sports Illustrated* had filed a lawsuit to require that she be admitted to the New York Yankees' dressing room along with male reporters so she could compete fairly with them as a sportswriter.

"It's one of those things you just knew had to happen in today's climate," Reagan said. "It seems . . . she doesn't have the same sports reporting rights the male reporters have. And, of course, she is barred simply because of her sex. Or maybe it's because of the ball players' sex.

"I have one suggestion. Why don't they grant her permission, then tell the ball players' wives what they've done and see if she could make it as far as the locker room door?"

The plaintiff, Melissa Ludtke, a twenty-seven-year-old graduate of Wellesley, won her lawsuit. A federal judge ruled that the Yankees could keep reporters away until the players dressed, or the players could get behind curtains or wear towels, but if men reporters were admitted women reporters could not be barred. A court of appeals upheld the ruling and by 1979 women reporters had some access to about half the major league clubhouses.

In his comment on her case, says the journalist (who is now working for *Time*), Reagan "was doing what I would have expected him to do, he's overlooking the question of access. No woman demanded to be admitted to a locker room, but if a story was to be reported in the locker room, we wanted an equal right to go in."

Had one judged by the Republican platform of 1980 one would have concluded that the Grand Old Party palpitates with concern for working women who need their children taken care of during the day. Inadequate child care for working women is a critical problem, according to the platform, and "as champions of the free enterprise system, of the individual, and of the idea that the best solutions to most problems rest at the community level, Republicans must find ways to meet this, the working woman's need."

Federal support for community-controlled day-care centers, perhaps? Federal funding for day-care centers complete with public health nurses and social workers? No. President Reagan says let's rely, for the working woman's need, on church volunteers. He told Saul Pett of the Associated Press: "What would be more logical than to say, 'You working mothers and you who want to help, let's meet Monday afternoon and see if we can't work out a solution'? And what better solution than the working mothers drop their kids off at the church and there are volunteers to take care of them—and there would be no government involved."

At the Justice Department, as we have seen, Bradford Reynolds has halted federal advocacy and enforcement of affirmative action goals and timetables to achieve reductions in racial and sexual discrimination. Class action suits have been discontinued, and underpaid women will not be able to afford to file expensive suits individually. At the EEOC Reagan's new general counsel told a group of the agency's people that he wanted them to stop pursuing lawsuits by women complaining that they are paid less than men for equal work. Mary Thornton of the *Washington Post* quoted one lawyer who had been present as recalling: "He told us he was a believer in the marketplace and that we would no longer pursue those cases." Employer discrimination against women?—to hell with it. "It is clear," declared Thomas Sowell, who was a member of Reagan's economic policy board and is black, "that marriage and childbearing have more to do with women's career prospects than employer discrimination." And sexual harassment on the job? Presently an employer can be held liable for sexual harassment of an employee by either management or another employee; the new EEOC staff chief told his subordinates that he did not want management held liable any more for what employees do.

Late in the second year of Reagan's term several incidents further betrayed the direction of the administration on women's rights. The Army, which has been giving men and women recruits their basic training together, decided that women will be trained in women-only groups. The Office of Personnel Management, which had maintained the government's entry-level salaries for the male-dominated professions of accountants, chemists, foresters, and auditors at $20,256 a year, proposed to

lower the entry-level pay for librarians with masters degrees to
$16,659. Of the librarians who work for the government 64
percent are women. By aggressive questioning of Reagan at a
press conference, reporter Sarah McLendon smoked out the
news that the Justice Department had informed him that problems of sex-biased practices have been identified in thirty-four
federal agencies.

Even full rights to education, a pathway to a better situation
for all historically oppressed groups, have been imperiled. Title
IX of the Education Amendments of 1972 guarantees women
equal access to educational resources, including athletic programs; under Reagan, Bradford Reynolds has resisted applying
this title to employees of federally funded schools. Reagan has
named as his executive director of the National Advisory Council on Women's Educational Programs a substitute teacher who
was a state director of the anti-ERA leader Phyllis Schlafly's
Eagel Forum.[4]

In defense of his record on women Reagan says he is *for* their
equal rights—the E and the R, but not the A. He favors a statute-
by-statute approach, wiping discriminatory laws off the books
one by one. He assigned a special assistant to work with the states
on the "Fifty States Project" to eliminate such laws, and he appointed an interagency task force, two-thirds women, to carry
out "the President's directives" concerning federal sexually discriminatory practices. While these initiatives have been criticized
as ineffective and window dressing, it may be too early to evaluate them.

In addition, Reagan says often that as governor of California
he signed new state laws that developed and improved child-care
centers; prohibited sex discrimination in employment, real
property transactions, and private accommodations and services; established a married woman's right to credit in her own
name; gave wives equal rights in the management and control of
community property; extended unemployment disability benefits to pregnant employees, and increased penalties for rape and
for using firearms in a rape.

Anita Miller, whom Reagan had appointed to the California
Commission on the Status of Women and who ran it for six
years, has taken some of the gloss off this apparently shining

record. Signing fourteen bills in eight years did not amount to so much, she said, when you recall that the legislature was considering 75 to 200 bills on women's rights every year and that Reagan "was not in a position of leadership" in initiating women's rights legislation.[5] Still, he did submit to those bills, and but for his reversals of his earlier positions on two issues he would get more credit for his California record than he does.

As far as feminists are concerned, on abortion and the ERA Reagan started out right and winds up wrong. Possibly he has simply caved in across the years to the intense opposition to abortion and ERA in the fundamentalist right wing that is a main source of his political strength. Perhaps his course was affected by the fact that his wife is opposed to abortion. Whatever the reasons, his change of direction on these two issues has discredited him with feminists of both genders and can hardly have pleased the two-to-one majorities of the general public who, according to the polls, favor legalized abortion and the ERA.

Likening abortion to murder, Reagan calls it the taking of a human life that can be justified only in self-defense, when the mother's life is in danger. Running in 1980 he endorsed the "human life" amendment to the Constitution that would prohibit abortion except in such extreme circumstances.

As governor, however, he had signed a law that liberalized abortions, particularly by letting doctors perform them if a pregnancy endangered the mental health of the mother. He worked on this law's terms with its sponsors—he was in the center of the controversy.

Reagan contends now that he didn't see the loophole; he explains that "some of our psychiatrists are particularly willing to declare the mother-to-be to have suicidal tendencies, and they do this on a five-minute examination." He acknowledges that the sponsor was going for "abortion on demand," but he explains that he was trapped by his own position that abortion is all right for self-defense because when legislators asked him about mental health, "they happened to have me there." Letters he wrote while still governor do show that he was appalled by how the law was applied. The safeguards he thought were in the law were regularly violated by medical professionals, he said. Writing a constituent about a ruling of the California Supreme Court that he believed loosened up the law's safeguards, he said he believed that "the decision was a license to murder and that we are committing murder on a wholesale scale."

Yet it is part of the record that in his press release as he signed the law he had said, "I am fully sympathetic with attempts to liberalize the outdated abortion law now on the law books of California," and he spoke of the new law's "humanitarian goals." He said he had objections to the law, but the only two he specified concerned his fears that California might become a haven for abortions and hospitals might be created mainly to perform them. In this release, as he signed the law, he said nothing at all about taking a human life, or murder, or morality.

Six Republican legislators allied with then President Ford said that the strong legal presumption against abortion which Reagan later advocated was the state of the law when he signed the proabortion statute. They also said that in 1967 there were 518 legal abortions in California, but between 1968 and 1974 there were 608,691 (and they were one cause of the reduced welfare rolls that Reagan credited to his welfare reform). By 1980 the twelve-year total was 1,440,778, with 172,000 abortions for that year alone.

Reagan, in 1980, flayed the Supreme Court for refusing to block the use of federal funds for medicaid abortions. "This time," he said, "the court's majority has gone too far. Its unprecedented grasp for power over the federal treasury must be blocked." Governor Reagan had signed legislation that funded about a third of the California abortions ("more than 200,000 potential births," as the six legislators said) with state Medi-Cal funds, which triggered matching federal funds.

On abortion, Nancy Reagan is emphatic. "I can't get beyond the point," she says, "that you're killing somebody." She recalls that her daughter Patti was asked once by a teacher in school, "Suppose a pregnant woman had a window in her tummy through which she could see her baby grow and take it out and hold it. At what point do you think she'd decide it was all right to kill it?" (Patti Reagan, though, differs with her parents on the abortion issue.)[6]

As President, Reagan has faithfully fulfilled his promises to curb abortion. His chief personnel officer announced that he would disapprove any health plan for federal workers that paid for an abortion except in cases that endangered the mother's life (a U.S. judge ruled that the bureaucrat had acted illegally). In an Ohio case the administration in effect supported making abortions much more difficult to get. Federal courts had ruled that localities in Ohio had created unconstitutional impediments to abortions by requiring, for example, that during the second trimester of pregnancies they had to be performed in hospitals and that doctors had to warn pregnant women seeking abortions that the fetus "is a human life from the moment of conception." The solicitor general of Reagan's Justice Department, in proceedings before the highest court, opposed the lower court rulings and thus supported the local restrictions, arguing that the courts should not "constitutionalize" so many issues but rather should defer to the decisions of elected representatives.

In mid-1982, after having stalled the Right to Life movement while economic and military priorities were dealt with, Reagan declared that the time had come for Congress to consider "the national tragedy of abortion"—the 1.5 million abortions that occur in America each year, he said, are "an assault on the sacredness of life." Within a month the Senate was mired down in a momentous debate on whether abortion is murder.

Senator Garn, one of the Republican senators from Utah, had proposed that "unborn offspring at every stage of their biological development" have a right to life, and Senator Hatch, the other one, wanted to prohibit constitutional protection of a right to abortion. With resistance rising, though, the Senate debate narrowed down to a weakened proposal by Jesse Helms which said life begins at conception, but did not try to give this statement the force of law. Helms wanted to declare that the Supreme Court had "erred" in *Roe v. Wade,* in which women were held to have a constitutional right of access to abortion, and he proposed to permanently prohibit federal funding of abortions, medical education on how to perform them, and health insurance coverage for them.

Test votes soon showed that even the Republican Senate

would not go this far. Evidently the senators reflected their constituents' views. In separate reputable polls taken during the first two years of Reagan's term, 78 percent of respondents believed that the decision about an abortion should be left to the woman concerned and her physician, 67 percent favored permitting legalized abortions under all circumstances, and a 62 to 31 percent majority opposed a constitutional amendment to ban legalized abortion. Nevertheless in 1983 Reagan returned to the offensive, endorsing legislation that was substantially similar to the Helms bill and speaking of "the excruciating pain the unborn must feel as their lives are snuffed away." In June the Supreme Court reaffirmed *Roe v. Wade* in the Ohio case, and a constitutional amendment to invalidate *Roe v. Wade* fell 18 votes short of approval in the Senate, but the issue will no doubt figure in the 1984 elections.[7]

Even if Reagan's switch on abortion between Sacramento and Washington is put to one side, his flipflop on the ERA is mystifying.

"I am in full support of the Equal Rights Amendment and will be pleased if you are able to find a use for my name in attracting additional support," he wrote a leader for the ERA on his governor's stationery in 1972. Ratification was a quivering question mark in the California Senate when he issued a well-timed statement that "the simple declaration that 'Equality of rights under the law shall not be denied or abridged by the United States or any state on account of sex' is morally unassailable." ERA was ratified in California shortly thereafter.

Was he pacifying his own right wing or his own wife as he pitched his tent in the right-wing encampment which had formed to do battle with the ERA? In 1976, a few years after his California performance, he said ERA could force women into "restrooms, barracks, and shower rooms" with men. "I do not want," he said, "to see sex and sexual differences treated as casually and amorally as dogs and other beasts treat them. I believe this could happen under ERA." When Congress refused to let states rescind votes for ratification of ERA, Jake Garn contended that an earlier federal law had permitted rescission and on radio in 1978 Reagan agreed: "Senator Garn has rightfully called attention to a pretty glaring inconsistency."

The religious right was warning by this time that ERA would lead not only to unisex toilets, but also to homosexual marriages, husbands freed of the duty to support their families, and women killing and dying alongside the men on the front lines of war. Reagan was not going to be the circus barker for such unholy sideshows. ERA opens the door to mischief, he said in 1980, "not from the ladies," but from men who, instead of running away to Canada to escape the draft, "would file a class action suit that they didn't have to fight if the girls didn't have to fight." Acting upon additional elucidations from Reagan and his staff, the Republicans in national convention dropped support for ERA from their platform, reversing their recent history, as had their candidate. But Reagan wasn't just hands-off, he was opposed, and for two main reasons, he now said: ERA would override essential statutes such as those based on the physical abilities of men and women, and it would give the responsibility for eliminating sex discrimination to judges who are not elected.

Phyllis Schlafly, the antifeminist leader, said Reagan's election "kills the ERA." Thirty-five states had ratified it, but five had tried to take it back. With only six months left for three more to ratify, a federal judge in Idaho issued a ruling that, if upheld, meant that it was already too late. The judge said Congress had not had the power to extend the deadline for ratification, which it had voted to do in 1979. Furthermore, he said, the five states that had rescinded their ratifications should be counted as nays, not yeas: in effect, the ERA needed, not three more states, but eight. At first Reagan's Justice Department, maintaining the continuity of the government's previous positions, said it would appeal this decision. But then a letter of protest arrived in the White House from Schlafly, Jerry Falwell of the Moral Majority, the right-wing mass-mail king Richard Viguerie, and assorted allies of theirs. In just one day, the supposedly august Justice Department ducked its head and announced that it would stand neutral on the decision from Idaho. The few more months passed, and time ran out.

Now a new generation of feminists have started the crusade for ERA all over again. The National Organization of Women, which had 100,000 members when Reagan took office, had 180,000 as ERA died; the amendment has been reintroduced as

HR 1. Perhaps in the longer view the victory over ERA for
Schlafly, Falwell, and their associates was only an historical aber-
ration. For the time being, though, the fundamentalists rejoiced
in the conviction that they had scored an important victory. In
the same hours during which the AFL-CIO, the YWCA, the
American Jewish Committee, NOW, the National Women's Political Caucus, and 450 other national organizations mourned
for their cause, Phyllis Schlafly praised the Holy Lord and
Ronald Reagan.[8]

As the administration embarked on its third year there were
signs of a White House decision to curry women's support with
new gestures. At the outset Reagan had fulfilled his promise to
appoint a woman to the Supreme Court, Sandra Day O'Connor.
Kirkpatrick held a Cabinet-level job, Burford had run EPA, and
Steorts was chairwoman of the Consumer Product Safety Commission, but the Cabinet itself had been all-male for two years.
Then within one week Reagan named two women Cabinet members, Dole and Heckler. Insurance companies regularly pay
women smaller annual retirement benefits than men on the
ground that women live longer than men; the administration
supported a private lawsuit contending that this practice violates
the federal civil rights laws. But it was probably too late for such
gestures to offset the record the administration had made. In
the summer of 1983 the country's first woman astronaut, Sally
Ride, joined men in piloting the space shuttle in orbit around the
earth. Although she had been chosen for astronaut training during Carter's term, she had been given her actual assignment
during the Reagan administration.[9] Since the Reaganists did
not seem to be able to come up with a compassion issue, perhaps
outer space would do.

13

The Liberties of the People

How fares the First Amendment under President Reagan? And the Fourth? Alas, not well; 1984 is upon us.

Reagan's record on civil liberties is not totally illiberal. As governor he signed a bill protecting newsmen who refused to disclose their sources. He would not identify for the press a staffer whom he had fired for homosexuality. During the Vietnam war he opposed the drafting of dissenters just because they were dissenters. His stated, although now-abandoned opposition to standby draft registration was rooted in his dislike of "the assumption that your kids belong to the state." But one quickly runs out of examples of Ronald Reagan's contributions to the defense of the Bill of Rights. The main current of his career and his presidency runs in the opposite direction.

His predecessor, Jimmy Carter, handed over the presidency to Reagan by briefing him on fifteen or twenty issues of the moment and other subjects, but Carter attests that "his only reaction of substance was to express admiration for the political circumstances of South Korea that let President Park close all the colleges and draft all the demonstrators. That was the only issue on which he came alive." Reagan "expressed with some enthusiasm his envy of the authority" of President Park, Carter said.

As the press is the fourth estate in the American governmental system, the American Civil Liberties Union, tirelessly defending the Bill of Rights, has become yet another essential element—the fifth estate. Yet Ed Meese, Reagan's close counselor, charged in 1981 that the ACLU helps the nation's criminals and is a "criminals' lobby" because the organization takes positions that make it more difficult to arrest and prosecute criminals.

Since Reagan's election the ACLU's membership has increased about 75,000, to 275,000. In some ways, according to its executive director, Ira Glasser, the Reagan administration is more dangerous to civil liberties than either the late Senator Joe McCarthy or President Nixon. "Those men were not ideologically committed to making fundamental changes in our legal structure," Glasser said. "But for this administration, the erosion of the Bill of Rights seems to be a primary goal, not a side effect. This administration seeks to make structural changes in our system of government."[1]

Right on the surface of events, the central government led by Reagan has again begun deploying federal agencies against the liberties of the citizens, returning to the pattern that was exposed in the many wakes of Watergate.

The Social Security Administration has announced that it will check the reports of dividend and interest income that are filed with the IRS by banks and corporations. The purpose is to ferret out welfare recipients who are not eligible for their benefits. If the recipients do not waive their right to keep their tax records private, the government threatened, they might lose their benefits.

Under a program Congress authorized in 1981, an office in the Department of Health and Human Services sends the IRS lists of parents who are behind in their child support payments and whose children are getting welfare. The IRS withholds tax refunds from any of the delinquent parents who are entitled to them (an average $630 from 270,000 taxpayers in the first eight months of the program) and gives all or some of the money to state and local governments.

In mid-1982 the Social Security Administration, using the records that were entrusted to it by the citizens so they could get jobs and participate in the retirement system, turned over to Selective Service the names of about nine million men between 18 and 22 years old so that Selective Service could conduct a computer match-up to identify the more than 500,000 young men who had not preregistered for the draft. "A government computer surveillance system," an ACLU lawyer called it. This new practice, too, was authorized in 1981 by the Reaganized Congress.

The government's early prosecutions of a few of the young men who did not preregister came under suspicion of malicious and manifestly unconstitutional motivation: to punish outspoken critics of the draft. In one case in which the government was accused of such discriminatory prosecution, the administration refused to let defense lawyers see relevant documents or question Ed Meese about his possible role in the matter.

Drawing lines between apparently remote events, one sees the outline of the Watergate pattern of using the government to punish persons and activities that the administration detests. The Education Department issued proposed rules to deny federal education loans to students who fail to register for the draft. The administration employed the Trading With the Enemy Act of 1917 to seize tens of thousands of periodicals mailed to the U.S. from Cuba and to require the few thousand U.S. subscribers who were affected to obtain a license from the Treasury Department to get their magazines. Congress passed and Reagan signed a law that made anyone who publicly advocates violent overthrow of the federal government ineligible for federal job training under the lapsing CETA law.[2]

Hidden out of the public's view, the Reagan administration has been restoring, how and to what extent is not yet known, the apparatus of state spying on private citizens and organizations that the government regards as unacceptably left of center. Reagan has already reversed the post-Watergate emergence of a more open central government: the use of secrecy to advance the administration's political purposes has been renewed.

The First Amendment's guarantee of freedom of assembly is the constitutional right against which Reagan first exercised himself in California. Governor Reagan's role in the crisis in the California colleges and universities during the Vietnam demonstrations is the background against which the seated President's actions now can be seen for what they are and can become.

"Preservation of free speech," Reagan said in California, "does not justify letting beatniks and advocates of sexual orgies, drug usage, and filthy speech disrupt the academic community." Campaigning for governor, he said he wanted a commission headed by a former CIA director to "investigate the charges of communism and blatant sexual misbehavior on the Berkeley campus," but elected, he did not pursue this. When booing by black militants caused Hubert Humphrey to break off a speech, Reagan likened them to the "jack-booted young monsters" of the Hitler Youth Corps. The question about more vocal critics of Nixon's Vietnam policy, Reagan said, was "whether what they want more is victory for North Vietnam or peace."

Concerning the marches and rallies that changed the course of American history during the Vietnam war, Reagan said, "We'd be pretty naive to rule out the part Communists play in these demonstrations." He condemned "the Vietnam sit-in, the using of the university to launch literally law-breaking expeditions and demonstrations out into the community." One reason he wanted to formally declare war on North Vietnam, he said, was the fact that "if we are officially at war, the anti-Vietnam demonstrations and the act of burning draft cards would be treasonable." Granted, laws against treason cannot be used against people who assemble peacefully in peacetime, he said, but "there would be plenty of laws to cover them if we were technically in a state of war."

During his reelection campaign in California he called demonstrators against him "those cowardly little fascist bands out there." Bearing down on "troublemakers" trying to make the campuses "staging grounds for insurrection," he supported the university regents as they refused the request of an antidraft organization for permission to meet in honor of 866 Berkeley students who had pledged not to answer the draft call. (The chancellor at Berkeley crossed him and the regents about this, and 3,000 or so people held an orderly meeting.) After the invasion of Cambodia and the killing of four students at Kent State University in Ohio, Reagan closed all the universities and colleges in the California system for the duration of a week of planned demonstrations—280,000 students were affected.

During one regents' meeting the governor looked out the window, saw demonstrating students, and reportedly shot them the finger. The same temper flared up in him again during his 1980 campaign. As a group of young protesters chanted "Reagan Wants War," he said to them, "I'll tell you something, you jokers. If I did want war, you'd be where I'd start it." On election eve, when he knew from polls that he was a certain winner, he was addressing a large crowd. A heckler called out something. "Aw, shut up," Reagan said.[3]

In California the uncommon unrest of the sixties came to three climaxes: the San Francisco College strike, the People's Park riot, and the firing of philosophy instructor Angela Davis, a Communist.

The strike was tripped off by the suspension of an English instructor who was an official of the Black Panther party. S. I. Hayakawa, the college president, countered the militants and became a folk hero and a U.S. senator. Reagan said those who wanted to teach or learn "should be protected in that at the point of a bayonet if necessary. The college has to be kept open. I don't care what force it takes. That force must be applied." If necessary the police would surround campuses, he said. Plans should be made, he added, to "get rid of" professors who were "more interested in closing the school" than in teaching and "the militant leaders" among students and their nonstudent friends.

At Berkeley, a group occupied a tract of unused university land and proclaimed it "the People's Park." Reagan sent in highway patrolmen, and more than 2,500 National Guard troops converged on the campus area. The troops manned machine gun emplacements, and moved around in heavy weapons carriers with fixed bayonets on their rifles. Helicopters buzzed over the campus; tear gas was dropped on demonstrators.

When a crowd of students and street people tried to stop the authorities from fencing the tract, police fired buckshot into them. About 50 were injured, including five policemen and two reporters. On the radio in 1979, Reagan said: "A mob of 2,000 armed with broken chunks of concrete and footlong pieces of steel reinforcing rod, which were thrown end over end, with horrifying results, swept down on the Berkeley police. . . . Armed with shotguns, [sheriff's deputies] fired the lightest of birdshot into the mob. . . ."

A black student, James Rector, died from gunfire wounds. Reagan said Rector probably had been hit by police shots. Reagan no doubt regretted his death, but he also said, "It's very naive to assume that you should send anyone into that kind of conflict with a flyswatter." Robert Scheer reported that Rector's death came up among Reagan staffers who were having a beer at the Mayflower Hotel in Washington during the 1980 campaign, and Ed Meese said lightly, "James Rector deserved to die."

The regents fired twenty-five-year-old Davis because she was a Communist. There was no showing that she taught anything in the classroom except philosophy. Reagan said the prevailing policy that prohibited political requirements concerning faculty members did not apply to Communists. Certainly a person whose teaching is subservient to and propagandizes for an organizational fount of political or religious dogma poses serious problems for educators, but the courts told the regents they could not fire Davis just because she was a Communist. The regents then refused to rehire her on grounds that she was making inflammatory statements outside the classroom. (Later she was charged with complicity in a courtroom shootout, but was acquitted, and this turned her, like Hayakawa, into a kind of folk heroine.)

In his official capacity Reagan did all he could to punish the demonstrators and their faculty allies. He proposed a law to expel students or fire teachers who interfere with the educational process and to make it a criminal trespass if a student, after being suspended or expelled, reentered a campus. He signed laws permitting the suspension of students and faculty who disrupt normal campus activities, cutting off scholarship aid to students convicted of participating in disturbances, and making it a misdemeanor to fail to leave college property when ordered to leave by an administrator or to willfully disturb the peace or quiet of a campus.

Amazingly, he proposed that, in the decision of whether or not to hire an applicant for a faculty job, the applicant's garden-variety politics should be considered. Administrators, he said, were concerned about the "one-sided ideological viewpoint" among professors, and whether a potential teacher is a conservative or a liberal "must be a consideration [in] hiring of faculty." As a regent he made a motion to do away with the faculty's right to establish and supervise courses, but the motion failed.[4]

Reagan was acting out a part in all this, and to good effect: his standing at the polls zoomed upward. But something very real was forming in him, too: he had become convinced, to some extent, that the issue in the United States was revolution and, therefore, its suppression. Provoked by disturbances at the Santa Barbara campus, he went before a council of growers in Yosemite National Park and said the militants want to "prove this system of ours, faced with a crisis, will not work. If there's going to be a bloodbath, let's get it over with."

His Democratic rival Jesse Unruh called this stunning remark a "deliberate invitation to violence." Reagan said it was only a figure of speech—"I didn't advocate a bloodbath." However, in the *New York Times* Wallace Turner reported a sequel. Meeting with a group of chamber of commerce executives in his office, Reagan did not disavow what he had said nor suggest he should not have said it; rather, he told the executives with a smile that to solve some problems, "I could advocate another bloodbath."[5]

In an interview during the worst of the turmoil in 1968 he said, "I don't know that we need the complete regimentation that we knew in World War II. Here again I would want the advice first of all of military men with regard to what is lacking and how much more they need." Asked about "guerrilla warfare in the cities of America," he replied, "When you say this, we're talking about crime, we're talking about violence such as the anti-Vietnam-war demonstrations, we're even talking about the growing tendency in legitimate disputes of labor, or whatever it is, to resort to violence more quickly. . . . We must make it perfectly plain that there will be no toleration of lawbreaking of any kind, that we will meet, with whatever force and power is necessary, those who do take the law into their own hands."

As Nixon took over the White House in Washington, Reagan charged that there was "growing evidence" of a student or international conspiracy behind the student unrest, "a nationwide plan or organization" that was behind it all. According to a report in the London *Observer,* a Reagan task force on riots and disorders—headed by a counterinsurgency expert—was visualizing a California intelligence network as the center of an apparatus that would be aimed at "those bent on destroying the system." The methods being discussed were electronic surveillance, deeper penetration of dissenting groups, probability models on future outbreaks, and national data banks on dissenters.

Reagan was not, of course, alone: in the White House Nixon set forth on a similar course. Reagan defended Nixon on Watergate as long as he could, granted as little as he could, upheld his pardon, and was with him on the main issue.

During the 1972 campaign Reagan berated George McGovern for trying to make a campaign issue out of the burglary of the Democratic National Committee at the Watergate. The initial attitude of Americans about the break-in, Reagan said in 1973, was "not one of shock so much as it was just of expecting this in campaigns." The bugging of the DNC was illegal, but the burglars should not be considered criminals because they "are not criminals at heart," and they were "appointive people." As late as September that year Reagan was saying the Watergate investigations might be attempts to cancel Nixon's mandate.

A year later, though, on August 7, 1974, Reagan said Nixon should resign. The lesson, he said, was that big government is the enemy of freedom and tends to become tyrannical. Learning that Nixon's health had taken a turn for the worse, Reagan said, "maybe that'll satisfy the lynch mob," and he approved of Ford's pardon of Nixon. The pardon, he said, "fit the crime," it was "Napoleon to Elba."

The overriding issue in the Watergate scandal was whether the President can break the law. Reagan's answer was yes, he can and he should be able to. In 1977 in a TV interview Nixon said that any President is entitled to order some actions that might normally be considered illegal to protect national security. Reagan agreed, commenting: "When the Commander-in-Chief of a nation finds it necessary to order employees of the government or agencies of the government to do things that would technically break the law, he has to be able to declare it legal for them to do that."

The conclusion should not be avoided: Ronald Reagan, like Richard Nixon, believes that it is all right for the President or his agencies to break the law in the cause of national security. Pertinent here is a remark Reagan made after having taken part in the Rockefeller commission study of the CIA: although there had been violations, he said, he had no serious misgivings about the CIA's domestic operations. Yet during these operations the CIA had illegally opened more than 200,000 letters which American citizens had dispatched to parties abroad.

If Reagan did not make himself perfectly clear on Watergate itself, he has on some of the players in it. His first secretary of state, Haig, who was White House chief of staff during Watergate, advised Nixon to reply to questions that he "just can't recall," defended the burglary of the office of Daniel Ellsberg's psychiatrist, transmitted Nixon's order to commit seventeen wiretaps that were later found to be illegal, and effectuated Nixon's order to fire special prosecutor Archibald Cox in what became the "Saturday Night Massacre."

According to the former head of a subsidiary of Grumman Corporation, in 1972 Richard Allen, who became Reagan's first national security adviser, suggested the company contribute $1 million to Nixon's campaign as they were discussing the administration's efforts to help Grumman get sales contracts in Japan. Allen denied it.

Fred F. Fielding, the conflict-of-interest counsel for Reagan's transition team and then his White House counsel, was deputy counsel to Nixon and an assistant to John Dean. In his book *Blind Ambition,* Dean wrote that after the Watergate break-in he and Fielding went through the contents of the safe of E. Howard Hunt, who was implicated in the break-in. In Dean's account, Fielding said, "John, this stuff is sensitive," left saying he was going to see a doctor, and "returned triumphantly with two pairs of transparent rubber gloves, the kind used for rectal examinations. 'Here,' he said. 'Put these on. We won't leave any prints.'"

Reagan nominated Frederic V. Malec, the author of the famous "government responsiveness" memo of 1972, to the board of governors of the U.S. Postal Service, and Maurice Stans, finance chairman of Nixon's Committee to Re-elect the President (CREEP), to the Overseas Private Investment Corporation. The third official Haig approached to deliver Nixon's dismissal order to Cox, Robert H. Bork, delivered it. Reagan made Bork a federal appeals judge. According to the Senate Watergate committee report, Lyn Nofziger, Reagan's adviser, defended the practice of having government agencies "review carefully the projects of individuals who were unfriendly to the administration."

A very political man, Reagan can be fairly presumed to know about at least some of these matters. Keeping Watergate players close to him, apparently he is willing to overlook the deeds in question, is indifferent to them, or approves of them.[6]

Several signs in 1980 gave warning that Reagan and his people meant to carry through in Washington something akin to the California intelligence network that has been discussed. The Associated Press reported in June 1980 that six senators who were advisers in Reagan's campaign, notably including Paul Laxalt, then the national campaign chairman, had drafted and planned to introduce a charter that would restructure U.S. intelligence agencies "and remove restrictions on spying on Americans," in the words of the AP story. The AP reported that the draft charter would:

"Establish a new National Office of Counterintelligence with the power to have any intelligence agency investigate any American who may be engaged in clandestine intelligence activity, terrorism, drug trafficking, or international organized crime.

"Allow intelligence agencies to write their own guidelines, in consultation with Congress, for using mail-opening, burglary and electronic surveillance against American and foreign intelligence targets without court warrants.

"Create a director of national intelligence who would be appointed by the President without Senate confirmation to oversee the agencies."

As introduced, the charter did not renew the prohibition in previous law against the CIA performing internal security work.

The Reagan-connected Heritage Foundation proposed to exempt the FBI from the privacy and freedom-of-information acts, restore the attorney general's list of subversive organizations and loyalty checks on federal employees, and establish "central files on . . . internal security." The President should emphasize "the un-American nature of much so-called dissidence," the report said, and there should be tighter surveillance of radical and New Left groups and "antidefense and antinuclear lobbies," among others. The foundation recommended abolishing restrictions that prevent the FBI from opening mail, investigating political groups that are not suspected of criminal activity, and conducting break-ins without advance permission from the President and the attorney general.

Finally, Reagan's transition team on the CIA proposed the creation of a central records system on the activities of suspected foreign agents and their dealings with Americans, obviously defensible in itself, which was to be used, however, not only by the CIA, but also by the FBI and domestic law-enforcement agencies.[7]

Certainly the stage was fully set by all this for a plunge back into the cold war jungles of loyalty oaths, McCarthyism, surveillance, and illegal break-ins. One witch-hunting project was foredoomed: a move to revive the House Un-American Activities Committee, which got nowhere in the House run by liberal Tip O'Neill. Senator Jeremiah Denton (R.–Ala.) became chairman of the Senate's new security and terrorism subcommittee. He proceeded, at first, cautiously, although he condemned "a narrowly focused concern for individual rights" and advocated in some cases "a limited relinquishment of some individual civil rights."[8]

Reagan's first signal seemed to be a portent: he pardoned two former FBI agents who had been convicted of authorizing illegal entries into the homes of friends and relatives of the Weather Underground. Reagan said that the two agents, believing they had grants of authority from the highest levels, had acted "not with criminal intent," but "on high principle to bring an end to terrorism." Correlatively, the administration has proposed that federal employees who are accused of violating individual citizens' rights should be made in effect immune from personal liability. The government would substitute for the accused official as the defendant; jury trials would be abolished in such cases; there could be no punitive damages, and if the government lost it would not have to pay attorneys' fees for the plaintiff.

Under the rubric of fighting internal terrorism, the FBI prepared public opinion for new guidelines which—as Attorney General Smith put it —"will remove unnecessary obstacles to the FBI's efforts in protecting us. . . ." FBI Director William Webster told Denton's panel that the FBI would not violate free speech and the right to "legitimate political dissent." He also remarked, during his discussion of terrorism, that groups which "produce propaganda, disinformation and 'legal assistance' may be even more dangerous than those who actually throw the bombs." When the President issued the new guidelines it was obvious that the FBI had been given a broader mandate to spy on disapproved organizations. Informers and infiltration now can be used before there is enough evidence to justify a full investigation; the FBI can continue an investigation even though there is not "any immediate threat of harm"; FBI agents may investigate statements advocating criminal activity, leading Rep. Don Edwards (D.–Calif.) to charge that the FBI "wants to investigate speech."

The will to use the black arts of spy work against U.S. citizens, organizations, and corporations prevailed at two of three stages in the struggle within the administration to draw up a new charter for the intelligence agencies. The extent to which that same determination prevailed in the new executive order, itself, remains to be seen.

In March 1981 the Reaganists circulated the first of three drafts of the new order. Under Carter's 1978 guidelines the President had to approve in general the use of break-ins, bugging, wiretapping, and the like; the attorney general had to approve each specific use. Targets had to be reasonably suspected of being agents of a foreign power. Infiltrating domestic groups and trying to alter their purposes were prohibited. Under Reagan's first proposal, circulated by CIA Director William Casey, the CIA could resort to mail-openings, break-ins, and electronic surveillance with only the attorney general's approval, and the CIA could use infiltration against U.S. residents, organizations, and companies even if they were not suspected of committing any crime or of being foreign agents. The CIA and other intelligence agencies, Reagan first proposed, should be able to secretly, and with no authorization but their own chiefs' decisions, infiltrate some democratic groups that have foreign ties (including multinational corporations) and try to alter their purposes. Under Carter, CIA covert actions like bribing politicians and running small armies were authorized only if they were "conducted abroad." Reagan's proposal dropped the words, "conducted abroad."

The problem for the Reaganists was not the expected outcries from civil libertarians, but the opposition of Deputy CIA Director Bobby Inman, who told a reporter that he was resisting "a series of repugnant changes for which I would not stay in this administration." In May, draft two basically retained the Carter restrictions and was warmly supported by Inman, but it was blocked by Richard Allen. After more months of infighting, the administration circulated draft three, a return to the key provisions of draft one with a few additional ideas: the President was asserted to have an inherent authority to authorize wiretaps and electronic surveillance without a court order, and agency heads were to be excused from being required to report possible federal crimes committed by those under them.

Having prevailed within the administration, the hard-liners now ran into angry objections from members of the House and Senate intelligence oversight committees, some of which became public. Backing down on some points, Reagan announced in

December 1981 his seventeen-page executive order, which has the force of law.

Assassination is still prohibited, as it was under Carter. But the President is no longer required to give his general approval for the use of the black arts. Approval by the Attorney General is required, and he cannot authorize the use of techniques that otherwise would require court orders unless there is probable cause to believe that the target is a foreign power or its agent. The President's inherent power to order intrusive surveillance without a court order is no longer explicitly claimed, and agency heads are still required to report possible crimes by their subordinates. But for the first time the CIA is given the right to collect "significant foreign intelligence" from American citizens either inside the U.S. or abroad.

Issuing the order, Reagan said it was designed to strengthen defenses against espionage and terrorism. While he is President, he vowed, no intelligence agency would be given the authority to violate rights guaranteed by the Constitution. But the loophole that gapes from his order is the recurrent use of "purpose" or "intention" as the key term in a restriction or an authorization.

The intelligence agencies may not collect significant foreign intelligence "for the purpose of acquiring information concerning the domestic activities of United States persons." Yet they *may* collect, retain, and disseminate information "acquired by overhead reconnaisance not directed at specific United States persons" or "incidentally obtained information that may indicate involvement in activities that may violate federal, state, local or foreign laws." Covert activities (which need be only "in support of national foreign policy objectives abroad" and thus can be conducted in the U.S.) may not be "intended to influence United States political processes, public opinion, policies, or media." All a smart federal snooper has to do is devise and commit to writing a purpose or intention that is permitted and then go ahead and spy on U.S. citizens.

The broadest authorization of black arts (cleverly worded negatively as if it is a prohibition) is qualified by a flat, but unspecific requirement that citizens' rights be respected. The language permits all of the intelligence agencies of the government "to use such techniques as electronic surveillance, unconsented physical search, mail surveillance, physical surveillance, or monitoring devices." ("Unconsented physical search" is bafflegab for breaking and entering.) The attorney general must approve the use of the described methods, and that use must conform to the agencies' own guidelines that "shall protect constitutional and other legal rights and limit use of such information to lawful government purposes." Presumably the government may penetrate and influence domestic organizations and companies. Meese, Inman, and a third official, briefing the press, said the entire executive order would be augmented by about thirty pages of guidelines that were not yet final and would be secret.

One may imagine Reagan's intelligence planners adapting to the objections from Inman and the congressional committees by asking themselves and each other what they could get done anyway without the proposed authorizations that were coming under harsh attack. Probably their thoughts turned often to the National Security Agency (NSA), the highly secret outfit that was created by President Truman in 1952 without an act of Congress or any public knowledge. The NSA intercepts the electronic messages of foreign governments at several thousand listening posts around the world. A Senate committee has reported that the agency's computer system gives it the capability of listening to all the electronically transmitted messages that are sent to or from the U.S. Currently there are 74 million messages that enter, move within, or leave the U.S. every year by telegram or telex, and millions more are transmitted on leased lines. William Casey, as the CIA director, is also in general command of the NSA. Under Reagan's order the three critical authorizations for the NSA are linked in identical language to "purposes." NSA may collect, process, and disseminate to "authorized elements" of the government what is described as "signals intelligence information for national foreign intelligence purposes." Late in 1982 a federal appeals court ruled that the NSA can legally eavesdrop on messages between U.S. citizens and people abroad and give summaries of the messages to the FBI even if there is no cause to believe the Americans are foreign agents.

In broadening the CIA's license for covert actions the admin-

istration perpetuated another problem for democracy. If federal
activities are to be (in the language of the Reagan order authorizing them) "planned and executed so that the role of the
United States Government is not apparent or acknowledged
publicly," how is public opinion supposed to judge or affect
them? Reagan rightly said, in promulgating the new guidelines,
that U.S. adversaries, whether totalitarian nations or international terrorists, pay no attention to the human rights the U.S. is
committed to protect. But does this mean that we should or that
we should not continue to protect these rights?

On its face the order seems to be a compromise between
Inman's moderates and the advocates of less restrained use of
the black arts in the United States. Inman evidently concluded
that the standoff would not last. Early in 1982 Reagan approved
a new general review of counterintelligence gathering and organization, and a few months later Inman resigned. Unidentified
sources told the *Wall Street Journal* that Inman "felt the new
procedures allowed intelligence agencies to get too heavily involved in spying activities in the U.S." Philip Taubman, also
relying on vaguely identified sources, reported in the *New York
Times*: "The sources said he [and allies of his on the subject]
feared a result might be a consolidation of counterintelligence
responsibility in a new organization vested with broad authority
to collect information within the United States. In addition, they
were concerned that a central records system would be created
that might threaten the civil liberties of American citizens, officials said." Increased spying on citizens in the United States? A
central records bureau on Americans? There, uneasily, the questions and the answers ended for the time being.[9]

The greater public access to government information that
has developed in recent years would have alleviated such concerns except for the fact that under Reagan secrecy has become
the norm again in Washington.

Information obtained under the Freedom of Information
Act (FOIA) formed a basis for such news stories as illegal FBI
harassment of political groups, CIA plots in Cuba and Chile, the
My Lai massacre, consumer hazards, and nuclear power dangers. The Reagan administration, however, has formally advo-

cated changes that would totally exempt from FOIA the CIA, the NSA, and the Defense Intelligence Agency and would let the attorney general keep secret selected FBI information on terrorism, organized crime, and foreign counterintelligence.

The administration has sought to let the government withhold information that was recorded by an official or bureaucrat "for personal convenience" (such as a President's tapes or notes on an important conversation?) or that would "tend to disclose" a confidential source; to let business specify exempted business records that would hurt the competitive interests of "any person"; to let agencies withhold technical information that may not be exported without government permission; and to keep secret information on law enforcement investigations that officials say are "ongoing." In 1982 a Senate committee rebuffed Reagan on most of this by a 15–0 vote, but he had at least two more years to keep trying, and he was proceeding on his own anyway.

Asked what his biggest first-year disappointment was, Reagan said, "the inability to control the leaks." Meese said a reporter who uses leaked information is like a fence, dealing in stolen property, and as for the leakers themselves, Meese spoke of finding out "who is betraying this country." He was reflecting the views of his boss. While governor, in a letter to William Buckley, Reagan described the *New York Times* role in the Pentagon papers case as "receiving stolen property and selling it for profit."

In various ways the Reaganists have put the pressure on the press. Attorney General Smith rescinded Carter administration rules that restrained the prosecution of whistleblowers inside the government. Reagan ordered all bureaucrats' and officials' discussions of classified matters with reporters to be cleared in advance with a senior official. In the various departments orders went down requiring the middle-level bureaucrats to get permission for important contacts with journalists. All or some of these rules were rescinded, to be succeeded by a rule requiring all press interviews to be cleared by the White House communications office. Thirteen reporters attending a Pentagon briefing on Soviet military strength were asked to sign a secrecy pledge (they all refused). The administration devised new freedom-of-information guidelines that levy high fees for providing government information unless bureaucrats decide it's in the public interest and the person asking for it has the "qualifications" to handle it.

Reagan's criticism of TV news—that it was emphasizing bad economic news and hard-times horror stories—was fair enough: the press is too powerful to be sacrosanct. Reagan's aides have tried to head off unfavorable stories they read as soon as they come over the White House news wires, and that's understandable, too. But Reagan showed a serious misunderstanding of the press when he told *TV Guide* that reporters should "trust us, and put themselves in our hands." Clearly the President, like other Presidents (including Lyndon Johnson) before him, sees the press as an instrument that should carry out the government's purposes in foreign policy, not as an independent source of information, perspective, and opinion.

TV news was always saying, Reagan complained, that the U.S. is intervening in El Salvador. He wished reporters would "call [us] and say, 'I have this story' . . .." He could tell them, he said, " 'If you use that story, it will result in harm to our nation, and probably will make it impossible to do what we're trying to do.' But they just go ahead with the story." The press, he said, had covered the Vietnam war from the perspective "that the war was wrong," and "had that been done in World War II, in behalf of the enemy that was killing American military men, I think there would have been a revolution in America."

If reporters and writers can't be shut up, they can be shut out. A revelatory book about the NSA, *The Puzzle Palace,* by James Bamford, was published in 1982. During his research in 1979, Bamford had won release of two documents that bore in part on the NSA's Operation Minaret, which was directed against American citizens and which the Rockefeller commission said "presents prima facie questions of criminality." In 1981, though, the Justice Department ordered Bamford to return the documents, which it had reclassified, and not to publish anything from them. Knowing that Carter's order prohibiting such reclassification was in full force, Bamford refused to comply and went ahead.

In several cases, Interior and Environmental Protection

Agency officials came to loggerheads with Congress for refusing to provide its committees with domestic policy information. Senator Joseph Biden of Delaware, a Democrat high up on the Senate Intelligence Committee, told the *New York Times* that the administration is cutting back on secret information for the congressional committees that are designated to receive it. If he asks the CIA now about El Salvador, Biden said, he gets, not a full and candid account, but "what they want to tell me."

In muzzling the government, just as in unleashing the spooks, Reagan has used his power as President to issue executive orders that have the force of law. By executive fiat he reversed Carter's previous requirements that government officials who classify documents balance the public interest against national security interests and that they certify, when classifying information, that its release would cause "identifiable" damage to national security. Now officials, when in doubt, are to overclassify rather than underclassify. Reclassification of released information is now permitted. Abandoning Carter's program of a review of classified documents every six years and the release of almost all of them after twenty years, Reagan deliberately reversed the strong trend toward a freer flow of information from the government to the people.

Heretofore officials of the CIA have been subjected to "prepublication agreements," binding them for life to submit anything they write bearing on the subject of their duties for approval. Reagan issued an order extending this system to the White House, the National Security Council, and the State, Justice, Defense, and some other departments. Morton Halperin, a former Defense official now working with the ACLU, charged that this order "proposes a censorship system that will cut off most of the information that Americans rely on to understand foreign affairs." A special committee of administration officials proposed that any government employee who improperly discloses classified information be subject to three years in prison and a $10,000 fine.

If critics emerging from inside the government are to be gagged, so, under Reagan, are those trying to come into the country from outside. The State Department denied an entry visa to the widow of the late President Salvador Allende of Chile, who had been invited to speak in San Francisco by the Catholic Archdiocese there. The government said her entry would be "prejudicial to U.S. interests." American citizens, guaranteed free speech and the free thought that lies behind it, were thus denied the right to hear the widow of the only parliamentary socialist who has attained national power in Latin America.[10]

Following the recommendations of the administration, Congress passed, during Reagan's second spring as President, the first law in American history which authorizes the prosecution of journalists as criminals for publishing public information. The law prohibits the use of any printing press to publish any information, whether part of a public record or already published elsewhere, which identifies U.S. intelligence agents. The penalty for offending journalists is up to four years in prison and a $15,000 fine for each offense.

The ostensible targets were ex-CIA agents Philip Agee and publisher Louis Wolf, who have systematically publicized the names of U.S. agents. Both the House and Senate rejected, on Reagan's lead, proposals to limit the crime to those who intend to impair or impede U.S. intelligence work. Instead, all that is required to violate the law is "a pattern of activities" to expose agents "and with reason to believe" that U.S. intelligence will be impaired or impeded. If the government warns a journalist who is writing an exposé of intelligence malpractices, naming agents, that the story will impair or impede U.S. intelligence, the government will be in position to put the journalist in prison unless the story is killed.

Conferees on the bill at the last moment issued a report stating that the exposure of ex-agents Edwin Wilson and Frank Terpil, who allegedly helped train terrorists in Libya (Wilson has been convicted on some charges), would not have been a crime under the law and that only journalists who are "in the business of ferreting out agents," foreseeably damaging an intelligence agency, would be prosecuted.

But that is not what the law says, and that is not what the sponsor of the "reason to believe" language in the Senate, John Chaffee (R.–R.I.), said. Asked if a reporter might be prosecuted even if his or her intention was to expose illegal conduct, Chaffee replied: "I'm not sure that the *New York Times* or the *Washington Post* has the right to expose names of agents any more than Mr. Wolf or Mr. Agee. They'll just have to be careful about exposing names of agents." The courts will have to decide: the ACLU called the law unconstitutional and said it would bring a lawsuit against it. Attorney Floyd Abrams, who has represented great newspapers in press freedom cases, wrote that the law imperils the ability of the press to expose such things as the CIA-Mafia conspiracy to assassinate Fidel Castro. Philip B. Kurland, a prominent and conservative constitutional expert at the University of Chicago, called the measure "the clearest violation of the First Amendment attempted in this era."

On a warm and sunny day in June the press was invited to the CIA headquarters in McLean, Virginia, near Washington. In the open, across a greensward, some hundreds of CIA people gathered. Reporters were served punch; the Army Band played patriotic music. Apparently President Reagan first spoke secretly to about a thousand of the secret people inside. Then he came outside, and before those gathered on the grass he praised the CIA employees as "heroes in a grim twilight struggle" and signed the Intelligence Identities Protection Act into law.[11]

Lie detectors—polygraph machines—are not reliable (results from their use are not admissible in court), but they have been spreading as insidiously as fire ants, and now Reaganized federal bureaucrats are realizing that they may be stung by the machines at any time, at their superior's pleasure or even a computer's random spit-out.

During a Pentagon meeting, an under secretary of defense said that Reagan's $1.5 trillion military buildup would actually cost half again as much. This leaked, and before the displeasure at the White House was appeased the twenty-five officials who were strapped into the lie-detecting contraption included the chairman of the joint chiefs of staff, two under secretaries of defense, the secretary of the Navy, and assorted admirals and other generals. Reagan implied that he approved of lie detector tests, and at the end of 1982 the Pentagon announced that it had 100 polygraph operators and would give lie tests to randomly

selected military and civilian "personnel" in all the military services. On March 11, 1983, Reagan ordered that every federal
employee with a security clearance, in whatever agency, "may be
required to submit to polygraph examinations, when appropriate, in the course of investigations of unauthorized disclosures of
classified information" and warned that an agency might decide
that "adverse consequences will follow an employee's refusal."[12]
All of a sudden, with a mere exertion of his pen, Ronald Reagan
had institutionalized mandatory lie detector tests throughout the
federal government. High officials and lowly bureaucrats all
over Washington, except the President, would find themselves
strapped into the machines well before the arrival of 1984.

14

Prayer, Sex, Innocence and Guns

"**W**hen I hear the First Amendment used as a reason to keep traditional moral values away from policymaking," Ronald Reagan says, "I am shocked." What this means, he makes clear.

The President claims to believe in the separation of church and state, but he condemns the 1962 Supreme Court decision that prohibits public schools from conducting organized prayer in class. An "affirmative action" for atheism, he calls that ruling.

"I don't believe we should have ever expelled God from the classroom," he says. "And who knows, if we get the federal government out of the classroom, maybe we'll get God back in." His wife writes in her memoirs, "God really is there in the classroom, as He is everywhere."

Both the Reagans have publicly discussed the storefront atheist Madalyn Murray O'Hair. Concerning O'Hair's suit alleging that the motto on U.S. coins, "In God We Trust," violates church-state separation, Reagan said on radio that she should mind her own business and he hoped she lost. It was one woman, Mrs. Reagan writes, who "took prayer out of the schools," and one person (presumably her husband) can "put Him back into our schoolrooms. . . ."

The Bible story about the creation should also be taught in the public schools, Reagan believes. He does not explicitly repudiate the huge body of scientific information which shows that homo sapiens evolved from lower forms of life, but during his 1980 campaign he told an evangelical Christian meeting in Dallas that he saw "great flaws" in the theory of evolution and if it was to be taught in the public schools, "the biblical story of creation" should be taught there, too.

The administration asked Congress to submit to the states for adoption the following constitutional amendment: "Nothing in this Constitution shall be construed to prohibit individual or group prayer in public schools or other public institutions. No person shall be required by the United States or by any state to participate in prayer." That was the law before 1962, when group prayer could be conducted in class, but no youngster could be "required" to participate.

However, the Senate's conservatives, led by Helms, decided instead to try to strip the courts of jurisdiction—simply to prohibit the federal courts from ruling on school prayer cases. Defenders of the independence of the judiciary and the separation of church and state tied up the Senate over this proposal for weeks, and Helms could not pass it (although it was close, 51–48 on his last try). This left Reagan's proposal outstanding, and he told a convention of broadcast preachers, "I am determined to bring that amendment back again and again and again and again."

The United States government has begun broadcasting various religious services, a different one each week that is repeated six times during the week. The Voice of America sends these programs around the world on the government's radio service. A fourth of the programming is devoted to Jewish culture and the rest consists of religious services of other denominations, according to a spokesperson for VOA. Reagan not only knows about this, he boasted to the broadcast preachers that "the Voice of America broadcast a religious service worldwide."

Reagan's proposal for a tuition tax credit for the parents of children attending private schools came under attack as a violation of the separation of church and state. Since 85 percent of private elementary and secondary schools in the U.S. have religious affiliations, David Landau of the ACLU argued, federal tuition subsidies to the parents of the schools' students would violate the constitutional prohibition against state-supported religion.[1]

Getting government "off our backs" is one of Reagan's pervasive rhetorical themes. He said in 1982 that before he came to the White House, "Government intrusion into the life of the family and the local neighborhood . . . on many matters that government had no business dealing with" had reached unparalleled heights. Yet as President he has moved the federal government toward an active role in the regulation of sexual activities.

His public attitudes toward sex have always been straitlaced. Running for governor, he dwelled on "sexual orgies" he said were going on among students at Berkeley, with behavior "so vile I cannot describe it to you." No, he wrote one citizen, he did not favor relaxing present laws on sexual conduct: "I am deeply concerned," he said, "with the wave of hedonism—the humanist philosophy so prevalent today." To another constituent he wrote: "On the higher law of morality we know that premarital sex or promiscuity in our entire Judeo-Christian tradition is a sin." He objected to "teaching sex as a purely physiological function, like eating when you are hungry." Such teaching on sexual matters in public schools is divorced, he said, from "moral behavior" and thus implants in young minds the question, "so why not?"

Reagan was attacked for his alliance with the bluenoses in an unusual column by Albert Hunt, a *Wall Street Journal* reporter. "On one level," Hunt said, "it's irritating to see Ronald Reagan pandering to the 'Moral Majority' fundamentalists, for there's a certain hypocrisy involved. In talking about restoring the old values, he presents himself as a positive prude; the best form of birth control, he has said, is to 'say no.' This comes from a man who was divorced and, before his second marriage, was one of Hollywood's well-known ladykillers. . . . It's disingenuous for the Gipper to pretend he's a moral cousin of the Rev. Jerry Falwell."

In California Reagan vetoed a bill that would have permitted doctors to prescribe contraceptives for minors. His statement that the bill would be an "intrusion into the prerogatives of parents" foreshadowed his administration's present attempt to cast the federal government in the role of an informer on teenage girls.

According to the government's figures, 615,000 girls seventeen years old or younger are obtaining prescriptions for birth control measures every year from 5,000 clinics that receive federal funds. Early in 1983, just before he resigned his post, HHS Secretary Schweiker said that his agency would promulgate a new rule: when any government-funded clinic prescribed the pill, intrauterine devices, or diaphragms for a female seventeen or younger, within ten working days the clinic would be required to tell her parents or guardians by registered letter or some other method that verified their receipt of the information. (Teenagers who are married or already supporting themselves would be excepted.) In short the government would inform on millions of girls to their families. As Mo Udall of Arizona quipped at a gridiron dinner, the Reagan administration was conducting, not a war on poverty, but a war on puberty.

First proposed almost a year earlier, the rule had stimulated 120,000 comments from the public. The government's people avoided giving any figures on how opinion ran, but it was one recurring objection that the notifications inevitably would reduce the number of sexually active teenagers who used birth control and, therefore, would increase the number of teenage pregnancies (350,000 teenagers bore children out of wedlock in 1982).

"Now big government comes in," said Representative Waxman of California. "This is Big Brother getting into the bedroom of people." "Do you think kids will give up sex?" Representative

Tom Downey (D.–N.Y.) asked Schweiker at a congressional hearing. Reagan's Cabinet member thought teenagers might discuss sex with their parents more. "That doesn't comport with the Jordache jean society. . . . Your view of what the world is doesn't comport with reality," Downey told him. The Planned Parenthood Federation of America, charging that "the Squeal Law" was intended to "destroy services to teenagers," filed suit charging that it contravened federal birth control law and violated the privacy of the teenagers and their families. New York's Attorney General Robert Abrams planned to fight the regulation in court, too.

Schweiker made the rule final, pending the court reviews, just as he was resigning his post. Clinics must tell parents or guardians unless the news would "result in physical harm to the minor by a parent or guardian." "In effect," commented columnist James A. Wechsler, "the only way for a teenager to prevent the government from squealing on her to her parents is for her to squeal on her parents to the government. In the real world, that isn't how things will happen. . . . Thousands of the young will instead revert to the risks of pregnancy and multiply the business of abortion." Schweiker's successor as HHS Secretary, recently defeated Congresswoman Heckler, had signed a letter with twenty-nine other congresspersons in 1982 which stated: "We fear that . . . such a regulation would discourage many young people from utilizing their services and would result in a drastic increase in the number of teenage pregnancies." (The final rule was rushed into the Federal Register just before she replaced Schweiker.)

A federal judge in Manhattan declared the rule invalid because Congress, in establishing family-planning clinics, had intended to combat "the problems of teenage pregnancy," but the rule, in "blatant disregard" of this purpose, would "cause increased adolescent pregnancies." At this writing the pitched battle between the Moral Majority and the facts of life was continuing.

Concerning divorce Reagan has been more modern, perhaps because of the broken marriage in his own life. Although divorce weakened the presidential prospects of candidates Adlai

Stevenson and Nelson Rockefeller in the recent past, Reagan's did not hurt him politically—Wyman initiated it, and there was no public gossip about other women. Despite Reagan's emphasis on the family in a time when one out of two marriages in California were ending in divorce, he signed a law that established no-fault divorce there, eliminating as grounds extreme cruelty, adultery, desertion, willful neglect, habitual drunkenness, and conviction for a felony.[2]

Homosexuality Reagan condemns as "a tragic illness" that should continue to be illegal. "In the Bible it says that in the eyes of the Lord, this is an abomination," he told Robert Scheer. The latter retorted: "It's the conservative who wants to keep government out of everything; why don't you keep it out of private morality?" and Reagan replied: "No one is advocating the invasion of the private life of any individual. I think Mrs. Patrick Campbell said it best in the trial of Oscar Wilde. She said, 'I have no objection to anyone's sex life so long as they don't practice it in the street and frighten the horses.'"

Gays should be barred from public life, he said in response to a question in 1967, but he added that he should limit his answer to the California state government, and he conjectured, making a joke, that perhaps service in the department of parks and recreation might be all right. His assistants investigated rumors that he had gays on his staff at Sacramento and he fired one or two of them quietly, but when his press secretary let that fact be known Reagan became angry on their behalf, saying, "I refuse to participate in trying to destroy human beings with no factual evidence," and their names were not given to reporters. More recently, in 1978, Reagan publicly opposed the Briggs proposition in California that would have prohibited homosexuals from classroom teaching. "Innocent lives could be ruined," he said, and the proposition was defeated.

During Reagan's presidency a conflict about homosexuality developed between the Army and six universities. Under Department of Defense regulations homosexuals may not serve in the armed forces, but law schools at the six universities (Harvard, Yale, Columbia, NYU, UCLA, and Wayne State) bar from their campuses recruiters for employers which discriminate on the basis of sexual orientation. The Army's judge advocate general informed the six schools in 1982 that he was "considering recommending" that no further Defense Department contracts be awarded to them and their ROTC units be abolished because of their position on the matter. If Reagan played a role in this controversy it was not evident. When the House of Representatives rejected, 281–119, a measure adopted by the local government in the District of Columbia that would have legalized sexual acts between consenting adults in the District, he said nothing.[3]

In the broader realm of the criminal law, Reagan's famous one-liners have become the themes of new tendencies in national policy. When he was questioned in 1966 on a Supreme Court ruling that placed new limits on police interrogation of suspects, he said he was "opposed to the spread of the philosophy that the criminal must be protected from society instead of the other way around." Or, as he put this on another occasion, "government's function is to protect society from the criminal, not the other way around." But what about, not the convicted criminal, but the accused standing in the dock? The Reagan administration is seeking to narrow the rights of the accused in significant ways.

At present, in pursuance of the Fourth Amendment's prohibition against "unreasonable searches and seizures," evidence which the authorities obtain during an illegal search cannot be used in a criminal trial. This is called "the exclusionary rule." In a 1961 ruling, *Mapp v. Ohio*, the Supreme Court said that without the exclusionary rule the Fourth Amendment would be "an empty promise," that police had to be deterred from misconduct in obtaining evidence and that the judiciary must not abet such misconduct by legitimizing its fruits. The Reagan administration has formally proposed that evidence be admissible in a criminal trial even if it was obtained illegally, provided that the officer in question "acted in the good faith, reasonable belief" that his actions were lawful. At the Justice Department's request, the Supreme Court agreed to consider creating such a rule in state as well as federal prosecutions.

This fresh drive against the exclusionary rule originates with

Reagan himself. He says he proposed in California that in cases of technical violations by a law enforcement officer, the citizen whose rights were thereby infringed be permitted to sue the government body that employs the officer, with the government paying the legal costs, "but that any evidence found by the officer be admissible in court." Reagan told his radio audience in 1978 that the use of what he called the exclusionary rule goes like this:

"An arresting officer is held to be in technical violation of someone's constitutional rights, therefore no evidence found on him can be used in court. It is so contrary to common sense that officers have complained that if they stopped a man for running a red light and found a bleeding body in the rear seat they could still only charge the man with a traffic violation."

The administration wants to empower judges to imprison accused people without bail and without trial on grounds that they are dangerous. An anticrime bill enacted in the Senate in 1982 (but not the House) would have put the legal burden on the accused to prove that he or she would not commit a crime if released on bail before trial, turning the traditional presumption of innocence until proved guilty into a presumption of guilt until proved innocent.

After a jury found the man who tried to assassinate Reagan, John Hinckley, Jr., not guilty by reason of insanity, Attorney General Smith asked Congress to eliminate the insanity defense, in effect. Under the legislation he supported, Smith testified, "Mental disease or defect would constitute a defense only if the defendant did not even know he had a gun in his hand or thought, for example, that he was shooting at a tree." Subsequently Reagan suggested that the law could be changed "perhaps from not guilty by reason of insanity, to guilty but insane." Reminding everyone that punishment should be based on moral responsibility, the American Psychiatric Association then recommended that only the seriously ill (meaning, mainly, psychotics) should be acquitted on the insanity defense, and they should not be released by doctors, but only by agencies that are part of the criminal justice system.

Hinckley had bought his cheap pistol in Dallas, but not even the near-fatal shots he fired from it into Reagan's body shook the President loose from his opposition to requiring the registration of firearms. Although Reagan was reportedly hit by a "Devastator" bullet that fortunately failed to explode inside him the way it was manufactured to do, he made no move toward outlawing either man-maiming or armor-penetrating cop-killer ammunition. Gun control is a part of crime control, but many citizens insist on their right to own firearms, including pistols. If one agrees that such a right to bear arms is an important constitutional privilege, then despite Reagan's terrible record on most civil liberties, he must be put down as a loyal supporter of that one. Shot with a pistol, he still defends the citizen's right to go buy one at the corner gunshop.[4]

15

Reagan's McCarthyism

McCarthyism, with its guilt by suspicion and its implications of treason, broke out in the second year of the Reagan adminis- tration with the President himself leading the vigilantes out the White House gate.

There had been a warning it was coming. In October and November, 1981, perhaps 2 million people marched in the capi- tals of Western Europe protesting the Soviet-American nuclear arms race. "Oh, those demonstrations," President Reagan said in an interview. "You could have used newsreels from the '60s in America. Those are all sponsored by a thing called the World Peace Council, which is bought and paid for by the Soviet Union."

Responding to the European inspiration, antinuclear groups in the United States launched a campaign for a verifiable mutual nuclear freeze and began a pattern of winning many local plebiscites despite the Reaganists' ardent protests. In an entirely peaceful demonstration on June 12, 1982, in Central

Park, New York City, an awesome multitude, three-quarters of a million Americans, marched, and the House of Representatives narrowly missed endorsing the freeze in a 204–202 vote.

Slipping badly on the issue and going into the November election, the Reaganists struck, first on the Senate floor, then in the President's own voice. After the election Reagan made the charge an explicit position of the administration: Soviet agents had been sent to help instigate, create, and sustain the freeze movement and some of the big demonstrations, including "the one in New York." According to articles on a reading list recommended by the White House, millions of Americans were guilty of serving Soviet purposes. Joe McCarthy of Wisconsin was moldering in his grave, but Ronald Reagan of Illinois was carrying on his work.

Although many were surprised, no one should have been. In the early sixties Reagan had made it clear that his opinions on the main issues of domestic politics are rooted in his anticommunism. In his 1978 and 1979 radio broadcasts he said that the Americans campaigning against nuclear power were being manipulated by pro-Soviet forces that want to keep America weak, and he has used anti-Soviet arguments against U.S. politicians. Often he said that Jimmy Carter's and even the Senate's defense policies were pleasing the Soviets; he said the Soviets wanted Carter reelected in 1980.

In a GE speech in 1962, he called on his listeners to examine "each domestic policy to see wherein it helps the enemy fulfill his goal." He was seeing Communists behind liberal domestic programs that he opposed. "The Communists in America boast," he claimed, "that they can put 50,000 letters in Washington in seventy-two hours on any issue they choose." It was his recurrent theme that liberal government programs were "a foot in the door." He argued, "We can lose our freedom all at once by succumbing to Russian aggression, or we can lose it gradually by installments. The end result is *slavery*."

Liberalism, then, is an early stage of communism? This was certainly the meaning of a John Birch Society poster of the period that said, "Beware of these 3 steps! 1 Liberalism 2 Socialism 3 Communism." In 1962 Reagan said, "I don't equate liber-

alism with socialism and socialism with communism, but . . .
they do have in common one characteristic—collectivism." On
another occasion he said, "All three seek the answer to human
problems through government. The liberal campaigns for more
and more participation by the federal government. . . . The
only common denominator needed to win his support for any
proposed legislation is the extent to which it will strengthen the
power of our federal government." Reagan conceded that
the three doctrines' reliance on government "is shared in common, though differing in degree," but clearly he asserted their
linkage.

Consider the implications of this approach for political
thought. All social forms can now be positioned on a right-to-left
spectrum, from the good, the conservative, on the right, to the
bad, liberalism-through-socialism-to-communism, on the left.
Advocates of federal aid to education are allies of the leftist
police state. Defenders of the progressive income tax are con-
sorts in Marxism. Socialists rub shoulders with the anti-Christ, the
Communist devil himself. This was guilt by association, but what
were being associated together in guilt were ideas.

In this early period Reagan quoted Khrushchev as saying
that "communism grows from Socialism and is its direct continuation," as if Soviet ideological doctrine could settle the nature of
democratic socialism by claiming its respectability for Soviet totalitarianism. Reagan granted that a socialist is "a bloody enemy"
of the Communists—Communists have shot down many socialists, he knew—but again he associated the two guiltily by his
association of their ideas (ignoring both political democracy and
the many sources and permutations of socialism): "The socialist
is an enemy of the Communist but not necessarily of the theory
of communism because both believe in the teachings of Marx
and Engels and both are dedicated to the government ownership of the means of production and the elimination of ownership of private property."

Here, in Reagan's thinking, was a pattern: grant that there
are differences in disapproved philosophies only to argue that
they come to the same thing. He next conceded there is hostility
in socialist traditions toward the police state, but then somehow

found liberals upholding communism! "There is a liberal philosophy," he said, "that seems to think that communism is simply an extension of extreme liberalism and that Soviet police-state brutality is not an integral part of communism. . . . Those liberated by this so-called liberal philosophy believe the solution to the cold war is to refrain from any overt act that would anger the men in the Kremlin." By whatever involuted reasoning came into his mind Reagan was determined to coat all his adversaries with the slime of the totalitarians. "Regardless of their humanitarian purpose," he told the nation in his 1964 plea for Goldwater, "those who would sacrifice freedom for security have, whether they know it or not, chosen this downward path" to "the ant heap of totalitarianism."

In 1979 he directly evaluated the tactics of the late Joe McCarthy. "It's true," Reagan said on the radio, "that the senator used a shotgun when a rifle was needed, injuring the innocent along with the guilty. Nevertheless, his broadsides should not be used today to infer that all who opposed Communist subversion were hysterical zealots."[1] But throughout his own career Reagan himself had used, not a rifle, but a shotgun.

When he was the GOP nominee for governor in 1966, his party's platform supported the use of loyalty oaths for public employees. As a candidate he demanded a legislative investigation, with public hearings, into alleged communism and sexual misconduct at the University of California at Berkeley. It is clear from the memoir of the chancellor of the University of California at San Diego, William J. McGill, that Reagan wanted the Marxist philosopher on the faculty there, Herbert Marcuse, denied reappointment. McGill, who reappointed Marcuse, regarded him as a utopian theorist, not a political revolutionary.[2]

In 1975 Reagan declared himself displeased about the disbanding of local police "red squads," the term that came to be applied to the programs of local police officers to spy on people and organizations that they regarded with suspicion. The New York police department, for example, kept dossiers on 250,000 people. In Chicago the police spied on individuals and groups that opposed the Vietnam war or criticized Mayor Richard Daley or the police. In Los Angeles in 1975 the police, jittery about lawsuits and unconstitutionality, destroyed six tons of their red squad files on more than 50,000 people. In 1983, however, the same police department has been exposed for having continued to spy on such people as Mayor Tom Bradley, members of the city council and the police commission, and judges. Los Angeles policemen have also now been caught spying on and infiltrating police-monitoring, antinuclear, and school desegregation organizations and other peaceful citizens' groups, some of which are genuinely radical. In Michigan a state police surveillance unit compiled about 38,000 files on organizations and persons, including some who are now prominent in business and public life, until judges declared the activity to be unconstitutional. In 1975, on radio, Reagan had said about the red squads:

"Let's not forget the outraged editorials with which much of the press greeted the discovery that police intelligence units in cities such as Washington, New York, and Los Angeles had accumulated files on people known to have potential for arson, murder, and starting riots. . . . The U.S. attorney general has called for limiting the ability of the FBI to proceed with domestic intelligence." In 1976 Reagan declared: "Piously claiming defense of civil liberties and prodded by a variety of bleeding hearts . . . we have dismantled much of the intelligence operations of law enforcement."

That year even Henry Kissinger found himself floodlit by Reagan's baleful anti-Communist spotlight. The provocation was a passage in a book by Admiral Elmo Zumwalt quoting Kissinger as having said to him, while they were on a train going to a football game, "The day of the U.S. is past and today is the day of the Soviet Union. My job as secretary of state is to negotiate the most acceptable second-best position available." Zumwalt said Kissinger compared the U.S. to Athens and Russia to Sparta. The secretary of state denied having said these things.

"Henry Kissinger's recent stewardship of U.S. foreign policy has coincided precisely with the loss of U.S. military supremacy," Reagan said. On the basis of Zumwalt's charges Reagan remarked: "Now we must ask if someone is giving away our freedom." Responding to a question, Reagan said, "I don't think Dr. Kissinger is in any way unpatriotic and I don't think that maybe there's any conspiracy or plot on his part." But reciting again Zumwalt's quotes and obviously not accepting Kissinger's denial, Reagan added, "So, therefore, his attitude is one of bowing and scraping to the Soviet Union, saying they're going to be No. 1, and, therefore, I must make these concessions that'll have them treat us nicely when they're once in charge."

After a majority of the members of the Senate voted to delay a decision on building the B-1 bomber until the newly elected President could review it, Reagan commented, "The action in the Senate must have been good news in Moscow. They must be toasting in the Kremlin."[3]

In his 1978–1979 prepresidential buildup Reagan plunged even deeper into the political paranoia of McCarthyism. During the 1978 Panama Canal debates he jestingly denounced one of the late McCarthy's favorite targets, the parlor pinks and striped-pants cookie pushers of the diplomatic corps. "You know," Reagan said, "giving up the Canal itself might be a better deal if we could throw in the State Department." He wasn't laughing in 1980 when he called for a "housecleaning" of the State Department and said the diplomatic service was a leading voice for appeasement.

From what he said in a May 1978 broadcast, he appeared to believe that traitors seriously endangered the government. In the decade after World War II, he said, "Communists in a great many critical agencies created a massive subversion problem in our government." On the basis of what he said was testimony that Alan Campbell, chairman of the Civil Service Commission, and the commission's director of personnel investigations gave to a Senate subcommittee, Reagan alleged that "known members of terrorist organizations and even Communist party members can not only become civil servants in government but can rise to the most sensitive government positions. Their subversive connections are deliberately left out of the [Civil Service] Commission's files" because membership in any organization is protected by the privacy act.

In other 1978 broadcasts Reagan told his listeners that during the cold war an international Communist meeting in Moscow decided on "a subtle campaign to make anticommunism unfashionable" in the U.S., using "well-meaning liberals and others. . . . And so, today most people in public life are afraid to hint at a Communist conspiracy." He quoted Professor Jeffrey Hart of Dartmouth concerning alleged facts revealing "a network of organizations once prominent in the protest against the Vietnam war" whose goal in 1978 was "support of the Salt II treaties and unilateral disarmament in the United States."

Quoting the same professor, Reagan passed on the allegation that in 1977 a member of the "Soviet-dominated . . . World Peace Council" (WPC) visited the U.S. "to set up a new combine of antinuclear power plant people and advocates of disarmament. We now have the MFS—Mobilization for Survival, based in Philadelphia." Reagan said in this context that the 1977 MFS conference was attended by Dr. Benjamin Spock, Barry Commoner, Sidney Lens, and Daniel Ellsberg and was supported by the War Resisters League, American Friends Service Committee, Women's Strike for Peace, and others.

Lou Cannon wrote in 1982, "I know of no one, either publicly or privately, whom Reagan has called a Communist other than those who have proclaimed their own communism." Yet, if Reagan's broadcasts on the Communist conspiracy and the MFS weren't McCarthyism, what is? No one could seriously deny that the WPC is a Soviet front. Speaking on hundreds of radio stations, Reagan associated Benjamin Spock, Barry Commoner, Sidney Lens, Daniel Ellsberg, and the hundreds of thousands of people in MFS, the War Resisters League, the American Friends Service Committee, and Women's Strike for Peace with a Soviet-originated Communist conspiracy.

Norma Becker, the founder of MFS, says that the organization won an equal-time right of reply on the approximately 500 stations on which Reagan's attack was aired. "It was nonsense," she says. A Soviet agent had not had a role in founding MFS? "No way, no way. I organized and founded the Mobilization for Survival and I know all the individuals who were involved," she said. "It was done because of a TV program I saw on Channel 13 the night of August 5, 1977, a roundtable of excerpts on the anniversary of Hiroshima the next day. I heard these guys and my blood turned to ice. I was sitting there absolutely in terror."

She went to work and the founding meeting was held on March 12, 1978.

Presumably still quoting the professor, the fortieth president of the United States said two years before his election: "The MFS works closely with the National Center to Slash Military Spending, which is an American arm of the World Peace Council and has in its upper crust a number of veteran members of the United States Communist party. . . .

"You could call these Americans a suicide lobby, but for heaven's sakes don't say 'conspiracy.'"

In this same context Reagan indicated that the antinuclear power movement is Communist-inspired. In a succession of radio broadcasts on this theme in 1978 and 1979, he said: "The Kremlin is going ahead with nuclear power and weapons development full-tilt, without so much as a peep of protest from the American left." Those who protest U.S. nuclear power safety standards "are the unwitting victims of Soviet designs." "The whole antinuclear movement is infiltrated by some of the same disruptive elements which sent so many young people into the streets to riot during the Vietnam war." "I've already spoken about the antinuclear power people and the fact that behind the scenes they are being manipulated by forces sympathetic to the Soviet Union." The antinuclear power movement "is run by strategists who are cynical and not sincere and have a motive not announced. . . . I wonder how many of our demonstrators would like to protest in Red Square."

Revving up on radio for his 1980 race against Carter, Reagan said that in delaying deployment of the neutron bomb the President was caving in to Soviet pressure and "bowing to Kremlin propaganda." When Carter canceled the program (styled "YC-14") for the Advanced Medium Short Takeoff and Landing Transport, Reagan said on radio, "By some strange coincidence the Soviet Union just happens to be going full-speed ahead" building a plane that "looks for all the world like a mirror image of the YC-14." When Carter vetoed a defense bill because it provided for a nuclear aircraft carrier which he thought should not be funded, Reagan, again on radio, said that responding to this veto, "the Soviets smile happily."

Reagan wrapped up this line of thought when he said in the newsletter of Citizens for the Republic in February 1979, "To the Communists and those others who are hostile to our country, President Carter and his supporters in the Congress must seem like Santa Claus. They have given the Panama Canal away, abandoned Taiwan to the Red Chinese, and they're negotiating a SALT II treaty that could very well make this nation NUMBER TWO."

Thus Reagan had built up gradually, step by step, to his climactic declarations in the spring and summer of 1980 that the Carter administration was committing "hypocrisy at its worst in cozying up to the Soviets" and that the Soviets wanted Carter elected to keep him—Reagan—out of the White House. On CBS's *60 Minutes* he said, "I think very definitely the Soviet Union is going to throw a few bones to Mr. Carter during the coming campaign in order to help him as President." The Russians were for Carter, Reagan said, "because, for one thing, I opposed a SALT II treaty." And the man who would be President said further with reference to the man who was, "I would be very worried about me if the Soviet Union wanted me to be President."

With such a background it was only a matter of time until McCarthyism would flash forth from the Oval Office occupied by President Reagan, and the moment came in December 1981 when he said that the antiwar demonstrations were sponsored by a thing called the World Peace Council, "which is bought and paid for by the Soviet Union." He had set his administration's course. When the McCarthy revival was in full flood a year later, a writer in *New Republic* found himself having to point out that the U.S. branch of WPC is not part of the elected leadership of the American nuclear freeze campaign.

Reagan's aides seemed to know that their chairman would not be displeased if they took out after the pinkos as in the days of yore. Interior Secretary Watt, meeting privately with a group of farmers (one of whom taped what he said and later gave it to the press), told them, "I never use the words Republicans and Democrats. It's liberals and Americans." Offered a chance to say liberals are "good Americans," he replied, "I suppose some of them are." The implications of this attitude resonated out of control when Watt later warned the Israeli Ambassador to the U.S., in writing, that American support for Israel could suffer if "liberals of the Jewish community join with the other liberals of this nation" in opposing what Watt described as the Reagan administration's energy program to accelerate the development of U.S. resources.

Reagan's radio theme in 1978 and 1979 that the antinuclear-power movement is Communist-inspired was echoed in the public statements of three of the men to whom he delegated portions of his official power as President. "What is the real motive of the extreme environmentalists?" Watt has asked. "Is it to weaken America?" They are, he said, "a left-wing cult" seeking to destroy "our very form of government." Secretary of Energy Edwards charged that "subversive elements" are using environmentalists to weaken nuclear power and that many of "these strident voices . . . wish us harm." Assistant Secretary of Agriculture Crowell told a reporter he was "sure" that the Sierra Club and the Audubon Society were "infiltrated by people who have very strong ideas about socialism and communism." Embarrassed by the ensuing outcry—Audubon President Peterson equated the remark with McCarthyism—Crowell made it worse, saying the two large organizations are open to anyone who pays dues, "and maybe there were people who felt strongly in favor of communism and socialism."[4]

In 1982 Betty Bumpers, wife of Senator Bumpers of Arkansas, was struck by the fact that a woman had said to her, "We can't use the word peace because it has a bad connotation." "Yeah, that's right," she had replied. "And then," she told the *New York Times*, "it hit me, to think that we had reached the point of thinking in this country that the word peace was unacceptable. What the heck, we said, we'll use it anyway."

Calling themselves "Peace Links," and with the help of grants from the Winthrop Rockefeller Foundation and the Rockefeller Family Fund, Betty Bumpers and her friends started in. The volunteers included Rosalyn Carter; Sharon Rockefeller, the wife of West Virginia Governor Jay Rockefeller; Barbara Levin, the wife of Democratic Senator Levin of Michigan; Teresa

Heinz, the wife of Republican Senator Heinz of Pennsylvania;
Nicola Tsongas, the wife of Democratic Senator Paul Tsongas
of Massachusetts . . .

"Peace Links is guided by a fourteen-organization advisory
board," Senator Jeremiah Denton told the Senate on a Friday
night, October 1, 1982. "Four organizations on the Peace Links
advisory board are either Soviet controlled or openly sympathetic with, and advocates for, Communist foreign policy objectives. These are the Women's Strike for Peace, an affiliate of the
Soviet-controlled Women's International Democratic Federation
which is based in East Germany; the Women's International
League for Peace and Freedom; the radical United States Student Association; and the Committee for National Security,
which was established by the radical, left-oriented Institute for
Policy Studies."

"Peace Links," Senator Bumpers retorted, "was not founded
in the Kremlin dining room—it was founded in my kitchen. And
by a group of mothers and housewives who were and are increasingly concerned about whether their children are going to
survive or not."

Earlier Denton had placed in the *Congressional Record* an article Bumpers now said had impugned the integrity of such people as George Ball, Averell Harriman, and William Fulbright by
suggesting that, favoring a nuclear freeze, they "are somehow
being manipulated by the KGB." Denton had attacked, Bumpers
said, "the patriotism of literally millions of people," not to mention the 202 representatives who had voted for the freeze and
the 30 senators then cosponsoring the Hatfield-Kennedy freeze
resolution. Pointedly Bumpers added that he had always favored a strong military defense "because there is always a bully
around who will try to silence his adversaries."

Senator after senator took the floor, most to defend Betty
Bumpers or their own wives, Gary Hart of Colorado to point a
finger at Denton and say "Shame on you," Jesse Helms to defend Denton, Barry Goldwater to implore his colleagues to "let
this thing calm down." Denton agreed there was no question of
Betty or Dale Bumpers' loyalty and complained, "This is the first
time in my life I have been called a bully." But Betty Bumpers,
listening in her husband's Senate office on the Capitol's televi-

sion system, believed that Denton had questioned her loyalty to the United States. Speaking of the fourteen advisory organizations, she asked later, "Who would have thought that I had to get State Department clearance?"[5]

The weekend passed, and then on Monday, speaking in Columbus, Ohio, President Reagan said of protesters who favor a nuclear freeze: "They were demonstrating in behalf of a movement that has swept across our country that I think is inspired by not the sincere and honest people who want peace but by some who want the weakening of America, and so are manipulating many honest and sincere people."

While Senator Baker, the Republican majority leader, called Reagan's remarks "broadbrush comments . . . common on the campaign trail," Senator Kennedy asked what exactly Reagan was suggesting about millions of people, and a cosponsor of the freeze resolution, Representative Edward J. Markey (D.–Mass.), said the President was guilty of "mud-slinging and McCarthy-like smear tactics." "I did not have any Americans in mind," Reagan hedged. A spokesman for the American Friends Service Committee (AFSC) thought there might be an orchestrated effort to discredit the freeze movement—there had been an article by John Barron in the *Readers' Digest,* then Denton, now Reagan. *Barron's,* the weekend companion to the *Wall Street Journal,* fired off a cheap shot at the involvement of senators' wives in Peace Links: "Evidently, bedfellows make strange politics." The *New York Times* said to Denton and Reagan, "The purpose of such ugly defamation can only be to prevent debate. . . ." In the same paper columnist Tom Wicker remarked that Reagan was suggesting that the profreeze Common Cause, the National Education Association, the United Auto Workers, and many members of Congress are dupes. Hodding Carter, formerly Carter's State Department spokesman, said Reagan meant the freeze movement was "made in Moscow."

"The image of a friendly but bumbling Reagan suddenly blurred into one of a mean and menacing Joe McCarthy," wrote columnist Richard Cohen. "All the statement lacked was a list of purported dupes or traitors." Becker, the founder of MFS and outgoing president of the War Resisters League, said, "I understand we're all Soviet agents. It's a time-tested method—label the opposition as being foreign spies or agents of the enemy. Unfortunately it works with some people."

An editorial in the *Washington Post* contributed to the burgeoning controversy. The *Post* editorial first condemned Reagan's statement as "a misstatement and a smear," but then added: "It is true, however, that one Peace Links advisory group, Women's International League for Peace and Freedom [WILPF], is a Soviet front and another, Women Strike for Peace [WSP], has connections to a second front, the Women's International Democratic Federation. They have the right. But why does Peace Links abide the taint that even the slightest connection to a Soviet stooge group imparts?"

The *Post* had based this editorial, as it subsequently stated, on a State Department report that was soon enough to become part of the White House's recommended reading list on Soviet influence in the peace movement. The report included WILPF in a list of thirteen Soviet front groups. The *Post* in a second editorial said it no longer believed WILPF was a Soviet front and that when its members or members of WSP participated in meetings conducted by Soviet-dominated groups abroad, they contended that was innocent attendance and entailed no Soviet funding or control. The State Department now backed off, too, telling the *Post* that its characterization of WILPF "was not directed toward the American section."

Yet the situation was degenerating rapidly. First Denton, then Reagan himself, and then the *Post*, relying on a Reagan-era State Department report. The WPC affiliate, the U.S. Peace Council, had been permitted to have a representative on the June 12 Rally Committee, and in the *Nation* and *New Republic* a dispute broke out whether the freeze movement should exclude Soviet fronts. "I can think of nothing more contemptible," declared elder statesman George Kennan in the wake of the outbreak, "than this effort to pin a communist label on a movement which is actually overwhelmingly motivated by nothing other than a deep concern for the security of this country and this civilization in the face of a volume of weaponry quite capable of putting an end to both."

Nonetheless, the revival of McCarthyism had one healthy effect on the peace movement, alerting it to the dangers of what

E. P. Thompson, a leader of the European movement, called "sleepwalking" into a de facto subservience to the interests of the totalitarian Soviet state. The passionate debate continued in left-wing American periodicals—it was the old "popular front" argument all over again.[6]

In the November election, nuclear freeze plebiscites passed in all the eight states and almost all of the localities where they were pending. Reagan's reaction: he dug in with the new statement that foreign agents were sent to help instigate the freeze movement and some of the big demonstrations, he cited Barron's *Readers' Digest* article to support his position, and he alluded guardedly to intelligence reports. The movement, he said, "might be carrying water that they're not aware of." In Texas the State Republican Executive Committee, responding to the President's signals, called on the FBI "to expose the credentials, aims, and allegiances" of the movement's leaders and to determine whether they were helping "godless aggressors."

An FBI spokesman commented, "the President's remarks are persistently consistent with what we have learned." In more exact truth, however, in subsequent open congressional testimony neither the FBI nor the CIA would allege that Soviet agents have inspired or manipulated the U.S. nuclear freeze movement nor that they control (although they have certainly influenced parts of) the European movement. The deputy director of the CIA said the Soviets had tried to exploit and manipulate the movement and had thereby "enabled it to grow beyond its own capabilities," but the FBI stated: "We do not see Soviet active measures in the United States as having a significant impact on U.S. decision makers."

Larry Speakes, the deputy White House press secretary, released on November 12 what has to be regarded as the White House reading list on this topic. The three magazines on the list are the *Readers' Digest*, the mass-circulation monthly with right-wing politics; *Commentary*, the formerly liberal, now right-wing magazine of the American Jewish Committee edited by Norman Podhoretz; and *The American Spectator*, another rightist monthly. There were also State Department reports and a 1980 congressional hearing.

It is the thrust of the government reports that the Soviets

have tried to infiltrate and exploit the U.S. peace movement and the freeze campaign. It is argued that in 1977–1978 the Soviets conducted an orchestrated propaganda campaign against U.S. manufacture of the neutron bomb because it would invalidate their huge advantage over NATO nations in numbers of tanks in Europe. Soviet attempts to whip up sentiment in Europe against new U.S. weapons are reviewed. A public 1980 report of the CIA lists thirteen Soviet front groups, obviously including the most notorious one, which is the World Peace Council, but not WILPF. No government document cited by the White House says, as Reagan did, that the Soviets *inspired* the freeze campaign—a word that has to mean in some important way that the Soviets originated it.

Two Reagan-era State Department reports recite the various dishonest and nefarious practices of the KGB, the Soviet secret police agency—forgeries, disinformation, lies, fronts, the use of prominent figures in a nation as collaborators to influence policies of the nation. "Of course," one report says, "not all opposition [to NATO weapons plans] is inspired by the Soviet Union." Another convincingly identifies WPC as an "instrument of Soviet foreign policy." But the one dated July 1982 (on which the *Post* relied to its regret) says, "The Communists and their supporters are all attempting to channel the peace and antinuclear movements to serve Moscow's purpose," and its list of thirteen Soviet fronts ends with the name of WILPF.

The magazine articles cited by the White House go all out. In *American Spectator*, Raul Jean Isaac and Erick Isaac have an article entitled, "Who's Behind the Politics of Nuclear Neurosis? The Crabshell-Kremlin Alliance?" The title tells the tone. Communists and Soviet agents have attended U.S. freeze meetings; Communists, being disciplined, dominate coalitions in which they participate; peace organizations have "shown so little resistance to Soviet manipulation"; peace organizations have been transformed into "channels that, for all practical purposes, serve Soviet interests"; there is "hardly any gap between the peace movement's perspective and that of the Soviet Union on how to create a more just global society"; "for all their fraudulence, the American peace organizations . . ." and so on.

The White House–recommended article in *Commentary*, written by Soviet émigré Vladimir Bukovsky, who spent twelve years in Soviet prisons because the Soviets did not like his writings, is a long, sarcastic anti-Soviet tirade, no doubt well justified. On the question at issue, however, Bukovsky simply asserts, giving no evidence, that the U.S. peace movement "is manipulated by a handful of scoundrels instructed directly from Moscow." Adopting an epithet of Lenin's about useful idiots, Bukovsky gives his opinion of the U.S. freeze campaign: "The Soviet rulers have scored a spectacular victory: they have recruited millions of useful idiots to implement their bankrupt foreign policy."

In the first two of three articles cited from *Readers' Digest*, students of the schoolmaster in the White House learn that "the small minority of Communists in the peace movement do not control it," but the peace groups "now mushrooming around Europe either have been created or are being manipulated by pro-Soviet apologists." The third article, by John Barron, is another matter.

Barron writes frequently on the KGB. In a preface, the *Digest* says the nuclear freeze movement is "largely made up of patriotic, sensible people," but has been "penetrated, manipulated and distorted to an amazing degree" by people promoting "Communist tyranny." Barron opens up, after this introduction, with an undocumented declaration that the KGB's current campaign is persuading the U.S. to abandon new weapons systems and "the name of the campaign is 'nuclear freeze.'"

All the cited magazine writers agree with Reagan's thesis on nuclear weapons that the Soviets are ahead of the U.S. and the U.S. must build the new weapons. In the context of this view, Barron alleges that the Soviet front the WPC, its affiliates, and local Communist parties were "the principal organizers" of the mass demonstrations in Europe (in Bonn, Amsterdam, Madrid, Athens)—a charge nowhere else advanced and here not documented. Because two Soviet agents attended an early freeze strategy meeting of 250 to 300 people in Washington, Barron concludes that "the KGB helped organize and inaugurate the American 'nuclear freeze' campaign." Barron charges that Senators Kennedy and Mark Hatfield (R.–Oreg.), by their nuclear

freeze resolution, "did significantly augment the Soviet campaign to prevent the United States from producing the weapon
that would ensure a balance of strategic power."

Such exercises in right-wing magazines are nothing new, but
the White House recommending such a reading list in support
of the seated President's charge that a great American mass
movement was inspired in Moscow is unprecedented. Polls
showed that 39 percent of Americans agreed with him that the
movement was led by people who have been "duped" by foreign
Communists.

The FBI had been pressed by the House Committee on Intelligence for a straightforward and understandable conclusion
on the charge. In the spring of 1983, then, the FBI produced a
written report informing the Congress that it had determined
that the Soviet Union does not "directly control or manipulate"
the American movement.

"Based on the information available to us," the FBI report
concluded, "we do not believe the Soviets have achieved a dominant role in the U.S. peace and nuclear freeze movements, or
that they directly control or manipulate the movement."[7]

The June 12th rally in Central Park for a mutual nuclear
freeze was the largest demonstration for a social cause in the
history of the world. Losing the argument and with a panoply of
new megadeath weapons at risk, the American President had
defamed many millions of his good and loyal fellow citizens. He
had let his accusative convictions burst forth from the Presidency itself and McCarthyism was loose again in the land.

For freshman Democratic Representative Bob Mrazek, it was
to laugh. During the Washington Press Club's 1983 "Salute to
Congress," the New Yorker regaled the 1,400 guests with an
account of his recent visit to the White House. "The President
had just finished his light after-dinner remarks on Communist
imperialism when he and Nancy invited us into the Red Room,"
Mrazek said. "I knew the President and I had much in common
when Ed Meese toasted McCarthy as the true great senator.
. . . The President turned to me and said, 'Isn't it a shame what
happened to McCarthy and Roy?' and I said, 'But I thought
Senator McCarthy's wife's name was Abigail.'"[8]

16

Punishing the Poor

Although nothing else in national politics is as difficult to understand as the federal budget, nothing else is remotely as important, either. The budget is "who gets what"—and who doesn't.

The subject is complicated and elusive. The President's proposals are different from what Congress resolves to spend, which is different from what Congress authorizes be spent, which is different from what Congress appropriates. Everything changes often, and the steep-sided figures, the "$12 billion," or "$300 million," or "$1.5 trillion," can be confusing or meaningless even to the well informed. "None of us really understands what's going on with all these numbers," Reagan's budget director Stockman confessed to Greider. "You've got so many different budgets out and so many different baselines and such complexity now in the interactive parts of the budget between policy action and the economic environment and all the internal mysteries of the budget, and there are a lot of them."

At the least, proposals must be kept separate from outcomes and one must look for actual consequences for people and programs. To hold a President accountable, the point must be clear, too, that he is responsible for his proposals whether Congress enacts them or not. "I dream of the day," Reagan said, "when maybe Washington gets smart enough to give a President the right of a line-item veto" (that is, the right to veto separate items on any line of the budget). His proposed constitutional amendment for a balanced budget would give him vast power, the right to "ensure" that expenditures not exceed income.[1] The point, though, is that a President is politically and ethically as responsible for his budget as he would be if he had a line-item veto. What the President proposes is either fully or partially passed or at the least creates pressures in the directions he recommends.

In the federal budget as we discuss it in this book, a reference to the budget for any given year always means that *fiscal* year. The federal fiscal year is the first nine months of its number's calendar year and the last three months of the preceding calendar year. Congress works on the budget for the fiscal year just ahead. "The 1984 budget" means the one that runs from October 1, 1983, through September 1984.

In dedicating his administration to cutting the federal budget for the poor and for the general public's health and education, Reagan has shown a certain courage: he has opened himself to the accusation and belief that he is mean and callous. Nothing more surely establishes the fact that he is the most right-wing President of this century than the relentlessness of his budget cutting. Bleeding-heart liberals are accused of going too far in condemning him as a Scrooge, and cold-hearted conservatives are accused of going too far in hailing him as the Pritikin of federal fat. The facts themselves tell their many stories—stories that radiate into tens of millions of lives.

Reagan has slashed government programs that benefit the poor, especially the working poor. There is nothing accidental or random about this. These programs are his targets. He and his people have cut them again and again and again, knowingly, coldly, with determination.

His theory is straightforward. If you can work the government should not help you, even if you are very poor. The government should help only those who cannot work, the "truly needy." The way to help the working poor is to intensify their self-reliance by cutting off their benefits.

The Reaganists' rhetoric, being multipurpose like most political rhetoric, asserts that by reducing inflation, reviving the economy, and creating more jobs, Reagan's budget cuts will help everyone, including the poor. The persuasive image is borrowed from President John Kennedy: rising water lifts all boats. The problem is that a lot of people don't own boats.

Programs for the poor use up only one-tenth of the federal budget, but under Reagan they have been cut much more harshly than any other federal activities. The programs that are designed specifically for the poor are Aid to Families with Dependent Children (AFDC), medicaid (medical care for the poor), Supplemental Security Income for the aged and disabled poor, free school meals, money for fuel bills, low-income housing, job and compensatory education programs, legal services, food supplements for pregnant mothers, infants, and children under five, and social services for the poor. Federal spending on medicare, Social Security, and the other retirement programs is three times as large as all these programs for the poor.

According to the Congressional Budget Office, Reagan's first budget proposed to take income, in-kind benefits, or public-service jobs from between 20 million and 25 million people who live just above the poverty line. Poor people make poor lobbyists, and with the newly elected President after them they had few defenders. The cuts Congress made in the programs for low-income people for 1982 were two and a half times larger than the cuts in all the other federal payments to individuals and families. That one year, food stamps were cut 11 percent, child nutrition programs 28 percent, AFDC 13 percent, student financial aid 25 percent, and fuel assistance for the poor 28 percent. Of the total $11 billion that was cut from federal entitlement programs, 60 percent came from programs for the poor. In Carter's budget for 1981 federal spending for the poor was scheduled at $100 billion. In Reagan's first two years he proposed to reduce this to $62 billion and Congress gave him cuts that brought it down to $82 billion. In real dollars, all this meant that during his first two years Reagan tried to cut federal aid to the needy almost in half, by 45 percent, and did cut it 28 percent.

By the fall of 1982, thanks to President Reagan and Congress, 660,000 children had lost medicaid; 1 million people had lost food stamps, and food stamp benefits had been reduced for another 20 million. About 365,000 families with dependent children had lost their monthly checks, and the AFDC checks had been reduced for another 260,000 families. About 3.2 million children no longer participated in the school lunch program; about 750,000 low-income children lost their eligibility for school lunches, and 500,000 children had been dropped from the summer meals program.[2]

The cruel effects of these cuts in the darkened lives of the poor were inherent in the instructions Reagan and his men gave Stockman and the way Stockman went about carrying them out. As Stockman told Greider, he was given the task of cutting out $40 billion, so:

"I put together a list of 20 social programs that had to be zeroed out completely, like Job Corps, Head Start, women and children's feeding programs, on and on. And another 25 that had to be cut by 50 percent: general revenue sharing, CETA manpower training, et cetera, et cetera. And then huge bites that would have to be taken out of Social Security. I mean really fierce, blood-and-guts stuff—widows' benefits and orphans' benefits, things like that. And still it didn't add up to $40 billion."

Supply-side economist Jude Wanniski, an ardent, but neo-populist Reaganist, was shocked when he heard Stockman and Republican economist Alan Greenspan discussing such cuts as the two of them were seated together in a corner at the Harvard Club in New York City. According to Wanniski:

"A hundred million here, a hundred million there, in cuts— that's how they were talking. So I walked over and picked up some peanuts from a bowl and began to drop them in, one by one. 'Peanuts,' I said. 'Here's $100 million worth of widows, here's $100 million worth of orphans you'll drive into the snow.'"

Reagan himself denied again and again that he would hurt

the "truly needy," but he knew what he was doing. On the Friday before his first budget was presented to Congress, he turned to Stockman and said, "We won't leave you out there alone, Dave. We'll all come to the hanging."[3]

The battles over the budget have filled the newspapers and television screens for two and a half years. The politics of the matter are essentially obvious.

His first year Reagan, strong in his recent victory, was assured of success because of congressional pliancy and the demoralization and opportunism among the Democrats. The President had public opinion with him, he had a thin majority in the Senate, and the first year in the Democratic-majority House he was given control by the "boll weevils," about 40 Democrats who vote like Republicans.

The Reaganists' strategy had two parts: move very fast, and make Congress vote on one package of cuts all at once, permitting no amendments to be considered. "It is my intention," said Senate Majority Leader Howard Baker of Tennessee, "to move these budget cuts in less than a month." In the course of attacking the proposed GOP cuts, House Majority Leader Wright made the fundamental admission about the House Democrats: "Our budget committee," he said, "has acceded to about three-fourths of all the spending reductions requested by President Reagan. This, it seems to me, amounts to substantial cooperation." Using what is called the "reconciliation" process, the House decided to take up the entire budget in one package and vote it up or down without amendments so that no member would have to vote specifically on cutting specific programs. The showdown came on June 26 on the House floor over a pasted-together 800-page bill of cuts. Representative Panetta of California protested, "We are dealing with more than 250 programs with no hearings, no deliberation, no debate." Exactly: that was the point. The bill was passed, and with the House Democrats in his sack Reagan had his limit for the year.

In effect the President, not Congress, wrote the 1982 budget, and the first signs of the counterreaction took the form of reasserted congressional prerogatives. The reconciliation process "is a potent recipe for despotism," the House Rules Committee

chairman, Representative Richard Bolling (D.–Mo.), warned.
Congress was also just beginning to realize that it could never
quench Reagan's thirst for more and more cuts. After the first
year's blood-letting Stockman told the House Budget Committee,
"There's no final vote. . . . We're going to have to go at it again
and again. . . ." Reagan's chief economist at the time, Murray
Weidenbaum, said in 1982, "Last year was the first round of
spending cuts, this year was the second, and there will be a third
and a fourth and so on." A weary lobbyist for the National Education Association said, "This business never ends. What one
gains today you have to defend tomorrow." The President was
an ideologue who would come back every year for more cuts.

People around the country and in Congress were learning,
too, that Reagan was targeting the poor—working and otherwise—and when his 1983 budget plunged ahead in the same
venture, the revolt began. Senator Dole said the widespread belief that Reagan's economic program was unfair was in some
respects "correct." Reagan's second budget was dead soon after
it reached the Hill, forcing him into negotiations with the House
Democrats. "Your [1981] budget was unfair and had no equity,"
Speaker O'Neill told him to his face (in conversations at the
White House reconstructed by reporters). "I've heard all that
crap," Reagan replied. "We haven't thrown anyone out in the
snow to die." "How can you say that people aren't hurt?" O'Neill
said to him. When Wright proposed halving the third year of
Reagan's tax cut in exchange for domestic and defense cuts,
Reagan replied: "Well, you may make me crap a pineapple, but
you won't make me crap a cactus." With alternatives like that
there was no compromise.

In the House the black caucus proposed the kind of liberal
budget that Democrats used to espouse while the committee
chairmen and the leadership patched together a proposed
schedule of spending that still gave Reagan most of his cuts.
Instead of following the Democratic leadership, the "Democratic" House adopted a Republican-drafted program that was
even stingier than the Democratic leadership's or the Senate's.
When these two measures were combined into one in the House-
Senate conference, however, the House conferees (probably re-

flecting the wishes of the more liberal House leadership) acceded to the terms of the more generous Senate bill in most cases. Then the House refused to vote the budget up or down in one package again; the Great Reaction was winding down. His first year Reagan had obtained an estimated 85 percent of 90 percent of his cuts; by the end of 1982 he had only 30 percent of his second-round cuts. He had been able to prevail against the "big spenders" by veto before (shutting the government down one day in 1981, killing another bill in mid-1982), but now when he vetoed a bill because he objected to money in it for low-income students, jobs for the elderly, and housing for the poor, Congress defied him: the House overrode him 301–117 and the Senate did, too, 60–30. By the autumn of his second year he was losing the Congress.

Just at this time, by his selection of Martin Feldstein to be the new chairman of his Council of Economic Advisers Reagan communicated his determination to stay his own course whether Congress would or not.

Feldstein, a Harvard professor who had been educated at Oxford, fit into the dominant pattern among Reagan's insiders. Before he became the White House economist he was an economic adviser to Dean Witter Reynolds, the stockbrokers, and a director of TRW, which makes aerospace, auto, and industrial products. Although he told a Senate committee his net worth was less than $1 million, in the written statement he had submitted to the committee (following, he said, the advice of his lawyer) he had put the figure at $1.2 million.

Before his appointment Feldstein had been expressing his views frequently in newspaper columns. He had proposed the cancellation of the 20 percent increase in Social Security benefits that was enacted in 1972; he had proposed a 13 percent cut in Social Security benefits by 1987, exempting the poor by introducing a means test or (less exactly) by exempting the smallest benefit checks. For medicare and what he called "other so-called entitlement programs" he proposed the same kind of treatment. "Why should the federal government spend $4 billion a year subsidizing school lunches?" he asked in the *Wall Street Journal.* He scorned, too, the federal programs for local sewage treatment, community development grants, and public service employment. "Why should elementary and secondary education . . . receive nearly $4 billion of federal funds?" he asked. "Why should Congress not . . . reduce the benefits" under medicare? Turning to the disability program under Social Security, he continued: "In 1980, about 3 million individuals who were classified as 'disabled workers' received benefits of over $12 billion. . . . A return to the old eligibility rules would probably eliminate one-half to two-thirds of current beneficiaries. . . ." Congress, he said early in 1981, should make spending cuts "that are at least as large as the President has requested." Yet, he complained early in 1982, "Every proposed spending cut brings howls from those who would lose benefits. . . ." Reagan's selection of Feldstein in the fall of 1982 demonstrated the President's personal accountability for his program cuts almost as vividly as his budgets themselves did.

The country was moving in the opposite direction. Reinforced by their 26-seat gain in the 1982 elections, in 1983 the House Democrats composed and passed their own more conventional budget, restoring some of the programs Reagan had cut (but reversing only 28 percent of the cuts in the programs for the poor). The Senate Budget Committee rebelled against Reagan's third-year demand for a 10 percent jump in military spending, voting half that instead, and then produced so mild a budget it pleased the House Democrats. Reagan had not only lost his ability to win in the House with his "Boll Weevils," he was losing control of his own party's Senate.[4] By the spring of 1983 he had set his basic pattern: if at first you don't cut, cut and cut again, and the elements were falling into place for a 1984 rerun of his 1980 crusade against the big spenders. But this time he would have to explain his own big spending for weapons and the Reaganists would have to explain why so many heavyweight Republicans had deserted their President.

Reagan not only embodies hostility toward "welfare" in the politics of the 1980s, but as much as any other public man he generated it. The welfare state, he says, is "a faceless mass waiting for handouts." Running for governor in California he spoke of newcomers loafing on the welfare rolls under regulations that "encourage divorce and immorality." Not for him, "those who would trade our freedom for the soup kitchen of the welfare state." In a 1970 memo to his Cabinet, distinguishing "the truly needy as opposed to the lazy unemployable," he called on his staff to declare "all-out war on the taxtaker."

Bothered by criticism that as governor he lacked compassion, he said in a letter: "I'm sure everyone feels sorry for the individual who has fallen by the wayside or who can't keep up in our competitive society, but my own compassion goes beyond that to those millions of unsung men and women who get up every morning, send the kids to school, go to work, try to keep up the payments on their house, pay exorbitant taxes to make possible compassion for the less fortunate, and as a result have to sacrifice many of their own desires and dreams and hopes. Government owes them something better than always finding a new way to make them share the fruit of their toils with others." In another letter he said, "A man may choose to sit and fish instead of working—that's his pursuit of happiness. He does not have the right to force his neighbors to support him (welfare) in his pursuit because that interferes with their pursuit of happiness."[5] Welfare is not, he said, an "inalienable right" of the poor. "Isn't it something of a gift granted by people who earn their own way . . . ?"

In California medicaid, the program of medical care for the poor, is called Medi-Cal. In 1966, while discussing Medi-Cal with his Cabinet, Reagan remarked: "I venture to say that there isn't anyone in the U.S. that was ever let go without medical care." "Absolutely," replied Spencer Williams, his chief of the California human resources agency. Twice Reagan cut medical benefits for the poor, and both times courts ruled he had done so illegally. In 1967 his administration cut back Medi-Cal services to the 1.5 eligible poor Californians in the total sum of $210 million, limiting surgery to injuries and life-threatening conditions, restricting dental care to emergencies, and eliminating nonemergency foot care, chiropractic and physical therapy services, psychotherapy, eyeglasses, and hearing aids. California courts, holding that the cuts violated welfare statutes and were not required by shortages in available funds, canceled them. Three years later Reagan tried again, and again the California courts swept his cuts aside.

Lyndon Johnson's war on poverty attracted Reagan's derision and official opposition from the West Coast. A week after his inauguration as governor, Reagan announced the elimination of eight of the thirteen agency service centers in poverty areas in the state. "Take the war on poverty—a matchless boondoggle," he said. "Under the combat rules, I have the option of vetoing those various projects. . . . All told, we have in several months successfully vetoed seven projects and caused more than half of all the rest to be substantially changed. . . ."

As his director of California's antipoverty agency (called the Office of Economic Opportunity like its counterpart in Washington) Reagan appointed Lewis K. Uhler, the former member of the Birch Society. An Assembly committee voted to abolish the agency on grounds that making Uhler the director was "like putting arsonists in charge of the fire department," as one assemblyman said.

According to the *Los Angeles Times*, Reagan ordered cutbacks in about 100 areas of service in the program for the care of crippled children, denying care to about 5,000 children who would have otherwise qualified. Benefits were denied to those whose conditions were not considered "chronic." In 1969 the legislature approved a $5 million school lunch bill, but Reagan cut it 90 percent, to $500,000.

In the summer of 1970 he triggered a $25 million cut in aid to the aged, blind, and disabled, but backed down when a lawsuit was threatened. That fall a U.S. judge ruled that California had to increase its payments under AFDC—an examiner said California was violating a U.S. law requiring cost-of-living increases in the payments. Reagan called the court ruling "absurd and ridiculous." A Superior Court judge in Sacramento ordered Reagan's state government to immediately increase welfare grants to thousands of needy children by 21.4 percent; Reagan's office announced an appeal because the state had not had a full and adequate hearing.

Reagan had asked the Nixon administration to give California (and him) full control over antipoverty programs in the state. Far from doing so, at one point the Nixon administration disclosed an intention to cut off $700 million worth of annual welfare payments for California because of the Reaganists' failure to pay AFDC benefits as required by law.

State mental hospitals are charged to care for mentally ill citizens who cannot afford costly private mental treatment. Reagan announced a plan to phase out California's state mental hospitals in favor of local treatment programs. According to former Governor Pat Brown, who was watching, distraught, from the sidelines, Reagan ordered a 3,700-employee reduction in the mental health program and called for the closing of 14 outpatient psychiatric clinics, the elimination of the Mendocino hospital's 400-bed alcoholism treatment center, and deactivation of 80 wards in ten state hospitals. He refused to visit the hospitals to evaluate the effects of the cuts. Faced with parents' bitter accusations that the state was dumping patients into communities that were not prepared for them, he backed down. He said his program had been designed to transfer patients from large state hospitals that were only custodial warehouses to smaller, localized treatment centers and hospitals. There were some closings and consolidations, he said, but there was no intention to eliminate the state hospitals.[6]

Reagan's trouble with the courts over his welfare cuts stemmed in part from lawsuits brought by California Rural Legal Assistance (CRLA), a legal service program for the poor that was funded by the federal OEO. Reagan had to be able to justify his vetoes of the poverty programs—if he could not, they could be overridden at the federal level. Ex-Bircher Uhler's staff produced a 283-page report charging CRLA with incompetence and with encouraging prison riots and engaging in radical and revolutionary acts; on the basis of this report Reagan vetoed a $2 million grant to CRLA. His aide William Clark (now the National Security Adviser) said: "The encouragement of litigation has perhaps opened the door too wide to the indigent client."

Former national OEO director Donald Rumsfeld, a Republican, had complimented CRLA, and the Nixon administration was not inclined to accept the veto. Nixon's head of OEO appointed three retired state-level Supreme Court justices to examine the charges. Uhler refused to participate in the hearing or present witnesses or evidence. The judges concluded that the Uhler study, the basis of Reagan's veto, was "totally irresponsible and without foundation," and the Nixon administration overrode the veto. Meanwhile, other federal studies concluded that Reagan's California OEO was "using the majority of its staff to perform investigative functions" and in 1972 had misused $133,000 to conduct "specifically prohibited" undercover investigations of welfare recipients, including surveillance and tailing.[7]

Much of this information will be news to most readers. Reagan glossed it over and the national press did not review it to any substantial extent. Reagan's 1971 welfare reform was a foundation of his 1980 campaign—but what he advocated before accepting the legislature's compromise program is little known to this day.

Governor Reagan proposed to tighten eligibility requirements for the totally disabled, deduct federal food-stamp and housing subsidies from state payments to all recipients, limit adult recipients' job training, open up welfare records between different agencies of government, and set an overall welfare spending ceiling which, if touched, would then cause all welfare payments to go down. "One look," Pat Brown said of the proposal, "and it was apparent that it would never pass." Bob Moretti, the Assembly speaker, told Reagan his program would hurt many deserving people badly. As quoted by Brown, Moretti told Reagan that 85 percent of the recipients of welfare are the aged, the blind, the disabled, or dependent children, another 14.9 percent are the mothers of the dependent children, and only about one-tenth of one percent are able-bodied men.

Moretti said Reagan "wanted that welfare 'scalp' so badly that he was willing to make a deal." The Democrats balked especially at the welfare ceiling and in their counterproposal proposed a 15 percent increase in welfare grants, which Reagan opposed.

Reagan also cast himself against Nixon's plan of a $2,400 floor under welfare families' income, a kind of guaranteed annual income for the poor. Although Nixon was the seated GOP President, Reagan said he feared that the Nixon plan would add as many as 20 million people to the welfare rolls and create a new federal bureaucracy.

At the same time Reagan sought authority from Washington to impose a wide range of changes in federal welfare regulations. He made seventy requests, thirty-nine of which were approved on the spot. The thrust of all of it was to cut benefits. He wanted a statewide waiver that would permit reduced welfare benefits under the Social Security Act, which he planned to use in California to require welfare recipients to pay $1 for each office visit to a doctor, $1 for each prescription at a drugstore, and $3 a day for hospital and nursing care. He said California had imposed or was seeking to impose the following rules: make a family eligible for welfare only if the dependent child was 18 or younger, not 21 or younger; permit the state to attach the wages of soldiers and other federal employees who were not supporting their families; deny aid to strikers and their families; and deny aid to a family where a stepfather or consort was living in the house and could be putting in support.

According to a report by the Urban Institute, a nonprofit Washington research group, the California welfare reform of 1971 tightened eligibility restrictions and required each welfare household to mail a signed postcard form every month certifying income. The maximum welfare grant for a family of three was increased from $204 to $235 a month. A "work or else" program, knocking people off welfare if they were qualified to work and would not, was also part of the changes. The report called the reform "a major policy success," on balance helping more recipients than it hurt. The "work or else" feature, however, failed, with only 9,600 people assigned to jobs in three years even though there was an average of 350,000 cases on the rolls, according to the study.

Reagan makes a number of standard claims about the reform. He says, for instance, "our caseload was increasing by 40,000 people a month. We . . . achieved an 8,000-a-month reduction in the rolls for more than three years." According to a study in the *Los Angeles Times*, the average increase was 26,000, and the average decrease 3,500. Reagan claimed $2 billion was saved, but this was based on inflated welfare projections; the actual savings were about $40 million a year (one-fiftieth of $2 billion).

The Urban Institute study showed the number of AFDC clients declining by 268,000, but agreed with other sources that the causes for this included economic decline and the existence of fewer poor people because of sharply increasing numbers of abortions. According to a group of Reagan's Republican colleagues in the legislature, "the total number of recipients on welfare in California nearly doubled during the Reagan years while the state's population growth rate decreased from 3 percent to 1 percent a year." Reagan says, "we increased grants to the truly needy by 43 percent." The maximum welfare grants were increased, but this was the work of the Democrats, not Reagan.[8]

The fortieth American President does not scruple against making people laugh at the poor with funny stories about welfare cheats. On radio in 1978 he jested that it's not so bad to be poor when "you can get subsidized housing, health and dental care, university scholarships and other welfare benefits, provided you're poor enough." Then he played out for his listeners an imagined conversation between an employee, Smedley, and his boss, Mr. Goodie. Smedley asks for a $25 cut in salary.

"If I made $25 less," he tells his boss, "we'd be eligible for an apartment in the city's new development, the one downtown with a pool, sauna and tennis court. Besides, my son would qualify for a government scholarship and we would get his teeth fixed at government expense."

Mr. Goodie says OK, "on this condition. If your work slips, you'll get a $10 raise, no questions asked."

"Bless you, Mr. Goodie."

"And Smedley, will you invite me over for tennis and a swim some night when you get into your new place?"

"Certainly, sir," Smedley replies. "I believe the poor should share with the less fortunate."

When the U.N. General Assembly proclaimed "The International Year of the Child," Reagan complained—on radio in August 1979—that "many liberal activists are using the U.N. proclamation as a moral mandate for new Big Government programs such as compulsory national health insurance and fully funded daycare centers." What really angered him was the U.N.'s declaration that "the child shall have the right to adequate nutrition and medical care, including prenatal and postnatal care, to child and mother." Of this he said: "Of course, we want our children to have those things. . . . But to speak of necessities such as medical care as 'rights' is . . . to say that it is the job of government. . . ."

Reagan brought to Washington his two top welfare surgeons, Ed Meese and Robert Carleson. The latter, who had been city manager of a small town, had become Reagan's welfare director in California and originated changes in the rules there which reduced the number of beneficiaries. Perhaps Carleson's most noteworthy addition to the California regulations required that payments made to a pregnant poor woman for her and her unborn child had to be reduced by the "in-kind" benefits the fetus was deemed to be receiving in its mother's womb in lieu of food, clothing, and shelter. As Reagan's commissioner of welfare in Washington, Carleson declared that income belongs by right to the people who earn it, and "it does not belong to the state, nor does it belong by right to any other segment of the population." Another state welfare director under Reagan in California, David B. Swoap, in Washington became his under secretary of HHS and formulated changes in welfare rules that reduced benefits more than $1 billion the first year. After yet another Californian, John Svahn, Reagan's U.S. commissioner of Social Security, had systematically savaged the disability program in accordance with the wishes of his boss, Reagan sent him over to HHS as the No. 2 official to keep an eye on the wishy-washy moderate, Margaret Heckler, who had replaced Schweiker as the secretary.

As Reagan never tired of lamenting, by 1981 22 million people received food stamps at a rising cost of $10 billion, 18 million received medicaid at a rising cost of $31 billion, and 11 million received AFDC at a rising cost of $13 billion. He was not interested in expatiating upon certain other realities. As states had failed to adjust aid to needy children for inflation, AFDC benefits measured in constant 1981 dollars had dropped from $558 a family in 1969 to $394 in 1981, a decline of 29 percent. One in six families received help from one or more of the in-kind bene-

fit programs (medicaid, food stamps, school meals, and subsidized housing), but these benefits were not reaching two-fifths of
the nation's poor people. When the recession began in July
1981—increasing unemployment to 12 million the next year—
the need for federal benefits would increase, too, as more people
fell into poverty.[9]

In Reagan's recitations of the rising costs of the government
transfers to individuals he also neglected to mention the fact that
as a result of these transfers poverty was decreasing dramatically. The number of poor households had dropped from 12
percent in 1965 to 4 percent in 1980; for every three American
citizens who were poor in 1965, only one was poor in 1980. The
percentage of elderly households in poverty had plummeted
from 35 percent in 1965 to less than 4 percent, from one in
every three to one in twenty-five! Most of this progress had been
caused by the cash and in-kind government payments, because
when only "market income" is considered for the same period
the numbers of the poor decline only slightly, from 21 percent
of the population to 20 percent. Poverty had increased among
blacks in the central cities, but Carter had been preparing programs to work on that.

Reagan's first priority was to finally kill off Johnson's war on
poverty entirely. Nixon had closed the OEO and merged its
surviving programs into the Community Services Administration (CSA), which was the sole surviving federal agency devoted
entirely to the problems of the poor. Now Stockman said the
United States could not afford the Great Society, and "substantial parts of it will have to be heaved overboard." "Block grants"
were the Reagan administration's standard deck-shuffle to dis-
tract attention from this over-the-side activity, and the first year
Reagan proposed to cut CSA a fourth and block-grant its programs out to states and municipalities. CSA was the kind of
agency where there were photographs on the walls of old
women and hungry children, and signs beside the pictures said
"10,200,000 poor Americans are children," and "6,400,000
Americans work but are still poor." On September 30, 1981,
CSA closed its doors and Johnson's "unconditional" war on poverty ended in unconditional surrender.[10]

"Our spending cuts will not be at the expense of the truly needy," Reagan said on February 5, 1981. "All those with true need," he promised solemnly on this solemn subject, "can rest assured that the social safety net of programs they depend on are exempt from any cuts." He announced that Social Security's mainline benefits, medicare, veterans' programs, school meal programs, Head Start education services for preschool and inner-city children, and the summer youth jobs program would not be cut. Spokesman for him said that a program for the "truly needy" was one which people needed to survive and without which they would find it "very difficult to survive."

Notably, though, the Reaganists reserved the right to tighten eligibility requirements for these programs, and there were even trickier hedges. Notice the italicized words in the "social safety net programs" as defined in Reagan's 1981 budget document (the italics are provided): "social insurance benefits *for the elderly*; *basic* unemployment benefits; *cash* benefits for *dependent* families, elderly, and disabled; and social obligations to veterans." Reagan thereupon proposed to cut Social Security benefits for early retirees and dependents, extended unemployment benefits, and in-kind benefits for the poor. The Urban Institute (whose chairman, William Ruckelshaus, has since returned to government as the head of the EPA) produced a sober book-length report, *The Reagan Experiment*, on the first two budgets. As this report stated, "Thus the 'safety net' did not in fact include early retirees; disabled workers or retirees' dependents under Social Security; workers unemployed longer than thirteen weeks; the typical welfare recipient (who has income other than welfare); and recipients of noncash aid regardless of their income." It did not include medicaid, the basic medical program for the poor, nor school meals nor food stamps. The Urban Institute report observed: " 'Safety net' proved to be a term that categorized people neither by their degree of current financial need nor by their vulnerability to future economic insecurity. Rather, it appears to have been used primarily to delineate and protect the benefits of those for whom cutbacks would likely have aroused the strongest reaction in Congress."

Even the safety net riddled with holes was disvalued

within the year. In September the White House press officer said
of the seven exempt programs that it would be "premature to
make guarantees." Stockman began replacing the term "truly
needy" with a new one, the "dependent poor," whom he defined
as persons too old to work, the physically disabled, and, perhaps,
mothers with small children. Almost everyone else, he told
Edward Cowan of the *New York Times*, was deemed to have
"some capacity" to earn a living and might lose some federal
benefits. As for the seven programs Reagan had said would be
exempt from cuts, Stockman now said they were "not exempt
from efforts to review, reform, or tighten" them—in other
words to cut them.

Reagan's next two budgets made it obvious why his men,
knowing what was coming, had tried to shift away from his guarantees to the "truly needy." For 1983 Reagan proposed cutting
medicare and housing assistance for the poor; he wanted food
stamps, medicaid, and AFDC cut back absolutely from $37 bil-
lion to $32 billion. For 1984 he proposed to cut the cost-of-living
adjustment in half on veterans' disability and pension benefits
and federal aid to the aged, blind and disabled and to cut all the
federal programs for the poor by a total of 19 percent in real
dollars.[11] He had ravaged the federal Treasury with his tax cuts
for the wealthy, and rather than curb these bonanzas to reduce
the deficits he decided to deprive the truly needy of money,
food, and medical care.

Program by program, here is what Reagan has done so far to
the poor.

He said food stamps increased 16,000 percent over the last
fifteen years. That was true, but went back for the statistical base
to 1966 when the program was in effect in only several hundred
American counties. He said 57 percent of stores checked were
accepting food stamps to pay for prohibited items. This was
true, for such items as toothpaste, soap, and beer, but the stores
checked were a group of them that were under suspicion.

His opposition to food stamps may contain an element of
hostility toward the recipients themselves, or so one might conclude from his reaction to the free food distribution program that
was demanded by the kidnappers of newspaper heiress Patricia

Hearst. While deploring the situation before an organization of aides to Republican congressmen, Reagan said, "It's just too bad we can't have an epidemic of botulism." Botulism is a poison that may infect preserved food. The statement was publicized, and a spokesman confirmed that Reagan had said something like "sometimes you wonder whether there shouldn't be an outbreak of botulism," but was only joking. Explaining later in a letter to a congressman, Reagan said his remark "was uttered in a private gathering and certainly not as a joke. . . . It was one of those exaggerations we all at times utter to express frustration, and we do so with the confidence that no one takes us literally."

Reagan's eagerest congressional ally in cutting food stamps is Senator Helms of North Carolina, who believes that food stamp officials should have access to recipients' tax returns. This has not happened yet, but the Agriculture Department authorized states to match food stamp applications with Social Security and unemployment compensation records, and recipients in seventeen big cities were required to obtain photographic identification cards.

Food stamps are the only wholly federal aid program for the American needy in two respects: Washington pays for all of it, and it is available to all the poor. About 87 percent of the recipients are poor and most of the others are "near poor," just above the poverty line. The average gross income of food stamp households is $325 a month. In 1981 Reagan proposed cuts reaching 20 percent in the fifth year and eligibility changes that would remove hundreds of thousands of households from the program. The first year the program was reduced $2.3 billion, about 1 million people lost their benefits, and most others took cuts. Reagan wanted to reduce a family's food stamps by the value of their children's free or subsidized school lunches, but Congress would not do that. At his motion Congress did slash the separate food stamp program for impoverished Puerto Rico (where more than half the people received food stamps) by 25 percent.

In Reagan's 1983 budget he wanted food stamps struck out or cut for 85 percent of the recipients, 17 million people; he wanted 3 million dropped from the rolls entirely. The families of the working poor would have lost $2 of every $5 in benefits, an average yearly loss of $684. According to the Congressional Budget Office (CBO), Reagan's budget would have either reduced or terminated food stamps for 92 percent of all households with elderly or disabled members (dropping 26 percent of them entirely). "Nearly all participants . . . would be cut an average of $262 a year," wrote Senator Leahy of Vermont. "Working households stand to lose about 40 percent of the food stamp benefits they now receive. . . . If the compassion of his program is measured by its direct effect on millions of needy human beings, it can indeed be charged that the President is turning his back on the poor and the elderly in this country." Reagan also wanted to make it mandatory that food stamp recipients work for public agencies, at no salary, in exchange for their stamps, but Congress refused. The program's spending shrank another $2 billion, though.

His third year Reagan asked for another $1.1 billion cut, and the CBO estimated that of the 8 million families still receiving food stamps, about 4.9 million, or 62 percent, would lose average benefits of $178 a year if the proposal was enacted. Two million food-stamp households that have incomes of under $3,800 a year, less than half the poverty line—that is, four out of five of all such truly impoverished households—would lose an average of $100 a year in benefits, the CBO said. Furthermore, according to the CBO, "among households losing benefits, those with elderly or disabled members would experience the greatest average benefit reduction, nearly $21 per month," or 26 percent of their benefits. Despite this responsible forecast that Reagan's proposed cuts for 1984 would snatch food away from most of the poorest of the poor people who receive food stamps, the administration continued to contend that under its third-year plan "to simplify and standardize the food stamp program," more food stamp families would gain than lose. An Agriculture Department official admitted to Congress that under Reagan's budget the food stamp cuts for 1985 would be almost four times greater than those budgeted for 1984.[12]

"What can you say about a plan to take food away from poor kids?" asked the *Washington Post* in an editorial. The pattern was the same in the school lunch program. For 1982, Reagan persuaded Congress to lower the amount of money a family can earn if their children are to be permitted free school lunches and to double the cost of reduced-price school lunches to 40 cents. Although the Agriculture Department had to back down from its proposals to abandon the requirement that school lunches provide a third of minimum daily nutrients and to count ketchup and relish as a vegetable, other ways of scrimping were found. In the 1981–1982 school year the school lunch program cost the government 40 percent less than it would have under pre-Reagan law. There had been 26 million children in the program, but 3.2 million of them stopped receiving free or subsidized school lunches in 1981–1982. Of these, 1.1 million children belonged to families defined as poor. The fact that middle-class children also dropped out because of the higher prices was one cause of the withdrawal of 2,700 schools from the program.

The administration's hostility to government paperwork has not protected poor and near-poor Americans from an ever-tightening federal red tape. In 1982 the Reaganists began requiring that all adults in the households of children in the school lunch program provide the government with their Social Security numbers. Starting in 1984 school districts must verify the eligibility of 3 percent or 3,000 of their applicants for school lunches every year. To do this the school authorities may ask for paycheck or welfare check stubs; notices of unemployment, alimony child support, or veterans' benefits; and the names of landlords, employers, social workers, or others who can then be asked financial questions. And the administration wants to take the program's operation from the schools and turn it over to local welfare offices. Ronald Reagan is getting government not off, but on the backs of the poor.

Senator McGovern had been the principal champion of federal nutrition programs, but he had been defeated in 1980, and in Reagan's first year the school lunch program was cut 30 percent, the school breakfast program 20 percent, the summer school-child feeding program 50 percent, and a special milk-buying program for the schools 80 percent. In 1981, 1.9 million children received summer lunches; in 1982, only 861,000. His second year Reagan proposed to end the summer and milk programs and reduce the breakfast program, provoking Nick Kotz, a reporter who has specialized in hunger in America, to explain plainly: "Hundreds of thousands of poor children would lose their free school breakfasts." Congress was balking now, refusing to give the President more deep cuts in child nutrition. Nevertheless, in his third year Reagan was trying to combine the various child nutrition programs into one block "child feeding" grant for the states with 15 percent less money.

Speaker O'Neill told reporters that Reagan had regaled a congressional delegation with a story about a woman who makes $75,000 a year, yet has a child in the free lunch program. "Mr. President, it can't happen," O'Neill said he replied. Furthermore, the Speaker said he continued, the cuts were devastating: in his own home state of Massachusetts 640,000 children who were eating school lunches in 1981 did not qualify for them in 1982. But the President persisted, asking, "Do we honestly believe that someone whose parents earn in six figures is entitled to have food stamps because they're going to college?"[13]

Under the women's, infants', and children's (WIC) program, needy pregnant and lactating mothers and their infants and small children up to age five who are deemed to be vulnerable to poor nutrition are provided foods rich in protein and other nutrients. WIC benefits about 2.4 million people in all. According to congressional testimony, a Massachusetts study showed that the cost of food aid and medical expenses for those in the WIC program totaled $230,000, whereas the cost of medical care only for those who had applied for WIC aid but could not be accommodated totaled $716,000.

His first year Reagan proposed cutting $224 million out of the Department of Agriculture WIC program, a chop of about a fourth which so shocked a Senate committee that even in 1981 the vote no was 15 to 4. Congress gave him only a 4 percent cut that first round. For 1983 Reagan proposed to slash WIC and a second program for maternal and child health from $1.3 billion to $1 billion, another 25 percent cut. Pressed to explain this humanly and politically incredible persistence in trying to cut nutritional benefits for pregnant mothers and infants, Reagan denied there had been any reduction and said that more money was being proposed; he had to be corrected by one of his own budget officers. Under his 1983 budget between 700,000 and 800,000 low-income infants, children aged five or younger, and indigent, pregnant, and lactating mothers would have lost their food supplements.

Organizations acting for poor pregnant women in Georgia and New York accused the Agriculture Department of ignoring a law that required the agency to redistribute unspent WIC money to states that needed it. In fiscal 1981, they charged, the WIC caseload had declined 200,000 while $51 million had been left unspent. In the fall of 1982 federal judge Charles R. Richey of Washington, D.C., felt it necessary to order Secretary of Agriculture John Block to reallocate $10 million in unspent WIC funds to states that needed it. He told the government's lawyer in open court, "I don't think a secretary of agriculture ought to have any excuse. Let him wash the blood off his own hands and get it done." By the time the government got around to disbursing the money, he said angrily, some of the children might be dead or retarded. He thundered at the government, "These are little human beings who have no constituency but their parents."

So ordered, the secretary of agriculture got it done. But five months later Reagan proposed to freeze the WIC program with no increases for inflation, which would deny food supplements to another 100,000 needy women, infants, and children in 1984 and prospectively could cause the program to lose $800 million in purchasing power in a five-year period. In its attempts once, twice, and thrice to cut back WIC, the administration's priorities could not be mistaken. The acting chief of the Department of Agriculture Food and Nutrition Service told Congress in April 1983 that the program was reaching only about 40 percent of those who need the help, that "We do have waiting lists in many states," and that it would cost two or three times present spending to provide the food aid to all mothers, infants, and children who need it.[14] But as Stockman said, the United States can't afford it.

"The single most important federal program dealing with

children," writes Senator Moynihan of New York, "is the Aid to Families with Dependent Children program, provided under Title IV of the Social Security Act. For this reason, the most radical change the Reagan administration has proposed in existing social programs is to abolish Title IV and, under the rubric of the 'new federalism,' to turn the care of dependent children over to those states that give a damn—and to those states that don't."

Moynihan, who was a welfare policy official in the Kennedy, Johnson, and Nixon administrations, says new data indicate that one-third of all children born in America during 1980 will likely spend some time on welfare before reaching the age of 18. This fact, he writes, "shows that the descent into welfare dependency is so chronic a condition that how we deal with it can legitimately be thought of as the question of how the nation will care for its children." In his view, "the federal government should bear the cost of income maintenance for dependent children, much as it does for the dependent aged."

Reagan first proposed that states be permitted to require that AFDC recipients enter "workfare," working for public agencies; his budgeteers thought this would save $1 billion of the $8 billion program as people dropped out rather than work for no pay except their welfare checks. He also initiated a series of technical changes designed to reduce benefits and drop 10 percent of the beneficiaries: persons in about 4 million households were receiving benefits, but this declined by 900,000 persons in 1982. Then, however, the rolls began growing again, perhaps because of the recession. Reagan's 1982 cuts ended AFDC support and medicaid in most states for a mother of three who earned as much as $5,000 a year.

On his second run at the program, Reagan proposed changes that he estimated would reduce costs a stunning 28 percent, from $7.6 billion to $5.5 billion. He advocated, for example, making workfare mandatory; reducing payments to reflect aid received for buying fuel; rounding benefits down to the next lowest dollar; reducing benefits to recipients who receive income from public programs for crippled children. And he wanted to reduce or end benefits for another 700,000 beneficiaries. Generally Congress balked this time, although it made some smaller cuts. So he was back a third time, not only to make workfare mandatory but to end AFDC benefits once children reach 16 (the present cutoff age is 18). Given Reagan's reelection and a more willing Congress, there is no telling what would happen to this program that is now the principal source of income for 4 million families.[15]

Reagan's "workfare" failed in California, but he has pushed it nationwide anyway. In his home state an official review of the program published by a state agency in his government concluded that it did "not appear to be administratively feasible or practical." At the peak year of the program in California, 183,000 people were eligible for "workfare," but only 4,760 of them were assigned jobs. Following Reagan's lead about two-thirds of the states have made cautious, limited experiments in requiring welfare recipients to work for nothing except their welfare checks. In West Virginia, for instance, 4,000 people were so entailed, and four months into the Georgia experiment 120 people were working for their welfare payments (out of 237,000 on welfare in that state).

The *Atlanta Constitution* said editorially: " 'Workfare' provides neither job placement nor skills training at a time of skyrocketing unemployment. It is rather a system of forced labor, dreamed up by people who persist against all reason in attributing unemployment to sheer laziness, in which those who are unable to find 'real' employment are assigned to menial, make-work tasks in which they receive no wages, pensions, health insurance, grievance procedures, collective bargaining, workmen's compensation benefits—and no support in finding real jobs."[16] In fact the Reaganists advanced workfare as a substitute for job training. His first year Reagan killed off demonstration projects to help welfare recipients find jobs in fourteen cities, and his 1983 budget proposed to replace training and job placement for AFDC recipients with workfare.

In determining to cut welfare benefits for the working poor the Reaganists were enacting what they took to be a reform of an injustice that had long irritated Reagan. "Working welfare families," Stockman said, "are almost always better off than those employed in the same job who have never been on welfare." The first-year budget proposed to reduce the spendable income of a working welfare mother in New York to only $15 a month more than a nonworking welfare mother. According to a university study of the second-year budget, if fully enacted it would have caused working welfare mothers to have less money than non-working welfare mothers in 24 of the 48 states that were in-included in the study. For welfare families with earnings, as a result of congressional enactments, disposable income for a sin-gle parent with two children declined in every state in 1982 (in Connecticut, from $731 to $534 a month; in Louisiana, from $449 to $371). The U.S. Civil Rights Commission said in the spring of 1983 that welfare recipients in thirteen states lost money if they went to work.

"You will make a mother choose between her children and her job," Moynihan berated Secretary Schweiker. "You really like to abuse these people, don't you?" California's Representa-tive Waxman said the policy "discourages people from the work incentive." Congressman Gonzalez of San Antonio said: "They're hitting the working poor who were getting food stamps—they've made them actually cut out working and get on the full 100 percent rolls."

The administration argued that its policy was vindicated by a study that was presented as representative of the 237,000 fami-lies with earnings who had been removed from the welfare rolls as a result of the 1982 budget. In 40 counties and 27 states, the study found that of the working people dropped from welfare from October 1981 to April 1982, about 15 percent, one in seven, were back on the welfare rolls in September 1982. This, however, showed that although about 45,000 of them had sunk back into welfare, most working people prefer to work; it did not show that the denial of their welfare benefits had not hurt them. The study granted that (since most of the families had lost medi-caid as well as AFDC) their medical needs "may not be met." Nevertheless, Reagan's special assistant for welfare, Robert Carleson, taught the moral: "They are removed from depen-dency."[17]

In 1974, under Nixon, Congress established the Legal Services Corporation (LSC), which provides 85 percent of the money for local legal-aid clinics for the poor. Remembering Reagan's trouble in California with CRLA, it was no surprise that he proposed total abolition of the federal program to help the poor use the courts. Congress refused, but gave him a cut from $321 million to $241 million, forcing the departure of a fourth of the lawyers from the program and the closing of 300 field offices. Unable to kill LSC outright, Reagan tried to take it over with appointees who were basically opposed to its work and indeed, its existence, but in a running and bruising fight Congress kept the wrecking crew at bay. The moderate columnist David Broder exclaimed: "I find it shameful that in a $750 billion budget, Reagan would propose the total elimination of the legal services program that, in my experience, is the first and only guarantee many people have found for securing the law's protection against those who chisel and prey on the poor and helpless. The $150 million cost of that program is the price of 10 of the newest armored attack helicopters. . . ." The director of the Los Angeles County and Beverly Hills bar associations' project to enlist lawyers for the poor, Cheryl Mason, told the *Wall Street Journal*: "I think the great tragedy will be silent. People will take default judgments, they'll lose their jobs, or their houses. It's not as though people will line up at our door and say, 'Give us legal services; we're suffering.' They will simply suffer."[18]

Gradually a network of federal laws and regulations has been developed to assist physically disabled people, mentally retarded adults, and neglected children. For two years, the administration made plans to reduce requirements that federal grant recipients accommodate the physically disabled in the construction of new facilities. Proposals of the Office of Management and Budget, leaked to the press, stated that in some cases the recipients of grants could weigh the cost of accommodation against the "social value" of the handicapped person concerned. Organizations of the disabled rallied and lobbied; the administration dropped the effort.[19]

Federally sustained social services for the disabled, retarded adults, and neglected children include vocational rehabilitation, day care, Head Start (to give poor children a preschool boost), local nutrition programs and social services for the elderly, family planning for the poor, and programs to help abused children, battered spouses, pregnant teenagers, and disoriented older widows. Reagan proposed to bunch forty such programs into one block grant to the states and cut them a fourth. Congress block-granted only two of the programs to the states, but cut them overall a fifth. For 1983 Reagan was back asking for a new 38 percent cut. While Head Start was spared, he wanted to cut community services 83 percent. The Urban Institute, taking Texas as an example of the impact of the cuts, said that the child day-care case load there dropped about 8,800 children in 1982 (from 47,000) and the child welfare cuts eliminated services to more than 40,000 Texas children who were at high risk of abuse and neglect or were unmarried, school-age parents. Late in 1982 the Children's Defense Fund said that 2 million of the 3 million seriously disturbed children in the United States under the age of 18 are not receiving social services.[20]

Reagan and his men point out that the safety nets erected by the New Deal and the Great Society are still there in the great ring of the national circus: Social Security, AFDC, food stamps, medicaid, medicare, and in this they are, after all, correct. The question, however, is, would the nets still be there if Reagan could work his will on the Congress? His direction has never changed: reduce, phase out, fold under, cut, cut, cut, and but for the Democratic House how much faster might he have moved—and how much more radically? Re-elected with, say, a Republican House as well as a strengthened Senate majority, Reagan and his men well might strike down the programs they despise as deftly and as suddenly as circus roustabouts who, acting together at a sign, collapse the real safety nets to the sawdust floor.

Housing, Education, and Health; Workers and Farmers

Although the fact is not broadly understood, Reagan has halted and reversed forty years of federal aid to the construction of housing for the poor. In plain magnitude this may affect the poor more than all the welfare cuts. At the same time, Reagan has begun to dismantle the celebrated federal mortgage programs that have subsidized home ownership for the middle class.

The American dream of self-reliant families that own their own homes has dissolved since World War II. The private housing industry has failed to continue providing new homes in a price range which average people can afford. The federal government's programs have mitigated the housing problems of the poor to a limited extent, but Congress would never spend

enough money to solve these problems. Most new families starting out cannot buy homes in the U.S. any more, and for the first
time since 1940 the rate of home ownership is dropping. Reagan
is aware of these developments. "What has happened to that
American dream of owning a home?" he asked in his first economic address as President. "Fewer than 1 out of 11 families can
afford to buy their first new home." But it is his position that this
is the fault of the government, not of private industry.

Two decades ago, for a time, he held that public housing was
needed although people with better-than-average incomes
should not be permitted to live in it. However, his position hardened. "Public housing . . . cannot be the answer," he said in
1967. He believes that federal housing programs have failed by
drying up private low-cost housing. He also complains, inaccurately but with some justification, that government-supported
housing has benefited "only the upper middle class." But nothing else so pungently conveys his personal attitude toward federal housing programs as his occasional references to the White
House as "public housing."

What, then, is his plan to revive the dream? Basically he says
let's free the private housing industry of regulation and give it
another chance. Roll back regulations that impede building
houses, deregulate lending institutions, bring down interest
rates, open national forests to timber harvesting to lower the cost
of lumber, provide tax incentives to encourage investment in
home construction. He ordered changes in federal regulations
to free billions of dollars in pension funds for residential construction.[1] Meanwhile he is destroying federal housing programs.

About 9 million families qualify for federal housing assistance now, but only about 3.4 million receive it; Reagan's presidential commission on housing estimated that as of 1977, 5.6
million families lived in inadequate housing. Carter had proposed a housing budget of $29 billion for 1982; Reagan cut it to
$18 billion. That just gives a hint of the havoc.

Carter wanted to authorize 260,000 new subsidized housing
units for the poor (the program inaugurated in 1975 as the
Section 8 rent subsidy program); Reagan cut this by 45,000 units
and argued for the total elimination of the program. For 1983,

New York State Commissioner of Housing Richard A. Berman charged that Reagan "proposed to renege on the federal government's commitment to allocate $12 billion over the next thirty years to support low- and moderate-income housing programs under the Section 8 program." Landlords of housing constructed with the Section 8 subsidies were to be permitted to ask the government to end the subsidies and then to raise their rents—in effect simply throwing out the poor.

Rents in public housing were raised from 25 percent of tenants' income to 30 percent at Reagan's behest. Reagan also proposed to raise the rents even more for the poorest of the poor in these units by counting 30 percent of the food stamps they receive as part of their income on the basis of which their rents would be computed. This Congress would not do, but Reagan tried for it again for 1984. There are 2.4 million families living in these units; their incomes average less than $6,000 a year. Reagan also obtained a reduction in the fuel assistance program, which subsidizes fuel purchases for poor families, from $2 billion to $1.3 billion in 1983, and he sought another cut of one-third for 1984.

The administration declared that the government would no longer finance construction or major rehabilitation of subsidized housing for the poor and dropped the $17 billion program for this from its 1983 budget. "Democrats and liberals believe you should build new semiluxury buildings for poor people," said Reagan's Deputy Federal Housing Commissioner Philip Abrams. "They would rather see everybody in brand-new semi-luxury units. . . ." Reagan set a goal of reducing the number of Americans in subsidized housing by 300,000 by 1985. Under the Reaganists' plans, according to Cushing N. Dolbeare, president of the National Low-Income Housing Coalition, "once the units authorized under the Carter administration are built and occupied, there will be no additions to the supply of low-income housing." The general manager of the New York City Housing Authority, John Simon, said: "It seems they have declared World War III on public housing." The authority's chairman, Joseph J. Christian, added: "I think they're trying to eliminate government's responsibility for housing, period." After a number of false starts, HUD came forth with a new accounting system that would reduce the money spent on major repairs and daily maintenance at the public housing developments.

Reagan took out after the federal housing program for the rural poor, too, proposing to slash funding through the Farmers Home Administration from $3.7 billion to $1.1 billion—a two-thirds cut. He would reduce the number of rural home owner-ship loans from 90,000 to 3,000; low-income repair loans from $24 million to $1 million; rural rental housing aid from $940 million to $16 million.

As if to make sure that there won't be much low-rent housing left anywhere, Reagan's presidential commission on housing proposed to end rent control laws and to deny the right of local governmental authorities to control rents on any properties fi-nanced by federally insured or guaranteed mortgages.

The only substantial federal housing programs which Secre-tary Pierce succeeded in preserving from the devastation were community development block grants, which fund sewer sys-tems and parks, and urban development action grants, which pay for hotels, shopping centers, and other commercial projects. Even these were to be broken free of federal oversight to make sure that the welfare of the poor is taken into account.

With much fanfare the administration advanced its plan to replace the federal programs with a rent voucher system under which the poor would get vouchers they could use to pay their landlords. This was quickly and easily identified as part of Reagan's scheme to abolish the established federal programs. The much cheaper system of rent stamps would do nothing to increase the supply of low-rent housing; according to the Urban Institute, the voucher program would reduce rent subsidies to participants, "over time possibly dramatically."

Probably Reagan's most radical housing initiative is implied (though not yet declared) in his meat-cleaver approach to the two programs for federally supported home mortgages. Late in 1981 he ordered federal agencies to cut Government National Mortgage Association (Ginnie Mae) support for home loans by $16 billion, or 25 percent. For 1983 he proposed to cut proper-ties financed through Ginnie Mae from $64 billion to $38 billion, to eliminate the interest-rate ceiling for Federal Housing Authority loans (which would eliminate the reason for such loans' existence), and to cut new Farmers Home Administration loans 58 percent. The Urban Institute report concluded that Reagan probably wants to abolish the Federal Housing Authority and Ginnie Mae altogether—a step, the report added, that would most hurt people whose ability to buy homes is marginal.

In 1982, led on the issue by Republican Senator Richard Lugar of Indiana, Congress voted to subsidize home mortgages with $3 billion in a five-year plan to reduce interest rates on such mortgages by up to four percentage points. Reagan denounced "multibillion dollar bailout schemes" and vetoed the bill. Despite Lugar's contention that each billion spent on such subsidies would build 400,000 new homes and put 700,000 people back to work, the House fell seventeen votes short of overriding the veto.

All this was going on as Congress also freed savings and loan associations from regulations that had made these institutions the primary source of home loans. Late in 1982 the chairman of the U.S. League of Savings Associations, Leonard Shane, was impelled to cry out: "We are in the process of dismantling the finest housing delivery system in the world, and we are doing it without any debate on what will replace it."[2]

Federal aid to education has been wicked in Reagan's ideology for two decades. "A nationalized school system . . . is the entire basis for the federal aid program," he declaimed in 1962. On the same reasoning he condemned the National Defense Education Act of 1958, the forerunner of later federal programs for education.

Judging from his California record he is hostile, not toward adequate funding for education, but toward *federal* funding for it. During his eight years in Sacramento spending for secondary and elementary schools went up 89 percent, compared to the antecedent administration's 71 percent. In 1969, however, he vetoed bills to help the gifted children of poor families and to raise the minimum salaries of teachers.

Similarly, higher education spending in California increased 136 percent during his years, compared to a 100 percent increase in all state spending. Funding doubled for the state university system and tripled for the state colleges; scholarships and loans rose by a multiple of nine. However, Reagan breached the state's tradition of free higher education: he requested the inauguration of college tuition and obtained what in effect amounted to the same thing, a doubling of student fees. He vetoed college grants for poverty-area youths and a 10 percent pay raise for university faculty.

His substantial role in the firing of the chief of the university system, Clark Kerr, and his superheated rhetoric against the student demonstrations made Reagan unpopular in some academic circles. When University of California regent Fred Dutton accused him of using the board of regents for political purposes, reporters heard the governor replying, "You're a liar. You're a liar. You're a lying son of a bitch." Kerr's successor, Charles Hatch, said near the end of Reagan's period in Sacramento: "On balance the Reagan impact has been quite negative. We have had eight years of inadequate budget in maintenance, libraries, and research support. Even more important . . . he adopted an adversary stance toward the university. And this resulted in bitterness and missed opportunities."

Some of his attitudes toward universities were philistine. He said he would not ask taxpayers to help "subsidize intellectual curiosity" in the universities. (A professor at UCLA asked "What the hell does he think a university is all about?") In 1976 Reagan contended that corporations should be allowed to influence the direction of university research which they pay for. "The intellectuals for some time have been antibusiness," he said. "They're more than willing to take the money business makes for university endowments and research grants. But if a businessman wants to suggest how his money might be used, he's violating 'academic freedom.' How gauche and uncivilized of him! . . . [Businessmen] deserve to be listened to by the so-called intellectuals."

On radio Reagan opposed the creation of the U.S. Department of Education. He perceived the new agency as a mere creature of what he regards as the left-wing National Education Association (NEA), which is of course the dominant organization in U.S. education. The creation of the department,

Reagan said, "means, of course, federal regulation of our schools under the domination of the National Education Association, which is in truth a very powerful union. . . . The National Education Association has a long-standing dream of a federal school system with everything from curriculum to textbooks dictated by Washington." What the NEA and others really seek, he said, is "a nationalized school system." In his 1980 campaign he advocated the abolition of the department and the transfer of federal education programs to states and local districts, along with the tax resources to pay for them.[3] It took a while for people to realize what his proposals of this kind meant, but in the case of education Congress caught on during his first year in Washington.

Federal education programs, which began to be enacted in force under President Johnson's leadership, were working. Programs for disadvantaged children in the primary and secondary schools had been clearly shown to be increasing children's reading and mathematics proficiencies. In 1960 only 41 percent of American children had finished high school, but by 1980, 66 percent had. Dramatic progress was being made among minorities. In 1960 only 20 percent of blacks had finished high school; by 1980 more than half the blacks, 51 percent, were high school graduates. Studies by the College Entrance Examination Board showed that minorities had been closing the racial gap in Scholastic Aptitude Test scores since 1976.

Reagan asked Congress to merge the federal education programs for disadvantaged, handicapped, bilingual, and other special children into two block grants and to reduce the money a fourth. He also wanted cuts of 20 to 25 percent in other programs—vocational education and aid to federally impacted areas—and by 1986 he wanted overall federal aid to education cut in two. For 1982 alone he asked for a 33 percent cut; while balking on the major block grant, Congress gave him a 26 percent cut. But when he came back the next year for another 30 percent cut Congress began to ignore him. His education budgets became, in fact, almost irrelevant: by 1983 the actual budget for the Department of Education was $15 billion compared to his request for $10 billion. His plan to abolish the department (replacing it with a foundation which would have no civil rights enforcement powers) got nowhere. When the department under Secretary Bell announced regulations to loosen present requirements that the nation's 4 million handicapped children be given mainstream education where that is feasible, the Senate by a vote of 93–4 ordered the department to hold up the new rules, and two months later Bell withdrew them.

Concerning higher education, Reagan seemed to be acting on the belief of Martin Feldstein that "we probably induce too many people to go on to college." In the stated reasoning of Reagan's chief economist, college students "acquire no particularly useful technical skills, but they think of themselves as not in the technician class but in the more status-carrying management, sales group. I don't think fifteen years ago I would ever have thought that I would be saying there's too much higher education. Yet look at what has actually happened as a result of government subsidies."

The system of Pell grants, initiated under Nixon for disadvantaged college students, inevitably attracted Reagan's interest. By late 1981 he had proposed reducing the 2.7 million students who receive them by 750,000; by 1983 he wanted to cut the program in half. Congress was providing interest-rate subsidies for Guaranteed Student Loans for students while they were in college; Reagan proposed to do away with these, and Congress gave him a fee students must pay which in effect halved them. For 1984 he wanted to subject all Guaranteed Student Loans to a means test and to require Pell grant recipients (which he had given up trying to cut) to first pay 40 percent of their education costs after taking family contributions into account. The administration cut off student aid to about 400 or 500 proprietary schools because more than 25 percent of their students were delinquent in repaying their loans.

The consequences for college-age students are hard to quantify, but there were some signs. Harvard noted a drop in new applications from poor families, Wesleyan decided to resume rejecting students because they cannot afford full tuition, first-year enrollment at forty-two historically black colleges dropped 12 percent in 1982, and education writers reported that colleges and universities have returned to granting student aid more on the basis of scholastic merit than on need. Former Democratic U.S. Senator Ralph Yarborough of Texas, who was a leader in the enactment of most of the federal education legislation, predicted that after four years of Reagan, "they will have ripped off aid to higher education." In 1983, as the country became alarmed by a serious shortage of math and science teachers, Reagan—responding to both the economic and the military implications—proposed a small federal program to stimulate their training. But otherwise it was his whole tendency to cut federal aid to public education.

By contrast he championed such help for private schools. He would give up to $300 a year in tax credits ($500 if Congress would have it) to families that pay tuition to private elementary and secondary schools. This would cost the Treasury billions, but for some reason that particular fact does not concern the President. Friends of the public schools who suspect on the whole record that he is seeking to build up the private schools at the expense of the public system are correct. If there was much doubt of it, he dispelled it in 1983 when he proposed to replace the effective Title I (now Chapter 1) aid program for disadvantaged children with a school stamp program. The money that now goes to public school districts for programs to help the poor children would go instead to the parents of the children as vouchers which they could "spend" at schools of their choice, public or private.[4] One may reasonably and fairly anticipate that this voucher system, like food stamps and housing vouchers under Reagan's ministrations, would reduce aid for the poor in the schools.

If anything worries the average American more than housing and education, it is probably health, and in this realm, too, Reagan opposes government programs. In the sixties he crusaded against the enactment of medicare. From the White House he advanced his program to curb it hesitantly, but suddenly burst forth into the open on the subject in 1983. From the first he worked at reducing medicaid for the poor, and with some success.

Medicare, Reagan said during the great debate on it, would

"force into a compulsory program all citizens of this country regardless of whether they are protected by insurance, have their own savings, or are blessed with an income." For the American Medical Association he recorded a speech against medicare which the association sent out to be played at meetings in what it called its "Operation Coffee Cup." On radio in 1979 he disparaged "medicaid and medicare and several other health programs, all of which constitute a gigantic wasteful government medical monopoly." He opposed the idea of national health insurance as "compulsory socialized medicine."

Some of his administration's proposals on medicare in 1983 were prefigured in his prepresidential notions. In California he proposed a plan to withhold $3 a month from everyone's paycheck to pay for buying everyone private-company insurance policies for protection against the costs of catastrophic illness. Closer to his presidency he proposed: "Let government approve a certain bracket of insurance policies with the private companies" and then pay the insurance premiums for poor people.

Reagan's complaints about waste and fraud in government medical programs were borne out after the 1980 election by a report from the House Select Committee on Aging which charged that medicare was losing about $2 billion a year in fraud and was paying less than 40 percent of the average beneficiary's medical bills. One common scam was the provision of unnecessary services, matched to cash kickbacks for doctors and the operators of nursing homes. A spokesman for the FBI said: "Corruption has permeated virtually every area of the medicare and medicaid health care industry."

But using private companies has its problems, too. Dr. Lester Breslow was the state health director in California until Reagan fired him. In 1975, when he was dean of the School of Public Health at UCLA, Breslow testified that profit-making health companies took, for administrative expenses and profit, more than half of the state and federal funds they received to provide health care to the poor in California, and the care they provided was lower in quality than that available elsewhere.[5]

Enacted in 1965 under Johnson, medicare is a national system of medical care for 26 million older persons and 3 million disabled ones. Its cost in 1983 was running at $57 billion a year. Part of the Social Security system, it covers everyone over 65 (like the system's retirement benefits it is insurance, not welfare). By 1983 the attack on medicare, orchestrated from Reagan's White House, seemed to be merely a continuation of his war on Social Security.

Medical costs have been rising out of control—11 percent in 1982, three times the (now much reduced) rate of inflation— and unless the system's income is increased *or benefits are cut,* the relevant trust fund will not be able to pay all of medicare's bills by the end of the decade. The situation is ready-made for Reagan's budgeteers. Outcries of "crisis" began to be heard in 1982, and only an aroused House of Representatives prevented Reagan from cutting medicare $5 billion for 1983.

For 1984 Reagan proposed to sharply increase the cost of medicare to patients. His main change was camouflaged by its linkage with a new plan to provide catastrophic health insurance for about 170,000 patients a year. The main cut, which would affect about 7 million medicare patients, would increase the patient's cost for an average hospital stay by 80 percent (from $350 to $630 for less than two weeks). Monthly medicare premiums, which now cover 25 percent of program costs, would be increased to 35 percent. Payments to doctors would be frozen, "saving" $6 billion in five years, but the doctors could pass on to patients some or all of the charges for which they are not reimbursed (as the Urban Institute's report said doctors usually do). Reagan asked Congress to abolish a program under which physicians evaluate the quality of care provided by their peers in the government health programs. Moreover, he proposed to make medicare "voluntary" by giving patients vouchers with which they could buy private health insurance in place of medicare. It seemed likely that Congress would adopt a flat-fee system he proposed to contain hospital costs in 467 categories of treatment, but as for the rest it was the Social Security fight all over again. Senator Max Baucus (D.–Mont.) said the 1983 proposals could "cut the heart out of medicare benefits" for millions of old people.

Medicaid, of course, is the program to provide medical care for the poor. His first year Reagan sought a medicaid cut that would have amounted to 19 percent by the fifth year. Congress gave him, not that, but overall cuts of 4.5 percent in federal medicaid payments to the states. For 1983 Reagan proposed to pass more medicaid costs to the states by refusing to pay them for payments made in error; to permit the states to require the parents of medicaid patients in nursing homes to help pay their costs (a requirement for which there is no authorization in federal law); and to charge $1 and $2 fees to the poor for various medical services to deter them from seeking treatment frivolously.

In general Congress resisted Reagan on medicaid, although changes made have reduced federal spending for the program by about $1 billion a year. However, according to the Children's Defense Fund, in the eighteen months after mid-1981 every state reduced health services for poor people. Almost 700,000 children lost medicaid coverage, and the cuts in community health centers cost 725,000 people medical services. In forty-four states prenatal and delivery services for pregnant women and preventive health services for women of childbearing age and for infants and children were reduced; in twenty-seven states services for crippled children were reduced.

There were cuts for other federal health programs. The administration proposed to reduce medicare payments to clinics for kidney dialysis and announced that it was simply stopping all federal grants and loans to health maintenance organizations. The Mental Health Systems Act, which required states to spend money on specified mental health programs, disappeared into one of Reagan's block grants. In 1982 the administration tried to cut the federal program for children's immunizations by about a third, driving Nancy Amidei, director of the Food and Research Action Center, to the blackest humor: "Reagan admires Franklin Roosevelt, who was a cripple, so what more fitting way to honor FDR's centennial than to bring back polio?"

At present workers do not pay income taxes on their employers' contributions to their private health insurance. One might presume that as an advocate of private enterprise Reagan would be seeking to expand the purview of private medical coverage. But the deficit was still mounting, and in 1983 the administration proposed—as a means, it said, of discouraging the overuse of health care—that workers start paying taxes on employer health insurance contributions that exceed $2,100 a year for a family. An increase in the tax burden of about 16.5 million workers, this would mean that a family of four with $25,000 taxable income and health benefits worth $4,100 would pay $500 more in tax.[6]

Reagan's austerity placed serious pressures on the budgets of the states and on state and local tax bases. Funding for mass transit was in short supply; states were cutting services and raising taxes. The President's ballyhooed "New Federalism" proposals, with which he had diverted attention from the cruelties of his 1983 budget, came to naught because the states feared they would be shortchanged—saddled with more services to deliver and unable to pay for them. His emphasis on voluntarism— his appeals to people to increase their charitable contributions— evoked assertions from corporate and religious leaders that there was just no way they could make up for the federal cuts, and the Reagans' own example, giving not 10 but 2 or 3 percent to charity, hardly set the pace.

As Reagan cut federal programs for the poor and the middle class, unemployment rose to the highest levels since the Great Depression. In December 1982 the rate was 10.8 percent. Twelve million Americans were classified as out of work, an additional 1.6 million were also out of work but were not counted on the odd ground that they were so discouraged they had stopped looking for jobs, and another 6.5 million were working shorter weeks than they wanted. Among blacks the unemployment rate was 20.2 percent, double the general rate; among teenagers it was 24 percent. The "full-time job deficit"— the number of people who were available to fill jobs that were nowhere to be had—was about 15 million. The United States had seen nothing like this since the spring of 1941, just before World War II ended the unemployment of the Depression.[7]

For the unemployed worker—and for the person on the job but afraid of losing it—Ronald Reagan was the wrong man in the wrong place at the wrong time.

Many economists now seriously fear that capitalist economies may have fallen into a chronic alternation between inflation and unemployment whereby one can be relieved only by increasing the other. Reagan was bringing down inflation as he had promised, but the cost turned out to be an appalling waste of productive potential that could never be recovered in the lives of the jobless or the prosperity of the nation. Democrats had long accused Republicans of conspiring to raise unemployment in order to weaken workers' security and to strengthen corporations against unionism, but in the jujitsu of politics the Republicans' 1980 platform had proclaimed: "Our party specifically rejects the philosophy of the Carter administration that unemployment is the answer to inflation." With unemployment skyrocketing from Carter's already high 7.4 percent and with public anxiety about it high, Reagan sympathized copiously with the jobless and asked them to wait for the rising water that would lift all the boats, but he had set down his attitudes on the subject long before.

On the radio in 1978 Reagan said people who had been polled "no longer consider unemployment a top priority." Inflation was first, while "Unemployment is down with the also rans," and in this judgment, Reagan said, "the people are right."

He persistently depreciates the seriousness of unemployment figures. Many of the 6 million shown to be unemployed in 1978, he said then, were "first-time job seekers," and the figure included "even more who are voluntarily unemployed. And it is estimated that possibly 2 million . . . are working for cash to avoid taxes."

As President he downplayed the figures by a reference to the entrance of many women into the job market; this was not a new idea in his mind. Originally, he said on radio in another late-1978 broadcast, the government's unemployment index "was used to measure one thing: the number of unemployed male adult heads of households," but the current index considered also "those who hold second jobs, officially retired people, and a good many young adults. . . . I think it's time to concentrate on the heads of households."

Generally Democrats had sought to define full employment

as 4 percent unemployment (this being regarded in the consensus as a liberal position). Reagan said the Kennedy administration had created "an illusion . . . that 4 percent was full employment," where in fact, he argued, three-fourths of the 4 percent may be accounted for by normal turnover, leaving only 1 percent actually unemployed. Reagan would also, he said, subtract from the unemployment total "the number of jobs that are open. Many jobs go begging because there's no penalty for being unemployed. . . . Today welfare says we can't make people move to find jobs: we've got to bring the jobs to them." Discussing jobs called menial, Reagan said, "Maybe we need to get back to the Depression mentality, where there were no menial jobs. A job was a job, and anyone who got one felt lucky."

As if obligingly to confirm liberals' darkest suspicions, Reagan in his 1976 campaign book said:

"The main reason we don't reduce the national debt, the main reason we have government-produced inflation, is that no politician can stand up to an increase in unemployment. . . . Several economists—hard-headed ones who aren't afraid to draw unpopular conclusions from logic and history—have said that higher unemployment is the necessary evil we must face if we are going to stop inflation. If it is . . . I'm confident [the American people] will be able to bear the burden."

Feldstein, President Reagan's top economist, has indeed argued that to end inflation there might have to be unemployment for as long as six years. "The current recession," Feldstein said in March 1982, "is an unavoidable cost of slowing inflation." Indeed, defeatism about unemployment characterizes Reagan and his administration. "We have to realize," the President said, "that we actually only solved unemployment by way of World War II." His 1984 budget assumed the jobless rate would not go below 10 percent until well into 1984. Treasury Secretary Regan said that a rate of 6 to 6.5 percent "is permanent." Feldstein told the public that it would take five or six years to bring the rate down to 6 or 7 percent and that 6 to 6.5 percent is "full employment."[8]

Reagan supports unemployment compensation for "the legitimate worker," but not for people who quit their jobs or are fired. In 1966 in California he said jobless benefits were being used "to provide benefits for those who quit voluntarily or are fired for legitimate cause," as well as to augment the earnings of those in seasonal jobs, providing "prepaid vacations for a segment of society which has made this a way of life." He sees the system as insurance against only "involuntary unemployment."

In 1981 at Reagan's request Congress sharply cut back unemployment benefits for the twenty-seventh through thirty-ninth weeks of unemployment. His most revealing proposal, though, was his request that Congress see to it that beginning in 1983, after three months of regular unemployment insurance workers would be required to look for jobs that paid less than their previous work. Under the present system they can refuse positions that are not comparable with what they did before. The association in his mind between unemployment compensation and shiftlessness was vividly obvious in some remarks he ad libbed after his visit to Barbados and Jamaica during Easter 1982. "I am convinced they haven't been spoiled by as much welfare as we have in our country," he said of the residents of those islands. Some Californians, he added, prefer surfing to working and "have worked out a system where unemployment insurance could be manipulated to make it possible for them to do that a great deal of the time." As unemployment soared Congress was obliged to cover its and the President's tracks and restore the extended unemployment benefits, but this could not be done before many states had dropped them.[9]

In a second spectacular example of poor timing, Reagan killed a number of federal job programs in 1981. He persuaded Congress to cancel $1.2 billion in subsidies to state and local governments for the hiring of poor people under the Comprehensive Employment and Training Act. This $4 billion program was employing 306,000 people when Reagan came in, but soon closed. In 1980, 532,000 workers were receiving cash benefits because they had lost their jobs in part or wholly because of import competition. Reagan got Congress to cut this trade adjustment assistance program so sharply, it covered only 29,000 workers in 1982. Reagan and Congress totally shut down the Youth Adult Conservation Corps, which in 1980 had provided jobs for 60,000 young people aged sixteen to twenty-three.

In 1982 he asked Congress to slash the Job Corps residential training program for the poor by a third. He vetoed a job program for 60,000 elderly workers, but Congress overrode the veto.[10]

Reagan's contention that much unemployment is voluntary may derive from the convictions of his long-time adviser Feldstein, who believes that unemployment compensation has led to unemployment by making joblessness less painful financially. Feldstein wants unemployment compensation taxed to discourage voluntary unemployment, and shortly after he became Reagan's top economist precisely this idea was floated into the press by high administration officials. Taxing jobless benefits, press aide Larry Speakes explained to a public appalled by rising unemployment, would be intended "to make it less attractive to stay out of work." Other unnamed officials said current benefits may be too "lucrative" for some people. As it happened the idea was suggested on Thanksgiving Day, and the outraged outcry in response quickly caused the administration to drop it amidst professions that Reagan had never even seen the paper on which it was proposed. Shocked by the revelation that in 1982 alone 11 million Americans had lost their health insurance (leading to estimates that 25 million people lacked health insurance because of unemployment), Congress moved to provide such benefits for the jobless, but quite predictably the administration, through Stockman, opposed any such program that would cost any federal money.[11]

The federal air controllers should have known that Reagan as governor had replaced striking workers on the California Water Project, but evidently they did not, and when they went out on an illegal strike in August 1981 he fired 11,400 of them and the administration stripped their union of its status as their bargaining agent. These highly trained professionals had been receiving an average of $33,000 a year, but confronted with Reagan's stubborn refusal to permit them to return to their jobs they took lower-paying work and started living on less. Meanwhile, according to Representative William D. Ford (D.–Mich.), Reagan's penny-pinching administration was spending more than $1 billion to train new controllers.[12]

In his autobiography Reagan presents himself as a hard-core

unionist. Ever since he joined the Screen Actors Guild, he wrote, "I have considered myself a rabid union man." His role in the settlement of a 1959 SAG strike has been a subject of some disagreement: whether, as he says, he won a victory for his members, or, as for example actor Gary Merrill believes, he "sold us down the river" for the benefit of the studios. Until 1976 Reagan favored the union shop (under the rules for which all workers at a jobsite must belong to the union if a majority of them vote for it), but that year he began to speak out for "right-to-work" bills that prohibit this arrangement. Only in the last month of his 1980 election campaign did he promise not to support a national "right-to-work" law. Neither, he added then, would he seek to make unions subject to antitrust laws. However, since without the weapon of the strike unions would be mere discussion clubs, Reagan's successful campaign as President to deny strikers food stamps may bear on his underlying attitudes toward unions, as well as toward welfare.[13]

Early in his campaign for President he staked out the implausible position that he favors the abolition of the minimum wage, and if he cannot get that he wants a lower minimum wage for young and old workers. ". . . The high unemployment of youth . . . is in large part due to the minimum wage," he said. "I think the minimum wage is not a blessing to needy people at all and could be eliminated. But at the very least if you can't force that through the stubborn proponents of the minimum wage at least then have a two-step minimum wage—a lower one for young people who are entering the work force for the first time. . . ." At a press conference he said, "The minimum wage has caused more misery and unemployment than anything since the Great Depression" and is not "much of an advantage to anyone anywhere."

His wish that his subminimum apply to older workers is also clear. "There are marginal jobs," he said, "that could be held by young people, or elderly people who cannot do a full day's work. And if you make the price for those jobs too high, the employer just cancels them out." Reagan also has in his mind some exemptions of employers' contributions to Social Security funds for teenage, and perhaps old-age, workers.

The minimum wage, $3.35 an hour since Jan. 1, 1981, is paid to about 5 million American workers. Another 4 million work legally at less than the minimum—high school and college students, workers in retail outlets, handicapped workers, domestic workers, and farm workers. Under an exemption for students created in 1961, retail places like fast-food chains can have up to six exempted students per workplace. Perhaps 1 million workers are paid less than the minimum wage illegally. But even for those paid less than the minimum, it is an important guidepost. All told, about one in ten American workers, about 10 million of the 105 million people in the civilian labor force—the poorest, the youngest, the oldest, the least skilled, the most handicapped—are directly affected by the minimum wage. Sar A. Levitan, an economist and director of the Center for Social Policy Studies at George Washington University, argues that while the minimum wage may have caused small employment losses, the increase in income for the working poor which the minimum wage requires has more than compensated for the lost jobs. Levitan argues that a minimum wage for many workers is an alternative to welfare.

In his 1983 budget message Reagan proposed to reduce the minimum wage to $2.50 an hour for summer jobs for teenagers which the government finances. One could assume, from the broad applicability of his reasoning, that this was a foot in the door, for he said: "Inexperienced youth cannot produce enough of value to make it worthwhile for employers to pay them the full minimum wage during short periods of employment." Or, as he put it while on the stump in Pittsburgh in April 1983 (where the unemployment rate was then 16 percent), employers "simply can't afford" to pay $3.35 an hour "to kids with no work experience."[14]

Other positions Reagan takes amount to antiunionism in construction work. His opposition to common-situs picketing bills led union forces, in realism, to abandon pursuit of their passage during his presidency. His stand against requiring the payment of prevailing wages on federally assisted construction jobs has focused antiunion opposition to the Davis-Bacon Act, which requires that the prevailing wage rates be paid.

"The big international unions have wanted for a long time to eliminate any nonunion workers from construction jobs," Reagan said on radio in 1975. "If the 'common situs' picketing bill passes . . . they'll get their way."

In 1976 a common-situs bill passed and Ford said he would sign it, but Reagan opposed that and Ford vetoed it instead. Reagan scored his party's President for appointing two secretaries of labor who favored both the common-situs idea and granting public employees the right to strike.

Attacking the Davis-Bacon Act during three broadcasts in 1978 and 1979, Reagan said its requirement that prevailing wages be paid "amounts to a sort of 'super-minimum wage.' . . . Because the 'prevailing wage' determinations are based mostly on union wage scales in large urban areas, the act tends to 'import' these high rates into rural areas where wages—and the cost of living—are lower. . . . Local contractors are often excluded. . . ."

Part of Reagan's October 1980 "switcheroo" to curry favor with union voters was a promise not to try to repeal Davis-Bacon. However, his administration tried to change rules so that prevailing wages would not be required on construction jobs outside of urban areas. Labor went to court and blocked these changes.[15]

With more than 13 million Americans actually out of work, Congress felt required to appear to do something. At first Reagan resisted, standing behind his standard rhetorical position that he opposes federal "makework" jobs. During the lame duck session Representative Conte of Massachusetts quoted the President telling congressional leaders, "I don't give a damn whether it's Friday night and the whole government is brought to a standstill, I will not sign a continuing resolution [to keep the government financed] with a jobs bill in it." Congress went ahead and appropriated about $4.4 billion (from the gasoline sales tax increase) for highway construction, which provided jobs for mostly male workers, and in 1983 passed another $4.6 billion "jobs bill" to create an estimated 400,000 public-service and public construction jobs. Reagan actually submitted to Congress a version of the second measure, so far was he in 1983 from persisting in his job-killing crusade of 1981.[16]

Government production controls and price supports for farm products—the New Deal programs for farmers—have provoked some of the purest free-market rhetoric of Reagan's career, but the farm belt votes Republican as a rule, and as Reagan approached the 1980 election his arguments took a wide meander. By 1983 he was conducting himself on these issues like a converted New Dealer.

When he was speaking for General Electric, he said: "Eighty percent of the farm economy is still out in the free market—regulated only by the law of supply and demand. Common sense would indicate the answer should be to get that subsidized 20 percent out into that same free market." Farmers had developed their craft to the point of genius and the thing to do was "turn this genius loose." The farm program "should be temporary and should be aimed at putting the entire farm economy back out into the free market." As governor he vetoed a bill he said would have let owners of cling-peach orchards in California keep anyone else from entering the business.

In 1967, though, and again in 1976, he said the farmers' return to freedom should not be too sudden: he favored "gradual elimination" of government supports. And 1980 was his color-changing time. In March he said: "The 100 percent of parity [price supports] . . . could create an enormous government subsidy, and my whole philosophy is I want to see farms out in the free market as much as it possibly can be." In April: government has an "obligation" to "provide a fair return" for the farmer. And on September 30, with the election fast approaching: "We will not turn our backs on programs that have sought to assure the farmer a reasonable income. . . . I believe improvements can be made without abandoning the programs that have proved themselves in the past."[17]

In 1981, the last year for which Carter was responsible, government farm subsidies cost $4 billion. They had never been higher than $6 billion a year. In 1982 under Reagan they not only broke the previous record, at $12 billion they doubled it. The administration then forecast that as a result of a voluntary production-limitation program which it had initiated among farmers, the government would pay out only $1.8 billion in farm subsidies in 1983. By the spring it had become clear that the outgo would reach ten times that, $18 billion, by the end of the fiscal year. The farmers were doing just what Reagan said they should, they were practicing their genius, but reduced demand abroad and reduced meat consumption at home were ruining farm prices, tripping off the payment of more government subsidies but also leading to farm foreclosures and a farm depression that an administration spokesman conceded was the worst since 1933. As the Farmers Home Administration tightened up on farmers' credit (part of the budget cutting), Reagan was sowing himself a political brier crop for 1984.

He made a hard run at the dairy industry's price subsidy, and the way things turned out was instructive. He succeeded in persuading Congress to hold the supports at 1980 levels through 1982, and he pushed a bill to give the secretary of agriculture absolute power to reduce milk price supports at will. But the administration's prediction that the $1.2 billion subsidy would fall to $509 million did not exactly turn out: Milk producers, responding to cheaper feed prices, produced more milk and the subsidy rose to $2.1 billion in 1982. Reagan persuaded Congress to charge the producers 50 cents per 100 pounds of milk every six months if production didn't go down; the fee began to be charged, and the farmers increased their production further to make up for the fee.

By November 1982 the U.S. owned 425 million pounds of butter, 883 million pounds of cheese, and 1.3 billion pounds of dried milk. The government has to pay the costs of storing these commodities, and in an act which no doubt took that into account but nevertheless ran counter to his budget cutting against the poor, Reagan authorized the distribution of 224 million pounds of these foods to poor Americans in 1982. Senator Dole came up with legislation in 1983 designed to make these giveaways permanent, administering them through charitable agencies at the level of $1 billion worth of surplus commodities every year. "Rather than pay millions of dollars on storage," he said, "it would be better to spend that money on distribution and processing." The administration resisted making the plan mandatory, but went along with the basic idea. Far from being able to return milk producers to the free market, the government under Reagan was institutionalizing the distribution of their price-supported surplus production to the poor.

Despite his uniform hostility toward trade with the Soviet Union, Reagan kept his word to the farmers and lifted Carter's partial embargo on grain sales to the Russians (who nevertheless reduced their purchases from the U.S.). He made the signing of long-term grain contracts with the Russians conditional on the reduction of the Soviet-induced repression of Solidarity in Poland, but still, in 1983 he announced that he would go along with legislation that would somewhat limit the President's power to use food exports as a weapon in foreign policy. He was walking a thin line with the farmers, and he knew it.

In April 1980, according to the *Greensboro Daily News* of tobacco-growing North Carolina, Reagan supported a rather specific exemption from his free-enterprise values: he favored tobacco price supports, which provide half a billion dollars of taxpayers' money each year to a closed monopoly of tobacco producers. Their champion, Reagan's fellow free-enterpriser Senator Helms, became somewhat unpopular personally in the Senate in 1982, and partially in consequence the tobacco lobby was barely able to fight off attempts to kill this subsidy.[18]

After two years of total failure in reducing farm price supports, Reagan decided to try out, not a new program, but one that had been first devised by the New Deal in 1933 to reduce the planting of cotton. "It's a crazy idea, but we've got to do something," Secretary of Agriculture Block said. In 1983 farmers are being given surplus grain, cotton, and rice from government storage bins in payment for removing from the production of grains and cotton any amount of their land that exceeds 20 percent of the acreage they usually plant in these crops. They can sell the commodities they receive from the government; they can feed the grain to their livestock. By the March deadline American farmers had signed up with the government not to plant more than 81 percent of the land they usually use for the target crops, a vast area of 186 million acres. While this looks free to the taxpayers and will help Stockman with his deficits, in fact Department of Agriculture officials admitted that the 1983

payment-in-kind (PIK) program could cost the taxpayers $9 bil-
lion in the market value of the federally owned commodities.[19]
But even though PIK was not original with Reagan, it was a
refreshing change because it was a positive attempt to solve a
problem.

"I've always thought," Reagan has said, "that the best thing
government can do is nothing." The California political publicist
Bill Roberts has said, "Reagan has a little blank spot, a fatal flaw.
He never initiated anything." He is said to have once joked with
a California legislator, "I look at everything with an open mind
before I vote no." Men around him now jest that they're not his
yes men—when he says no, they say no. His negativism runs
deep and controls his entourage. "I used to fantasize," Reagan
said in 1979, "what it would be like if everyone in government
would quietly slip away and close the doors and disappear. . . .
I think that life would go on . . . and we would get along a lot
better than we think."[20]

He looks upon civil servants as a class and holds them in
contempt. The 1.2 million federal "bureaucrats" are, after all,
just citizens who work for the government, but they have been
for the President a target almost as vulnerable as the working
poor. He has squeezed their pay and their pension programs,
and he has reduced their numbers by attrition and outright
dismissals. While this must please all foes of big government, it
can hardly enhance the quality of government service.

He would, in fact, abolish much of that service altogether.
Under the rubric of "privatization" he celebrates the sale to private businesses of such municipal services as trash collection,
some police work, street maintenance, and fire fighting.[21] During his presidency private companies have entered the rocket
business, which has heretofore been a government monopoly.
His administration has proposed to sell, not only millions of acres
of public land, but also some public housing developments and
the government's weather satellites, which, it is expected, might
well lead to commercialization of parts of the nation's weather
service. Of course he favors using the government to fight crime,
but his unyielding opposition to pistol control makes dramatic
reductions in violent crime unlikely during his tenure.

His crusades against certain kinds of government spending are not to be mistaken for a real crusade against big government. Like every President he has his priorities, and the battleships, intercontinental missiles and bombers, exotic command systems, chemical and biological weapons, and civil defense schemes which characterize his presidency have required the government to expand faster than it has in recent years. When he took office the federal budget was 23 percent of the gross national product. He said he was going to get it down to 19 percent by 1986. In 1983 it was 25 percent. His requested $849 billion for 1984 was $120 billion more than the government spent in 1982; Carter's last budget had called for $664 billion. On the radio in 1978, using the kind of simplification that made him President, Reagan complained that the government was spending "$57 million an hour round the clock every day including Sundays and holidays." In March 1983, after two years of Reaganism, the government was spending $93 million an hour. As Joseph D. Duffey, Carter's chief of the National Endowment for the Humanities, said, "This government is not reducing spending; what they're doing is going on a military binge."[22] The administration had billions for the overextended banks, but not for indigent pregnant women, billions for the military corporations, but not for the working poor, billions for the already rich, but not for federal aid to health and education. "We keep pointing out," said Dr. Eugene Bautilier of the Southern California Council of Churches, "that we're not experiencing budget cuts but budget transfers." Even after Carter became a born-again hawk, defense spending cost the taxpayers $133 billion in 1980, but for 1984 the total is about $230 billion. In real dollars military spending has grown 40 percent since 1980, and the new money comes from the taxpayers and from the budget cuts Reagan has made. In a speech in his home state of Oregon, Republican Senator Hatfield said exaggerated military spending is being authorized while "60 percent of the population living under the poverty line have no federal assistance for food, shelter, or clothing." Little wonder, then, that the public's response was not too kindly when Reagan showed off four pairs of new $1,000 boots that were embossed with the presidential seal in 14-karat gold, Mrs. Reagan presented herself in designer dresses, mink, and jewels, the secretary of commerce spent more than $118,000 to redecorate his office, and a foundation received the customary tax break as it gave $210,000 to pay for a 220-place setting of gold-bordered china for the White House.[23]

Like "the truly needy," "the safety net," and "the New Federalism," "Reaganomics" was a catch-phrase that missed. Although he subscribed to "supply-side economics," Reagan did not have a coherent economic theory, he just wanted to cut government benefit programs for the poor and middle class, lower taxes on the wealthy, and build up the nation's nuclear striking force. Like any politician he would blame inflation on Carter and the Democrats, he would deny responsibility for the deep recession that began in July 1981, he would take credit for plummeting inflation and interest rates, and he would lament the calamitous unemployment, but he was just as much at the mercy of unpredictable economic events as any stockbroker predicting the next turn in the Dow. If Reagan ran again many people would vote for or against him according to the state of the economy at the time, but that would happen just because people vote on that basis, not because it would be logical. Indeed, Reagan's spectacular failure to fulfill his vow to balance the budget could well be a main cause of economic recovery; Keynesians, out of fashion but not therefore wrong, have always contended (with various qualifications) that government deficits stimulate the economy.

The primary issue in all this is not how the economy is doing and why, but whether Reagan is mean. If one concludes that he is, then there must arise the question of what to think about the corporations, the party, and the politicians who have sustained and supported his election and his programs and who stand ready now to regroup into phalanxes to drive their Reaganism deeper and deeper into the body of humane government.

The question of meanness presents itself despite the abundant testimony and evidence that Reagan is a nice guy, amiable, good natured, quick with a jest. The paradox of his likability is wrapped up in a sentence written by columnist James Reston: "He has a tendency to say the most hardhearted things in the most lighthearted way." Speaker O'Neill called him "Herbert Hoover with a smile." Witticist Andy Rooney wrote seriously, "I

don't offhand remember a President whose policies were de-
tested by so many people whose personal popularity was as high
as Ronald Reagan's. . . ." Returning from an anti-Reagan meeting among workers in a steel town with high unemployment,
Representative George Miller (D.–Calif.) said that somehow
people kept liking the President personally: "They can't believe
that he is doing something that is hurting them." "We rise to
denounce the charm of Ronald Reagan," the *New York Times*
opened an editorial. "The President's irrepressible cheer and
courtesy take . . . all the fun out of criticizing his policies,"
which are "charming but chilling."

Such a nice guy would not have a meanness problem if he
had not done the things Reagan has done. O'Neill says a group
of nuns approached him and said in effect: "Stop calling Reagan
a decent man. Anyone who is doing what he's doing to old people and handicapped children is not decent." A citizen wrote
columnist Haynes Johnson from Maryland: "I don't think
Reagan is nice. He has worried old people on Social Security half
to death. . . . Reagan is cold, callous, and mean. . . . Even
Nixon did not try to starve the old and the sick." On January 28,
1982, having a hamburger at Jake's Barbecue in Austin, Texas, I
heard two workingmen and a woman, seated in the booth behind me, discussing Reagan.

First man: "He was gonna cut interest rates, cut inflation,
employment was gonna be real good. And whadda we get? Free
cheese."

Second man: "That son of a bitch Reagan."

Woman: "Take from the poor and give to the rich."

First man: "–From the needy to the greedy."

They were speaking with concentrated anger.

Reagan's aides heard talk like this, too, and by mid-1982 they
were worrying aloud about "the fairness thing," which press aide
David Gergen called "a weight that's pulling him down." Michael Horowitz, counsel to Stockman in the budget office, wrote
in a bitterly ironic memo circulated in the White House: "We are
being savaged by the fairness issue. . . . 'Fairness,' 'compassion'
and 'decency'—catchwords eroding our support—are not defined by the bond traders and chief executive officers to whose

sensibilities we have exquisitely attended." Horowitz himself believed all the administration had to do was explain itself better, but he said the precipitous disenchantment among women was "significantly rooted in the perception of this administration as uncaring, perhaps even cruel." Could a tightly suppressed self-hate be breaking out among some of the Reaganists? The *New York Times* printed a joke James Baker made about Stockman during a dinner party: "We saved a lot of air-conditioning in the White House this summer. We kept cool by huddling around Dave Stockman's heart."

"I know an image has been created that I don't care about the underprivileged," Reagan has said. "Anyone who knows me knows that's not true; I'm a pushover for a hard-luck story." In a letter to a constituent who asked for a prescription for living, he replied, "Always do and say the kindest thing." His former secretary, Helene von Damm, told a story about him when he was governor. A nine-year-old boy whose mother had been cut off welfare wrote him that it wasn't fair. After an investigation he concluded the boy was right and had his mother reinstated. Then Reagan had his friend Frank Sinatra provide the family with special gifts at Christmas.

A White House aide was quoted as saying that the charge Reagan is hard really gets to him—that he is "genuinely upset" that people think he's a racist or antielderly. He believes, however, in personal, and not in governmental help for the out-of-luck, and he can be cruel with those leading liberal Democrats who excite his animosity. Speaking about Senator Edward Kennedy in 1972 not long after Chappaquiddick, he said Kennedy was "bridging the gap—if you'll forgive the expression. . . ." The loquacious liberal Hubert Humphrey, Reagan said, had a windup watch: "You wind the Hubert Humphrey watch and you never have to wind it again." Speaking in Texas in 1982, President Reagan ad libbed that someone had asked him what Pac-Man is, "and somebody told me it was a round thing that gobbles up money. I thought that was Tip O'Neill."

Neither is Reagan a nice guy when he's crossed. There was the night his 1980 campaign ended when he snapped at some hecklers, "Aw, shut up." He said to critics of his 1983 budget,

"Put up or shut up." When a right-wing Republican congressional candidate interrupted him during a speech in the White House and started berating him, the President of the United States colored with anger and told him: "Shut up."

His statements can be, to say the least, unfeeling—time for a bloodbath, botulism for the recipients of free food. "The air is filled with liberal voices talking big talk about fairness and compassion," he said in the autumn of 1982. "And to listen to their horror stories about budgets, you'd have to like horror movies." Critics of his budget were "sob sisters." His cuts had removed from government benefit rolls "people who had no moral right to be receiving benefits from the taxpayers." Being in Texas seems to bring out the harshness in him. In Houston in May 1983 he said: "I get a little irritated with that constant refrain about compassion. I got an unsigned valentine in February and I'm sure it was from Fritz Mondale. The heart on it was bleeding." Reagan may be a sucker for a hard-luck story, but not if the government helps. Senator David Durrenberger, the Minnesota Republican, told the *Wall Street Journal:* "It just isn't fair for him to get up and say the medicare program went from $11 billion to $60 billion and imply it was due to fraud, waste, and abuse. And why doesn't he ever say something nice about food stamps? There's a lot of nice things to say about food stamps."

In 1976 former Governor Pat Brown of California, whom Reagan had unseated a decade earlier, said there is "the dark side of Mr. Good Guy . . . the radical, superficial, and compassionless man behind the perpetual Mr. Nice Guy facade." Those who have come to the opinion that there is a meanness at the base of Reaganism may say so impersonally, as in columnist David Broder's reference to "the moral meanness of the Reagan administration," or personally, as in Speaker O'Neill's remark that Reagan has "ice water for blood" when it comes to poor people. But the implications of this conclusion are terrible for Reagan, for the Republicans, and for the country. Former Senator Yarborough of Texas said: "I think this is the most vicious administration in United States history. Hoover didn't will that people go hungry. Hoover realized it's got to be done by the government or people will go hungry. This is the only government in our history that would deliberately go out and deny food to people." Nor did Yarborough stop there. "We're starving children," he said, "dooming hundreds of thousands every year to the slow lines in school, maybe mental retardation, maybe crime."[24]

18

Parking Stripes and Moonscapes

In trying to imagine how President Reagan might conduct a "conventional" war if the United States became involved in one during his remaining time in office, we may use as a benchmark his public performance concerning American participation in the Vietnam war.

From the first day of 1967 onward he was the governor of the dominant state in the western United States. His opinions counted in the highest places. Obviously he was in touch with some of the country's military leaders. From his redoubt in Sacramento he was the most bellicose of the hawks on the Vietnam war, an influential and disturbing spokesman for the very Pentagon generals President Johnson kept saying he was muzzling.

So far as is known, Reagan did not publicly express any disapproval of President Kennedy's commitment of 16,000 American troops to the jungles of Vietnam. In 1980, during the presidential campaign, Mrs. Reagan said: "He never was in agreement with Kennedy on sending troops into Vietnam. He didn't think we should be fighting a land war there. But once they were there. . . ."

Ronald Reagan went as far as anyone holding high office in calling for all-out war on North Vietnam. He wanted the U.S. to invade the country if the military so advised. He contemplated the use of nuclear weapons if that was necessary to end the war quickly.

In a little-remembered passage in his nationally televised speech for Goldwater in 1964, Reagan said, "As for the peace that we would preserve, I wonder who among us would like to approach the wife or mother whose husband or son has died in Vietnam and ask them if they think this is a peace that should be maintained indefinitely."

This was early autumn. The United States was not yet committed heavily to the war, and many people had turned away from Goldwater because they feared he was trigger-happy. Yet Reagan told them in this broadcast, "There can be no real peace while one American is dying someplace in the world for the rest of us. We are at war with the most dangerous enemy that has ever faced mankind in his long climb from the swamp to the stars."

In October of 1965, after Johnson had ordered regular bombing raids against North Vietnam and committed U.S. troops to the war, Reagan said, "We should declare war on North Vietnam. We could pave the whole country and put parking stripes on it and still be home by Christmas."[1]

One of Reagan's advisers, Richard J. Whaley, has said that the U.S. should have bombed the dikes in North Vietnam to put "90 percent of the country under water," and Reagan himself has spoken approvingly of an Air Force plan to bring North Vietnam to its knees early in the war by saturation bombing. "The Air Force," Reagan said, "had a plan at the beginning of the war that would have saved all the bloodshed: a ninety-day plan to hit sixty-five targets, all vital to the military, industrial, and transportation capabilities of North Vietnam. At the time the North Vietnamese didn't have antiaircraft missiles and radar to fend off our air attacks. And there would have come a point during those ninety days, as we destroyed their capability to make war, at which they would have given up. But the plan was vetoed in Washington."

Reagan advocated that the harbor of Haiphong be mined and the bombing be increased in order to close (or "interdict," as the generals put it) the supply routes between Red China and North Vietnam. He advocated the "hot pursuit" of enemy troops into their sanctuaries in Cambodia.

Johnson opposed invading North Vietnam for fear of bringing in China—even Russia. In the fall of 1967, Reagan said that the decision to invade should be left to the military. "That's a military decision," he said. "If this would bring the war to a quicker end, then yes," the governor added.

This reminded Robert J. Donovan, the Washington bureau chief of the *Los Angeles Times,* of Senator Goldwater's remark in 1964 concerning Vietnam: "I would turn to my joint chiefs of staff and say, 'Fellows, we made the decision to win, now it's your problem.' "

Reagan said he was not advocating that the generals assume all direction of the war: civilian control of the military should be preserved. "But once the shooting starts," he asserted, "we should accept the generals' advice about where the enemy is best attacked." On the question of whether to invade, no one but military officers had the information "to make that kind of decision." At one point he also said the decision about invasion should be made by "the government and the people," but he never did state that the Congress, under the American Constitution, would be the only proper source of such a grave undertaking. By 1968 he was saying, "I don't see anything wrong with invasion of North Vietnam." He was clearly implying—at the least—that if he were President and the military said "invade," he would order the invasion.

"Certainly it is a radical view," Donovan retorted, "that an invasion of a sovereign country like North Vietnam should be a military decision. . . . On these terms situations could develop where vital national policy could be set by the uniformed military leaders—for example, in an attack on Haiphong harbor where Soviet ships unload."

Once the killing starts, Reagan said, the nation should "impose its full resources to end it as soon as possible"—it should "commit all the power we need to win a victory as quickly as possible."[2] This language created the impression that his thoughts were turning to nuclear weapons, and he was asked if he proposed that they be used in Vietnam.

"No one would cheerfully want to use atomic weapons," he replied. "But the last person in the world that should know we wouldn't use them is the enemy. He should go to bed every night being afraid that we might." The Korean War was halted, he recalled, after the U.S. "let the word get to the enemy by way of certain neutral sources that we were considering the use of atomic weapons."

In this recollection he was correct. In fact, as author Joe Goulden reported in his recent book on the Korean War, on May 19, 1953, the joint chiefs of staff recommended air and naval operations "directly against China and Manchuria," including the use of nuclear weapons. The necessary operations, including "extensive strategical and tactical use of atomic bombs," should be undertaken, said the joint chiefs, in ways that would "obtain maximum surprise and maximum impact." The next day the National Security Council approved these recommendations. Eisenhower's secretary of state, John Foster Dulles, sent word to Chinese Premier Chou En-lai, through Prime Minister Nehru of India, that if the war did not end quickly the U.S. would bomb Manchuria north of the Yalu River. Moreover, Dulles warned, the United States had successfully tested nuclear artillery shells, which he implied the U.S. would not hesitate to use in North Korea. Fortunately for all—including the only country which had ever used atomic weapons in warfare—the message was heeded and the war ended shortly thereafter.

Trying to fight in Vietnam with foot soldiers was wrong, Reagan said, "when there are forces like Russia and China— Asia, generally, that can outman us." Instead, "the full technological resources of the United States" should be used, he said. Again, necessarily, he was asked: Did he mean we should use nuclear weapons? "Well . . . nuclear weapons, we hope, would not be resorted to," he said in 1967.[3]

To Johnson's program for both guns and butter Reagan rejoined, "We must have more guns and less butter." In 1967 Reagan helped to block the governors' conference from endorsing the government's course of action in Vietnam with the argument that Johnson was escalating not too much, but too little. After the shock of the Tet offensive in 1968, Reagan complained bitterly against what he regarded as Johnson's gradual escalations. "If this had happened all at once," Reagan said, "the evidence of our willingness to go all out" would have broken the enemy. "It's sort of like the frog in the boiling water: You know, if you just heat it up a degree at a time, he'll stay there till he boils." When Johnson, in quitting politics, also announced a partial suspension of the bombing, Reagan said: "I am disappointed. . . . I would favor a step-up of the war."

Reagan had never wanted the peace negotiations, and he did not like them once they started. Late in 1965 he had said, "I am concerned about negotiations. What is there to negotiate? The enemy must get absolutely no gain." He opposed Senator Robert Kennedy's contention that the Viet Cong should be a party to negotiations, and he opposed a coalition government with the National Liberation Front. As for the actual peace talks with the North Vietnamese, he said the U.S. should set a deadline in the talks and if it wasn't met, "kick the devil" out of them—if they didn't cooperate we should threaten to "kick the hell" out of them. Invasion would be "a pretty good threat to hold over their heads" in the Paris peace talks, he said, and he unmistakably implied that there should also be a nuclear threat. Alluding again to Eisenhower's having passed the word to the enemy in 1953 that the U.S. was going to "review its options with regard to weapons, theaters of operation, manners of fighting, and so forth," Reagan said, "the same thing . . . should be true in the Paris negotiations." That is to say, Reagan wanted the U.S. to threaten to use nuclear weapons unless the Vietnam war was ended promptly. As the summer opened he added that while nuclear weapons were "neither necessary nor desirable in this conflict, if they are to be a deterrent, we should not have gone so far as we have to assure everybody they would not be used."

"I can hope for peace," he said that same summer, "but I don't hope for the kind of peace" that would let the Viet Cong into the Saigon government. "This would be about the same as the United States government taking the Cosa Nostra in as partners." He declared at this time, after three years of fighting, death, anguish, and national division: "We are in Vietnam because it is in our national interest, and whether it offends friend or foe, we are going to do what has to be done."[4]

When the Nixon Republicans took over the war, the governor on the west coast fell relatively quiet about it. As Nixon's envoy to the far east in 1971 Reagan delivered Nixon's congratulations to President Thieu on his reelection in a one-candidate-only vote and told the press he "couldn't understand why there was such an uproar" over Thieu's having had no opponent. In 1972 he labeled Senator McGovern "super-dove." Senator Edmund Muskie (D.–Me.), while contesting with McGovern for that year's Democratic presidential nomination, proposed an immediate ceasefire in Vietnam. Reagan said of that, "Senator Muskie has a two-point plan of his own: Bug out now, and let the last man to leave shoot President Thieu. I think really he's been playing Lincoln so long in this campaign that he wants us to surrender at Appomattox." And Governor Reagan opposed broad amnesty for deserters from the Vietnam war.

The collapse of the American forces in Vietnam and the chaotic pullout reactivated Reagan's belligerency. Congress had lost Vietnam by acting "more irresponsibly than any Congress in our history" and had "blood on their hands," he said early in May 1975. At the end of that harrowing month he said the country should have met North Vietnam's final thrust in South Vietnam with B-52 bombers. President Ford, he said, was failing to provide "a strong, lasting, consistent foreign policy," and he asked, "Can anyone think for one moment that North Vietnam would have moved to the attack had its leaders believed we would respond with B-52s?" Reagan's thoughts also swept up across the China Sea toward Korea: "B-52s should make a moonscape out of North Korea if South Korea is attacked," he said.[5]

Reagan never accepted the widespread view that the war was a mistake. The post-Vietnam War Powers Act, by which Congress tried to put a check on the President's independent war-making power, "tied the President's hands," he said. "American public opinion," he said in 1976, "will no longer tolerate wars of the Vietnam type, because they no longer feel a threat, thanks to the liberal press, from communism, and they cannot interpret those wars as being really in the defense of freedom and our own country."

Two years later on radio it was the import of his rhetorical questions that he refused to accept the loss of the war. "How now," he asked, "do we negotiate with the North Vietnamese unless we begin with . . . the release of half-a-million South Vietnamese now in concentration camps and the North Vietnamese withdrawal from South Vietnam? For that matter, how did we agree to North Vietnam's entry into the United Nations . . . ? Until South Vietnam is freed, North Vietnam is still an outlaw among nations." His one surest crowd rouser on the war harked back to his theme that Johnson was too restrained. The wrong is done, he would say, "When a government asks its young men to fight and die in a war the government is afraid to let them win."

Shortly before he was nominated for President in 1980, Reagan was cudgeled in the national press for having made what was characterized as some kind of blooper. What he had done was go before the Veterans of Foreign Wars convention in Chicago and say, "For too long, we have lived with the 'Vietnam syndrome.' . . . It is time we recognized that ours was, in truth, a noble cause." That was no blooper: he said later that he personally wrote the passage into his speech.[6] There is not a scrap of evidence that Ronald Reagan ever wavered in his belief that Vietnam was a noble war. Now he is President.

19

Reagan and the World

President Reagan has stealthily but steadily returned the United States to its postwar role as the world's policeman. To achieve this he has proceeded covertly, given reasons other than the real ones for his actions, internationalized his McCarthyism, and fully exploited the vacillation and confusion of American progressives on the momentous issue of civil liberties in newly emerging revolutionary states.

Seeing the near and middle east as an important source of oil for the west that is jeopardized by Soviet ambitions, he has long wanted a U.S. military beachhead in the area, and in September 1982, without placing his action within reach of the authority of Congress as the War Powers Act seemed to require, he dispatched U.S. Marines to Lebanon. In the summer of 1983 1,800 of them were holding on there despite having taken casualties and despite the deadly terrorist bombing of the U.S. embassy in Beirut. President Carter, hoping to encourage the prodemocratic groups among the revolutionaries in Nicaragua, persuaded Congress to send aid to the revolutionary Sandinista government there. Reagan has used the CIA to foment a war and an invasion from Honduras against that same Nicaraguan government. In other ways and in other episodes he has demonstrated that the use of military force abroad is the means that becomes the end of his foreign policy. In 1980 Carter had tried to warn the voters of the bellicosity that was inherent in his opponent's statements and policies. The Reaganists countered with the most ingenious ploy of the campaign: They accused Carter of implying that Reagan was a warmonger, and rather than press the point with the facts Carter backed away. Reagan's prepresidential record does show him to be a Teddy Roosevelt–type nationalist who often impulsively advocated the use of military force. His record so far as President shows that he has moderated the rhetoric but not his preference for force over diplomacy and negotiations.

Reagan's strength on the stump when he speaks of foreign policy questions derives from the fact that most Americans share both his pride in the United States and his anticommunism. The concern about and opposition to his foreign policy which are registered in public opinion polls are probably in the main expressions of fear of another Vietnam and the dread of nuclear war. There is an extremism at the base of his views that makes many people uneasy about having him in the White House.

On the issue of communism, Reagan is categorical. In his basic General Electric speech back in 1962 he said, "Now there are many people among us who deny that we are at war. But war was declared a hundred years ago by Karl Marx and reaffirmed fifty years later by Nikolai Lenin," and then by Khrushchev. (Lenin's name was Vladimir, not Nikolai.) "The inescapable truth is that we are at war, and we are losing that war simply because we don't or won't realize we are in it. . . . It is a declared war." And, "There can only be one end to the war we are in. . . . Wars end in victory or defeat."

In his 1964 speech for Goldwater he declared that "we are at war with the most dangerous enemy ever known to man. . . . The guns are silent in this war but frontiers fall while those who should be warriors prefer neutrality." The "final step" in "the

Communist master plan," he said in 1976, "is to conquer the United States."

Nine days into his presidency Reagan raised questions about his ability and will to negotiate nuclear arms treaties with the Soviets when he said during his first press conference that those very Soviets "reserve unto themselves the right to commit any crime, to lie, to cheat, in order to obtain" their objective. Two years later he told reporters that he had just read an article that quoted "the Ten Commandments of Nikolai Lenin. . . . And they are all there, that promises are like pie crust, made to be broken." This theme was one of the drumbeats of the Christian Anti-Communist Crusade rallies in the 1950s, and whatever implications the fact has for arms talks, Reagan believed it then and still does.

In his 1978 radio broadcasts he asked why the U.S. should ratify the SALT II treaty when "the Soviets don't keep their word even when they understand the meaning." He also said on radio that year, while discussing the fact that Castro lied by saying he was not a Marxist-Leninist: "Calling a Communist a liar when he is one is pretty frustrating. How do you insult a pig by calling it a pig? Communists are not bound by our morality. They say any crime, including lying, is moral if it advances the cause of socialism. That is Karl Marx as interpreted by Lenin." Disvaluing the Helsinki accord, he said "the Russians make promises; they don't keep them." Two years before he assumed the presidency he said, "I wouldn't trust the Russians around the block. They must be laughing at us because we continue to think of them as people like us."

In 1978 he reasoned, again on radio, that Russia should be denied its vote in the United Nations. The Soviets and their satellites had refused to pay about $100 million in U.N. assessments for activities of which they disapproved. "If a club member or, in many cases, a union member is delinquent in his dues," Reagan said, "he loses privileges, including the right to vote till he pays up. Why shouldn't our ambassador officially move that voting rights be denied to the Soviet Union? And this time make it stick. If they threaten to pack up and go home—what will have been lost? Can anyone remember a single instance in which the

Soviet Union has contributed anything of lasting value? . . . If the United Nations would take such an action it might acquire a soul. If it refuses, then we could take a walk and discover we still have one."

Reagan has what can best be understood as a devil theory of the Soviet Union. In his mind Moscow is not only the capital of communism, it is the capital of everything revolutionary in the world. "The Soviet Union underlies all the unrest that is going on," he told the *Wall Street Journal* in 1980. "If they weren't engaged in this game of dominoes, there wouldn't be any hot spots in the world." It follows from this doctrine that Israel is a deterrent to Soviet expansion, the U.S. should give military aid to the anti-Marxist guerrillas in Afghanistan and Angola, Cuba is the Soviet Union in the Caribbean, Nicaragua is a bear's paw, and whatever quarrels Russia has with China, "both are Communist, and both want to take over the world."

"There is sin and evil in the world," President Reagan told the National Association of Evangelicals on March 9, 1983. For example, he said, "racism, antiSemitism." And that brought him to his final point. At his first press conference, he recalled, he had said that "the Soviet leaders have openly and publicly declared that the only morality they recognize is that which will further their cause, which is world revolution." He then quoted Lenin in 1920 to that effect. Next he condemned the proposed nuclear arms freeze as "a very dangerous fraud." And then he said: "Let us pray for the salvation of all those who live in totalitarian darkness, pray they will discover the joy of knowing God. But until they do," and while they preach what they preach, "they are the focus of evil in the modern world." This remarkable speech seemed like a declaration of a holy war or at least a holy arms race, and later Reagan had to add that what he was pointing out "is not the inevitability of war," but just the differences between the two sides.

The implications of Reagan's devil theory for any revolutionary movement are clear. No matter how rotten and murderous a right-wing dictator may be, no matter how corrupt and repressive a military junta, any revolutionaries rising up against it are Communists directed by Moscow. All leftism and even mere reformism are equated with communism just as they are in domestic McCarthyism. No middle ground is left for the emergence of democratic states from national upheavals and revolutions.

An example of this is Portugal. In 1975 in a speech he made in Atlantic City, N.J., Reagan exclaimed that the U.S. should have acted *"in any way* to prevent or discourage" what ' e called Portugal's slide toward Communist control. (The italics are provided.) He said that the Communist takeover of the country threatened the U.S. military base in the Azores. There were, he said, two possibilities: "One would be an outright Soviet takeover of the NATO ally, with all that means. Or—this is possibly worse—the Soviets stay in the background, pulling the strings, while Portugal puts up a front on independence, remaining in NATO, not as an ally of the western nations but of the Soviet Union." As it turned out, of course, Portugal was on its way to democracy.

Reagan's devil theory also lays the basis for internationalized McCarthyism. In the first month of the Reagan administration, Secretary of State Haig said the U.S.S.R. as part of a "conscious policy" was "training, funding, and equipping" international terrorists. In their writings Claire Sterling and John Barron weave some substance and much anonymously provided information into the same conclusion. Yet officials in the CIA, the Defense Intelligence Agency, and the State Department said they could not substantiate the charge. They told the *New York Times* that it was based on ten-year-old testimony from a Czechoslovak defector and added, "There is no substantial new evidence." In April 1981 FBI director William Webster said the U.S. has "no real evidence" that the U.S.S.R. is financing, training, or encouraging terrorists in the U.S., and in April 1983 Frederick Kempe reported in the *Wall Street Journal*: "A good many experts who have had first-hand experience with terrorism sharply disagree with [the theory that worldwide terrorist activity is all part of a comprehensive Soviet-conceived and Soviet-executed plan to undermine the west]. For example, Israeli intelligence officials . . . contend that the many proven ties among terrorist groups are much more of a series of pragmatic, mutually beneficial business arrangements. . . ." Added Ambassador Robert M. Sayre, head of the U.S. State Department Office for Combating Terrorism: "I don't think the intelligence is there to establish an overall (Soviet-supported) network." Yet so securely have been laid the foundations of international McCarthyism, Vice President Bush said that he could not understand how Catholic priests in Central America can reconcile their faith with Marxist ideas and tactics, as if poverty could have nothing to do with the revolutionary ferment there.

Perhaps nothing else so dramatically illustrates a certain heedlessness in Reagan concerning the Soviet Union than one of his 1979 radio broadcasts. Even though he knew that he was going to run for President again the next year, Reagan publicly expressed his suspicion that the Soviet Union put Lee Harvey Oswald up to the assassination of President Kennedy. "Have we hesitated," he asked, "to investigate the possibility that Oswald might have been carrying out a plot engineered by an international agency? . . .

"Former Marine Lee Harvey Oswald gave up his American citizenship and moved to Russia. He had learned the Russian language before he defected. Someone must have helped him do this. Once in Russia, he married the niece of a colonel in the Soviet spy organization, the KGB. . . .

"After his arrest his wallet was found to contain the addresses of *'The Communist Daily Worker'* and the Soviet Embassy in Washington.

"It has been reported . . . that President Johnson and the (Warren) Commission were fearful that evidence of a Communist conspiracy, involving as it would the Soviet Union and/or Cuba, would anger the American people and lead to a confrontation, possibly even to war. . . .

"Maybe some day a new investigation will start down that trail."[1]

The Soviet Union had such a dark history of state crime and terror under Stalin and it continues to this day to be such a harsh dictatorship, it has long been fair game for politicians, and in ordinary times one might just think, well, the President has a good thing going there. But these are nuclear times.

Having such a demonology concerning the Soviet Union, Reagan naturally set out at once from the White House to cut off trade with the enemy. His tenacious but ill-fated campaign to prevent the completion of the natural gas pipeline from Siberia to western Europe and his repeatedly rebuffed attempts to enlist the Europeans' participation in other schemes to cut off the Soviets commercially need no detailed review here. What explains the whole affair is the fact that he had been musing about quarantining the U.S.S.R. for at least twelve years before he became President.

In 1968 reporter Bill Snyder wrote in the *Springfield Daily News* in Missouri, in his story on a Reagan speech: "What a nation in a position of leadership might have done after the Russians invaded Czechoslovakia, he said, was to ask friendly nations to join us in quarantining Russian borders. Russian planes should not land at our airports, he said, and this country should not trade with them."

On his radio program in 1975, discussing the sale of American wheat to Russia, Reagan said, "Maybe . . . we simply do what's morally right. Stop doing business with them. Let their system collapse." On radio in the summer of 1979 he condemned U.S. assistance in the building of a truck plant in Russia and the U.S. sale to Russia of ball bearings which, according to Reagan, were "just the kind needed for multiple warheads on nuclear missiles." During the alarmism about the Soviet brigade in Cuba he said, "I think our government shouldn't have any further communications with the Soviet Union. There can be no discussion of those (issues) as long as the Soviet troops are in Cuba."

After the Soviet invasion of Afghanistan by which the Kremlin installed its own puppet regime in Kabul, Reagan opposed President Carter's retaliatory grain embargo against Russia. But a week later Reagan suggested that the U.S. and its allies should suspend trade with the Soviets until their troops were withdrawn. "Why shouldn't the western world quarantine the Soviet Union until they decide to behave like a civilized nation should?" he asked. In the summer of 1980 he went a bit further: "Maybe the U.S. should have said, 'Look, don't talk to us about trade. There will be none. Don't talk to us about treaties, like SALT II,' until the troops were withdrawn."

Two weeks before his election, Reagan reasoned that a quarantine of Russia might save the peace. "I think the farmer would be the first one to volunteer," he said, "if, in the interest of national security, we were forced to say some day to the Soviet Union, 'That's all, quarantine, no trade, we're going to have no more trade with you until you do such-and-such or so-and-so.' " The embargo would follow any provocation, he suggested—it might be a response to "some kind of aggression that threatened our national security, such as a move in the Persian Gulf or something."[2]

Reagan is actively seeking to advance his world view through his presidency. "We must . . . resist any unpeaceful act wherever it may occur," he said in 1979. In the 1980 campaign he said, "We did not seek leadership of the free world, but there is no one else who can provide it." Believing in the domino theory, he wants the CIA to engage in covert political activity abroad. "I think we would be stupid not to help the people in those countries being subverted," he said. He complained in 1980 that we decided to treat the CIA "like some Virginia gentlemen's club." As for congressional oversight, away with it: "Senseless restrictions requiring the CIA to report any and all covert actions to eight congressional committees must be eliminated."

Reagan's sponsorship, through the CIA, of an invasion army in Honduras falls into place in the light of a story written in 1967 by reporter Ward Just after he had listened to a Reagan speech. "The governor implied," Just wrote, "that the United States might consider promoting wars of its own on Communist territory." What Reagan had said, without elaboration, was: "We are always reacting. . . . Next time we might have a few spots of our own in their backyard picked out." He returned to this theme in the mid-1970s, telling *U.S. News & World Report*: "I think this nation should have a master plan, if you want to call it that, based on what we believe is the enemy's master plan. . . . Maybe part of the answer in a hot spot such as Vietnam is to give the enemy something else to worry about in another corner of the world. . . . Maybe he [the enemy] ought to have some unrest in some corner of his realm to worry about."[3]

President Reagan has been developing two military concentrations that could foment unrest abroad or, alternatively, extinguish it. Carter developed the 200,000-man Rapid Deployment Force (RDF); Reagan is doubling that and spending $4 billion a year on it, plus $11 billion by 1987 to increase airlift capability and about as much again to increase sealift capability. The RDF commander announced in 1981 that the U.S. was negotiating with several nations in the Middle East to establish "a forward headquarters" for RDF in the region. In 1983 it emerged that the U.S. has a secret base in the desert in southern Egypt with 100 airmen stationed there.

A secret five-year defense guidance plan promulgated by Secretary of Defense Weinberger and leaked to the press ordered that Special Forces be ready "to exploit political, economic, and military weaknesses within the Soviet bloc" and said that "other opportunities for counteroffensives against Soviet interests, forces, and proxy forces worldwide will be exploited to the extent possible."

In 1982 the Army announced the formation of a Special Operations Command to respond to leftist insurgencies in Asia, Africa, and Latin America. According to reporter Richard Halloran in the *New York Times*, this new command's primary mission "is insurgency, particularly in making contact with dissidents behind enemy lines and training them in guerrilla operations, sabotage, and terror." The command includes the secret antiterrorist unit at Fort Bragg and other contingents there and in Massachusetts, Georgia, Washington, Panama, and West Germany. Units are also to be prepared to engage in psychological warfare and clandestine assault. A Pentagon official told a reporter that the men in the force are "the best there are at the rough stuff."[4]

Under Reagan and his 1980 campaign manager, William Casey, the CIA is putting emphasis on acquiring clandestine agents. Casey told Suzanne Garment of the *Wall Street Journal* that "lots of the little countries of the world are under pressure" from Soviet-backed forces, and the CIA helps them in communications, metal detection, photographic information, sensors, "or training for antiterrorist forces." Also, he said, "we helped in (an) El Salvador election." *Newsweek* said in the fall of 1982 that it had learned that the CIA was then running paramilitary operations in about ten countries in addition to Nicaragua.[5]

The U.S. is now the world's leading supplier of arms, measured by dollar value. Carter, who had promised to reduce the arms trade, increased U.S. sales from $9 billion to $15 billion a year. According to a book commissioned by the Council of Foreign Relations on the arms trade, in Reagan's first three months in office he offered foreign nations $15 billion worth of arms sales. In 1982 total U.S. sales leapt to $21.5 billion, compared to the Soviet Union's $9 billion. James Buckley, under secretary of state for security assistance, contends the Soviet Union is the top arms seller because of its cut-rate prices and other factors, and obviously the Soviets are furnishing weapons to a large part of the world. Still, by 1983 the U.S. had quadrupled its weapons sales in the western hemisphere. Reagan was pushing Japan to rearm more thoroughly, and Weinberger said U.S. help to Persian Gulf nations in building an arms industry was "a very real possibility."

Reagan was also increasing the sophistication of the weapons the U.S. sells to friendly nations. For instance, the F-16 fighter was sold to Venezuela and Pakistan. India, Pakistan's uneasy neighbor, at once began planning to obtain something comparably menacing. Frank Carlucci, the deputy secretary of defense (who later resigned), instructed the military services to "actively plan with the [friendly] nations for sensible acquisitions" of U.S. weapons. A vice president of an investment bank told a gathering of military industry executives in Washington that the administration, following a new policy, encouraged foreign nations to buy top-of-the-line U.S. weapons. Senator Thomas Dodd (D.– Conn.) said the U.S. is acquiring a reputation as "a discount house for arms."

With worldwide military spending totaling $130 a year for every person in the world ($521 billion in 1979), Senator Charles Mathias (R.–Md.) called the world arms trade "truly frightening." How crucial the trade is to Reagan's practice of foreign policy was indicated when a senior official of the State Department was quoted as saying in 1981 that arms sales are "the currency in which foreign policy now deals." As Representative Michael Barnes (D.–Md.) said, "The Reagan administration has not so much a foreign policy as an arms policy."[6]

Reagan's world view finds its focus closest to home in Cuba. David L. Aaron, Carter's deputy assistant for national security affairs, said Carter, if reelected, would "see if a broad accommodation is possible with the Cubans." Reagan has no interest in this. In a 1978 radio broadcast he declared, "Fidel Castro is a liar and he's been lying on a regular basis since before he seized power." This was an undoubted truth, but it was not a basis for accommodation. Speaking to Cuban exiles in Miami in 1980, Reagan said, "I do not believe relations can be normalized until Cuba is out from under Soviet domination. . . . My policy would be based on my longtime view that captive nations must once again know freedom."

During the campaign he suggested "that we might blockade Cuba and stop the transportation back and forth of Russian arms, of Soviet military. . . . A blockade of Cuba could be an option." Bush, running against him then, said, "That's a lot of macho." But Reagan persisted: "Suppose we put a blockade around that island and said, 'Now, buster, we'll lift it when you take your forces out of Afghanistan'?"

Would not such a blockade lead to a confrontation with Russia similar to the 1962 Cuban missile crisis? As in 1962, Soviet ships, steaming across the high seas for Cuba, would have to turn back or be turned back. Even though the 1962 crisis was the closest the world has come to the nuclear precipice, Reagan believes President Kennedy failed to do something he should have. "We have seen," Reagan said in 1972, "an American President walk all the way to the barricade in the Cuban missile crisis and lack the will to take the final step to make it successful." What final step would that have been? Invasion, presumably.

"We have got to get at Cuba," wrote right-wing columnist William F. Buckley, Jr., in 1982. "A declaration of war . . . could plausibly be framed." That sounds like something the pre-presidential Reagan might have said. Secretary of State Haig urged him to blockade both Cuba and Nicaragua, but in November 1981 he decided to support the secret war against Nicaragua instead. As for Cuba, so far the President has contented himself with using the Trading with the Enemy Act to prohibit American tourists and businessmen from going there. His objective seems to be to try to squeeze Castro economically. Reagan's attempt to establish a government station in Florida, Radio Marti, to send a strong broadcast signal into Cuba foundered in Congress because of the likelihood that Castro would respond by jamming American channels.

Reagan's friend, Senator Steve Symms (R.–Idaho), acting with the President's support, succeeded in winning Senate passage of a resolution favoring the use of any means, "including the use of arms," to contain Cuban aggression or subversion in the hemisphere. Senator Charles Percy (R.–Ill.), chairman of the Senate Foreign Relations Committee, tried after the vote to get the reference to force deleted—the Symms proposal, he said, was "a Gulf of Tonkin resolution for Cuba"—but he lost, 52–47. The Senate did add the afterthought that it did not mean to authorize invasion under the War Powers Act. The resolution did not pass the House.[7]

Grenada, a tourist island of 110,000 people that lies close to Venezuela, has been ruled since an armed coup in 1979 by socialist Maurice Bishop and his Jewel movement, which has held no elections and appears to be aligned with Cuba and the U.S.S.R. to a considerable degree. The administration considered a covert operation against Grenada in 1981, but desisted because of the opposition of the Senate Intelligence Committee. The Grenadan government charged that a group was training in Miami in preparation for a coup against it. On national television Reagan displayed photographs of a long runway Grenada is constructing; Cuba has more than 200 Russian MIG bombers.

(With Cuba and Grenada the spurs, Reagan proposed a "Caribbean Basin Initiative" to provide economic aid to the region. Congress granted him $350 million, but not his request to allow duty-free access to the U.S. market for Caribbean and Central American goods. Meanwhile he approved the nation's first sugar import quotas since 1974, engendering concern in the

Caribbean that this would cancel the benefits of the new U.S. aid.)[8]

Reagan does not always need an anti-Communist reason to justify the use of U.S. power; statements he made about Ecuador and Panama show that any challenge to national pride may arouse his belligerency.

In 1975 he proposed sending a destroyer to Ecuadoran waters to protect U.S. fishermen. Ecuador had declared its territorial limit to be 200 miles out to sea, although international law sets 12. Unless the U.S. itself adopted a 200-mile standard, Reagan wrote in his column, the U.S. "should send along a destroyer with the tuna boats to cruise, say, 13 miles off the shore of Ecuador in an updated version of Teddy Roosevelt's dictum to 'talk softly, but carry a big stick.'"[9]

During the debate on the Panama Canal treaty, under which Panama takes control of the canal in the year 2000, Reagan said "We bought it, we paid for it, it's ours and we're going to keep it." He was asked, what if guerrilla warfare was launched by the Panamanians? "We would have to take the same approach as a police department when it goes to quell a riot: Take whatever force is necessary to control the situation," he asserted. He would go to war if necessary to protect the canal, he said, and in this context he criticized a provision in the U.N. Charter which prohibits a member nation from using armed force to prevent expropriation of its property abroad (such as U.S. property in Panama under the treaty). "This," Reagan said of the provision, "rules out the practice of *force majeure*, the idea that because we have the size and strength, why we just move."

Senator Goldwater, who supported ratification, made a grave observation about his friend and fellow westerner. He did not do so lightly. "It took me all night to decide," he said. "I think I wrote that thing six times." Finally he carried his statement to a Senate press room and read it out: Reagan's position on the issue contained "gross factual errors" that could "needlessly lead the country into open military conflict" and perhaps reflected "a surprisingly dangerous state of mind, which is that he will not seek alternatives to a military solution when dealing with complex foreign policy issues."[10]

Costa Rica, just north of Panama, is the only stable democracy on the Central American isthmus. North of Costa Rica lie three army-backed governments, El Salvador (which has held an election), Honduras, and Guatemala, and the revolutionary government of Nicaragua, teetering on the brink of becoming either a Marxist-Leninist dictatorship or a socialist democracy. Upon this tiny strip of the world, holding apart as it does the two great oceans, Ronald Reagan has set the sights of his world view. As of June 1983 his administration, with the increasingly balky complicity of Congress, was continuing to provide arms to the El Salvador government for its war against Communist-backed guerrillas, was arming and aiding Guatemala, whose general-dictator in 1982 slaughtered thousands of persons deemed to be leftists, and was promoting, training, and paying an army which invaded Nicaragua from Honduras and which by May 1983 numbered 7,000 guerrillas, many of whom had been soldiers for the deposed Nicaraguan dictator Anastacio Somoza.

In the first forty months of civil war in El Salvador, a country of 5 million, government security forces have killed more than 35,000 civilians and another 2,000 have "disappeared," according to the Catholic Archdiocese of the country. In 1982, said this same source, 6,000 died there. Despite this and the reversal of the country's land reform, Reagan has "certified" (as Congress requires if aid is to be given) that El Salvador is making sufficient progress in human rights. As they had concerning South Vietnam, officials in Washington began to say that the war might be lost by the government in San Salvador; despite the level of U.S. aid at $60 million a year, the guerrillas were mysteriously winning. Reagan asked that the sum be raised to $110 million and hinted he might increase the number of U.S. military advisers there. The U.S. ambassador there predicted a long war lasting perhaps 7 to 10 years. On February 2, 1983, the U.S. suffered its first casualty in El Salvador when a Green Beret, while flying in a Salvadoran-piloted helicopter near an important bridge, was wounded.[11]

In Guatemala a junta seized power and suspended all political parties; one month later Reagan officials said that the administration intended to end the U.S. arms freeze against that country and approve the sale of spare parts for American-made helicopters. That was April 1982. According to Amnesty International, between March 23, when General Efrain Rios Montt had seized power, and July, 2,600 unarmed civilians were killed by death squads that were "pacifying" northern and western parts of the country said to be dominated by Marxist guerrillas. Reagan remarked that Rios Montt had gotten a "bum rap" on human rights violations and early in 1983 lifted the five-year-old ban on arms sales to Guatemala.[12]

The U.S. Constitution gives Congress the power to declare war, but the framers did not contemplate the present period when American Presidents covertly foment wars abroad by providing foreigners military training, weapons, intelligence, and other logistical support. At first the U.S. encouraged Argentina to mount an attack on the Sandinista government in Nicaragua. The U.S. officially knew about and tolerated a training camp for Nicaraguan, Cuban, and Panamanian exiles in Miami and another one in southern California for foes of the Sandinistas. The *Washington Post* reported in February 1982 that Reagan had authorized the encouragement of political and paramilitary operations by other governments against Nicaragua. Subsequently Leslie H. Gelb revealed in the *New York Times* that on March 9, 1981, Reagan had authorized covert military action for the stated purpose of intercepting arms moving through Nicaragua to El Salvador and Guatemala. Then, on November 18, 1981, in what came to be known as Document 17, Reagan granted the CIA authority to conduct and support "political and military operations against Cubans and Cuban supply lines" in Nicaragua and elsewhere in Central America and to work with other governments, mainly Argentina and Honduras. Document 17 authorized $20 million for all covert actions in Central America, including the financing of a 500-guerrilla force of Latin-Americans (a force that was to increase 14-fold in eighteen months).

However, understandings that Argentina would take the lead deteriorated when Reagan sided with Britain against Argentina in the Falklands war. The U.S. then took the lead itself, in tandem with the government of Honduras. Moreover, a U.S. destroyer began intelligence monitoring off the coasts of Salvador and Nicaragua.

The House, fearing that Reagan was going to "Vietnam"

them (the verb was coined by Senator Laxalt of Nevada), specified that monies for the anti-Nicaragua effort could not be used
"for the purpose of" overthrowing the government there, and
through April 1983 Reagan maintained: "We are not doing anything to try and overthrow the Nicaraguan government." But
then in May he let down his guard against candor and made an
all-out case for the U.S.-sponsored guerrillas as "freedom
fighters" and against the Sandinistas as totalitarians who had
betrayed their revolution. Under Reagan the United States was
all but admittedly sponsoring the overthrow of the government
of Nicaragua without a declaration of war by Congress and in
explicit defiance of the charter of the Organization of American
States.

While there was much official palaver about discussions between the U.S. and Nicaragua, by 1983 the Sandinistas were
saying that it was the U.S., not they, who had shut off the dialogue. When, during a hearing, members of Congress told Secretary of State Shultz that the U.S. should sponsor negotiations
between the Salvadoran rebels and the government there, Shultz
exploded: "And to now say, let them shoot their way into that
government. No dice!" Mexico and Venezuela came up with a
peace plan, and states in the area met to try to end the region's
turmoil without inviting the U.S. to attend. But when Ambassador Kirkpatrick returned from visiting government officials in
El Salvador, she quoted them as opposing a negotiated settlement.

The U.S. was thus helping to polarize the situation within
Central America, destroying the middle ground. It was also in-
tensifying the antigringo hostilities that are a feature of ordinary
discourse in Latin America. Even the president of friendly Venezuela said gently that the U.S. "should make an effort to com-
prehend" Latin America's problems "in order to act in a realistic
way." During a special U.N. Security Council debate on Nicaragua the U.S. found itself almost alone. The country's moral authority was once again suffering self-inflicted wounds; for how
could the American President say, as he did in his 1983 State of
the Union address: "Responsible members of the world community do not threaten or invade their neighbors and they restrain
their allies from aggression." He meant, of course, the Soviets

and Afghanistan, but his secret war in Nicaragua was violating his own norms.

There is a failure of social imagination and moral responsibility at the basis of U.S. foreign policy which Reagan's crystallization of that policy's gravest tendencies makes more costly than ever. In Haiti, the state that lies fewer than 100 miles eastward of Cuba across the Caribbean's Windward Passage, "Baby Doc" Duvalier continues the tyrannical ways of his notorious father, terrorizing and repressing the country's impoverished 5 million people. The Reagan administration declaims against the human rights abuses of Cuba and Grenada, but not of Haiti. Not that Duvalier is regarded as clean; the point is that he's on our side. "Only America can save Haiti from Moscow," said Haiti's foreign minister in a flight of inspiration late in 1981. The failure of imagination is leaving these situations to fester as they may until Leninist one-party-dictatorship movements develop to remedy and exploit them, leaving the U.S. once again forced to choose between right-wing and Communist dictatorships. (Sure enough, in 1983 there appeared in Haiti the Riobe Brigade, allegedly trained in Libya and by the Palestine Liberation Organization in Lebanon.)

Judging from public opinion polls that show sharp hostility toward Reagan's Central American interventions, an increasing number of Americans may have become aware of this failure in U.S. policy abroad. Representative Gonzalez, a native-born American whose forebears fled from Mexico to San Antonio to escape the Mexican Revolution, supported the Vietnam war, but he will not support Reagan in Central America. The U.S., he says, has allied itself with the forces of oppression there: "We're identified, as the United States, with all of the oppressors, all of the dictators, all of the upper classes who have exploited the masses for hundreds of years. . . . All of a sudden it's our arms they're facing. They're not going to take it any more." Alluding to the Salvadoran generals' complaints in the spring of 1983 that the government troops were not willing to fight, Gonzalez said from his sad experience as a friend at Johnson's side during the Vietnam war: "That's what they told us in Vietnam. We've learned nothing."

Not only did the U.S. under Reagan find itself allied once again with dictatorships abroad, the U.S.-backed war to subvert Nicaragua made it easier for the world's most powerful dictatorship, the Soviet Union, to justify its invasion of Afghanistan. Nor did the Soviet leader, Yuri Andropov, miss the opportunity. "Would the United States not care what kind of government rules in Nicaragua?" he asked. "Nicaragua is an enormous distance from America. We have a common border with Afghanistan."

Probably the real sources of the administration's actions in Central America are concealed in Reagan's multipurpose anticommunism. He means by anticommunism not only what most American people mean by it—down with totalitarianism, up with civil liberties—he means by it down with the liberals, or as people in Europe and Latin America might formulate it, down with the leftists. Alan Riding, the Mexico City bureau chief of the *New York Times,* reached the hidden heart of the matter when he wrote: "The Reagan administration's unwavering objective in fact, would seem to be the cleansing of leftists from Central America."[13] Not for President Reagan the distinction between reformers and democratic socialists, on the one hand, and Marxist-Leninists on the other. The same animus in him toward Americans who support a nuclear freeze and oppose nuclear power (they are manipulated by Moscow, giving the Kremlin joy) finds similar targets abroad. And abroad—where there really are a lot of Communists mixed in among the democratic leftists—he can deploy guns, helicopters, and bombs and send destroyers offshore to gather intelligence. Reagan's foreign policy is not only military anticommunism, it is also military McCarthyism.

If the foe is outright Communist and it is giving serious offense to the American flag, Reagan inclines toward acts of war. He violently disagreed with President Johnson's restraint in 1968 when the North Koreans seized the intelligence ship U.S.S. *Pueblo,* killing a member of its crew in the course of the seizure. "I cannot for the life of me understand," said the governor of California, "why someone in the United States government, particularly the President, has not said, 'That ship had better come out of that harbor in twenty-four hours or we are coming in after it.'" Asked a few days later if there might not be retaliation against the crew, Reagan replied, "What number do we set the limit on? How many of our citizens can be kidnapped by a foreign power before . . . (we) do something about it?" As far as he was concerned, he said, the limit was one.

On second thought, a week later, he said he had not meant that he would send American warships into Wonsan Harbor to take back the *Pueblo* by force. Possibly, he said, the U.S. should have at once blockaded North Korea's shipping or seized one of its ships on the high seas. But Johnson's decision not to act immediately was, he said, "appeasement." Johnson continued to forebear, and the members of the crew were safely returned.

Reagan had eight more years to think about the matter before he next discussed it—and his opinion then was even more belligerent than his initial, impulsive one. "Even today, eight years after the *Pueblo* was captured, some people in this country will think what I'm going to say is jingoistic," he began. "I say the only defensible action, the only moral action, was to move our Seventh Fleet into position outside the harbor and then say to the North Koreans: 'Send our ship and our men safely out of that harbor within six hours or we're coming in to get them, and we'll use planes, guns, torpedoes, whatever it takes.'"

To save South Korea from communism, 52,246 Americans died in the Korean War. South Korea was and still is a right-wing police state that matches the left-wing police state in North Korea. In 1978, arguing against Carter's decision to withdraw some U.S. combat troops from South Korea (a decision which Carter later reversed), Reagan reviewed a State Department report on the situation in a curious way. The report, he told his listeners, "says steps must be taken" to replace the combat capability we were withdrawing. In fact it said that agreement had been reached with South Korea to do so. Then, after a series of phrases reviewing what else the report recommended, for his own part Reagan—without saying that it was his opinion—added: "And still—with all that—they would need our active participation if war should come."[14]

In October 1979 South Korea's dictator-president Park Chung-hee was assassinated, and a general named Chun Doo-Hwan seized power in a bloody coup. Chun had the leading opposition politician, Kim Dae Jung, arrested, and he banned more than 800 other politicians from running for office or engaging in political activities. He closed newspapers and news agencies. Dissidents charged that authorities systematically tortured the more than 500 political prisoners in custody. In 1980 Kim Dae Jung was condemned to death for sedition by a military court that called no prosecution witnesses. West Germany and Japan threatened to stop economic aid to the country if he was killed; Secretary of State Edmund Muskie took a personal interest, Secretary of Defense Harold Brown told Chun in Seoul that the U.S. opposed the execution, and President-elect Reagan joined in the efforts to stop it. Chun had by this time been "elected" president by a rubber-stamp electoral college. On January 22, two days after Reagan was inaugurated, Chun received an invitation to meet with him in Washington on February 2. On January 23 Chun commuted Kim Dae Jung's sentence to life in prison; on January 24 he ended 456 days of martial law, while keeping control of the press and leaving the political prisoners where they were.

During their meeting in the White House, Chun promised Reagan he would work for "a freer, more abundant and democratic society" (or so George Bush later said). Reagan and Chun issued a joint communiqué renewing full diplomatic, military, and economic cooperation between the two countries. Reagan also marked the occasion by announcing that all the 40,000 U.S. troops would stay in South Korea and the U.S. would sell South Korea sophisticated F-16 fighter planes. In late February and early March 1982 Chun reduced Kim Dae Jung's sentence to twenty years and said he was lifting the ban on 250 politicians. At the end of that March Defense Secretary Weinberger visited Seoul to join Chun in a concrete bunker equipped with bullet-proof glass to review a military exercise in which South Korean forces and U.S. helicopter gunships and jet fighter-bombers participated. The U.S. has tactical nuclear weapons in South Korea, and in a joint communiqué with Chun, Weinberger "confirmed that the United States' nuclear umbrella will continue to provide additional security to the Republic of Korea."

At year's end, by prearrangement between South Korea and the Reagan administration, Kim Dae Jung was released from prison and deported to the U.S. with an announcement that he was being received here for medical treatment, which he needed for an arthritic condition. The administration took a measure of credit for achieving his release. From another point of view, the former director of the State Department's Office of Korean Affairs, Donald L. Ranard, said the State Department could be open to criticism as "an accessory to Kim's exile." Kim himself said on arriving in the U.S. that he would return to South Korea to fight for democracy and help his "many colleagues" in prison. Chun continued to ban 567 leading politicians from politics. Kim was grateful to be welcomed by the Americans, he said, but he added, in an interview with the *New York Times*: "In reality, America has helped dictatorial regimes in the name of anticommunism, security, and economic rehabilitation. But in so many of these countries, like South Korea, democratic forces are still of minority weight and are pressed from both sides, by the Communists on one side and on the other by fascist power elites supported by the United States. We feel sad and betrayed by this."[15]

Reagan has long been associated with the cause of Taiwan, the island nation of 18 million people off the coast of China. When Communists took over mainland China in 1949 Nationalist leaders retreated to Taiwan, which they have ruled dictatorially ever since. In the early 1970s President Nixon, contrary to what had been expected of Republicans for two decades, forged a friendly new U.S. relationship with Communist China. If a Democrat had been making Nixon's trip to China, Reagan said in 1972, "I'd be up on the wall screaming, because . . . a Democratic President would be appeasement-minded," but Nixon "only intends to establish communication." On Nixon's return, Reagan said he had asked him what would happen if Red China tried to take Taiwan by force and Nixon had replied, "This country will protect and defend Taiwan." In a 1975 interview, discussing U.S. treaty commitments to South Korea and Taiwan,

Reagan said North Korea and China "must know that they risk involvement and confrontation with the United States if they start any adventuring."

Beginning in 1977 the public relations firm of Michael Deaver and Peter Hannaford, which was handling Reagan's radio broadcasts, was listed as an agent of the Taiwan government at a fee of $5,000 a month. Reagan said "we should accept" the work, Hannaford wrote later. Deaver, Hannaford, and Reagan certainly discussed the country during this period—"Hell," Reagan jested, "I was the one who was selling them on Taiwan." In his radio broadcasts in 1978 and 1979, with another presumptively appeasement-minded Democrat in the White House, Reagan fulminated as Carter established diplomatic relations with Communist China and abrogated the U.S. defense treaty with Taiwan. The new U.S. relationship with Red China, Reagan said, was "based on betrayal of the Free Chinese on Taiwan"; the world's nations "have seen us cold-bloodedly betray a friend for political expediency."

In his campaign he began to feel the political heft of the public's acceptance of the new U.S. relationship with China—a bully state like all Communist states, yes, but also a baby born every two seconds, 1 billion people, almost a fourth of the human race. He proposed to convert the informal American liaison office on Taiwan into an official U.S. office. Predictably the Communist Chinese took offense; Reagan sent Bush to Peking in an attempt to pacify them, but they were not pacified. Sensing, probably, that he was toying with an issue that could activate fears that he was an extremist, Reagan abandoned his proposal and accepted the informality of U.S.-Taiwan relations.[16]

As President, seeking to bring about a worldwide quarantine of the Soviets, he has found himself occupied with a much more momentous Chinese puzzle than how to strike a balance on the subject between his own right wing and an electoral majority. It was Nixon's geopolitical motive in his opening to China to exploit that nation's natural rivalry with the Soviet giant, which it faces to its north and northwest across the 4,500 continuous miles of frequently disputed borders between them. As Nixon saw it in 1982: "Will China continue its hostility toward the Soviet Union, or will the new Soviet overtures lead to a *rapprochement* between the two Communist powers?" The ranking Democrat on the Senate Armed Services Committee, Senator Henry Jackson (D.–Wash.), said it would be a "serious mistake" to provide additional arms to Taiwan: "There is a faction within the Chinese establishment that would like to make an accord with the Russians. And we could wake up one morning and find another 1939 Hitler-Stalin pact with a new group in power in China." If China felt its only real defense against the U.S.S.R. was a pact with it, he added, "the whole balance of power could shift overnight."

With the Red Chinese warning that U.S. arms sales to Taiwan would be the "litmus test," Reagan announced that the U.S. would sell the Nationalist government more F-5 jet fighters (the number turned out to be sixty) and $60 million worth of military parts, coproducing the jets in Taiwan. To stave off the Communists' anger, the U.S. signed an almost inscrutable communiqué with the People's Republic. The U.S. agreed to "reduce gradually" the quality and quantity of its arms sales to Taiwan, "leading over a period of time to a final resolution." For its part Peking said it was its "fundamental policy to strive for a peaceful solution to the Taiwan question." Fending off attacks from the right, Reagan and his spokesmen said in effect that if Peking used force against Taiwan the agreement was off. But the Communists in Peking took this as a grave offense: They had not promised not to use force. A wrangle broke out over Peking's charges that Reagan was increasing arms sales to Taiwan from the levels of recent years. In an interview with *Human Events* (again seeking to appease his special constituency) Reagan said the communiqué meant merely that if the day ever came when Taiwan was peacefully reunified with China there wouldn't be any need for arms sales to Taiwan—"Nothing was meant beyond that," he said. The official Chinese news agency charged that Reagan "totally disregarded" the meaning of the accord.

Then, onto this strife-ridden stage lumbered the long-expected Russian bear. "A Soviet-China Thaw?" "Soviet Aide Hints at a Cut in Troops on Chinese Border." "Soviet Reporting a Chinese Détente." "Peking, in Message to Moscow, Urges Each

Side to Bend." The world's top Communist leaders were not likely to disclose to western reporters what was really happening, but Soviet officials did inform Leslie Gelb in March 1983 that Moscow had reached "substantial détente" with Peking and was prepared to make concessions on border disputes because the Soviets did not think that relations between Peking and Washington would ever again be as cordial as they were at their high point, in 1980.[17]

What appears to be happening in U.S. foreign policy is a series of collisions between the President's predictable and primitive ideology and the unpredictable complexities of the world. Few situations are so simple that Reagan can play good-guy gunslinger. And since foreign policy may be set by the President but is administered by others who may know a great deal more about the real situation than he does, outcomes vary.

In Libya Reagan found his easiest target: a small nation of 3 million geopolitically somewhat isolated in North Africa and led by the sinister dictator-executioner, Kaddafi. The American President accused Kaddafi of sending squads into the U.S. to assassinate him (which may have been so but was never proved), ordered all Americans to withdraw from the country, and challenged Kaddafi's claims of sovereignty in the Gulf of Sidra (a challenge which led to U.S. planes shooting down two Libyan planes). After the assassination of Egypt's Anwar Sadat, acting on an alleged report that Libyan forces were massing for an invasion of their neighbor to the east, Reagan sent four AWACs planes to Egypt and put the Rapid Deployment Force on alert. He then withdrew the planes and called off the alert, and Secretary of State Shultz said that as a result of Reagan's action "Kaddafi is back in his box where he belongs." Yet even concerning so ripe a target as Kaddafi's Marxist Libya, events took their own ironic turn. *Newsweek* learned that CIA agents in Chad, one of Libya's southern neighbors, were stirring up trouble for him there and that the CIA was also working with Libyan dissidents in exile to encourage a "legitimate opposition" to him; the magazine also said that CIA director Casey had told one congressional committee that the anti-Kaddafi activities might lead to Kaddafi's "ultimate" removal.[18]

When criticizing Carter's active human rights policy, Reagan asserted that we must "accept the world" as it is. But this did not characterize his convictions on the subject; he meant that we must anathematize the human rights abuses of left-wing dictatorships while we tolerate the human rights abuses of right-wing dictatorships. Back in 1964 he criticized "the hypocrisy of assailing our allies because here and there they cling to a colony" while we never, he said, protest "the millions of people enslaved in Soviet colonies." Communist governments do not honor rights, he said, so how can Carter criticize our friends who do not do so, either? Reagan dramatizes and excoriates left-wing repressions and atrocities while he minimizes and justifies right-wing repressions and atrocities.

On the record, the administration has evolved a transparent have-it-both-ways position: It professes support for human rights everywhere while admitting that it avoids causing any public difficulties for friendly dictatorships. Speaking spontaneously at a press conference the second week of the administration's existence, Secretary of State Haig blurted out: "International terrorism will take the place of human rights in our concern. . . ." But this was succeeded by the more politic formulations, for instance, that human rights concern us, but "we must take into account the pressures a regime faces and the nature of its enemies." The administration also contends that it has continued Carter's human rights policy but with one difference: The Reaganists are working for progress with our friends in private rather than making public statements and employing sanctions against offending nations.[19] Despite this obfuscation, the drift is clear. We can best see the assumptions and purposes of Reagan's policies and the power of reality to frustrate them by comparing his attitudes toward the two great southern continents with the trends of actual events there.

Southern Africa is a perfect trap for Reagan's ideas. White-ruled South Africa remains the strongest nation in the region. African Marxists have taken over its neighbors to the northeast and north, Mozambique and Zimbabwe (formerly Rhodesia). Rebels in South Africa's territory Namibia on the south Atlantic, led by African Marxist Sam Nujoma, have been fighting for that territory's independence since 1966. To Namibia's immediate north, covert CIA support for the Savimbi rebels in Angola's civil war failed to prevent Angola's takeover in 1975 by a pro-Soviet Marxist faction. Only seven or eight of Africa's fifty or so nations are Marxist, but the concentration of several of them around South Africa occupied Reagan at the radio microphone many a time in the late 1970s.

Now, South Africa is a racist police state. The government's official policy of racial apartness is called apartheid. The nation's 4.5 million whites enjoy civil liberties within their social and political enclaves, but the 23 million blacks cannot vote and are totally excluded from all political life. The whites have reserved for themselves 87 percent of the land and are forcing the blacks into impoverished enclaves called "black spots." As workers the blacks are regimented by a pass system of enforced migrant labor (beyond a time limit they must show official authorization to be in "white" areas), and they are exploited at a white-to-black wage differential that now averages about 4 to 1. For helping blacks organize unions, whites have been imprisoned indefinitely without trial and cruelly interrogated. Blacks and whites are sent to prison or put under house arrest for years for political offenses. Tortures and assaults during interrogations are frequently alleged. Recently the security police searched the home of a *Washington Post* reporter looking for evidence that he had illegally quoted the wife of an imprisoned leader of the outlawed revolutionary African National Congress. A black South African journalist got two and a half years in jail for owning a copy of a book published by another outlawed resistance organization, the Pan Africanist Congress. One can readily imagine how many of the blacks on this continent of half a billion people feel about the 4.5 million whites who run the avowedly racist nation that dominates their southern area.

Five American states and some local governments in the U.S., as well as some corporations and universities, now scruple against investing in South Africa. The reason for the movement against doing business in South Africa, Reagan said on the radio before he became President, was, "of course, apartheid, and the protesters insist the corporations are supporting injustice and exploitations of the black majority by maintaining operations there. I've pointed out . . . that we all find apartheid repugnant. I've also pointed out that South Africa's problem is quite a bit more complicated than our own struggle with bigotry and prejudice."

Reagan devoted the rest of that broadcast to repeating appreciatively some arguments for U.S. trade with South Africa that had been advanced by Chief Gatcha Buthelezi, the leader of ZwaZulu, the Zulu homeland, who spoke, Reagan said, "in warmest praise of American employers in his country." This same chief was saying something quite a bit different by 1983. The white government of South Africa had proposed a token sharing of power with Indians and mixed-race, or "colored" Africans, while leaving the black majority entirely unrepresented. A party of the mixed-race group had decided to accept the offer and to participate, and Reagan's State Department had endorsed that party's decision. Buthelezi called this endorsement "a slap in the face of black South Africa."[20]

Until 1979 Zimbabwe, South Africa's northern neighbor, was her sister republic of Rhodesia, ruled by the whites led by Ian Smith. Once black Marxists took over Mozambique and shut Rhodesia off from the Indian Ocean, though, the days of Smith's Rhodesia were numbered. In 1976, three years before the founding of Zimbabwe, Reagan recommended an idea that he advanced: The U.S. should send troops to Rhodesia.

He had been speaking to the Sacramento Press Club. The U.S. and Britain, he was saying, should try to mediate an agreement on a transition to democratic majority rule in Rhodesia and should try to prevent bloodshed. How could bloodshed be prevented? he was asked. In a rambling answer, he said perhaps the agreement would do it, or "Whether it will be enough to have simply a show of strength, a promise that we would supply troops, or whether you'd have to go in with occupation forces or not, I don't know." Then, in a choppy sentence with a syntactical gulp toward the end of it, he said that sending troops would be justified: "But I believe, in the interests of peace and avoiding bloodshed, and to achieve a democratic majority rule which we all, I think, subscribe to, I think would be worth this for us to do it."

President Ford, whom Reagan was then running against, said at once that sending troops to Rhodesia would be "irresponsible." Senator Baker, then the GOP Minority Leader in the Senate, said Reagan was "too reckless to be President." Flaring back, Reagan said his remarks had been hypothetical, but then talked himself into much more trouble. Here is Robert Lindsey's account of the occasion in the *Los Angeles Times:* "Mr. Reagan said there had been 'many instances' where the United States had sent a 'token military force['], such as to Lebanon during the Eisenhower administration, and suggested that the United States should have done this during the recent Cyprus crisis that also involved Turkey and Greece, and during the current Lebanese civil war, and said that he would favor such troop actions as President."

Reporting the same remarks, Cannon of the *Washington Post* wrote that Reagan "used as an example of effective foreign policy President Eisenhower's sending of 'a battalion' of Marines into Lebanon in 1958. 'They never fired a shot,' " Reagan was quoted.

The Carter administration had refused to accept an interim government in Rhodesia unless it included the two tribal leaders of the blacks in the rebellion, Robert Mugabe and Joshua Nkomo. They led separate guerrilla armies that were allied in the Patriotic Front. Nkomo was regarded as the country's patriarch, but Mugabe's army and tribe were much the larger, and in the first election in the new country Mugabe won 57, and Nkomo 20, of the 100 seats in the new Zimbabwean parliament. The white minority was guaranteed another 20 seats under the peace agreement. Mugabe became the prime minister, replacing Smith, and Nkomo became a member of Mugabe's Cabinet.

To Reagan in the late 1970s, though, Mugabe and Nkomo were nothing but murderous leftists. A man Reagan did not identify, who had just returned from a trip to Rhodesia, sent him a full-page advertisement from a St. Louis newspaper, and this was the basis for his broadcast on the situation.

"There were pictures of Rhodesian citizens—always black and always dead—their hands tied behind their backs," he said. "They lay sprawled on the ground where they had fallen when Russian-made automatic weapons mowed them down.

"In one photo the innocent victims had been burned alive. There was a hard-to-look-at picture of a village chief. He was still alive. His lips, ears, and hands had been cut off. The caption said his wife had been forced to cook and eat them.

"There was only one picture of a white Rhodesian, a tiny baby girl . . . bayoneted a dozen times.

"These guerrillas are the forces of Joshua Nkomo and Robert Mugabe who call themselves and their murderous gangs, 'The Patriotic Front.' . . . Since 1972 they have killed an estimated 9,000 of their fellow Rhodesians—mainly blacks."

By holding out for Nkomo and Mugabe, Reagan concluded, the Carter administration continued to cause "hardship and more guerrilla killings."

Prime Minister Mugabe earned much international respect. He set about trying to improve living standards in the new country, especially in an arduous and agonizing land reform. He spoke quietly, and he refused to let Zimbabwe become an outpost of either the Soviets or the Americans. Administration officials began to see Zimbabwe as a bulwark against Soviet influence in Africa Reagan changed course and continued U.S. aid to Mugabe's government at about the same level Carter had provided, $75 million a year. Hopes soared that Zimbabwe might become a model of progress in Africa.

Late in 1982, however, a new civil war broke out between the tribes of Mugabe and Nkomo, the Shona and the Ndebele. Mugabe, calling those fighting him "dissidents," said chillingly: ". . . in a war zone the price of supporting dissidents is death. People who feed dissidents . . . should not complain when their relatives die." At the same time Mugabe informed everyone that if he is re-elected in 1985, he will then convert Zimbabwe into a one-party state.[21]

In Namibia, Sam Nujoma leads the Southwest Africa Peoples Organization (SWAPO), which he is frank to admit is funded by the U.S.S.R. and East Germany. Ostensibly Namibia became independent in 1978 under a U.N. agreement. On radio in 1979, calling Nujoma the "leader of a Marxist terrorist band," Reagan contended the agreement had been violated when the parties to it declared that the South African seaport of Walvis Bay had to be integrated into Namibia. This port on the south Atlantic is the only possible one for the new country; as some analysts see the situation, South Africa's control of the port would mean its continued economic control of Namibia.

Reagan said that "Nujoma's SWAPO forces—like the bandits of Nkomo and Mugabe in Rhodesia—were busily murdering and pillaging." He complained that the U.N. Commission for Namibia, the U.N. Council for Namibia, the U.N. Fund for Namibia, UNICEF and UNESCO regarded Nujoma as the country's only legitimate spokesman and were giving his movement financial assistance. "Our country," Reagan said, "is going along with this in spite of Nujoma's declaration . . . that he isn't fighting for majority rule, but is fighting to seize power. . . . It boggles the mind to think that our government believes it is in our best interest to turn Namibia over to a procommunist government."

Six months into the Reagan administration, the President's powerful aide William Clark, acting then as deputy secretary of state, journeyed to Pretoria for talks with the South Africans on Namibia. In these talks, the U.S. refused to join the South Africans in jettisoning the agreement on Namibia's independence, but Joseph Lelyveld of the *New York Times* was told that late one night in a Cape Town hotel the U.S. side did propose that Washington would undertake to guarantee that if the South Africans would withdraw their troops from Namibia, the 20,000 or so Cuban troops in Angola would likewise be withdrawn. Despite the obvious question, how could the U.S. guarantee this, South Africa, which wants to keep control of Namibia one way or another, must have seen the offer as a no-lose proposition: Either the Cubans would leave Angola or South Africa would stay in Namibia.[22]

Angola, too, though a one-party Marxist state, is a complicated case. The government derives much of its income from the Gulf Oil Corporation, which produces oil off its coast. Reagan asked Congress to repeal the Clark amendment by which the covert aid to the Savimbi guerrillas in Angola had been cut off, but Congress refused. Nevertheless, the antigovernment forces of Jonas Savimbi still operate in southern Angola. Savimbi says he wants socialism, but also multiparty government. Visiting Washington he was warmly received and met with Haig. He acknowledges that he is receiving aid from South Africa, which has troops of its own in southern Angola. Pretoria is also training and financing guerrillas who are seeking to destabilize the Marxist government in Mozambique.[23] The whole situation in southern Africa is a cauldron of war, reform, terror, subversion, racism, in a word: danger.

How distant all of this is, though, from what we know. Many of the new nations in Africa arose from and are still only the new forms of ancient tribes, a fact which may create an indigenous bias for one-party government. Moreover, David Rockefeller, the retired chairman of Chase Manhattan Bank, remarked in Zimbabwe in 1982: "The more I've seen of countries which are allegedly Marxist in Africa, the more I have a feeling it is more labels and trappings than reality." The primary interest of the leaders of these countries, he said, "is to improve the lot of their people and strengthen the economies of the countries," and he did not think African Marxism was a threat to the U.S. or to American business interests on the continent. But maybe this is just the way Marxists talk to the most powerful banker in the world. When Joseph Lelyveld asked South Africa's successor to Cecil Rhodes, Harry Oppenheimer, whose group controls the world's principal gold and diamond deposits, about Rockefeller's remark that African Marxism is no threat to American business interests, Oppenheimer replied, "I think that's obvious nonsense, don't you?" He also told Lelyveld, "I think this is a very risky time."

Carter had decided that U.S. relations with South Africa could not be normal until there was racial justice for blacks in that country. This policy, fashioned in part by Carter's Georgia friend Andrew Young, obviously had the whole African continent in view, not just South Africa. Reagan, reversing Carter, has relaxed restrictions on trade with South Africa. The Commerce Department actually approved selling the country 2,500 batons about the size of police nightsticks. The Treasury Department supported a $1.1 billion loan to South Africa from the International Monetary Fund. Early in the life of the administration the fifty-one-nation African Group at the U.N. issued a statement that it "will not accept the development of the policy by the present American administration in favor of the racist regime of South Africa." After two more years of Reagan, Kenneth Kaunda, the president of Zambia, who is a friend of Harry Oppenheimer's, said during a state visit to Washington: "If you do not act on apartheid, that thing is going to explode. It's going to happen, and as I have said before, when it does, it will make the French Revolution look like a child's picnic. All of the things that you believe in will go up in flames."[24]

Both the nations that dominate the South American land mass have been ruled by military dictatorships, but in Brazil the general-president permitted elections in 1982 for the first time in seventeen years and some centrist democracy was developing. Reagan conducted himself carefully there during his South American tour and extended about as much aid as the touchy Brazilians seemed willing to accept.[25]

In Argentina in 1976 a junta overthrew the populist government of Isabel Martínez de Perón and conducted a military operation against what it said were terrorists and leftists. By 1979 between 6,000 and 15,000 people had disappeared, and it is widely presumed that the *desaparecidos,* as they are called, were arrested, tortured, and killed by the government. The security forces had been set loose to carry out the junta's announced purpose, the "annihilation of subversive delinquents." The *New York Times* reported in July 1976: "The bullet-riddled bodies of some who disappeared have turned up in ditches or empty lots. . . . Armed youths painting slogans on walls have been shot by the police."

The junta appointed as its economic czar, with the title of the minister of economy, José Martínez de Hoz, who had been chairman of the country's largest private steel company. At the time of the takeover most national union headquarters were occupied by troops and the leaders of the unions were arrested or went into hiding. Martínez de Hoz controlled wages, but left prices free; strikes and collective bargaining were outlawed.

In broadcasts in 1978 and 1979, relying on Martínez de Hoz for his information, Reagan justified the junta's "process of bringing stability" to Argentina. "The armed forces stepped in," he said, "as Martínez de Hoz explained, as a last resort, to keep the country together. He said that his country had been facing a well-equipped force of 15,000 terrorists. . . . The situation is virtually under control today. . . .

"[Martínez de Hoz] points out that in the process of bringing stability to a terrorized nation of 25 million, a small number were caught in the crossfire, among them a few innocents. Today, the number of people detained for suspicion of terrorist links is steadily declining."

President Reagan asked Congress to lift the ban on aid to Argentina which had been in force since 1978, and Congress obliged him, provided he certified that progress was being made on human rights there. After the Falklands war the Argentine government scheduled elections for 1983, and Reagan lifted economic, but not yet military sanctions. A few months later, though, the junta banned the reporting of human rights issues on television and shut down three magazines. About 1,500 unidentified bodies had been found in six cemeteries. In 1983 the junta said its crackdown on terrorists and leftists had been a military one and was exempt from action by the civilian courts. As for the vanished persons who were not otherwise accounted for, the junta said they were "considered dead, for all legal and administrative purposes."[26]

Reagan's imperviousness to indignation about right-wing dictators is even more remarkable in the case of Chile, the Andean nation that has had a strong and respected democratic tradition. Salvador Allende, a Marxist who opposed violence and may have been committed to democracy, was elected president of the country in a free election and thus established the first democratic socialist government in South America. If there is to be a democratic middle way for nations that want socialism, Allende had created the possibility of it in Chile. In 1973 the CIA helped the Chilean military overthrow him (Allende died in the action), and General Augusto Pinochet became the dictator. The vigorous democracy which the country had enjoyed was closed down. All political parties were banned, including, for example, the centrist party which had elected pro-American Eduardo Frei president in the 1960s. According to Amnesty International, the torture of political prisoners was commonplace: During five months of 1980, for instance, 2,000 people were arrested on political charges and most of them were tortured. Victims were tied to a metal grid while electric shocks were administered to different parts of their bodies. Pinochet also drove tens of thousands of Chileans into exile because of their politics.

"Allende was a Marxist and took Chile down the road to socialism," Reagan said on the radio in 1979. "Businesses of all kinds were nationalized. Journalists who have made an honest effort to talk with the Chilean man-in-the-street report that there would have been a people's revolt if the military overthrow of the Allende regime had not taken place."

Pinochet, Reagan said, "promised to restore democratic rule also and to allow elections. True, they haven't taken place as yet, but there is reason to believe that if and when they do the general might just be the favorite candidate if he chooses to run." Reagan cited a Gallup poll in Chile which showed that more than two-thirds of the people approved of the Pinochet government, wanted no election then, and found Pinochet "decent and humane." All in all, Reagan said, Chile under Pinochet sounded like a good country "to be friends with."

A year later, while Reagan was busy running for President in the United States, Pinochet submitted to the people of Chile a new constitution that specifically called for the continuation of his rule until 1989. The people could vote yes or no, but the military would choose the next president until 1997, when at last democracy would start and there would be free presidential elections again. Former President Frei, bereft of his banned party, fought the constitution's adoption, but the police prevented him from holding public rallies during the last days of the campaign. The vote was announced as about two-to-one for the constitution.

One of the thousands exiled from Pinochet's Chile was Orlando Letelier, who had been a member of Allende's Cabinet and had become associated with the leftist Institute for Policy

Studies in Washington. In 1976 a bomb exploded under his car in Washington, killing him and a young woman who was with him. The Pinochet government was suspected, but in two broadcasts on these murders Reagan advanced doubts that the suspicion was correct. In fact, he suggested, perhaps Marxists had planted the bomb to make Letelier a martyr (see the Appendix). An American named Michael Townley, who worked for the Chilean secret police, was indicted for the crime and convicted. During his trials U.S. prosecutors presented evidence that he was a senior agent in Chile's intelligence service and had planted the bomb under its direct orders. Three former senior officers of the intelligence service were indicted by a U.S. grand jury for complicity in the murders, but the Pinochet government refused to extradite them to the U.S. for trial.

All in all Reagan struck out in his broadcasts on Chile, but if he noticed, it did not affect his course of action. Congress had banned trade and military aid to Chile in 1976 because of the human rights situation. Reagan asked Congress to lift this ban. Despite accusations that Chile harbored international terrorists, Congress said all right, but this time required, not only that he certify that Chile had made "significant progress" in human rights, but also that the Pinochet government had cooperated in bringing the three Chilean agents to justice for the assassination of Letelier. The assistant U.S. attorney in charge of the Letelier case had told the press that Chilean officials "haven't done spit since the day this thing happened." For the time being, it seemed, Reagan was stymied.[27]

A potentially more positive feature of Reagan's policy abroad is his "crusade for freedom," which he announced during an anti-Soviet speech he made in London. The objective, he said, would be "to foster the infrastructure of democracy—the system of a free press, unions, political parties, universities" in the world. Back home he asked for $65 million to finance what first occasioned a classified presidential memorandum and the inclusion of the CIA for management of covert aspects of "Project Democracy." The CIA was then allegedly cut away from the project, which was described as a governmental effort to advance democratic values abroad. This would include intensifying information programs beamed into Communist countries. Representative Stephen J. Solarz (D.–N.Y.) asked Secretary of State Shultz during hearings whether the U.S. would be prepared to help democrats in places like South Korea, the Philippines, and Taiwan, where democracy is regarded as a subversive idea. Shultz replied that no, the purpose was not to destabilize governments (he meant, of course, right-wing dictatorships). Oddly, in his London speech Reagan had remarked defensively that his proposal "is not cultural imperialism." Yet lurking in the background of this project is gathering pressure to set up a mechanism for sending private U.S. money into elections and political movements abroad; conceivably this is the principal objective of "Project Democracy."[28]

All the dominant strands in Reagan's foreign policy formed a tapestry in the Middle East. There he extended Carter's increasing reliance on military solutions toward deeper involvement and a U.S.-Soviet confrontation. He transformed Carter's general declaration that Persian Gulf oil is a vital national interest of the U.S. into a specific pledge, later hedged but still strongly implied, to defend the princes of Saudi Arabia against internal rebellion as well as external threat. And he sent in the Marines for what was said to be a short time, and nine months later, the Marines still there, the evidence gathered that the Soviets were responding with more military people of their own to match them.

After the Soviet invasion of Afghanistan, Carter had deployed U.S. warships, drawn from the Seventh Fleet in Asian waters, in the Indian Ocean area. Shortly before the 1980 election Carter said the U.S. had "prepositioned equipment for 12,000 Marines and munitions for 500 aircraft" in the Persian Gulf region. Perhaps he was just trying to keep pace with his electoral opponent. Reagan had said he wanted U.S. aircraft stationed in Pakistan and perhaps also in Saudi Arabia and elsewhere in the region. In January 1980 Reagan had suggested that these aircraft be manned by U.S. pilots and serviced by U.S. ground personnel. "I think," Reagan said, "this might be a very, very good time for the United States to show a presence in the Middle East. . . . with the consent of, say, Egypt, Israel, Saudi Arabia to have a presence there." The U.S. should move into bases in Egypt, he said, and if possible get Saudi Arabia to join in. The *Wall Street Journal* reported that many of Reagan's advisers had been "urging him to advocate basing U.S. soldiers in Israel or Egypt." The Reagan administration was not yet a month old when Weinberger said that if Israel ever requested that the U.S. base troops on its soil, the request would be considered "sympathetically." By 1982 Congress was funding new air bases, ports, and barracks for the Rapid Deployment Force in Egypt, Kenya, Oman, Portugal, Diego Garcia, and Somalia.

During the Afghan crisis Reagan had called for the stationing of U.S. troops in Pakistan—but had pulled back. To prevent further Soviet moves, he said, "We have every reason to be there." He also urged ("we are in a power game with the Soviet Union") the establishment of air and naval bases in east Africa and southwest Asia. What would the U.S. advisers do in Pakistan? "They would go to the country we have a treaty with, Pakistan, and that training could be provided there." We might station a squadron of warplanes there, too, he said. Finally, however, he drew back somewhat: "I never thought of it as actually stationing a force of ground troops there. But I thought that . . . we must provide the arms and the technicians . . ." and "we ought to be funneling weapons through there that can be delivered to those freedom fighters in Afghanistan."[29]

Carter had laid the doctrinal basis for a war for oil, declaring that any effort to block U.S. access to Persian Gulf oil would be regarded as "an assault on the vital interests of the United States" and would "be repelled by use of any means necessary, including military force." Reagan thought the U.S. "can survive without it (Persian Gulf oil), but it is absolutely essential to our allies in western Europe and Japan," and on radio in the fall of 1979 he stated: "Any American government which allowed oil supplies to its allies to be placed in question would almost certainly invite the neutralization of western Europe and Japan, the encirclement of China, and—eventually—the isolation of our own country." At first Secretary Weinberger declined to reaffirm Carter's commitment (calling it "clumsy and ill-advised"), but by 1982 the press learned that the Pentagon's five-year secret "defense guidance" document said: "It is essential that the Soviet Union be confronted with the prospect of a major conflict should it seek to reach oil resources of the gulf. Because the Soviets might induce or exploit local political instabilities, their forces could be extended into the area by means other than outright invasion. Whatever the circumstances, we should be prepared to introduce American forces directly into the region should it appear that the security of access to Persian Gulf oil is threatened."

Reagan believed that the overthrow of the pro-American Shah in Iran had "increased Israel's value as perhaps the only remaining strategic asset in the region on which the United States can truly rely. . . . Her facilities and airfields could provide a secure point of access if required in . . . emergency."[30]

Reagan first spoke in 1980 of not letting the Saudi princes be overthrown. "We should let (the Soviets) know," he said, "that we are not going to let Saudi Arabia fall, either from trouble within or from aggression without," and that "if they . . . decided to go in there, they would be running into the possibility— the probability—of a confrontation with us." In the midst of the 1981 debate on his successful proposal to permit the sale of $8.5 billion worth of military aircraft to Saudi Arabia, he stated during a press conference: "I have to say that Saudi Arabia we will not permit to be an Iran." That was so bald, he drew back a few weeks later, saying that what he "had in mind" was that if the U.S. had backed the Shah all-out, he would not have been overthrown. But before this additional instance of too much candor was retracted, Secretary Weinberger had been entirely explicit: "We would not stand by, in the event of Saudi requests, as we did before Iran, and allow a government that had been totally unfriendly to the United States and to the Free World to take over." Furthermore: "President Reagan would intervene if there should be anything that resembled an internal revolution in Saudi Arabia. . . ."[31]

Reagan believes the U.S. should have aborted the Khomeini revolution in Iran (just as we overthrew the oil-nationalizing Mossadeq government there in the early 1950s). "I believe," he said, "at the time the (Khomeini) revolution was just riots in the streets, we vacillated. . . . I believe there was a time this revolt could have been halted. . . . There were certain leaders who could have been separated from their followers and they weren't." In the White House he added that he had been told by a "knowledgeable" person that the revolution "could have been headed off with the arrest of 500 individuals," but Carter had advised against it. In 1982 Leslie Gelb reported that according to western intelligence officials and other sources, the U.S. was covertly aiding Iranian paramilitary and political exile groups and broadcasting propaganda into Iran—but not, the sources insisted, with the purpose of destabilizing the Khomeini government.[32]

In the summer of 1982 Israel invaded Lebanon on the stated ground that it needed to clear a 25-mile security zone of Palestine Liberation Organization (PLO) terrorists in order to prevent them from shelling villages inside Israel. However, in pursuit of the PLO guerrillas the Israeli forces swept right up the country and shelled Beirut, eventually entering and capturing the city. Later the most respected newspaper in the Arab world, Beirut's *An Nahar,* tabulated the war's casualties from police and hospital records: 17,825 persons killed and another 30,203 wounded. In Beirut and its suburbs 5,515 people were killed, but there was no breakdown between the military and civilian deaths there. The Israeli dead numbered about 500. These events put U.S. relations with Israel to a severe test from which they did not emerge undamaged.

In a statement with grave implications, former President Carter said sources of his in Israel had told him the U.S. had approved the invasion in advance. He said he did not have "any way to know" if the information was correct, and "the only thing I can say is that the word I got from very knowledgeable people in Israel is that 'we have a green light from Washington.' " Shultz said that was "not correct." His understanding, said the secretary of state, was that "the U.S. government was not informed and the U.S. government was and is on the record as having opposed the invasion." But Shultz added it was possible that "somebody came through here and talked about (the invasion) as a possibility." Israel's Defense Minister Ariel Sharon had visited Washington in May, but Weinberger said Sharon had never alluded to the fact that Israel was going to invade.

In any event Reagan took an active role in discouraging the Israeli venture as its extent became evident. He had played a similar role just before Argentina invaded the Falkland Islands, telephoning that nation's president in an attempt to restrain him. Evidently when Reagan's own national pride and ideological convictions are not challenged he is a peacemaker. When Israel bombarded guerrilla positions and residential areas of West Beirut for fourteen hours, Reagan said he had "lost patience a long time ago. . . . This must be resolved and the bloodshed must be stopped." Administration spokesmen gave the press their opinion that Israel had been responsible for the violation of most of nine cease-fires to that date. The press also learned that Reagan had told the Israelis he was flatly opposed to the siege of Beirut. On August 5 Reagan sent Israeli Prime Minister Menachem Begin a message that reportedly made it clear that U.S.-Israeli relations would be jeopardized unless Israel stopped "unnecessary bloodshed" in Lebanon. Israeli jets bombed West Beirut for eleven hours on August 12; the deputy White House press secretary told the press Reagan had phoned Begin and "expressed his outrage. . . . The result has been more needless destruction and bloodshed." On September 16, as the massacre of more than 300 Palestinian men, women, and children was being committed by Lebanese Christian Phalangist militia at the Shatila refugee camp in Beirut, unbeknownst as yet to the world, Reagan demanded that Israel withdraw its military forces from West Beirut immediately. With the worldwide revulsion against the massacre, for which an Israeli state investigating committee later assigned "indirect responsibility" to Israel, the war shuddered to an end. Israel admitted having used U.S.-provided cluster bombs, so-called "antipersonnel" weapons, each one of which consists of hundreds of bomblets that explode into flying sprays of steel pellets or shards. Since the U.S. and Israel had an agreement that Israel would not use U.S.-provided equipment in "any act of aggression against any other state," the State Department held that a violation of the agreement "may have occurred" and cluster-bomb shipments to Israel were indefinitely suspended.[33]

Under the Israeli-Egyptian peace treaty of 1979, 1,200 U.S.

troops were already on duty as part of the Sinai peacekeeping force. Tens of thousands of troops of Israel and Soviet-backed Syria, as well as PLO guerrillas, were in Lebanon; no peace could be expected to last unless these forces were withdrawn. Israel agreed to accept a three-nation peacekeeping force for Lebanon composed of troops from the U.S., Italy, and France. The U.S. sent 1,200 Marines to Lebanon itself and another 600 were assigned to ships offshore. There was "no intention or expectation" they would become involved in hostilities, Reagan said. Administration sources said they would be home "soon," or by the end of 1982 (this was late September). Reagan dismissed the chance of "a long entanglement," as in Vietnam. But there were some circumstances that seemed to reflect his fundamental desire to station U.S. troops in the Middle East.

The Marines would stay, Reagan said on September 28, until Israeli and Syrian forces were withdrawn from Lebanon. On the face of it this made their departure subject to indirect veto by both Israel and Soviet-backed Syria. When Reagan's policy was clarified, it turned out their withdrawal might also require Lebanon's approval because the host country's establishment of its military security was the ultimate stated objective of their deployment.

On November 1 Reagan agreed to a Lebanese request that the Marines be assigned to patrol a highway and watch out for PLO infiltrators, thus placing the U.S. troops at much greater risk. One U.S. Marine had already been killed and another three wounded when they encountered undetected explosives at Beirut Airport; now the Marines were to get involved in regulating the heavily armed population in the country. The toll was rising. A French Marine was slightly wounded by a grenade hurled at him from a passing motorcycle. Five U.S. Marines and nine Italian soldiers were wounded while on patrol when a hand grenade was thrown from a second-story window. Then, in April 1983, fifty-seven persons were killed, including a Marine and sixteen other Americans, when a terrorist bombed the U.S. Embassy in Beirut.

Some members of Congress had noticed at the outset that, while notifying Congress he was sending the Marines, Reagan had not done so under the provision of the 1973 War Powers Act which required withdrawal of the Marines after sixty days if Congress had not formally approved their deployment by then and if the troops had been introduced "into situations were imminent involvement in hostilities is clearly indicated." Reagan said that did not apply, and not until the spring of 1983 did committees of Congress begin to caution him seriously—a House committee, for instance, said congressional approval would be required before more Marines were sent in.

More might have to be, Weinberger said. The administration went so far as to pledge to take "all necessary measures" to guarantee the security of Israel's northern border if Israel withdrew its troops, and in May, nine months into the Americans' tour of duty in this dangerous situation, officials began to hint that even if all other foreign troops were withdrawn the Marines might not come home. In pursuit of a withdrawal agreement Shultz barnstormed the Middle East, but Syria was balking, and as he said, "None of these things come easy in the Middle East." Indeed not. The Israelis informed the U.S. that about 200 Soviet military experts had entered Lebanon itself from Syria. Villagers told reporters they had seen Soviet advisers touring Syrian lines within sight of the Mediterranean coastline north of Beirut. The U.S. Sixth Fleet cruised off Lebanon; the U.S.S.R., too, had about forty vessels standing off the Lebanese and Israeli coasts. Soviet officials in Moscow told Leslie Gelb that the long-range surface-to-air missiles installed in Syria would continue to be manned by Soviet troops as a "calculated decision" to draw a line against possible Israeli attack, with the implication, Gelb thought, that the Soviets might respond in some way against Israel. Lebanon and Israel agreed to a security pact that was meant to be the basis for the withdrawal of Israel's troops from Lebanon if Syrian troops and PLO forces also withdrew, but this was mere shadowboxing: Despite a five-hour confrontation with Shultz, President Hafez al-Assad flatly refused to withdraw. The U.S. asked Israel to withdraw its forces unilaterally, and the Israelis refused. Reagan had pledged that the Marines would stay in Lebanon until the other foreign troops left, and the other foreign troops weren't leaving. In the last month of 1980 the

Soviet leader Leonid Brezhnev had invited the U.S. and other world powers to join the U.S.S.R. in a treaty to forego military and naval intervention in the Persian Gulf; two and a half years later such an idea seemed like a fantasy. Reagan's major (his most presidential) foreign policy initiative, his proposal that Palestinians should achieve "full autonomy" under Jordanian supervision in the Israeli-occupied West Bank and Gaza Strip, had been vetoed by the prevailing hardliners in the PLO; 1,200 U.S. Marines and 4,000 Soviet military advisers faced each other from Lebanon and Syria, only 60 or so miles apart, and Soviet military officials themselves were probing to the edge of the eastern Mediterranean.[34] In unquestionably sincere moral shock Reagan had sought to restrain the Israelis during their invasion, but he had not succeeded, and he had volunteered then to be responsible for the defense of Israel's northern border, a task which would certainly be a full-time occupation. The United States Marines were positioned conveniently nearby.

20

Reagan and Nuclear War

"This debate is about the end of the world and how we can prevent it, or at best delay it." So said the Archbishop of York, the Right Reverend Stuart Blanch, as the governing body of the Church of England came to its decision to oppose the first use of nuclear weapons. "U.S. security has been diminished by each new round of weapons systems," declared the science adviser to Presidents Kennedy and Johnson, Jerome B. Weisner. "No President, no Congress, has foreseen the ultimate security consequences of their actions." Said Congressman John J. Rhodes, the former Republican leader in the House: "This whole idea: the more they build, the more we build, the more we both build, the more dangerous it gets. I'm worried about the economy and, well, I'm worried about the future of mankind." "The next round in the arms race," warned Senators Kennedy and Hatfield, "threatens to become the last chapter in modern history." "The question before the human species, therefore," Jonathan Schell wrote in *The Fate of the Earth*, "is whether life or death will prevail on the earth."

President Reagan has propelled the United States into an unprecedented lurch forward in the nuclear arms race. In every major controversy about a new weapons system, from the neutron bomb to binary poison gas, he has committed himself and his administration to the manufacture of the system. The arguments he uses are almost interchangeable: the Soviets are ahead of us, or we need it for deterrence, or we need it for defense. In some cases, as with the MX and the long-range cruise missile, he is carrying forward initiatives from Carter; in others, as with the B-1 bomber and space weapons, he is setting a new course for the nation. Invariantly, though, he wants the new weapons systems—all of them anywhere in sight or on the drawing boards.

Like almost everyone else he expresses abhorrence toward nuclear war. He says that it cannot be won and should never be fought, and he prays to God the weapons will never be used. But he jokes about the subject occasionally. After the all-out nuclear war drill, Operation "Ivy League," at the White House, in which the Vice President survived longer than the President, Reagan protested to George Bush that he thought *he* had won the 1980 election. In a story the President tells, an old farmer is asked where he would like to be if a nuclear bomb goes off. The farmer replies, "Someplace where I could say, 'What was that?'"

"The other day," presidential counselor Ed Meese said during an address to the Veterans of Foreign Wars in Washington, "Cap Weinberger came in to see the President, and he said, 'Mister President, you know, the press has been giving us a hard time on the MX missile. I suggest that we rename it the Hallmark missile.' And the President said, 'Well, why would you want to do that?' He said, 'Well, Mister President, I hope we never have to do it. But if we do, I want the Russians to know we cared enough to send the very best.'" Meese repeated this terrible jest in March 1982. A year later Reagan, during a picture-taking session with members of his commission on the MX, quipped: "Some of my best friends are MX missiles."[1]

Because of the intervention of his liberal daughter, Patti, in 1983 the President met with Dr. Helen Caldicott, the prime mover in Physicians for Social Responsibility, the organization of doctors who teach that the only treatment possible for nuclear war is prevention. Caldicott says Reagan told her: "I believe in building more bombs."

It is possible that Reagan is relatively ignorant about the different nuclear weapons systems. In the written opinion of George Kistiakowsky, Eisenhower's science adviser, George Rathjens, an arms control expert who has served in the government, and Herbert Scoville, a former deputy director of the CIA, Reagan "is far less informed on nuclear weapons—their capabilities, their characteristics and strategy for their use—than any President since the nuclear era began."

"I spent more than an hour with President Reagan, along with his daughter," Helen Caldicott says, "and I tell you that he doesn't understand much of this. We argued about all these strategies and almost every single thing he said to me was incorrect. . . . We talked about strategic systems and almost everything he said to me was wrong."

Reagan contends that the U.S. has fallen behind the Soviets in the arms race, that they have "a definite margin of superiority." This assertion is the basic argument for his nuclear buildup. In 1976 he said his goal was military parity, but the Republican platform in 1980 called for "overall military and technological superiority over the Soviet Union." Well-informed specialists in general do not support the proposition that the U.S. is behind the U.S.S.R. militarily. Reagan's own Department of Defense annual report for 1982 said, "The United States and the Soviet Union are roughly equal in strategic nuclear power."

During his 1980 campaign Reagan said that the United States "is in greater danger today than it was the day of Pearl Harbor," and he proposed that the country embark on a "catch-up program which would not be completed until 1990, if then." What he seems to have in mind, however, is not catching up, but winning the arms race. In a 1978 speech he had said, "The Soviet Union cannot possibly match us in an arms race." During one of his radio broadcasts the same year he said: "In his June 28 column, journalist Ben Stein summed it up very well: 'An unrestrained arms race which the U.S. could not possibly lose given our industrial superiority, or a treaty (SALT II) which says that the arms race is over and that we have lost it.' And he asks—

'which is worse?'" On the radio Reagan did not explicitly answer the journalist's question, but he has now.

One of the deeper puzzles posed by Reagan's buildup is the question: Why are we building these new weapons of mass extermination when we should know that the Soviets will respond by building new genocidal systems of their own? This has been the history of the nuclear arms race. In 1952, we tested the H-bomb; in 1955, the Soviets tested one. In 1957 they launched Sputnik; we had a rocket up the next year. In 1964 we went to work to put multiple warheads on our missiles; they copied this in 1973. In 1970 we "MIRVed" our missiles, making their multiple warheads "independently targetable"; the Soviets followed suit in 1975. Why now would we build a new generation of Trident submarines and thousands of long-range guided missiles knowing the Soviets will match us? The solution to the puzzle is the fact that Reagan, contrary to experience, does not believe the Soviets can match us.

His response to the obvious accusation that he is accelerating the arms race is a side step. "We're already in an arms race," he says, "but only the Soviets are racing." To anyone who argues that a new nuclear arms race is madness, he replies head-on that such a race is our strategy.

In 1977 he said Carter should have been willing to use "one trump card," that is, the "threat" of "an arms race." Only then, he said, would the Soviets "become interested in legitimate arms control." The month before the election he repeated: "The one card that's been missing in these negotiations has been the possibility of an arms race." Carter charged that Reagan would start "a massive nuclear arms race" which could lead to war with Russia—that playing the trump card might move us to "the nuclear precipice." But Nixon and elements in the military rushed in to support the proposition that the U.S. was behind the Soviets, and the postelection polls showed that among the voters Reagan won the argument. Thus it came to pass that in 1982 the Pentagon's five-year defense guidance plan said that the United States should develop weapons that "are difficult for the Soviets to counter, impose disproportionate costs, open up new areas of major military competition, and obsolesce previous Soviet investment."[2]

Reagan's nuclear buildup, as announced in October 1981 and subsequently modified, called for 1,000 warheads on 100 MX missiles, 100 B-1 bombers, the development of an advanced radar-eluding Stealth bomber, the placement of larger and more accurate D-5 missiles on Trident submarines, the deployment of more than 3,000 cruise missiles on B-52s and B-1s and several hundred more on submarines, the rebuilding of the nuclear command and control systems, and a civil defense program based on the evacuation of cities and the construction of blast shelters for essential workers.

He wanted four new Army divisions, $2.5 billion for the expanded Rapid Deployment Force, and five more Air Force wings. The Navy's 456 ships would be increased to 600, its 12 aircraft carriers to 15 (at $2.5 billion each). World War II battleships have been brought back into action, armed with cruise missiles. The Navy is also preparing a hospital ship against the eventuality of casualties from the Persian Gulf in a war for oil, which the Pentagon's defense guidance postulates if the Soviets or pro-Soviet groups or nations threaten the Western supply.

For 1982 Reagan asked for the largest peacetime increase in military spending in U.S. history. From $160 billion in 1981, Reagan proposed a 58 percent increase in three years and more than a doubling, to $368 billion, by 1986. For 1983 he proposed an 18 percent increase, 10.5 percent after inflation, from $183 billion to $216 billion. Budgeted weapons purchases that one year went up 37 percent, nuclear weapons forces 43 percent, Navy shipbuilding costs by more than double. Under Reagan's plans the military's share of the federal budget went from 24 percent under Carter to 32 percent by 1984. His 1984 budget included $6.9 billion for the B-1 bomber, $6.6 billion for MX, $3 billion for a Trident 1 sub, $600 million for 52 Trident 1 missiles, $1.5 billion for Trident 2 missiles, $450 million for 95 Pershing 2 missiles, $1.7 billion for 224 cruise missiles, $3.7 billion for three cruisers, $2.2 billion for three nuclear attack subs, $12 billion for 270 miscellaneous Navy, Air Force, and Marine planes, $1.5 billion for 112 Army attack helicopters, $1.8 billion for 720 M-1 tanks. In 1980, U.S. weapons programs cost $35 billion; in Reagan's 1984 they will cost $94 billion, which is more than $250 million a day. For the five years 1985–1989 Reagan seeks $2 trillion in military spending.

When the government orders a new weapons system it only pays for part of it at first; the contract and the payouts continue. Reagan has locked the government into many weapons contracts for the years ahead. Senator Levin of Michigan says, "we are creating military entitlement programs." What the *Washington Post* calls "a giant bow wave" of defense costs will hit the taxpayers in the second half of the 1980s. To critics of Reagan's $100 billion expansion of the Navy, Navy Secretary Lehman said: "Sorry . . . it's too late to stop it . . . we've got the 600-ship Navy."[3]

Fourteen years ago, in 1969, Nixon stopped U.S. production of poison gas and pledged to abide by the 1929 Geneva Protocol against its first use in war. The U.S. had 3 million poison gas artillery shells, and Nixon thought that was enough. Ford signed the Protocol on behalf of the U.S. On February 8, 1982, Reagan told Congress that production of new lethal binary nerve-gas weapons "is essential to the national interest" to deter possible Soviet use of chemical warfare.

During the ensuing month, the U.S. accused the Soviets and their allies of having killed 10,000 people in nearly 400 chemical warfare attacks in Laos, Cambodia, and Afghanistan since 1975. Reagan said the U.S. had "conclusive evidence" of these crimes. A team of scientists appointed by the U.N. Secretary-General studied U.S. data for nine months and concluded that certain U.S. allegations were "well supported" by "circumstantial evidence," but drew no definite conclusions. Even though the controversy about the truth of this matter continued to rage, the Democratic-held House refused through mid-1983 to provide Reagan the money for the new nerve gas. The administration showed no sign of dropping its campaign. Discussion of "the use of poison gas frightens people," a senior defense official told Drew Middleton of the *Times,* "but it could be considered a cheaper substitute for nuclear war that would do far less damage outside the battlefield." The Pentagon's defense guidance orders the services to be sure they could "rapidly employ existing chemical munitions in retaliation worldwide" by 1985 and to develop advanced chemical weapons for all the services by the 1990s.[4]

President Eisenhower expected and planned to use nuclear weapons in a war, but as the superpowers settled into the stand-off of mutual nuclear terror ("mutual assured destruction," or MAD), actual nuclear war came to be regarded as "unthinkable"—morally hideous and national suicide, as well. In the 1960s, however, doctrines of "limited nuclear war" gained currency on the reasoning that leaders should not have to choose between surrender and the mass murder of civilians. The thinkability of limited nuclear war led, in the 1970s and 1980s, to elaborated plans for actually "fighting" a nuclear war through its guessed-at stages. As the comment of the senior defense official on poison gas shows, nuclear war is now often quite thinkable in the minds of defense strategists. Although it is subtle and elusive, this transformation of nuclear war from unthinkable to thinkable is the most portentous development in the history of the nuclear era.

In a 1978 radio broadcast, Reagan in effect argued for thinkability by contending that the Russians were thinking about it. "We say 'thermonuclear war is unthinkable by either side,'" stated the future President. "The Russians have told their own people that while it would be a calamity, it is not unthinkable; that it very well might happen and if it does, the Soviet Union will survive and be victorious." Four years later Senators Kennedy and Hatfield wrote: "The thought has taken hold that nuclear weapons might actually be used. A decision to do so, once considered to be insane, has now been seriously contemplated under certain conditions. Thousands of people stand ready to execute such a decision."[5] As Reagan was rising in national politics during those four years, two doctrines had caught on: first, that nuclear war can be won, and second, that since nuclear war may be only regional (that is, "limited"), nuclear war-fighting plans should be laid.

Are the superpowers both now planning to fight and win a nuclear war? A military strategy review presented to Carter in

1977 said that in such a war the U.S. would suffer 140 million deaths and the Soviets 113 million, and both economies would be about 75 percent destroyed, so neither side could be "a winner." Early in 1980, however, during interviews with Robert Scheer, George Bush said that a nuclear war could be won and Reagan said that "some of your people and some of your facilities" would survive one.

"I don't believe," Bush said, that "there is no such thing as a winner in a nuclear exchange." "How do you win in a nuclear exchange?" Scheer asked the future Vice President. He replied: "You have a survivability of command [and] control, survivability of industrial potential, protection of a percentage of your citizens, and you have a capability that inflicts more damage on the opposition than it can inflict on you. That's the way you can have a winner. . . .

Some weeks later Scheer asked Reagan, on the basis of the candidate's premise that the U.S.S.R. was ahead militarily: "Let's say we get stronger than them again. Do you think we could survive a nuclear war?" Reagan replied: "It would be a survival of some of your people and some of your facilities that you could start again. It would not be anything that I think in our society you would consider acceptable. . . ."

In 1976, when Bush was running the CIA, his hawkish "Team B," estimating comparative Soviet and U.S. strength, evidently concluded that the Soviets were seeking a nuclear war-fighting capability. In 1977 Richard Pipes, a professor who was to help shape the Reaganists' policies as the senior Kremlinologist on the National Security Council staff, wrote an article whose title told its tale: "Why the Soviet Union Thinks It Could Fight and Win a Nuclear War." Richard Burt, when still at the *Times* before he joined the Reagan administration, wrote about "the apparent Soviet drive to acquire a 'first-strike capability' against American land-based rockets." Carter's secretary of defense, Harold Brown, noted that some Soviet circles visualized "a relatively prolonged" nuclear war and "a theoretical possibility of victory." The stage was set.

From his post at the heart of national security, Pipes said that "there is no alternative to war with the Soviet Union if the Russians do not abandon communism." The White House press secretary disavowed this statement, but Pipes was not fired and continued his work as a member of the administration's inner circle. In the spring of 1982 he told the *Post* that the probability of nuclear war was 40 percent and that his strategy, which reflected official thinking, was a winnable nuclear war, but that nonetheless, "The worst thing to do is to be afraid. . . . Europe . . . is so frightened." The task, in Pipes' opinion, is to convince Americans not to fear nuclear war. Some Washington insiders contended that Pipes had little influence, but certainly as he returned to Harvard he could feel that administration policy was consistent with many of his views.

It was a textbook case of mirror-imaging as the Reaganists' program to prepare to fight and win a nuclear war developed out of their perceptions that this was what the Soviets were doing. Weinberger told Congress that the administration's plan was "to prevail should deterrence fail." Reagan said reassuringly, "I don't think there could be any winners—everybody would be a loser." But in the administration's first five-year defense guidance, extensively summarized by Richard Halloran in the *Times* on May 30, 1982, U.S. armed forces were ordered to prepare for nuclear counterattacks against the Soviet Union "over a protracted period of time" and the Pentagon said twice in this document that in such a war U.S. nuclear forces "must prevail."

It is implausible that a British émigré who thinks about nuclear war, Colin S. Gray, should have a role in the Reaganists' plans, but he does. In 1980 Gray had written: "Victory or defeat in nuclear war is possible, and such a war may have to be waged to that point. . . . The United States should plan to defeat the Soviet Union and to do so at a cost that would not prohibit U.S. recovery." Subsequently Gray was made a member of the general advisory committee of Reagan's arms control agency, and in that new capacity he wrote: "What is wrong with the United States 'planning' to prevail, or win, in war? . . . The idea of a U.S. victory in nuclear war encompasses everything from . . . restoring the territorial *status quo ante* in Europe to—*in extremis*—destroying the Soviet state . . . achieved at a social cost to the west that, though heavy, does not preclude rapid recovery." From his seventh-floor office in the State Department, Gray told the *Post* that "no one can possibly design a nuclear strategy that entails anything less than somewhere between 5 and 20 million front-deaths," and his point was that while this is "horrific," it is not the holocaust. In fact, he has said concerning 20 million U.S. casualties, "it is damage from which we could recover."

"It is madness," in the opinion of former Secretary of State Cyrus Vance, "to talk about trying to fight a continuing nuclear war as though it were like fighting a conventional war, and that one could control the outcome with the kind of precision that is sometimes possible in a conventional war situation." Yet in the Reaganists' defense guidance they officially plan for "forces that will maintain, throughout a protracted conflict period and afterward, the capability to inflict very high levels of damage" upon the Soviets; that will be "capable of supporting controlled nuclear attacks over a protracted period"; and that during "post-attack reconnaissance" will target "enemy means of reconstitution and waging protracted nuclear war." The 1983 version of the defense guidance, Halloran has reported, commands that the services integrate their various plans for firing long-, medium-, and short-range nuclear weapons because "we must not impose any arbitrary division between categories of nuclear weapons systems which could constrain their effective, coordinated employment in retaliation." In April 1983 Reagan made his declaration that "a nuclear war cannot be won and must never be fought," but the word games (win or prevail, prepare to fight or plan to fight in order to deter) could not and did not obscure the fact that the superpowers have somehow challenged each other into a contest to develop the ability to win a nuclear war.[6]

During Reagan's first summer, the chief of the Army's tactical and chemical weapons policy-making division, General Niles J. Fulwyler, discussed, on a CBS report that was shown in Europe, "an attempt to have limited-use nuclear weapons" and to get the adversary to understand "that in a case like this it would be a restrained use." In the autumn Reagan further alarmed many people in Europe by saying that it is possible to have a limited nuclear war without having the holocaust. "I could see," the President said, "where you could have the exchange of tactical weapons against troops in the field without it bringing either one of the major powers to pushing the button." Trying to repair the damage this statement had done, he made things worse by repeating his thought and tying it now to an apparent reference to the European continent: U.S.–Soviet nuclear war might be avoided, he said, "if there had been battlefield (nuclear) weapons troop-to-troop exchanged there."

During that same autumn Secretary Haig, a former commander of the North Atlantic Treaty Organization (NATO), testified in Washington: "There are contingency plans in the NATO doctrine to fire a nuclear weapon for demonstrative purposes to demonstrate to the other side that they are exceeding the limits of toleration in the conventional (weapons) area. . . ." Backing him up, the State Department explained that the idea is to explode a low-yield weapon high enough above the ground to cause little damage or else to explode it in an uninhabited area or at sea. (Presumably Weinberger's fervent denial of Haig's statement was cosmetic; two years later a NATO report referred to plans for "a controlled demonstrative use.") It was Brezhnev's position that "even one nuclear bomb dropped by one side over the other would result in general nuclear exchange—a nuclear holocaust," but the U.N. Secretary-General has concluded, in a report on nuclear weapons, that Soviet strategists do contemplate local nuclear wars. As if only to underscore the profound uncertainty among the superpower leaders, in 1983 the U.S. NATO forces commander, General Bernard Rogers, said: "A nuclear war in western Europe is going to escalate to a strategic exchange."

The contemplation of "constrained nuclear warfare," confined to Europe or some other locality (and by implication not touching the U.S.), has been official U.S. policy since the Nixon administration and was refined and ratified by Carter in his Presidential Directive 59. Reagan and Haig were just spelling out what this policy means, but to many Europeans and Americans, it was news. Catholic Bishop Roger Mohony of California told a fellow bishop that when he read Haig's comment about a warning shot, "It hit me. They're really planning to use those things. And I suddenly became aware. This is not a game. This is serious business." By so publicly and vividly visualizing the use of nuclear weapons in war, Reagan and others in his administration were generating volatile fears that U.S. policymakers do expect this to happen.[7]

In March 1982 a worldwide nuclear war game was directed from the White House as Reagan, Bush, Haig, Weinberger, Clark, and other members of the NSC looked on. Former Secretary of State William Rogers, playing the President, was informed that the Soviets had used tactical nuclear weapons against a U.S. ship and chemical weapons against U.S. troops. Rogers authorized the use of tactical nuclear weapons in response. On the fourth day of the game the Soviets hit the U.S. with an all-out nuclear strike of 5,000 megatons. "The President" having been killed, control shifted to the Vice President, played by former CIA director Richard Helms; a little later control shifted to Cabinet members Baldridge and Watt, playing themselves. The game ended with the U.S. launching a retaliatory strike against the U.S.S.R. in accordance with the current "Single Integrated Operations Plan" (SIOP). Accounts of this game, which was the first one conducted from the White House since 1956, were given to the press deliberately "to make sure" that the Soviets knew that the U.S. was ready. Later in the year, according to U.S. intelligence sources, Soviet backfire bombers made their first simulated missile strikes against two U.S. aircraft carriers during major U.S. naval maneuvers in the northern Pacific.[8]

Leaders in the West appear to have become increasingly resigned to the likelihood of a nuclear war. Kistiakowsky, the science adviser to Eisenhower, said in 1980: "It would be a miracle if no nuclear warheads were exploded in anger before the end of this century and only a bit smaller miracle if that did not lead to a nuclear holocaust." Said the Swedish leader Olof Palme: "We are being driven toward nuclear war by the sheer momentum of military technology. We live in the days of madness." The commander of the Air Training Command at Randolph Air Force Base in Texas, General Bennie L. Davis, said late in 1980: "We estimate that as early as 1985, we will be at the highest level of danger for nuclear confrontation," and the Air Force was getting "ready to fight." Lamenting the death of the SALT II treaty, outgoing Senate Foreign Relations Committee Chairman Frank Church said it would take six or seven years to recover the lost ground, "and I don't think we have that much time."

In 1981 the highest military officer on Reagan's NSC, Major General Robert L. Schweitzer, having informed his superiors in general terms what he was going to say, spoke before several hundred Army officers about "a drift toward war" and told them that the Soviets had nuclear superiority over the U.S. and "are going to strike." The White House reacted disturbingly: Schweitzer's statements were said to be "at some degree of variance with Reagan's views." The two-star general was relieved of his White House duties, but a year and a half later Reagan promoted him to three stars and made him chairman of the Inter-American Defense Board.

"Nuclear war appears more likely to happen," said former Secretary of State Muskie. George Kennan said in 1982 and 1983, "I do think that we are on a collision course with the Soviet Union at this time," and the conditions between the two superpowers "are the familiar characteristics of a march toward war—that, and nothing else." Arthur Macy Cox, the former CIA official, believes that "the new Reagan policies, if carried out, will substantially increase the risk of nuclear holocaust." A leader of the European peace movement, E. P. Thompson, says nuclear war "is probable within our lifetimes" because "we are preparing to be the kind of societies which go to war. I doubt if there is any way out." "Is nuclear war possible?" General Brent Scocroft the chief of Reagan's commission on the MX, was asked in the spring of 1983. "The potential is there," he replied. The U.N. Secretary-General, Javier Perez de Cuellar, said that with the new and more accurate weapons, the possibility of such a war "seems to have increased."

During an appearance Defense Secretary Weinberger made at Harvard, a student asked him, "Do you believe the world is going to end, and, if you do, do you think it will be by an act of God or an act of man?"

"I have read the Book of Revelation," Weinberger replied, "and, yes, I believe the world is going to end—by an act of God, I hope—but every day I think that time is running out."

"Are you scared?" another student asked him.

"I worry," Weinberger replied, "that we will not have enough time to get strong enough to prevent nuclear war. . . . I fear we will not be ready. I think time is running out . . . but I have faith."[9]

Increasing belief that a nuclear war is coming is itself very dangerous. Officials of the superpowers, knowing the calamity that being hit by a first strike would be, are likelier to strike first if they think such a war is coming anyway. Yet defeatism about preventing nuclear war is spreading just as the world is entering what Senators Kennedy and Hatfield call "the impending era of first-strike temptations."

"First-strike capability" (as defined, for instance, in a 1969 CIA study) is one nation's ability to launch a surprise nuclear attack against another one without receiving in retaliation damage that it would regard as "unacceptable." A superpower that achieved first-strike capability might decide to destroy its adversary nation, but a nation so threatened might strike first to avoid being struck first. In 1983 former Senator Jacob Javits, the New York Republican, wrote, in an aside, that there are suspicions in both the U.S. and the U.S.S.R. that the superpowers are plotting atomic war. "Weapons are about to be deployed," according to Kennedy and Hatfield, "that would compel one side to strike first in a crisis. . . . Both sides could pass beyond the 'first-strike' threshold, where either side might assume that it had first-strike capability and first-strike vulnerability simultaneously. The inexorable development of nuclear technology is heading inevitably to a world . . . governed by a 'use them or lose them' nuclear psychology."

Seen over a five-year span, Reagan's statements that the Soviets are preparing to fight and win a nuclear war are doubly alarming because they are resonant with so many implications. In 1975 he said that SALT II "guarantees the Soviets a clear missile superiority sufficient to make a first strike possible with little fear of reprisal." On radio in 1978 he said that "while we are trying to avoid a war the Soviets are preparing to win one should it occur." His 1979 formulation of this same idea was: "While we plan to prevent a war, the Soviets plan to win a war." In 1980 he said "the Soviet Union decided some time ago that a nuclear war was possible and was winnable." He appeared to believe that the U.S. did not have the ability to inflict unacceptable damage on the U.S.S.R. after absorbing a Soviet first strike, telling *Business Week* that we needed either a defensive system or "an offensive weapon that would give us a second-strike capability."

On radio he quoted Brezhnev and Soviet military and propaganda officials to the effect that world socialism would be victorious in a nuclear war and that civil defense was a decisive factor in "the attainment of victory." None of the Soviets' statements threatened to start a nuclear war, but perhaps Reagan was conveying a suspicion that they might do it. If so, he was only mirroring Soviet suspicions about the U.S.

One of his Soviet authorities, the late Marshal Nikolai Krylov, who had been chief of Soviet missile forces, had charged that the U.S. was "preparing for a surprise attack on the Soviet Union and other socialist countries." Brezhnev said in 1981 that in the U.S., "scenarios for a surprise preemptive nuclear strike are being rehearsed," and in 1983 Andropov said U.S. strategic forces are being developed "along quite a definite line . . . of acquiring a first-strike nuclear capability."

This mutual suspicion entails, for the secret thinking on each side, a paranoid question and a suicidal answer. The question: "If they think we are planning a first strike, what are they planning to do about it?" The answer: "If we thought they were planning a first strike against us, we would plan one against them."[10]

How, one might ask, could Reagan reason that the Soviets might hit the U.S. land missiles first even though they would then definitely face the U.S. missiles that would still be intact on submarines and B-52s? "The window of vulnerability" of which Reagan warned was based on "a scenario" that was outlined, for instance, for Michael Getler of the *Post* by Pentagon sources during the closing weeks of the 1980 election: Soviet leaders might risk striking U.S. land-based missiles on the presumption that the American President would not make the gruesome decision to counterattack against Russian cities from submarines and planes when he knew that such a counterattack would also ensure a second Soviet attack on American cities.

Administration and military spokesmen, selling Reagan's military budget, conjured up the first strike. In 1981 Major General James L. Brown of the Air Force said that Soviet forces, "structured to fight, survive, and win a nuclear war," might "attempt a first strike." Reagan's first director of the Arms Control and Disarmament Agency (ACDA), Eugene Rostow, said: "There is a very real potentiality for a (Soviet) first strike." Unidentified U.S. intelligence analysts announced that in 1982 the Soviets conducted test firings that simulated a first strike, first knocking out U.S. reconnaissance satellites that could warn of an attack, then "ripple-firing" land and submarine missiles, and finally launching antimissile missiles as if against an incoming retaliatory strike. "The Soviets look like they believe they can win a nuclear war, or they can prevail in a first strike," Weinberger declared.

The Soviets could not deny that their gigantic land-based missiles are targeted on U.S. cities—Krylov had once written that they were—but they did deny that their nuclear doctrine is anything but "unalterably defensive." The more convincing testimony, though, came from the U.S. side. Harold Brown said: "A Soviet nuclear attack on the United States is the least likely military contingency we face." Robert McNamara, Johnson's secretary of defense, said that even if the Soviets took out U.S. land-based missiles, "that doesn't give them a first-strike capability, not when they are facing our Polaris submarines and bombers." McNamara dismissed as "incredible" the idea that the Soviets could plan to kill, say, 20 million Americans and assume the U.S. would not retaliate. "At least half of the thirty-two U.S. submarines would be available to strike back after a first strike," wrote Kennedy and Hatfield, and since a Poseidon sub carries 160 nuclear warheads, "a single submarine alone is capable of mounting a war larger than any conflict in human history." The joint chiefs, in 1982, and the Scocroft commission, in 1983, in effect agreed with these positions.

Unfortunately, while the closed nature of Soviet society prevents outsiders from knowing whether Kremlin leaders have seriously considered a first strike against the U.S., there is information in the historical record that American political and military leaders have considered a first strike against the U.S.S.R.

For example, a military reporter, Fred Kaplan, disclosed in a book in 1983 that the commander of the Strategic Air Command, the late General Curtis E. LeMay, told a fellow official that U.S. spy planes could detect military activity in the U.S.S.R. and "if I see the Russians are amassing their planes for an attack, I'm going to knock the shit out of them before they take off the ground." The official remonstrated that this was not national policy; Lemay replied, "I don't care. . . . That's what I'm going to do."

McNamara, in discussions with Scheer, revealed that on November 21, 1962, he informed President Kennedy that the Air Force had said in a report to him, McNamara: "The Air Force has rather supported the development of forces which provide the United States a first-strike capability." McNamara opposed such an objective and said it was rejected.

Roger Molander, a nuclear analyst for the NSC until he left the government to run the peace organization "Ground Zero," has written that when he worked for a defense think tank in 1969 he became aware of "a small but not uninfluential community of people who violently opposed SALT for a simple reason. It might keep America from developing a first-strike capability against the Soviet Union. I'll never forget being lectured by an Air Force colonel about how we should have 'nuked' the Soviets in the late 1940s before they got The Bomb. I was told that if SALT would go away, we'd soon have the capability to nuke them again—and this time we'd use it."

The question arises: Have elements in the military who want the U.S. to attain a first-strike capability found their President in Ronald Reagan? In the spring of 1982, McNamara indirectly and cautiously addressed this subject. "There has always been a nuclear hard-line group, you saw it reflected in that quote from the Air Force," he told Scheer. "That was 1962. There has always been a hard-line nuclear group, and there is today. But in the past, it didn't have the influence that it does today."

Although Colin Gray holds only an advisory role with the ACDA, it is a serious matter that his advocacy in authoritative publications of a U.S. first-strike capability must be known to the Reaganists who brought him into the administration. The commitment to preserve western Europe from aggression, he wrote in *Foreign Policy* in the summer of 1980, "requires American strategic forces that would enable a president to initiate strategic nuclear use for coercive, though politically defensive purposes." In March 1981, in the *Journal of the U.S. Army War College,* Gray wrote: "The United States requires the capability to strike first with strategic forces and dominate any subsequent process of escalation."

In 1983 columnist Jack Anderson quoted directly from what he identified as a secret ACDA report which contained a chart with the title: "Outcome of Hypothetical U.S. First Strikes, 1993." Assuming that the Soviets would not launch their missiles at the first warning of the U.S. attack and predicating technically favorable conditions, the ACDA chart indicated that after a U.S. first strike with nuclear weapons now on line, not a single Soviet missile silo would survive. Anderson reported that the report also said: "Under extreme crisis conditions, Soviet leaders might perceive pressures to strike first."

This background is the reason citizens may well be disturbed when the respected former CIA official, Arthur Macy Cox, writes: "The Reagan administration is pressing ahead to build and deploy first-strike weapons."[11]

Soviet submarine-launched missiles can reach the U.S. mainland in ten minutes, and the Soviet Union is similarly vulnerable. The Pershing 2 missiles that are scheduled to be based in West Germany in December 1983 have a fly time to the U.S.S.R. of four to six minutes or so. Warning systems would alert either nation of an attack, but there have been false alarms in U.S. watch stations and presumably in the Soviet stations, too. In case of an attack reported on the instruments, would the U.S. or the U.S.S.R. at once launch their missiles against the other side, or might they launch them as soon as the first incoming missile exploded? In the logic of the hair-trigger to Armageddon, these alternatives are called "launch on warning" and "launch under attack."

"It is terrifying," writes Cox, "that we are prepared to run the risk of building first-strike weapons" when our command, control, and communications systems can be destroyed. Paul

Warnke, Carter's first SALT negotiator, says: "If we end up with a situation in which either side operates on the doctrine of 'launch on warning,' then a nuclear war could start because of panic. . . . I think that's the risk."

U.S. doctrine provides that we will not "rely" on quick launch, but we will not rule it out. As an official of the Reagan administration testified: "Launch under attack is a good capability . . . but a dangerously destabilizing strategy to depend on. We do not, and we will not, depend on it." For several years, however, the U.S. side has practiced how to "launch on warning." Discussing a hypothetical Soviet attack on MX missiles, Reagan's chairman of the joint chiefs, General John W. Vessey, Jr., told Congress: "The Soviets have no assurance that we would ride out the attack." The deputy director of the Air Force MX program said in the spring of 1983 that the Scocroft commission would recommend that the U.S. adopt "launch on attack," but a Pentagon spokesman repeated that the U.S. "does not rely on its capabilities for launch on warning or under attack," and the commission did not recommend launch under attack.

The chief of the Soviet general staff, Marshal Nikolai Orgakov, said that same spring that Moscow had not adopted launch on warning, but added, "We are approaching a dangerous line." The president of the Soviet Academy of Sciences, discussing a five-to-seven-minute warning time for the Pershing 2 missiles, stated: "What remains is only automatic retaliation, with all available means, on all targets on the territories of all potential opponents." The only possibility, he said, would be "a counterattack that must be launched in two or three minutes." According to General Scocroft, the head of the MX commission, U.S. strategists do not think a Soviet first strike is very likely, but "as nearly as we can figure, they do believe in preemption should they once decide that war is inevitable." That is, we suspect that if the Soviets decide a strike is coming they will strike first.[12]

Since 1949 the United States and its NATO allies have relied on the first use of nuclear weapons for the defense of western Europe against Soviet invasion. Until the Reagan administration, the morality of basing the defense of western Europe upon launching nuclear weapons, rather than upon sufficient conventional military defenses, was not generally considered because the truth was hidden behind secrecy, euphemisms and the weird metaphor, "the American nuclear umbrella."

The Soviets and the Chinese have pledged not to use nuclear weapons first. "Our doctrine," according to a Soviet expert on nuclear strategy, General Mikhail Mihlstein, "is that we will never use nuclear weapons unless an aggressor uses them first." In 1982 Brezhnev pledged that the Soviets would not commit first use, and his successor Andropov repeated, in a letter to an American schoolgirl, that the U.S.S.R. "will never, but never, be the first to use nuclear weapons against any country."

But to whatever extent Americans have assumed that it is their government's policy never again to initiate a nuclear attack, they have been mistaken. Four prominent Americans confronted the truth in a stunning article in *Foreign Affairs* in the spring of 1982. A third of a century earlier one of them, George Kennan, then a U.S. policy planner, had proposed an announcement that the U.S. would never again use nuclear weapons first, but this was ignored and he left Washington. Now, in the second year of the Reagan administration, Kennan was joined by McNamara, McGeorge Bundy, the national security adviser to Kennedy and Johnson, and Gerald Smith, Nixon's chief delegate to the SALT talks, in a declaration that urged movement toward a U.S-NATO doctrine of "no first use."

Once a nuclear conflict was initiated, these four men argued, it could not reliably be expected to remain limited. They advocated a conventional military buildup in Europe and maintenance of second-strike nuclear capability so that the West can "escape from the need to plan for a first use that is credible" and "from the pressure to seem willing and able to use these weapons first." Subsequently the American Catholic bishops, in their historic pastoral letter on war and peace, stated that "the danger of escalation is so great that it would be morally unjustifiable to initiate nuclear war in any form." First use, the bishops added, "involves transgressing a fragile barrier—political, psychological and moral—which has been constructed since 1945."

Reagan fairly clearly projects a willingness to use nuclear weapons first. His eventual position that they should not have been used in Vietnam ("I don't think they were needed") implied that they should be used in a conventional war if they are needed. Scheer raised the question with him whether the U.S. is not setting an example that other nuclear nations may follow— "Doesn't that just leave open the possibility for another nation to justify its preemptive use of a nuclear strike?" Reagan fobbed off the question with another one that was oddly illogical: "Don't you open up the possibility of being hit by a surprise nuclear attack far more if you assure the rest of the world that under no circumstances would you ever be the first to fire those bombs?"

Rostow said on network television that it is "plausible" that the U.S. might use nuclear weapons first in a conflict with the Soviets, as in Europe. Haig, trying to reduce the impact of the Kennan group's article, made the official U.S. position unmistakable for the first time. "A pledge against the first use of nuclear weapons," he said, would be "tantamount to making Europe safe for conventional aggression." He opposed "an American decision not to pose and accept the risk of nuclear war in the defense of Europe." In fact, he said, "a 'no first use' policy would be the end . . . of the very credibility of the Western strategy of deterrence."

U.S. planning for prospective first use was ordered in the 1982 defense guidance document. In a passage in which "TNF" means theater nuclear forces and "NCA" means the national command authority, the document, distributed to about 30 top Pentagon officials, said: "Plans for the first use and possible follow-on uses of TNF should be developed which give the NCA the flexibility to use the TNF at a variety of levels. If widening the war by conventional means and total mobilization are insufficient to ensure a satisfactory termination of war, the United States will prepare options for the use of nuclear weapons."[13]

"First use" should not be confused with "first strike," even though both terms refer to an initial use of nuclear weapons. First use generally means the first use of tactical nuclear weapons for the "limited" or "restrained" purpose of avoiding defeat in a theretofore conventional regional conflict. First strike generally refers to one nation launching a concerted nuclear attack on another, ranging from a "counterforce" strike aimed at military targets (many of which are in or near cities) or an all-out strike that is intended to destroy a whole nation and all or most of its people. The U.S. has about 6,000 tactical nuclear weapons in Europe now—bombs, artillery shells, mines—and these are the kinds of weapons that might be employed in "first use." In a first strike, a nation would use its "strategic" weapons, such as the ICBMs.

The 96-ton, 71-foot-long MX missile, carrying ten independently targeted 300-kiloton nuclear warheads, can fly 8,000 miles and place its bombs within a circle 600 feet wide. Kennedy and Hatfield say it will be "the most powerful and accurate missile ever constructed."

Carter, convinced that the Soviets would attain the ability to destroy the land-based leg of the U.S. nuclear triad in the 1980s, proposed that 200 MX missiles be rotated among 4,600 concrete shelters in Utah and Nevada so the Soviets could not know exactly where they were. Reagan rejected this, and for a time he favored "dense packing" the missiles in a small "missile field." It was the theory of "dense pack" that Soviet missiles coming in to blow up the MX field would have to bunch up and would knock each other off course, letting some of the MX missiles be fired off. Late in 1982 Congress temporarily denied Reagan the funding for MX flight testing. In one of a set of moves that persuaded Congress to let him have the money, Reagan adopted his Scocroft commission's recommendation that instead of "dense pack," 100 of the missiles replace existing Minuteman missiles in their "hardened" underground launching silos in Wyoming and Nebraska. But, as everyone admitted, this left the land-based missiles still vulnerable. What was the point? What was going on here?

President Reagan says the MX will be deployed "not as a means to fight a war, but as a deterrent to conflict and an incentive to peaceful negotiations." He calls it "the Peacekeeper" ("Is it armed with peaceheads?" asked columnist Molly Ivins). What the MX does, says George Bush, is give the U.S. "an ability to retaliate against hard silos."

The Soviets call MX a "fundamentally new-generation weapon designed . . . for launching the first strike," "a nuclear first-strike weapon." More sobering (because of the need to make allowances for propaganda in responding to superpower rhetoric) are statements from the American side to the same effect.

The distinguished military reporter for the *Washington Post*, Michael Getler, wrote a month before the 1980 election that the MX missiles "will give the United States for the first time a real possibility of knocking out most if not all of the entire Soviet land-based force of 1,400 missiles in a first strike."

A secret report prepared by Reagan's ACDA, quoted by Jack Anderson in 1983, warned of fears which it said the MX might cause among the Soviets: "If MX were deployed in substantial numbers . . . the U.S. would have acquired . . . an apparent capability to destroy much of the Soviet ICBM force in a first strike, just as the Soviet Union (develops) one threatening the Minuteman force."

Kistiakowsky said the only justification for MX "is to be extremely effective against Soviet ICBM silos. There is no point in destroying empty silos. Therefore, clearly we are talking about a first strike, before the Soviets have launched their ICBMs." Hans Bethe, the Nobel prize-winning nuclear scientist, says: "The MX is a first-strike weapon. It makes no sense in any other way." William Colby and Stansfield Turner, CIA directors in the Nixon and Carter administrations, respectively, say Congress should stop the MX "and put to rest any prospect that we would go for a first-strike strategy." Cox writes that "the MX is a first-strike weapon" and "Moscow will probably adopt a policy of launch on warning," and Warnke believes MX would pose a first-strike threat to Soviet forces and invite a first-strike attack. Gerald Smith says MX "risks encouraging both sides to move to a 'launch on warning' system." Senator Mark Andrews (R.–N.Dak.) said he and Senator Moynihan warned members of the Scocroft commission that MX threatened to make it acceptable strategy to fire U.S. missiles at the first warning of attack. Striking first is against national policy and the MX would not survive a Soviet attack, so "why the hell are we spending $20 billion on this thing?" asked Representative Les AuCoin (D.–Oreg.).

During the administration's attempts to influence the American bishops' deliberations, Reagan's aide William Clark assured them that U.S. weapons are not first-strike weapons. Weinberger, alluding to the years of planning how to make the MX invulnerable, said, "If it was a first-strike system we wouldn't worry at all about protecting it." Yet, the *Post* has reported, the Air Force estimates that by 1989 the Soviets could have so many accurate nuclear warheads of their own, they could destroy 99 percent of the U.S. land-based missile force. Presumably then there might be only one of Reagan's 100 MX missiles left in existence after "a well-executed Soviet first strike."

McGeorge Bundy has cast his formidable standing and influence with the American establishment against what he calls "the first-strike multiple-warhead MX." He berated the Scocroft commission for proposing contradictory steps to slow down the arms race at the same time it was recommending MX. The "real purpose" behind the commissioners' MX recommendation, Bundy said, is that they "want these first-strike weapons because the Soviet Union has them. . . . Because the Russians do have weapons that can strike first at hard targets, the commission concludes that we must have them, too. . . . The commissioners neglect to tell us that we have plenty of weapons already that can strike hard targets second. . . ."

In the most penetrating analysis of the Reagan administration's nuclear policy that has come from any leading figure in the defense elite, Bundy concluded: "For almost thirty years, we have made survivable second-strike strength our central strategic standard. Are we now to move, in a cloud of consensus prose and good intentions, to a nonsurvivable first-strike system?"[14]

The long-range cruise missile, a pilotless 21-foot-long guided missile with a wingspan of 12 feet, can fly 500 miles an hour as low as 50 feet above the ground, hugging and zig-zagging across the terrain. By using computer-programmed contour maps of the target area, a cruise can hit targets accurately with warheads of 100 to 200 kilotons. It is so small, can be so easily hidden, and is so similar to its conventionally armed version, it may make arms control literally impossible—that, says Arthur Macy Cox, is the very reason why "opponents of arms control are eager to have the weapons deployed."

Reagan has been enthusiastic about the long-range cruise missile since 1976, when he exclaimed: "You can shoot it down a pickle barrel at 2,000 miles." Its development, he said, was "a bright spot for us." Eight years later he is presiding over an $18 billion program to deploy 8,458 cruise missiles on bombers, submarines, battleships, and destroyers and on the ground in Europe. In December 1982 they began to be placed on B-52 bombers; in December 1983, if NATO's plan holds, the first 16 of 464 of them for Europe will be installed on trucks in Britain. The Soviets are said to be five years behind us in these weapons, but following; when they catch up the west will be just as threatened by them as the east.

Reagan has now shifted the cruise program into the manufacture of "the stealth cruise," a highly secret program to make perhaps 1,300 radar-evading versions. According to a *New York Times* report, the first of these extremely threatening devices was to be deployed in 1982. A writer warned in *Newsday* that the stealth cruise will have devastating accuracy and ranges of 6,000 to 8,000 miles (thus they can be fired from almost anywhere). As Reagan might say, you can shoot them down a pickle barrel at 6,000 miles.[15]

The original U.S. nuclear-weapons submarine carried one Polaris missile that could hit within a mile or two of a target 1,200 miles away. Each of the 16 missiles on the successor Poseidon sub can send ten warheads 2,500 miles to within 1,800 feet of their targets. Poseidon's successor, Trident 1, can send 24 missiles with eight to ten warheads each (at least 192 in all) 4,500 miles to within 1,500 feet of their targets. The U.S. has 34 older Polaris and Poseidon subs; 15 Trident 1's were planned by the Carter administration, and the first three of them have been christened under Reagan. Archbishop James Hunthausen of Seattle calls Trident submarines that operate in waters near his city "the Auschwitz of Puget Sound." They are second-strike, not first-strike weapons because their missiles still are not accurate enough to destroy Soviet missiles in silos for sure. For this reason they are staunchly upheld by arms control specialists like Bethe and Scoville as an invulnerable deterrent.

Reagan's nuclear submarine program has a total price tag of

about $60 billion. First, he increased the Trident 1 program to
20 subs (they cost about $1.5 billion each). Carter had funded
research on Trident 2 subs that would be able to send their
missiles 6,000 miles to within 400 feet of their targets and destroy Soviet missiles in silos. But this clearly suggests first-strike
capability, and Carter did not make the decision to build. In
October 1981 Reagan announced that the U.S. will make and
deploy the Trident 2 subs, too; they are to be ready, along with
their D-5 missiles, in 1988.

The Trident 2 is expected to be able to destroy Soviet land-
based missiles within ten minutes of a launch. Kennedy, Hatfield, and Arthur Cox all denounce it as a first-strike weapon
capable of driving the Soviets to launch on warning. Reagan's
Undersecretary of Defense Richard DeLauer was quoted saying
that Trident 2 could even provide the capability for a preemptive strike. Representative Downey of New York, who is a member of the defense task force of the House Budget Committee,
stated: ". . . the Trident 2 will be the most destabilizing first-
strike weapon ever built, far more than the MX. . . . The Trident 2 will . . . be a quick-strike surprise-attack weapon. . . . Its
sole significance will be to initiate nuclear war by delivering a
uniquely effective first strike against the Soviet Union's deterrent forces. . . . Here is the central flaw of any first-strike strategy: The adversary can always prevent our first strike by beating
us to the punch. . . . Most probably, the Russians will have to
give a computer the authority to launch ICBMs . . . whenever
the computer thinks it perceives a United States launch. It is not
in our interest to force such a course of action." Kennedy and
Hatfield add: "It is probable that, in the absence of a freeze or
other restraints, Soviet submarines will eventually achieve a first-
strike potential against American ICBMs."[16]

The neutron bomb is a small hydrogen bomb that releases six
to eight times more life-killing radiation and destroys somewhat
less property than a fission bomb of the same size. Carter backed
off from building it and deploying it in Europe because of a
great outcry against it there. In this context, on radio in 1978,
Reagan, erroneously saying that the bomb would not destroy
property, expressed an enthusiasm for it that was exultant.

"Very simply," he said, "it is the dreamed-of death ray weapon of science fiction. It kills enemy soldiers but doesn't blow up the surrounding countryside or destroy villages, towns, and cities. It won't even destroy an enemy tank—just kill the tank crew.

"Now some express horror at this and, charging immorality, portray those who would use such a weapon as placing a higher value on property than human life," Reagan continued. "This is sheer unadulterated nonsense. It is harsh sounding, but all war weapons back to the club, the sling and the arrow are designed to kill the soldiers of the enemy. With gunpowder and artillery and later bombs and bombers, war could not be confined to the battlefield. And so came total war with noncombatants outnumbering soldiers in casualties.

"Here is a deterrent weapon available to us at much lower cost than trying to match the enemy gun for gun, tank for tank, plane for plane. . . . Indeed the neutron bomb represents a moral improvement in the horror that is modern war."

In 1980 Reagan favored building and deploying neutron bombs "for U.S. theater nuclear forces including ballistic missiles, cruise missiles, artillery and bombs." Extraordinarily and dangerously, he also said—in March 1980—"I consider the neutron warhead conventional because it is a deterrent where the Soviet Union outnumbers us tremendously in eastern Europe." Although the neutron bomb is a nuclear weapon of great destructiveness, the Democrats made no objection to this remark, and six weeks later candidate Reagan again said, "I suppose an offensive weapon that could bridge (the gap between U.S. and superior Soviet arms) for conventional weapons could very easily be the neutron warhead."

The explosion of a neutron bomb would be regarded as nuclear by almost everyone, although apparently not by the American President. A weapon in which a nuclear fission reaction sets off a nuclear fusion reaction, it is officially called "the enhanced radiation warhead." Its inventor, Samuel Cohen, says it is a tactical nuclear weapon the development of which President Kennedy opposed "because he was scared to death that it would lead to a trading of thermonuclear strikes." A Carter-era ACDA report said it might help deter nuclear war, but "could increase

Soviet propensities to initiate the use of nuclear weapons if they
have decided to go to war." The Army's tactical and chemical
warfare planner, General Fulwyler, who told a reporter in 1981
that neutron bombs "offer even greater possibilities for use than
the weapons of the past," of course regards the neutron bombs
as nuclear weapons.

At his first press conference as secretary of defense, Weinberger said the U.S. would "probably want to make use of" the
neutron warheads and advocated deploying them in Europe. "I
think it's a very good addition," he said. These remarks revived
the hostility toward the weapon in much of Europe and concern
in the administration that this hostility might reduce the prospects for deployment of Pershing 2 and cruise missiles in Europe
in 1983. Reagan ordered that the neutron bombs be made, but
stored in the U.S. Weinberger said they can be sent to Europe in
a matter of hours if necessary or to "any theater where the
necessity of repelling overwhelming force may be required" (the
Middle East and South Korea are often mentioned in this connection). By mid-1983, according to Walter Pincus in the *Washington Post*, about 300 neutron bombs for Lance missiles had
been made and stored in this country and 1,000 neutron-bomb
shells for Army and Marine 8-inch howitzers were being made.
Congress, having twice refused to do so, was again considering
authorizing a third type of neutron weapon, a 155-mm shell,
which Britain, West Germany, and Italy have asked the U.S. to
produce for their new cannons.[17]

Carter had canceled the B-1 bomber on grounds that the B-
52s would serve. Reagan berated him for this on radio and on
the stump, and during the 1980 campaign the secret information was leaked to the press (no doubt by the Carter administration) that a radar-eluding Stealth bomber was being developed
to replace the B-52s. As President, Reagan has pressed the "two-
bomber" strategy (actually three, counting the B-52s) of building
100 B-1s until the "invisible" Stealth bomber comes on line. The
B-1 program costs from $28 to $40 billion; B-1 and Stealth together may cost $80 billion. Weinberger told Congress that pen-
etrating the U.S.S.R. with a B-1 after 1990 would be "a suicide
mission," but this testimony did the B-1 so much damage he took
it back. "We can't afford two bombers," according to Senator

Sam Nunn (D.–Ga.) of the Senate Armed Services Committee. "It's obsolete," says Nixon's secretary of defense, Melvin Laird. "Now you could go from the B-52s to the Stealth bomber." But Reagan says the B-1 is needed now and skipping it would make people think that U.S. resolve had weakened.[18]

A race for space-based weapons has been going on for at least several years. Before he took office Reagan expressed strong interest in such weapons, and during his administration between $1 billion and $2 billion has been spent annually for research on laser and particle-beam devices that would shoot down enemy missiles. The Pentagon's top research official warned in 1982 that the Soviets planned to put a laser weapon in space in the next few years; in the administration's first defense guidance plan preparations were ordered to "project force" and "wage war effectively" from space and to deploy antisatellite weapons within five years. "We should acquire the capability," the Pentagon guidance says, "to negate, as well as disrupt, hostile space systems." In 1982 also Reagan formally militarized the U.S. space program. That year the National Aeronautics and Space Administration was spending about a fourth of its research money on military work, and the space shuttle flew its first of many secret missions.

All this was already happening when Reagan went on TV in 1983, in what became known as his Star Wars speech, to call on U.S. scientists to develop a space-based missile defense system. Reagan, who is advised on this subject by the father of the hydrogen bomb, Edward Teller, held forth the ostensibly visionary, but far-fetched hope that space-based weapons might make nuclear weapons obsolete. Andropov naturally saw and said that rendering the U.S.S.R. "incapable of dealing a retaliatory strike is a bid to disarm the Soviet Union." Reagan replied mildly that a future President could share defensive space weapons with the Soviets, but one would need the imagination of a saint or a fool to believe that this reassured the men in the Kremlin. These events amounted to the public declaration of the race between the superpowers for the use of space for military power. *Business Week* called Reagan's Star Wars address "the most radical change in strategic policy since the end of World War II."[19]

Back here on earth, the Pershing 2 missiles scheduled for

West Germany will have a range of 1,100 miles, which will let them penetrate the western U.S.S.R. in four to six or eight minutes, although they cannot reach Moscow. They will have unprecedented accuracy, almost four times that of the MX: half the warheads will land in a circle 240 feet across. Designed to destroy command bunkers and hardened missile silos, the Pershing 2 will be able to do what no other U.S. nuclear weapon can yet do, strike accurately deep inside the Soviet Union giving almost no warning.

E. P. Thompson of the European peace movement writes: "Putting Pershing 2s in West Germany is an exact analogy with Khrushchev's freighters steaming toward Cuba." In the Soviet's perception, their spokesmen say, "Pershing 2s can reach Soviet territory in a matter of minutes, whereas no counterpart weapons are sited near the U.S." Thus, they reason, Pershing 2s are "forward-based" American first-strike weapons that can destroy virtually all Soviet command and control points throughout European Russia.

The State Department's leading arms control specialist under Reagan, Richard Burt, calls the Soviets' first-strike charge "ludicrous." Moscow-based command and control and 90 percent of Soviet strategic forces will be outside the Pershing 2s' range, Burt contends, and there will be only 108 Pershings compared to the 1,053 warheads on 351 Soviet SS-20s. In 1983 Congress funded Pershing 2 with only 73 no votes in the House.

But some U.S. weapons experts believe the Soviets might well fear that the Pershing 2s could take out their early-warning system, some command centers, and some ICBM sites as the first stage of an all-out attack and that the 108 missiles might later be MIRVed or made replaceable by reloading and their range extended. The U.S. is building, not 108, but 311 of them. "Only the Pershings," wrote Getler in the *Post*, "could hit the Soviets 'out of the blue,' in a surprise attack with essentially no warning." According to a Pentagon official, "We wouldn't be too surprised if the Russians moved some of their own SS-20 missiles close enough to strike the northwestern U.S. when the first Pershing 2s are deployed." That is to say, if the U.S. puts Pershing 2s in

West Germany, the Soviets may put SS-20s in northeastern Siberia, throwing the U.S. into or close to launch on warning.[20]

Civil defense against nuclear war was a dead issue in the U.S. for 20 years. In the early 1960s about a million U.S. homemakers built civil defense shelters and some citizens stocked theirs with guns to shoot anyone else who might try to get in, but the Kennedy administration decided to kill the program itself because the growing Soviet arsenal made it impractical.

In recent years there have been reports, some of them apparently exaggerated, concerning Soviet preparations for civil defense. Reagan says, "they have gone very largely into a great civil defense program, providing shelters, some of their industry is underground, and all of it is hardened to the point of being able to withstand a nuclear blast. . . . They have practiced evacuation." Now Reagan has called for a seven-year $4.6 billion program to prepare to evacuate 150 million Americans from 400 cities and military areas and to build shelters for "essential workers."

His reasoning appears to be contradictory. In 1978 on the radio he said: "The truth is there is no defense against a nuclear attack. If the Soviets should push the button . . . there is no defense against them—no way to prevent nuclear devastation of their targets here in the United States." But eight months later he said: "A renewed emphasis on civil defense preparedness is necessary."

He may regard civil defense as a necessary part of defense strategy whether it can protect people or not. In March 1982 he issued a civil defense directive that said: "Civil defense . . . is an essential ingredient of our nuclear deterrent force." In announcing the President's plan the Federal Emergency Management Agency (FEMA) carried forward a Carter administration document which listed the purposes of civil defense in this order: first, to "enhance deterrence and stability," second, to "reduce the possibility that the U.S. should be coerced," and, third, to protect the population in an attack.

Carter's FEMA had said the U.S. could recover from nuclear attack "within a relatively few years." Reagan's undersecretary of defense for strategic and nuclear forces, T. K. Jones, said that with proper civil defense in the U.S. (including enough shovels to go around) the U.S. could fully recover from all-out nuclear war in two to four years. Although Jones denied making the statement about two to four years, Scheer had it on tape.

Reagan's plan assumes that the President would have at least a week's advance notice for the evacuation. FEMA says that, provided there is no follow-up bombing after the first attack, provided nuclear power plants are not hit, and provided everyone has nearly perfect protection from fallout, 80 percent of Americans would survive. FEMA working papers plan that "hard-core" hospital patients will be left behind and assume that others will choose to stay behind, "addicts and alcoholics, antiwar idealists, pet lovers and individuals—perhaps those from minority communities—who might not be willing to tolerate the cultural shock of a relocation." As for how the 150 million people in the countryside are to eat and survive, in the plan that's up to them and the "host areas."

The serious argument for such a program is that under unlikely circumstances it might save some lives. By one FEMA estimate, given a week's warning and evacuation, the number of survivors would be doubled. The serious argument against it is that it will make nuclear war more likely by creating an illusion that it may well be survivable and by inviting an attack.

Senators Kennedy and Hatfield, who charge in their book *Freeze!* that Reagan's civil defense program is part of a strategy which assumes that nuclear war can be fought and won, warn: "A mass evacuation of target sites could well provoke precisely the nuclear war from which it purports to protect us. Can you imagine how strategic planners in Moscow would react if their spy satellites saw streams of cars crawling along clogged highways, fleeing from New York City toward the Adirondacks?" Nor can this logical flaw in the program have escaped Soviet attention. Dr. Bernard Lown of Harvard Medical School stated on Soviet TV during a discussion of nuclear war: "If any nation begins to evacuate its people it means it's preparing to strike and it invites preemption."

The Soviets and the Americans have plenty of bombs to totally destroy each other if they decide to do it. Harold Brown said: "If you target cities, they are not going to be saved by civil defense." Warnke is just as blunt. "What kind of civil defense program is going to protect you against 6,000 nuclear warheads?" he asks. "It depends upon whether you want to die in the field or die in a hole. Would you rather be roasted or boiled? . . . There *is* no civil defense against the number of warheads that we and the Soviet Union have deployed against one another." Oddly this is just about what Ronald Reagan said on the radio in 1978.[21]

As the Soviets have declared openly and repeatedly, they plan to match whatever we do—it's tit for tat. Behind all the rhetoric and involuted logic there is the plain reality: Reagan is fiercely accelerating the nuclear arms race and the Soviets will seek to keep pace. Jonathan Schell estimates that the 50,000 nuclear warheads which now exist in the world have a total explosive power of about 20 billion tons of TNT, which is 1.6 million times the power of the Hiroshima bomb. The Nobel scientist Linus Pauling calculates that the destructive potential in the world's stockpile is about 100,000 times the power of all the explosives used in World War II. In personal terms, the nuclear stockpile amounts now to about 4 tons of TNT for every man, woman, and child alive.

The United States has about 30,000 nuclear warheads. Carter authorized substantial planning increases for new nuclear bombs before he left office, and Reagan has now approved the production of about 17,000 new nuclear warheads in the next five to eight years, the highest rate of such production in more than twenty years. Since 11,000 of the older warheads will be retired, the American government will possess about 35,000 warheads by the end of the decade. According to Assistant Secretary of State Burt, both the U.S. and the U.S.S.R. "have over 10,000 warheads, deliverable on short notice, to any location in the other's country."

"Where are we headed for?" asks Meg Greenfield, the editor of the editorial page of the *Washington Post.* "An MX missile in every garage? An SS-18 in every dacha?" In 1979 Carter said that just one Poseidon submarine, constituting less than one-fiftieth of our nuclear forces at that time, "carries enough warheads to destroy every large and medium-size city in the Soviet Union." The total U.S. "throw-weight" of nuclear power is said to be 3,500 megatons compared to the Soviets' 9,000 (until now the U.S. has opted for relatively smaller "payloads"). Schell estimates that 60 percent of the American people could be killed by just 300 megatons—300 one-megaton bombs. Weisner, the science adviser to Kennedy and Johnson, writes: "A single modern nuclear weapon exploded on target can obliterate one city, and 200 of them would destroy an entire civilization." As Professor of Industrial Engineering Seymour Melman has summarized this basic situation, the U.S. "can overkill Soviet cities more than 40 times; the Russians can destroy our cities about 40 times over."

The Soviets have built up SS-20 overkill against Europe; the U.S. prepares to plant Pershing 2s and cruise missiles in Europe and to build and deploy the MX and Trident 2; both sides race to spawn easily concealable cruise missiles and to threaten the world and each other from space. The logic of the situation was addressed by a heading on an article in a recent number of the *Bulletin of Atomic Scientists*: "If the answer is more weapons, what was the question?" After passing along an estimate he had received that 5.2 percent of the Trident fleet's warheads could destroy the Soviet Union, *New York Times* Associate Editor Tom Wicker wrote: "Should the Government not be asked to tell us just how many times over they are planning to destroy the Soviet Union, and why, or, if this striking force suffices for one such destruction, what they propose to do with the remaining 94.8 percent?"[22]

Reagan is fatalistic about the spread of nuclear weapons to other nations. Officially the administration continues to oppose nuclear proliferation, but by its deeds it has helped other nations' nuclear programs in a variety of ways. Reagan simply does not share the widespread concern that as more and more nations get the bomb, its use becomes ever more likely. There is enough evidence about his attitude, in fact, to justify the conjecture that having accepted the spread of the weapons, he wants to help U.S. allies get them or has no real objection to their doing so.

When he was talking to reporters about his notion of sending troops and planes to Pakistan, Reagan remarked that he would be willing to abandon U.S. efforts to prevent nuclear development in Pakistan if the Pakistanis would let our planes in. Did this mean he would agree to the Pakistanis' work on a nuclear bomb? "Yes," he replied. "I don't think it's any of our business."

Two hours later, attempting to reduce the chagrin this statement had caused (for he was opposing U.S. policy of twenty years' standing), he merely made it even clearer that he believes we might as well stop fighting the spread of nuclear weapons. According to Richard Bergholz in the *Los Angeles Times,* he denied he had answered "Yes," but then he went into the reporters' workroom to explain.

"I suppose in my mind, when I answered that question," Reagan said, "I was thinking in terms of if they were going ahead with such a thing as that that it would not be our position to say we won't send them (fighter planes) unless you stop what you were doing. We don't have the right to tell them, as a sovereign nation, what they can do. . . .

"Would the symbolism of a squadron of planes be worth making an exception to our nonproliferation policy—and particularly because it hasn't worked very well?" he asked. He said he did not have the information to answer that question, but he continued: "India next door has them (nuclear weapons). And India is very hostile to Pakistan. . . . What I am saying is that we have not succeeded (in regard to nonproliferation). The U.S. seems to be the only nation that is trying to stop the proliferation of nuclear weapons."

The Soviets' brutal invasion of Pakistan's neighbor Afghanistan was the context as President Reagan persuaded Congress to provide Pakistan with $3.2 billion in military and economic aid and to sell the country 40 F-16 fighter planes. President Zia of Pakistan, a military dictator who assented to the killing of his predecessor in office, claimed repeatedly that Pakistan had no intention of developing nuclear bombs, but U.S. intelligence reported that the country has developed the capability to do so. The administration's stated theory was that U.S. aid to Pakistan would "reduce the incentive" to develop the bomb.

Various administration spokesmen, including Shultz, have professed their opposition to proliferation, but early in 1983 Reagan's candor once again escaped his aides' control. "I think," he told a group of high school students, "we are pretty well on our way to, if not entirely eliminating nuclear proliferation, holding it down to where a country might have a weapon or two, but they're not going to have enough to threaten the world."

In his actions Reagan had already done more than any other President in the nuclear era to foster the spread of these weapons. As noted earlier, he committed his administration to the commercial reprocessing of nuclear fuel, a process which abets weapons-making abroad. He has systematically loosened restrictions on U.S. exports of nuclear fuel and technology, even though, according to a Government Accounting Office report in 1982, the government's programs for monitoring and protecting exports of weapons-grade fuel are "inaccurate and incomplete." Argentina is widely believed to be reaching for nuclear weapons and refuses to submit to international norms to prevent proliferation, yet in 1981 the administration secretly authorized the export to that country of an element critical to one way of producing weapons-grade materials. Argentina's rival, Brazil, has not signed the nuclear nonproliferation treaty, yet Bush announced that the U.S. had made a "special-case exemption" to let Brazil buy fuel for its nuclear reactor. Fifteen months later Brazil was able to breed plutonium by using U.S.-supplied enriched uranium in a U.S.-supplied research reactor. Although India does not comply with international nuclear safeguards, the administration consented not to object when the French supplied fuel for the reactors at Tarapur. With extensive technical assistance from the U.S. as well as France and West Germany, South Africa has probably built nuclear weapons (in reaction to which a black African leader has proclaimed "the duty of the African states that can . . . to resolutely embark on the nuclear path"), yet the Reagan administration has explicitly changed U.S. policy in order to increase U.S. sales of nuclear materials to South Africa.

When he was fighting Communists in Hollywood, Reagan became a friend of a lawyer named Lawrence Beilenson, who was an ally of his in the fight. Beilenson has written several books on international subjects, and he says Reagan has read them all. They also talk together fairly frequently, Beilenson says. It is the opinion of the self-taught Beilenson that the U.S. should help its allies get nuclear weapons and then leave them to defend themselves, thereby reducing the chances of U.S. involvement in a nuclear war. Reagan as President has decided to offer Australia access to highly classified centrifuge technology that can be useful in making nuclear bombs. According to a *Washington Post* report, the administration secretly approved the export to West Germany and France of lasers which can make it easier to produce fuel for nuclear bombs. The administration denied that the equipment in question has such a potential use.

Reagan is certainly correct that the outlook for controlling the spread of the weapons is bleak. In 1982 a U.S. intelligence survey predicted that thirty-one countries will be able to make the bomb by the year 2000. But rather than resisting this trend as effectively as he can, the 40th American President has abetted it and has told schoolchildren that it's nothing to worry about.[23]

On John Mitchell's principle that one should watch what politicians do rather than what they say, we have concentrated here on the arms race and the nuclear weapons, even though public attention is more usually concentrated on international maneuvers, declarations, and negotiations. From the White House Reagan has often expressed an ardent desire for treaties with the Soviets that will reduce the level of nuclear armaments on both sides. Unfortunately his previous public career provides convincing grounds for the widespread doubt that treaties with Communist nations are one of his priorities.

Reagan did more than any other public figure to shatter détente with the Soviets, which Presidents Johnson, Ford, and Nixon had constructed out of the opportunities provided by the Sino-Soviet split. Reagan was the leading politician in the successful campaign against Senate ratification of the SALT II treaty which Carter and Brezhnev had negotiated. And it is the starting point of Reagan's arms policy that the U.S. must build more nuclear weapons before the Soviets will agree to the arms reductions that Reagan says he fervently wants.

The President spelled out his "less by more" doctrine in his 1982 State of the Union address: "We're working for reduction of arms and military activities. . . . It is essential that we negotiate from a position of strength. . . . This requires that we rebuild our military forces." The practical meaning was that the

U.S. will build big new nuclear weapons systems before signing any agreements to reduce armaments. This is what Kennedy called "voodoo arms control."

Behind the tricky rhetoric there is the plain reality. Arthur Cox informs us that in July 1980 Paul Nitze and Edward Rowny, two of the key figures among Reagan's arms control officials, were members of a group meeting at the National Defense University which agreed that no weapons program should be deferred on grounds that it would interfere with future control of strategic arms. They also agreed that the U.S. should not "fiddle with systems in order to make them more inspectable, verifiable, or countable." In May 1981, several months before he became Reagan's negotiator for European-theater missiles, Nitze told Scheer that "there could be serious arms control negotiations, but only after we have built up our forces" and that this could be done "in ten years."[24]

Reagan has been skeptical of international negotiations for years. "We are being told," he said during the first half of the 1960s, "that we can sit down and negotiate with this enemy of ours, that there's a little right and a little wrong on both sides. How do you compromise between good and evil? How do you say to this enemy that we can compromise our belief in God with his dialectic materialism. . . . How do you compromise with men who say we have no soul, there is no hereafter, there is no God?" During Nixon's presidency Reagan said he was sure everyone shared Nixon's desire that "an era of negotiations" replace the cold war, "but we are also aware (that) every nation in history which has sought peace and freedom solely through negotiation has been crushed." Asked in 1980 if he wanted to return to cold-war days, he responded: "When did the cold war ever end?"

His contempt for the United Nations forms a pattern extending across two decades. When friends of the U.N. wanted the U.S. to buy $100 million worth of U.N. bonds in 1962, he said, "Well, let me be a real right-wing heretic now . . . let them go into the open market and sell them." In his 1965 book he said he was "against subordinating American interests" to the U.N. when a two-thirds majority of the General Assembly could represent less than a tenth of world population. As governor he refused to proclaim U.N. Day. The U.N. vote in 1971 to oust Taiwan and seat China, he said then, "confirms the moral bankruptcy of that international organization." Provoked in 1975 by a U.N. resolution condemning Zionism as racism, he said he was tempted to call for U.S. withdrawal, but instead said that if the U.N. continued on its course the U.S. should serve notice that "we're going to go home and sit for a while." In the late 1970s he conceded that the U.N. World Health Organization does good work, but also suggested that if the Soviet Union was not denied its U.N. voting rights, "we could take a walk."

This, then, was the background when Reagan told the graduating class at West Point in 1981 that in his administration, "the argument, if there is any, will be over which weapons, not whether we should forsake weaponry for treaties and agreements." As its Secretary-General acknowledged in 1982, the U.N. was being defied or ignored by many nations, wars were breaking out everywhere, and "we are perilously near to a new international anarchy." The Reagan administration's refusal to sign the laboriously negotiated law of the seas treaty was a faithful expression of Reagan's underlying attitudes about diplomacy and international agreements.

Reagan recommends that people read his friend Beilenson's book, *The Treaty Trap,* in which Beilenson argues that treaties cannot enhance U.S. security in the nuclear age (see Appendix). In an article Beilenson and the inventor of the neutron bomb coauthored, they asked the rhetorical question, "why not take a chance on the treaty process?" and answered, "because reliance on that approach increases the chance of war by lowering our guard."

Some officials in the Reagan administration reportedly favor making arms control offers which the Soviets probably might regard as a basis for negotiation. Burt at the State Department is one such official. However, the leader of the opponents of arms control in the administration, Assistant Secretary of Defense Richard Perle, has prevailed with Reagan so far. Formerly the staff chief for the hawkish Senator Jackson of Washington State, Perle provides the rationale as Weinberger takes the hardest line on arms control. *Newsweek* reported in 1981: "As Perle explains it, the entire arms-control process of the past decade has so harmed American security that the United States will no longer make sacrifices to keep the process going. . . . The Reagan administration is not likely to waste much time in such pursuits." In mid-1983 "a high State Department official" told Leslie Gelb: "Shultz has told the Soviets in every meeting that we are prepared to talk to them about their agenda—arms control, trade technology—but if we are to make progress in theirs, we must also make progress in ours: human rights and Soviet international behavior."[25] Thus arms control, a priority for Nixon, Ford, and Carter, for the Reaganists is only an item on the Soviets' agenda.

Broadly speaking, through June 1983 the Reagan administration had not made arms control offers that the Soviets could reasonably be expected to consider seriously. U.S.-Soviet talks were under way in Geneva concerning strategic arms reduction and the reduction of nuclear weapons in Europe. One promising idea concerning low equal levels of the weapons in Europe, discussed between Nitze and his Soviet counterpart during a walk in the woods in 1982, had been rejected by the Reaganists and the Soviets, but the episode had illustrated the fact that agreement was not impossible. Brezhnev had clearly signaled his desire for a serious summit meeting with Reagan, but (the complex rhetoric aside) Reagan and his men did not want one, either with Brezhnev or his successor. For their part, by 1983 the Soviets did not seem inclined to send Andropov to a sideshow summit, with arms control off limits, which some of Reagan's aides had thought might help their man politically at home. Who was to say that Reagan and Andropov would not reach arms control agreements?—things as strange have happened (Nixon's détente, for instance). But the bitterness of the U.S.-Soviet rhetoric exceeded anything since the years of the cold war, and skepticism abounded about Reagan's desire for agreement as the months slipped by toward December. Ex-Chancellor Helmut Schmidt of West Germany told representatives of the *Washington Post,* who called on him in Bonn: "I am not, as yet, convinced that (the Americans) are negotiating seriously, but they still have time to do so." Senator Hart reviewed the administration's record on SALT II, abandonment of the goal of a comprehensive test ban treaty, and "launching a major 'Star Wars' arms race in space" and asked: "What now should give us confidence that this administration is serious about nuclear arms control?" And Jimmy Carter charged that neither the U.S. nor the Soviets were negotiating in good faith. Within a month of the time during which these remarks were made, there was one dark sign that the skeptics were right. Pressed by the Senate Foreign Relations Committee to say under what circumstances the U.S. would *not* deploy the MX, Reagan's new ACDA director, Kenneth L. Adelman, speaking for the administration, replied in writing: ". . . unless the Soviets are prepared to . . . forego their heavy and medium ICBMs, the U.S. will go forward with MX." Leading senators of both parties shot down this position as totally unrealistic even before the Soviets did.[26]

Shored up by the election of the conservative Helmut Kohl government in West Germany and the reelection of Margaret Thatcher's conservatives in Britain, the foreign ministers of NATO reaffirmed their decision to deploy the Pershing 2s and cruise missiles in December. Kohl's coalition would have to hold together to effect this purpose and there was a possibility that it would not, but the deployments seemed likely to begin on schedule. Discouragement, intensified by expectations of civil disobedience and violence, began to rack the European peace movement.[27]

Is it possible that President Reagan himself is defeatist about nuclear war—that he expects it to happen? His friend Beilenson thinks that such a war is probable and says, with his co-author, that "the fears of the American people that nuclear war may soon be upon them are more than justified." The President has expressed a similar pessimism. In support of his position that the U.S. must build the new weapons to pressure the Soviets to negotiate, Reagan said on May 16, 1983: "I can't believe that this world can go on . . . with this kind of weapon on both sides, poised at each other, without some day some fool or some maniac or some accident triggering a war that is the end of the line for all of us."[28]

The sources of the present situation lie in the darkest recesses of human nature. As Kennan has suggested, there may be some need in human beings organized into nations for a scape-goat, an external enemy to blame for their troubles and fears. Already in the Reagan years we have had rather too many indications of a readiness for war, even a will to war: Pipes saying the Soviets must change or go to war; Schweitzer saying they are "going to strike"; Haig telling the Senate Foreign Relations Committee "there are things worth fighting for"; Weinberger saying "if we go to war, it won't be fought with social services." In the opinion of Bishop Leroy Matthiessen of Amarillo, the administration is "gearing up, is spoiling for a war." The critic Alfred Kazin says that the Reaganists' "vision of America resembles that of a defense contractor." The Soviets match us in this; as Thomas Powers writes, "the principal undertaking of our time is the preparation for war.

It is Reagan's time-worn doctrine that if we are strong we will stay out of war, but speaking of superior power he also says: "We must have the will to use this if it becomes necessary." There is a passage in his autobiography in which he discusses the views of commentators who he said are opposed to war at any cost. "The fact is," he wrote in 1965, "we will all die. . . . What makes the difference in the matter is what we die for. . . . It is not war-mongering to say that some things are worth dying for. If this be not so—then write off the martyrs as fools. Christ . . . Moses . . . those men at Concord bridge. . . . He said in a 1971 letter hailing *Patton* as one of the all-time great movies: "It says something which needs saying today—that there are things for which men must be willing to die." In another letter about an address he made to a group of college-age youths, he wrote: "Each generation must learn that the things men prize the most, the things which make a civilization, are those things for which men have always been willing to die."[29]

All day and all night, on eight-hour shifts, a set of four field-grade officers stay as close as they can to President Reagan and carry for him a thick black leather briefcase that contains the codes and mechanisms by which he can order the firing of different combinations of U.S. nuclear weapons. The officers are under strict orders not to drop the briefcase, which is called "the football." Reagan usually carries his counterpart "code card" in his wallet. The football and the code card: this is the responsibility that he and every American President lives with.

Is it sane, or is it "almost hysterical," to fear a nuclear war? The question is not rhetorical. Senator Goldwater believes that since the Russians do not want a nuclear war the U.S. can take larger risks to achieve geopolitical purposes, and in the 1970s Reagan agreed with this position.

In 1962, when reports first began reaching the political establishment in Washington that the Soviets were installing nuclear missiles in Cuba, Goldwater called on President Kennedy to tell him that "we now had a reason to move on Cuba militarily" and that "considering our tremendous superiority over the Russians in the field of nuclear weapons, Khrushchev would not respond militarily." But, Goldwater complained, Kennedy "dwelt on the ultimate horror of nuclear war," and Goldwater concluded that no Soviet provocation would ever justify in Kennedy's mind "any action which might lead to the use of atomic weaponry." In his memoirs Goldwater condemned "the public's almost hysterical, unreasoned attitude toward nuclear war" and "the Communist propaganda that any strong opposition (to communism) . . . would inevitably lead to a nuclear holocaust."

In the mid-seventies Reagan, when renewing his earlier criticism of President Johnson for not having taken military action against North Korea after its seizure of the *Pueblo,* wrote: "The *Pueblo* case was a classic example of the folly of our own indecisiveness and the degree to which our people have been misled by the fear of nuclear war. The Communists don't want all-out war. . . ."

Reagan agrees with President Truman's decision to drop atomic bombs on Hiroshima and Nagasaki—this averted an invasion and prevented millions of casualties, Reagan says. The touchiest question a reporter can ask an American President is, would *you* fire nuclear weapons? In effect I asked President Johnson this, and he responded with a long yarn that seemed to mean: It's out of my hands. Hugh Sidey of *Time* and Barbara Walters of ABC asked Reagan.

"If driven to the wall," Sidey asked him, "could you press the

nuclear button?" ". . . I don't think any President could say that
he wouldn't," Reagan replied. The dialogue on the same subject
between Walters and Reagan was more revealing.

Walters: Mr. President, a week or so ago you rode in the
"doomsday plane" which would be the plane that you, any other
President would ride in should there be a nuclear attack. And
I've heard that if there is an attack you as President would have
something like 17 minutes to make up your mind what you do,
whether you press that button and fire back or what. I wondered
whether this is something you have nightmares about. . . .

Reagan: It is awesome. I don't have nightmares about it. . . .
Seventeen minutes is generous. If they start with those nuclear
missiles from the submarines off our coast—and right now there
are more submarines, Russian nuclear submarines, off our coast
than there have been in years—then you only have a very few
minutes.

Walters: But it's your responsibility.

Reagan: Yes.

Walters: . . . Doesn't that sometimes frighten the daylights
out of you?

Reagan: I can't say fear. There's a dread that we'd ever reach
that point. But remember, what you're talking about is the other
side would have already pushed the button. Those missiles
would be on their way. Now—

Walters: That would be the only way you'd do it?

Reagan: You have to assume that those missiles are aimed at
our own ability to fight back. And you acquire all the knowledge
you can, all the options that are available. . . .

Although one does not draw conclusions from such a discussion, its implications are momentous. For instance, when
Walters asked Reagan if "the only way you'd do it" would be if
the other side had already pushed the button, he did not answer
the question, but continued with what he had been saying
before.

"You know my fear of a Ronald Reagan presidency," Robert
Scheer told him in the course of the 1980 campaign. "My fear is,
are you going to push the button, are you going to get us blown
up, are you going to get us into a nuclear war?"

"No, I don't want it," Reagan replied, "but what I have seen in all of those [past] wars is that we have gone into those wars, backed our way into them, through weakness. I have never seen us get into one through strength. . . . I'm not a warmonger, I say that we are going into war if a man like Carter continues giving the wrong signals, backing away from the Soviet Union."

Reagan is a delegator, and according to John Sears, his campaign manager in 1976 and again for a while for 1980, "his decisions rarely originate with him. He is an endorser. It is fair to say that on some occasions he is presented with options and selects one, but it is also true that in other instances he simply looks to someone to tell him what to do. . . . He can be guided." His first appointments secretary in California, Thomas Reed, has been quoted: "He's startling in the way he's willing to delegate things." As we have seen, in 1967 Reagan contended that the military should decide whether the U.S. should invade Vietnam. "If nuclear war were suggested as one option to President Reagan," Sears says, "he'd pick something short of it." In a different context, Anthony Lewis has written in the *Times* that while Reagan would not want to hurt people in a war, he would be likely to defer to his advisers, "a group of hard liners." James David Barber, the specialist in presidential character, believes that "the character-rooted danger of the Reagan type in the presidency is that he will cave in to pressure."

The Catholic bishops of the United States lived under the nuclear sword uncomplainingly for a third of a century, but during the Reagan administration they chose to say "no to nuclear war." As they worked through drafts of a pastoral letter on the subject, the administration sought to prevent them from endorsing the nuclear freeze and opposing first use, but in substance they did anyway. The vote among them was 239 to 8.

The bishops had asked the administration what U.S. plans were, in the event of a nuclear war, concerning Soviet cities. William Clark replied for Reagan and the government that "the United States does not target the Soviet civilian population as such" and "our targeting policy does not call for attack on cities *per se*." This did not satisfy the bishops, for as they informed the public in their pastoral letter, the administration also told them that the U.S. "has identified 60 'military' targets within the city of Moscow alone, and that 40,000 'military' targets for nuclear weapons have been identified in the whole Soviet Union."

The government refused to give the church estimates of the number of civilian casualties that would be incurred in such attacks on cities, but according to the Rev. J. Bryan Hehir (who was a central figure in the bishops' deliberations), the administration did say that U.S. nuclear strategy is "open-ended." "We asked about civilian casualties," Hehir said, and the administration spokesman replied, in Hehir's paraphrase of what he said: "Please don't have any illusions on an all-out nuclear exchange, it's simply got no limits in terms of strategy."

In January 1983, five bishops and their assistants confronted an array of government officials on the issue of civilian casualties. The representatives of the church sat on one side of a long table, the representatives of the state on the other. The government people said at length that the U.S. is developing accurate counterforce weapons, apparently implying that these would minimize civilian casualties. But then, according to Edward Doherty, a member of the bishop's staff who was present, the truth came out. Ron Lehman, a Pentagon official, suddenly told the church people: "We don't want to deceive you. We don't want you to feel you have been deceived. Even if we did not target any civilian and even if our whole force was made up of systems that could hit military targets precisely, the distribution of targets in Russia is such that the civilian casualties would be virtually the same as if we were targeting cities. But there's nothing we can do about it. We didn't plan the location of their military targets."

As the Kennan group's paper on first use had clearly posed the ethical implications of that U.S.–NATO doctrine, now the bishops clearly posed the ethical implications of threatening to destroy cities in pursuance of the policy of deterrence. They denied, in their pastoral letter, that "the assertion of an intention not to strike civilians directly" constitutes "a 'moral policy' for the use of nuclear weapons." To the contrary, said the assembled hierarchy of the American Catholic Church, trying to justify killing a million innocent people because they happened to live near "a militarily significant target" would be "a perverted political policy or moral casuistry."

On the radio, in 1975, Reagan gave his overview. "The Russians have told us over and over again their goal is to impose their incompetent and ridiculous system on the world," he said. "We invest in armaments to hold them off, but what do we envision as the eventual outcome? Either that they will see the fallacy of their way and give up their goal, or their system will collapse, or (and we don't let ourselves think of this) we'll have to use our weapons one day."

In Reagan's traditional and patriotic view, each generation must learn that the things that make a civilization are those for which men have always been willing to die. For the second generation of the nuclear era, however, war between the superpowers means the extermination of hundreds of millions of people. The point in the present situation is not what men are willing to die for. As Jonathan Schell says, "life is the point."[30]

I fear that Reagan does not understand this well enough, or does not believe it with enough understanding. He has abetted the spread of nuclear weapons among other nations. He is determined that the United States shall build the MX, thousands of long-range cruise missiles that can be hidden even on trucks or in garages, and the D-5 missiles that will be able to destroy Soviet missiles in land silos from 6,000 miles away. He accepts and asserts the principle of the first use of nuclear weapons; he says he regards the neutron bomb as a conventional weapon. He is determined to deploy not only cruise missiles in Europe, but also the Pershing 2s in West Germany, despite the fact that the Pershing 2s obviously will be forward-based American strategic weapons that could be an effective part of a larger first-strike strategy. Finally he has sought to lead the nation into a civil defense program based on the evacuation of cities, a program that cannot save lives without sharply increasing the likelihood of nuclear war the moment the evacuation occurs. These are the plain facts. When one considers them together one must consider reaching the conclusion that Ronald Reagan is the leader of elements in the government who want the United States to obtain a first-strike capability.

Robert C. Aldridge, an aeronautical engineer who worked on sea-based nuclear missiles for Lockheed until he resigned as a matter of conscience in 1973, has concluded in a book in 1983 that the United States will have an unanswerable first-strike capability by the end of the present decade. He believes that this will come not only from MX and Trident 2, but also from the development of missile guidance systems, which, using atomic clocks, take fixes on satellites and can maneuver upon reentering the atmosphere for even greater accuracy; ingenious programs to track Soviet submarines so they can be destroyed on command; and clouds of small interceptor warheads that can destroy incoming missiles.[31]

Nuclear weapons are not in any ordinary sense political, but they are more important than all the political issues put together. As Mary Dent Crisp, a former co-chairperson of the Republican National Committee, has said, other issues have begun to pale compared to this one. The Reagan administration should of course be held accountable on Social Security, taxes, civil rights, the ERA, civil liberties, food stamps, medicare, unemployment, federal aid to education, the secret war in Central America. But above every other subject, the 1984 election in the United States should be decided on the basis of the profoundly unwise nuclear course upon which Reagan has launched the nation and the terrible likelihood that he and his men are now reaching for a first-strike capability. Not before in the nuclear era have so many experienced and distinguished public figures expressed such alarm. Representing them, William Colby, the former director of the CIA, warns that the nuclear arms race "is moving us toward a hair-trigger world with all this talk of launch under attack. My God, we're talking about the fate of the world." Our window of vulnerability is not the threat of a Soviet first strike, it is the nuclear arms race itself. Colby, who knows government from the inside of its most secret operations, tells us now that "we cannot rely on governments" to act in time. Yet as Mary Crisp says, if we do not prevent nuclear war "we won't be around for anything else."[32] We can deal with anything else if we have the time, but nuclear war will call time on us. We must put the issue of the nuclear weapons ahead of everything else because it is the issue of whether there is any more time for the human race.

21

Critics on Reaganism
1981–1983
A Selection of Newspaper Columns

As with every President nowadays, millions and millions of words are written about Ronald Reagan and his administration. Probably the freest form for newspaper comment on current affairs in the United States is the personal column, and for this closing chapter I have selected a baker's dozen of such columns, written from different stands and perspectives, but most of them critical of Reaganism. In the Appendix readers will find Reagan himself speaking extensively on Reaganism in previously unpublished excerpts from manuscripts of his radio broadcasts in 1975, 1978, and 1979.

SLOGAN OF REAGAN REPUBLICANS: "I'VE GOT MINE"
By Michael Kilian

NEWPORT, R.I. I have come to see the light as Ronald Reagan has shown me the light.

I'm not quite sure exactly when I came to see it. Perhaps it was when I was peering at the two-story-high golden dining room of Cornelius Vanderbilt's mansion at Newport, The Breakers, a chamber large enough to feed half of El Salvador in.

Or perhaps it was while looking at the peach bedroom of Mrs. William K. Vanderbilt's charming Newport cottage, Marble House, a room in which—to paraphrase the late Dorothy Parker—all the girls at the Harvard prom could recline end to end.

More likely, it was when gazing the length of society leader Mrs. Hermann Oelrichs' grand ballroom in Rosecliff. Mrs. Oelrichs was famous for giving many "brilliant entertainments" in this room. From the size of it, they must have included indoor polo.

But wherever it was, I now know that Ronald Reagan is right, and the wicked Democrats are wrong.

For some time now, I've been trying to figure out what kind of Republicans the Reagan Republicans are.

They are not at all like Dwight Eisenhower, who admonished the military-industrial complex to remember that every bomber built cost the same as a school. The bombers the Reagan people want to build cost as much as entire colleges.

They have nothing at all in common with Teddy Roosevelt, who believed in busting up trusts, fighting for the little man, and using the White House to do good. He would have had Interior Secretary James Watt deported.

And they certainly have nothing in common with Abraham Lincoln, who helped create the Republican party as a "Free Soil, Free Labor, Free Man" alternative to money-grubbing Whigs and conservative Democrats. You can't see Ronald Reagan using federal troops to stamp out racism.

But, gazing at the 10-ton front door, crystal chandeliers and 20-acre croquet lawns of Newport, I finally got the idea.

The Reagan Republicans are the Republicans of Grant, McKinley, Harding, and Coolidge, Reagan's greatest hero. They're like Cornelius Vanderbilt, who rose from captain of a Staten Island garbage scow to the wealth of Croesus by taking over other people's railroads and acquiring vast tracts of slum property.

Or like Gustavas Swift, who first sold smelly meat from an open cart and got rich from grisly packing plants.

Or like E. J. Berwind, who built his palatial "Elms" with the labor of several thousand starving Irish coal miners.

They're from the same cloth as the child labor employers and the Civil War profiteers whose products gave the language the word "shoddy," people who didn't have the government on their backs then and don't want it now.

They differ from Lincoln Republicans and Eisenhower Republicans because their chief interest in life is making money. They want to run government only to keep it out of the hands of those who might interfere with their making money.

Reagan is the white man's Reverend Ike. His ethic is the same: "I want you to have moneeeee!"

Which is why I'm signing up for the Reagan program. Maybe a 25 percent tax cut won't get me a house with a 20-acre croquet lawn, but it might get me into a new car—or into tax shelters that'll reduce my taxes even further.

Why should I worry about inflation, deficits, Social Security cuts, and the shift of federal subsidies from cities to B-1 bomber plants? Like Charles Z. Wick, Walter Annenberg, William Casey, Bebe Rebozo and the rest of them, I'll be able to say, "I got mine!"

With the Reagan plan, no one in America should complain that they don't have a chance to get theirs, too. They can just go out and hire several thousand starving coal miners.

The Reagan administration certainly won't stand in their way.

> —*From the* Chicago Tribune, *July 30, 1981. Copyright 1981,* Chicago Tribune. *Reprinted by permission.*

TRAGICOMEDY: ACT II
By John B. Oakes

As he raises the curtain on the second year of his presidential performance, Ronald Reagan's benign image partly masks but doesn't wholly conceal his deeply cynical role.

"I will not ask you to try to balance the budget on the backs of the American taxpayers," he told Congress last week as he promised "tax relief" to "the American people."

Who are these "American people"? They are the rich—individual and corporate. They are the boxholders at the Reagan theater, the top 6 percent of the economic elite. They will receive one-third of Mr. Reagan's projected "savings." The bottom 40 percent, the underclass in the second balcony, will share 9 percent of the "relief."

As a result of Mr. Reagan's sleight-of-hand in tax and spending cuts, those whose annual household income is less than $23,000 will be about $30 billion poorer by 1985; those above that level will be $350 billion richer.

The main beneficiaries of President Reagan's version of tax relief are also those who mainly profit from the more unconscionable loopholes that will cost the Treasury at least $20 billion annually: the depletion allowances, the speculative real estate tax shelters, the unlimited property tax and mortgage interest deductions. Reaganomics has no place for tax reform.

"We must cut out more nonessential government spending and root out more waste," says the President, overlooking the biggest source, by far, of waste and fraud. It is the ravenous appetite of the Pentagon and its defense contractors, represented by the next fiscal year's $260 billion military budget. Mr. Reagan's war against waste is fraudulent so long as he ignores the tens of billions that could be saved annually by management reforms in the Pentagon and by critical evaluation—instead of blind acceptance—of the entire weapons program.

No less an authority than Admiral Hyman G. Rickover, father of the nuclear Navy, said, on his retirement last week: "What's the difference if we have 100 nuclear submarines or 200? . . . You can sink everything on the oceans several times over with the number we have, and so can they. . . . Our leaders keep using scare words to get what they want."

Echoing President Eisenhower's historic warning against the military-industrial complex, Admiral Rickover noted that "defense contractors can do anything they want, with nothing to hinder them." Instead of trying to hinder them, Mr. Reagan now blandly offers his audience a spurious diet of unlimited guns and subsidized butter.

"The people with real dependency," said Mr. Reagan in last

week's masterly TV performance before Congress, are "deprived of what they need because available resources are going not to the needy but to the greedy."

Too true. Virtually every federal program to aid "the needy" (and also to protect the health, education, and basic quality of life for all the rest of us) is deprived of financial lifeblood. Virtually every program to help "the greedy" through corporate and agricultural subsidies, loan guarantees, and political payoffs (such as Westway in New York) has found ample sustenance in the same budget.

Meanwhile, Mr. Reagan deftly draws the curtain over the $100 billion deficit that will feed inflationary fires this year and a 9 percent unemployment rate that may well feed fires of another kind this summer. He shifts national responsibility for social programs to the states despite their proved unwillingness or inability to accept it. He has reinvented and now hastily unveils a synthetic early nineteenth-century federalism to meet the needs of a late twentieth-century society.

The cynical fatuity of this administration is not limited to domestic policy. "America will not conduct 'business as usual' with the forces of oppression," proclaimed Mr. Reagan, citing sanctions against the Soviet Union for interfering in Poland.

Yet the moral base for sanctions against forces of oppression is undercut by our interference, in increasing measure, in a bloody civil war in El Salvador, by our scrapping a once meaningful human rights policy virtually everywhere, and by permitting on United States soil troop training for subversive operations in Nicaragua, a country with which we are theoretically at peace. Mr. Reagan has promoted business (particularly the arms business) far greater than usual with "forces of oppression" anywhere, from Argentina to Pakistan, so long as they are nominally anti-Soviet.

Where is the morality, or even the realism, in substituting arms sales (50 percent greater last year than the year before) for diplomacy, and a nuclear buildup for nuclear negotiation? Where lies the wisdom in treating strategic nuclear arms talks as a favor to the Russians, or in "punishing" them for their despicable behavior, by deferring those talks—on which our fate, their fate, and the fate of all mankind depends?

Act II of the Reagan tragicomedy is proving to be more tragedy than comedy.

—John B. Oakes is the former senior editor of the New York Times. *From the* New York Times, *February 4, 1982.* © *1982 by the* New York Times *Company. Reprinted by permission.*

FLUNKING THE FAIRNESS TEST
By Norman C. Miller

WASHINGTON Those of us who are reasonably affluent can afford to be fairly relaxed about President Reagan's dangerously unbalanced budget.

Yes, the mindboggling deficits projected in the Reagan plan are theoretically worrisome. They'll probably be worse than the $345 billion the President projects over his four-year term. In Washington, deficits almost always grow bigger than administrations predict.

And yes, the enormous deficits might cause such havoc in the financial markets that the markets will collapse, businesses will go bankrupt, interest rates will stay at strangling levels, and the recession will deepen. But probably the prophets of doom are wrong, as usual, and the country will muddle through. If so, those of us with good to rich incomes will be all right.

But the needy among us will not be all right. They will suffer—and suffer badly—even if, as the President promises, supply-side economics eventually produces sound economic growth. For until the supply-side miracle occurs, if it ever does, the President's harsh social-program cuts will impose more pain and sacrifice on the poorest members of society—while the rest of us enjoy a bonanza of immediate benefits.

To refresh your memories, take inventory of what we—the affluent—get under the Reagan tax-cut law, which the President is determined to keep in place despite its failure to rapidly revitalize economic growth as the administration promised a year ago.

We get our income taxes cut 10 percent this year and next,

plus inflation-indexed cuts forever. The wealthiest among us get their tax rates cut to 50 from 70 percent. We get a sizable cut in our capital gains taxes. We can shelter substantial sums in IRAs and Keoghs and get big annual tax deductions to boot. We can invest in tax-free "All-Savers" certificates paying premium interest rates. If we have stock options, we'll get all our immediate gains free of tax when we exercise our new "incentive" options.

The corporations we work for and invest in will get stunning profit gains from liberalized depreciation rules and tax-rate cuts. Even if corporations lose money, they can cut losses by leasing unused tax credits to profitable companies, which can then lower their tax payments even more. The leasing gimmick is akin to food stamps for corporations.

The very few among the affluent who are members of Congress get the most dazzling tax bonanza of all under a law sneaked through the last day of the 1981 congressional session. They can claim annual tax deductions of $18,000 or more for their Washington living expenses! With other standard tax breaks, some of our lawmakers could wind up owing almost no taxes on their $60,662 salaries.

Contrast this bountiful array of tax benefits for the affluent with what the poor will suffer under the new Reagan budget, remembering that social programs were cut $35 billion last year. The new budget envisions $26 billion of additional cuts in direct aid for the needy, more indirect reductions, and further cuts in the year ahead.

With unemployment at 8.5 percent and threatening to worsen, the Reagan budget slashes job subsidies and training by nearly $2.7 billion. What's left of the shrunken public-service jobs program is destroyed; the Job Corps for poor youngsters is slashed by one third. The federal-state employment service is cut sharply, making it less able to assist job seekers. And in perhaps the meanest line in the budget, the administration proposes to take pennies from jobless people by rounding weekly unemployment compensation checks "down to the next lower whole dollar."

Housing subsidies for 3.4 million families will be slashed by $3 billion; their rents will rise as a result. Many of these families exist on welfare; their checks will be cut as the budget slashes $2.2 billion from the biggest welfare program, Aid to Families with Dependent Children. Some will also lose food stamp assistance; the program will be cut by $900 million. And the 22 million poor persons receiving medicaid assistance will have to pay more when they're sick if the administration gets its way; it wants Congress to enact a 10 percent program cut, totaling $1.9 billion.

Poor children will have a harder time. An array of social services aimed mainly at helping needy kids and their parents will be cut by $1.3 billion. Special reading and math programs in schools serving poor children also will be cut by $539 million.

College students and their parents will be hit hard, too, if Congress passes administration proposals. Grants to the neediest students will be cut $800 million; some of the 2.2 million students depending on these grants may have to drop out as a result. Loans to college students also will be cut sharply. Some 700,000 graduate students will be especially hard hit by sharply higher interest rates on their loans.

Now, nobody pretends that federal programs aiding the poor aren't riddled with inefficiencies as the Reagan administration constantly reminds us. But it is fundamentally unfair for the administration to concentrate almost exclusively on cutting assistance to the poor while simultaneously providing an excessive array of tax breaks—several of dubious equity—to affluent persons and corporations.

The imbalance of the administration's policies becomes more drastic when one examines its incredibly overstuffed military budget. There is, to be sure, a clear need to build up the nation's military strength to counter increasing Soviet might. But the size and pace of the administration's military spending increases go beyond reasonable military needs and will guarantee huge deficits gravely threatening hopes for controlling inflation and achieving sound growth.

Under the Reagan plan, Pentagon spending will zoom up 18 percent to $216 billion next year. Just about every weapon the Pentagon ever conceived—some of highly questionable military value—will be purchased at a sharply accelerated rate.

Some $5 billion will be spent to start producing B-1 bombers. These planes—costing at least $533 million each for this year's run—are designed to penetrate Soviet air defenses starting in 1986. By the Pentagon's own testimony, these new bombers will be good for their main mission for only four or five years. Then, they'll have to be replaced by an advanced Stealth bomber, for which development spending also is being accelerated. Some military specialists believe B-1s aren't needed even for a four- or five-year period; they think the current fleet of B-52s can be upgraded to serve as a credible threat to the Soviets until the Stealth is ready around 1990.

Another $5 billion is budgeted for developing and producing the new MX missile. This bigger missile is going into production despite the administration's failure to develop a militarily sound plan for basing it so it can't be destroyed by a Soviet attack. The administration's current basing plan is so flawed that the joint chiefs of staff publicly opposed it. Yet somehow the deployment of a vulnerable MX is supposed to enhance our sense of security against a possible Soviet attack.

The pell-mell buildup of conventional forces is equally questionable. The Navy will spend $18.7 billion building ships. Three cruisers will cost $1 billion each. Two nuclear aircraft carriers will cost $3.5 billion each. It will cost $776 million to renovate two battleships, which many naval experts think are dinosaurs. And this budget is just the first installment of a five-year plan to build 133 more ships at a cost of at least $96 billion. How the Navy is going to man the planned 600-ship fleet is an unanswered question.

The Army also will add weapons at a breakneck pace. For example, it will spend $2 billion for 776 M1 tanks, the first models of which have been breaking down regularly in field tests.

We would be better off if a good deal of the billions President Reagan is throwing at the military went unspent or were spent more slowly and carefully. The budget deficit wouldn't be so dangerously big. The administration might even be able to find a little more money to help poor people cope with the twin evils of unemployment and inflation.

President Reagan's budget, however, makes it clear that the needs of our poorest people are his least concern, notwithstanding his pious statements to the contrary. On that count, his budget flunks the test of fairness.

—From the Wall Street Journal, February 8, 1982.
Reprinted by permission of the Wall Street Journal.

ADRIFT IN THE TROPICS
By Russell Baker

The government's performance in the Central American mess is mysterious to me. I'm in no doubt that there are malcontents aplenty down there and they don't wish us any good, but on the other hand why should they?

What have we done for them lately? What have we ever done for them? There must be something, but Secretary of State Haig doesn't say what it is. I might be able to get sore at them if somebody would show that they're a bunch of ingrates like the Japanese.

After putting the Japanese on their feet, picking up their defense bills and letting them flood our markets with cars and TV sets, what thanks do we get? They make it as hard as possible for us to sell anything in Japan. That's what I call a bunch of ingrates, but it's not the Japanese I'm supposed to be sore at; it's the Nicaraguans.

Is Detroit going broke because every other American you know is buying a Nicaraguan car? Did we rebuild Nicaragua into one of the world's leading economic powers and then find that Nicaragua wouldn't let us sell Pac-Man on their territory?

Maybe we ought to be sore at Nicaragua because we haven't done anything for it and are therefore deprived of the self-pitying pleasure of thinking of the Nicaraguans as ingrates.

I know, I know: some of them are in cahoots with Fidel Castro, who doesn't wish us any good. On the other hand, why should he? We financed an invasion of Cuba to throw him out and when that failed we tried to have him murdered by the Mafia. Once the CIA even tried to slip a dipilatory chemical into his boots that would work its way through his body all the way up to his jaw and make his beard fall out.

Is that any way to make somebody like you?

Well, of course Castro is in cahoots with Moscow, which doesn't wish us any good, and having Moscow interfere in Central America is a challenge to us because Central America is our territory.

I can buy that, but it would help if somebody in Washington explained why it's all right for us to interfere in Poland, which is Moscow's territory, but all wrong for Moscow to interfere in Central America, which is our territory. Maybe it is, but why doesn't Secretary of State Haig explain why?

I'm more puzzled, though, about what the government wants to do in Central America. The usual leaks from Washington say that one thing the CIA is doing is pumping millions of dollars into the "moderate elements" down there.

Washington's idea of "moderate elements" in Central America is usually a group of men in uniforms who transfer Washington's millions to Miami bank accounts.

After immoderate elements chase them out of the palace, they fly to Florida, Spain, or Switzerland, cease being moderate elements and live like kings. On my money.

There's also talk of "paramilitary operations" to bounce the Marxists and restore order. Is this sound?

A "paramilitary operation" is a military attack conducted by professional soldiers wearing civilian clothes. It is often run by the CIA and usually results in putting a dictator in the palace.

We conducted a famous "paramilitary" operation in Guatemala in 1954. It was run by the CIA with the usual result: a dictator in the palace. Now, twenty-eight years after the CIA triumph, Guatemala is a place you wouldn't want to visit unless you were the kind of person who enjoyed smashing other people's kneecaps.

Sooner or later, I'll bet, somebody will fly from Guatemala to Miami and live like a king on my money while Washington tries to make me get sore because the palace has been taken over by Marxists who like Fidel Castro.

The leaks from Washington have it that Argentina is very

interested in supplying help for a "paramilitary operation" in Nicaragua. This is supposed to make us feel good about it, I guess, because it suggests American soldiers won't be involved.

What puzzles me is why Washington would want to get caught sponsoring Argentine military mischief in Central America. Argentina is a country where thousands of people have answered a nighttime knock at the door and never been seen again.

Why would we try to save Central America from the horrors of communism by sponsoring a visit by soldiers representing a country like Argentina? Isn't that like shooting a friend in the jaw to relieve his toothache?

Washington must have some better ideas for Central America than it's let anybody know about. Lately there has been talk of passing the problem to Mexico. That would free the State Department for things it's better at, like keeping us all from getting sore at those Japanese ingrates.

—*From the* New York Times, *March 17, 1982.* © *1982 by The* New York Times *Company. Reprinted by permission.*

DEFENDING REAGAN'S TRULY NEEDY
By Molly Ivins

In a file-keeping system chiefly notable for its eccentricity, I find the folder named Significant Mish-Mash has grown to proportions that demand response. . . .

Leading off the Mish-Mash list is my growing concern over the media's tendency to be unfair to the Reagan administration. Picky, picky, picky. You take that CBS documentary "People Like Us" that ran a few weeks back. Here CBS sets out to do a program about how the administration's policies are affecting Americans. So who does CBS interview? Poor people. Old folks. Folks who work for the minimum wage and folks who are out of work entirely. What kind of people is that?

Why doesn't CBS go out and interview some happy millionaires? People frisking off to Europe for the summer while their Jaguars depreciate here at home? There are lots of people who are happier now that Ronald Reagan is in office. Right here in Dallas, Bunker Hunt, the man who pays no taxes, would be a good interview. If the media want to talk about the Truly Needy, what about John McAtee, Jr., head of the U.S. Synthetic Fuels Corporation? McAtee's salary is $150,000 a year and he told a congressional committee it was such a terrible pay cut he might be forced to move out of Greenwich, Conn.

The media don't pay enough attention to the suffering of corporate executives. The head of General Motors got no incentive bonus at all in 1980, just because his company lost $1.5 billion. He did get his base salary of $400,000; you see, the administration has always said there would be a Safety Net for the Truly Needy. David Gergen, the White House spokesman, said the CBS documentary was "below the belt," and while I won't go that far, I do say it was unbalanced. Corporate executives can get the blues, too, you know. Environmental zealots brutally prevent them from dumping their poisonous wastes into handy rivers. Bureaucrats cruelly flail them with red tape. And the private sector never thinks up its own red tape, as you know if you have lately tried to return a dishcloth to a department store.

—Excerpted from the Dallas Times-Herald, *June 20, 1982. Reprinted by permission.*

A REPOPULARIZED PHRASE HAS STUCK . . . AND IS PROVING STICKY
By Haynes Johnson

ST. JOSEPH, MO. When the definitive history of the Reagan administration is written, assign David A. Stockman a major role. It appears more and more that Stockman, through his celebrated confessions to William Greider, has tagged the administration with a label that seems likely to endure.

Stockman's use of the expression "trickle down" to describe the President's so-called supply-side economic program has stuck. The phrase, in political/economic use decades before Stockman repopularized it, now crops up in conversations almost everywhere. And now it appears so deeply associated with the Reagan approach that people use it without apparent recognition of its source. History will have to remedy that lack of credit.

"Trickle down" is mentioned by all sorts of citizens in their casual comments. It forms the stuff of jokes, of commentary about events, of a way to describe what is happening. However it's employed, the phrase carries a barbed political message. It evokes an unflattering class connotation of rich vs. poor. That, too, more and more is associated with the Reagan presidency.

Examples, gathered here in St. Joe:

Morning, on a farm some ten miles outside town: "One of Reagan's mistakes was his tax cut," the farmer says. "He had to favor the rich. He's a little bit wrong in his thinking you can trickle down. It's not going to happen that way."

Afternoon, lunch in the graceful old Buchanan County courthouse: "That trickle down's not getting down to me," a county employee says with some anger.

Evening, over drinks in a lawyer's home: "Did you hear that Mark Russell joke, the one he told in Buffalo?" his wife says. "'Now we have the trickle-down theory. Give David Rockefeller a lot of money and it will trickle down to Laurence.'"

What follows here is offered as primary source material from the American midwest for a chapter in that forthcoming historical volume, "Ronald Reagan and the Trickle-Down Years."

Gathered in one room were leaders of the St. Joseph homebuilding industry. Recent years had been good to them. They all had prospered. Now their business has been devastated.

Tom Woods, for instance, has had to lay off 60 percent of his workforce. "We've had builders lose their own homes on foreclosures," he says. "I don't know what the rates are, but I'm sure foreclosures are at an all-time high. I'm the leading supplier of lumber and building materials to the home-building industry here, 100 percent to the homebuilder. I don't do any retail business whatsoever. As you can see from my figures there I'm not sending near the money back to Washington that I did in the past."

He handed over a sheet of paper containing his business data for the three-year period from May 1979 to the end of last month. His sales are off 73 percent. The amount of wages paid has dropped 55 percent. Sales tax revenues he's paid to the State of Missouri are off 85 percent. The amount of federal income taxes he has withheld has dropped 63 percent.

They all had similar stories to tell.

Jim Summers, Summers Realtors, a broker:

"The situation has reached the point where I think we have no in-town buying at all going on at this point. The statistics will show that we're off about 60 percent in the total dollar sale."

David Eldridge, who builds upper-bracket homes ranging up to $200,000: "In the last three years my production has gone from roughly fifteen houses a year to drop down to about five and then to one. This year it's zero."

Jim Holmes, David and Wayne Kerns, Reed Kline, Bob Cobb added their descriptions of deep trouble. The hardest thing, one said, was how their attitudes were being affected. "We all used to feel that we were winners, that we were in an economy that was fairly constant. Now it's upside down. From an emotional-psychological standpoint, there's a lot on the line. Are we winners or are we ultimately going to be losers?"

They all had been strong supporters of Ronald Reagan, and still admire him personally. But when they were asked to assess Reagan and Reaganomics now, the tape recorder picked up these words:

■ "As a nation as a whole we took a conscious approach through Reagan's leadership, and I voted for him the last time. I thought it would be good to reduce inflation. And I think the country as a whole felt that it was a goal, but now we've overkilled it. We're in a lot worse situation now than we were three years ago when we had inflation that was double digit, 13 percent or so in 1979 and it's probably 5 or 6 percent now, but the whole economy can't operate."

■ "I think Reagan's main policy was to bring down inflation at the same time he cut taxes and raised military spending. From an ideological standpoint, if it had worked it might have been fine. But it certainly is not trickling down to this level."

■ "I voted for him. I thought a lot of his policies, his ideas. Given a chance, I thought they would improve things overall. But like so many other people he doesn't get the opportunity to see the plans executed. I think the whole game is political and maybe it's beyond what I can understand."

▪ "I also voted for the man and thought his programs would be a lot better than what we'd seen in the past. It was the approach on the supply side that I had great hopes for. Downrange, into the program, we have not seen that great an effect. In fact, it's been a worsening. The future? I don't know exactly what should be done. The deficit is a major problem and, if given a chance to really work all the way through, I think it would have come on through, but, we've overkilled."

▪ "I agree totally with that. Sometimes the medicine is extremely bitter to take, yet if the medicine kills you who's going to win in a situation like that."

Something else Stockman said is having impact here. These are not old confessions, as told to Greider, but recent words of his from Washington. To beleaguered businessmen here, they are especially disturbing.

"There was an item in the paper the other day quoting David Stockman as saying that last year the federal government absorbed 34 percent of the available credit in the country and now for the fiscal year 1982 they're going to absorb 56 percent of the total available credit," one of the realtors remarked. "Knowing David Stockman and the federal government, I would say that's probably a conservative estimate."

A banker, who also cited that Stockman remark, commented, "If we're going to have 56 percent of available funds next year sapped up by government to finance this deficit, and those are the figures you're beginning to see, we've got some real problems out here. Obviously, something haywire has happened."

Indeed, it has. If that report of Stockman's is correct, our problem isn't over a lack of wealth trickling down. Our problem involves stopping a hemorrhage of the nation's economic blood supply.

—From the Washington Post, *June 20, 1982.* ©
Washington Post *1982. Reprinted by permission.*

"CAP'S" LAST LAUGH: WINNABLE NUCLEAR WAR
By Art Buchwald

People are constantly asking me, "Who is the man with the most humor in the Reagan administration?" They are surprised when my response is "Cap" Weinberger, our secretary of defense. Cap says things with a straight face that make you want to roll on the floor.

Just the other day he told newspapermen he is for a "protracted nuclear war." He doesn't want one of these hair-trigger wars which last 30 or 40 minutes. Cap said he has ordered everyone at the Pentagon to figure out not only how to keep a nuclear war going, but how to make sure the United States wins one when the missiles start flying.

Half the people in the Pentagon took Cap seriously. But those who knew what a deadpan comic Cap is just laughed and went back to doing the crossword puzzle.

The material for Cap's "protracted nuclear war" came out of a routine he did when he first took charge of the Defense Department and came up with a comic routine on "limited nuclear war."

He tried this one out in front of an armed services committee last year and had everyone in stitches. Cap, without cracking a smile, said he thought a "limited nuclear war" with the Soviets was not only feasible, but essential so the United States would have time to fight a conventional war.

Cap said if we let the Russians know that we were only going to fight a "limited nuclear war" then they would agree not to use their big stuff to attack us.

The only ones who didn't laugh were our NATO allies who figured out that if a "limited nuclear war" was going to be waged it would be on their turf, and even after Al Haig tried to explain to the Europeans that Cap was only joking, they still didn't find the secretary of defense's war routine very funny.

So Cap got his writers together and said, "I think my jokes are losing something in the translation. We're going to have to come up with a new monologue, and throw the 'limited nuclear war' stuff out."

One of the writers said, "I got it! What if you just stand up at the microphone and say you're no longer for a 'limited nuclear war,' but you've opted for a 'protracted' one instead? Say we're going to build offensive weapons that will make the U.S. prevail no matter what the Russians throw at us."

"That's pretty funny," Cap said. "Let's work on it. But keep it quiet or Johnny Carson will hear about it, and use it on his 'Tonight' show first."

The writers all went to work and came up with some memorable lines.

One was "you show me a secretary of defense who is not preparing to win a nuclear war, and I'll show you a secretary of defense who should be impeached."

Another one which was a real crowd pleaser: When he was asked if a nuclear war was winnable, Cap replied, again with a straight face, "I just don't have any idea; I don't know that anybody has any idea. But we're certainly going to give the armed forces everything they need to win one."

These are just a few samples of Cap Weinberger's humor. They may not sound as funny on paper, but when you see him standing up in front of the mike, looking like Woody Allen, delivering them, you could die laughing.

—*From the* Washington Post, *August 31, 1982.* © *Art Buchwald 1982. Reprinted by permission.*

DOES REAGAN REALLY CARE?
By Carl T. Rowan

Michael Horowitz, a key adviser to David Stockman, director of the Office of Management and Budget, has caused an uproar in the White House by putting an unpalatable truth on paper. In an internal memorandum, Horowitz observed that the Reagan administration is perceived by many Americans as "uncaring, perhaps even cruel."

This got into the media, provoking declarations from the White House press office that "Ronald Reagan is a fair man. He believes his policies are fair."

Well, let the White House tell that to the 4,508 people who

lined up in Hempstead, N.Y., a few days ago to apply for 296 jobs ranging from dishwashers to desk clerks at a new hotel. These applicants, and some 11 million other jobless Americans, remember Reagan's suggesting that the want ads are loaded with jobs for people who really want to work.

Let them give the fairness lecture to the 700,000 or more families that have been thrown into poverty since he took office—even as his administration has snatched food stamps out of their grasp on grounds that Reagan knows someone who used the change from the food stamps to buy vodka.

Let them give that speech to the thousands of children who used to get their major nutrition during school lunch, but now find that their district has abandoned the program in the face of federal budget cuts.

Or tell it to the millions of children long deprived by poverty and racism who see this administration slashing away at funds for compensatory education, or trying to cripple the public schools in general. The White House could distribute some "WE CARE" buttons to the kids whose dreams of going to college vanished in the reduction of federal scholarship funds.

Part of the administration's bad image is that it is insensitive to the needs of minorities and has declined to enforce civil rights laws. The President indicated irritation over this when he spoke recently to black Republicans. But he had hardly finished speaking before his Justice Department was announcing that it may encourage the courts to dismantle busing-for-desegregation programs in Boston and other cities.

Against this record, what does anyone in the White House expect the administration's image to be?

—*From the* Washington Post, *October 2, 1982. © 1982 by Field Enterprises, Inc. Courtesy of Field Newspaper Syndicate.*

DINNER AT THE WHITE HOUSE
By Charlotte Curtis

WASHINGTON President and Mrs. Reagan's State Dinner for Indonesia's controversial President and Mrs. Suharto was one of those routinely brilliant gatherings for which the White House is famous. Everything went exactly to plan, and the Suhartos, the blasé Washington regulars, and the dazzled first-timers went away suitably impressed.

As always, perhaps 125 of the formally clad rich, famous, accomplished, or politically useful arrived at the south entrance. Inside, guests went up the marble stairs, through the marble hallway where a string orchestra was playing, and into the East Room to sip drinks, study one another intently, and talk in little clusters.

Edwin Meese III, counselor to the President, and James A. Baker III, Mr. Reagan's chief of staff, were among the first to arrive, and across the room Alexis Smith, the actress, Craig Claiborne, the food critic, and Gloria Vanderbilt, the fashion designer, discovered Mabel Mercer, jazz singer *extraordinaire*, introduced themselves and asked if she were going to perform. "No," she said, she wasn't singing. Furthermore, she hadn't the faintest idea why she'd been invited. Several others said they didn't know either. Which is what guests who have no special tie to a President always say.

But that's the genius of White House dinners. Presidential invitations are like summonses, and knowing First Ladies always see that they go to (thereby honoring) a wide variety of influential Americans, whether they know them or not, and they are virtually never refused. Baseball players meet Nobel scientists they've never heard of, film stars gape at tycoons, and generals sit next to best-selling writers.

Eleanor Lambert, the fashion publicist, swept in and said hello to what was rapidly becoming a New York group and to Paige Rense, editor of *Architectural Digest*. Secretary of State George Shultz and Treasury Secretary Donald T. Regan appeared, and shortly thereafter the crowd formed a receiving line and, to a resounding blast of "Hail to the Chief," President and Mrs. Reagan and the Suhartos arrived.

Mrs. Reagan, a champion of classical American fashion, wore a Bill Blass black silk jersey with a diagonally hemmed white silk jersey top, a black and white silk choker fastened with mother-of-pearl and matching earrings. In her first months in the White House, close friends urged her to wear more makeup lest she look pale. She refused, and even in harsh lights she looks natural and ladylike. Shy as she is, she is exceedingly outgoing, and there is nothing perfunctory about her handshake.

"She's fabulous," said Selwa Roosevelt, the chief of protocol.

Mrs. Roosevelt stood with the Presidents and their wives to introduce the guests, and from there all proceeded to the State Dining Room, where pink tables were set with pink and coral floribunda roses, vermeil and the celebrated new red and gold presidential china. President Reagan and Mrs. Suharto sat beneath the Lincoln portrait, and Mrs. Reagan and President Suharto sat at a table facing them.

Mrs. Reagan and Miss Vanderbilt, smashing in bouffant black silk with a tiny waist, a rhinestone choker and chandelier rhinestone earrings the size of fists, talked fashion. When Miss Rense wasn't talking with Daniel J. Boorstin, the Librarian of Congress, at her left, she was smoking Sobranie cigarillos, lighted on her right by General Charles A. Gabriel, the Air Force chief of staff, who reminded Mrs. Reagan that when she'd rushed to Monte Carlo for Princess Grace's funeral, he'd been flying a B-1 bomber that landed just as her plane took off.

"That was a terrible time," Mrs. Reagan said. "Grace and I were old friends. We were in Hollywood together. We saw each other at Prince Charles's wedding, and we said, would anybody back then have believed she would marry a Prince and I'd end up here."

The dinner started with pampano, and included beef, béarnaise sauce, souffléd potatoes, a pretty endive and watercress salad and ended spectacularly with molded pear sherbet topped by pears dipped in chocolate.

President Reagan toasted the Suhartos and announced the nomination of John H. Holdridge, assistant secretary of state for east Asian affairs, as the new ambassador to Indonesia. President Suharto, pleased, returned the toast. Afterwards, the dinner adjourned for coffee and moved to the East Room where Frederica von Stade, the mezzo-soprano, sang a program ranging from Mozart to Charles Ives. As usual, the dancing was in the flower-banked marble hall, and by 11 P.M., Muffie Brandon, Mrs. Reagan's social secretary, looked at her watch.

"I'll give it another twenty minutes before 'Good Night Ladies,' " she said. Instead, twenty minutes later, the orchestra played the Brahms Lullabye, guests went down the marble stairs and out into the starry night. Pickets still marched their protest against Indonesia's seizure of East Timor.

"What a lovely dinner," President Suharto said on the way to his hotel.

"And the flowers were beautiful," Mrs. Suharto agreed.

—From the New York Times, *October 19, 1982. © 1982 by the* New York Times *Company. Reprinted by permission.*

THE OVAL OFFICE AESOP
By James David Barber

DURHAM, N.C. The election is over, the Republic stands, but how long can democracy stand the type of talk we are drifting into as the nation deliberates the choice of leaders?

Democracy is not only a structure of power, it is also a special kind of conversation: a deliberation meant to result in the consent of the governed—an informed consent, a persuaded consent, not just a sigh of thanks that all that jabber is over. If President Reagan's performance so far is any index, we are in for a long slide away from democratic deliberation as we mosey toward 1984.

Ronald Reagan is the first modern President whose contempt for the facts is treated as a charming idiosyncracy. Way back in 1976, those of us who watch presidential politics could deplore the news media's fascination with gaffes, such as Jimmy Carter's odd blurts about "ethnic purity" and "lust in the heart" and Gerald Ford's accidental liberation of Poland from the Soviet grip. These lapses were blown way out of proportion. The media seemed (unconsciously) to be aping Freud, treating any slip of the tongue as an important clue to the mind. The gaffe story graduated from a diverting episode of the day to a running drama of at least a week, featuring the candidate's denial, admission, defense and ultimate apology, in a tragic sequence signaling the victory of form over content. Those stories were trivial, but the exaggerated coverage made the candidates think twice about their words.

Comes Ronald Reagan. In the campaign of 1980, his counterfactual statements rolled forth so fast the news magazines had to bundle them together as a weekly feature. In a factual sense, be the subject air pollution or nuclear power, farm policy or foreign policy, he literally did not know what he was talking about. By now, he has shown that he does not care. As for the past, he has yet to retract his mythical version of Vietnam history, which, if he believes it, could easily misguide him when the next Vietnam pops up. In the present, despite the efforts of his fact checker (Misty Church, age 24), he continues to toss off spurious specifics with a cavalier abandon, as if to say he could have gotten them right, but why bother? As for the future and the policies he hopes to make work, we already have the testimony of his chief dream broker, David A. Stockman, that Mr. Reagan and his friends saw through their own flashy program from the start, knowing it to be as hollow as a Trojan horse. Now, his left hand offers record-smashing deficits as his right offers a constitutional bar to any deficit at all. Having come full circle on taxes, Mr. Reagan urged us to "stay the course" he himself had abandoned.

But it is not the hypocrisy or dishonesty of any particular politician that ought to disturb us. Rather, the chill descends when it becomes apparent that the President's fictional flights are being defended as a positive good and that the media are beginning to buy the idea that at least they are not a significant harm. David Gergen, Mr. Reagan's communications man, recently illustrated the new line. He applied a novel version of majority rule to the Reagan record: "Over the years, he's come out with many facts and figures and far more often than not, he was right." Anyway, "these stories have a parable-like quality to them," Mr. Gergen says. "He's trying to tell us how society works"—which, presumably, cannot be done with the straight story. The Gergen solution to remaining doubts? Since the press was making so much of the factual errors when expressed in afternoon press conferences, Mr. Reagan should shift to evening conferences and "let the public judge for themselves" when their President was telling them truth or falsehood.

It is not too far a leap from these new roles for presidential rhetoric to that of the President as the Aesop of the Oval Office, tossing off parables instead of argument. Parables challenge us at church or amuse us in the theater: they reach beyond the test of evidence. But in the White House, we need a President who lives in the real world—and knows it. Even more, we rely on public discourse in which proposals meet facts in a test clear enough for reason to grasp. What we are getting instead is a mockery of the consent of the governed.

Charles Peters of the *Washington Monthly* has noticed that, although the big newspapers still cover Mr. Reagan's fables, the story is slipping away from the front page as its news value fades. But it is just that retreat from national attention that may do more to corrupt political talk than the most vituperative of television ads. Mr. Gergen calls Mr. Reagan's storytelling a "folk art." Thomas Jefferson would have viewed it differently: "The whole of government is the art of being honest."

—*James David Barber, professor of political science at Duke University, is author of* The Pulse of Politics: Electing Presidents in the Media Age. *This article is reprinted from the* New York Times, *November 7, 1982.* © *1982 by the* New York Times *Company. Reprinted by permission.*

WATCH OUT!
By Dorothy Gilliam

Ronald Reagan was his old self again this week. He showed his true colors in the State of the Union address—heavy on defense, light on human concerns. He waved the tattered flag of waste and fraud in the food stamp program, never mentioning waste in military spending. He called for a freeze that amounts to another cut for social programs and a boost for defense.

Then he followed up that performance with the bizarre suggestion in Boston the next day that now is the time for corporations to pay no taxes at all. And no matter how his staff tries to clean it up, the statement rips away the conciliatory mask to reveal Vintage Reagan.

What's new is that it won't wash any more.

The polls now show a majority of Americans deep in doubt about Ronald Reagan's achievements. In a recent *Washington*

Post–ABC News poll, 54 percent of the people interviewed said they disapprove of the President's handling of his job. Many of those voicing discontent are the people who have seen their incomes plummet from joblessness, layoffs, or forced cuts in working time.

Jimmy Carter's midterm polls were about as bad as Reagan's. But Reagan's polls are dramatic, significant beyond mere percentage points when you consider the tenacious support many Americans gave him for so long.

Some Americans saw Reagan for what he was from the beginning. Women, organized labor, minorities, and education leaders have for some time been critical of $750 billion tax breaks and $2.2 trillion military spending in the face of record unemployment, attacks on affirmative action, and slashes in social programs.

Suddenly, these groups are not screaming alone.

And that raises a question: What will it mean that so many Americans from diverse backgrounds are coming to deeply distrust Ronald Reagan?

During the Great Depression, we had no television that made possible instant commiseration between an unemployed mechanic in Birmingham and a laid-off schoolteacher in Baltimore. But each day now people from Miami to Seattle see instantly the commonality of their plight, and it cuts across racial, territorial, and geographical boundaries.

History tells us that when Americans are possessed of a mammoth feeling that something is wrong, we take a brief hiatus from the divisions that are part of our warp and woof. We act decisively.

Such an interval occurred immediately after President Lyndon Baines Johnson utilized this willingness to act to push through a landmark civil rights bill. A similar interruption in divisiveness occurred in the aftermath of Watergate when the country united behind the need to establish a new morality, and the Congress instituted new rules and procedures.

The situation now in Detroit or Youngstown or any one of a dozen cities is just as much of a crisis as those earlier events. Record unemployment, small business failures and foreclosures on small farms have brought us—at least symbolically—to as much of a standstill as those shocks did.

The potential is there for a different political alliance to emerge from all of this discontent. Blacks and women have already declared they have too much at stake in fighting a common foe to worry about the things that divide them. An even broader kind of coalition of whites, Hispanics, and middle-class Americans could join these early critics.

Reagan capitalized on a liberal bankruptcy that had been long in building. He benefited from the frustration of a wide range of groups that had grown angry with the perceived failure of government to carry out the old liberal ideals.

His election looked like the beginning of a new conservative era, but his policies are producing the kind of drastic consequences that could revitalize the old coalitions, fast.

While Reagan continues to sing his old song, the ground is shifting around him. If his actions this week were any indication, he is ignoring the signs of change and paving the way for what could be a sharp, fundamental shift. When public opinion in this country unifies, things start to happen.

Watch out, Mr. President. America is losing patience.

—*From the* Washington Post, *January 29, 1983. © 1983
the* Washington Post. *Reprinted by permission.*

Patrick J. Buchanan, a staffer in the White House during the Nixon administration, struck a recurring theme in his syndicated column that the Reagan administration is tapping under to the international bankers. For instance, in his column of Jan. 21, 1983, Buchanan wrote:

"At Treasury, the men of principle with the sometimes prickly personalities, Paul Craig Roberts and Norman Ture, have gone. . . . Meanwhile, the remaining minions at Treasury are busy constructing a giant pipeline from Middle America through the International Monetary Fund into the looted vaults of the third world so that not a single extortionate interest payment will be missed at David Rockefeller's bank."

What follows is Buchanan's column on this subject for Feb. 4, 1983.

CONSERVATIVES JOIN BIG BAILOUT
By Patrick J. Buchanan

WASHINGTON Sad to report, but the conservatives have begun signing on to the Great Bank Bailout of 1983.

Senator Bill Armstrong of Colorado, who chairs a subcommittee on international institutions, suggests on national television that we have no choice but give the International Monetary Fund the largest national slice of the $50 billion it wants. Big John Connally of Texas, while conceding the folly of the big banks, reluctantly agrees.

Don Regan and Beryl Sprinkel of Treasury trek to Toronto, trepidatious Christians ready to face the lions rather than burn incense at the altar of the IMF, and return to the catacombs, new acolytes of Apollo, telling us we must now all burn incense to the pagan gods and it is not all that bad once you get the hang of it.

President Reagan sends the signal in his State of the Union address: "We will continue to work closely with the International Monetary Fund to ensure it has adequate resources to help bring the world economy back to strong noninflationary growth."

Look at it this way, Fed chairman Paul Volcker soothes the House Banking Committee. This is not a "bail-out" of the big banks; it is a "bail-in," heh-heh, since the big banks are being forced to shell out even more money to their debtor clients to get the IMF aid.

And so they are—with Yugoslavia the textbook case. With the U.S. government in the lead, eleven western governments agreed to give Communist Yugoslavia $1.3 billion in new money, but only if the western banks provided this insolvent regime with another $1 billion in new loans.

The same situation obtained in the great Mexican bailout. The U.S. and the IMF poured in billions, but the big banks were also required to send new billions chasing the tens of billions already gone.

Can no one see what is going on here? The ultimate in foreign aid machinery is being created with the consent and complicity of a conservative American government, a machine beyond the erotic imaginings of the Brandt Commission and the Socialist International.

The "New International Economic Order" under which the black and brown nations of the socialist south have a permanent moral claim upon the wealth of the white and capitalist west is being created before our very eyes—Regan & Reagan, Architects.

The transfusion of the precious investment capital of the U.S., blood bank of the west, into the anemic socialist economics of east and south is increasing at a geometric rate. Not a week passes without some new country declaring it cannot pay its debts and the IMF rushing to the rescue with western capital, dragging along the hapless banks.

Not a single insolvent regime, no matter how odious, appears to have been denied a seat at the sumptuous banquet table of the IMF—to be forever set by U.S. taxpayers.

In the desperate effort to save *all* the bad loans of the decade past, all the principles of sound banking are being abandoned. It is not the best of foreign enterprises that are first in line at the loan windows of the IMF. It is the worst—the bankrupts, the freeloaders, the deadbeats, the insolvent, the illiquid, walking away with the capital: Stalinist Romania, $10 billion in the hole; Yugoslavia, $20 billion and bust; Argentina, $40 billion in debt with wholesale prices rising at 300 percent; Mexico, $80 billion in debt, with foreign earnings collapsing by a billion dollars every time the price of a barrel of oil falls another $2.

If this massive transfer of American capital to the IMF and the third world is a wise, prudent investment, let us fairly ask: how much of the *personal* wealth of these affluent international bankers is invested in such loans?

How much of David Rockefeller's *personal* wealth was sent down to Mexico City—along with the savings of his Chase Manhattan depositors—*after* the threatened August default?

Not to worry, the follies of the past will not be repeated, we are assured. This time the IMF will place "conditions" on the loans. But the folly *is* being repeated!

The only condition that will make Yugoslavia and Romania sensible economic investments is to demand that both junk their ridiculous Marxist economic systems. Has the IMF done that? The only way Mexico and Tanzania can become prosperous nations is for the former to abandon its socialist nostrums and controls, and the latter to jettison the neo-Maoist kakistocracy that has ruined that country. Did the IMF tell them that?

After two years of immense economic hardship, we Americans have accumulated a savings pool upon which all our hopes for recovery depend. Why, when capitalism is desperate for credit, would intelligent capitalists ship their wealth off to subsidize any Communist and socialist failure?

—From the New York Post, *February 4, 1982.*
© *1983 by the* Chicago Tribune–New York News
Syndicate, Inc. Reprinted by permission.

ONWARD CHRISTIAN SOLDIERS
By Anthony Lewis

BOSTON When a politician claims that God favors his programs, alarm bells should ring. That is what Ronald Reagan has just done. Speaking to the National Association of Evangelicals in Orlando, Fla., he said that belief in God should make Americans join him in opposing a nuclear freeze and pressing a vast buildup in U.S. weapons.

"There is sin and evil in the world," the President said, "and we are enjoined by Scripture and the Lord Jesus to oppose it with all our might." Soviet Communism is "the focus of evil in the modern world," he said, and those who favor a mutual freeze on new nuclear weapons ignore "the aggressive instincts of an evil empire."

If there is anything that should be illegitimate in the American system, it is such use of sectarian religiosity to sell a political program. And this was done not by some fringe figure, but by the President of the United States. Yet I wonder how many people, reading about the speech or seeing bits on television, really noticed its outrageous character. Our political sensibilities have become so degraded.

Primitive: that is the only word for it. We laugh at stage representations of William Jennings Bryan, who used religion to argue against everything from the gold standard to Darwinian theory. The Ronald Reagan who spoke in Orlando could easily call it a sin to teach evolution.

But it is not funny. What is the world to think when the greatest of powers is led by a man who applies to the most difficult human problem a simplistic theology—one in fact rejected by most theologians?

Any President is entitled to give uplifting talks about moral or spiritual questions. But Mr. Reagan was doing something very different. He was purporting to apply religious concepts to the contentious technical particulars of arms programs. Can the concept of good and evil determine whether 10,000 nuclear warheads is enough? Whether this country needs a first-strike weapon against the Soviet Union? Whether a nuclear freeze is likely to make the world more or less safe?

Believers, Mr. Reagan said, should avoid "the temptations of pride"—calling both sides at fault in the arms race instead of putting the blame where it belonged: on the Russians. But there again he applied a black-and-white standard to something that is much more complex.

One may regard the Soviet system as a vicious tyranny and still understand that it has not been solely responsible for the nuclear arms race. The terrible irony of that race is that the United States has led the way on virtually every major new development over the last thirty years, only to find itself met by the Soviet Union.

The dramatic example was the introduction of MIRV's, the multiple-warhead missiles. It was a great U.S. technological breakthrough. But the Russians then copied it, building weapons systems that have been regarded with special alarm by the West. It is precisely such history that requires the United States and its allies, as a matter of self-interest, to think through arms-control issues—in concrete terms, not pieties.

What must the leaders of western Europe think of such a speech? They look to the head of the alliance for reasoning that can persuade them and their constituents. What they get from Ronald Reagan is a mirror image of crude Soviet rhetoric.

And it is more than rhetoric: Everyone must sense that. The

real Ronald Reagan was speaking in Orlando. The exaggeration and the simplicities are there not only in the rhetoric but in the process by which he makes decisions.

What must Soviet leaders think? However one detests their system, the world's survival depends ultimately on mutual restraint. What confidence can they have in the restraint of an American leader with such an outlook?

Perhaps most important, what view can Ronald Reagan have of his own country? He makes a political speech identifying himself with a particular sectarian view. He denounces the "value system" of secularism. He says that "freedom prospers when religion is vibrant." He cites Whitaker Chambers as a moral arbiter.

That audience cheered as an orchestra played "Onward, Christian Soldiers." But America is not a country of evangelicals alone. Not all or most Americans agree with conservative Protestant or Catholic theology. Many religious groups have in fact endorsed the nuclear freeze. But numbers are not the point: diversity is.

The American Republic has lasted nearly 200 years because it has a system in which people of fundamentally different views can coexist. The President is the symbol, as Jefferson understood when he said in his first inaugural: "We are all Republicans—we are all Federalists." For a President to attack those who disagree with his politics as ungodly is terribly dangerous.

Reagan on Reaganism
1975–1979

(Additional excerpts from Reagan's 1975, 1978, and 1979 radio broadcasts)

There follow here excerpts, additional to those in the text of this book, from some of Ronald Reagan's radio broadcasts in 1975, transcripts of which I obtained from the Democratic National Committee in 1982, and from a full set of the transcripts of his radio broadcasts in 1978 and 1979, which I obtained in October 1980 from Reagan's political action committee, Citizens for the Republic.

I have selected the excerpts, grouped them by subjects, and added the introductory titles (except for a few cases in which I have used the same titles given on the transcripts, which are also given with the date at the end of each excerpt).

The broadcasts were mailed to hundreds of radio stations in the U.S. in packets of fifteen with a cover sheet indicating the period during which they were to be presented. According to

Peter Hannaford, an aide of Reagan's at the time, Reagan recorded fifteen programs during each visit to the recording studio. The date given at the end of each excerpt in this Appendix is the period specified on the cover sheet for the broadcast from which the excerpt is drawn. For example, "10/78" at the end of an excerpt means that the broadcast was contained in a packet sent out for presentation in October 1978; "7–8/79" means the same for July–August 1979. Each of the 1975 broadcasts is dated, so the specific dates are given for the 1975 excerpts.

I have silently modified paragraphing, some sentence-opening capitalization, misspellings, and typing errors. I have silently omitted opening and closing portions of a broadcast and the words "quote" and "unquote" enclosing quotations that Reagan was reading. Otherwise I have indicated all omissions with the customary system of either three or four dots.

In many cases I have not introduced commas where ordinarily they would be needed because the shortage of commas in the transcripts reflects Reagan's rapid-fire delivery. My minimal editorial interventions in the transcripts are enclosed by brackets. My annotations are italicized in parentheses.

SECTION I: THE UNITED STATES

SOCIAL SECURITY

Private Insurance Would Be Better

(*Reagan's three broadcasts on Social Security in 1975 are reviewed fully in the text. In the opening months of 1978 he returned to the subject.*)

Right now more than half the people paying into Social Security will get less than they pay in—possibly as little as half. . . .

Truth is if we could invest your and your employer's share of the Social Security tax in savings or insurance we could make a much better return than that promised by Social Security. . . .

Now it's going to cost more than 7 percent [tax] on $42,600 [income] and it is, in effect, bankrupt.

—"Social Security," 1–2/78.

COMMERCE AND CONSERVATION

Allow More Cutting in National Forests

Dead trees are pure waste and are harmful to the forest. Take the example of Lassen National Forest in California. This preserve allows a cut of 150 million board feet a year. It could raise that to 268 million board feet if the timber cutters were allowed to harvest only the overmature and dying trees. Lassen would be a better national forest and one much safer from the threat of forest fire if the additional cutting were done. As it is, it's choked with rotting wood. . . .

So what's the federal government waiting for?

—"Lumber," 7–8/78.

Make Public Resources Available to Industry

Not only do public forests lag behind well-managed private ones in productivity, but the government is also adopting measures that remove large areas of land and volumes of timber from our industrial resource base. . . .

In addition, under these lands are coal and oil and natural gas and mineral deposits which, turned to productive use, could improve our economy and help strengthen the dollar.

The unavailability of these public resources to provide jobs, wages and yes, taxes, undermines the whole system that has made us prosperous.

—"Needed—Better Use of National Forest," 10/78.

Produce More Energy from Federal Lands

The Dean of the University of Arizona College of Mines . . . tells us that 50 percent of all known energy sources are in [the] federal lands. Yet, in 1976, they only accounted for 10 percent of our total energy production. According to Dean William Lesher, the federal government has been locking these lands up as fast as new energy sources are discovered on them, thereby preventing production which could make us less dependent on foreign sources. . . .

We're so used to calling this one-third of our nation federal land, isn't it time we remembered that the very term means it belongs to us—to the people of America?

—"Federal Lands," 10–11/78.

Wilderness Areas as a Lock-Out

Right now something called "Rare II" is going on. Rare stands for Roadless Area Review and Evaluation. It is a program by the Bureau of Land Management and the Forest Service to take about 62 million acres of national forest and national grasslands in 37 states and Puerto Rico and designate them as wilderness areas. This would mean, of course, the closing of all roads. In other words, only those robust enough to go backpacking would have access to those millions of acres of scenic land. . . .

I think we all should be [concerned] lest a handful of extremists plus these government agencies lock up in a preserve the great scenic areas of our land for the benefit of a privileged few.

—"Keep Off the Grass," 12/78–1/79.

No to Alaskan Lands Bill

Many Alaskans are furious these days over a bill sponsored by Representatives Morris Udall and John Anderson. The so-called Alaskan Lands bill would set aside an area of Alaskan land as big as California for the purpose of creating reserves, national parks, and wildlife refuges. . . .

The Alaskan Lands legislation will disrupt the lives of Alaskans and the development of the state's major industries. Seven major mines, which would produce various metals, will be blocked from developing. . . . Other major industries, such as oil and timber, will face economic hardship or ruin. . . . Alaskans have every reason to be angry.

—"Alaskan Anger," 9/79.
(Congress passed the bill and Carter signed it into law in 1980.)

THE Environment

Pollution and Faith in Technology

Back in the Depression years the factory smokestack belching black clouds of coal smoke skyward was a symbol of reassurance that the good life was still possible. Today it is an evil thing to be deplored and eliminated, symbol of everything that is wrong.

Now I'm not lobbying for air pollution, water pollution, or destruction of the environment in the name of progress. : . . . Yes, I'm aware of the problems accompanying the benefits, but do we throw away the benefits to get rid of the problems or do we have faith that the technology that gave us the benefits might first possibly rid us of the problems?

—"Technology," 9/78.

80 Percent of Air Pollution Comes from Plants, Trees

The American Petroleum Institute filed suit against the Environmental Protection Agency under the Freedom of Information Act. The institute charged that the agency was suppressing a scientific study for fear it might be misinterpreted. Possibly you are aware that the EPA has set ozone standards which industrial groups claim simply can't be met. Apparently, industry is right. The suppressed study reveals that 80 percent of air pollution comes not from chimneys and auto exhaust pipes, but from plants and trees.

—"Miscellaneous," I, 1–2/79.

Disney's Mineral King vs. "An Elite Few"

Thirteen years ago—in 1965—the United States Forest Service under a mandate from Congress and at the direction of President Johnson initiated an action to develop the recreation potential of a California beauty spot known as Mineral King which adjoins Sequoia National Park. . . . But suddenly a hue and cry was raised by a small group of ardent preservationists opposed to the developments. . . . Is public land really for the public or for an elite few who want to keep it for their own use?

—"Mineral King," 3–4/78.

Private Ownership of Ocean Frontage

California has 1,000-plus miles of coastline ranging from broad sandy beaches to mountains dropping steeply into the surf, and in the north redwood forests coming almost to the water's edge. What most Californians weren't aware of was that almost half—some 400 miles of ocean front—is already owned by government. . . .

In spite of all this the coastal commission, made up of appointees, and not elected representatives, almost from the very first assumed dictatorial powers and displayed what can only be described as hostility to any private ownership of ocean frontage.

—"Malibu," 7/78.

Environmentalists' Are Intimidating

Recently I received a letter from an old friend who backpacks into the high Sierra . . . and therefore is a true environmentalist with real love for the beauty of this earth. He had just completed a four-day hike to Yosemite Park, from Tuolomne Meadows to Glen Aulin.

He wrote that he was appalled at the condition of the lodgepole pines. . . . These trees have been attacked by an insect known as the Lodge Pole Needle Miner. . . .

There is a spray that will control those insects, but so far the forestry people are dragging their feet while the needles turn brown and fall from the trees. The environmentalists, vocal and well organized, are opposed to the spraying of the trees. The foresters, apparently, are intimidated.

—"Miscellaneous," III, 8/79.

The Absurdity of the Endangered Species Law

In California we have an environmental problem which could pit environmentalists against environmentalists. The Pacific Legal Foundation, a nonprofit organization consistently found on the side of common sense and fairness, has filed suit against the EPA. It seeks an injunction to stop EPA activities which violate the Endangered Species Act. . . .

The legal group actually has a serious and worthwhile purpose. They are trying to establish the absurdity of the present endangered species law which gives priority to tiny fish, weeds and spiders regardless of the merits of any proposed project.

—"Environment," 10–11/78.

(*The Reagan administration has supported renewal of the Endangered Species Act, but by the spring of 1983 had added only eight species to the protected categories.*)

No More Progressivity, Please

Yes, the tax system is a disgrace but not for the reasons usually given and no we don't need a "more progressive system of taxation." Let's take a look at the two ends of the scale. The lowest earning one-fourth of the population pay less than one-tenth of the total income tax. The top one-fourth pay 70 percent and you are part of *that* one-fourth if you earn $17,000 a year. . . .

Traditionally in Western religions it is accepted that the Lord's share of our earnings is a tenth and we have been told that if the Lord prospers us ten times as much we will give ten times as much. But it all comes out a little different when we "render under Caesar."

—"Tax Time," 4–5/78.

Business Lunches and Bologna Sandwiches

The administration in Washington is pretty upset about the tax deductibility of the business lunch. I don't know how much additional revenue the government would get by making such luncheons nondeductible, but I suspect there wouldn't be much, not after you figure the decline in restaurant business and the possible layoff of waiters and bartenders.

But, in touting their case, the tax collectors bleed and weep for the working man who can't deduct his bologna sandwich.

—"Three Martini Lunch," 4–5/78.

Income and Capital Gains Taxes

The labor leaders [in the California AFL-CIO convention] . . . raised the old cry—born of demagoguery—that income taxes should be more progressive, making those with higher earnings pay a bigger share of the tax. . . .

Finally the other proposal the convention made was to gain more revenue from the capital gains tax. . . .

I wish today's labor leaders had the statesmanship of the American Federation of Labor leaders in 1942 who demanded that the capital gains tax be reduced if not eliminated because it was preventing the investment of capital needed to create jobs for their members.

—"Economics," II, 8–9/78.

Proposition 13

In California, Howard Jarvis, a 75-year-old veteran battler of high taxes, stunned the spenders in Sacramento when his petition drive [for Proposition 13] netted more than 1.2 million signatures—an all-time record. . . .

Meanwhile, some of the spenders in the legislature—scared stiff that they will no longer be able to buy votes with other people's money—are sounding like a Greek chorus. They are crying "tax shift" and warning that state income and sales taxes will have to go up to make up for local budget cuts.

—"Tax Limitation 1978 Style," 3/78.

A National Proposition 13?

It's easy to see why Congress had to go through what has become an annual ritual—the raising of the debt limit a few weeks ago. In just eight years the debt has gone from $377 billion to $814 billion. If the present trends continue, we will have a trillion-dollar debt, a trillion-dollar budget, and $200 billion of that will be for interest on that debt—and all by 1985. Anyone for a national Proposition 13?

—"Government Payroll," 10/78.

Government Can't Tax Corporations

The economic fairy tale shows up . . . in the [California AFL-CIO] convention's decision to battle for reimposing the property tax Proposition 13 canceled back on business and industry. . . .

Whether it be corporation or corner store, taxes are part of business costs and must be recovered in the price of the product. Meaning that all of us consumers pay those taxes. . . .

Government can't tax things like businesses or corporations, it can only tax people. When it says it's going to "make business pay," it is really saying it is going to make business help it collect taxes.

—"Economics," I, 8–9/78.

Abolish Corporate Taxes

The fair answer, of course, would be a single tax. If there were no corporate tax, nontaxable funds such as union pensions, endowments for schools and hospitals, etc., would get twice as much money for their investments and would pay no tax on it. On the other hand, individuals would receive increased dividends and pay income tax at whatever rate was called for by their income-tax bracket. The retired couple with only a few dollars investment would pay no tax. As it is now they've been taxed at more than a 50 percent rate before they get their money. The high-salaried individual in a 40 percent or 50 percent bracket would pay that rate of tax on his dividends.

—"Business Tax," 12/78–1/79.

CAMPAIGN FINANCE

The Limits Are Part of a Pattern

Government is encroaching more and more into areas previously left to our own free choice. We ride in monopolized and government-regulated commuter railroads, taxicabs, buses, and airlines. Everything we use is delivered and shipped on regulated vehicles or through regulated pipelines. Our homes and places of employment are heated by government-regulated gas. We read by regulated light. Our food and drugs and vitamin supplements are government-inspected. We are limited as to how much we can spend per child on education, how much we contribute to political candidates, and even how much of his own money a candidate can spend on his own campaign.

—"More on Regulations," II, 10/7/75.

BUSINESS

Healthy Competition vs. Monopoly

Ed [Wimmer] knew that the liberty and prosperity of the American people depended critically upon the preservation of economic freedom. Ed's hero was the bold, daring, independent man or woman who cleaned and planted, dug and drilled, built and invented, invested and produced. . . .

Concentrated power has always been the enemy of liberty. Power widely diffused among the people means freedom. Thus the program of Wimmer's organization aims at encouraging a widespread distribution of capital and property ownership and discouraging the concentration of economic and political power in the hands of big business, big labor, and big government alike.

—"Healthy Competition," 1/78.

Oil Is No Monopoly

High on the list of things the oil industry is accused of is that it enjoys being a monopoly. . . . There are more than 10,000 companies competing with each other in oil and gas exploration and production; 133 companies operate 264 refineries and more than 100 pipeline companies transport crude oil, liquefied natural gas, and refined products.

In the wholesale side of the industry there are 15,000 companies selling petroleum products to over 300,000 retailers. . . . That's not much of a monopoly. . . .

There is an oil monopoly. It is made up of the OPEC nations. We can break that monopoly only by finding and producing more oil in these United States, thereby lessening our dependence on OPEC oil. And if our government will trust in the incentives of the marketplace we'll find and produce that additional oil.

—"Oil," 2–3/78, and "Oil," 5–6/79.

The Steel Industry's Problems

There are charges of dumping of steel on the United States marketed by Japan. . . .

Possibly there was some dumping—I don't know, but the problem of the United States steel industry is a little more complicated than that. For example in 1976 our labor costs averaged $12.22 an hour compared to Japan's $6.31. Since then, steel in our country agreed to a wage contract that will raise the hourly pay 30 percent over the next three years. In 1977 steelworkers' pay averaged $12.75 an hour compared to the workers in all manufacturing getting $7.79.

—"Steel," 3/78.

In the rest of this broadcast, Reagan discussed government regulations, the decline of capital investment, and other phenomena as factors in steel's decline.

Trade Should Be as Free as Possible

Protectionism, in the form of higher tariffs, quotas on imports and so forth, almost always leads to retaliation; sometimes even trade war. . . . When cries go up for protection, we need to remember that a great many American jobs are dependent on import-export trade. . . .

On balance, making trade as free as possible is the best course for any nation, especially one such as ours whose dealings have such a great impact on the world's economy.

—"Free Trade vs. Protectionism," 6/79.

If We Let the Price of Oil Go Higher . . .

In 1973 at the time of the embargo we had only been importing 23 percent of our oil; now it's 47 percent. . . . Economists have figured out that for every 5 percent increase in price we allow, we'll increase domestic supplies by 1 percent. They also tell us that because we are maintaining our domestic price at 30 percent less than the import price we are consuming about 3 million barrels per day more than we otherwise would. Now add 3 million barrels we'd save if the price were allowed to go higher and 2 million barrels more per day we'd pump domestically if the price were higher and you have a 5-million-barrel-a-day reduction in our imports.

—"Oil," 6–7/78.

Let Natural Gas Prices Rise

There are vast quantities of natural gas available in the U.S. if our own government regulations did not stand in the way of it being produced. This untapped natural gas would break the back of the OPEC cartel.

We had been warned in 1974 that we were in danger of running out of natural gas. Part of the problem is that deeper wells must be drilled. . . . These harder-to-get-at gas deposits cannot be delivered to the pipelines for the price the government allows them to charge. . . . You can't sell a pencil for a nickel if it costs a dime to make it. . . .

Decontrol now and production of the gas available in our own land would literally break up the OPEC cartel. What are we waiting for?

—"OPEC," 2/79.

A Happy Note Concerning Consumerism

Maybe some of those people in Washington should look at the last election results before they go on deciding they know what we want. The Consumer Federation of America targeted one senator and four congressmen they were out to defeat—supposedly because they weren't thoughtful enough of consumers. All five won. They named four senators they were going to help win—obviously friends of consumers—all four lost.

On that happy note I'll call it a day.

—"Miscellaneous," II, 12/78–1/79.

NUCLEAR POWER

Nuclear Power Is Necessary, Safe

We come down to the bottom line—nuclear power is necessary. Why is there such opposition in the face of this obvious fact? Well, in part it's emotional. We lump nuclear power and bombs together and try to ban both. Indeed some of the anti–Vietnam war crowd, lacking a cause, have decided this is a good one.

There is also the no-growth group who think that somehow we can return to a bucolic yesteryear. . . .

The safeguards required by law, including automatic shut-offs and back-up systems, make the odds against a fatal accident 300 million to 1. You have 75,000 times the danger of dying in an auto accident than you have of losing your life in a nuclear mishap. As for radiation, a coal-fired plant emits more radiation than a nuclear-powered plant. You even get more from watching TV or having your teeth x-rayed. . . .

Paper, not nuclear waste is our real storage problem. The legal work for the Seabrook plant in New Hampshire alone has generated a 5-foot shelf of state hearing transcripts; twenty 3-inch thick volumes of applications to the federal government, 12,522 pages of transcripts from the federal hearings; another 5-foot shelf of papers filed before the NRC licensing board; and an unmeasured mass of briefs, environmental impact statements and exhibits. Anybody got a match?

—"Nuclear Power," I and II, 11–12/78.

Regulation

OSHA Should be Abolished

The Senate Committee of Governmental Affairs made public a study by two Harvard professors who came to the conclusion that OSHA should go. In their report they said: "Rather than continue on the course of its first seven years, we would argue that OSHA should be abolished. Safety and health in the work place would not suffer measurably. Significant private and governmental resources (they mean money) would be saved and an agency perceived primarily as a tool of government harassment would be eliminated." Amen!

—"Miscellaneous," II, 4/79.

(Late in his 1980 campaign Reagan abandoned this position, advocating instead that the powers of OSHA be made advisory.)

The 20,000-Word Mousetrap

We used to believe that if you built a better mousetrap the world would beat a path to your door. Now if you build a better mousetrap the government comes along with a better mouse. But maybe we've gone a step beyond that. The federal government has drawn up specifications on how to build a mousetrap. It must be some trap. The plans and specifications all (20,000 words of them on 700 pages) weigh almost 3½ pounds.

—"Items," 3–4/78.

Torrents of Government Paper

The federal government goes to press more often than the *New York Times*. The United States Printing Office spews forth about 600 documents per day. Now I'm not talking about forms or questionnaires. These are truly documents supposedly designed to inform the citizenry and by so doing make our lives richer and fuller. . . .

But to get back to the total number of such documents, in 1976 alone there were 150,000 printed. There are several depositories in the country. At one, the main library of the University of Iowa, it takes one full-time employee just to open and sort the 14 boxes that arrive each day.

—"Paperwork," 8–9/78.

The Airline Cartel Is Ended

In the years since World War II the air cargo business has experienced steady growth. It has, however, been constantly and carefully regulated by the Civil Aeronautics Board, which also regulates the passenger airline industry. Actually, regulating is not quite the right term. What the CAB has done since 1938 is maintain a cartel. . . .

Now, only a few months after the air cargo deregulation act, we are beginning to see what can happen. . . . The whole field is humming with new activity. . . .

—"Air Cargo Deregulation," 5/78.

Repeal the Kefauver Amendment

Back in 1962 the late Senator Estes Kefauver tacked an amendment onto the Food, Drug, and Cosmetics Act. . . .

The Federal Drug Administration exists to protect us from drugs or medicines such as Thalidomide that could prove harmful to our health. Senator Kefauver's amendment stated that—in addition—the FDA had to establish that the drug was *effective*. This is a nearly impossible task. . . .

The result of the Kefauver amendment was a toboggan slide for the United States pharmaceutical industry. . . . We need the result that repeal of the amendment would bring.

—"Drugs," 6–7/78.

Our Children Are Underestimated

The Federal Trade Commission is considering a ban on TV advertising of toys to children. . . . They say children must be protected since they are too young to see the distinction between program and commercial. I think they underestimate our children.

Isn't this really an interference in the parent-child relationship? The FTC's concern should extend no further than insuring that the advertising is not deceptive or misleading and that the toy meets legal requirements as to safety, etc. From then on it is the parents' responsibility to decide whether a toy is or is not suitable for their child.

—"Toys," 12/78.

CIVIL RIGHTS

No to Statehood for D.C.

Now comes Senator Edward Kennedy of Massachusetts who says the citizens of the District of Columbia are victims of taxation without representation and that possibly they also suffer racial discrimination. His answer is to make the District our fifty-first state. . . .

If this were implemented, the District of Columbia would have two United States senators and one or two representatives in the House. Their constituency would be for the most part government employees and there is no way that the fifty-first state's representatives would free themselves from a built-in conflict of interest. They would undoubtedly vote for higher taxes and expansion of the government payroll.

—"District of Columbia," 7/78.

End Busing by Constitutional Amendment

The other day when I picked up my local Los Angeles newspaper, I saw a headline referring to the court-ordered school busing program scheduled to begin in September. I thought my eyes were playing tricks. The busing scheme, it seems, will involve bus rides of up to ninety minutes each way every day for some of the youngsters. That's three hours a day on a bus for a child, just to satisfy some federal judge's notion of how to achieve equal education. It sounds more like the Mad Hatter's Tea Party.

Federal judges still seem to be stuck on the notion that rigid forced busing schemes which disrupt family and neighborhood life (not to mention wasting thousands of gallons of gasoline and large numbers of tax dollars) are somehow the way to solve the problem. Yet, in case after case, such schemes have proved impractical, counterproductive, and divisive.

Meanwhile, there have been a variety of innovations designed to improve and equalize educational opportunities—such things as "magnet" schools, academic parks, open enrollment, and the flexible voucher system. Increasingly in recent years, public opinion has been running strongly against compulsory busing. Judges, however, are insulated against public opinion. . . .

There is a remedy that is coming closer to fulfillment. Back in 1975 a freshman congressman, Representative Ron Mottl, Democrat of Ohio, introduced a constitutional amendment to abolish forced school busing as a means of achieving racial integration. . . . His bill has two key provisions. One says "No student shall be compelled to attend public school other than the one nearest his residence." The other says, "The Congress shall have the power to enforce by appropriate legislation the provisions of this article; and to insure equal educational opportunities for all students wherever located." . . . By this summer, a net total of 201 members of the House have signed it, just 17 short of the needed number.

—"School Busing," 7–8/78.

(Mottl, a Democrat who was accused of being too supportive of Reagan's policies and was defeated for reelection in 1982, had introduced his busing bill every Congress since 1975. In 1979 it was defeated 216–209. In 1981 he had obtained signatures from 205 of his colleagues on a petition to force a vote on it again, but his defeat at the polls killed his bill. "It is effectively dead," he said.)

WOMEN'S RIGHTS

Speculations on Gender-free Sports

In a federal court in Ohio recently a judge ruled that state and federal guidelines providing for separate male and female sports are unconstitutional. . . . [This] brings all kinds of possibilities to mind. . . . Here comes "Joe Muscles," six feet four 225 pounds who didn't quite make the varsity. He still wants to play basketball and so he plays—on what used to be the all-girls' team.

You buy a ticket to see the championship girls' basketball team do its stuff and five hairy-chested male "rejects" from the varsity take the floor.

—"Sports," 5/78.

Foolishness about Women's Athletics

. . . some of the foolishness HEW [the Department of Health, Education, and Welfare] commits under Title IX of the Education Amendments of 1972.

The Oak Ridge Tennessee schools have, for example, been ordered to see that varsity cheerleaders cheer equally for boys' and girls' teams. Boston State College is on the carpet because the busy guideline writers at HEW have discovered that the corridors where trophies and pictures of athletic heroes and title-winning teams are displayed do not give equal space and publicity to women's athletics.

—"Nit Picking," 5/78.

Women, the Civilizing Influence

In spite of all the jokes men like to tell about women drivers, I think almost all men know in their hearts that women have been the single most civilizing influence in the world.

—"Women," 5–6/78.

For One-Gender Service Clubs

Just recently the Senate Committee on Banking, Housing and Urban Affairs launched what one man has called a vendetta against the social and service clubs of America.

The committee wanted to know if Kankakee Savings & Loan paid membership dues in private clubs for employees, directors, and officers. . . . Remember most of these clubs are strictly male or female. . . .

[James G. Schneider, the company president, wrote the committee chairman:] ". . . If your committee now finds that it has the time, the funds and the inclination to start harassing the financial institutions of America over their strong backing of such 'sexist clubs' as Rotary, Zonta, Kiwanis, Business & Professional Women, Lions, Jaycees. . . .

There was more but you get the idea. We should be grateful to Mr. Schneider.

—"No," I, 2–3/79.

CRIME AND CIVIL LIBERTIES

Short Sentences for Murderers

I have just received a letter from the father of a young man who was brutally murdered on New Year's Eve five years ago. His letter was a cry of protest because one of his son's two murderers has been free on parole after only two years in prison and now has been discharged from parole and is totally free. . . .

As Cicero said, "The safety of the people shall be the highest law." But in California, a father writes, "After two years the murderer of my son goes free, but my son is dead."

—"Crime," 1/78.

Pot Can Wreck Minds and Bodies

Not too long ago, forty-one scientists representing thirteen countries met in France to present new research findings [on "pot"]. . . . These scientists have found pot, grass, weed—whatever you want to call it—definitely bad news.

They linked its use with harmful effects on human reproduction, the brain, and other organs, including the lungs. . . .

Is anyone listening? Why aren't our young people made to read this scientific evidence before they wreck the bodies and minds they are going to have to live with the rest of their lives? . . .

The toxic ingredient which provides the effect pot smokers want has a jawbreaker of a name which I may not pronounce correctly—tetra-hydracannabinal—which I will henceforth refer to as T.H.C. This T.H.C. lodges in the body's fatty tissues and that includes the brain and the reproductive organs. Now, for those hard to sell souls who liken a "joint" to a martini, the difference is our body eliminates the martini in 24 hours. T.H.C. stays in the body for a month. . . . And it lowers the male hormone and sperm count in men which, if I may be blunt, leads to sterility.

—"Pot," 10/78, and "Marijuana," 9/79.

TERRORISM AND POLICE

Keeping Files on American Citizens

The House and Senate committees presently investigating intelligence activities have been hostile to the keeping of files on American citizens, even where there is evidence indicating possible danger. . . .

Let's not forget the outraged editorials with which much of the press greeted the discovery that police intelligence units in cities such as Washington, New York, and Los Angeles had accumulated files on people believed to have a potential for arson, murder, and starting riots. . . .

The U.S. attorney general has called for limiting the ability of the FBI to proceed with domestic intelligence. But, in the

meantime, it is admitted the foreign terrorist groups are moving closer to America, in addition to an estimated 15,000 terrorists already organized into twenty-one groups in the United States.
—"Secret Service," 10/30/75.

Millions of Files Destroyed

In a kind of hysteria about supposed violation of our civil liberties by the FBI and CIA, we have caused police intelligence units around the country to destroy millions of files on suspected subversives, terrorists and other criminals. . . .

Not by coincidence I'm sure the pro-Castro FALN (a Puerto Rican terrorist group) recently set off two bombs in New York. That makes the total sixty-three in that city alone. Police have been unable to track down the bombers. You see, a few years ago a New York mayor ordered the police department to destroy intelligence files on Puerto Rican extremists.
—"Items," 3–4/78.

(See pp. 271–272. A spokesman for Patrick Murphy, the New York City police commissioner during the period Reagan discussed in the above broadcast, says that while many intelligence files were discarded for constitutional and practical reasons, no information that pertained to terrorist groups was discarded.)

Prosecuted FBI Agents Justified?

The top ranking Soviet official at the United Nations, Arkady Shevchenko, a forty-seven-year-old protege of Foreign Minister Gromyko, has defected and refused to return to Russia. . . .

Who knows, Shevchenko might have information of possible ties between the Weathermen Underground and the Soviet Union which could prove that the FBI agents the Justice Department is prosecuting were right in doing what they did a few years ago. Those agents have based their defense on proving the Weathermen were working closely with Soviet agents.
—"National Security," 6–7/78.

(On this theory, President Reagan pardoned two former FBI agents convicted of authorizing illegal entries. See p. 248.)

U.S. Terrorist Contacts Mostly Left-Wing

International Terrorism is on the increase. . . .

Let me quote you a few sentences from a sobering new book just published by the American Council for World Freedom. . . . Here's how [the] study begins: "There is virtually no terrorist operation or guerrilla movement anywhere in the world today . . . with which Communists of one sort or another have not been involved. This includes noncommunist operations and movements . . ." As for terrorist groups in the United States, they make the point that most have foreign contacts and most of these are left-wing. . . .

—"Terrorism," 10/78.

The book entitled International Terrorism: The Communist Connection, *was written by Dr. Stefan Possony of the Hoover Institution at Stanford and Francis L. Bouchey, executive director of the Council for Inter-American Security.*

CIA, FBI Hands Are Tied

On February 18 an ad appeared in the *Los Angeles Times*. It was surrounded by a heavy black border—red might have been more appropriate. Its purpose was to sell a book written by Philip Agee and Louis Wolf entitled *Dirty Work*. The title aptly describes in my opinion what the authors are up to. . . .

This advertised book is Mr. Agee's second. He has violated his oath to not expose fellow workers he knew when he was an agent. He is hardly to be described as just an outraged citizen. If he is so opposed to counterintelligence, why does he exempt the Soviet Union from his wrath?

—"CIA," 3–4/79.

Communists in the U.S.

Moscow and Its U.S. Friends

Moscow has . . . asked the help of its friends on the left in the United States to try to build pressure [to get] a favorable SALT II agreement signed. Prompted by the Soviet-controlled World Peace Council, an ad hoc group met twice in October to work out a linkup between advocates of U.S. disarmament and the more hysterical elements of the antinuclear movement. Among groups supporting the Mobilization for Survival, the new ad hoc operation, are some old familiars on the left: the War Resisters League, Women Strike for Peace and the American Friends Service Committee.

The plan of this coalition is to fight new American weapons development tooth and nail (along with nuclear power) on the grounds that if we take the first disarmament steps unilaterally, the Russians are sure to follow. Heard that one before? It's been around for at least two decades. One of the things that caused so much controversy over Paul Warnke's appointment by President Carter as disarmament chief last year was Warnke's apparent belief in this theory.

You needn't ask whether there are any Moscow chapters of this antinuclear, prodisarmament lobby. There aren't. And the Kremlin is going ahead with nuclear power and weapons development full tilt, without so much as a peep of protest from the American left.

—"SALT II," 1–2/78.

Defectors and Nonpatriots

When a defector—sometimes one who held a fairly high rank in the Soviet social order or even a domestic Communist party member now disillusioned—wants to tell us the reason for his defection or disillusionment, he is dismissed by many liberals as no longer a credible source. Yet very often those same liberals will accept as gospel the complaints of an American who disavows patriotism and proclaims from podium and printed page—"What's wrong with America."

—"Blind on the Left," 3/78.

"Don't Say 'Conspiracy' "

Many years ago during the period called the "cold war," when Americans were very conscious of the threat of subversion, a huge Congress of the international Communist movement was held in Moscow. The meeting adopted a plan for fighting anticommunism. . . . The idea was to use well-meaning liberals and others until an anti-Communist would be ridiculed as some kind of right-wing nut guilty of "witch hunting" and looking for reds under the bed. And so, today most people in public life are afraid to hint at a Communist conspiracy.

Professor Jeffrey Hart of Dartmouth has documented some facts. . . .

There is a Soviet-dominated international organization known as the World Peace Council. . . . Last spring, Professor Hart says a Council member visited our shores to set up a new combine of antinuclear power plant people and advocates of disarmament. We now have MFS—Mobilization For Survival, based in Philadelphia.

Last October MFS held a conference at Yale and the ghosts appeared—in the flesh. There was Dr. [Benjamin] Spock, environmentalists Barry Commoner, Sidney Lens, who is hardly on the right side of anything, and Daniel Ellsburg. . . .

Supporting the conference was the War Resisters League, American Friends Service Committee, Women Strike for Peace, and others. . . .

The MFS works closely with the National Center to Slash Military Spending, which is an American arm of the World Peace Council and has in its upper crust a number of veteran members of the United States Communist party. . . .

You could call these Americans a suicide lobby, but for heaven's sake don't say "conspiracy."

—"Suicide Lobby," 3–4/78.

(MFS was granted an equal-time right to reply to this Reagan broadcast on more than 500 radio stations. For comments by the founder of MFS, see pp. 274–275.)

A Motive Not Announced

We continue to be treated to the spectacle of antinuclear power zealots demonstrating at sites where nuclear power plants are being built or planned or even where they have been in operation. . . .

I'm sure many of these demonstrators are true believers in their cause, sincere in their belief that nuclear power constitutes a great danger to the world. I'm also sure they are unaware that their movement is run by strategists who are cynical and not sincere and who have a motive not announced to the ground troops who go out and get arrested. Indeed some time ago the press carried stories of a coalition being put together to promote unilateral disarmament by the U.S. and opposition to further development of nuclear power in the U.S.

These two causes aren't as far apart as it might seem at first glance. A study by the Heritage Foundation finds that unless we go forward and fast with the building of more nuclear generating plants we may face the early 1980s with unemployment soaring above the seven million mark and around $90 billion a year in lost wages. Our industrial might would be severely crippled by brownouts and power shortages.

Where does this tie into disarmament? Well, obviously our industrial capacity is the greatest thing we have going for us in the contest with the Soviet Union, which is not only going forward with its military buildup, but is plunging full-speed ahead in the development of nuclear power. I wonder how many of our demonstrators would like to protest in Red Square. . . .

The Soviets are clearly planning to outstrip us in the nuclear arena. Since nuclear power has considerable military significance, Soviet dominance in this area could add to their lead in many areas of both conventional and strategic weaponry. Those who protest what must be—at least judging by Soviet standards—a meticulous regard for nuclear safety and environmental concerns by American companies are the unwitting victims of Soviet designs.

> —"Nuclear Power," 10/78, and "Soviet Nuclear Power,"
> 10–11/78.

McCarthyism

The Campaign to Revive the Term "McCarthyism"

From the Academy Awards performance (by way of one Oscar winner) to well-written dramas and documentaries on TV, feature motion pictures, novels and articles there is an orchestrated campaign to revive the term "McCarthyism" and to rewrite history. We are supposed to believe there was no Communist subversion, no use of communist fronts to lure innocent dupes in supporting Communist causes and no effort by Communists to infiltrate government, industry, and the news media. . . . I find the documentaries shamefully dishonest and the dramas based on falsehood. . . .

[Alger Hiss] is being presented as an innocent victim of the thing called "McCarthyism," martyred by intolerant witch hunters. But wait a moment—the late Senator McCarthy hadn't even been heard from when Alger Hiss was charged with being a member of the Soviet underground.

—"Alger Hiss," 5–6/78.

A Rifle, Not a Shotgun

Today all of those stormy years are lumped together by the history rewriters and laid on the doorstep of the late Senator Joseph McCarthy. Indeed, the term "McCarthyism" is used to identify that entire era. Actually the senator didn't make his charges and begin his investigation until several years after the Communist effort in Hollywood had been defeated. But it's true that the senator used a shotgun when a rifle was needed, injuring the innocent along with the guilty. Nevertheless, his broadsides should not be used today to infer that all who opposed Communist subversion were hysterical zealots, while the Communists were high-minded liberals, free thinkers, and not really Communists at all.

—"McCarthy," 5–6/79.

WELFARE

Welfare Is a Dangerous Drug

Welfare can be reformed by using common sense. The objective should be to care for those who can't help themselves, give temporary aid to those who can while you get them back into the private industry job market. But it looks as if the White House has given up on this objective before it begins. . . .

Welfare is really not the complex problem government pretends it is. All we have to do is think of it as a temporary helping hand until we can assist someone to become self-supporting. And that means we recognize it for what it is—charity, and "charity" is a noble word. We should judge our success by how much we decrease the need for welfare. The failure of the present programs is indicated by the vast increase in the number of recipients. Welfare is a dangerous drug destroying the spirit of people once proudly independent. Our mission should be to help people kick that particular drug habit.

—"Welfare," 1/78, and "Welfare Reform," 2–3/78.

Welfare Makes Permanent Clients

The General Accounting Office in Washington estimates that the federal government alone loses $25 billion a year in fraud. It is true, however, that many people believe welfare itself is a sinkhole where a lot of tax dollars disappear without doing any real good. . . . We aren't salvaging people; we are making them permanent clients of a professional group of welfarists whose careers depend on the preservation of poverty. . . .

—"Pay Raise," 9/78.

Close Down the Welfare Shop in Washington

. . . I am convinced the welfare mess is a Washington mess. It can be straightened out if Washington will close down its welfare shop and turn welfare over completely to the states and local government. This of course must include turning the necessary tax sources over to the states at the same time. . . .

—"Welfare," 11–12/78.

Housing Subsidy Programs

Most federally subsidized housing falls into two categories. The first is the traditional public housing program. The government owns the land and pays construction costs. Tenants pay only the operating costs of their units.

The other housing program—the one that is expanding at a breakneck pace—is called "Section 8." In this program, the housing remains in the hands of a private owner. . . . The tenant pays part of the rent, usually set at 25 percent of his income. The government pays the rest. . . . In this year's housing authorization bill, the House has voted to make some tenants of Section 8 housing pay 30 percent of their incomes in rent. . . .

Without careful monitoring . . . we will witness the uncontrolled growth of another federal welfare program.

—"Government Housing Programs," 9/79.

(In the first year of the Reagan administration, Congress raised rents for present public housing tenants to 27 from 25 percent of their annual incomes and for new tenants to 30 from 25 percent.)

Government

Government Programs Hurt Neighborhoods

We all know the importance of preserving strong urban neighborhoods. . . .

. . . foolish government policies over the past several decades have often worked to undermine, even destroy established neighborhoods[;] building codes, zoning laws, highway construction, urban renewal, federal mortgage insurance, the so-called model cities program, forced school busing—these and other factors have often combined to depress the value of neighborhoods. . . .

Wisconsin Senator William Proxmire, a member of the new [presidential National Commission on Neighborhoods], commented on this at a Senate hearing when he said to a witness, "You would probably have better neighborhoods today if there had been no federal programs at all!" Amen to that!

—"Neighborhoods," 3/78.

Tax-Dependent Americans Are a Majority

According to the Census Bureau there are 218 million men, women, children and babies in America—of which more than half—124 million—are dependent on tax dollars for all or most of their income. Let me hasten to say we shouldn't rise up in wrath automatically assuming they are all parasites. Many are legitimate pensioners, Social Security recipients and, of course, government employees.

But, with less than half the population supporting more than half (in addition to themselves and their own dependents) we need to make sure there are safeguards against extravagance, waste, and/or cheating. . . .

—"Salaries," 6–7/78.

Gargantuan Government Spending

The Brookings Institution puts the figure of those dependent on tax dollars for their year-'round living at 8.3 million people. Government's only source of revenue consists of 70 million citizens on private payrolls. . . .

It took the United States 173 years (until 1962) to hit the first $100 billion budget. . . . Some of you have children who won't even have gotten rid of their braces by the time it's a full trillion dollars.

Isn't it time we borrowed an expression from our fellow citizens of Latin descent—"Ya Basta"—we've had it.

—"Budget," 3–4/78.

Give the President an Item Veto

An amendment to the Constitution to give an item veto power to the President would eliminate an existing abuse of power by the Congress. The Congress, of course, would retain the right to override. But the taxpayers would have the protection of a President and a Congress, each able to restrain excessive spending by the other.

—"Budget," 4–5/79.

Fraud Costs Billions in Taxes

Prosecutors, government officials, and congressional investigators estimate that fraud in the multitudinous federal aid programs amounts to about $12 billion a year. John Ohls of the General Accounting Office doubles that estimate and puts the figure at nearer $25 billion. Come to think of it that's about the size of a tax cut Congress turned down a while back.

Mr. Ohls says the fraud ranges from nickel-and-dime chiseling on food stamps to million-dollar rip-offs. . . . Very little is being done about fraud. . . . Maybe tax limitation is the answer to fraud.

—"Fraud," 7/78.

MEDICAL CARE

Health Costs Have Not Skyrocketed

By saying it over and over and over again, proponents of government medicine have tried to make us believe that health care costs are spiraling out of sight. . . .

It is true that a dollar's worth of medical care ten years ago cost $1.85 today. But a dollar's worth of plumbing repairs ten years ago costs $2.10 today. . . .

Secretary of HEW [Joseph] Califano has said Britain's national health care program should be our model. . . . The secretary should find a better model—perhaps the system we already have.

—"Health Care," 5–6/78.

Abuses of Medicaid

The scene is an emergency room in a large midwest metropolitan hospital. An ambulance pulls into the emergency entrance. . . .

An elderly woman disembarks under her own power and walks into the Emergency to see a doctor about her chronic sinus condition. The doctor treats her and writes three prescriptions, fuming all the while. Ambulance rental is about $40 or $50. It costs $35 just to walk into the emergency room. Then the lady calmly called for an ambulance to take her home. Total bill? Probably $115 to $135. No, she was not an eccentric individual of great wealth. She is on medicaid. You and I paid the bill.

—"Foolishness," 6–7/78.

Government Funding of Private Health Premiums

I'm not belittling those . . . who [suffer] long and costly illnesses. Catastrophic injury or disease can strike any of us and the tremendous costs can go on for years. But this is a particular problem to be solved and it should not be used to justify compulsory government medicine for everyone.

Can any of us believe that total takeover by government would not vastly increase the paperwork, the regulations and the cost of health care? . . .

Medicaid . . . is far more costly than medicine as practiced in our traditional fee-for-service system. . . .

Beyond the cost factor, do we have a right to order all citizens into a compulsory program? And what kind of precedent do we set if government can tell members of any profession or craft that in order to practice they must become employees of the government?

Let me suggest a possible alternative. . . . About 130 million Americans are now protected by medical and/or hospital insurance policies. How many more would or could afford this if they received an income tax credit of their insurance premiums each year?

For those now enrolled in medicaid, what if the government paid all or part of their premiums (depending on their need) in the medical and hospital insurance plan of their choice?

—"Patent Medicine," I and II, and "Health Insurance,"
1–2/79.

EDUCATION

Educational Quality vs. Federal Aid

About 1950 funding of grade schools and high schools began to shift to the state with healthy increases also in federal grants. . . . At first glance you might say that's great for the local community—until you realize we, the same old taxpayers, are putting up the entire 100 percent—just funneling it through different tax collectors. And, the higher you go in government the greater the overhead. Now what has this change meant to us? Well for one thing our locally elected school boards don't have as much to say about content of textbooks, curriculum, and methods of teaching as they once did. . . .

Federal aid actually began about 1962, so did federal control over education and so did the decline in educational quality, as measured by the Scholastic Aptitude Tests. . . .

The only thing you can say for increased state and federal aid to education is that it will result in higher cost, more educational employees, and less supervision by the taxpayers.

—"Local Control" I and II, 3–4/78.

State vs. Local Control of Education

In California a court decision has outlawed the traditional financing of public schools by local property tax on the grounds that some school districts are poorer than others in real estate values. . . .

California doesn't face this problem alone. More than twenty states—perhaps your own—have switched from local property tax funding since 1971. That was the year a high-powered movement began to centralize school funding at the state level. Those pushing the move were very well aware that control of funding would also mean control of education and that was really their goal.

—"Taxes," 1/78.

An End to Social Promotion

Most of us have little or no reason to know anything about little Greensville County, Virginia. It has only 17,000 inhabitants and none of them is famous, except maybe Sam Owen. Sam is the county superintendent of schools. His fame comes from the fact that he is one of the first superintendents of schools in the country to put an end to social promotion. . . . And in the five years of the county's minimal competency program, achievement scores have climbed steadily and pupil retentions have declined sharply.

Sam Owen and the people of Greensville County believe their program may be the trend of tomorrow in public education. I hope they're right.

—"Greensville County Education," 5/78.

A Tax Credit for Private School Tuition

Tens of thousands of independent and parochial schools—elementary, secondary, and college level—have gone broke in recent years. . . . This is a tragic loss. The very existence of independent schools helps preserve academic freedom and diversity. To reverse this trend two senators sponsored a bill providing for an income tax credit for half the tuition up to a ceiling of $500 per child. . . .

The education lobby has risen up in wrath, calling this a plot to destroy the public schools. That's a bit hysterical when you consider that 90 percent of all students attend public schools.

—"Education," 5–6/78.

MASS TRANSIT

San Francisco's BART No Good

[So far] the San Francisco Bay Area Rapid Transit system known as BART . . . has cost double the planned amount, $1.6 billion. It has only attracted half the passengers it expected and serves only 2 percent of the trips in the district. It was supposed to reduce auto traffic but less than one-third of its riders came from automobiles. About half switched over from buses. Now the BART ride costs twice as much as the bus and half again as much as the private car. The transit system could buy a fleet of new buses capable of handling all of BART's passengers until 1980 for less than half of what BART is losing each year.

—"Government Cost," 9/78.

Amtrak and Conrail: Horrendous Losses

A good case can be made that the ills of railroading were brought on by excessive government interference in the running of the railroads. Now of course that same government has ridden to the rescue with Amtrak and in the east a combine called Conrail. Both are losing horrendous sums of taxpayers' money every day. . . .

Now I'm a train buff. . . . I'll admit to a great nostalgia for the conductor's "All aboard" and for seeing the country through a pullman window. But the numbers don't add up any more and maybe we should settle for nostalgia.

The average Amtrak passenger takes a 226-mile trip. This costs Amtrak $44 but the passenger pays $16, leaving $28 to be anted up by the taxpayers. . . .

If Amtrak quit and the government granted the railroad companies now hauling freight the right to carry passengers under the same regulations now applying to Amtrak, maybe we could have trains without the subsidy.

—"Trains," 7–8/78 and "Amtrak," 10–11/78.

FARMERS AND SUBSIDIES

Farmers and Food Prices

Twenty-five years ago one out of seven Americans farmed and each farmer raised food for sixteen people. Today only one out of twenty-two is a farmer and each one produces enough food for himself and fifty-five others. . . . During these twenty-five years the cost of food as a percentage of our after-tax income has fallen more than 30 percent. It now only takes 14.8 percent of our income after taxes to put food on the table. And only a little over a third of that 14.8 percent goes to the farmer. We eat better for less money than any other people on earth.

—"Farm Day," 3/78.

Farmers and the Free Market

Only a few years ago under then Secretary of Agriculture Earl Butz the farmers were getting out from under the federal program of direct regulation, control, and subsidy and back into the free market. Now there is a crisis caused by increased production costs and higher prices for equipment, machinery, and fertilizer. Much of the problem is caused by government restrictions on the free market.

I've been trying to find an answer that wouldn't increase government involvement in the farm market. . . .

—"Farm," 4–5/78.

Farm Subsidies Are a Sickness

In 1969, we began a move to put farming back into the free marketplace. The almost $5.5 billion farm subsidy dropped to less than $1 billion by 1975. The subsidies went down by 85 percent. . . .

But then we fell into the same old sickness. In three years the farm subsidy rose and last year it was bigger than it was in 1969. . . .

Government interference in agriculture hasn't held down food prices and it hasn't increased farmers' income. They are worse off, we're worse off, and government costs about $7 billion more than it did or should. Farm net income in constant dollars was almost twice as great in 1974 as it is now. When will we learn?

—"Agriculture," 4/79.

PRIVATIZATION

The Post Office Monopoly

I reported to you some time ago about the young housewife in Rochester, New York, who built a thriving business delivering business letters in downtown Rochester for 10 cents each—delivery the same day guaranteed. The Post Office obtained an injunction and halted this invasion of its monopoly on first class delivery even though it can't match price or delivery time. . . .

In Charleston, South Carolina, there is an enterprising young fourteen-year-old named Kenny Maguire. . . . Astride a bicycle, Kenny earned $10 delivering eighty wedding invitations. That was the beginning and the end of his delivery service. Postal authorities jumped in and grounded him for interfering with their legal monopoly over mail delivery.

—"Mail," 10/78.

Contracting Out City Services

Several years ago a couple of bright young men . . . began to accumulate information on good ideas for making municipal services more cost-effective, including especially the use of pri-

vate contracting for garbage removal, public works, and even
fire departments. . . .

Contracting out is not the only way a city can conserve scarce
tax dollars. The Local Government Center did a survey of user-
fee systems and found numerous examples of cities trying to
apportion the costs of recreation, tree trimming, library, street
sweeping and other programs directly to those who benefit from
the programs, instead of imposing the costs on all the taxpayers.

—"Local Government Center," 8–9/78.

States Can Contract Out, Too

The State of California would do well to review its own constitution which prevents private contracting for state work. Just
recently the New York State Court of Appeals upheld the right
of Westchester County to contract with a private protection
agency for security guards. One community immediately replaced its public sanitation force with a private one. The deputy
mayor said the savings was a full 25 percent with absolutely no
reduction in the quality of service

—"Miscellaneous," 9/78.

UNEMPLOYMENT

Planning Implies Control

In May [1975], Senate Bill 1795 was introduced into the U.S.
Senate under the title, "The Balanced Growth and Economic
Planning Act of 1975." . . .

Right now, government is actually disposing of 37 percent of
our total gross national product. We know that with this have
come thousands and thousands of regulations touching on almost every facet of our lives.

Every government in history with that kind of power has
ended political freedom for its people. Planning by its very nature implies control. There is no way to have blueprints if the
people aren't forced to follow them.

—"Economic Planning," 10/28/75.

Unemployment Is an "Also-Ran" Problem

Curiously enough "we the people" with an almost instinctive wisdom have given indications that we no longer consider unemployment a top priority. When polled as to what are our most important national problems, inflation is number one by an overwhelming majority. Unemployment is down with the also rans. And as is so often the case—the people are right. . . .

Now jobless people numbering 6 million would indicate that [we] do have a problem but that is not necessarily so. There are many of those who are first-time job seekers, even more who are voluntarily unemployed. And it is estimated that possibly 2 million actually have jobs but are working for cash to avoid taxes.

—"Employment," 8–9/78.

Unemployment Is Overestimated

When it comes time to measure unemployment in this country, we seem to be using . . . hyped-up thermometers. . . .

Originally, back in the 1930s, [the traditional employment] index was used to measure one thing: the number of unemployed male adult heads of households. But the *current* index takes into account not only adult heads of households, but those who hold second jobs, officially retired people, and a good many young adults not yet burdened with family responsibilities.

I think it's time we concentrate on the heads of households, make sure they have work and *then* turn attention to others. . . . Let's start using a good unemployment thermometer!

—"An Accurate Thermometer," 12/78.

PUBLIC-SECTOR JOBS

Private Jobs Cost No Taxes

In the last two years business and industry in the U.S. have actually created 7 million new jobs. The federal government is still talking about an $8.8 billion job program to put 1.4 million people to work in jobs the government will create. That prorates out to about 6,300 tax dollars per job. Yet, the 7 million I first mentioned didn't cost the taxpayers anything.

—"Miscellaneous," 2–3/78.

Public-Sector Jobs Are No Answer

Back in 1971 Congress—spurred by the recession of 1970—passed a measure called the Comprehensive Employment and Training Act. It was to be a temporary program, cost $1 billion. The money was to be doled out to state and local governments which would, in turn hire the hardcore unemployed in fields such as law enforcement, health, education, and so forth.

The "temporary" program is still with us, but now it costs $6 billion a year. . . . With one out of five workers in the United States already on the public payroll, more government jobs doesn't seem to be a practical answer to employment.

—"Jobs," 2–3/78.

Scandals in Public-Sector Employment

Some time ago on one of these broadcasts I mentioned some of the shortcomings of the CETA program. . . . It has $11 billion to spend and where the money is that big, a little scandal is not an unusual thing.

In Dade County, Florida, a grand jury has found waste, false recordkeeping, and criminal violations in the federally funded program. One CETA employer turned out to be a pool hall operator who hired his nephew with the federal money.

—"Spending," 6–7/78.

Shortcomings of CETA

From time to time on these commentaries I've pointed out the shortcomings of CETA. . . . The main criticism is that it simply has been used by local governments all too often to put people on the public payroll.

—"Miscellaneous," I, 7/79.

LABOR UNIONS

On Refusing to Join

Mrs. Margaret Ellers, assistant professor of engineering graphics at a tax-supported institution, Ferris State College in Michigan, has lost her position as a teacher with tenure and less than a year to go before being eligible for full pension. . . . Her crime (with consequent dismissal) was refusal to pay a $160 fee to a faculty union she refused to join. . . .

Now, some will say that the service fee was fair because even nonmembers would be getting the benefit of union representation. Some will say that, but it doesn't hold up. Of the $160 fee, only $22 covers service by the Ferris Association. The balance— $138—goes to the Michigan and the National Education Association to pay for their lobbying and political activities.

—"Academic Freedom," 10/2/75.

"Freedom to Choose"

On January 25th the Senate Human Resources Committee reported out and sent to the floor of the Senate the so-called labor reform bill which is a high-priority item on organized labor's agenda. . . . It is, in fact, a measure wherein government will give labor special advantages in its effort to recruit members and to organize workers in nonunion plants. Management will be given no comparable rights. . . . An enlarged National Labor Relations Board would, undoubtedly, have more power and a definite prolabor, antimanagement bias.

—"Labor," 3/78.

The Davis-Bacon Act "Imports" High Wages

The Davis-Bacon Act requires employees on all federally assisted construction projects to be paid what are known as "prevailing wages." This amounts to a sort of "super-minimum wage." . . . Because the "prevailing wage" determinations are based mostly on union wage scales in large urban areas, the act tends to "import" those high rates into rural areas where wages—and the cost of living—are lower. This insures that con-

struction costs in rural areas will be higher than they otherwise
would have been and local contractors are often excluded.

—"Davis-Bacon Act," 6–7/78.

Union Plumbers and Davis-Bacon

Consider what happened to the Interfaith Adopt-A-Building
project in Manhattan's Lower East Side. There, a group of
young Puerto Rican men decided to rehabilitate an abandoned
tenement building. . . .

The U.S. Labor Department insisted that for the first young
worker learning the ropes on the project, *twelve* union plumbers
had to be employed, and for the second trainee an additional
fourteen union plumbers were required! This is the so-called
work rules requirement under the Davis-Bacon Act. . . .

No wonder people are losing faith in government.

—"Davis-Bacon Act," 11–12/78.

(*Late in his 1980 campaign, Reagan reversed course and opposed repeal of
Davis-Bacon.*)

Cesar Chavez's Demands

California's lettuce strike has become a celery strike and
no matter how it ends up, you'll be paying higher prices for
produce.

At stake is a test of the federal government's wage-and-price
guidelines, as well as a test of strength of the mystique of Cesar
Chavez, founder of the United Farm Workers Union. . . .

Chavez's efforts to halt the winter lettuce harvest were only
partly successful. Volunteers from throughout the Imperial Valley pitched in to harvest the crop, though growers estimate they
still lost more than $2 million worth of produce.

—"Lettuce Strike," 3–4/79.

CHRISTIANITY

Santa Claus Expelled from the Classroom

With voluntary prayer banned from our public schools,
Christmas has been tolerated so long as there was no reference

to its religious significance . . . but children were permitted to decorate a tree and, of course, jolly old Santa Claus. But maybe his days are numbered.

The Rhode Island branch of the American Civil Liberties Union has decided even the present method of recognizing Christmas threatens the Constitution. A spokesman explains that Santa comes on Christmas Eve so he has acquired a religious significance and must be expelled from the classroom.

—"Miscellaneous," 2–3/78.

Christmas and the Divine Jesus

For many of us he is much more. He is the promised Messiah, the Son of God come to earth to offer salvation for all mankind.

It was disturbing therefore to read that in many Christian seminaries there is an increasing tendency to minimize his divinity, to reject the miracle of his birth and regard him as merely human. Meaning no disrespect to the religious convictions of others, I still can't help wondering how we can explain away what to me is the greatest miracle of all and which is recorded in history.

—"Christmas," 1–2/78 (following the capitalization in the transcript).

VOLUNTEERISM

Volunteerism Is Alive and Well

. . . anyone who lives in southern California has a certain fondness for that giant sign in the Hollywood hills that spells "Hollywood." . . . In recent years the old landmark has fallen into disrepair. . . .

Two young men decided not to wait any longer. Stuart Levine, seventeen, and Cory Slater, twenty, began in January to spend their spare time patching up the sign. Both work at night and in the daytime they don hardhats and carry nails and lumber (which have been donated) down the mountainside to repair the sign. . . .

Who says volunteerism isn't alive and well in America?

—"Snails & Signboard," 5/78.

Saving Cities Is Not a Federal Problem

Billions of dollars, thousands of studies, hundreds of experts—this is the formidable array of weapons the federal bureaucrats brought to the struggle to revitalize the cities.

And what did it all lead to? Failure. Failure so great, so costly, so devastating in its destruction of neighborhoods—all in the name of "urban renewal"—that it is all but unbelievable. . . .

You don't need billions of taxpayers' dollars to save a city. You need a sense of purpose, some pride, some hope, and a capacity for work. . . .

—"Hope for the Cities," 12/78.

That Great Sense of Private Generosity and Charity

To tell you the truth, a very real fear of mine is that government with its many social reforms may rob us of that great sense of generosity and charity which is our American heritage. . . .

Robert Young told me about "Children's Village," a modern residential facility near Los Angeles on 119 acres, where abused children can be cared for—where they will hear possibly for the first time a kind voice as they are tucked in bed with a teddy bear or a doll.

—"Charity," 7–8/78.

SECTION II: FOREIGN POLICY

VIETNAM

North Vietnam Is an Outlaw Nation

The Vietnamese war was a plain and simple effort by North Vietnam to conquer South Vietnam. We tried to prevent this in a long, bloody war which our government refused to win. But now how do we negotiate with North Vietnam unless we begin with step one—the release of half a million South Vietnamese now in concentration camps and the North Vietnamese withdrawal from South Vietnam, leaving it once again a free and independent nation?

For that matter how did we agree to North Vietnam's entry into the United Nations which specifically demands that its member nations do not take up arms against their neighbor? Until South Vietnam is freed, North Vietnam is still an outlaw among nations.

—"Human Rights," I, 1/78.

Dominoes in Southeast Asia

Remember when antiwar protesters and some well known public figures ridiculed the "domino theory," the idea that if South Vietnam fell to the Communists other southeast Asia nations would follow?

Well South Vietnam fell in 1975 and Laos shortly thereafter. Now Cambodia (already Communist) is faced with attack by the North Vietnamese Communists. . . .

The Mekong river which flows through Cambodia and southern Vietnam also winds between Laos and Thailand. . . . Control of the Mekong means control of the region and after all the ridicule, it seems the dominoes are really falling.

—"Desk Cleaning," 4–5/78.

Our Money Repairs the Dikes We Destroyed

The administration is still determined to normalize relations with the Communist tyrants of Hanoi. World Bank president Robert McNamara isn't waiting however. World Bank funds will provide a huge loan—largely of our money—to Hanoi for repair of irrigation dikes destroyed by our bombers—in raids Robert McNamara authorized when he was defense secretary.

—"Miscellaneous," 8–9/78.

Vietnam Was Not a Civil War

A few weeks ago the U.N. was asked to deal with the matter of China's attack on Vietnam and Vietnam's attack on Cambodia. . . .

The North Vietnamese, who broke their pledged word given in the Paris peace accords, conquered an independent neighbor, South Vietnam. The Vietnam war was not a civil war. They have been separate nations for centuries. Let the resolution be amended to read that North Vietnam will not only leave Cambodia, but will leave South Vietnam as well.

—"P.O.W.," 3–4/79.

The Soviet Union

"Let Their System Collapse"

The Russians have told us over and over again their goal is to impose their incompetent and ridiculous system on the world. We invest in armaments to hold them off, but what do we envision as the eventual outcome? Either that they will see the fallacy of their way and give up their goal, or their system will collapse, or (and we don't let ourselves think of this) we'll have to use our weapons one day.

Maybe there is an answer—we simply do what's morally right. Stop doing business with them. Let their system collapse, but meantime buy our farmers' wheat ourselves and have it on hand to feed the Russian people when they finally become free.

—"The Russian Wheat Deals," 10/29/75.

Détente: Communist Strategy

We are blind to reality if we refuse to recognize that détente's usefulness to the Soviet is only as a cover for their traditional and basic strategy for aggression.

Détente is for the Soviet Union a no-can-lose proposition. It fits their Communist dialectic. According to this dialectic, "opposites clash and become ultimately fused into a synthesis on a higher plane." Today the primary clash is between imperialist finance capitalists and revolutionary workers, the synthesis is the proletarian dictatorship led by the Communists. All Communist strategy is conceived against that doctrine or background—and that most assuredly includes détente.

—"Détente," 10/31/75.

Quoting Solzhenitsyn

Remembering the anti–Vietnam war sentiment of the late 60s and early 70s, some might find a bit of irony in the fact that Alexander Solzhenitsyn was this June's Harvard University graduation speaker. . . .

For those who think hopefully that Angola might become the Soviet Union's Vietnam or that Cuba's adventuring in Africa can be stopped by being polite to Castro, he has an answer. He describes their failure to understand the Vietnam war as "the most crucial mistake. Members of the U.S. antiwar movement wound up being involved in the betrayal of far eastern nations in a genocide and in suffering today imposed on 30 million people." . . .

If the west doesn't have the will to stand firm, Solzhenitsyn says, nothing is left then but concessions and betrayal to gain time. . . .

Then he said that while the next world war would probably not be an atomic one, still it might very well bury western civilization forever. . . .

Solzhenitsyn told the Harvard graduating class that since our bodies are all doomed to die, our task while on earth must be of a more spiritual nature.

—"Alexander Solzhenitsyn," I and II, 7/78.

The Marxian Denial of God

One of the more prevalent myths has to do with religious freedom and whether it does or does not exist in those lands where Karl Marx is hailed as the messiah. The World Council of Churches seems unable to believe that religion might be forbidden fruit in the Communist world. The fact that a few churches in Russia remain open and are attended by an ever-shrinking group of senior citizens makes the council ignore the uncompromising Marxian denial of God. He swore that his paradise could only be realized by destroying the church. He had a special hatred for the Hebrews, possibly because the God of Moses is also the God of Christianity. . . .

When President Carter and Leonid Brezhnev met at the summit in Vienna, Brezhnev is quoted as saying that God would never forgive them if they failed in their mission. I'm sorry that I can't believe in his sincerity. Indeed I think he was hypocritical and deliberately using the Lord's name to curry favor or soften up the President who does believe in God as Brezhnev does not.

Atheism is as much a part of communism as is the Gulag. Every kind of roadblock is thrown in the way of religion, up to and including imprisonment. Children in Soviet schools are indoctrinated from grade one with the falsehood that there is no God.

—"Religious Freedom," 8–9/78, and "The Pope in Poland," 7/79.

EASTERN EUROPE

The East German Police State

An American ex-G.I. and his German-born wife have made the perilous journey through the Berlin Wall almost a dozen times in the last few years to help people who have no human rights. . . .

Right now [the wife] is trying to help a man named Rolf Mainz and his family. Mr. Mainz held an executive position with a publishing company. Then one day he dropped his membership in the Communist party. Several days later he was fired but no one would say why. . . . So, after six months he wrote a letter to the editor of a West German paper—a sarcastic letter. . . . One week later the paper reported that he had been arrested four days after his letter appeared. He is now serving a fifty-four-month sentence in the worst, most brutal East German prison. . . .

It seems that unpopular prisoners have a way of dying on the operating table in Brandenburg prison. The conditions in Brandenburg are beyond description. Almost every day prisoners go on hunger strikes in protest against the brutality and inhuman treatment. . . . Rolf is in great danger of losing his life. His diet consists of a saltless watery soup.

—"Human Rights," II, 1/78, and "Helsinki Pact," 12/78–1/79.

Folly at Helsinki

In signing the Helsinki pact we gave the Russians something they've wanted for thirty-five years. In effect, we recognized the Soviet Union's right to hold captive the eastern and central European nations they have ruled since World War II. We signed the pact apparently because of one clause which had to do with human rights. Those making the decision to sign claimed the Soviet Union by its signature had agreed to let people have some (if not all) of the rights the rest of us take for granted. They are (for example) supposed to be able to leave the Soviet Union and the captive nations if they choose. But the Russians make promises; they don't keep them.

—"Human Rights," III, 1/78.

Western Europe

Strikes in England

A few weeks ago we took off for Europe. . . . England had been undergoing a bakers' strike for about three weeks before we got there. . . . To our surprise we never sat down to a meal that didn't include a variety of breadstuffs and pastries. . . .

The paper suggested there was evidently "an alarming degree of overmanning" in the bakeries and said, "it is time the leaders of the bread strike faced up to reality." Ironically the newspaper workers who voiced those thoughts were planning to go on strike themselves, before we left.

—"Bread," 12/78–1/79.

Rooting for Margaret Thatcher

I couldn't be happier than I am over England's new prime minister. It has been my privilege to meet and have two lengthy visits with Margaret Thatcher. I've been rooting for her to become prime minister since our first meeting.

If anyone can remind England of the greatness it knew during those dangerous days in World War II when alone and unafraid her people fought the Battle of Britain it will be the prime minister the English press has already nicknamed "Maggie."

I think she'll do some moving and shaking of England's once proud industrial capacity. . . . Bricklayers for example laid 1,000 bricks a day in 1937—today they lay 300. I think "Maggie"—bless her soul—will do something about that. . . .

Mrs. Thatcher has promised to turn away from the failures of Britain's brand of socialism and get the country moving again.

—"Miscellaneous," II, and "Investment Lag," 6/79.

Eurocommunism and Russia

. . . I hope you'll remember how often and how persistently the Communist parties in European countries like Italy and France deny any connection with the Soviet Union. They protest that Eurocommunism is independent of Russia. Well an enterprising French reporter has just uncovered the fact that the French Communist party keeps its money in the "Banque Commerciale pour L'Europe de Nord." That bank, it so happens, is owned by a Frenchman and the Soviet Union. Their partnership is like mule and rabbit stew—one mule to one rabbit. The Frenchman owns three-tenths of one percent of the bank; the Soviet Union owns 99.7 percent. So much for the independence of Eurocommunism.

—"Miscellaneous," III, 4/79.

CENTRAL AMERICA

Cuba and Nicaragua

. . . Congressman Steve Symms of Idaho . . . made a nine-day trip, touching shore in Jamaica (our newest Marxist neighbor), the Dominican Republic [and] Cuba. His summation is blunt and to the point. He says the Caribbean is rapidly becoming a Communist lake in what should be an American pond and the United States resembles a giant, afraid to move. . . .

I'm sure he would agree that the troubles in Nicaragua bear a Cuban label also. While there are people in that troubled land who probably have justified grievances against the Somoza regime, there is no question but that most of the rebels are Cuban-trained, Cuban-armed, and dedicated to creating another Communist country in this hemisphere.

—"Cuba," 3–4/79.

Castro Is Off and Somoza Is on Our Blacklist

Our State Department [has decided on] a cutback in economic aid to Nicaragua and the withdrawal of American personnel. This we are doing because, according to the State Department, President Somoza is in violation of our standards of human rights. He may be—I don't know. I do know, because it's a matter of record, that the revolutionary forces who are fighting against his regime are Marxists for the most part and many were trained and armed by Castro's Cuba. So it's one off and one on our human rights blacklist.

—"Human Rights," 3–4/79.

(Dictator Somoza fled the country and the Sandinista rebels took over shortly after Reagan made these broadcasts.)

Mexico's "Oil of Olé"

. . . the announcement by Mexico's President Jose Lopez Portillo that his country's possible oil reserves were being revised upward to 200 billion barrels . . . could put Mexico in the Saudi Arabia class as an oil supplier. . . .

Will the Mexicans give us access to the oil? That remains to be seen, but it will take patience and diplomacy on our part, plus an understanding of Mexico's fierce sense of national pride and its worries about foreign exploitation. The opportunity is there, as one magazine put it, to make it the "Oil of Olé."

—"Mexico's Oil," 10/78.

Jamaica: Totalitarian Socialism

The prime minister of Jamaica, who is taking that lovely island nation into totalitarian socialism, is discovering the price of such foolishness. The once-solid tourist trade and flourishing economy of Jamaica are virtually nonexistent now. But over the hill to the rescue comes the cavalry. The State Department is bailing him out with a little over $63 million of our money. It is reported the announcement of this was held up till after Fidel Castro's visit with the prime minister.

—"Miscellaneous," 1/78.

(The Manley government of which Reagan was here speaking was replaced in the fall of 1980 by a conservative administration with Edward Seaga the prime minister.)

Report from a Business Friend on the Canal

A builder friend of mine in California, knowledgeable about engineering and construction, went to Panama solely for the purpose of seeing for himself what the situation is. Then he wrote me a letter and sent a copy to every U.S. senator. He wrote. . . .

"Give Panama more money, but not our canal. It is said we can't defend it. If we can't defend it now, we can't take it back when the Communists control it. Thinking Latins don't want the Russians in there any more than thinking Americans do. Now is the time to show some backbone, not after the fact."

End quote of a letter from an American who went down on his own to see for himself.

—"Canal," 3–4/78.

(In April 1978 President Carter won the Senate fight for ratification of the Panama Canal treaties under which the U.S. and Panama run the canal together, with the U.S. the "senior partner," until the end of this century, when U.S. military forces are to be withdrawn with the permanent right to return to defend the canal's neutrality.)

SOUTH AMERICA

The Armed Forces Saved Argentina

Martínez de Hoz is the architect of what may turn out to be one of the most remarkable economic recoveries in modern history. By March 1976—the tail end of Peronism under the widow of Juan Peron—Argentina's people were being crushed by a 920 percent inflation rate. . . .

The armed forces stepped in. As Martínez de Hoz explained, as a last resort, to keep the country together. He said that his country had been facing a well-equipped force of 15,000 terrorists who were "destroying the social fabric" of the country. . . .

Though the situation is virtually under control today, some terrorists have quietly slipped back "above ground" and others have gone into exile. . . .

—"Argentina," 10–11/78.

A Small Number in the Crossfire

Today, Argentina is at peace, the terrorist threat nearly eliminated. Though Martínez de Hoz, in his U.S. talks, concentrates on economics, he does not shy from discussing human rights. He points out that in the process of bringing stability to a terrorized nation of 25 million, a small number were caught in the crossfire, among them a few innocents. . . .

If you ask the average Argentine-in-the-street what he thinks about the state of his country's economy, chances are you'll find him pleased, not seething, about the way things are going.

—"Common Sense from a Neighbor," 8/79.

(Martínez de Hoz was the economic czar designated by the military junta that seized Argentina's government in 1976. Union leaders were arrested or went into hiding; Martínez de Hoz controlled wages, but not prices.

(It has been widely alleged and reported that the Argentine junta Reagan defended in the two preceding broadcasts was responsible for the disappearance and presumed murder of between 6,000 and 15,000 persons. Demonstrations by mothers of the missing have been a continuing embarrassment to the junta. Mass graves containing an estimated 1,500 corpses were discovered in the country in 1982. The junta scheduled elections for October 1983.

(See Chapter 19.)

The Murder of Orlando Letelier

In Washington, on September 21, 1976, Orlando Letelier, who had been Chile's ambassador to the United States in the leftist Allende government, died in a bomb explosion in his automobile. A woman coworker died with him. . . .

First, the question of who killed Letelier has not been answered, though an American living in Chile, one Michael Townley, has confessed to U.S. authorities that he placed the bomb under the car. Townley implicated five Cuban anti-Castro exiles (who have been indicted) and in exchange for a promise in advance of a light sentence, he has claimed that the parties responsible for Letelier's death are the former head of Chile's disbanded security agency called DINA and two of his subordinates. . . . General [Mario] Contreras [Tapia], that former head of DINA, is close to General [Augusto] Pinochet, head of the Chilean government. . . .

Virginia Prewett, a veteran award-winning journalist who has specialized in Latin American affairs, is the author of the new report. . . .

Miss Prewett doubts that the Pinochet government had anything to gain by engineering the assassination of Letelier. On the contrary. The very day Letelier was killed, Chile's finance minister arrived in Washington to confer with then-Secretary of the Treasury William Simon on financial aid Chile needed to pursue its economic recovery plan. In fact, the Chilean embassy had scheduled a press conference to kick off the plan. The Letelier murder wiped it out. Virginia Prewett asks: "Why would Pinochet tell his right-hand man to kill Letelier on the very day when such a murder would torpedo the (finance minister's) conference, the key to Chile's hoped-for restoration to the good graces of international finance?" Why, indeed? . . .

Let's look at Letelier's own group, the Institute for Policy Studies, and just what Letelier was up to in Washington. According to Virginia Prewett . . . the IPS's Transnational Institute, which Letelier headed, had awarded a grant to Tariq Ali, an advocate of urban terrorism. And, among the IPS's leadership are Peter Weiss, chairman, a leading figure in the National Lawyers Guild which consistently follows a Marxist line, and IPS Fellow Roberta Salper, identified as a member of "the U.S. Zone of the Marxist Puerto Rican Socialist Party." That party, in turn, has extensive connections with Castro's international intelligence network.

Letelier's connections with Marxists and far-left causes became clearer when columnists Jack Anderson and [Rowland] Evans and [Robert] Novak revealed that among the contents of Letelier's briefcase on the day he was killed were documents showing that he was getting $1,000 a month from [the late Salvador] Allende's daughter in Havana "for his work."

According to Miss Prewett, what emerged from "The Briefcase Papers" was a picture of a man who was systematically taking advantage of the human rights impulses of liberal members of Congress in order to get an amendment added to the U.S. Foreign Assistance Act of 1976 imposing mandatory penalties on nations which allegedly violated human rights. This did become law.

The Prewett report says that "the briefcase documents identify Letelier with an intercontinental network of clandestine political activity, within an apparatus co-directed by Havana Communists and aided by the governments of East Germany and the Soviet Union." She adds, "The 'Briefcase Papers' further revealed that Havana was manufacturing propaganda on (so-called) 'human right violations' in Chile for Letelier to use at the U.N. and elsewhere." . . .

Miss Prewett raises the question of whether Letelier might have been murdered by his own masters. Alive he could be compromised; dead he could become a martyr. And the left didn't lose a minute in making him one. I don't know the answer, but it is a question worth asking. . . .

—"Letelier," I and II, 11–12/78.

(On the Letelier case and IPS, see pp. 383–384.

(Robert Borosage, director of IPS, provided a copy of an FBI document which showed that Letelier's briefcase contained nothing that would support an assertion that Letelier was an agent of a foreign government.)

THE MIDDLE EAST

The Palestinian Refugees

The general assumption is that the [Palestinian] refugees (and now they have descendants) were ousted from their homes to make room for the newly created state of Israel. You see the truth is there never was a nation called Palestine. Palestine was the name of an area populated by a variety of peoples or social groups. . . .

Has any effort been made (and if not, why not) to canvass the refugees and see where the families and individuals would like to live? About 10 percent are Christians; 90 percent are Sunni Moslems. Their language is Arabic, virtually identical to that spoken in Lebanon, Syria, and Jordan. What if the Arab States and Israel were to offer citizenship to any who wanted to emigrate? What if all of us helped to fund such emigrations? It might eliminate a vexing problem. It might be worth a try.

—"Palestine," 4/79.

A Visit to Iran in 1978

Ancient Persia is becoming as modern as tomorrow in an industrial way but still retains much of its cultural heritage. . . . We met with government officials and the Shah and Shahbanou. . . .

Iran must receive the worst press of almost any nation. Where have we read of the effort the government is making to upgrade the standard of living and eliminate poverty? A great reforestation program is turning barren hills and valleys into green forest lands. American industry is encouraged. . . .

But, above all, we should know that Iran has been and is a staunch friend and ally of the United States. It has a clear understanding of the Soviet threat. And it has the second longest border with Russia.

—"Hong Kong," 5–6/78.

(Three months after the antecedent broadcast the Shah declared martial law. Widespread uprisings forced his departure from Iran, never to return, on January 16, 1979.)

AFRICA

In Africa, One Man, One Vote, Once

A citizen of one of the new African states once assured me that Africans believe in one man, one vote—once. The newly elected then make sure there will be no need for another election by eliminating the opposition. . . .

It seems that Sierra Leone, once considered one of Africa's few relatively free nations, has verified that statement. . . . President Sioka Stevens has rammed through a new constitution for his country. It outlaws opposition parties. . . . The leader of the APC party (who happens to be President Stevens) is the only person eligible to run for president. No opposition is permitted.

—"Africa," 10/78.

Slaughter in Equatorial Guinea

There is word from another of the continent's new nations which has been largely ignored. Equatorial Guinea, the only Spanish-speaking nation in Africa, is, or, perhaps I should say, *was* 95 percent Catholic. It had a population of 350,000, give or take a few, when it became independent in 1968. Now there are 90,000 refugees in Spain and neighboring African nations and no one knows how many did not escape and were slaughtered.

Some time ago the president of Equatorial Guinea issued an edict that his picture would hang above the altar and that when crossing themselves the citizens would say his name as well as that of God. When the church refused, the persecution began.

The church has been outlawed, foreign priests expelled from the country. Native-born priests and nuns are in prison. . . .

—"Africa," 10/78.

The Emperor of the Central African Empire

Quite a while ago I did a broadcast about the coronation of Emperor Bokassa I of the Central African Empire. This is one of the newly emerging African states. It is also one of the poorest nations in the world.

Nevertheless, Emperor Bokassa spent about $25 million to mark his entry into royalty. As I recall he imported from France thirty-six matched horses to pull his gold-and-jewel-trimmed carriage. His bejeweled gold crown was also made in France as was his equally bejeweled golden throne. . . .

He allowed his cabinet to watch while several prisoners were executed by being clubbed to death with rifle butts. If they'd refused to watch they'd have joined the prisoners.

Just recently he bought a million-dollar villa in Switzerland. It will be a handy hideaway if his one-and-a-half million subjects ever decide to do a little clubbing on their own.

I thought you'd like to know that the administration in Washington has asked Congress for $658,000 in foreign aid for Emperor Bokassa's Central African Empire—which I'm sure means for Emperor Bokassa.

—"Miscellaneous," 3–4/79.

Nkomo's Guerrillas Slaughtered Civilians

The World Council of Churches has given Joshua Nkomo's guerrillas in Rhodesia [now Zimbabwe] a grant of $85,000. You remember Nkomo's guerrillas—they're the patriotic humanitarians who recently shot down the civilian passenger plane and slaughtered the survivors.

—"Africa," 10/78.

Namibia: U.S. Backs Terrorist Murderers

In 1978 South Africa accepted a plan drawn up by our country, Britain, France, Canada and West Germany by which Namibia would become an independent nation. . . .

Last year the U.N. Security Council by a 15 to 9 vote declared that Walvis Bay must be integrated into Namibia. This was in direct contravention to the agreement with South Africa. The bay is one of South Africa's major seaports. . . .

It now appears that the U.N. and the five western powers changed their minds on Walvis Bay in an effort to persuade Sam Nujoma, leader of a Marxist terrorist band, to accept the U.N. plan. . . .

It boggles the mind to think that our government believes it is in our best interest to turn Namibia over to a pro-Communist government when it is obvious that the people of that country prefer a government favorable to the west and certainly non-Communist. . . .

It's hard to understand our agreeing with a demand that Nujoma's murderous force be allowed to openly establish bases within Namibia. Possibly we think it is inconvenient for them to have to cross the border from their hideouts in Angola whenever they feel a murder coming on.

—"Namibia," I and II, 7–8/79.

CHINA AND TAIWAN

Taiwan Contrasted to the Mainland

Taipei is a modern, prosperous city complete with luxury hotels, smart shops, and congested rush hour traffic. Industries flourish and exports are counted in the billions of dollars. . . .

I renewed acquaintance with President Chian Ching-kuo, son of the late Generalismo Chiang Kai-Shek. He is a remarkable leader, dedicated to the welfare of his people. . . .

Today the mainland is totally regimented. There is no personal freedom and it can't feed its people without importing foods. The other part of China—Taiwan—has a prosperous, free economy. . . . Their military is superb and has very high morale. They have half a million men in uniform and can mobilize two and a half million on short notice. . . .

Thanks to the acting governor of Hong Kong, we had a helicopter tour around the colony and along the Communist Chinese border—that barrier to freedom which is penetrated constantly by refugees from the workers' paradise. So much so that Hong Kong is bursting at the seams with a population of four and a half million. . . .

Hong Kong could, of course, be swallowed by Communist China in a second, but it is a necessary window to the outside world. You can't help but wonder how the Communist leaders can look through that window at the miracle of free enterprise without realizing how stupid they are to stick with the idiocy of Karl Marx.

—"Taiwan," I, and "Hong Kong," 5–6/78.

"Normalization" with China Is Chancy

One result of the Brezinski trip to Peking in May seems to be an accelerated timetable by the Carter administration to complete the so-called "normalization" of diplomatic relations with Peking. The purpose of all this, we're led to believe, is to checkmate Russian expansionism and to make the Soviets more agreeable at the bargaining table.

Whether the strategy works remains to be seen, but it is a chancy game. . . . We have something [the Chinese] want: technology and sophisticated industrial equipment. Once they get it so they can industrialize by the end of this century, what will they do then?

Now, most Americans (according to many public opinion polls) favor being friends with the mainland Chinese, but they don't want to do it at the expense of our longtime allies and friends of the Republic of China on Taiwan. But the trouble is, we can't have it both ways. . . .

. . . the administration seems to be nudging its way toward accepting the Communists' terms. First, our government announced the closing of two popular U.S. information libraries on Taiwan. . . . Then, the word went out that our government would not object to our European allies selling Peking armaments even if these included American technology. . . .

—"Normalization" and "U.S. China-Relations," 7/78.

China Still Authoritarian

. . . The regime of Mao Tse-tung's successors is still authoritarian and repressive, a statist monopoly founded on violence and propaganda and destructive of the humane traditions of the Chinese people themselves.

—"Chinese Libertarians," 11–12/78.

(On December 15, 1978, the U.S. and China announced normalization of their relations, which meant U.S. diplomatic recognition of China. U.S. military sales to Taiwan would continue, but not the U.S.-Taiwan defense agreement. U.S.-Taiwanese relations would be maintained through nongovernmental means—a private organization to be established by Congress.)

China Says U.S. Must Be Destroyed Eventually

The United States for the first time in its history broke a treaty without cause. We callously betrayed a longtime friend and ally which had refused to betray us. And we did so with brutal rudeness.

During the two years of the Carter administration, there has been a deliberate snubbing of the government of Taiwan. . . . What our government did was entirely lacking in virtue. . . .

The nations of the world have seen us cold-bloodedly betray a friend for political expediency. That memory will not go away. . . .

The Peking regime—once allied with the Soviet Union—now sees the Russians as not being true to the principles of Karl Marx. Soldiers of the two great Communist powers face each other across a long border and China proclaims Russia is an enemy and a threat to peace.

But, in their speeches to their own comrades, Peking's leaders have repeatedly said *we* are an imperialist enemy which must eventually be destroyed. . . .

And if they should ever decide we're Enemy Number One, not Number Two, they can do so with a clear conscience. They'll only be doing to us what we've done to Taiwan.

—"Taiwan," I, II, and III, 1–2/79.

The Denial of Human Rights in China

We know of course that literally tens of thousands of mainland Chinese every year make their way to the British outpost, Hong Kong. Some of these swim through miles of shark-infested waters, so determined are they to escape their homeland. . . . I've talked of our betrayal of the 17 million Chinese on Taiwan—haven't we also betrayed millions and millions of Chinese on the mainland who lived with a dream of one day regaining freedom? We have legitimized the denial of their human rights.

—"Human Rights," 1–2/79.

KOREA

The Firing of General Singlaub

Last spring Major General John Singlaub, a most capable soldier with a distinguished military record, was abruptly and publicly removed from his job in South Korea by the Commander-in-Chief himself. The general had expressed his views in what he thought was a private conversation that the President's plan to withdraw our Second Infantry Division from Korea could tempt the Communists in the North to have another go at conquering the Republic of Korea. . . .

The presence of our troops in South Korea could very well mean the difference between peace and war.

—"Korea," 2–3/78.

(For discussion of Reagan's review in this broadcast [omitted above] of the State Department report on Korea, see p. 368 in the text and the associated source note.)

To Counter Communism at Any Cost

An executive with what must be the world's biggest news agency recently made a trip to Asia. . . .

He told me that he found, as I had this spring, an almost universal anxiety over our foreign policy. Everyone in South Korea was convinced that North Korea would attack if the United States presence was reduced. . . .

In all of his contacts in Korea he found no hostility toward the United States. He also found a resolve on the part of the people to counter communism at any cost. That's a little contrary to the view we're so often given that South Koreans are unhappy with their own leaders.

—"Asia," I, 7/78.

(Carter abandoned the idea of U.S. troop withdrawals from South Korea.)

JAPAN AND THE PACIFIC

A 1978 Visit to Japan

An American visiting Japan can't help being impressed by the vitality and energy of the people. You come away with an uncomfortable feeling that they have something we once had and took for granted but which, if we haven't lost entirely, we are in danger of losing. . . .

I met with Japanese business leaders who are also concerned about the trade imbalance even though it is in their favor. They are worried about the voices demanding protectionism and not from the selfish view that it will be directed against them alone. They hear Japanese voices demanding protection against our exports to Japan. Protectionism is a two-way street and they know that once started it ends in a demand for retaliation.

Japanese industrialists believe in free trade and they are not building their export supremacy on slave-labor wages. . . .

In . . . meetings [with Japanese officials] one topic was uppermost in the minds of each person I met. That is, is the United States withdrawing from the western Pacific? They quoted statements by our leaders, which seemed to indicate such a withdrawal was possible. They brought up our [contemplated] troop withdrawal from South Korea, the talk of normalizing relations with the mainland of China at the expense of Taiwan, and the growing strength of the Soviet navy in the northwest Pacific. . . .

Our presence in Japan, South Korea, Taiwan, and the Philippines is absolutely essential to the stability of the western Pacific and, actually, to peace and freedom in the world.

—"Japan," I, II, and III, 5–6/78.

The Navy and Our Asian Allies

Officers, who for obvious reasons can't be named, say that in a global war we would have to shift Pacific fleet units to support our undersized naval forces in the European theatre. That would reduce our Pacific fleet. . . .

Admiral [Maurice Franklin] Weisner, commander of U.S. forces in the Pacific, has warned that continuation of the present trends will give the Soviet Union supremacy in the Pacific within a decade. And, he adds, it will even threaten the United States' ability to defend itself. Some Seventh Fleet officers think the balance could tip within five years and they say the west coast is already less than impregnable.

—"The Pacific," 5–6/78.

FOREIGN AID

U.S. Foreign Aid to a Worthy School in Greece

A few months ago friends of mine in San Francisco told me of their interest in helping something called the American Farm School. Thanks to them, Nancy and I were visited by a young lady who works out of an office at 380 Madison Avenue, New York City. . . .

The American Farm School is about twenty minutes from downtown Thessaloniki in northern Greece. It is an agricultural and technical training center on 400 acres, with a girls school featuring home economics and crafts and a boys school with specialties in farm machinery, animal husbandry, and horticulture. . . .

The students get a total education—an academic program plus homemaking skills and crafts for the girls and modern farming for the boys. They pay $350 a year which is one-half of the cost per student. All the work is done by the students, the housekeeping chores and the farming. They have a shop where the girls' handiwork is sold. This, and the produce raised by the boys, provides almost one-half of the school budget.

A small percentage of help now comes from the Greek government which pays to send adult farmers to the school for special courses. Our own foreign aid program, AID [Agency for International Development], helps with some construction needs which leaves 37 percent to be raised by private donations, both in Greece and the U.S.

—"American Farm School," I and II, 1/78.

America Should Continue Helping Other Countries

God bless him, Gordon Sinclair [a Canadian commentator] went on the radio and said: "It is time to speak up for the Americans as the most generous and possibly the least appreciated people in all the earth." He said: "As long as sixty years ago, when I first started to read newspapers, I read of floods on the Yellow river and the Yangtze. Who rushed in with men and money to help? The Americans did. . . . When the franc looked to be in danger of collapsing in 1956, it was the Americans again who propped it up. . . ."

Mr. Sinclair said he wouldn't blame us if we thumbed our nose at the rest of the world. I'm grateful to him, but I hope there'll be no nose-thumbing. I hope we'll keep right on being the first to arrive when help is needed.

—"Our Country," 1/78.

THE UNITED NATIONS

Fight Two U.N. Treaties Carter Signed

For many years the United Nations has had before it two covenants, the Covenant on Civil and Political Rights and the United Nations Covenant on Economic, Social, and Cultural

Rights. Both specifically omit the right to own property or to be protected from arbitrary seizure without compensation. . . .

Presidents Truman, Eisenhower, Kennedy, Johnson, Nixon and Ford steadfastly refused to sign these covenants. . . .

What is apparently little known by the American people is that President Carter has signed both of these United Nations covenants. . . .

—"Treaties," 3/78.

(Neither treaty had been ratified by the Senate by the Spring of 1983, nor had President Reagan withdrawn them from consideration.)

SECTION III: THE NUCLEAR ARMS RACE

SALT II AND TREATIES IN GENERAL

Bargaining Away Our Cruise Missile

When it comes to the current Strategic Arms Limitation Talks (they're called SALT II for short), the Soviet Union seems to be resorting to a technique they've used with us before: bluster. . . .

American critics of the current negotiations are worried that our cruise missile will be bargained away. It's a new weapon system that could provide security for western Europe. . . .

Bear in mind the Soviet objectives. They want maximum flexibility for their mobile-launched missiles; they want to downplay the importance of their intercontinental Backfire bomber and, of course, they are firmly against on-site inspections. . . .

—"SALT II," 1/78.

Beilenson on Treaties

Lawrence Beilenson, a distinguished California lawyer and scholar, authored a book a few years ago that is unique. Called *The Treaty Trap*, it is, so far as I know, the only history of treaties and the observance and lack of observance of some—dating all the way back through biblical times. One thing stands out sharply: no nation which put its faith in treaties but let its military hardware deteriorate stayed around very long.

—"Treaties," 3–4/78.

(On the basis of the history of treaties, Reagan's friend Beilenson argues in the book that the destructive power of nuclear weapons does not increase the reliability or efficacy of treaties in protecting a nation against attack in the nuclear age. He contends in substance that the Soviets cannot be trusted not to store or manufacture nuclear weapons secretly.)

Eugene Rostow Calls SALT II Appeasement

On July 25th in this year of our Lord 1978, a man of unquestionable liberal credentials—Sterling Professor of Law, former under secretary of state for political affairs under the Johnson administration—Eugene V. Rostow addressed a conference on U.S. Security and the Soviet Challenge. There is no way Eugene Rostow could be called a hawk or a tool for military interests. . . .

Professor Rostow says, ". . . The Soviet Union is engaged in a policy of imperial expansion all over the world, despite the supposedly benign influence of SALT I and its various commitments of cooperation in the name of détente. . . ."

It is often said that the goal of our nuclear forces is to deter or make less credible the possibility of war. It is, however, a mistake to believe that deterrence is also the goal of Soviet nuclear policy. . . .

In Greece, Turkey, the Berlin airlift, Korea and the Cuban missile crisis, the nuclear weapon was always a decisive factor in the background. The Soviets knew that in a nuclear exchange, our casualties would have numbered ten million, theirs 100 million. By the middle 60s, their buildup had brought us to a stalemate. We could no longer hint at the use of nuclear weapons in places like Vietnam.

Now, "there can be no question," says Rostow, "that our position has slipped from stalemate to the borders of inferiority. . . ." . . .

Our secretary of defense has tried to reassure us by saying that a successful Soviet nuclear strike against our missile silos would be followed with an attack by our submarine-launched missiles against Moscow, Leningrad and other cities. The assumption is that Russia would never launch a first strike and risk our followup attack. This is hardly a credible assumption since the Russians have enough nuclear forces for a second strike against our cities. . . .

Our goal is a stable peace. Who has ever met an American who favored war with the Soviet Union? Rostow concludes with the warning that the Soviet rulers will expand their power as long as the risks are not excessive. . . .

—"Rostow," I to VI (six broadcasts), 10–11/78.
(President Reagan made Eugene Rostow director of the Arms Control and Disarmament Agency, but fired him in 1983.)

THE RUSSIANS ARE AHEAD

U.S. Nuclear Deterrent Is Fading

When it comes to the Soviet Union, no one denies they have assembled an offensive force of tanks, mobile artillery, support aircraft and armored personnel carriers on the western front in Europe that are superior to our forces and those of our NATO allies. Though correcting that imbalance is important, we could at least say, till recently, that we had the deterrent of nuclear superiority. That, if the Soviets attacked western Europe they would do so at the risk of nuclear destruction. That deterrent ability is fading rapidly and there are indications that the SALT II negotiations may leave us even worse off. . . .

If the Soviets attacked western Europe we could threaten Russia with nuclear destruction. That, of course, is no longer true.

—"Neutron Bomb," 3/78, and "War," 3–4/78.

The Russians Have Overtaken Us

You might be interested in some timetables as presented by former Secretary of the Air Force Thomas C. Reed. . . .

It was October 1962, when the world for six days hung on the brink of nuclear war. Then the Russians blinked and their missiles were removed from Cuba. . . . They were caught because we had overwhelming nuclear superiority at the time. . . .

By 1969 the Soviets had passed us in numbers of ICBM—Intercontinental Ballistic Missile—silos. . . . By 1971 they outnumbered us in tactical aircraft. By 1973 their surface navy outnumbered ours. Also in 1973 they flew their multiple independently targeted reentry vehicles—MIRVs. . . . By 1975 their spending on strategic offensive nuclear forces was double ours and seven times as much in the field of ballistic missiles. . . .

Quite a while ago I did a commentary which involved 1985. Our military intelligence had learned that Brezhnev told a secret meeting of Communist leaders that détente was a stratagem to allow the Soviets time to build up their military so that by 1985 they could exert their will wherever they wished.

—"SALT Talks," I and II, 8–9/78.

The Neutron Bomb

Soviet Brainwashing on Risk of Nuclear War

The Soviet Union must really be uptight about the neutron weapon. Seldom have we seen a campaign to kill off a weapon before it even goes into production. In our own country, well-intentioned people have joined in the campaign but without (and let me emphasize that "without") any realization that their own concern might possibly be the result of subtle, Soviet "brainwashing." . . .

Now we learn the Soviets have developed and field tested a new tank, the T-80, and according to all available information it is immune to our anti-tank missile. . . . But (and that explains Russia's anxiety about the neutron warhead) the new armor is no better against the neutron weapon than the present steel plate.

—"Brainwashing," I, 9/78.

On Equality and Superiority

Strategic Parity Is Giving In

While most Americans are deeply concerned about our falling behind the Soviets in strategic nuclear weapons, one American has a different worry. The President's strategic arms limitation adviser on the National Security Council, no less, declares that it is in our best interest to give up any remaining areas where we still have a strategic advantage. His reason? We might be tempted to throw our weight around in some risky ways if we think we're strong enough. Heaven forbid we should stand up to the Russians when it's so easy to give in!

—"Miscellaneous," 4/79.

Acknowledgments

I am deeply indebted to my wife, Patricia Blake, concerning this book. She read it in first draft during the summer of 1981 in Provincetown and spurred me on to finish it, and she has made many valuable suggestions as I have done so.

I acknowledge with thanks research assistance from Marty Franks, Eric Burke, and others at the Carter-Mondale Committee in Washington, D.C.; Robin Gray at the Reagan-Bush Committee in Arlington, Va.; Ben Bradlee and others at the *Washington Post*; Victor Navasky and Kai Bird at the *Nation* magazine; Wes McCune of Group Research, Inc., in Washington, D.C.; Bill Stetson of Citizens for the Republic of Santa Monica, Ca.; Kathleen Voigt and Bill Sinkin in San Antonio, and Robert Strauss in Washington, D.C., concerning 1980 inquiries; Frank Bierlein, research director of the Democratic National Committee in Washington, D.C., concerning 1982 inquiries; and Bob Eckhardt and Henry Gonzalez of Texas and their congressional office staffs in Washington.

I thank my old friends Bob and Mary Sherrill for letting me have their house in Washington when I was there working on this project late in 1980. I thank my new friends Nina and Herman Schneider for their hospitality and kindness as I have worked on the book in New York City. I thank Dr. Jonathan Fanton, Joan Dempsey, and the New School for Social Research for timely courtesies extended. I thank Leigh Hyams and the Djerassi Foundation for providing me sanctuary in California for the closing days of my work on this book.

My editor at McGraw-Hill, the estimable Gladys Justin Carr, Editor-in-Chief and Chairman of the Editorial Board, has been patient, supportive, and very helpful. She, her able aide-de-camp, Associate Editor Leslie Meredith, and their assistant Theodora Martin have made things much easier for me than they might have been under the intractable pressures of time which the subject and circumstances imposed. No author could possibly ask for a more responsive and adaptable publisher, under trying circumstances concerning a book of importance, than I have had in McGraw-Hill.

I am much obliged to my agent, Edward J. Acton of Acton Agency, for his understanding of the importance of this book and his skillful and purposeful representation; more than that, I count him among my new eastern friends. His associate Asher Jason has also been most helpful. I thank Andrew Wylie of JCA Literary Services for his assistance in the earlier stages of my work on Reagan.

As I stated in the introduction, in this book I have relied on many thousands of stories in periodicals and newspapers (notably the mainline dailies on the eastern seaboard) and on the other books on Reagan, as the notes reflect. Most serious cultural work is aggregative, and I am fully sensible of the extent to which this book stands on the work of many other reporters, writers, and scholars.

Professor Wilbur J. Cohen, Fred Schmidt, Frances Barton, Cliff Olofson, Susan Raleigh, and Roger Duncan gave me good suggestions about parts of the manuscript. Celia W. Dugger, my daughter; made many good suggestions about the entire manuscript. Gary Dugger, my son, gave me unstinted and extensive assistance in Texas without which I could not have given full time to this work. I would like to thank, too, my brilliant mother, Mary King Dugger of San Antonio and Glasgow, for her constant encouragement during this undertaking.

Gerald W. Barrett typed the final manuscript rapidly and accurately, making many trips to the Village from midtown in the best of spirit.

I close these acknowledgments doffing my cap cross-country to Bill Stetson of Reagan's political action committee in California. Spontaneously on the telephone Stetson promised me he would give me authenticated transcripts of Reagan's radio broadcasts if the Reagan campaign committee would not, and when the committee refused he stuck by his promise. Integrity is personal and has no politics.

Of course I alone am responsible for this book and for any errors in it.

Notes and Sources

ON REAGAN

ABBREVIATIONS IN THE NOTES

AP	Associated Press
CR	*Congressional Record*
CQ	*Congressional Quarterly*
DTH	*Dallas Times-Herald*
EGC	"Encroaching Government Controls," a Reagan speech, in *Human Events*, 6/21/61
GRI	Group Research, Inc. Wes McCune's research group in Washington, D.C., concerned with the American right wing
LAT	*Los Angeles Times*
LC	Lou Cannon
LOF	"Losing Our Freedom by Installments," a Reagan speech, undated but not earlier than 1960, distributed by National Research Bureau, Inc.

NR	Nancy Reagan
NYT	*New York Times*
Radio	Transcripts of radio broadcasts more fully styled "Viewpoint with Ronald Reagan, Reprint of a Radio Program . . . ," being copies of the scripts of Reagan's 1975 radio broadcasts, each with a separate title, and "Ronald Reagan Radio Commentary," being copies of the scripts of Reagan's 1978 and 1979 radio broadcasts, also each with a separate title. For the 1975 programs the date given is the one written on the face of each transcript which I examined; for the 1978–1979 programs the date given is the one on the set of fifteen programs of which the broadcast in question is a part.
RI	"The Tentative Reagan Index," a collection of cited quotations in the files of GRI, referred to in the notes when a primary source is a document that I have not examined myself.
RD	Ronnie Dugger
RR	Ronald Reagan
SAE	*San Antonio Express* (including the Sunday *San Antonio Express-News*)
SFC	*San Francisco Chronicle*
TFC	"A Time for Choosing," a Reagan TV speech for Goldwater for President, 10/27/64
UPI	United Press International
USNWR	*U.S. News & World Report*
WC	*Weekly Compilation of Presidential Documents,* Government Printing Office, Washington, D.C. Paginated continuously for each year.
WP	*Washington Post*
WPF	"What Price Freedom," a Reagan speech to the Los Angeles County Young Republican Club, Los Angeles, in *The Cross and the Flag,* 4/64
WS	*Washington Star*
WSJ	*Wall Street Journal*

Chapter 1. Swerving from Left to Right

1. RR with Hubler, *where's*, pp. 3, 7–10, 18, 23, 35, 117–122; RR with Hobbs, *Ronald*, p. 96; von Damm, *Sincerely*, p. 16; LC, *Ronnie*, pp. 1–2, 5, 7, 18, and LC, *Reagan*, pp. 25, 37, 39; Edwards, *Ronald*, p. 51; Hannaford, *The Reagans*, p. 100; Kenneth Harris, *SAE*, 11/8/80; James M. Perry, *WSJ*, 10/8/80; ABC, "RR"; Gene I. Maeroff, *NYT*, undated (on Eureka College); *CQ*, 7/28/67; *Newsweek*, 7/21/80; Eric Morgenthaler, *WSJ*, 12/2/80; *San Antonio Light* (UPI), 11/25/80; *SAE* (AP), 11/11/80.

2. RR with Hubler, *where's*, pp. 106, 123, 126, 138–139, 141–170, 174, 203, 233–243; Hayden, *The American*, p. 358; LC, *Reagan*, pp. 32, 37, 64, 72–83, 85, 86, 91, 96, and LC, *Ronnie*, pp. 18, 26, 38; Boyarsky, *The Rise*, pp. 83–89; Edwards, *Ronald*, pp. 51–54; Edwards, "Ronald"; John Sherwood, *LAT* Service in *SAE*, 11/9/80; *Current Biography*, 1967; *Time*, 7/7/80; *NYT*, 6/3/66, 7/16/80; Drew Pearson and Jack Anderson, *WP*, 10/27/66 (see also Drew Pearson, *WP*, 8/6/68); interview, Jack Anderson, 10/20/80; *Bill Moyers' Journal*, "A Conversation with Ronald Reagan," PBS, 7/10/80, transcript; Conaway, "Looking"; Litvak, "The Ronald"; *Newsweek*, 7/21/80; RR, EGC; ABC, "RR." (The Pearson column of 10/27/66 carried the byline of Pearson and Anderson, but Anderson says it was Pearson's work.) Cf., Leuchtenburg, "Ronald."

3. Eleanor Harris Howard, *SAE* (Special), 11/16/80; RR, *where's*, pp. 251, 257–273; LC, *Reagan*, pp. 89, 92, 94, 96, 141–142, 146, and LC, *Ronnie*, pp. 42, 158–162; NR with Libby, *Nancy*, pp. 14, 16, 18, 19, 51, 97, 112, 114, 116, 132–134, 145, 149–150, 175–177, 180; Weymouth, "The Biggest"; NR in *First Monday*, 11/12/81; Wanda McDaniel, *San Antonio Light*, 11/9/80; *WS*, 8/31/65, and Jurate Kazickas, *WS*, 10/31/80; Edward Cowan, *NYT*, 6/9/82 (on GE's political reputation); Oulahan and Lambert, "The Real"; Warner Bros. release cited in biography of RR by GRI; *Louisville Courier-Journal*, 6/17/66; Owens, "The President"; Edwards, *Ronald*, pp. 67, 122; Roy J. Harris, Jr., *WSJ*, 12/10/80.

4. *WS*, 10/28/64; *LAT*, 11/11/64; RR, *National Review*, 12/1/64; Carl Greenberg, *LAT*, ca. 1964; Rowland Evans and Robert Novak, *WP*, 9/23/66, and *WP*,

9/25/65, 6/2,9,13/66, 8/12,15/66, 4/27/71; *Time*, 10/7/66; *Meet the Press*, NBC, 9/11/66, transcript; RR form letter, 6/18/62 for YAF, undated handwritten letter for *National Review*, undated note for *Human Events*, in files of GRI; "Ronald Reagan, Extremist Collaborator, An Exposé," published by the California Democratic State Central Committee, 9/66, files of GRI; RR, *The Creative*, p. 136.

5. LC, *WP*, 4/26/80; Leroy F. Aarons, *WP*, 12/23/74; *WP*, 1/23/76; *Esquire*, March, 1976; *Miami Herald*, 1/18/76; LC, *Reagan*, pp. 158–163, 192, 222.

6. The transcripts of the 1978–1979 radio broadcasts were provided to me by Bill Stetson of Citizens for the Republic, Santa Monica, Ca., and bear the imprint of O'Connor Creative Services of Universal City, Ca., which sent out the disks and transcripts for fifteen programs in each batch, along with suggestions for when the programs should be aired and in what sequence. The transcripts were exact matches of a bootleg set I had already examined in the offices of the Democratic National Committee in Washington. The latter source also provided me in 1980 with a few scripts of Reagan's 1975 radio broadcasts and, in 1982, an additional set of the 1975 programs. Stetson told me he did not have any of the 1975 transcripts. Reagan's aide Peter Hannaford indicates Reagan also did radio broadcasts in 1977; I have not found any transcripts for that year.

The vice president for news at National Public Radio from March 1979 until the summer of 1983 was Barbara Cohen. "We never got anything like that," she said of the radio transcripts. "Maybe they kept waiting for us to ask for them and we were too dumb to do it. . . . I don't think we asked." Cohen is now in charge of coverage of the 1984 campaigns for NBC News.

Omaha World-Herald, 12/15/79; interviews, Robin Gray, Arlington, Va., 10/10/80, Maris Milas, Los Angeles (telephone), 10/13/80, Bill Stetson, Santa Monica, Ca. (telephone), 10/13,15/80, Frank Mankiewicz, 6/22/83, and Barbara Cohen, 7/1/83; Brownstein and Easton, *Reagan's*, p. 646; Rowse, *One*, p. 7; LC, *Reagan*, p. 230; Hannaford, *The Reagans*, pp. 15, 43, 53–54, 138, 141–142, 177; see *Miami Herald*, 4/9/75.

7. CBS Evening News, 10/7/80, transcript; *NYT*, 1/26/75, 1/25/80, 6/2/80, and Robert Lindsey, *NYT*, 1/14/80; LC, *WP*, 11/11/79, 1/25/80, and see 10/11/80; *WP*, 11/29/74, 12/12/75, 8/28/76, 10/10,21/80; Suzanne Garment, *WSJ*, 9/12/80; Drew, "1980"; *Business Week*, 9/15/80; *Newsweek*, 7/28/80; *Richmond News Leader*, 1/18/75; *USNWR*, 10/6/80; on avoiding remarks about intervention, see *Sterling Gazette*, 12/15/79.

8. *NYT*, 6/3/66, 10/9/80, 11/2,9,16/80; *SAE*, 11/6,23/80; Arthur Schlesinger, Jr., *WSJ*, 11/20/80; Lou Harris, *San Antonio Light*, 11/17/80; *Newsweek*, 11/17/80; Rowse, *One*, pp. 17–18; LC, *Reagan*, p. 323; remarks by Holmes Tuttle in Roy J. Harris, *WSJ*, 12/10/80. The availability of Carter's stolen briefing book to David Stockman when he was "playing" Carter in debate rehearsals with Reagan was first revealed in Laurence Barrett's book, *Gambling with History*, and was still being investigated in the summer of 1983.

Chapter 2. The Board of Directors of the United States

1. *Manchester Guardian*, 7/20/80; *San Francisco Chronicle*, 7/6/80; *Oakland Tribune*, 6/18/80; RR, *The Creative*, p. 141; *WP*, 12/5/69.

2. LC, *Ronnie*, pp. 70–75, 87, 132, 267; Robert Lindsey, *NYT*, 5/31/80; Steven B. Weisman, *NYT*, 11/30/80; *NYT*, 10/31/80, 8/24/82; Star, "What"; PBS, "The Reagan Transition," 1/21/81.

3. *USNWR*, 5/31/82; *Time*, 7/7/80; *NYT*, 5/4/76, 7/16/80, 8/1,2/80, 4/16/83; Edward T. Pound, *NYT*, 2/23/81; Douglas E. Kneeland, *NYT*, 10/6/80; *WP*, 10/21/70, 8/1/80, 4/16/83; *San Francisco Chronicle (NYT)*, 2/26/76; Jim Drinkhall, *WSJ*, 8/1/80; *WSJ*, 4/18/83. On the Malibu ranch, see also *Rolling Stone*, 8/26/76, and cf. LC, *Reagan*, p. 354 and 354*n*.

4. Weinberger: LC, *Ronnie*, pp. 132–133; *NYT*, 12/12/80; *WSJ*, 12/12/80, 5/10/81; *DTH*, 7/15/82. Haig-Shultz: United Technologies, *Annual Report*, 1982; *WSJ*, 9/7/82; *CQ*, 10/4/80; Brownstein and Easton, *Reagan's*, p. 545. Regan: *NYT*, 12/12/80; *SAE* (AP), 12/12/80. Smith: *NYT*, 10/6/80, 12/12/80; Mary Thornton and Elisabeth Bumiller, *WP*, 3/31/82; Brownstein and Easton, *Reagan's*, p. 352. Baldrige: *NYT*, 12/12/80; *WSJ*, 1/21/82; William Safire, *NYT*, 12/25/80. Donovan: *Business Week*, 12/29/80; Brownstein and Easton, *Reagan's*, p. 227; *WSJ*, 12/17/80; *NYT*, 12/24/80. Pierce: *NYT*, 12/23/80; *WSJ*, 12/23/80; Molly Ivins, *DTH*, 6/20/80. Brock: *NYT*, 7/19/80. Lewis: *NYT*, 12/12/80, 12/29/82; *Fortune*, 1/24/83; see *WSJ*, 12/12/80. Dole: *SAE* (AP), 12/21/80; *NYT*, 1/6/83. Watt: Charles Mohr, *NYT*, 12/23/80, and *NYT*, 1/8,9/81; Mike Kilian, *San Antonio Light*, 1/2/81; Andy Pasztor, *WSJ*, 12/23/80, 1/8/81; *Time*, 8/23/82; Zwerdling, "The Power." Block: *NYT*, 12/23/80; *WSJ*, 12/23/80; William Robbins, *NYT*, 4/18/83. Schweiker: *NYT*, 12/12/80, and Robert Pear, *NYT*, 1/13,14/83; *WSJ*, 12/12/80; *WP*, 1/12/83. Heckler: *NYT*, 1/13/83. Casey: *NYT*, 4/22/80, 12/12/80; *WSJ*, 7/7/80, 12/12/80. Edwards-Hodel: *San Antonio Light*, 12/25/80; *NYT*, 12/23/80, 11/6/82. Bell: *NYT*, 1/8/80; *Newsweek*, 1/19/81. Kirkpatrick: *NYT*, 12/1,23/80; Kirkpatrick, *Dictatorships*, passim. Stockman: *NYT*, 12/12,29/80; on NLF and SDS, Jack W. Germond and Jules Witcover, *DTH*, 12/14/80. Burford: *WSJ*, 2/20/80; Rowse, *One*, p. 66; Brownstein and Easton, *Reagan's*, pp. 205–208. Baker: Kornheiser, "Reagan's Chief"; Germond and Witcover, "The Rise"; LC, *Reagan*, p. 307; *NYT*, 11/15/80; *WP*, 5/20/82. Meese: PBS, "The Reagan Transition," 1/21/81; *Oakland Tribune*, 7/18/80; *NYT*, 11/15/80; see *Time*, 7/12/82. Deaver: LC, *WP*, 6/3/75; LC, *Reagan*, p. 233; *USNWR*, 2/9/81; *Newsweek*, 2/2/81. Darman: see Elisabeth Bumiller, *WP*, 10/21/81, and LC and David Hoffman, *WP*, 1/9/83. Allen: Jonathan Kwitny, *WSJ*, 10/28/80, and *WSJ*, 11/16/81; *NYT*, 10/31/80, 8/17/82; *WP*, 4/11/83. Clark: see LC, *Reagan*, p. 400.

5. According to Barrett in his insider's book on the administration, Haig opposed the AWACs sale, but faltered in presenting that opposition.

Casey's financial disclosure statements showed that in 1981 he sold more than $600,000 in oil company stocks as the world oil glut developed, and that in 1982 he bought stock worth between $1.9 million to $4.5 million and sold stock worth between $1 million and $2.1 million. The CIA's deputy director and general counsel review Casey's financial transactions to determine whether he should step aside on certain CIA decisions to avoid a conflict of interest in his exercise of his official duties.

NYT (AP), 1/26/81, 6/1/83; Brownstein and Easton, *Reagan's*, pp. 5, 37, 149, 230, 252, 296, 332, 438, 546, 632, 649–50; *WP* (AP), 6/9/82; *WP* (UPI), 7/2/82; *WSJ*, 2/2/81; *WP*, 6/2,3/83; see USNWR, 6/13/83.

6. Managing directors of Dillon, Read & Co. bought back controlling interest in the firm from Bechtel in 1983.

Part of my argument concerning Bechtel and conflict of interest was suggested to me by a column by Bill Porterfield in the *Dallas Times-Herald*.

NYT, 12/5/80, 1/12/81, 2/14/81, 8/13/81, 5/26/82, 3/8/83; Richard D. James, *WSJ*, 4/10/79, and *WSJ*, 3/26/81, 4/30/81, 5/1,12/81, 9/4/81, 8/2/82, 3/8/83; *WP* (especially work of Ward Sinclair), 7/26/82, 3/9/83, and see *WP*, 8/4/82; Robert D. Shaw, *DTH* (Knight-Ridder), 7/15/82; *DTH*, 7/26/82; Bill Porterfield, *DTH*, 7/30/82; on United Technologies lobbying, Jack Anderson, *New York Post*, 10/26/81; Brownstein and Easton, *Reagan's*, pp. 150, 153, 437; *Business Week*, 3/7/83; see Cordtz, "Bechtel," and Dowie, "The Bechtel."

7. LC, *Ronnie*, pp. 139n., 262; Wallace Turner, *NYT*, 2/2/70, and *NYT*, 5/15/82; *WP* (UPI), 11/17/82; *WP* (AP), 5/15/82; *WP*, 1/4/82, 5/15,16,26/82, 9/15/82; Herbert H. Denton, *WP*, 5/18/82; Donnie Radcliffe and David Remnick, *WP*, 7/31/82; Elisabeth Bumiller and Donnie Radcliffe, *WP*, 1/23/83; Robert G. Kaiser, *WP*, 1/2/83; RR, *Sincerely*, pp. 29–30; NR with Libby, *Nancy*, pp. 171–173, 221; *SAE* (*NYT*) 12/27/81; *SAE* (AP) 1/16/82; *USNWR*, 2/23/76.

8. Smith: Jo Thomas, *NYT*, 5/12,29/82, 6/8/82; Bob Woodward et al., *WP*, 5/12,14,15,20/82, 6/5/82, 7/22/82, and *WP*, 5/25/82; Cohen, "Post-Post-Watergate." Reed: Kosterlitz, "The Thomas Reed Affair"; *WSJ*, 3/15,16,23/83; *NYT*, 3/15,23/83, 5/8/83; *WP*, 3/12,16,22,23,27/83; *Time*, 3/28/83. Lehman: Judith Miller and Jeff Gerth, *NYT*, 12/25/82, and *NYT*, 12/28/82; *WSJ*, 12/28/82. Regulating own industries: Rowse, *One*, pp. 66–68; *WSJ*, 3/4/81, and Andy Pasztor, *WSJ*, 3/18,19/81; Peterson, "Laissez-Faire"; *NYT*, 2/10/83, and on the surface mining case, cf. Brownstein and Easton, *Reagan's*, pp. 142–143. Dixon: *WSJ*, 11/6/80.

Chapter 3. The War on Social Security

1. Myles, "The Trillion"; *NYT*, 1/15/81.

2. Of all sources of income for the 65-and-older population in 1978, 38 percent came from Social Security and 8 percent from private pensions. *NYT*, 12/6/81, citing the Bureau of the Census.

RR, LOF, speech, San Antonio, 1962, and speech, Amarillo, 1962, text; *St. Louis Globe-Democrat*, 1/26/62; interviews, Wilbur J. Cohen; *WP*, 1/6,11/76, RR, TFC; Colvin, "How Sick"; LC, *WP*, 10/11/80; see Myles, "The Trillion."

3. RR, radio, "Strengthening Social Security," I, II, and III, 9/24,25,26/75, basically repeated in RR, *Ronald*, 105–110, with Feldstein identified. On the disputed 1974 study: Karen W. Arenson, Dean R. Leimer and Selig D. Lesnoy and Martin S. Feldstein, *NYT*, 10/5/80; *WP*, 8/21/82; *NYT* (UPI), 8/21/82; Golden, "Superstar," and see Feldstein, *WSJ*, 9/24/81.

4. After the election, Caspar Weinberger, Reagan's secretary of defense, supported changing the retirement age from 65 to 68, but Reagan's May 12, 1982 proposals did not include that one. In 1983 Reagan supported changing it to 66.

WP, 1/30/76, 2/17,18,27/76, 8/14/80, 9/8/80, 10/12,16/80; *NYT*, 3/5/76; "RR on the Issues," Reagan-Bush Committee, 10/10/80; *USNWR*, 7/28/80, 10/6/80; *CBS Evening News*, 10/7/80, transcript; *Time*, 6/30/80; *WS*, 10/3,10,11,21/80; Brooks Jackson, *WSJ*, 10/24/80, and *WSJ*, 8/4/82; *SAE*, 11/24/80; *Newsweek*, 12/1/80.

5. *Forbes*, 12/8/80; Michael J. Boskin, *NYT*, 1/11/81; David Broder in *SAE*, 3/13/81; *Houston Post*, 3/31/82; *Dallas Morning News*, 3/31/82; *San Antonio Light*, 2/8/81; *DTH*, 3/7/81; Document, U.S. Senate, *Staff Data*, table 6, pp 12–15; press release, Rep. J. J. Pickle, 9/17/81; *NYT*, 1/31/83.

6. Document, Library of Congress, Koitz, *Major*, pp. 4, 5; statement, Richard Schweiker, 5/12/81, and Document, Dept. of HHS, *HHS Fact Sheet*, 5/12/81; document, U.S. Senate, *Staff Data*, pp. 53–68; Greider, "The Education"; *WP*, 12/31/81; *Houston Chronicle*, 5/20/81, 7/8/81, 5/13/82; Rep. Martin Frost, "Washington Report," July 1981; press release, J. J. Pickle, 9/17/81; *Fort Worth Star-Telegram*, 8/1/81.

7. Moynihan included the Senate Budget Committee in his stricture concerning terrorizing old people.

NYT, 12/2/81, 3/11/82, 11/17/82; *DTH*, 5/22,29/81, 7/8/81; *Houston Chronicle*, 7/7,8/81; *USNWR*, 7/20/81; *WSJ*, 7/7/81; Jack Anderson, *SAE*, 7/11/81; *SAE* (AP), 2/18/81; *SAE* (AP), 2/22/81; *Houston Post* (AP), 8/1/81; *Time*, 5/24/82.

8. Peter A. Brown, *Dallas Morning News* (UPI), 3/19/81; Robert Reno, *Houston Chronicle* (Newsday), 3/20/82; *Houston Post*, 6/6/81; *USNWR*, 6/7/82; Ann Crittenden, *NYT*, 6/9/82, and *NYT*, 11/12/82; Myles, "The Trillion"; *WP*, 12/2/81, 11/12/82; David Broder, *WP*, 11/12/82.

9. In May 1983 the Social Security Administration actually issued new regulations providing that when a person who has been threatened with loss of disability benefits threatens to commit suicide, "it is important that he or she be treated with the utmost sensitivity, patience, compassion, and understanding. . . ."

The president of the Association of Administrative Law Judges, Charles N. Bono, said the Social Security agency has told some administrative law judges that they have allowed too high a percentage of disability claims. By mid-1983, 781,000 cases had been reviewed and 355,000 people taken off the disability rolls, of whom 88,000 were put back on after they appealed.

In one highly publicized case, a retired Army master sergeant whom Reagan had given the Medal of Honor in February 1981 said he was cut off Social Security disability when officials concluded that he could work even though he had two pieces of shrapnel in his heart, both arms and legs were "severely impaired," a lung was punctured, and he had "constant pain." This Vietnam veteran, Roy P. Benavidez, was wounded when he braved heavy gunfire to rescue eight comrades in a jungle fight in 1968.

In June 1983 Secretary Heckler of HHS announced administration actions that she said were designed to increase the number of disabled beneficiaries who would be permitted to continue to receive benefits. She said that under the new rules more people would be exempted from the eligibility reviews.

WSJ, 1/4/82, 6/8/83, and Martin Feldstein, *WSJ*, 2/2/81; *WP*, 11/13/82, 1/23/83, 2/26/83, 6/8,20/83, and letter in *WP*, 6/14/82; Robert Pear, *NYT*, 5/9/82, 5/8/83, 6/8,9,21/83; *NYT*, 5/19,22/82, 8/23/82, 11/9/82, 12/22/82, 2/19/83 (editorial), 4/7/83; *Time*, 12/29/80; *DTH*, 6/5/82; *USNWR*, 6/28/82; interview, Jim Wright, fall, 1981; *Miami Herald*, 12/2/82. See Aaron, "Social."

10. *WP*, 6/18/82; *WP* (AP), 8/24/82; *New York Post*, 6/18/82; Thimmesch, "The Cashing"; *San Antonio Evening-News*, 10/1/81; *WSJ*, 10/5/81, 7/20/82, and see 7/7/82; *NYT*, 3/2/82, 6/17/82, 8/14/82, 10/31/82; *NYT* (AP), 8/29/82; Jack Anderson, *WP*, 7/1/82.

11. *Houston Post*, 3/14/81; *SAE*, 7/22/81; *NYT*, 9/11,20,25/81, 2/6/82, 7/9/82;

WP, 9/18,23/81, and see Spencer Rich, *WP*, 9/11/51, and Jane Bryant Quinn, *WP*, 9/14/81; *WSJ*, 12/15,17/81.

12. *WP*, 2/13/82, 4/26/82, 11/19/82; *Fort Worth Star-Telegram*, 7/17/81; *SAE*, 6/29/81, 10/3/81; *Business Week*, 5/31/82; *DTH*, 8/9/82; *NYT*, 1/9/83.

13. Burt Schorr, *WSJ*, 11/27/82, 12/1,4/82; Lawrence Meyer, *WP*, 11/26, 30/81, 12/2,3,4/81, 10/29/82; Warren Weaver, *NYT*, 12/1–4,6/81, and *NYT*, 11/28/81, 12/2/81, 6/3/82; *Time*, 12/12/81.

14. *NYT*, 5/6,14,18,19/82; *WP*, 5/12,13,18,19/82; Edward Cowan, *NYT*, 6/26/82.

15. *NYT*, 7/1,7,16,19/82, 10/28/82; *WSJ*, 8/4/82; *WP*, 9/8/82, 10/29/82; *Time*, 6/1/81, 8/10/81; Martin Feldstein, *WSJ*, 2/2/81, and Feldstein, *WP*, 3/14/82; see Ehrbar, "Martin."

16. Greider, "The Education"; *NYT*, 11/13/82, 1/17/83, 2/3/82; Sylvia Porter, *New York Daily News*, 11/3/82; *WP*, 8/9/82, 10/29/82, 11/1,8,14,28/82, 12/4/82, 1/8,14,22/83, 2/8/83, 3/26/83; *WSJ*, 11/9,15/82, 2/8/83, 3/25/83; *Miami Herald* (AP), 12/16/82; Peterson, "No More," "Social," and "The Salvation"; *DTH*, 11/21/81; *CR* 1983, p. H183; *USNWR*, 4/4,18/83. See Fallows, "Entitlements."

Chapter 4. "A Wholesale Giveaway to Private Interests"

1. Hollander, "The Greening"; interview, Steve Wilder; advertisement of Friends of the Earth in *NYT*, 2/2/82.

2. RR, *Las Vegas Sun*, 6/2/78; RR, radio, "Land," undated, "Bugs," 10/78, "The Delaney Amendment," 6/79; Carter, *Keeping*, pp. 582–583; Brownstein, ed., *Selecting*, p. 96; Felicity Barringer, *WP*, 1/26/83; Joanne Omang, *WP*, 10/9/80; *WP*, 6/3/75, 4/24/80, 8/14/80, 10/10/80; Kramer, "Reagan's"; *NYT*, 7/14/80; *WS*, 10/9,14/80; LC, *Reagan*, pp. 287–289. On NO_2, see Conservation Fdtn., *State*, p. 54, 54*n*.

3. LC, *WP*, 4/26/80; Brownstein, ed., *Selecting*, pp. 71–72, 96; LC, *Ronnie*, p. 221, and LC, *Reagan*, pp. 167, 352–353; RR, Radio, "Miscellaneous," 4–5/78, "Malibu," 7/78; *WSJ*, 1/19/83; *NYT*, 10/27/80.

4. *NYT*, 2/19/82, 7/25,29/82, 3/16/83; *WP*, 6/9/82, 7/29/82, 3/18/83; Tucker, "The Chemistry"; see Peterson, "Laissez-Faire."

5. Philip Shabecoff, *NYT*, 12/4/80, 1/2/82, 3/1,13,17/82, 7/24/82, 12/20/82, 4/9/83; Andy Pasztor, *WSJ*, 2/5/81, and *WSJ*, 3/3/82, 3/25/83; "Poison at the EPA," editorial, *New Republic*, 3/24/82; Sandra Sugawara, *WP*, 3/18/82; John McMullan, *Miami Herald*, 12/19/82; Dale Russakoff, *WP*, 10/27/82; *Fortune*, 9/20/82, 1/24/83; *Newsweek*, 1/3/83; *WP*, 6/27/82, 12/18/82; *NYT*, 12/10/82, 2/19/83, 3/3,17/83; see Conference on Alternative State and Local Policies, *The Issues*, pp. 123–127. On the Reagan administration and Love Canal, see *NYT*, 7/15/82, 8/10/82.

6. *NYT*, 7/25/82, 8/19/82, 10/13,17/82; Stephen Barlas, Independent News Alliance in *WP*, 8/14/82; *WP*, 2/1/83; *Miami Herald* (AP), 12/22/82; Pete Earley, *WP*, 1/11/83.

7. Peterson, "Laissez-Faire"; *WP*, 10/5/81, 7/11/82, 8/24/82; Michael Waldholz, *WSJ*, 5/27/82; Robert D. Hershey, *NYT*, 2/19/82, 5/26/82; Philip Shabecoff, *NYT*, 1/8/82, 8/1,24/82; *NYT*, 5/15/82, 7/31/82, 10/29/82, and editorials, 4/18/82, 7/10/82.

8. Conservation Fdtn., *State*, pp. 65–70; Peterson, "Laissez-Faire"; Philip Shabecoff, *NYT*, 4/3/82; *NYT*, 3/10,26/82, 8/17/82; Sherrill, "Reagan Inc."

9. *WP*, 11/4,18/81, 3/25/82, 4/8/82, 7/31/82, 8/2,11/82, 11/8/82, 7/1/83; *WSJ*, 3/16/82, 8/12,20/82; *NYT*, 1/4/82, 2/5/82, 7/8,11,23/82, 10/23/82, 12/2/82; LC, *Reagan*, p. 370; Rowse, *One*, pp. 84–85; *Fortune*, 5/30/83, pp. 33, 36; on chlorofluorocarbons, see *WSJ*, 2/16/82, Conservation Fdtn., *State*, pp. 74–76, and Symonds, "Washington"; cf. Alan K. Simpson, *WP*, 2/20/83.

10. Andy Pasztor, *WSJ*, 2/5/82, 10/6/82, 2/10/83, and *WSJ*, 5/27/82; Philip Shabecoff, *NYT*, 1/15/82, 4/9/82, 6/29/82, 10/20/82, and *NYT*, 5/28/82, 10/12/82, 2/18/83; Sandra Sugawara, *WP*, 3/30/82, and *WP*, 4/9/82, 3/23/83; *DTH* (AP), 7/8/82.

11. Andy Pasztor, *WSJ*, 10/20/81, and *WSJ*, 8/24/82; Peterson, "Laissez-Faire"; Philip Shabecoff, *NYT*, 4/4,13/82, 7/23/82; Anne M. Gorsuch, *NYT*, 8/13/82; *NYT*, 2/9/82, 7/22/82, 11/13,23/82, 12/11/82; Russell E. Train, *WP*, 2/2/82; Sandra Sugawara, *WP*, 4/3/82; *WP*, 4/9,21/82, 5/20/82, 1/21/83; Conservation Fdtn., *State*, p. 60; *CQ Almanac 1981*, p. 504; *DTH*, 10/11/82; *SAE* (AP), 10/5/81.

12. *Dallas Morning News*, (AP), 6/7/81; LC, *Reagan*, p. 362; Andy Pasztor, *WSJ*, undated (on parks "probably too big"); Conaway, "Wilderness"; *WSJ*, 9/16/82; *DTH*, 11/2/82, 12/10/82; *NYT*, 8/17/82, 10/19/82, 12/10/82; *SAE*, 12/28/82; *WP*, 8/17/82, 10/9/82, 1/14,20/83.

13. Rowse, *One*, p. 88; Brownstein and Easton, *Reagan's*, pp. 120–123; *Time*, 8/23/82; *WP*, 11/21/81, 3/21/82; Jane Perlez, *NYT*, 8/18/82; on "mine more," etc., *Denver Post*, 3/1/81, cited in LC, *Reagan*, p. 359; Philip Shabecoff, *NYT*, 11/25/81, 12/24/81, 1/19/82, 8/10/82; *CR 1983*, pp. S25, E 48; Dale Russakoff, *WP*, 4/23/82; *NYT*, 11/12/80, 5/15/82, 11/15/82; *WSJ*, 11/10/80, 3/15/82, 6/2/82, 11/21/82; Deni Greene, *NYT*, 7/19/82.

14. Philip Shabecoff, *NYT*, 2/22/82, 4/6/82, 12/28,31/82, and *NYT*, 11/13,20/81, 8/13/82; Dale Russakoff, *WP*, 4/7/82, and *WP*, 2/22/82, 3/19/82, 9/24/82, 12/28,31/82; *Time*, 8/23/82; Brownstein and Easton, *Reagan's*, pp. 120–123; LC, *Reagan*, pp. 363, 367; *USNWR*, 6/14/82; *Austin American-Statesman*, 2/23/82; *WSJ*, 12/31/82; *CR 1983*, p. H118. Cf. Watt, "Ours."

15. LC, *Reagan*, p. 367; Norman L. Dean, *NYT*, 8/8/82; Conservation Fdtn., *State*, pp. 403–404; *WP*, 6/3,6/82, 7/16/82, 1/21/83; Russell Peterson memo in *NYT*, 2/5/82; *Time*, 8/23/82; *NYT*, 1/19/81, 7/16/82, 11/22,23/82 and editorial, 7/24/82.

16. RR, radio, "Clearcutting," 11/13/75, "Redwoods," 3/78, "Lumber," 7–8/78, "Needed—Better Use of National Forest," 10/78; Brown, *Reagan*, pp. 202–203; LC, *Ronnie*, pp. 135, 140–141, and LC, *Reagan*, pp. 115, 349; Conservation Fdtn., *State*, p. 398; Ward Sinclair, *WP*, 3/10/82, 5/21/82, and *WP*, 8/13/82; Philip Shabecoff, *NYT*, 2/2/83; Jeffrey H. Birnbaum and Andy Pasztor, *WSJ*, 6/19/82; *WSJ*, 4/1/83; Peterson, "Laissez-Faire." On clearcutting, see *Encyclopaedia Britannica* (1965) on "Forests and Forestry."

17. *NYT*, 6/15/82, 7/2/82, 2/18/83, and Philip Shabecoff, *NYT*, 7/3/82; *WP*, 3/29/82, 4/1/82, 6/18/82, 8/12/82; Conservation Fdtn., *State*, pp. 408, 429; *CR 1982*, pp. S13357–S13358; *WSJ*, 6/18/82; George Will, *WP*, 8/19/82; see *Time*, 8/23/82.

18. Philip Shabecoff, *NYT*, 1/31/81, 10/10/81, 2/7/82, 3/9/82, 4/14/82, 6/9/82, 7/4/82, 1/5/83, and *NYT*, 2/5/82, 8/12/82; *CR 1983*, p. E48; Peterson, "Laissez-Faire"; Richard Kazis and Richard Grossman, *NYT*, 1/15/82; *WP*,

4/10/82, 7/15/82, 8/9,16/82, and see 5/24/82; *WSJ*, Andy Pasztor, 7/2/82, 8/9/82; Hollander, "The Greening"; *Business Week*, 1/24/83.

19. Philip Shabecoff, *NYT*, 12/17/82, 1/23/83, 3/8,13,27/83, 4/28,29/83, 5/5/83; Howard Kurtz, *WP*, 3/26/83; *NYT*, 2/12,13,16–18,20,21,23–25/83, 3/2–6,8,11,13,14,16–18,22,23,25–27,30/83, 4/1,3,20,30/83, 5/15/83; *WSJ*, 2/24,25/83, 3/8–10,17,18,22,27,28/83, 5/5/83; Andy Pasztor, *WSJ*, 5/4,6/83, 6/2,15/83; *WP*, 2/17–20,22,24,25,27,28/83, 3/1,2,5,6,9,11,12,15–17,19,22,23, 30,31/83, 4/29/83; *Business Week*, 2/28/83; *Newsweek*, 3/7/83; Rugenstein, "Ruckelshaus' Record."

Chapter 5. Riding Down the Marxist Income Tax

1. Reagan's record in California both and did not fit his convictions about taxes.

In 1967 he recommended almost $1 billion in new taxes, the largest tax hike in the state's history. Adjusted for inflation, total per capita state and local taxes increased during his governorship from $426 to $557. The billion-dollar hike alone raised personal income taxes 60 percent, taxes on cigarettes from three to ten cents a pack, and others. He sponsored and signed two other bills raising taxes by half a billion and a billion dollars a year.

Reagan claims, "We gave back $5.7 billion in tax rebates and credits to the people of California," but as *Los Angeles Times* reporters have explained, these were caused by overtaxing one year, rebates the next, "a fiscal roller coaster." By the end of Reagan's term state income tax collections had nearly tripled, from $7.68 of personal income to $19.48.

His record thus did not wash with his rhetoric and is one reason he was regarded as having been a pragmatic governor. But as governor he also did what he could to advance his views.

His 1968 tax reform, he told the legislature, was designed to "see that each citizen pays the same percentage of his income in state and local taxes after payment of his federal taxes. Local or state taxes should not be used to redistribute the earnings of the citizenry. The federal government has preempted that field." When there was a surplus, he tried to rebate taxes on the flat-rate principle, which would have given rich people more than otherwise and took no account of the fact that poor and middle-income people pay proportionally more of their income in sales taxes than the wealthy.

After a five-year fight with the Democrats Reagan achieved one of his goals, hiking the sales tax and lowering taxes on property owners, a $1 billion "tax shift." This fit his flat-rate tax philosophy, reversing progressivity by raising taxes on sales and lowering them on property owners. According to writers in *Rolling Stone*, "Reagan's property tax bill . . . cost the owner of a $15,000 house $78 more each year but saved owners of $700,000 mansions as much as $4,000 a year." That fits, too.

On Reagan's record in California: *WSJ*, 5/11/67 and see 5/6/80; Brown and Brown, *Reagan*, p. 57; *WP*, 7/30/67, 1/10/68, 12/3/72; Bill Stall and William Endicott, *LAT*, 4/12/80, and see John Fialka, *WS*, 3/2/80; Kohn and Berman, "Reagan's"; Witcover and Cohen, "Where's"; see LC, *Reagan*, pp. 155–157, 171, 184, 185.

On the discussion in the text on Reagan's views: *Time*, 2/1/82; Sen. Russell B. Long in *WP*, 7/13/82; RR, EGC, LOF, speech in Amarillo, 3/2/62, speech in Detroit 5/15/80 (text); RR, radio, "Tax Time," 4–5/78, "Taxes Again," 6–7/78,

"Proposition 13," 7–8/78, "Economics," II, 8–9/78, "Taxation," 12/78, "Taxes," 1/2/79; RR, *where's*, p. 245; Wallace Turner, *NYT*, 6/13/71, 10/6/80; *NYT*, 4/7/76, 1/2/80, 1/27/83, 4/16/83; Robert Strauss, *NYT*, 7/12,20/80; *WP*, 6/15/71, 4/20/76, 7/5/80, 5/18/82, 1/27/83; *WSJ*, 3/27/80; 4/19/82; *St. Louis Post-Dispatch*, 1/25/62, 5/5/71; *WS*, 6/13/71; *CQ*, 7/28/67; *Springfield* (Mo.) *Leader Press*, 9/12/72; Brown and Brown, *Reagan*, p. 67; *Sacramento Bee*, 11/15/79; *LAT*, 7/11/80; *Boston Globe*, 1/13/80; CBS Evening News 10/8/80, transcript; "RR on the Issues," Reagan-Bush Committee, 10/10/80; *Des Moines Register*, 1/11/80; *Face the Nation*, CBS, 5/14/78; Drew, "1980"; *USNWR*, 10/6/80.

2. Greider, "The Education"; *WSJ*, 2/17/81; *WP*, 6/11/81, Thomas B. Edsall, 11/8/81, and David Broder, 3/23/82; *DTH* (AP), 6/11/81; *SAE* (AP), 6/14/81; Karen W. Arenson, *NYT*, 9/16/81; Barrett, *Gambling*, p. 166; see Deborah Rankin, *NYT*, 2/1/82. The calculations on the income tax cut are derived from a table provided the *NYT* by Deloitte Haskins & Sells. On the continuation of the 50 percent maximum rate on earned income, see *NYT*, 2/17,18/81.

3. *DTH* (UPI), 6/11/81; Edward Cowan, *NYT*, 3/18/82; Caroline Atkinson, *WP* in *DTH*, 5/12/81; Thomas B. Edsall and Hobart Rowen, *WP*, 2/16/82; Robert W. Merry, *WSJ*, 10/7/81. See Carson-Parker, "The Capital Cloud."

4. The 1981 tax bill also reduced the "marriage penalty" in the income tax laws. The "all-savers" experiment that was intended to aid savings and loan associations originated in the 1981 law, too, but did not work.

DTH (*WP* wire), 7/24,25,27/81, 8/4/81; *Dallas Morning News*, 7/10/81, 8/2/81; *NYT*, 7/7/81; *Time*, 2/1/82; *WP*, 7/28/82, and see Art Pine, *WP*, 6/12/81. On estate taxes: Deborah Rankin, *NYT*, 6/2/82, Karen W. Arenson, 7/2/82, and see Daniel F. Cuff, *NYT*, 2/27/82; *WSJ*, 10/5/81; Newsletter, Rep. J. J. Pickle, 8/14/81. For a careful report on the outbreak of bidding, see Drew, "Politics."

5. Thomas B. Edsall, *WP*, 11/6,11/81, 3/16/82; *WSJ*, 11/6,19/81; Scott R. Schmedel, *WSJ*, 3/15/82; *NYT*, 11/14/81, 2/20/82, 7/2/82; Robert Wagman, *SAE*, 3/9/82; *Time*, 2/1/82; Stuart, "Leasing."

6. The federal budget is based on the fiscal year beginning Oct. 1.

Edward Walsh, *WP*, 7/24/81; Bob Dole, *WP* (in "Outlook"), 8/8/82; Dan Rostenkowski, *WP*, 8/3/82; David Broder, *WP*, 2/2/83; *Austin American-Statesman*, 4/9,10/81, 7/30/81; *Dallas Morning News*, 8/2/81; Brown and Brown, *Reagan*, p. 204; *WSJ*, 1/28/81; *NYT*, 2/4/81, 10/15/82; *WC* 1981, p. 615–616.

7. With special acknowledgement of the work of Karen W. Arenson, Marjorie Hunter, Deborah Rankin, and Edward Cowan in the *Times* and Thomas B. Edsall in the *Post*: *NYT*, 12/22/81, 5/22/82, 7/24,29/82, 8/2,15,16,20/82, 9/20/82, 10/10/82; *WP*, 12/28/81, 1/28/82, 7/20,22,23,29/82, 8/8/82; *WSJ*, 2/2/82, 4/1/82, 7/2,6,14,23,26/82, 8/4,16/82; *DTH*, 6/29/82, 8/6/82.

8. On user fees: *Dallas Morning News*, 6/13/81; *WP*, 6/9/82; *NYT*, 2/9/82; *WSJ*, 4/1/82. On the gasoline tax: *NYT*, 11/1,10,13,23,24/82; *WSJ*, 11/9,11/82.

9. *NYT*, 5/25/82, 6/6/82, 9/29/82, (AP) 11/21/82, 6/7,8,15,24,30/83; Joseph Pechman, *NYT*, 1/30/83; *WP*, 5/8,28/82, 6/22/82 (David Broder), 7/4/82, 1/20/83; Thomas B. Edsall, *WP*, 1/26/83; *WSJ*, 7/8/82; Maurice Zeitlein, *DTH*, 1/5/83; *DTH*, 6/27/82; Dole in *Village Voice* interview, 2/8/83; Susan Lee, *WSJ*, 6/30/82; Russell Long, *WP*, 7/13/82; Kirkland, "The Flatter Tax"; Galbraith and Davidson, "Flattening." On the progressiveness of the present income tax, see statement of Jerome Kurtz, *CR* 1982, pp. E4636–E4638. For the current libertarian-Republican case against the income tax, see Paul, "Taxes."

Chapter 6. Big Money and Big Business in the White House

1. *WP*, 12/14/79, 8/1/82; *WSJ*, 8/1/80, 11/30/81, 8/19/82, 11/4/82, 2/24/83; Norman C. Miller, *WSJ*, 2/17/83; LC, *Ronnie*, p. 197, and LC, *Reagan*, pp. 175n., 300n.; Hannaford, *The Reagans*, p. 175; Drew, "Politics"; Green, "Political" (quoting Laxalt and RR in 1978 and Panetta); *NYT*, 11/16/81, 4/16/83; Adam Clymer, *NYT*, 11/5/82, 1/11/83; Fenwick on ABC News, 11/2/82; see Hogan, et al., "The New."

2. There was one occasion during Reagan's presidency when he criticized powerful business interests. He was quoted by Senator Dole as having said he had had it up to his keister with the bankers because of their organized campaign to repeal the 1982 law requiring them to withhold 10 percent of dividend and interest payments. Despite Reagan's expressions of displeasure, Congress repealed the law by huge margins in both chambers.
Baltimore Sun, 12/15/77; RR campaign letter, 11/20/75, cited in RI; *New York Daily News*, 3/21/79; *WP*, 8/25/74, 4/19/80, 6/3/80, 8/26/82; LC, *Reagan*, p. 242; *WSJ*, 3/27/80; *NYT*, 5/14/75, 3/22/80, 7/16/80; RR, radio, "Phone," undated, "Government," 4–5/78, "Agriculture," 4/79, and "Utilities," 10/78; Brownstein, ed., *Selecting*, p. 72; Kohn and Bergman, "Reagan's"; Agran, "Adding"; *Nashua Telegraph*, 9/29/79.

3. *WP*, 5/27/82, 8/7/82; *NYT*, 1/23/82, 5/19,27/82, 6/29/82; *WSJ*, 5/27/82.

4. *WP*, 4/7/76, 10/15/80; *NYT*, 5/9/76; *LAT*, 12/1/77; *New Orleans Times-Picayune*, 11/15/78; *Sterling Gazette*, 12/15/79; *WSJ*, 8/5/80.

5. *NYT*, 1/27,29/81; Richard L. Hudson, *WSJ*, 1/14/81; *WSJ*, 1/28/81, 2/4,5/81; *Common Cause*, April 1981.

6. Drew, "Politics"; *Houston Post* (AP), 3/7,21/81; *SAE* (AP), 3/26/81; *DTH* (UPI), 3/21/81; Paul West, *DTH*, 3/25/81, quoting Hodges; Nikki Finke Greenberg, *Dallas Morning News*, 3/30/81.

7. Andy Pasztor and John R. Emshwiller, *WSJ*, 4/19/82, 11/10/82, 3/7/83; *DTH* (AP), 4/12/81; *Houston Chronicle* (AP), 6/12/81; *WP*, 3/9/83; see *WP*, 11/10/82, and Rowse, *One*, p. 196.

8. RR, radio, "OPEC," 2/79; Steve Mufson, *WSJ*, 11/11/81, 11/11/82; Andy Pasztor, *WSJ*, 12/7/81, 1/21/83, 4/21/83; *WSJ*, 2/28/83; Hobart Rowen, *WP*, 12/17/81; Mary McGrory, *WP*, 1/14/82; Martha Hamilton, *WP*, 1/25/82, 1/14/83; *WP*, 11/4/81, 2/10,18,26,27/83, 3/1,4/83; Robert D. Hershey, Jr., *NYT*, 3/1/82, 3/1,4/83; *NYT*, 1/23/83, 2/27/83, 4/30/83; Larry Green, *DTH* (*LAT*), 2/27/82; *Dallas Morning News* (AP), 4/4/81; *New York Post*, 3/1/83; *SAE* (AP), 3/7/81; *CR* 1983, pp. H387, H400, H403, S722–S724; DeParle, "Old"; Schwartz, "Reagan."

9. Danny J. Boggs, *NYT*, op-ed, 5/1/82; *SAE* (AP), 4/26/82; *Houston Post* (Knight-Ridder), 3/15/81; Andy Pasztor, *WSJ*, 7/20/82, 8/24/82; *WSJ*, 12/5/80, 8/11/82, 11/22/82; *NYT* (esp. the work of Robert D. Hershey, Jr.) 11/10,26/80, 10/1/81, 3/21,25/82, 5/5/82, 11/9/82; *WP*, 3/14,21,27/82; Milton R. Benjamin, *WP*, 4/2/83; Gold, "Synfuels"; Stuart E. Eisenstat, *NYT*, op-ed, 6/1/82; Jody Powell, column, *DTH*, 10/17/82; see Daniel Yergin, *DTH*, 6/18/82.

10. *NYT*, 3/22/80; *San Antonio Light*, 12/7/80; *DTH* (John M. Berry, *WP*), 3/25/81; *SAE* (AP), 1/12/82; Milton R. Benjamin, *WP*, 10/28/82; *WP*, 1/12/83, 3/9/83.

11. American Enterprise Institute, *The Candidates 1980*, cited in RI; report by League of Women Voters on a 1979 radio spot, from RI; *NYT*, 3/22/80,

2/5/82, 11/12/82; Brownstein and Easton, *Reagan's*, p. 162; Friends of the Earth ad, *NYT*, 2/2/82; *WP*, 11/6/82, 1/19/83; *WSJ*, 12/30/82; see Harris, "Solar."

12. *WSJ*, 1/12/81, 5/24/82, 6/18/82; *Business Week*, 1/31/83; Cass Peterson, *WP*, 12/8/82; *NYT*, 1/29/82, 6/24/82.

13. *WP*, 4/20/76; *SAE*, 5/14/82; *Houston Post*, 5/15/82; *Newsweek*, 7/21/80; *CR* 1982, pp. H8423–H8439; *NYT*, 5/21/82, 9/30/82; *WSJ*, 10/30/81, 3/4/82; Nancy L. Ross, *WP*, 8/5/82, 10/12/82; *DTH*, 9/30/82, 10/16/82; Quirk, "The Baleful."

14. Brooks Jackson, *WSJ*, 2/22/83; Norman C. Miller, *WSJ*, 7/15/82; *Business Week*, 3/31/80 (cited at Brownstein, ed., *Selecting*, p. 98) and 4/18/83; *WSJ*, 1/16/81, 11/24/81, 2/25/83; *Austin American-Statesman*, (*NYT*), 5/21/81; *DTH*, 5/22/81; Bill Brock, *Houston Chronicle*, op-ed, 5/28/81; *NYT* (AP), 9/18/82.

Chapter 7.   Uranium, Plutonium, and Bechtel

1. John R. Emshwiller, *WSJ*, 12/15/80; Mark Hertsgaard, *NYT*, op-ed, 10/9/81; *NYT*, 10/11/81; *WP*, 10/11,12/81; *SAE* (AP), 12/26/82; *Houston Post* (UPI), 2/5/82; Alexander, "America's"; *Business Week*, 6/28/82; Curtis, "$10 Billion."

2. RR, radio, "Nuclear Power," II, 11–12/78, "Nuclear Power," I, 3–4/79; *WP*, 3/2/80, 11/27/81, 12/21/82, 1/8/83; *NYT*, 10/11/81, 7/11,25/82, 10/24/82 (AP), 12/22/82; Barnaby J. Feder, *NYT*, 2/4/82; Judith Miller, *NYT*, 12/25/82; Shapiro, "Nuclear"; Polgrove, "Where."

3. *Newsweek*, 1/12/81; Jack Anderson, *SAE*, 1/30/81; *WSJ*, 10/9/81, 12/7/82; Milton R. Benjamin, *WP*, 7/2/82, 9/23/82, and *WP*, 12/20/82; *NYT*, 7/9/82, 2/16/83, 5/13/83, 6/23/83.

4. *Lebanon Valley* (N.H.) *News*, 2/19/80; RR, radio, "Nuclear Power," II, 11–12/78; Ford, "The Cult"; Matthew L. Wald, *NYT*, 12/15/81; Janet Lowenthal, *NYT*, op-ed, 12/20/82; *NYT*, 10/9/81.

5. RR, radio, "Three Mile Island," I and II, 5–6/79; *NYT*, 11/2,24/82, 12/3/82, 1/11,14,20,25/83; William Robbins, *NYT*, 3/29/83; Susan Q. Stranahan, *WP*, 2/20/82.

6. Janet Lowenthal, *NYT*, op-ed, 12/20/82; Matthew L. Wald, *NYT*, 2/16/83; *NYT*, 4/14/82, 10/10/82; *WSJ*, 8/11/82; S David Freeman, *WP*, 11/28/82; Kern, "The Nuclear"; McKean, "The Mounting Crisis."

7. Milton R. Benjamin, *WP*, 10/16/82, 11/1/82; Matthew L. Wald, *NYT*, 12/6/81, 7/6,9/82, 8/8/82; Demetrios L. Basdekas, *NYT*, op-ed, 3/29/82; *NYT*, 3/16/83; *NYT*, editorial, 3/20/83; Stu Henigson, *DTH*, 8/8/82.

8. Matthew L. Wald, *NYT*, 3/13/82, 5/9/82, 1/19/83, 4/16/83; *NYT* (esp. the work of Judith Miller), 10/1/81, 11/20,21/81, 12/2,15/81, 2/12/82, 3/5/82, 6/23/82 (AP), 7/29/82 (AP), 10/4/82, 11/13/82, 12/12/82 (AP), 1/11/83, 2/18,23, 27/83; Nunzio J. Palladino, *WP*, op-ed, 12/9/81; *WP*, 11/20/81, 1/6/83; *WSJ*, 7/29/82, 12/15/82; Brownstein and Easton, *Reagan's*, p. 197.

9. *Business Week*, 6/28/82; Curtis, "$10 Billion"; Alexander, "America's"; Janet Lowenthal, *NYT*, op-ed, 12/20/82; Robert D. Shaw, Jr., *DTH* (Knight-Ridder), 7/15/82; Eric N. Berg, *DTH*, 7/3/82; Richard D. James, *WSJ*, 4/10/79; *NYT*, 10/9,19/81, 7/23,30/82, 11/17,22/82; *Christian Science Monitor*, 7/7/82; *WSJ*, 1/2/81, 5/23/81, 10/26/81, 1/1/82, 8/5/82; Iver Peterson, *NYT*, 11/17/82; *WP*, 6/2/82, 7/14/82, 9/9/82, 3/23/83; Brownstein and Easton, *Reagan's*, p. 150;

Joseph Albright and Andrew Alexander, Cox Newspapers, in *CR* 1982, p. S13359.

10. *NYT*, 11/29/82, 2/15/83; *WSJ*, 1/18/82, 11/8/82, 1/19/83 (editorial), 2/16/83, 3/4/83; Bernstein, "A Nuclear."

Chapter 8. Unleashing Free Enterprise

1. *CQ*, 11/13/75; *Business Week*, 3/9/81; Philip Shabecoff, *NYT*, 11/7/81, and see Winston Williams, *NYT*, 3/1/81; Rowse, *One*, p. 78; Stuart M. Statler, *WP*, 1/10/82, and *WP*, 8/5/82.

2. Michael deCourcy Hinds, *NYT*, 1/23/82; Sally Bedell, *NYT*, 2/22/83; *NYT* (esp. the work of Ernest Holsendolph), 11/1/81, 1/6,10/82, 3/19/82, 7/17/82, 11/14,24/82; *DTH* (AP), 10/25/82; *WP*, 7/18/82, 10/30/82; *WSJ*, 3/19/82, 6/14/82, 8/6/82, 11/5,29/82, 3/4/83; *CR* 1983, pp. S306–307, S1289–S1293; Guzzardi, "Reagan's"; see Pertschuk, "Reaganism."

3. RR to board of directors, American Trucking Assn., 10/16/74, cited in RR Index, GRI; McMenamin, "The Teamster-ICC Partnership"; *NYT*, 1/10,24/82; *WSJ*, 12/31/81, and James C. Miller III, *WSJ*, 3/8/82; Howard Kurtz and Douglas B. Feaver, *WP*, 12/18,19/82; Guzzardi, "Reagan's"; Lindley H. Clark, *WSJ*, 7/27/82.

4. In the spring of 1983 the Justice Department was investigating the travel agents' ticketing system.

Melvin A. Brenner, *NYT*, 4/14/82; Alfred E. Kahn, *WP*, 11/5/81, and *WP*, 9/21/82, 3/13/83; see *WSJ*, 1/25/83; Cieply, "Hardball."

5. *WSJ*, 8/2/82; *NYT*, 9/21/82, 10/3/82, 2/21/83; *USNWR*, 4/18/83.

6. In mid-1983 Fedders became a subject of a federal grand jury investigation into circumstances surrounding the indictment of Southland Corp. on charges of its involvement in a bribery and cover-up conspiracy. Fedders had provided the company with legal assistance concerning the subject matter of the indictment. He testified before Congress that he had done nothing wrong or improper in the matter. (See *WP*, 5/30/83, 6/29/83; *NYT*, 6/3,6/83.)

Richard L. Hudson, *WSJ*, 2/25/82, 3/22/82, 7/2/82, 8/10/82, 12/27/82; *WSJ*, 10/18/82; Jeff Gerth, *NYT*, 2/18/82, 9/13,14/82, 6/24/83; Rowan, "The Maverick"; William M. Carley, *WSJ*, 9/14/82; *WP*, 9/14,17/82, 1/14/83; Kenneth B. Noble, *NYT*, 1/25/83; see Ehrbar, "Upheaval."

7. *WSJ*, 10/6,20/81, 9/30/82, 12/10,13/82, 3/21/83, 4/12/83; Brownstein and Easton, *Reagan's*, pp. 16–17; Rudnitsky and Blyskal, "From one pocket"; Hector, "The Banks"; *SAE* (AP), 4/7,8/82; Gordon Williams, *NYT*, 10/18/82; *DTH* (AP), 10/6/82; *NYT*, 5/19/82, 1/8/83, 4/18,19/83; *Barron's*, editorial, 10/4/82; *Business Week*, 4/11/83; see *NYT*, 10/4/82, and *WSJ*, 11/18/82.

8. Hobart Rowen, *WP*, 5/27/82, 8/22/82, 2/10,27/83; *WP*, 3/14/82, 8/1/82, 10/1/82, 2/16/83; James Gipson, *WP*, 1/2/83; *NYT*, 11/22/81, 5/7/82, 7/19/82, 8/16,23/82, 9/18/82, 1/31/83, 2/8,12,22/83, 4/8,12/83; Jeff Gerth, *NYT*, 8/6,14, 17/82, 11/11/82; *WSJ*, 6/1/82, 7/26,30/82, 8/17,20/82, 2/15,16,24/83, 3/4/83, 4/11,15/83; *DTH*, 8/2,16/82; Dince, "Why"; Rescigno, "Why"; Ehrbar, "Toil"; *Barron's*, editorial, 10/4/82; *Business Week*, 3/14/83; see *CR* 1983, p. H179.

9. *WP*, 1/18/83. On power generation, see Susan Lee, *WSJ*, 3/23/82, and Sherrid, "Live." *In re* ICC, see, *e.g.*, *WP*, 1/18/83.

Chapter 9. Trusting Business with Health and Safety

1. Joan B. Claybrook, *WP*, 6/29/82; Thomas W. Lippmann, *WP*, 11/21/81.

2. Peck resigned in April 1983, before the Supreme Court had invalidated his rescission of the auto safety standard.
DTH (AP), 4/7/81; *WP*, 10/13/82, and undated clip; *NYT*, 11/1/81, 2/3/83. Airbags: *NYT*, 2/10/81, 10/18/81, 1/23/82, 6/2/82, 8/5/82, 4/10,23/83, 6/25/83; *WP*, 6/2/82, 8/5/82, and see 1/31/83; *DTH*, 5/1/81. GM recall: David Burnham, *NYT*, 1/5,15/83, 2/10/83, 3/2,3,31/83; Letter, Rep. Tim Wirth to Hon. Charles A. Bowsher, 1/5/83, in *CR*, 1/6/83; *WP*, 3/3/83; see *NYT*, 3/2/83, *WP*, 3/3/83.

3. In the spring and summer of 1983, Auchter was indicating he was considering stricter controls on asbestos and benzene, and attracting publicity because of his victory over the budget office concerning the continuation of a requirement that engineering controls be part of the program to protect textile workers from cotton dust. (See *WSJ*, 5/20/83, 7/6/83; *NYT*, 6/8/83.)
Joann S. Lubin, *WSJ*, 2/12/81, 3/2,5/81, 11/23/81, 12/20/82; RR, radio, "Miscellaneous," 12/78–1/79, and "Miscellaneous," II, 4/79; *WP*, 6/5/80, 10/11/80, 3/10/82, 4/3/82, 5/25/82, 7/2/82, 1/7,19,26/83, 2/23/83; Philip Shabecoff, *NYT*, 12/24/80; Seth S. King, *NYT*, 10/29/82; *NYT*, 1/10/82, 6/2,9/82, 8/27/82, 10/31/82, 11/15/82, 1/7/83, 4/15/83; *WSJ*, 2/19/81, 8/27/82, 11/15/82, 3/4/83; Vicky Cahan, *Business Week*, 1/19/81, 4/11/83; *UAW Washington Report*, 5/18/82, 7/30/82; *DTH* (UPI), 6/4/82; Alter, "Reagan's."

4. Harvie, "Cooperation"; Alter, "Reagan's"; Paul J. Hyden, *NYT*, 2/24/82; *NYT*, 2/20/81, 5/8/82, 8/2/82; *WSJ*, 2/19/81, 3/9/81; *WP*, 4/23/82.

5. Robert Pear, *NYT*, 1/8/82, 3/21/82, 8/5/82; *NYT*, 5/25/82; Spencer Rich, *WP*, 3/31/82; *WP*, 8/5/82; Alter, "Reagan's."

6. Robert Pear, *NYT*, 12/31/82, and see *NYT*, 10/30/82; Sidney M. Wolfe, *NYT*, op-ed page, undated.

7. *USNWR*, 7/12/82; Michael deCourcy Hinds, *NYT*, 1/23/82, 3/13/82; *WSJ*, 7/1/82; *WP*, 4/9/83.

8. Alter, "Reagan's"; *NYT*, 2/1/83; Joan B. Claybrook, *WP*, 6/29/82; *WP*, 2/24/83; Kathleen A. Hughes, *WP*, op-ed, 3/2/83.

9. *WP*, 5/28/82, 1/29/83; *NYT*, 12/4/82; *WSJ*, 12/4/82; see *WP*, 8/6/82.

10. Peter Navarro, *WP*, 1/4/82; Joan B. Claybrook, *WP*, 6/29/82; *WP*, 10/18/81, 3/10/82, 8/6/82, 9/22/82, 1/3,5/83, 2/10/83; Stone, "Dumping"; *WSJ*, 6/10/82; William B. Schultz and Katherine A. Meyer, *NYT*, 2/3/83; *NYT*, 1/5/83, 4/4/83; Alter, "Reagan's"; Cohn, "Patient."

11. Guzzardi, "Reagan's"; *WSJ*, 12/31/81, 8/5/82, 12/31/82; *NYT*, 1/10, 23/82, 1/21/83; Mark Green, *WP*, op-ed, 11/24/81; *WP*, 8/9,22/82; Alter, "Reagan's."

Chapter 10. The Turn Against Antitrust

1. RR, *where's*, pp. 126, 286–293; *Berkeley Gazette*, 2/22/66; RR, radio, "Federal Trade Cmsn.," 2/79.

2. Green, "The (Anti) Trustbusters"; Brownstein and Easton, *Reagan's*, pp. 359, 390, 392, 395, 397; interview with William Baxter by Robert H. Bork, Jr., in *Fort Worth Star-Telegram*, 6/7/81; Charles Babcock, *WP*, 2/7/82; *WSJ*, 3/20/81.

3. RR, radio, "Oil," 2–3/78; Steve Lohr, *NYT*, 2/15/81; Ralph Nader, *NYT*, op-ed, 3/4/82; Caroline E. Mayer, *WP*, 10/30/82; see Stone, "Investigation."

4. William M. Carley, *WSJ*, 3/4,31/82, 4/2/82; *WSJ*, 1/11/82, 6/18/82; *NYT*,

2/15/81, 1/9/82, 5/20/82, 6/18,19/82, 8/14/82; *DTH* (AP), 6/20/82; Merrill Brown and Peter Behr, *WP*, 1/10/82.

5. RR, radio, "The Federal Trade Cmsn.," 2/79; *WSJ*, 1/18/82; *NYT*, 1/16/82; *USNWR*, 8/2/82.

6. *NYT* (esp. the work of Ernest Holsendolph), 1/1,9,10,11,26/82, 7/21/82, 8/12,13/82, 10/5/82, 11/21/82, 1/13/83, 2/12,21/83, 3/1/83; *WSJ*, 1/11,19/82, 4/12/82, 6/25/82, 8/12,16,20/82, 10/12/82, 3/3,21/83, and see 2/11/83; Hobart Rowen, *WP*, 1/14/82; *WP*, 12/27/82; Kosterlitz, "The Heavy-Handed"; Uttal, "Life"; *USNWR*, 8/30/82; *DTH*, 7/25/82; Paul W. MacAvoy, *NYT*, 1/17/82; *Newsweek*, 4/4/83; on long-distance subsidy complexities, see, *e.g.*, Ben Johnson, *NYT*, op-ed, 2/13/82.

7. *NYT*, 4/9/82, 9/25,26/82, 12/2/82, 2/24/83; *WP*, 5/12/82, 6/5/82, 8/10/82, 9/24/82, 2/24,26/83; Michael Wines, "Reagan's Antitrust Line," *National Journal*, 7/10/82, cited in *Wilson Quarterly*, Special Issue, 1982, p. 21; Margaret Garrard Warner, *WSJ*, 8/19/82, 3/2/83; Frank, "Poor"; Angoff and Maasen, "Just"; see David A. Clanton, *NYT*, op-ed, 9/22/82.

8. *Fort Worth Star-Telegram*, 6/7/81; Robert E. Taylor, *WSJ*, 3/4/82; David A. Wise, *WP*, 8/13/82; *DTH* (AP), 5/6/81; *WSJ*, 3/16,28/82, 4/4/83; *NYT*, 10/18/81, 3/1,23/83, and *in re* FTC, cf. *NYT*, 7/8/82; *Business Week*, 4/18/83.

9. *Business Week*, 3/31/80, quoted in Brownstein, ed., *Selecting*, p. 98; *Fort Worth Star-Telegram*, 6/7/81; *NYT*, 10/5,9/82; *WSJ*, 10/8/82; *CR* 1982, pp. H8459–H8464.

10. *CR* 1983, pp. S1483–S1498 (esp. p. S1490), and subsequent; *NYT*, 3/2/83.

11. Ford and Chrysler spokespersons objected to the proposed GM–Toyota joint venture, and as this book was closing the FTC was expected to rule soon on whether the venture would violate antitrust laws.
WP, 10/6/81; *NYT*, 10/6/81, 12/31/82, 2/18/83, 4/29/83; *WSJ*, 3/7/81, undated (ca. 10/81), 2/18/83, 3/4/83, 4/28/83, 6/10/83.

12. Robert E. Taylor, *WSJ*, 3/4/82; Robert D. Hershey, Jr., *NYT*, 1/10/82, 6/15/82; *WSJ*, 3/20/81, 3/4/82; *NYT*, 2/7/81; Brownstein and Easton, *Reagan's*, p. 715; Rowse, *One*, pp. 108–109; see *Fort Worth Star-Telegram*, 6/7/81.

13. An eighteen-member panel appointed by the SEC recommended that surprise takeover offers and the "golden parachutes" (which protect corporate officials financially against the consequences of takeovers for them personally) be curbed.
NYT, 12/1,15/81, 1/7/82, 5/27/82, 6/15,21/82, 7/31/82, 8/7,10,14,16,17/82, 9/22,23,24,27/82, 1/8/83, 3/30/83, 6/11/83; *WSJ*, 11/12,23/81, 3/13/82, 6/18/82, 8/10/82, 9/24/82, 1/3/83 (Tim Metz), 2/2,9/83, 3/29/83; *WP*, 10/4/81, 2/7/82, 7/29/82, 8/14/82, 9/26/82, 10/31/82; Meadows, "Deals"; Steyer, "Deals"; Wayne, "The Corporate Raiders."

14. Sherrill, "The Decline"; *WP*, 2/7/82; Wayne, "The Corporate Raiders"; Louis, "The Bottom Line"; Robert E. Taylor, *WSJ*, 3/4/82; Howard Metzenbaum, *NYT*, 10/18/81.

Chapter 11. "All These Beautiful White People"

1. *NYT*, 11/19/80; RR, *where's*, pp. 63–64, 146, passim; LC, *Ronnie*, p. 6, and LC, *Reagan*, pp. 27, 38, 142; *Des Moines Register*, 12/6/67.

2. LC, *Reagan*, p. 91; *CQ*, 7/28/67; *Look*, "Old Pro Up Against the Old

Star," 7/1/66; *Springfield* (Mo.) *News and Leader*, 4/25/65; Boyarsky, *The Rise*, p. 143; Litvak, "The Ronald"; *Louisville Courier-Journal*, 6/17/66 (Broder); Lewis, *What*, p. 102; LC, *Ronnie*, p. 86; on red-headed Kiwanians, Brown and Brown, *Reagan*, pp. 138–139, and cf. Julius Duscha, *WP*, 6/2/66; *NYT*, 6/1/66, 7/16/80, 4/13/83; *Des Moines Register*, 9/29/67; *Meet the Press*, NBC, 9/11/66, transcript; Scheer, "The Reagan"; Barrett, *Gambling*, p. 426; *WSJ*, 5/20/83.

3. *Newsweek*, 10/11/65; *NYT*, 4/10/68, 2/20/75, 2/5/76, 8/8/80, 9/19,27/80; Lewis, *What*, p. 143; LC, *Ronnie*, pp. 271–272; *WP*, 8/12/66, 7/28/67, 3/31/68, 7/17/68, 11/18/73 (LC), 3/23/75, 1/28/76, 2/18/80 (UPI), 8/6,7/80, 1/17/82 (Haynes Johnson); *Time*, 5/17/76; LC, *Reagan*, p. 250*n*. On bayonets, *Detroit Free Press*, 5/12/80, and cf. Robert Lindsey, *NYT*, 1/2/80. On Puerto Rico and the District: *Fresno Bee*, 11/14/79; *NYT*, 1/13/82; RR, radio, "District of Columbia," 7/78, "District of Columbia," 10–11/78, "Miscellaneous," 12/78, "District of Columbia," 4/79; Document, U.S. Dept. of Commerce, 1980 Census, *District*.

4. RR, radio, "Bakke," 3/78; some quotations from, and see, *NYT*, 11/16/81; John Herbers, *NYT*, 1/24/82; Stuart Taylor, Jr., *NYT*, 3/10/82; William French Smith, speech, 8/5/82, text; see James F. Blumstein, *WSJ*, 11/28/80.

5. Both as an educational and a civil rights issue, bilingual education is too complex to be adequately considered here. For views with tendencies contrary to mine, see, e.g., George F. Will, *San Antonio Light*, 11/30/80, and James Reston, *Corpus Christi Caller-Times*, 2/7/81.

RR, radio, "Bilingualism," 12/78, and "Bilingual Education," II, 4–5/79; *WC* 1981, p. 836; *WSJ*, 2/3/81; *WP*, 2/12/82, 4/24/82; Ernest Holsendolph, *NYT*, undated, but fall, 1982.

6. Robert E. Taylor, *WSJ*, 7/28/82; *NYT*, 11/20/81; *WP*, 9/15/70, 4/6/76, 6/3/76, 4/24/80, 10/3/80; *WS*, 4/6/76; RR, radio, "Busing Amendment," 8/79; on "ridiculous," Brown and Brown, *Reagan*, p. 76, cf. Agran, "Adding"; RR, press release, 12/14/79, cited in RI.

7. RR, *Reagan's*, pp. 64–65; *NYT*, 2/5,13/82, 3/3/82, 5/17/82, 10/13/82, 12/11/82, 1/7,8/83; *WP*, 7/16,23/82, 2/19/83; Charles Babcock, *WP*, 7/27/82; *WSJ*, 8/10/82, 12/13/82; see *NYT*, 9/7/82.

8. Because the fired whites in Boston were rehired, the Supreme Court ruled that the case was moot.

Seligman, "Affirmative"; Gartner, et al., eds., *What*, p. 174; John H. Bunzel, *WSJ*, 1/21/83; *NYT*, 7/7/76, 12/8/81, 1/4/82, 10/10/82, 11/24/82, 1/8/83, 5/17/83; *USNWR*, 10/6/80; *DTH*, 5/23/81; *WSJ*, 1/30/81, 7/28/82, 12/17,18/82, 1/8/83.

9. American Civil Liberties Union, *Voting Rights*; *NYT*, 10/6/81, 11/1,7, 13/81, 12/3,22/81, 3/2/82, 4/28/82, 5/4,5/82, 6/18,19/82, and see 11/14/82; *WP*, 10/6,20/81, 5/4/82, 6/18/82, 10/30/82; *WSJ*, 1/28/82, 5/4/82, 6/21/82; William French Smith, *NYT*, 3/26/82, and *WP*, 3/29/82; *SAE*, 1/28/82, 7/2/82.

10. *NYT*, esp. the work of Stuart Taylor, Jr., and Gregory Jaynes: 1/9,10, 12(Tom Wicker),13,14,17,18,19/82, 2/3,4,12,20,26,27/82, 4/20/82, 10/13, 16/82, 5/25/83, and see Anthony Lewis, 1/21/82, 10/14/82; *WP*, 4/30/76, 1/17, 20/82, 2/3/82, 10/13/82, including Haynes Johnson, 1/17/82; *WS*, 8/23/80. Concerning the impact of the tuition tax credit proposal, see Chester E. Finn, Jr., and Neal E. Devins, *WSJ*, 2/2/82, and *NYT*, 7/17/82.

11. *WP*, 10/6/81, 3/8/82, 4/4/82, 5/28/82, 12/19/82; *NYT*, 11/20/81, 1/27/82, 2/13/82, 3/17/82, 4/6/82, 8/14/82; speech, Father Drinan, Washington, D.C., 3/13/82; and concerning allegations about EEOC and fair housing enforce-

ment, Joann S. Lublin, *WSJ*, 7/29/82, Colman McCarthy, *WP*, 3/20/82, and Robert E. Taylor, *WSJ*, 7/28/82.

12. *NYT*, 5/29/82, and see Sydney H. Schanberg, *NYT*, 6/5/82; *WSJ*, 6/1/82; *WP*, 4/22/82; Brownstein and Easton, *Reagan's*, p. 402; John Shattuck and David Landau, *NYT*, 2/14/82.

13. *WSJ*, 7/28/82, 3/15/83; *WP*, 3/25/76, 1/29/82, 5/21/82, 6/28/82, 10/12/82, 1/26/83, 4/16/83; *NYT*, 1/18,28/82, 5/3/82, 9/17/82, 12/1/82, 1/22/83, 4/3/83; Richard Cohen, *WP*, 4/22/82; LC, *Reagan*, p. 280; William Raspberry, *WP*, 1/15,20/82; Carl T. Rowan, *WP*, 1/19/82, 5/19/82.

14. *WP*, 1/20/82.

Chapter 12. Sneering at the Women's Movement

1. Piven and Cloward, *The New*, pp. 140–141; Gartner, et al., eds., *What*, p. 187; *NYT*, 10/27/82; Judy Mann, *WP*, 7/2/82; *WP*, 11/6/82; *Time*, 7/12/82; Albert R. Hunt, *WSJ*, 5/6/82; Ann Hulbert, *NYT*, 12/10/82; Judis, "The Right"; Adam Clymer, *NYT*, 1/6/83.

2. Von Damm, *Sincerely*, pp. 62–64; RR, *where's*, p. 297; Domhoff, "Politics"; RR, radio, "Miscellaneous," 5/78, "Sports," 5/78, "Miscellaneous," 4–5/79; RR to Barbara Walters on ABC, 11/26/81; Molly Ivins, *DTH*, 10/10/82; *SAE*, 1/5/81; Ellen Goodman, *San Antonio Light*, 2/1/82; Brownstein and Easton, *Reagan's*, p. 352; Judy Mann, *WP*, 8/11/82; Wallace Turner, *NYT*, 1/12/81; *NYT*, 1/16/81, 5/21/82, 9/10/82.

3. Weymouth, "The Biggest"; NR with Libby, *Nancy*, pp. 7, 18–19, 21, 90–91, 95, 113, 125–127, 131, 132, 148, 183; *Newsweek*, 3/9/81; Wanda McDaniel, *San Antonio Light*, 11/9/80; *Time*, 7/12/82; *USNWR*, 11/29/82, 1/31/83; see Rader, "Reflections."

4. Lynn Hecht Schafran, *NYT*, 10/13/81, and see her chapter in Gartner, et al., eds., *What*, pp. 162–189; *NYT*, 7/13/80, 10/30/82; Judy Mann, *WP*, 5/28/82; *Time*, 7/12/82; Osborne, "Rich Doctors"; Mary Thornton, *WP*, 1/20/82; *WP*, 7/22/82; *Houston Chronicle*, 4/26/81; RR, radio, "Miscellaneous," 2–3/78; Interview, Melissa Ludtke; Angell, "The Sporting"; Molly Ivins, *DTH*, 10/10/82; Saul Pett, *NYT* (AP), 10/18/81; Lynn Rosellini, *NYT*, 5/21/82; Cass Peterson, *WP*, 11/15/82; on Justice report to RR, David Hoffman, *WP*, undated; see Brownstein and Easton, *Reagan's*, pp. 400–402.

5. *NYT*, 10/21/80; *WS*, 10/21/80; *WC* 1981, pp. 836, 1100, 1395–1397; see *WP*, 7/5/82.

6. *WP*, 6/14/67, 1/22/80, 2/22/80, 4/24/80, 1/20/82; *NYT*, 3/22/80; Scheer, "The Reagan"; Reagan-Bush Committee, 10/10/80; RR, press release, 6/13/67; letter, State Sen. Robert S. Stevens and five GOP colleagues, for general release, 7/15/76; LC, *Ronnie*, pp. 179–182, and LC, *Reagan*, p. 132; *Boston Globe*, 1/13/80; von Damm, *Sincerely*, p. 94, passim; NR on "Sixty Minutes," CBS, 7/14/80; NR with Libby, *Nancy*, p. 132.

7. *NYT*, 2/15/81, 3/7/81, 3/11/82, 5/25/82, 7/30/82, 8/10,17/82, 9/20/82, 2/1/83, 6/16,29/83; and see editorial pages, 8/4,13/82; *WP*, 10/9/81, 7/21/82, 8/9,17,18,19/82, 1/22/83; Gartner, et al., eds., *What*, p. 183; *SAE*, 10/6/81.

8. *NYT*, 6/21/80, 10/27/80, 1/7,8/82, and Tom Wicker, *NYT*, 1/8/82; *Time*, 7/12/82; *San Antonio Light* (UPI), 11/16/80; Brownstein, ed., *Selecting*, pp. 75–76; *USNWR*, 3/1/76; RR, *Call*, pp. 136–37; RR, radio, "Miscellaneous," 12/78;

Yonkers Herald Statesman (Westchester, N.Y.), 1/18/80; *WP*, 7/4/80, 1/4/83; on polls, see *NYT*, 10/23/80, and *WP*, 8/9/82.

9. *WP*, 1/12/83, 5/8,10/83; *USNWR*, 11/29/82; *NYT*, 6/25/83.

Chapter 13. The Liberties of the People

1. RR, radio, "The Draft," 10–11/79; *WP*, 12/5/67, 12/15/71, 8/23/82; Carter in *Time*, 10/11/82, and Carter, *Keeping*, p. 578; *NYT*, in *SAE*, 5/18/81; *Dallas Morning News*, 5/17/81; *NYT*, 10/25/82.

2. *NYT*, 5/19/82, 6/7,9/82, 7/13/82, 8/4/82, 10/28/82, 11/16,17/82, 12/5/82; *WP*, 6/3/82, 8/18/82, 1/11,22/83, and see 11/25/81; Vernon Guidry, Jr., *Baltimore Sun* in *DTH*, 8/1/82; Hentoff, "Killing"; Rowse, *One*, p. 113.

3. Brown and Brown, *Reagan*, pp. 72, 103; LC, *Ronnie*, p. 230; *WP*, 1/10/68, 4/21/68, 5/18/68, 7/29/68, 5/7/70, 4/21/72, 3/22/77; *Meet the Press*, NBC, 9/11/66, transcript; Robert Scheer, *LAT*, 6/26/80; Witcover and Cohen, "where's"; *NYT*, 3/20/80. On "Aw, shut up," CBS News, week of 11/3/80.

4. Edwards, "Ronald"; *WP*, 12/8/68, 1/8/68, 2/26/69, 3/4,22/69, 5/1, 16,21,27/69, 9/20/69, 6/20/70; Brown and Brown, *Reagan*, pp. 74, 81, 84; *LAT* in *WP*, 9/4/69; RR, radio, "People's Park," II, 6/79; Robert Scheer, *LAT*, 6/26/80; LC, *Reagan*, pp. 151–152.

5. Five years after the "bloodbath" remark, Reagan offered this tortured explanation: He had meant that besieged college administrators were going to have to "stand firm and take their bloodbath, meaning that they were going to have to undergo whatever repercussions . . . there would be."
Leroy F. Aarons, *WP*, 4/16/70, 12/23/74, and *WP*, 1/5/75; Wallace Turner, *NYT*, 4/19/70.

6. RR in *USNWR*, 3/25/68; *WP*, 3/7/69, 10/1/72, 5/2,13/73, 9/10/73, 3/31/74, 10/30/74, 5/21/77; Charles Foley, *London Observer* reprinted in *Atlas*, July 1970; *NYT*, 8/5,7/74, 1/26/75, but see 3/19/76; *St. Louis Globe-Democrat*, 9/12/74. On Haig: Anthony Lewis, *NYT*, 12/8/80; William Safire, *NYT*, 11/24/80; Tom Wicker, *NYT*, 4/27/82. Allen: *NYT*, 11/14/81. Fielding: *NYT*, 12/7/80; the Dean passage is cited by Elisabeth Bumiller in *WP*, 11/23/81. Malek: Mary McGrory, *WP*, 3/25/82. Stans: see Mary McGrory, *Boston Globe*, 6/18/82. Bork: *NYT*, 12/8/81. Nofziger: *NYT*, 6/8/73; Document, U.S. Senate, *The Final Report*, pp. 100–101.

7. *WP*, 8/3/75; Jeffrey Klein and Brian McTigue, *Mother Jones*, 9–10/80; *SFC (AP)*, 6/29/80; Heatherly, ed., *Mandate*, passim, e.g., pp. 941–942; *SAE*, 11/16/80; *NYT*, 12/8/80.

8. *Dallas Morning News*, 5/15/81, 8/12/82; *NYT*, 5/18/82; Judis, "Setting"; Sherrill, "Opening Day"; see Don Edwards, *NYT*, 2/19/81.

9. LC, *Reagan*, p. 383; speech, William French Smith, text, 8/5/82; *DTH*, 3/1/81, *DTH* (AP) 5/31/81; *Newsweek*, 3/23/81; *Corpus Christi Caller-Times* (AP), 4/16/81; *NYT*, 10/14,16/81, 11/5,9,13,15 (Judith Miller)/81, 12/5/81, 11/23/82 (Philip Taubman), 6/25/82, 7/4/82, 11/7/82, 3/7/83; *WSJ*, 10/6/81, 4/22/82; *WP*, 12/5/81; George Lardner, *WP*, 10/13/81, 11/13/81; Bamford, *The Puzzle*, pp. 1–4, 365; see Tom Wicker, *NYT*, 4/23/82, and Taubman, "Casey."

10. *NYT*, 10/4,16,22/81, 11/13,27/81, 1/14/82, 2/3,6/82, 3/11,17/82, 4/3, 4/82, 5/1,21,22/82, 8/10/82, 11/15/82, 12/15,16/82, 1/12/83, 3/4,12,14/83, 4/21/83; *DTH*, 6/8/81, 5/5/82; von Damm, *Sincerely*, p. 30; Brownstein and

Easton, *Reagan's*, pp. 359–360; Robert J. Wagman, *SAE*, 10/6/81; Bamford, "How"; *WP*, 11/13/82, 1/13/82, 3/16/82, 4/3,27/82, 11/11/83, 12/15/83; *Time*, 1/25/82; Unterberger, "Burying"; *WSJ*, 3/19/82, 12/15/82.

11. *NYT*, 9/24/82, 10/4,7/82, 11/17/82, 3/4,18,19/82, 6/11,24/82; Stuart Taylor, Jr., *NYT*, 3/3/82; Floyd Abrams, *NYT*, 6/11/82; *WP*, 6/4,24/82; Mac-Kenzie, "Darker Cloaks."

12. Late in June 1983, the Senate Armed Services Committee voted to prohibit the Department of Defense from penalizing military or civilian employees solely because of lie detector test results or refusal to submit to such tests.

Richard Halloran, *NYT*, 1/24/82, 12/10/82; *NYT*, 3/12/83; *SAE* (*LAT*), 10/8/81; *WP*, 3/12/83, 6/30/83; see *USNWR*, 4/4/83.

Chapter 14. Prayer, Sex, Innocence, and Guns

1. *Baltimore Sun*, 4/30/80; *WP*, 6/3/76, 9/13/80, 10/3/80, 5/18/82, 2/4/83; *NYT*, 8/23/80, 10/4/80, 5/18/82, 7/17/82, 9/22,24/82, 2/1/83, and see Yale Kamisar, *NYT*, 5/17/82; *CR* 1983, p. S994; RR, radio, "A Tale of Two Countries," 7/79; and "Miscellaneous," 4–5/79; *USNWR*, 7/28/80; NR with Libby, *Nancy*, pp. 134–135.

2. Von Damm, *Sincerely*, pp. 84, 95; *WP*, 9/6/69, 12/28/72, 2/20/82, 3/29/82, 8/4,8/82, 1/11/83; David Broder, *NYT*, 6/6/66; *NYT*, 2/5,10/82, 3/29/82, 1/25/83, 2/15/83; RR, radio, "Sex Education," 5–6/79; *WSJ*, 4/2/82, 1/11/83, and Albert Hunt, *WSJ*, 11/3/80; James Wechsler, *New York Post*, 1/27/83.

3. In a newspaper column before the voting on the Briggs proposition in California, Reagan wrote: "Whatever else it is, homosexuality is not a contagious disease like the measles. Prevailing scientific opinion is that an individual's sexuality is determined at a very early age and that a child's teachers do not really influence this."

LC, *Ronnie*, pp. 182–188, 242, and LC, *Reagan*, p. 133; Scheer, "The Reagan"; *WP*, 10/2/81, 7/23/82, and William Raspberry, *WP*, 10/8/81; *NYT*, 7/25/82; Hannaford, *The Reagans*, pp. 185–186.

4. *WP*, 6/17/66, 7/21/82, 1/20/83, and William W. Greenhalgh, *WP*, 3/30/82; *CQ*, 7/28/67; RR, radio, "Crime," 4–5/78; Wayne R. LaFave, *DTH* (*LAT*), 12/9/82; Ira Glasser in Gartner, et al., eds., *What*, pp. 243–244; Stuart Taylor, Jr., *NYT*, 1/26/83, and *NYT*, 7/2/82, and see editorial, "The Presume-'Em-Guilty Act," *NYT*, 10/13/82. On "Devastator" bullets, see Philip M. Stern, *WP*, 8/9/82.

Chapter 15. Reagan's McCarthyism

1. LC, *Reagan*, p. 87; Birch poster displayed in John Birch Society document, GRI; RR, speech, San Antonio, 1962, and LOF, WPF; RR, *where's*, p. 303; RR, radio, "McCarthy," 5–6/79. For my account of the June 12 demonstration at Central Park, see RD, "Marching."

2. *NYT*, 5/16/66, 8/8/66; Edwards, "Ronald"; McGill, *The Year*, pp. 59, 80–83, 99–100, 104, 108–111.

3. *NYT*, 12/31/80, 1/7/81; RR, radio, "Can You Persuade a Leftist?" 10/16/75, "Secret Service," 10/30/75; *WP*, 3/5/76, 4/1,2/76, 5/22/76, 12/31/80, 1/7/81, 1/20/83; *NYT*, 3/27/76, 4/1/76, 12/29,31/80, 1/7/81, 1/17/83; Kenneth Reich, *LAT*, 4/16/76; Cooper, "Spies"; *Newsweek*, 1/24/83.

4. RR, radio, "Canal," 4–5/78, "Government Security," 5/78, "Suicide Lobby," 3–4/78, "Salt II," 1–2/78, "Soviet Nuclear Power," 10/78, "Nuclear Power," 7/79, "Miscellaneous," 7–8/79, "Planes," 6–7/78, "Nuclear Carrier," 11–12/78; Radosh, "The 'Peace Council' "; interview, Norma Becker; LC, *Reagan*, p. 86; *WP*, 7/14/80, 11/30/81, 3/24/82; *NYT*, 2/29/80, 3/18/80, 5/10/80; Reagan-Bush release, "Deployment of Nuclear Warhead in Europe," handed to me 10/10/80, describing RR's position; Newsletter, Citizens for the Republic, 2/79, in RI (capitals in original); Kenneth Reich, *LAT*, 4/16/76; Brownstein and Easton, *Reagan's*, pp. 109, 123, 147; *NYT*, 2/29/80, 3/26/82, 7/24/82; *WSJ* 6/2/82.

5. Barbara Gamarekian, *NYT*, 5/26/82; *CR* 1982, pp. S13138–S13147; *NYT*, 10/2/82; Mary McGrory, *WP*, 10/5/82; Donnie Radcliffe, *WP*, 10/7/82. *NYT*, 10/5,6/82; Tom Wicker, *NYT*, 10/8/82; Hodding Carter, *WSJ*, 10/7/82; Richard Cohen, *SAE*, 10/12/82; *WP*, 10/6,9,12/82; speech, George Kennan, Oct. 25, 1982, at Union Theological Seminary in New York City; Donner, "The Campaign"; Radosh, "The 'Peace Council'", Thompson, "END" and "Peace"; Solomon, "Europe."

6. In a *Nation* article, Frank Donner, in the course of condemning the revival of McCarthyism, wrote that the U.S. Peace Council (USPC) "has some Communist party members in its midst, but it also has members from Congress, state legislatures, city councils, and legal and religious groups." Donner's article provoked impassioned rejoinders in subsequent numbers of the *Nation*.

New Republic countered with a well-aimed argument written by Ronald Radosh. The executive director of USPC, he pointed out, is a Communist party activist, Michael Myerson, and USPC "was established by the American Communist party two years ago as a vehicle to consolidate its 'peace work,' and as a way to reach the newly emerging broad peace movement with pro-Soviet arguments." USPC, Radosh said, is "an old-fashioned Communist front," and he concluded: "There is no good reason to collaborate with Communists, and plenty of reason not to."

For this perfectly sensible position Radosh has been roundly abused, as has been E. P. Thompson, also. The long-standing failure of the American left to insist and act on the distinction between revolutions for economic justice and civil liberties and revolutions for economic justice and a police state was reducing it to impotence again.

7. *NYT*, 11/12,13/82, 3/26/83; *Newsweek* (Periscope), 11/22/82; *WP*, 11/13/82, 12/10/82, 3/26/83; *Time*, 12/27/82; interview, Norma Becker; documents, Department of State, *Soviet* and *Soviet . . . An Update, Expulsion*, and *World Peace Council*; U.S. House of Representatives, intelligence subcommittee, *Soviet Covert Action*, and Central Intelligence Agency, *Soviet Covert Action*. Isaac and Isaac, "The Counterfeit"; Bukovsky, "The Peace Movement"; Griffith, "Perspective . . . I"; Chappie, "Perspective . . . II"; Barron, "The KGB's Magical War." See Graves, "Are These."

8. Roy Cohn was an investigator for and sidekick of the late Senator Joe McCarthy of Wisconsin; Abigail McCarthy is the wife of former Sen. Eugene

McCarthy of Minnesota. Mrazek was quoted by Lois Romano and Phil Mc-
Combs in *WP*, 1/28/83.

Chapter 16. Punishing the Poor

1. Greider, "The Education"; *NYT*, 10/18/81, 9/10/82; speech by Rep. Jim
Wright in Washington, 9/30/83.
2. Greenstein, "Revising"; Palmer and Sawhill, *The Reagan*, pp. 373, 496;
Houston Chronicle (UPI), 4/17/81; *Newsweek*, 4/5/82; Schoen, "Once"; Nicholas
Ashford, *London Times*, 10/14/82.
3. Greider, "The Education"; Brownstein and Easton, *Reagan's*, p. 54; LC,
Reagan, p. 331.
4. *NYT*, 1/12/81, 2/24/81, 10/2/81, 3/11,27/82, 4/30/82, 5/26,28/82, 6/3/82,
7/18/82, 8/22,29/82, 9/10,11/82, 3/24/83, 4/9,14,22/83; *WP*, 10/7/81, 11/24/81,
3/5/82, 5/2/82 (Martin Tolchin), 5/30/82 (David S. Broder), 6/11,12/82, 7/14,
29/82, 8/29/82, 9/11/82, 3/24,27/83, 4/8,9,22/83; *WSJ*, 4/13/83; *Fort Worth Star-
Telegram*, 7/4/81; Brownstein and Easton, *Reagan's*, p. 52; speech, Rep. Jim
Wright, Washington, 5/4/81; *Dallas Morning News* (UPI), 3/1/82; *SAE*, 3/5/81.
On Feldstein: *NYT*, 11/8/81, 8/6/82, 12/6/82, and see 1/23/81; *New Republic*
("Flush But Coy"), 10/25/82; *WSJ*, 7/16/82; *WP*, 9/23/82; Martin Feldstein
columns, *WSJ*, 2/2/81, 3/12/81, 1/19/82, and 2/2/82, and *WP*, 3/14/82.
5. Jack Germond and Jules Witcover, *San Antonio Light*, 11/17/80; *San
Diego Union*, 5/30/65; *NYT*, 6/6/66; *WS*, 6/23/80; von Damm, *Sincerely*, pp. 86,
90; LC, *Reagan*, p. 166.
6. *WP*, 9/9,20/67, 10/21/67, 1/10/68, 7/26/70, 10/8/70, 1/8/71, 4/16,27/71,
11/22/72; Brownstein, ed., *Selecting*, pp. 79–80, 88–89; *CQ*, 7/28/67; RR, *The
Creative*, p. 17; *NYT*, 9/25/67; von Damm, *Sincerely*, p. 58; LC, *Ronnie*, pp. 137,
141–142, 145, and LC, *Reagan*, p. 127.
7. *WP*, 11/5/70, 4/18,27/71, 5/6/71, 7/1/71; *NYT*, 4/25,27/71; Brownstein,
ed., *Selecting*, pp. 89–91; von Damm, *Sincerely*, p. 48; LC, *Ronnie*, p. 302.
8. *WP*, 5/7/70, 1/13/71, 3/4/71, 5/1/71 (Nick Kotz), 5/2/71, 6/11/71, 7/12/71,
2/2/72, 12/23/74; *NYT*, 5/12/71, 7/24/80; von Damm, *Sincerely*, p. 49; Bill Stall
and William Endicott, *LAT*, 4/12/80; John J. Fialka, *WS*, 3/2/80; RR, radio,
"Welfare," 1/78, and "Welfare," 11–12/78; Agran, "Adding"; Brown and
Brown, *Reagan*, pp. 126–129, 131–132; letter, State Senator Robert S. Stevens
and five GOP colleagues, 7/15/76; *USNWR*, 10/6/80; PBS, "A Conversation";
LC, *Reagan*, p. 183; Hannaford, *The Reagans*, p. 18.
9. RR, radio, "Pity the Middle Class," 2–3/78, and "International Year of
the Child," 8/79; *NYT*, 11/3/81, 1/10/82, 4/26/82, 9/12/82; LC, *Reagan*, pp. 177,
181*n*., 182–184; Spencer Rich, *Austin American Statesman* (WP), 4/3/81, *WP*,
7/7/82, and *WP*, undated; *WSJ*, 2/19/81.
10. *Business Week*, 9/29/80; Danziger and Haveman, "The Reagan"; *NYT*,
9/29/80, 10/2/81 (editorial quoting Stockman); Kathy Sawyer, *WP*, 9/30/81,
from whose story I obtained the details about the CSA photographs and signs;
see *WP*, 8/2/82.
11. *WP*, 2/6/81, 2/7/82, 2/1/83; *USNWR*, 3/2/81; *SAE (NYT)*, 2/11/81; *NYT*,

2/12/81, 9/11/81, 10/6,28/81, 12/27/81 (editorial), 2/14/82, 1/29/83; Palmer and Sawhill, eds., *The Reagan*, p. 383; *WSJ*, 1/26/83.

12. Leroy F. Aarons, *WP*, 12/23/74; von Damm, *Sincerely*, pp. 34, 79; Robert Pear, *NYT*, 10/19/81, 3/30/82, 4/2,13/82, 8/25/82, 10/1/82, 1/31/83, 4/13/83; *NYT*, 2/19,20/81, 10/1/81, 5/16/82 (UPI), 1/29/83, 3/12/83; Spencer Rich, *WP*, 2/12/82; *WP*, 2/7/82, 8/19/82, 2/28/83 (editorial), 3/28/83, 4/14,23,28/83; *WSJ*, 1/31/83; Kotz, "The War"; Representative James Jones (D.–Okla.) on *Meet the Press*, NBC, 2/1/81; *Newsweek*, 4/5/82; *USNWR*, 2/7/82; Patrick J. Leahy, *WP*, op-ed, 3/7/82; see Colman McCarthy, *WP*, 2/12/82.

13. Robert Pear, *NYT*, 10/21/81, 11/18/81, 8/25/82, 11/1/82, 1/31/83, 2/3/83; *NYT*, 2/20/81, 7/4,29/82, 11/29/82, 1/29/83; Les Lescaze and Helen Dewar, *WP*, 2/9/82; *WP*, 11/18/81, 2/7/82, 9/5/82, 11/16/82 (letters to the editor); *WSJ*, 3/11/81; Kotz, "The War"; *Newsweek*, 4/5/82; see Katherine Hayes, *Atlanta Journal*, 11/1/81.

14. *WSJ*, 3/11,19/81, 1/31/83; *Newsweek*, 4/5/82; Greenstein, "Revising"; Robert Pear, *NYT*, 4/2/82, 8/28/82; *NYT* (AP), 4/6/83; Kotz, "The War"; *WP*, 2/7/82, 9/11/82, 7/10/82, 2/28/83 (editorial).

15. Moynihan, "One-Third"; Robert Pear, *NYT*, 11/28/81, 8/25/82, 10/1/82, 1/31/83; *NYT*, 2/20/81, 9/8/81 (AP), 10/1/81, 7/21/82, 8/23/82, 1/29/83; *WP*, 10/1/81, 2/7/82; Robert Isikoff, *WP*, 4/1/83; *WSJ*, 2/19/81, 3/11/81, 2/7,8/82, 1/31/83; *Houston Chronicle*, 2/5/82; *Newsweek*, 4/5/82; Kotz, "The War."

16. Brownstein, ed., *Selecting*, p. 70; *NYT*, 10/1/82; *WP*, 5/9/82; Doron P. Levin, *WSJ*, 10/28/82; Celia W. Dugger, *Atlanta Constitution*, 1/25/83; *Atlanta Constitution* (editorial), 1/27/83.

17. *WP*, 10/1/81, 4/28/83; Kotz, "The War"; *NYT*, 11/10/81, 3/10/82, 5/16/82, 4/29/83; Danziger and Haveman, "The Reagan"; *Newsweek*, 4/5/82; Palmer and Sawhill, eds., *The Reagan*, p. 384; *USA Today*, 4/3/83; interview, Henry B. Gonzalez; see Burt Schorr, *WSJ*, 10/21/81, Leslie Bennetts, *NYT*, 4/6/82, and Norgren, "Heaven."

18. *NYT*, 1/1/82, 2/14/82, 7/16/82, 10/28,30/82, 12/2,9,15,17,19/82, 1/22/83; David S. Broder, *WP*, 2/10/82; *WP*, 11/11/82, 12/9,15,18/82, 4/12/83, 4/13/83 (editorial); Scot J. Paltrow, *WSJ*, 1/28/82; *Time*, 11/23/81, 12/27/82; see Gerald L. Caplan, *WSJ*, 12/9/82, and Drew, "Legal."

19. Felicity Barringer, *WP*, 12/2/81, 11/23/82, 4/12/83; *NYT*, 1/7/81, 12/2,30/81, 5/1/82, 1/5/83, 4/26/83; *Newsweek*, 2/8/82.

20. Palmer and Sawhill, eds., *The Reagan*, pp. 307–319; *NYT*, 1/31/83; *WP*, 12/19/82.

Chapter 17. Housing, Education, and Health; Workers and Farmers

1. RR, speech, San Antonio, 1962; *CQ*, 7/28/67; LC, *WP*, 1/10/76; *WP*, 2/5/81, 12/4/81; *WSJ*, 8/6/80, 8/11/82; Brooks Jackson, *WSJ*, 10/24/80; RR, speech, Green Bay, Wisc., 10/2/80, text; "RR on the Issues," Reagan-Bush Committee, 10/10/80. For the computations that are the basis of the widely accepted estimate that only one in eleven families starting out can buy a new home, see *CR* 1983, p. S728.

2. Robert Pear, *NYT*, 10/1/81, 1/3/82, 3/5/82, 4/16/82, 9/5/82, 1/31/83;

Palmer and Sawhill, eds., *The Reagan*, pp. 403–405, 408, 410; *NYT*, 10/1/81, 10/28/81 (AP), 11/1,6,15/81, 12/2/81 (AP), 1/3/82, 2/5,7/82, 3/13/82 (letters to editor), 3/30/82, 4/3,30/82, 6/15,25/82, 7/14/82, 10/19/82 (editorial), 1/29/83, 3/22/83 (UPI); Ward Sinclair, *WP*, 1/14/83; *WP*, 2/14/82, 6/5/82, 10/16/82 (editorial), 10/20/82, 3/2,29/82, 4/2/83; *WSJ*, 2/19/81, 3/11/81, 10/5/81, 11/6/81, 12/23,24/81; *DTH*, (James O'Shea, *Chicago Tribune*), 11/8/82; *Time*, 2/15/82, *Newsweek*, 4/5/82; Diane Granat, *SAE* (*CQ*), 12/29/82.

3. "RR on the Issues," Reagan-Bush Committee, 10/10/80; *NYT*, 12/14/79; RR, radio, "Education," 5–6/78, "Department of Education," 10–11/79; RR, speech, San Antonio, 1962, and EGC; *LAT*, ca. 2/72; *WS*, 10/3/80; Brown and Brown, *Reagan*, pp. 74, 85; Leroy F. Aarons, *WP*, 12/23/74; *WP*, 1/30/67, 2/21/70, 10/19/70, 7/7/71; RR, "An Equal"; LC, *Reagan*, pp. 154, 184, 23–240; von Damm, *Sincerely*, pp. 37–38; RR, *Ronald*, p. 74.

4. *NYT* (especially work by Edward B. Fiske and Marjorie Hunter), 2/19,20,22/81, 10/20/81, 11/1,8,15/81, 2/16,18/82, 3/3,26/82, 4/13,16,20/82. 7/29/82, 8/4,11,29/82, 9/9,30/82, 10/5/82 (AP), 10/12,14,21/82, 11/28/82, 1/31/83, 2/1,13/83, 3/3/83, 4/25,29/83; *WP*, 4/16/82, 8/11/82, 9/9/82, 10/15/82, 1/3/83, 2/1/83, 3/13/83 (UPI), 3/5,18/83; *WSJ*, 2/19/81, 3/11/81, 2/8/82, 11/12/82, 12/21/82, 1/31/83; David S. Tatel, *NYT*, op-ed, 3/23/83; Greenstein, "Revising"; *SAE* (AP), 2/5/82; Palmer and Sawhill, eds., *The Reagan*, pp. 336–338, 351–356; *Time*, 5/2/83; Ralph W. Yarborough, speech, Austin, Tex., 2/27/82.

5. Drew Pearson, *WP*, 6/17/61; RR, speech, San Antonio, 1962; *NYT*, 10/18/80, 11/17/80; RR, radio, "Health Insurance," 1–2/79, "Miscellaneous," II, 4/79, "Health Care," 10–11/79; *USNWR*, 3/1/76; *Politics Today*, 1–2/80; Brownstein, ed., *Selecting*, passim; *Time*, 5/17/76; *WP*, 2/7/72, 11/22/73; Stuart Auerbach, *WP*, 3/14/75.

6. Robert Pear, *NYT*, 4/18/82, 8/29/82, 10/1/82, 12/5/82, 1/17,24,27,31/83, 2/3,21,25/83, 3/1,30/83, 5/2/83; *NYT*, 2/19,20/81, 10/15/81, 2/5,7/82, 7/9/82, 10/2/82 (editorial), 1/29/83, 2/1/83, 2/7/83 (editorial); *WP*, 2/7/82, 5/25,28/82, 1/12/83, 2/8,25/83, 4/10/83, 4/14/83 (UPI); *WSJ*, 5/28,82, 10/18/82, 1/31/83, 2/1,25/83; *USNWR*, 9/6/82, 2/7/83; Starr, "The Laissez-Faire"; Palmer and Sawhill, eds., *The Reagan*, pp. 283, 285; *Business Week*, 2/7/83.

7. For example, *NYT*, 12/4/82, 4/2/83; *WP*, 12/4/82; Levitan and Johnson, "The Politics."

8. RR, radio, "Employment," 8–9/78, "An Accurate Thermometer," 12/78; *USNWR*, 5/31/76; RR, *Ronald*, pp. 56, 80–81; *NYT*, 7/13/80, 6/11/82, 9/30/82, 10/18/82 (AP), 11/30/82, 1/27/83; *WSJ*, 3/30/82.

9. *NYT*, 10/17/80, 9/12/82, 1/31/83; *San Francisco Chronicle*, 4/22/66; RR, speech, 1966, in Reagan for Governor speakers' manual; *USNWR*, 10/6/80; *WSJ*, 2/19/81; *WP* (UPI), 4/29/82; see *NYT*, 7/14/80, and Palmer and Sawhill, eds., *The Reagan*, p. 378.

10. *NYT*, 3/25/82, 9/8,10/82, 1/31/83; *USNWR*, 10/25/82; *WSJ*, 2/8/82.

11. Golden, "Superstar"; *NYT*, 11/26,27,28/82, 3/7/83, 4/17,22,28/83; *WP*, 11/27/82.

12. *NYT*, 10/23/81, 11/2/81, 12/2,10/81; *Atlanta Journal*, 11/1/81; *WSJ*, 10/4/82; *WP*, 8/3/82.

13. RR, *where's*, 132, 133, 138, 178, 198, 276–283; *WP*, 8/16/66, 1/13/76; letter to editor, *Rocky Mountain Journal*, 12/20/61; von Damm, *Sincerely*, p. 104;

CBS, *Face the Nation*, 5/14/78; *San Francisco Chronicle*, 6/26/79; *Business Week*, 9/15/80; *USNWR*, 3/25/68; *CBS Evening News*, 10/7/80; *NYT*, 4/23/80; *CQ*, 7/28/67; RR, *The Creative*, pp. 6, 7, 85–86; RR, radio, "Davis-Bacon Act," 6–7/78, "Davis-Bacon Act" (same title), 11–12/78; see *NYT*, 10/2/81.

14. *WSJ*, 1/30/80; *NYT*, 1/2/80, 3/22/80, 2/1/83; Robert Scheer, *LAT*, 3/6/80; *Business Week*, 3/31/80; William Serrin, *NYT*, 11/18/80; Michael P. Smith, *NYT*, 12/1/80; RR, *Ronald*, p. 73; Joann S. Lublin, *WSJ*, 11/28/80; *NYT*, 4/7/83.

15. RR, radio, "Common-Situs Picketing," 11/5/75, "Davis-Bacon Act," 6–7/78, "Davis-Bacon Act," 11–12/78, "Miscellaneous," II, 1–2/79; *NYT*, 1/4/76, 2/29/76, 11/27/80, 1/4/83 (editorial); *Business Week*, 12/1/80; *WSJ*, 11/28/80; Alter, "Reagan's."

16. *NYT*, 1/2/83, 2/11,15/83, 3/25/83; *WP*, 12/15/82.

17. RR, LOF, EGC; von Damm, *Sincerely*, pp. 60–61; Drake Mabry, *Des Moines Register*, 9/29/67; *LAT*, 3/9/76; RR, radio, "Agriculture," 4/79; *Christian Science Monitor*, 6/3/76; *WP*, 3/24/80; *WSJ*, 3/28/80; *Austin American-Statesman*, 4/19/80; RR, speech, 9/30/80, in Nevada, Iowa, text; *NYT*, 10/1/80.

18. Seth S. King, *NYT*, 4/18/82, 7/6,11/82, 10/21/82, 1/19,22/83, 2/13/83, 3/17/83; *NYT*, 8/3/82, 1/12,31/83, 5/4/83; Ward Sinclair, *WP*, 9/2/82, 1/13/83, 3/27/83; *WP*, 5/6/82, 1/12,26/83, 2/16/83, 3/4,17/83; *WSJ*, 1/31/83, 3/17/83; McMenamin, "Feeding"; *Milwaukee Journal*, 8/22/82; Dole in *Village Voice* interview, 2/5/83; Elizabeth Wear, *SAE (CQ)*, 12/30/82; *Greensboro* (N.C.) *Daily News*, 4/8/80.

19. Ward Sinclair, *WP*, 12/10,17/82, 5/2/83; Seth S. King, *NYT*, 12/10/82, 3/23/83; *WSJ*, 1/19/83.

20. Brown and Brown, *Reagan*, p. 45; *WP*, 3/5/76, 4/20/76, 6/3/76, 10/15/80; CBS, *Face the Nation*, 6/1/75, transcript; Murray, "Ronald"; *NYT*, 1/29/75; RR, radio, "Left and Right," 9/78; *Time*, 11/26/79; Witcover and Cohen, "Where's"; John Fialka, *WS*, 3/2/80.

21. RR, radio, "Cities," 7/78.

22. RR, radio, "Economy," 3,78, "Budget," 3–4/78, "Proposition 13," 7–8/78; Cutter, "The Battle"; Rudolph G. Penner, *NYT*, 2/22/81; "RR on the Issues," Reagan-Bush Committee, 10/10/80; *LAT*, 4/12/80; *CQ*, 7/28/67; *USNWR*, 10/6/80; Brownstein, ed., *Selecting*, pp. 66–67; *NYT*, 3/6/76, 7/16/80, 9/8/82, 1/31/83, 2/1,6,7/83; *WP*, 1/6/67, 3/13/67, 8/3/72, 9/25/73, 11/8/73, 6/19/80, 10/12/80, 1/30/83; see Ehrbar, "Reagan." Concerning my computations on spending per hour in 1983, see *WSJ*, 4/26/83.

23. *NYT*, 12/8/81, 1/22/82; *NYT* (UPI), 9/10/82; Patricia O'Brien, *Philadelphia Inquirer*, 9/20/81; Brownstein and Easton, *Reagan's*, p. 38; LC, *Reagan*, p. 340; Donnie Radcliffe, *WP*, 2/4/82.

24. James Reston, *NYT*, 11/11/81; Robert Pear, *NYT*, 9/27/82; *NYT*, 2/11/82, 3/3,21/82 (editorials); *NYT*, 9/17/82, 10/5,7,12,22/82; Haynes Johnson, *WP*, 10/4/81; David S. Broder, *WP*, 1/20/82; *WP*, 5/1/81, 9/8,22/82, 10/7,12/82; Rich Jaroslovsky, *WSJ*, 6/10/82; *WSJ*, 10/12/82; Andy Rooney, *DTH*, 10/5/82; *Newsweek*, 10/1/79, 11/15/82; RR, speech, *CR*, 4/20/72; *Time*, 11/17/80; *LAT*, 10/1/82; von Damm, *Sincerely*, pp. 82–84, 120–122; CBS, *Face the Nation*, 6/1/75, transcript; Brown and Brown, *Reagan*, pp. 107, 135; Ralph W. Yarborough, speech, Austin, Tex., 2/27/82; see RR, radio, "Charity," 7–8/78.

Chapter 18. Parking Stripes and Moonscapes

1. RR, TFC; on parking stripes, *SFC*, 10/15/65, and cf., "Old Pro," *Look*, 11/1/66, *Fresno Bee*, 10/10/65, and *Newsweek*, 7/21/80; Weymouth, "The Biggest."

2. *WP*, 11/21/66, 9/29,30/67, 10/10,16/67, 11/12/67, 1/18/68 (including work by William Chapman, Davis S. Broder, and Robert J. Donovan); *USNWR*, 3/25/68; *Kansas City Times*, 6/24/67; *Des Moines Register*, 10/1/67; *Christian Science Monitor*, 5/27/66; Litvak, "The Ronald"; *LAT*, 6/26/80; RR, *Ronald*, p. 42.

3. *WP*, 12/10/66, 7/3/67; *WS*, 9/13/67; *NYT*, 9/13/67; Goulden, *Korea*, pp. xxv–xxvi, 628–631.

4. Edwards, "Ronald"; Litvak, "The Ronald"; *WP*, 10/20/67, 1/18/68, 3/1/68, 5/19,21,22,27/68, 6/17,24/68, 7/21/68; *WS*, undated, probably around mid-1967; *USNWR*, 3/25/67.

5. Peter Osnos, *WP*, 10/16/71, and *WP*, 8/25/74, 5/3/75, 6/1/75; RR, speech, 3/29/72, in *CR*, 4/30/72; *LAT*, 6/1/75.

6. RR, radio, "Human Rights I," 1–2/78; RR, speech to VFW, Chicago, 8/16/80, text; *NYT*, 2/14/76; *WS*, 5/27/80, cf. *WSJ*, 11/15/79; *Denver Post* (AP), 8/24/80.

Chapter 19. Reagan and the World

1. RR, radio, "Human Rights," III, 1–2/78, "No Pay, No Vote," 4–5/78, "Conspiracy," 2–3/79; RR, speech in San Antonio, 2/21/62, text; EGC; *NYT*, 1/23/65, 3/18/80, 6/16/80, 1/30/81, 2/9/81, 10/18/81, 1/22/83, 3/9,18/83; *WP*, 4/24/80, 3/3,23/83; Goldwater, *With*, pp. 152–153, 155; RR, *where's*, p. 302; RR, *Ronald*, pp. 40–41; leaflet, Christian Anti-Communist Crusade, files of GRI; Karen Eliott House, *WSJ*, 6/3/80; *Dallas Morning News* (UPI), 4/26/81; Frederick Kempe, *WSJ*, 4/26/83; see Smith, "Reagan," Sterling, "Terrorism," Strobe Talbott, *Time*, 6/9/80, Richard A. Allen, *WP*, 1/23/83, and Arthur Schlesinger, Jr., *WSJ*, 3/17/83.

2. RR, radio, "The Russian Wheat Deal," 10/29/75, and "Soviet Trade," 7–8/79; Bill Snyder, *Springfield* (Mo.) *Daily News*, 10/12/68; *LAT*, 9/11/79, cf. *SFC*, 9/11/79; *St. Petersburg Times*, 9/20/79; *WP*, 1/8/80; *Time*, 6/30/80; Howell Raines, *NYT*, 10/23/80.

3. *Fresno Bee*, 11/14/79; *NYT*, 2/29/80, 6/2/80, 7/18/80; RR, speech, 3/17/80, in *Human Events*, 4/5/80; *WS*, 1/8/80, 10/19/80; *Kansas City Times*, 5/9/75; RR, radio, "CIA," 3–4/79; *WP*, 2/6/77, 2/16/80; *Des Moines Register*, 9/29/74; RR on *CBS Morning News*, 4/9/80; Ward Just, *WP*, 12/8/67; *USNWR*, 3/25/68.

4. Manning, "America's"; George C. Wilson, *WP*, 9/17/82; Richard Halloran, *NYT*, 2/9/81, 12/18/81, 1/21/82, 7/19/82, 9/17/82, 6/24/83; *NYT*, 12/10/80, 3/31/82; Walter Pincus and Fred Hiatt, *WP*, 6/23/83; see Walter Pincus, *WP*, 2/7/82, and Klare, "An Army."

5. Gerald F. Seib, *WSJ*, 3/5/82; *NYT*, 2/1/82, 4/28/82; Suzanne Garment, *WSJ*, 7/16/82; Russell Watson and David C. Martin, *Newsweek*, 11/8/82; see Taubman, "Casey."

6. *DTH* (WP), 5/22/81, (Knight-Ridder) 1/2/83; *NYT*, 12/2/81, 1/31/82, 2/7/82, 8/3/82 (AP), 8/8/82, 10/15/82; *WP*, 11/18/81, 1/24/82, 4/29/82 (UPI), 8/13/82 (editorial), 8/15/82 (letters to editor); *CR* 1983, pp. S2052–2074; Christopher J. Dodd, *NYT*, op-ed, 4/9/82; *Business Week*, 3/14/83.

7. *WP*, 1/28/80, 3/1/80, 8/12/82; Martin Schram, *WP*, 10/19/80; *NYT*, 1/29,30/80, 4/4,17,20/82, 8/12/82; Richard Burt, *NYT*, 10/19/80; Robert Scheer, *LAT*, 6/26/80; *CQ*, 10/4/80; *USNWR*, 10/6/80; *Business Week*, 3/31/80; RR, speech, 3/29/72 in *CR*, 4/20/72; RR, radio, "Castro," 7–8/78, "Cuba," 7–8/78, "Brainwashing," II, 9/78, and "Cuban Conditions," 10–11/79; RR article in *CR*, 1/25/75; William F. Buckley, *WP*, 3/26/82; *New York Post* (UPI), 3/7/83; Don Oberdorfer and Patrick E. Tyler, *WP*, 5/8/83 (on Haig and blockades); RR in *Reader's Digest* interview, Feb. 1982; see Goldwater, *With*, pp. 148–149, 151.

8. Grenada: Patrick E. Tyler, *WP*, 2/27/83; Edward Cody, *WP*, 4/22/83; *Newsweek*, 4/11/83; "Grenadian Menace," *Nation*, 4/16/83; *NYT* (AP), 4/5/83. Caribbean Basin Initiative: *e.g.*, *NYT*, 2/25/82, 5/5,22/82, 2/23/83; *WP*, 6/13/82.

9. RR, *San Diego Union*, 3/7/75.

10. Spencer Rich, *WP*, 5/14/76; *WP*, 3/10/76, 4/22,24/76, 5/3,5/76, 6/6/76, 8/13,17,26/77, 9/7/77, 1/24/78, 4/20/78, 3/5/80; *USNWR*, 3/31/76; *NYT*, 3/3/76, 3/22/80; *LAT*, 8/12/77; *Sanford Journal Tribune*, 8/12/77; *Atlanta Constitution*, 1/18/80.

11. Anthony Lewis, *NYT*, 4/28/83; *NYT*, 1/24/81, 2/20/81, 5/24,30/82, 7/27/82, 1/22/83, 2/13,27/83, 3/1,5,9,25/83, 3/28/83 (Reuters), 4/22/83, 5/5/83; *WP*, 7/28/82, 2/4/83, 3/5/83, 4/18,22,28/83; Don Oberdorfer and Patrick E. Tyler, *WP*, 5/8/83.

12. *NYT*, 3/24,25/82, 4/25/82, 12/19/82, 1/8/83, 3/23/83; Christopher Dickey, *WP*, 1/3/83; *WP*, 10/21/82, 1/2/83; Nairn, "The Guns."

13. Philip Taubman, *NYT*, 3/10/82, 11/1/82, 12/3/82; Stuart Taylor, Jr., *NYT*, 12/24/81; Robert Lindsey, *NYT*, 1/18/82; Raymond Bonner, *NYT*, 4/7/83; Leslie H. Gelb, *NYT*, 4/8/83; *NYT*, 11/30/80, 12/1,5,10,15/80, 11/19/81, 12/3/81, 3/13/82, 4/10,15/82, 7/8/82, 10/7/82, 1/23/83, 2/10,17,25/83, 3/6,18,20,23,29/83, 4/3,6,11,13–15,24,27,30/83, 5/4,5/83; Jackson Diehl, *WP*, 11/6/81, 3/24/82; Don Oberdorfer and Patrick E. Tyler, *WP*, 2/14/82; *WP*, 12/10/81, 7/8/82, 1/26/83, 4/15,20,28/83; *Newsweek*, 11/8/82; George C. Cotter, *NYT*, op-ed, 3/17/81; Payne, "'Baby Doc'"; *Business Week*, 4/18/83; Robert D. Tomsho, *SAE*, 4/10/83; Riding, "The Central"; see White, "The Problem," and Riding, "Revolution."

14. In November 1980 I wrote Senator Frank Church, then chairman of the Senate Foreign Relations Committee, reviewing the content of Reagan's 1978 broadcast and requesting a copy of what Reagan in that broadcast described as the "12-page report to Congress on Korea" from the State Department. Church sent me "Report on Korea 1977," dated December 1977, 11 not 12 pages long. Although this is the report Reagan was reviewing, discrepancies suggest either that he saw a somewhat different version of it or that he reviewed it inaccurately (or perhaps both).

Twice he directly quoted from it. "The report points out 'the sizable military advantage' the North [North Korea] has over the South [South Korea]," Reagan said. The report Church sent me said the North Korean Army had "a sizable advantage . . . in armored personnel carriers, multiple rocket launchers and artillery," but that the military forces deployed on the ground in the two nations "are roughly comparable." (Reagan also, not directly quoting, said: "In tanks, armored personnel carriers, rocket launchers, artillery, and so forth, the South is outnumbered more than two to one." The report said what I have just quoted about the carriers, launchers, and artillery, but that the North Koreans had "a 2 to 1 edge in tanks.") Reagan directly quoted the report again:

"The report," he said, "goes farther and says steps must be taken to 'replace the combat capability of the U.S. ground forces we are going to withdraw.'" The report Church sent me says variantly: "We have reached agreement with the ROK (Republic of Korea) concerning the augmentation of its defenses to replace the capabilities of the U.S. ground combat forces which will be withdrawn."

Immediately after Reagan's statement on the radio that the report said steps had to be taken to replace the withdrawn capability, he continued: "We must build up South Korea's stores of ammunition and equipment, send more and better tanks and anti-tank weapons; there must be an increase in South Korea's capability to utilize sophisticated weaponry and still—with all that— they would need our active participation if war should come." The State Department report recommended everything Reagan in this sentence said it did up to his closing phrase, but nowhere in the report is it stated that South Korea would require "the active participation" of the U.S. if war should come. That must have been Reagan's own statement.

LAT, 1/25/68; *NYT*, 1/31/68, 5/8/76; Boyarsky, *The Rise*, pp. 30–31; RR, *Ronald*, pp. 45–46; RR, radio, "Korea," 2–3/78; letter, RD to Frank Church, 11/11/80; undated memorandum, Frank Church to RD, received 12/4/80, enclosing "Report on Korea 1977."

15. Henry Scott Stokes (whose work is particularly important in understanding the situation in South Korea), *NYT*, 8/9,14/80, 10/25/80, 12/7,12,14,26,27/80, 2/2/81, 3/3,4/82, 5/30/82, 7/15/82, 12/16,17,24/82; *NYT*, 8/13/80, 11/13/80, 1/24,25,27/81, 2/1,3/81, 3/30/82, 12/27,29/82, 1/11/83; Michael Getler, *WP*, 4/1/82; *WP*, 4/27/82, 2/26/83; Donald L. Ranard, *DTH*, (*LAT*), 12/29/82; *SAE* (AP), 8/16/80; see Chinoy, "Chun."

16. *WP*, 10/9,24/71, 8/20/80; Rowland Evans and Robert Novak, *WP*, 3/5/72; LC, *WP*, 6/1/75; *Des Moines Register*, 2/23/72; RR, speech, 3/29/72, in *CR*, 4/20/72, and cf. *WP*, 3/10/72; RR, radio, "China," 4–5/78, "Normalization," 7/78, "China," 12/78, "Taiwan," II, 1–2/79, "Taiwan," III, 1–2/79, "Human Rights," 1–2/79, "Taiwan's Future," 3–4/79; *WSJ*, 11/6/80; *SAE*, 11/18/80; Philip Geyelin, *WP*, 9/1/80; *NYT*, 8/21,25–27/80, 10/19/80, 7/19/82; Leslie L. Gelb, *NYT*, 3/30/83; *Houston Post*, 9/28/80; *WS*, 1/30/80. On Deaver-Hannaford: Robert Scheer, *LAT*, 6/26/80; *CQ*, 10/4/80; *WP*, 6/19/80; Hannaford, *The Reagans*, p. 156n. For Goldwater on Taiwan, cf. Goldwater, *With*, pp. 241, 246–247, 250.

17. *NYT*, 11/12/81, 1/12,13/82, 3/25/82, 4/14/82, 5/5,9,25/82, 7/6,17,29/82, 8/17,18,29/82, 8/17,18/82, 10/18,28/82, 11/18/82, 12/1/82 (Reuters), 12/27/82, 3/18/83, 5/3/83; *WP*, 2/13/82 (UPI), 8/18,19/82, 10/19/82, 2/23/83; Richard Nixon, *NYT* (op-ed), 10/11/82; William Safire, *NYT*, 10/18/82.

18. *NYT*, 10/12/81, 11/12,28/81, 12/11,12/81, 1/14,31/82, 2/17–19/83; *WP*, 12/6,8/81, 2/10,20,24/83; *WSJ*, 2/18/83; *Newsweek*, 11/8/82; *Time*, 12/21/81.

19. *NYT*, 1/29/81, 11/5/81, 1/20/83; interview with Haig in *First Monday*, May 1982.

20. RR, radio, "South Africa," 1–2/79, and cf., concerning the views of Ernest Lefever, Alexander Cockburn, *WSJ*, 2/12/81; Joseph Lelyveld, *NYT*, 10/30/80, 6/24,27/82, 12/6/82, 1/5/83, 3/17/83, 5/8/83, and Lelyveld, "Oppenheimer"; Anthony Lewis, *NYT*, 5/8/83; *NYT*, 8/21/82, 10/21/82 (AP), 1/11/83; *WP*, 4/25/82, 7/31/82, 1/23/83, 3/17/83; June Kronholz, *WSJ*, 12/31/82.

21. RR, radio, "Rhodesia," 5–6/78, "Nigeria," 7–8/79; Robert Lindsey,

LAT, 6/4/76; *WP,* 4/29/76, 5/1/76, 6/4,6,8/76, 8/5/82, 10/7/82; Jay Ross, *WP,* 2/18/82, 3/5/82, 4/18/82, 8/5/82, 10/7/82, 2/26/83, 3/27,30/83, 4/27/83; June Kronholz, *WSJ,* 9/10/82; *WSJ,* 3/24/81, 4/19/83; Davidow, "Zimbabwe"; Smiley, "The Cracks"; Manning, "So Far"; Burns, "A Delicate"; Gordimer, "Letter"; Donovan, "A Continent."

22. Joseph Lelyveld, *NYT,* 1/12,18/81, 7/15/82, 9/25/82, 10/17/82, 11/21/82, and 1/19/83, and Lelyveld, "Inside"; Anthony Lewis, *NYT,* 2/3/83; *NYT,* 7/14/82, 8/26/82, 11/18/82, 11/22/82 (AP), 2/9/83 (UPI), 2/16/83, 4/22/83; Jay Ross, *WP,* 10/31/82, 1/11/83; *WP,* 10/7/81, 12/10/82, 4/22/83; June Kronholz, *WSJ,* 10/20/82.

23. *LAT,* 1/6/76; *NYT,* 1/8/76, 10/1/81, 7/1/82, 9/26/82, 10/6/82, 11/11/82, 4/14/83; Jay Ross, *WP,* 1/6–8/83, 5/4/83; *WP,* 1/6/76, 11/20/82; Anthony Lewis, *NYT,* 1/25/81.

24. Lelyveld, "Oppenheimer"; Alan Cowell, *NYT,* 3/28/83; Dorothy Gilliam, *WP,* 10/18/81; *NYT,* 8/8/82, 4/2/83 (Reuters); Jay Ross, *WP,* 3/3/82; *WP,* 2/27/82, 9/24/82, 10/15/82; *WSJ,* 3/21/81; *Houston Post,* 3/25/81; see also sources in note 20 above.

25. Jackson Diehl, *WP,* 9/14/82; Warren Hoge, *NYT,* 1/14/81, 11/25/82, 12/1/82, 4/10/83; *NYT,* 12/2,3/82; *Time,* 11/29/82.

26. RR, radio, "Argentina," 10–11/78, "Common Sense from a Neighbor," 8/79; John B. Oakes, *NYT,* 5/15/79; Juan de Onis, *NYT,* 3/27/76, 4/3,6/76, 7/28/76, 3/25/77, 7/10/77, 11/17/77, 8/17/80, 3/8/81; Edward Schumacher, *NYT,* 11/11/80, 6/24/82, 9/11/82, 11/6,7/82, 4/29/83, 5/9/83; *NYT,* 3/23, 29/76, 6/27/76, 1/13/81, 6/4/81, 4/3,16/82, 7/13/82, 8/12/82 (Reuters), 5/9/83; *WP,* 4/29/82, 4/29/83, 5/6/83; Agostino Bono, *WSJ,* 4/5/76; Everett G. Martin, *WSJ,* 4/30/80, 7/30/80, 4/17/81; *London Times,* 4/30/83.

27. RR, radio, "Letelier," I and II, 11–12/78; "Chile," 8/79; Jackson Diehl, *WP,* 3/12,27/82, 9/12,16/82, 3/12,24/83; *WP,* 3/5/82, 4/29/82, 10/13/82; Patrick E. Tyler, *WP,* 2/23/82; Edward Schumacher, *NYT,* 12/6/82, 1/2/83, 4/25/83; *NYT,* 3/11/82, 3/11/82 (UPI), 8/30/82, 9/12/82 (AP); *WSJ,* 9/15/80; Anthony Lewis, *NYT,* 2/4/82; *SAE* (AP), 12/1/80; *Daily Texan* (Austin, Tex.: UPI), 3/11/81. But on Allende, see Geyer, *Buying,* pp. 96–98, 111–115.

28. Jeff Gerth, *NYT,* 2/4/83; *NYT,* 6/9/82, 2/24/83; *WP,* 1/21/83, 2/24/83, 3/4/83; Robert J. McCloskey, *WP,* 2/20/83; William Safire, *NYT,* 8/19/82; see Gardner, "Selling."

29. *NYT,* 1/11,14/80, 7/17/80, 10/19,20/80, 11/7,9/80; *WS,* 1/11,31/80, 10/19,20/80; RR in *WP,* 8/15/79; Martin Schram, *WP,* 1/10/80; *WP,* 1/10,11,25/80, 8/12/82; *Boston Globe,* 1/13/80; *St. Louis Globe Democrat,* 1/11/80; *Nashville Tennesseean,* 1/31/80; Louis Berney, *Rutland* (Vt.) *Herald,* 1/19/80; *WSJ,* 2/4/81.

30. *USNWR,* 10/6/80; RR, radio, "Palestine," 4/79, "Israel," I and II, 10–11/79; RR in *WP,* 8/15/79; Hedrick Smith, *NYT,* 5/25/80; Hedrick Smith, *SAE,* 11/17/80; *NYT,* 1/7/81; Rothbard, "The Two"; Klare, "Is Exxon"; George C. Wilson, *WP,* 5/27/82.

31. *WP,* 5/10/80, 10/29/81; George C. Wilson, *WP,* 10/5/81; *NYT,* 5/10/80, 3/7/81, 10/1,18,29/81; Richard Halloran, *NYT,* 4/4/83; *Time,* 6/30/80; *Corpus Christi Caller* (AP), 4/17/81; Joseph Kraft, *WP,* 10/6/81; Philip Geyelin, *WP,* 10/12/81.

32. *SFC,* 11/15/79, cf. *LAT,* 6/26/80; *NYT,* 10/18/81; Leslie H. Gelb, *NYT,* 3/7/82.

33. *NYT*, 6/7,12,28/82, 8/2,3,6,13/82, 2/9,11/83; *WP*, 6/28/82, 7/19,27/82, 8/4/82, 8/21/82 (AP), 9/3/82; Wright, "Israeli" (Weinberger on Sharon); see Thomas L. Friedman, *NYT*, 9/26/82, and *NYT*, 12/15,16,22/81, 9/17/82.

34. *NYT*, 11/25/81, 9/2,3,6,22,29,30/82, 10/1,20/82, 11/2/82, 1/8/83, 2/8,23,24/83, 3/2/83, 4/9,11,12,19,20,29/83, 5/7,8,10–12,14,16–18/83, 7/1, 7/83; Jacob K. Javits, *NYT* (letters to editor), 11/22/82; *WP*, 8/26/82, 9/26/82, 10/1,4/82, 11/4/82, 12/28/82, 1/16,30/83, 2/25/83, 3/17/83, 4/21,24/83; Clement J. Zablocki, *WP* op-ed, 10/3/82; Karen Elliott House, *WSJ*, 4/15,20/83, 5/6/83; David Ignatius, *WSJ*, 10/11/82, 4/12/83; *WSJ*, 10/11/82, 2/23,25/83, 3/17/83; *Time*, 5/2/83; see *NYT*, 4/1,2,14,17/83.

Chapter 20. Reagan and Nuclear War

1. Rita Dallas, *WP*, 2/11/83; Weisner, "George"; Bernard Weintraub, *NYT*, 4/19/82; Kennedy and Hatfield, *Freeze!* p. 111; Schell, "The Fate"; *CBS Evening News with Dan Rather*, 3/29/82, transcript (Meese on the Hallmark MX); LC, *WP*, 4/18/83 (RR on some of his best friends). I read a report of Reagan's joke about the vice president surviving in the *New York Times* "Briefing" on its "Washington Talk" page, but did not clip it.

2. Thomas Oliphant, *Boston Globe*, 5/24/83 (quoting Caldicott, who also confirmed the Reagan remark to me); *USNWR*, 7/28/80; *Boston Globe*, 1/13/80; RR, speech, Chicago, 8/18/80, text; RR, radio, "SALT II," 2–3/78, and "Salt Talks," 7/78; *Eugene* (Ore.) *Register-Guard*, 3/3/79; *Manchester Union Leader*, undated; RR, statement, Reagan-Bush Committee, 10/10/80; *WP*, 4/17/77, 10/11,12/80; RR, speech, Boston, 8/20/80, text; *WS*, 10/17,19,20/80; John J. Fialka, *WS*, 10/21/80; *WSJ*, 9/3/80; Michaels, "Why"; *NYT*, 1/31/76, 8/19/80, 10/18,20/80; Adam Clymer, *NYT*, 11/9/80; Philip Geyelin, *SAE* (*WP*), 11/14/80; *Time*, 4/12/82; Richard Halloran, *NYT*, 5/30/82; *Common Cause*, 8/82, p. 47.

3. *NYT*, 2/19/81, 10/3/81, 6/26/83; George C. Wilson, *WP*, 9/18/81, 11/28/82; Walter Mossberg, *WSJ*, 1/12/81, 2/8/82, 1/31/83; Michael Getler, *WP*, 12/2/82; *Newsweek*, 3/16/81, 6/8/81; *USNWR*, 9/13/82; Ross Corson in *Progressive*, 9/82; *Business Week*, 2/14/83; see Smith, "How Many," Seligman, "Why Cuts," White, "Weinberger," and Drew, "A Political."

4. Richard Halloran, *NYT*, 3/9/82, 7/23/82, 3/22/83; *NYT*, 1/21/82 (editorial), 3/14,23/82, 5/2/82, 11/30/82, 12/5/82, 2/20/83 (AP); *SAE* (AP), 2/9/82; *WSJ*, 2/9/82, 12/3/82; *Time*, 6/28/82; *WP*, 5/6/82; Drew Middleton, *NYT*, 2/5/82.

5. Rosenberg, "The Origins"; RR, radio, "Salt Talks," 7/78; Kennedy and Hatfield, *Freeze!*, p. 79.

6. Rosenberg, "Nuclear"; Richard Burt, *NYT*, 1/6/78, 8/7/80; Robert Scheer, *LAT*, 1/24/80, 8/15/82; Scheer, *With*, pp. 12, 29–30, 33, 60, 140, 241; Pipes, *U.S.-Soviet*, pp. 135–168; *NYT*, 8/21/81, 11/4/81, 4/18/82, 5/25/82; Arkin, "Why"; Hodding Carter, *WSJ*, 4/8/82; Richard Halloran (the leading reporter on U.S. defense guidance plans), *NYT*, 5/22,30/82, 6/4,17,19,21/82, 7/22/82, 8/10,24/82, 2/1/83, 3/22/83; Richard C. Gross, a UPI dispatch (provided to me by the author), 1/16/83; George C. Wilson, *WP*, 10/5/81, 6/19/82, 8/25/82; Charles Fenyvesi, *WP*, 4/11/82; Cox, *Russian*, pp. 92–93; Draper, "Dear"; Gray, "Nuclear"; James Lardner, *WP*, 5/14/82; *Time*, 3/29/82; Michael Getler, *WP*, 11/10/82; Thompson, "A Letter"; Zacharias, "Common."

7. *NYT,* 10/21,22/81, 11/5,6/81, 3/11/83 (UPI), and see Drew Middleton, *NYT,* 11/18/81; *WP,* 10/16,21/81, 11/6,12/81; Cox, *Russian,* pp. 20, 115, 127, 140–143; Gray, "Nuclear"; Powers, "Choosing"; Michael Getler, *WP,* 11/10/82; Walter Pincus, *WP,* 3/14/83; Jack Anderson, *WP,* 10/12/80, 5/22/83; Report of the Secretary-General, *Nuclear,* pp. 121–124; *DTH* (*Newsday*), 11/29/82.

8. John J. Fialka, *WSJ,* 3/26/82; *WSJ,* 3/26/82; *Newsweek,* 4/5/82; *WP* (AP), 11/9/82.

9. Cox, *Russian,* p. 28; Palme, "The Slick"; *SAE,* 12/20/80; *San Antonio Light,* 12/20/80; McNeil-Lehrer Report, PBS, 12/4/80 (Church); *WP,* 10/20, 21/81, 3/19/82, 4/30/83 (AP), 5/18/83; PBS special, 10/13/82 (Kennan); *NYT,* 8/23/82, 2/16/83, 5/18/83 (AP); *Business Week,* 4/11/83; Arthur Macy Cox, *NYT* (op-ed), 11/2/82; Thompson, *Beyond,* pp. 22–23.

10. In his 1978 broadcast Reagan quoted, as well as Krylov, Rear Admiral Vasili Shelyag, a career propagandist for the Soviet armed forces, and General Aleksandr Altunin, the Soviet deputy minister of defense for civil defense. Reagan quoted Shelyag as denying that everything living on earth would be annihilated in a nuclear war; Krylov as saying that "Victory will be on the side of world socialism"; and Altunin on civil defense and victory.

In an article in the newspaper *Sovietskaya Rossiya* in 1969, Krylov, who died in 1972, had written that Americans "actively prepare for a new world war. . . . They are preparing to plunge mankind into a rocket-nuclear war." He had characterized statements in the west that there would be no victors in a future nuclear war as attempts to "lull" the other side and then had said, in the passage from which Reagan apparently drew: "Victory in war, if the imperialists succeed in starting it, will be on the side of world socialism."

At the time U.S. planners were quoted as doubting that Krylov had spoken for Soviet political leaders, and subsequently Soviet spokesmen said in effect that they could not control their generals any better than the U.S. could and that the generals said such things to keep up their troops' morale.

Kennedy and Hatfield, *Freeze!* pp. xiii, 111, 131; Jacob Javits, *NYT* (op-ed), 5/28/83; Krylov, "Strategic"; *WP,* 11/25/69, 2/16/75, 3/27/83; RR, radio, "Spaceships," 3/73, "Salt Talks," 7/78; *Normal* (Ill.) *Vidette,* 4/7/79; Scheer, *With,* p. 31; *Business Week,* 3/31/80; *NYT,* 4/15/63, 2/23/64, 11/19/67, 8/31/69, 9/12/69, 2/11/72, 11/4/81; Bialer, "The Men"; see RD, "Ronald."

11. Other examples of U.S. leaders' positions on a first strike:

Truman confided to his diaries either draft plans or fantasies—one cannot tell which—about destroying the Soviet Union and China with atomic bombs if they did not fold up the Korean War. A new study by a historian at the University of Houston, David Alan Rosenberg, shows that from 1947 to 1950 it was U.S. policy "to strike the first blow if necessary." In 1950 the NSC rejected preventive war, but allowed for nuclear attack "as soon as we are attacked, and, if possible, before the Soviet blow is actually delivered." In 1953 Eisenhower stated in a memorandum to Secretary of State John Foster Dulles that in the event of an indefinitely prolonged U.S.-Soviet nuclear competition threatening the U.S. with a first strike, "we would be forced to consider whether or not our duty to future generations did not require us to initiate war at the most propitious moment we could designate." In 1954 Eisenhower rejected preventive war. In 1956 he provided the joint chiefs with assumptions he had approved that "if general war should be forced upon us, the U.S. will employ atomic weapons from the outset of hostilities," and this requirement of a nuclear response in a general war was incorporated into the military's plans.

Kaplan also discovered that in 1961 a study was presented to President Kennedy showing how the U.S. could successfully commit a first strike against the U.S.S.R. Doing it was rejected.

The memorandum McNamara sent to Kennedy was dated just one month after the Cuban missile crisis. McNamara told Scheer that "one possible explanation" for the Soviets' installation of nuclear missiles in Cuba was that they "may have heard talk that we were trying to achieve a first-strike capability" and may have believed it when they looked at "the substantial numerical superiority" of U.S. nuclear forces. "I have no doubt," McNamara said, "but that the Soviets thought we were trying to achieve a first-strike capability. . . . If I had been the Soviet secretary of defense, I'd have been worried as hell about the imbalance of force. . . . It would have just scared the hell out of me!"

"Counterforce" is a misleading term in the nuclear lexicon. It sounds as if it should mean the use of nuclear weapons in retaliation. Actually it means the capability to attack the military force of an adversary nation, and according to some nuclear logicians it is closely tied to first-strike doctrine. A former official in the office of the secretary of defense, Earl C. Ravenal, explains: "Counterforce and first nuclear strike are mutually dependent. . . . Counterforce targeting implies (at the strategic level) a first strike, indeed a preemptive attack, because a second strike against the enemy's missiles is useless since our missiles, for the most part, would hit empty holes." It appears that both superpowers are now close to developing strategic counterforce capabilities. The U.S. has been drifting in this direction since the early 1970s, when Secretary of Defense Schlesinger spoke openly of a "selective first strike" policy.

Michael Getler, *WP*, 10/8/80, 2/10/82; *DMN* (AP), 5/13/81; Robert Scheer, *LAT*, 9/29/81; *WP*, 6/21/82; Krylov, "Strategic"; *NYT*, 9/3/67, 11/7/81; Cox, *Russian*, pp. 17–28, 70–71, 223; Scheer, *With*, pp. 10, 31, 214–217, 220; Reeves, "How"; Kennedy and Hatfield, *Freeze!* pp. 82, 104–105; RD, *The Politician*, pp. 371–372; Rosenberg, "The Origins"; Kaplan, *The Wizards*, pp. 132–133; Ravenal, "No"; Roger Molander, *WP*, 3/21/82; Jack Anderson, *WP*, 5/19/83.

12. Cox, *Russian*, pp. 9, 27, and Arthur Macy Cox, *NYT* (op-ed), 5/17/83; Robert Scheer, *LAT*, 9/29/81; *NYT*, 5/6/82, 3/17/83; *Newsweek*, 5/30/83; *WP*, 4/11/82, 7/13/82, 5/18/83; Zacharias, *et al.*, "Common"; see *NYT*, 4/8/83.

13. Under Eisenhower, it was explicit although secret U.S. policy to "consider nuclear weapons to be as available for use as other munitions." Eisenhower told the joint chiefs that if nuclear war broke out in western Europe, the U.S. would use tactical nuclear weapons, and he instructed the military to assume their use in less-than-general conflicts "whenever it is of military advantage to do so." As the Soviets acquired the nuclear capability to destroy the U.S., the American policy of "massive retaliation" was abandoned, but in 1967, under the euphemism of "flexible response," the willingness of the U.S. and NATO to start nuclear war over western Europe was explicitly approved as basic policy.

Bundy, *et al.*, "Nuclear"; Kennan, *Memoirs, 1925–1950*, pp. 471–476, passim; Rosenberg, "The Origins"; Kaiser, *et al.*, "Nuclear"; statement by Gen. David C. Jones, chairman, joint chiefs of staff, in 1982, quoted in *Foreign*

Affairs, summer, 1982, at p. 1173; Richard C. Gross, UPI dispatch, 1/16/83 (provided by the author); *NYT,* 4/7/82, 6/17/82, 4/26/83, and cf., 11/4/81; U.S. Catholic Bishops, "The Pastoral"; Scheer, *With,* pp. 240–241; *WP,* 6/21/82; *SAE* (*NYT*), 3/9/81.

14. MX characteristics: *NYT,* 6/17,24/83; Michael Getler, *WP,* 6/4/83; Kennedy and Hatfield, *Freeze!* p. 106; cf., *NYT,* 10/9/81, *WP,* 2/24/82, and Chuck Bell, *SAE,* 6/30/82. Carter and MX: see, *e.g.,* LC, *Reagan,* pp. 387–393. Basing mode: national press, 1978–1983 (a vast literature). Reaganists' rationales: RR, *WP* (op-ed), 11/23/82; Molly Ivins, *DTH,* 11/23/82; Robert Scheer, *LAT,* 1/24/80; Jack Anderson, *New York Post,* 4/19/83. Soviet views: Scheer, *With,* p. 78; *NYT,* 11/23/82; *WP,* 11/24/82. U.S. views: Thompson and Smith, eds., *Protest,* p. 129; Scheer, *LAT,* 4/11/82; *WP,* 4/8,21/83, 5/17–19/83; Stansfield Turner, *DTH,* 3/29/81; *NYT,* 4/13/83 and editorials on 5/25,29/83; Arthur Macy Cox, *NYT* (op-ed), 11/2/82, 5/17/83, and cf., Cox, *Russian,* p. 20; Paul C. Warnke and Alan B. Sherr, *NYT* (op-ed), 5/29/83; Gerald C. Smith, *NYT* (op-ed), 5/23/83, and cf., Gerald C. Smith, *Newsweek* ("My Turn"), 1/31/83; Michael Getler, *WP,* 10/8/80; Niles Lathem, *New York Post,* 11/29/82 (quoting Weinberger on MX not first-strike weapon); McGeorge Bundy, *NYT,* (op-ed), 4/17/83; and cf., Anthony Lewis, *NYT,* 10/5/81, Tom Wicker, *NYT,* 10/6/81, 5/14/82, 4/15/83, 5/13,14/83, and John B. Oakes, *NYT,* 10/21/80.

15. Kenneth Reich, *LAT,* 4/16/76; RR in *WSJ,* 2/13/76; Walter S. Mossberg, *WSJ,* 6/3/83; Leslie H. Gelb, *NYT,* 9/2/82; *WP,* 11/18/81, 2/16/83, 6/11/83; Charles Mohr, *NYT,* 2/27/83; *USNWR,* 6/13/83; *NYT,* 10/19/82, 2/16/83, 4/17/83 (AP); James M. Perry, *WSJ,* 12/22/81; Honan, "Return"; *Newsweek,* 1/3/83; Cox, *Russian,* pp. 126, 146; Kennedy and Hatfield, *Freeze!* p. 109; *WSJ,* 4/18/83; Richard Halloran, *NYT,* 8/4/82; David C. Morrison, *DTH* (*Newsday*), 2/16/83.

16. *Business Week,* 11/24/80; Richard Burt, *NYT,* 11/25/80; *Time,* 7/27/81; *WP,* 11/12/81, 9/12/82; *NYT,* 11/12/81, 8/13/82 (AP); Hans Bethe, testimony to Senate Foreign Relations Committee, printed in *New York Review,* 6/10/82; Richard Halloran, *NYT,* 5/30/82, 2/6/83; Drew Middleton, *NYT,* 2/15/83; Philip M. Boffey, *NYT,* 7/13/82; Scheer, *With,* pp. 32, 73; Walter S. Mossberg, *WSJ,* 5/18,19/83; *WSJ,* 12/9/82; Kennedy and Hatfield, *Freeze!* p. 107; Arthur Macy Cox, *NYT* (op-ed), 12/2/82; *Business Week,* 5/16/83; Thomas J. Downey, *NYT* (op-ed), 2/11/82.

17. RR, radio, "War," 3–4/78; Biddle, "Neutron"; *WP,* 4/24/80; "Neutron Warhead," Reagan-Bush Committee release, 10/80; *Boston Globe,* 3/30/80; *NYT,* 5/6/80, 2/15/81 (Reuters); Cohen, *The Truth,* pp. 30, 38, 68; *SAE,* 2/6/81 (*NYT*), 2/11/81 (*WP*); *WSJ,* 2/4/81; Walter Pincus, *WP,* 12/11/81, 8/3/82, 5/29/83; Cohen, *The Truth,* pp. 113–125; cf., Paine, "Reagatomics."

18. *NYT,* 8/21/80, 9/7/80, 10/3,8,11/81, 11/10/81, 4/8/82, 6/17/82; *WSJ,* 10/29/81, 3/2/82; *WP,* 10/11,29/81, 11/10,18/81, 12/4/81, 4/15/82, 6/17/82, 11/30/82; *Business Week,* 2/21/83; *USNWR,* 9/13/82; Drew, "A Reporter"; Paine, "The Selling." On Stealth see also Grambart, "The Stealth"; *WSJ,* 3/17/82; *WP,* 5/5/82; Drew Middleton, *NYT,* 5/13/83.

19. *SAE* (*WP*), 12/27/80; *NYT,* 6/22/82, 3/3,24,26,27,30/83; LC, *WP,* 3/28/83; Richard Halloran, *NYT,* 6/6,22/82, 10/17/82, 5/18/83; Richard C. Gross, UPI dispatch, 1/16/83; Patrick E. Tyler, *WP,* 4/3/83; Judith Miller, *NYT,* 10/29/82; *WP,* 6/27/82, 7/5/82; *Business Week,* 6/20/83; and see, *e.g.,* Edward

Teller, *NYT* (op-ed), 3/30/83, Aldridge, "Missile," Tonge, "The 'Space Beam,'" Jastrow, "The New," and Karas, "The Star."

20. Charles Mohr, *NYT*, 2/27/83; *WP*, 11/18/81, 3/19/83; *Time*, 11/29/82; *Business Week*, 5/16/83; Dusko Doder, *WP*, 1/24/83; letter to editor, *NYT*, 6/8/83, from commentator for Novosti Press Agency, U.S.S.R.; Thompson, *Beyond*, p. 17; *NYT* (AP), 6/17/83; Richard Burt, *WP* (Insight), 4/10/83; Michael Getler, *WP*, 3/17/82. On Soviet SS-20s in Siberia, see, *e.g.*, Karen Elliott House, *WSJ*, 6/16/83.

21. RR, radio, "Defence IV," 2–3/78, "SALT Talks," 7/78; Santa Rosa Press Democrat (quoting RR on civil defense), 11/1/78, cited in Brownstein, ed., *Selecting*, p. 100; David Binder, *NYT*, 1/3/77; *NYT*, 10/9/72, 3/17,30/82; Drew Middleton, *NYT*, 10/11/76; John F. Burns, *NYT*, 6/11/82; Judith Miller, *NYT*, 4/4/82, 6/10/82; Kennedy and Hatfield, *Freeze!* pp. 86, 87, 90–93; Scheer, *With*, pp. 21–26, 105–106; Leaning, *et al.*, "Programs"; *WP*, 1/29/82, 3/30/82, 4/1,23/82, 7/22/82; Bernard Weintraub, *NYT*, 4/8/82; Sen. William Proxmire in *CR* 1982, p. S12654; Howard L. Rosenberg and Howard Kohn, *SAE*, 4/25/82; Robert Scheer, *LAT*, 9/29/81, 1/16/82; "Inside Story," PBS, 10/13/82, including a broadcast on Soviet TV; Tom Wicker, *NYT*, 8/1/82; Cox, *Russian*, p. 102.

22. Schell, "The Fate"; Flora Lewis, *NYT*, 4/4/82; *Time*, 3/29/82; Richard Burt, *WP* (Insight), 4/10/83; Richard Burt, *NYT*, 9/27/80; Judith Miller, *NYT*, 2/28/82, 3/22/82; Paine, "Reagatomics"; Meg Greenfield, *WP*, 4/14/82; Draper, "How"; Anthony Lewis, *NYT*, 12/10/81; Zacharias, *et al.*, "Common Sense"; Jerome B. Weisner, *NYT* (op-ed), 4/12/83; Seymour Melman, *NYT*, 10/17/80; *Bulletin of the Atomic Scientists*, April 1983, p. 3; Tom Wicker, *NYT*, 3/18/83; and cf., Paul C. Warnke, *NYT* (op-ed), 1/26/83; Report of the Secretary-General, *Nuclear*, p. 8; Walter Pincus, *WP*, 10/11/81, 6/7/83; Milton R. Benjamin, *WP*, 11/20/82.

23. Richard Bergholz, *LAT*, 2/1/80; *NYT*, 6/27/80, 10/16/81, 5/19/82, 7/10/82, 12/7/82, 1/4/83, 6/10/83 (UPI); *WP*, 12/8/82; Judith Miller, *NYT*, 11/20/81, 1/24/82, 8/10/82; *Newsweek*, 12/20/82; Kraft, "Letter"; W. Kenneth Davis, *WP*, 8/21/82; Milton R. Benjamin, *WP*, 7/9,19,20/82, 2/3/83; Rep. Charles B. Rangel in *CR* 1982, p. E4493–94; Richard Halloran, *NYT*, 11/15/82.

24. Détente was useful to the Soviets, Reagan said, only as a cover for aggression. In the same speech during his drive against Ford in 1976, Reagan professed an intention to seek peace through détente and said, "The Soviet Union is using détente to further its aim for world conquest." On March 3, 1976, Ford said, "I don't use the word 'détente' any more," and the word dropped out of the Republicans' lexicon. Four years later Reagan officiated at détente's funeral, saying, "It's time to stop pretending that détente with the Soviet Union is still alive. . . ." (In 1982 Nixon, calling for a resumption of détente, said pointedly that critics of it "would deprive us of many of our most effective diplomatic weapons" and that détente "is better than the alternatives of either sterile confrontation or nuclear conflict.")

NYT, 1/31/80, 2/29/80, 11/4/81, 6/22/82 (UPI), 8/18/82; *Kansas City Times*, 5/9/75; *LAT*, 11/17/75; RR, radio, "Detente," 10/31/75, "Two Worlds," 9/78; *Wilmington* (Del.) *News*, 11/15/79; Joseph Kraft, *WP*, 11/24/75; Evans and Novak, *WP*, 11/24/75; Jules Witcover, *WP*, 1/6/76; on Ford dropping "détente," *WP*, 3/3/76, cf. *NYT* 1/4/76; Cox, *Russian*, p. 23.

25. RR, WPF; RR, speech to World Affairs Council, 10/11/72, text; *WSJ*, 6/3/80; RR, speech, San Antonio, 1962; *WP*, 8/2/68; RR, press conference, 10/26/71, transcript; RR, radio, "Treaties," 3/78, "No Pay, No Vote," 4–5/78, "Another Side of the U.N.," 8/79; RR, *where's*, p. 307; von Damm, *Sincerely*, p. 108; Reagan, *The Creative*, p. 52; Beilenson and Cohen, "A New"; Barrett, *Gambling*, pp. 309–324; Scheer, *With*, p. 83; Leslie H. Gelb, *NYT*, 6/17/83.

26. The literature on the START and TNF negotiations between the U.S. and the U.S.S.R. is extensive and ubiquitous. Sources for specific items in this passage: *WP*, 5/22,27/83, 6/6,22/83; *NYT*, 6/1,2/83; *WSJ*, 6/16/83; Gary Hart, *WP* (op-ed), 5/25/83.

27. John F. Burns, *NYT*, 6/13/83; James M. Markham, *NYT*, 6/12/83; Charles Mohr, *NYT*, 2/27/83; Cox, *Russian*, pp. 120–121; *WP*, 1/20/83, 6/3, 11,26/83; *NYT*, 6/3,11,12,26/83; Thompson in *Protest*, p. 11, and Thompson, *Beyond*, p. 74; see Michael Getler, *WP*, 6/27/83.

28. *SAE* (AP), 11/16/80; Robert Scheer, *LAT*, 9/28/81; Beilenson and Cohen, "A New"; *WP*, 5/17/83.

29. *NYT*, 2/20/79, 1/10/81; *WP*, 6/1/75, 4/18/82; *Austin American-Statesman*, 3/31/82; Kazin, "Saving"; Thomas Powers in a book review, *New York Review*, 2/3/83; Rothbard, "The Two"; RR, radio, "Textbooks," 12/78–1/79; RR, *where's*, p. 298; von Damm, *Sincerely*, pp. 21, 87.

30. Football and code card: Strobe Talbott, *Time*, 3/29/82; *WP*, 12/13/81. Risking nuclear war: Goldwater, *With*, pp. 145–149, 155; RR, *Ronald*, p. 45. Questioning the President: Scheer, *With*, pp. 253, 256, 258; RD, *The Politician*, pp. 22–24; PBS, "The Reagan Transition," 1/21/81; *Barbara Walters Special Report*, ABC, 11/26/81, transcript. Reagan as delegator: John Sears, *WP* (op-ed), 7/16/80; Conaway, "Looking"; Witcover and Cohen, "Where's"; Anthony Lewis, *NYT*, 10/20/80; James David Barber, *NYT* (op-ed), 9/8/80. Bishops and the bomb: *NYT*, 5/4/83; U.S. Catholic Bishops, "The Pastoral"; "The Bishops and the Bomb," NBC, 5/15/83 (transcript); interview, Edward Doherty. RR's overview; RR, radio, "The Russian Wheat Deals," 10/29/75.

31. Robert C. Aldridge, *First Strike! The Pentagon's Strategy for Nuclear War* (Boston: South End Press, paper, 1983, not in the bibliography of this book), pp. 37, 66–67, 118–125, 163–183, 200–201, 272. Aldridge should also be consulted concerning variant details on the annex at pp. 118–135, cruise missiles at pp. 141–154, and nuclear submarine warfare at pp. 44, 49, 80, 88, and 95–99.

32. *WP*, 6/4/83 (Crisp); *NYT*, 6/14/83 (Colby).

Bibliography

Books

Bamford, James: *The Puzzle Palace: A Report on America's Most Secret Agency.* Boston: Houghton Mifflin, 1982.

Barrett, Laurence: *Gambling with History: Ronald Reagan in the White House.* Garden City, N.Y.: Doubleday, 1983.

Bartlett, Bruce R.: *Reaganomics: Supply-Side Economics in Action.* Foreword Jack Kemp. New York: Quill (paper), 1982.

Beilenson, Lawrence W., assisted by Bernard M. Dain: *The Treaty Trap: A History of the Performance of Political Treaties by the United States and European Nations.* Washington: Public Affairs Press, 1969.

Boyarsky, Bill: *The Rise of Ronald Reagan.* New York: Random House, 1967.

Broder, David, Lou Cannon, Haynes Johnson, Martin Schram, Richard Harwood, and the staff of the *Washington Post*, Richard Harwood, ed.: *The Pursuit of the Presidency 1980.* New York: Berkley Books (paper), 1980.

Brown, Edmund G. (Pat), and Bill Brown: *Reagan, the Political Chameleon.* New York: Praeger, 1976.

Brownstein, Ronald, ed.: *Selecting a President, A Citizen Guide to the 1980 Election.* (Citizens Research Group, Ralph Nader, chairman.) Thornwood, N.Y.: Caroline House, 1980 (distributed by Farrar, Straus & Giroux). Section on RR written by Mike Calabrese.

Brownstein, Ronald, and Nina Easton: *Reagan's Ruling Class: Portraits of the President's Top 100 Officials*. Intro. Ralph Nader. Washington, D.C.: The Presidential Accountability Group, 1982.

Cannon, Lou: *Ronnie and Jesse, A Political Odyssey*. Garden City, N.Y.: Doubleday, 1969. *Reagan*. New York: Putnam's, 1982.

Carter, Jimmy: *Keeping Faith: Memoirs of a President*. New York: Bantam, 1982.

Cohen, Sam: *The Truth About the Neutron Bomb: The Inventor of the Bomb Speaks Out*. New York: Morrow, 1983.

Conference on Alternative State and Local Policies: *The Issues of 1982: A Briefing Book*. Washington: Conference on Alternative State and Local Policies, 1982.

Congressional Quarterly, Inc.: *Congressional Quarterly Almanac*, 97th Cong. 1st Sess. 1981, vol. 37. Washington, 1982.

Congressional Quarterly, Inc.: *Reagan's First Year*. Washington (paper), 1982.

Conservation Foundation: *State of the Environment 1982*. Washington, 1982.

Cox, Arthur Macy: *Russian Roulette, The Superpower Game*. New York: Times Books, 1982.

Dugger, Ronnie: *The Politician: The Life and Times of Lyndon Johnson, From the Frontier to Master of the Senate*. New York: W. W. Norton, 1982.

Dunn, Lewis A.: *Controlling the Bomb: Nuclear Proliferation in the 1980s*. New Haven: Yale University Press, 1982.

Edwards, Lee: *Ronald Reagan: A Political Biography*. Foreword William Buckley, Jr. Houston: Nordland (paper), 1981.

Fallows, James: *National Defense*. New York: Vintage (paper), 1982.

Ferguson, Thomas, and Joel Rogers: *The Hidden Election: Politics and Economics in the 1982 Presidential Campaign*. New York: Pantheon (a *Nation* book, paper), 1982.

Gartner, Alan, Colin Greer, and Frank Riessman, eds.: *What Reagan Is Doing to Us*. New York: Harper & Row (Perennial Library, paper), 1982.

Geyer, Georgie Anne: *Buying the Night Flight: The Autobiography of a Woman Foreign Correspondent*. New York: Delacorte/Lawrence, 1983.

Gilder, George: *Wealth and Poverty*. New York: Bantam (paper), 1981.

Goldwater, Barry: *With No Apologies: The Personal and Political Memoirs of United States Senator Barry M. Goldwater*. New York: Berkley (paper), 1980.

Goulden, Joe: *Korea, The Untold Story of the War*. New York: Times Books, 1982.

Green, Mark: *Winning Back America*. New York: Bantam (paper), 1982.

Greenfield, Jeff: *The Real Campaign, How the Media Missed the Story of the 1980 Campaign*. New York: Summit, 1982.

Greider, William: *The Education of David Stockman and Other Americans*. New York: Dutton, 1982.

Ground Zero (the organization): *Nuclear War: What's in It for You?* New York: Pocket Books (paper), 1982.

Hannaford, Peter: *The Reagans: A Political Portrait*. New York: Coward-McCann, 1983.

Hayden, Tom: *The American Future, New Visions beyond the Reagan Administration*. New York: Washington Square Press (paper), 1982.

Heatherly, Charles L., ed.: *Mandate for Leadership, Policy Management in a Conservative Administration*. Foreword Edwin J. Feulner, Jr. Washington, D.C.: Heritage Foundation (paper), 1981.

Herman, Edward S.: *The Real Terror Network, Terrorism in Fact and Propaganda*. Boston: South End Press, 1982.

Holloway, David: *The Soviet Union and the Arms Race*. New Haven: Yale University Press, 1983.

Jordan, Hamilton: *Crisis: The Last Year of the Carter Presidency*. New York: Putnam, 1982.

Kaplan, Fred: *The Wizards of Armageddon*. New York: Simon & Schuster, 1983.

Kennan, George F.: *Memoirs: 1925–1950*. Boston: Atlantic Monthly Press, 1967. *The Nuclear Delusion: Soviet-American Relations in the Atomic Age*. New York: Pantheon, 1982.

Kennedy, Edward M., and Mark O. Hatfield: *Freeze! How You Can Help Prevent Nuclear War*. New York: Bantam (paper), 1982.

Kirkpatrick, Jeane J: *Dictatorships and Double Standards: Rationalism and Reason in Politics*. New York: American Enterprise Institute, Simon and Schuster, 1982.

Leamer, Laurence: *Make-Believe: The Story of Nancy and Ronald Reagan*. New York: Harper & Row, 1983.

Lekachman, Robert: *Greed Is Not Enough: Reaganomics*. New York: Pantheon, 1982.

Lewis, Joseph: *What Makes Reagan Run? A Political Profile*. New York: McGraw-Hill, 1968.

Lifton, Robert Jay, and Richard Falk: *Indefensible Weapons: The Political and Psychological Case against Nuclearism*. New York: Basic Books, 1982.

McGill, William J.: *The Year of the Monkey: Revolt on Campus, 1968–69*. New York: McGraw-Hill, 1982.

Moore, Jonathan, ed.: *The Campaign for President, 1980 in Retrospect*. Cambridge, Mass.: Ballinger, 1981.

Morris, Roger: *Haig: The General's Progress*. New York: Playboy Press, 1982.

Obert, John C., ed.: *Democratic Fact Book: Issues for 1982*. Washington, D.C.: Democrats for the 80's (paper), 1982.

Ornstein, Norman J.: *President and Congress: Assessing Reagan's First Year*. Washington, D.C.: American Enterprise Institute (paper), 1982.

Palmer, John L., and Isabel V. Sawhill, eds.: *The Reagan Experiment, an Examination of Economic and Social Policies under the Reagan Administration*. Washington: Urban Institute Press, 1982.

Pechman, Joseph A., ed.: *Setting National Priorities: The 1983 Budget*. Washington: Brookings Institution (paper), 1982.

Pertschuk, Michael: *Revolt against Regulation: The Rise and Pause of the Consumer Movement*. Berkeley: University of California Press, 1982.

Pipes, Richard: *U.S.-Soviet Relations in the Era of Détente*. Boulder, Colo.: Westview Press (paper), 1981.

Piven, Frances Fox, and Richard A. Cloward: *The New Class War: Reagan's Attack on the Welfare State and Its Consequences*. New York: Pantheon, 1982.

Reagan, Nancy, with Bill Libby: *Nancy.* New York: Berkley (paper), 1981.

Reagan, Ronald: *The Creative Society: Some Comments on Problems Facing America.* New York: Devin-Adair, 1968.

Reagan, Ronald, with Charles D. Hobbs: *Ronald Reagan's Call to Action.* New York: Warner Books (paper), 1976.

Reagan, Ronald, with Richard G. Hubler: *where's the rest of me?* New York: Duell, Sloan and Pearce, 1965.

Rowse, Arthur E.: *One Sweet Guy and What He Is Doing To You.* Washington, D.C.: Consumer News, Inc., 1981.

Scheer, Robert, with the assistance of Narda Zacchino and Constance Matthiessen: *With Enough Shovels: Reagan, Bush and Nuclear War.* New York: Random House, 1982.

Schell, Jonathan: *The Fate of the Earth.* New York: Knopf, 1982.

Secretary General of the United Nations: *Nuclear Weapons, Report of the Secretary General of the United Nations.* Brookline, Mass.: Autumn Press, Inc. (paper), 1980.

Shultz, George P., and Kenneth W. Dam: *Economic Policy Beyond the Headlines.* New York: Norton (paper), 1977.

Smith, Hedrick, Adam Clymer, Leonard Silk, Robert Lindsey, and Richard Burt: *Reagan the Man, the President.* New York: Macmillan, 1980.

Thompson, E. P.: *Beyond the Cold War: A New Approach to the Arms Race and Nuclear Annihilation.* New York: Pantheon (paper), 1982.

Thompson, E. P., and Dan Smith, eds.: *Protest and Survive.* New York and London: Monthly Review Press (paper), 1981.

Ulam, Adam B.: *Dangerous Relations: The Soviet Union in World Politics, 1970–1982.* New York: Oxford University Press, 1983.

van der Linden, Frank: *Reagan: What He Believes, What He Has Accomplished, What We Can Expect from Him.* New York: Morrow, 1981.

von Damm, Helene E. *Sincerely, Ronald Reagan.* Ottawa, Ill.: Green Hill Publishers (paper), 1976.

Wead, Doug, and Bill Wead: *Reagan in Pursuit of the Presidency—1980.* Plainfield, N.J.: Haven Books (paper), presumably 1980.

White, F. Clifton, and William J. Gill: *Why Reagan Won: A Narrative History of the Conservative Movement, 1964–1981.* Intro., Paul Laxalt. Chicago: Regnery, 1981.

Woodruff, Judy, with Kathleen Maxa: *"This Is Judy Woodruff at the White House."* Reading, Mass.: Addison-Wesley, 1982.

Articles

Aaron, Henry J.: "Social Security Can Be Saved," *Challenge,* 11–12/81.

Adams, Gordon: "Congress Begins the Debate," *Bulletin of the Atomic Scientists,* Apr., 1983.

Agran, Larry: "Adding up the Damage," *Nation,* 6/22/74.

Aldridge, Robert C.: "Missile Killers: The Hidden Arms Race," *Nation,* 10/18/80.

Alexander, Tom: "The Reaganites' Misadventure at Sea," *Fortune,* 8/23/82. "America's Costliest Boondoggle," *Fortune,* 11/1/82.

Alter, Jonathan: "Reagan's Regulatory Report Card," *Washington Monthly,* Nov., 1982.

Alterman, Eric R.: "An Alternative to Zero Option," *Nation,* 3/5/83.

Angell, Roger: "The Sporting Scene: Sharing the Beat," *New Yorker,* 4/9/79.

Angoff, Jay, and Elizabeth Maasen: "Just What the Doctors Ordered," *Public Citizen,* Spring, 1982.

Arbatov, Georgi: "View from Moscow," *Bulletin of the Atomic Scientists* (reprinted from *Daily World*), Nov., 1982.

Arkin, William: "Why SIOP-6?" *Bulletin of the Atomic Scientists,* Apr., 1983.

Arkin, William, and Peter Pringle: "C^{3}1: Command Post for Armageddon," *Nation,* 4/9/83.

Ball, George W.: "The Case against Sanctions," *NYT Magazine*, 9/12/82.

Ball, Robert: "Nuclear Weapons: Suppose We Froze?" *Fortune*, 5/17/82.

Bamford, Hames: "How I Got the N.S.A. Files . . . How Reagan Tried to Get Them Back," *Nation*, 11/6/82.

Barron, John: "The KGB's Magical War for 'Peace,' " *Reader's Digest*, Oct., 1982.

Beilenson, Lawrence W., and Samuel T. Cohen: "A New Nuclear Strategy," *NYT Magazine*, 1/24/82. "Foreswearing a First Nuclear Strike," *National Review*, 10/29/82.

Bennett, Philip W.: "Adding to the Numbers Game," *Bulletin of the Atomic Scientists*, April, 1983.

Bernstein, Peter W.: "A Nuclear Fiasco Shakes the Bond Market," *Fortune*, 2/22/82.

Bialer, Severyn, "The Men Who Run Russia's Armed Forces," *NYT Magazine*, 2/21/65.

Biddle, Wayne: "Neutron Bomb: An Explosive Issue," *NYT Magazine*, 11/15/81.

Blechman, Barry M., Janne E. Nolan, and Alan Platt: "Pushing Arms," *Foreign Policy*, Spring, 1982. "Is There a Conventional Defense Option?" *Washington Quarterly*, Summer, 1982.

Blitzer, Wolf: "Reagan's Saudi Link," *New Republic*, 7/26/80.

Bonner, Ray: "Bailing Out Bolivia's Junta," *Nation*, 11/29/80. "Bolivia: Once More, the Generals Take Over," *Atlantic*, 12/80.

Bonner, Raymond: "The Agony of El Salvador," *NYT Magazine*, 2/22/81.

Borgese, Elisabeth Mann: "The Law of the Sea," *Scientific American*, Mar., 1983.

Breckenfeld, Gurney: "Has Reagan Hurt the Poor?" *Fortune*, 1/24/83.

Bruck, Connie: "Springing the Haitians," *American Lawyer*, Sept., 1982.

Brzezinski, Zbigniew: "What's Wrong with Reagan's Foreign Policy?" *NYT Magazine*, 12/6/81.

Bukovsky, Vladimir: "The Peace Movement and the Soviet Union," *Commentary*, May, 1982.

Bundy, McGeorge, George F. Kennan, Robert S. McNamara, and Gerald Smith: "Nuclear Weapons and the Atlantic Alliance," *Foreign Affairs*, Summer, 1982.

Burnett, Nicholas: "Subsidies for Big Business: The Export-Import Bank," *Inquiry*, 12/24/79.

Burns, John F.: "A Delicate Balance in Zimbabwe," *NYT Magazine*, 7/7/80.

Butterfield, Fox: "Anatomy of the Nuclear Protest," *NYT Magazine*, 7/11/82.

Capozzi, Robert: "Social Security: Why It's Going Bankrupt," *Inquiry*, Oct., 1982.

Carson-Parker, John: "The Capital Cloud over Smokestack America," *Fortune*, 2/23/81.

Carver, Michael: "No first use: a view from Europe," *Bulletin of the Atomic Scientists*, Mar., 1983.

Chappie, Frank: "Perspective on the Peace Movement: II: Masters of Manipulation," *Readers' Digest*, June, 1982.

Chinoy, Michael: "Chun 'Purifies' South Korea," *Nation*, 10/25/80.

Ciephy, Michael: "Hardball," *Forbes*, 2/28/83.

Cohen, Toby: "The Medicaid Class Struggle," *Nation*, 2/21/81. "Voodoo Medical Economics," *Nation*, 3/19/83.

Cohen, Richard: "Post-Post-Watergate Morality," *Harper's*, Apr., 1983.

Cohn, Diane: "Patient Package Inserts," *Public Citizen*, Spring, 1982.

Colvin, Geoffrey: "How Sick Companies Are Endangering the Pension System," *Fortune*, 10/4/82.

Conaway, James: "Looking at Reagan," *Atlantic Monthly*, Oct., 1980. "Wilderness Held Hostage," *WP Magazine*, 7/18/82.

Cooper, Marc: "Spies over Los Angeles," *Inquiry*, Jan., 1983.

Cordtz, Dan: "Bechtel Thrives on Billion-Dollar Jobs," *Fortune*, Jan., 1975.

Curtis, Carol E.: "$10 Billion Question," *Forbes*, 2/14/83.

Cutter, W. Bowman: "The Battle of the Budget," *Atlantic*, March, 1981. "The Budget of Oz," *New Republic*, 3/24/82.

Danziger, Sheldon, and Robert Haveman: "The Reagan Budget: A Sharp Break with the Past," *Challenge*, May–June, 1981.

Davidow, Jeffrey: "Zimbabwe Is a Success," *Foreign Policy*, Winter, 1982–1983.

Davis, D. K.: "Natural Gas Decontrol: A Sound Principle Is Bent Out of Shape," *TIPRO Reporter*, Spring, 1981.

Day, Samuel H., Jr.: "The New Resistance," *Progressive*, Apr., 1983.

Dean, Jonathan: "Beyond First Use," *Foreign Policy*, Fall, 1982.

Dellums, Ronald V.: "Defense Sense," *Nation*, 8/21–28/82.

DeParle, Jason: "Old Gas, New Gas," *New Republic*, 4/11/83.

Didion, Joan: "In El Salvador," 3 parts, *New York Review*, 11/4,18/82, 12/2/82.

Dince, Robert B.: "Why Bank Examiners Fail," *Fortune*, 8/23/82.

Doctorow, E. L.: "The Rise of Ronald Reagan," *Nation*, 11/19–26/80.

Donner, Frank: "The Campaign to Smear the Nuclear Freeze Movement," *Nation*, 11/6/82.

Donovan, Hedley: "A Continent in Trouble," *Fortune*, 11/29/82.

Dorgan, Bryan: "America's Real Farm Problem: It Can Be Solved," *Washington Monthly*, April, 1983.

Dowie, Mark: "The Bechtel File," *Mother Jones*, Sept.–Oct., 1978.

Draper, Theodore: "How Not to Think about Nuclear War," *New York Review*, 7/15/82. "How Not to Think About Nuclear War," *New York Review*, 9/23/82. "Dear Mr. Weinberger: An Open Reply to an Open Letter," *New York Review*, 11/4/82.

Drew, Elizabeth: "1980: Reagan," *New Yorker*, 3/24/80 and 9/29/80. "Politics and Money," *New Yorker*, 2 parts, 12/6,13/82. "A Reporter in Washington, D.C.: Sketchbook," 6/21/82. "A Political Journal," *New Yorker*, 5/9/83.

Dugger, Ronnie: "The Imperial Reagan," *Nation*, 11/1/80. "Marching in New York: This Day Was Beautiful," *Texas Observer*, 7/9/82.

Edwards, Lee: "Ronald Reagan: Spokesman for Conservatism," *Human Events* (special supplement), 2/2/74.

Ehrbar, A. F.: "Martin Feldstein's Electric-Blue Economic Prescriptions," *Fortune*, 2/27/78. "How to Cut Those Deficits—And Why," *Fortune*, 2/22/82. "Upheaval in Investment Banking," *Fortune*, 8/23/82. "Toil and Trouble at Continental Illinois," *Fortune*, 2/7/83. "Reagan Steps Back from Reaganomics," *Fortune*, 2/21/83.

Eisenstein, Maurice: "Third World Missiles and Nuclear Proliferation," *Washington Quarterly*, Summer, 1982.

Emerson, Steve: "New Salaams to the Saudis," *New Republic*, 3/21/81.

Fallows, James: "Reagan's MX Surprise," *Atlantic*, Dec., 1981. "Entitlements," *Atlantic*, Nov., 1982. "The Ordeal of Kenneth Adelman," *Atlantic*, July, 1983.

Farer, Tom J.: "Reagan's Latin America," *New York Review*, 3/16/81.

Feiveson, H. A.: "Thinking About Nuclear Weapons," *Dissent*, Spring, 1982.

Fishlow, Albert: "The United States and Brazil: The Case of the Missing Relationship," *Foreign Affairs*, Spring, 1982.

Ford, Daniel: "The Cult of the Atom," *New Yorker*, 10/25/82, 11/1/82.

Frank, Allan Dodds: "Poor Prescription," *Forbes*, 8/30/82.

Freedman, Lawrence: "Arms Control: No Hiding Place," *SAIS Review*, Winter–Spring, 1983.

Gardner, Richard N.: "Selling America in the Marketplace of Ideas," *NYT Magazine*, 3/20/83.

Gaylor, Noel: "How to Break the Momentum of the Nuclear Arms Race," *NYT Magazine*, 4/25/82.

Galbraith, James K.: "Short Changed: The Decline and Fall of Monetarism," *Working Papers*, Sept.–Oct., 1982.

Galbraith, James K., and Greg Davidson: "Flattening the Progressive Tax," *New Leader*, 8/9–23/82.

Gelb, Leslie H.: "Keeping an Eye on Russia," *NYT Magazine*, 11/29/81. "The President's Options: Nuclear Bargaining," *NYT Magazine*, 6/27/82.

Gerjuoy, Edward: "Embargo on Ideas: The Reagan Isolationism," *Bulletin of the Atomic Scientists*, Nov., 1982.

Germond, Jack W., and Jules Witcover: "The Rise of Jim Baker," *The Washingtonian*, Oct., 1982.

Gold, Michael: "Synfuels Stall Out," *Science 82*, July–Aug., 1982.

Golden, Soma: "Superstar of the New Economists," *NYT Magazine*, 3/23/80.

Goldsborough, James O.: "The Roots of Western Disunity," *NYT Magazine*, 5/9/82.

Gordiner, Nadine: "Letter from the 153rd State," *New York Review*, 11/6/80.

Gore, Albert, Jr.: "The Fork in the Road," *New Republic*, 5/5/82.

Grambert, James: "The Stealth 'Secret,'" *Progressive*, Dec., 1980.

Granelli, James S.: "Reagan Judges: In His Image?" *National Law Journal*, 9/15/80.

Grass, Günter: "Solidarity with the Sandinists," *Nation*, 3/12/83.

Graves, Florence: "Are These Men Soviet Dupes?" *Common Cause*, Jan.–Feb., 1983.

Gray, Colin S.: "Nuclear Strategy: A Regrettable Necessity," *SAIS Review*, Winter–Spring, 1983.

Green, Mark: "The (Anti) Trustbusters," *Nation*, 1/3–10/81. "Political Pac-Man," *New Republic*, 12/13/82. "The Gang That Can't Deregulate," *New Republic*, 3/21/83.

Greenstein, Robert: "Revising the Budget: Bad News for the Poor," *Christianity and Crisis*, 6/21/82.

Greider, William: "The Education of David Stockman," *Atlantic*, Dec., 1981. "The Budget's Bottom Line," *Rolling Stone*, 6/24/82.

Griffith, William E.: "Perspective on the Peace Movement: I: Ban Whose Bomb?" *Readers' Digest*, June, 1982.

Grigsby, Jefferson: "Apocalypse Deferred," *Forbes*, 2/2/81.

Gupte, Pranay: "Nigeria: Oil Rich and Nervous," *Atlantic*, Jan., 1981.

Guzzardi, Walter, Jr.: "The Mental Gap in the Defense Debate," *Fortune*, 9/8/80. "Reagan's Reluctant Deregulators," *Fortune*, 3/8/82. "Who Will Care for the Poor?" *Fortune*, 6/28/82.

Hand, Douglas: "Portrait: Dr. Helen Caldicott," *Life*, June, 1982.

Harris, Bryan: "Solar Energy: No Profit in Politics," *Atlantic*, May, 1982.

Hart, Gary: "What's Wrong with the Military?" *NYT Magazine*, 2/14/82.

Harvie, Chris: "Cooperation Kills the Coal Miners," *Public Citizen*, Spring, 1982.

Hector, Gary: "The Banks Invade Wall Street," *Fortune*, 2/7/83.

Hentoff, Nat: "Killing the First Amendment Softly in the Congress," *Village Voice*, 2/10–16/82.

Hogan, Bill, Diane Kiesel, and Alan Green: "The New Slush Fund Scandal," *New Republic*, 8/30/82.

Holdren, John P.: "Nuclear Power and Nuclear Weapons: The Connection Is Dangerous," *Bulletin of the Atomic Scientists*, Jan., 1983.

Hollander, Ron: "The Greening of Conservation," *Town & Country*, Oct., 1982.

Honan, William H.: "Return of the Battleship," 2 parts, *NYT Magazine*, 4/4,11/82.

Horne, Jed: "The Nuclear Trigger," *Life*, Aug., 1980.

Hulbert, Mark: "Will the U.S. Bail out the Bankers?" *Nation*, 10/16/82.

Isaac, Raul Jean, and Erich Isaac: "The Counterfeit Peacemakers: Atomic Freeze," *American Spectator*, June, 1982.

Jastrow, Robert: "The New Soviet Arms Buildup in Space," *NYT Magazine*, 10/3/82. "Why Strategic Superiority Matters," *Commentary*, Mar., 1983.

Jenkins, John A.: "Who Owns the Sky?" *Student Lawyer*, Nov., 1980.

Joffe, Josef: "The Greening of Germany," *New Republic*, 2/14/83.

Judis, John B.: "The Rights and the Wrongs of Reagan," *Progressive*, Jan., 1983. "Setting the Stage for Repression," *Progressive*, April, 1981.

Kahn, Herman: "Thinking about Nuclear Morality," *NYT Magazine*, 6/13/82. "Refusing to Think about the Thinkable," *Fortune*, 6/28/82.

Kaiser, Karl, Georg Leber, Alois Mertes, and Franz-Josef Schulze: "Nuclear Weapons and the Preservation of Peace," *Foreign Affairs*, Summer, 1982.

Kalb, Madeleine G.: "The U.N.'s Embattled Peacekeeper," *NYT Magazine*, 12/19/82.

Kaplan, Fred: "'New Look' from the Pentagon," *Inquiry*, 9/22/80. "Missile Envy," *New Republic*, 10/11/82.

Karas, Thomas H.: "The Star Wars Scenario," *Nation*, 4/9/83.

Kazin, Alfred: "Saving My Soul at the Plaza," *New York Review*, 3/31/83.

Kennan, George F.: "Cease This Madness," *Atlantic*, Jan., 1981. "America's Unstable Soviet Policy," *Atlantic*, Nov., 1982.

Kern, Edward: "The Nuclear Industry Begins to Die," *Life*, May, 1982.

Kesler, Charles R.: "Jeane Kirkpatrick: Not Quite Right," *National Review*, 10/29/82.

Keisling, Phil: "The Tallest Gun in Foggy Bottom," *Washington Monthly*, Nov., 1982.

Kirkland, Richard I., Jr.: "The Flatter-Tax Movement Picks Up Steam," *Fortune*, 7/26/82.

Kissinger, Henry A.: "Nuclear Weapons and the Peace Movement," *Washington Quarterly*, Summer, 1982.

Kitman, Jamie: "A Nerve Gas We Can Love," *Nation*, 7/5/80.

Klare, Michael T.: "Is Exxon Worth Dying For?" *Progressive*, July, 1980. "An Army in Search of a War," *Progressive*, Feb., 1981. "U.S.S.N. Nimitz: Cruising on the Edge of War," *Mother Jones*, April, 1982. "The Weinberger Revolution," *Inquiry*, Sept., 1982.

Kohn, Howard, and Lowell Bergman: "Reagan's Millions," *Rolling Stone*, 8/26/76.

Kondracke, Morton: "Ronnie's for Real," *New Republic*, 4/5/80.

Kornheiser, Tony: "Reagan's Chief of Staff: Jim Baker," *DTH* (*Westward*), 3/1/81.

Kosterlitz, Julie: "The Heavy-Handed Ma Bell," *Common Cause*, Dec., 1981. "The Thomas Reed Affair," *Common Cause*, Jan.–Feb., 1983.

Kotz, Nick: "The War on the Poor," *New Republic*, 3/24/82.

Kraft, Joseph: "Letter from Pakistan," *New Yorker*, 8/10/81.

Kramer, Michael: "Reagan's Moment?" *New York*, 10/27/80. "Dense-Think on Defense," *New York*, 11/29/82.

Krylov, Nikolai I.: "Strategic Rockets," *Military Review*, Dec., 1964 (reprinted from *Izvestia*, 11/17/63).

Larrabee, Stephen F.: "Papandreou: National Interests Are the Key," *Atlantic*, Mar., 1983.

Latiner, Leigh S.: "The Law of the Sea: A Crossroads for American Foreign Policy," *Foreign Affairs*, Summer, 1982.

Leaning, Jennifer, Matthew Leighton, John Lamperti, and Herbert L. Abrams: "Programs for Surviving a Nuclear War: A Critique," *Bulletin of the Atomic Scientists*, June–July, 1983.

Lelyveld, Joseph: "Inside Namibia," *NYT Magazine*, 8/1/82. "Oppenheimer of South Africa," *NYT Magazine*, 5/8/83.

Leontief, Wassily W.: "The Distribution of Work and Income," *Scientific American*, Sept., 1982.

Leuchtenberg, William E: "Ronald Reagan's Liberal Past," *New Republic*, 5/23/83.

Levitan, Sar A., and Clifford M. Johnson: "The Politics of Unemployment," *New Republic*, 9/20–27/82.

Litvak, Leo: "The Ronald Reagan Story," *NYT Magazine*, 11/14/65.

Loomis, Carol J.: "The Madness of Executive Compensation," *Fortune*, 7/12/82.

Louis, Arthur M.: "The Bottom Line on Ten Big Mergers," *Fortune*, 3/3/82.

Lowenthal, Abraham F.: "The Caribbean," *Wilson Quarterly*, Spring, 1982.

Lubar, Robert: "Reaganizing the Third World," *Fortune*, 11/16/81.

MacKenzie, Angus: "Darker Cloaks, Longer Daggers," *Progressive*, June, 1982.

McKean, Kevin: "A 'Safer' Poison Gas," *Discover*, Sept., 1981. "The Mounting Crisis in Nuclear Energy," *Discover*, May, 1982.

McMenamin, Michael: "Feeding the Dairy Lobby," *Inquiry*, July, 1982. "The Teamster-I.C.C. Partnership Unltd.," *Inquiry*, Nov., 1982.

Magnet, Myron: "Grumman's Comeback," *Fortune*, 9/20/82.

Manning, Robert A.: "So Far, So Fair in Zimbabwe," *New Republic*, 4/4/81. "America's Newest Tripwire," *Inquiry*, Jan., 1983.

Marsh, Gerald E.: "No Evidence of Cheating," *Bulletin of the Atomic Scientists*, Mar., 1983.

Martin, Benjamin: "Spain's Charismatic Socialist and His Party: The Felipe Factor," *New Republic*, 11/8/82.

Meadows, Edward: "Deals of the Year," *Fortune*, 1/25/82.

Mearsheimer, John J.: "Maneuver, Mobile Defense, and the NATO Central Front," *International Security*, Winter, 1981–1982.

Medvedev, Roy A., and Zhores A. Medvedev: "A Nuclear Samizdat on America's Arms Race," *Nation*, 1/16/82.

Melanson, Philip H.: "The C.I.A.'s Secret Ties to Local Police," *Nation*, 3/26/83.

Michaels, Marguerite: "Why Nixon Believes We're Losing the Race on Land, on Sea, and in the Air," *Parade* in *WP*, 10/4/80.

Minard, Lawrence: "Embracing the Bear," *Forbes*, 7/7/82.

Moore, Didi: "American's Neglected Elderly," *NYT Magazine*, 1/30/83.

Moynihan, Daniel Patrick: "One-Third of a Nation," *New Republic*, 6/9/82.

Mueller, Milton: "Making Waves at the FCC," *Inquiry*, July, 1982.

Murray, Jim: "Ronald Reagan to the Rescue!" *Esquire*, Feb., 1966.

Myles, John: "The Trillion Dollar Misunderstanding," *Working Papers*, July/August 1981.

Nacht, Michael: "ABM ABCs," *Foreign Policy*, Spring, 1982.

Nairn, Allen: "The Guns of Guatemala," *New Republic*, 4/11/83.

Nathan, James A.: "Return of the Great White Fleet," *Nation*, 3/5/83.

Newhouse, John: "A Sporty Game," 4 parts, *New Yorker*, 6/14,21,28/82, 7/5/82. "Arms and Allies," *New Yorker*, 2/28/83.

Nickel, Herman: "OPEC's Billions," *Fortune*, 11/17/80.

Norgren, Jill, and Sheila Cole: "Heaven Help the Working Mother," *Nation*, 1/23/82.

Nossiter, Bernard D.: "The United Nations: Rules of the House," *Atlantic*, Apr., 1982. "Questioning the Value of the United Nations," *NYT Magazine*, 4/11/82.

Nunn, Sam: "NATO: Saving the Alliance," *Washington Quarterly*, Summer, 1982.

Osborne, David: "Rich Doctors, Poor Nurses," *Harper's*, Sept., 1982.

Osborne, John: "Preferring Johnson," *New Republic*, 6/14/80.

Oulahan, Richard, and William Lambert: "The Real Ronald Reagan Stands Up," *Life*, 1/22/66.

Owens, Patrick: "The President from GE," *Nation*, 1/31/81.

Paine, Christopher: "The Selling of the B-1," *Common Cause*, Oct., 1982. "Nuclear Combat: the Five-Year Defense Plan," *Bulletin of the Atomic Scientists*, Nov., 1982. "Free Verification: Time for a Fresh Approach," *Bulletin of the Atomic Scientists*, Jan., 1983. "MX: Too Dense for Congress," *Bulletin of the*

Atomic Scientists, Feb., 1983. "Reagatomics, or How to 'Prevail,'" *Nation,* 4/9/83.

Palme, Olaf: "The Slick Slide into Armageddon," *Nation,* 1/3–10/81.

Pastor, Robert: "Sinking in the Caribbean Basin," *Foreign Affairs,* Summer, 1982.

Paul, Ron: "Taxes: The Flatter the Better?" *Inquiry,* Sept., 1982.

Payne, Karen: "Purge in Haiti: 'Baby Doc' Takes Charge," *Nation,* 12/27/80.

Pertschuk, Michael: "Reaganism Is Harmful to Your Health," *Nation,* 7/24–1/3/82.

Peterson, Peter G.: "No More Free Lunch for the Middle Class," *NYT Magazine,* 1/17/82. "Social Security: The Coming Crash," and "The Salvation of Social Security," *New York Review,* 12/2,16/82.

Peterson, Russell W.: "Laissez-faire Landscape," *NYT Magazine,* 10/31/82.

Peterzell, Jay: "Unleashing the Dogs of McCarthyism," *Nation,* 1/17/81. "The Government Shuts Up," *Columbia Journalism Review,* July–Aug., 1982.

Petras, James: "Terrorism in El Salvador: The Junta's War against the People," *Nation,* 12/20/80.

Polsgrove, Carol: "Where Will We Dump the Nuclear Trash?" *Progressive,* Mar., 1983.

Powers, Thomas: "Choosing a Strategy for World War III," *Atlantic,* Nov., 1982.

Pringle, Peter: "Putting World War III on Ice," *Inquiry,* July, 1982.

Quirk, William J.: "The Baleful Bailout Bandwagon," *Fortune,* 6/14/82. "The Big Bank Bailout," *New Republic,* 2/21/83.

Rader, Dotson: "Reflections of a Woman in Love," *Parade (WP),* 11/8/81. "'What I Would Have Done,'" *Parade (WP),* 4/4/82.

Radosh, Ronald: "The 'Peace Council' and Peace," *New Republic,* 1/31/83.

Raskin, A.H.: "Unionist in Reaganland," *New Yorker,* 9/7/81.

Raskin, Marcus: "Abolitions & Prudentialists," *Nation*, 8/7–14/82. "War, Peace, and the Bishops," *Nation*, 1/29/83.

Ravenal, Earl C.: "No first use: a view from the United States," *Bulletin of the Atomic Scientists*, Apr., 1983.

Reagan, Ronald: "Business Ballots and Bureaus," *Western Underwriters' Life Edition*, June, 1960. "An Equal Education Plan Through Tuition," *Compact*, Feb., 1968.

Reeves, Richard: "How Safe Are We?" *Parade (San Antonio Light)*, 3/20/83.

Regenstein, Lewis: "Ruckelshaus' Record," *New Republic*, 7/11/83.

Reich, Robert B.: "Ideologies of Survival," *New Republic*, 9/20–27/82.

Rescigno, Richard: "Why Penn Square Failed," *Barron's*, 8/23/82.

Riding, Alan: "Guatemala: State of Siege," *NYT Magazine*, 8/24/80. "The Central American Quagmire," *Foreign Affairs*, Vol. 61, No. 3 (1982). "Revolution and the Intellectual in Latin America," *NYT Magazine*, 3/13/83.

Rips, Geoffrey: "A Block Grant Bill of Rights," *Texas Observer*, 2/25/83.

Rogers, Bernard W.: "The Atlantic Alliance: Prescriptions for a Difficult Decade," *Foreign Affairs*, Summer, 1982.

Rosenberg, David Alan: "The Origins of Overkill: Nuclear War and American Strategy, 1945–1960," *International Security*, Spring, 1983.

Rothbard, Murray: "The Two Faces of Ronald Reagan," *Inquiry*, 7/7,21/80.

Rowan, Roy: "The Maverick Who Yelled Foul at Citibank," *Fortune*, 1/10/83.

Rudnitsky, Howard, and Jeff Blyskal: "From One Pocket into the Other," *Forbes*, 2/28/83.

Scheer, Robert: "The Reagan Question," *Playboy*, Aug., 1980.

Schell, Jonathan: "The Fate of the Earth," 3 parts, *New Yorker*, 2/1,8,15/82.

Schlesinger, Stephen: "Reagan's 'Secret' War on Nicaragua," *Nation*, 1/1–8/83.

Schoen, Elin: "Once Again, Hunger Troubles America," *NYT Magazine*, 1/2/83.

Scott, Barbara Ann: "Playing Favorites: Federal Aid to Higher Education," *democracy,* Spring, 1983.

Schwartz, Herman: "Reagan Uncaps Natural Gas," *Nation,* 3/19/83.

Seligman, Daniel: "Affirmative Action Is Here to Stay," *Fortune,* 4/19/82. "Why Cuts Will Be Hard to Come By," *Fortune,* 4/4/83.

Shapiro, Fred C.: "Nuclear Waste," *New Yorker,* 10/19/81.

Shapley, Deborah: "The Fragile System," *Nation,* Aug., 1980. "The Army's New Fighting Doctrine," *NYT Magazine,* 11/28/82.

Shattuck, John: "National Security a Decade After Watergate," *democracy,* Winter, 1983.

Sherrid, Pamela: "Live Wire," *Forbes,* 9/27/82.

Sherrill, Robert: "Opening Day at the Subcommittee," *Nation,* 5/9/81. "Reagan Inc. Dumps on Canada," *Nation,* 9/4/82. "The Decline and Fall of Antitrust," *Nation,* 3/19/83.

Singham, A.W.: "The Illegal Exploitation of Namibia," *Nation,* 10/18/80.

Smiley, Xan: "The Cracks in Zimbabwe," *New Republic,* 1/31/83.

Smith, Hedrick: "Reagan: What Kind of World Leader?" *NYT Magazine,* 11/11/80. "How Many Billions for Defense?" *NYT Magazine,* 11/1/81. "How Reagan Rode out 1981," *NYT Magazine,* 1/10/82.

Smith, Lee: "The Military Contract the Big Firms Shun," *Fortune,* 5/17/82.

Solomon, Norman: "The Atom-Weapons Lobby Is Gaining," *Nation,* 10/11/80. "Europe, Russia, and the U.S. Missiles," *Nation,* 4/16/83.

Specter, Michael: "Is the Volunteer Army a Failure?" *Nation,* 6/19/82.

Stacks, John F., Jack Germond, and Jules Witcover: "How the Democrats Gave Us Reagan: The Ten Key Moments of the 1980 Campaign," *Washington Monthly,* Feb., 1982.

Star, Jack: "What about Ronald Reagan?" *Look,* 7/23/68.

Starr, Paul: "The Laissez-Faire Elixir," *New Republic,* 4/18/83.

Steel, Ronald: "NATO's Bad Boy," *New Republic,* 3/21/83.

Stein, Daniel L.: "Electromagnetic Pulse—the Uncertain Certainty," *Bulletin of the Atomic Scientists*, March, 1983.

Sterling, Claire: "Terrorism: Tracing the International Network," *NYT Magazine*, 3/1/81.

Steyer, Robert: "Deals of the Year," *Fortune*, 1/24/83.

Stone, I.F.: "Behind the Reagan 'Start,' " *Nation*, 5/22/82. "Imbalancing Act," *Nation*, 6/5/82.

Stone, Jane: "Investigation Challenges Reagan Antitrust Policies," *Public Citizen*, Fall, 1981. "Dumping, Delaney, and Food Safety," *Public Citizen*, Spring, 1982.

Stuart, Alexander: "Leasing Leaves the Harbor," *Fortune*, 1/24/83.

Symonds, William: "Washington in the Grip of the Green Giant," *Fortune*, 10/4/82.

Tabb, William K.: "Social Security Goes Private," *Nation*, 1/30/82.

Taubman, Philip: "Casey and His C.I.A. on the Rebound," *NYT Magazine*, 1/16/83.

Thimmesch, Nick: "The Cashing of Social Security Checks for Dead Relatives," *Saturday Evening Post*, Jan.–Feb., 1982.

Thompson, E.P.: "A Letter to America," *Nation*, 1/24/81. "Deterrence and 'Addiction,' " *Yale Review*, Autumn, 1982. "END and the Soviet 'Peace Offensive,' " *Nation*, 2/26/83. "Peace Is a Third-Way Street," *Nation*, 4/16/83.

Tonge, David: "The 'Space Beam' Race," *World Press Review* (reprinted from *Financial Times* of London), Dec., 1980.

Tower, John: "The Politics of Chemical Deterrence," *Washington Quarterly*, Spring, 1982.

Tuchman, Barbara W.: "The Alternative to Arms Control," *NYT Magazine*, 4/18/82.

Tucker, William: "The Chemistry Is Getting Better at the EPA," *Fortune*, 9/20/82. "Public Radio Comes to Market," *Fortune*, 10/18/82.

Ullman, Richard H.: "Out of the Euromissile Mire," *Foreign Policy*, Spring, 1983.

Unterberger, Betty Miller: "Burying the Diplomatic Record," *Nation*, 5/8/82.

Uttal, Bro: "Life after Litigation at IBM and AT&T," *Fortune*, 2/8/82.

Van Atta, Dale: "Inside a U.S.-Soviet Arms Negotiation," *Nation*, 12/19/81.

Vinocur, John: "The German Malaise," *NYT Magazine*, 11/15/81. "German's Season of Discontent," *NYT Magazine*, 8/8/82.

Watt, James: "Ours Is the Earth," *Saturday Evening Post*, Jan.–Feb., 1982.

Wayne, Leslie: "The Corporate Raiders," *NYT Magazine*, 7/18/82.

Weiler, Lawrence D.: "No First Use: a History," *Bulletin of the Atomic Scientists*, Feb., 1983.

Weisman, Steven R.: "Reaganomics and the President's Men," *NYT Magazine*, 10/24/82.

Weisner, Jerome B.: "George Kennan's Case for Ending the Arms Race," *Book World* (*Washington Post*), ca. Nov., 1982.

Weltman, John J.: "Managing Nuclear Multipolarity," *International Security*, Winter, 1981–82.

Weymouth, Lally: "The Biggest Role of Nancy's Life," *NYT Magazine*, 10/26/80.

Whalen, Richard J.: "Peace-Pit Conservative or Closet Moderate?" *NYT Magazine*, 2/22/76.

Whitaker, Jennifer Seymour: "Outside the Mainstream," *Atlantic*, Oct., 1982.

Williams, Juan: "Bob Dole Wants to Raise Your Taxes Again," *Fortune*, 10/18/82.

Witcover, Jules, and Richard M. Cohen: "Where's the Rest of Ronald Reagan?" *Esquire*, March, 1976.

White, Robert E.: "Central America: The Problem That Won't Go Away," *NYT Magazine*, 7/18/82.

White, Theodore H.: "Weinberger on the Ramparts," *NYT Magazine*, 2/6/83.

Wolfe, Alan: "Europe in Search of Autonomy," *Nation*, 2/27/82.

Wright, Claudia: "Israeli Attack No Surprise to Pentagon," *In These Times*, 9/8–14/82.

Wright, Michael: "The Marine Corps Faces the Future," *NYT Magazine*, 6/20/82.

Zacharias, Jerrold R., Myles Gordon, and Saville R. Davis: "Common Sense and Nuclear Peace," *Bulletin of the Atomic Scientists*, Apr., 1983.

Zwerdling, Daniel: "The Power of James Watt," *Progressive*, Mar., 1981.

Documents

American Civil Liberties Union: *Voting Rights in the South: Ten Years of Litigation Challenging Continuing Discrimination Against Minorities*. A special report from the ACLU by Laughlin McDonald, Jan., 1982. *Civil Liberties in Reagan's America: A Special Two-Year Report on the ACLU's Defense of the Bill of Rights Against the Attacks of the Administration and Its Allies*. Oct., 1982.

American Federation of Labor and Congress of Industrial Organizations: *Transcripts of press conferences held by AFL-CIO President Lane Kirkland . . .* 2/15,16,18,19/82; 5/26,27/82; 8/3–5/82. Department of Information, AFL-CIO, Washington. *The Reagan Recession*, AFL-CIO Department of Economic Research, July, 1982.

Americans for Democratic Action: *500 Days: ADA Assesses the Reagan Administration*, 6/3/82.

Central Intelligence Agency: *Soviet Covert Action and Propaganda* (a report presented to the House Permanent Select Committee on Intelligence, Subcommittee on Oversight), 2/6/80.

Congressional Quarterly, Inc., Editorial Research Reports series:
Prentice Bowsher, "Housing the Poor," 11/7/80.
Richard C. Schroeder, "Retirement Income in Jeopardy," 3/6/81.
William Sweet, "MX Missile Decision," 6/5/81.
William Sweet, "Controlling Nuclear Proliferation," 7/17/81.
Marc Leepson, "Affirmative Action Reconsidered," 7/31/81.
William Sweet, "Banking Deregulation," 8/7/81.
Jean Rosenblatt and Hoyt Gimlin, "Tuition Tax Credits," 8/14/81.
William Sweet, "Labor Under Siege," 11/6/81.
Robert Benenson, "Reaganomics on Trial," 1/8/82.
William Sweet, "Business Mergers and Antitrust," 1/15/82.

Defenders of Wildlife, Environmental Action, Environmental Defense Fund, Environmental Policy Center, Friends of the Earth, National Audubon Society, Natural Resources Defense Council, Sierra Club, Solar Lobby, Wilderness Society: *Hitting Home: The Effects of the Reagan Environmental Policies on Communities across America*. Washington, Oct., 1982.

Democratic Congressional Campaign Committee: *The 1980 Campaign Promises of Ronald Reagan*, May, 1981.

Department of Health, Education and Welfare: Dean R. Leimer and Selig D. Lesnoy, "Social Security and Private Saving: A Reexamination of the Time Series Evidence Using Alternative Social Security Wealth Variables," Division of Economic Research, Social Security Administration, Nov., 1980.

Department of Health and Human Services: HHS Fact Sheet, "Provisions of the Social Security Proposal," 5/12/81.

Department of State: *Report on Korea 1977*, Dec., 1977 (mimeographed), *Soviet "Active Measures": Forgery, Disinformation, Political Operations*, Special Report No. 88, Bureau of Public Affairs, Oct., 1981. *Expulsion of Soviet Representatives from Foreign Countries, 1970–1981*, "Foreign Affairs Note," Feb., 1982. *World Peace Council: Instrument of Soviet Foreign Policy*, "Foreign Affairs Note," April, 1982. *Soviet 'Active Measures': An Update*, Bureau of Public Affairs, Oct., 1982.

Friends of the Earth, Natural Resources Defense Council, Wilderness Society, Sierra Club, National Audubon Society, Environmental Defense Fund, Environmental Policy Center, Environmental Action, Defenders of Wildlife, and Solar Lobby: *Indictment: The Case Against the Reagan Environmental Record*, Mar., 1982.

Government Printing Office: *Weekly Compilation of Presidential Documents*. A serial.

Group Research, Inc.: *The Tentative Reagan Index* (consulted in 1980).

House (U.S.) Democratic Caucus, Caucus Committee on Party Effectiveness: *Rebuilding the Road to Opportunity: A Democratic Direction for the 1980s*, Sept., 1982.

House of Representatives, U.S.: *Soviet Covert Action (The Forgery Offensive)*, Permanent Select Committee on Intelligence, Subcommittee on Oversight, *Hearings*, 2/2,19/80.

Library of Congress: David Koitz, "Major Social Security Financing Packages Now Before the Congress," Congressional Research Service, 6/1/81.

National Bureau of Economic Research, Inc.:

NBER Reprint No. 40, Martin S. Feldstein and Anthony Pellechio, "Social Security Wealth: The Impact of Alternative Inflation Adjustments" (1979).

NBER Reprint No. 46, Martin Feldstein, "The Effect of Social Security on Private Savings: The Time Series Evidence" (1979).

NBER Reprint No. 56, Martin Feldstein and Anthony Pellechio, "Social Security and Household Wealth Accumulation: New Microeconometric Evidence" (1979).

Working Paper No. 477, Martin Feldstein, "Social Security Benefits and the Accumulation of Preretirement Wealth," May, 1980.

O'Connor Creative Services: *Ronald Reagan Radio Commentary,* being copies of the scripts of Reagan's 1978 and 1979 radio broadcasts. Also, though not identified as from O'Connor Creative Services: *Viewpoint with Ronald Reagan, Reprint of a Radio Program,* etc., being copies of scripts of Reagan's 1975 broadcasts, obtained from the Democratic National Committee.

Reagan, Ronald: Early speech texts: "Encroaching Government Controls," *Human Events,* 7/21/61. Address to San Antonio, Tex., Chamber of Commerce and Downtown Lions Club, 2/21/62. Address at Municipal Auditorium, Amarillo, Tex., 3/2/62. Address to World Affairs Council, place not specified, 10/11/72. "Losing Our Freedom by Installments," distributed by National Research Bureau, Inc., not dated. "What Price Freedom," *The Cross and the Flag,* April 1964.

Republican National Committee: *Promises: A Progress Report on President Reagan's First Year,* Katherine Blake and Richard Hansen, eds. Communications Division, Jan., 1982.

Ronald Reagan for Governor Committee: *Reagan for Governor Official Speakers Manual,* 1966.

Senate, U.S.: *The Final Report of the Select Committee on Presidential Campaign Activities,* Washington, GPO: 1974. *Report on Korea,* mimeographed, Dec., 1977 (provided by office of Sen. Frank Church, Chairman, in 12/80). *Staff Data and Materials Related to Social Security Financing,* Committee on Finance, U.S. Senate, GPO; Sept., 1981.

U.S. Catholic Bishops: "The Pastoral Letter of the U.S. Bishops on War and Peace: The Challenge of Peace: God's Promise and Our Response." U.S. Catholic Conference, Inc., 1983. Published in *Origins,* NC Documentary Service, Washington, D.C.

U.S. Commission on Civil Rights: *The Voting Rights Act: Unfulfilled Goals,* Sept., 1981.

White House: *America's New Beginning: A Program for Economic Recovery*, along with *The Economic Plan*, 2/18/81. *The Reagan Presidency: A New Beginning: A Review of the First Year 1981*, Barbara Gleason and Christopher Rizzuto, eds., Office of Public Affairs, 1982.

Miscellaneous

American Broadcasting Company (ABC), "Ronald Reagan: At Home on the Ranch," Barbara Walters Special Report, 11/26/81.

Anderson, Jack, interview, 10/20/80.

Becker, Norma, interviews, 9/11/82, 12/7/82, New York City.

Bierlein, Fred, interview, 10/1/82, Washington, D.C.

Borosage, Robert L., letters to RD, 8/16/82, 1/13/83.

Burton, Phil, interview, 9/30/82, Washington, D.C.

Caldicott, Helen, interview, 6/16/83, Boston (phone).

Church, Frank, memorandum to RD, undated, ca. Dec., 1980, enclosing "Report on Korea 1977."

Cohen, Barbara, interview, 7/1/83, Washington, D.C., (phone).

Cohen, Wilbur J., interview, 9/9/82, Austin, Tx. (phone).

Doherty, Edward, interview, 7/1/83, Washington, D.C., (phone).

Feinstein, Fred, interview, 9/30/82, Washington, D.C.

Franks, Marty, interview, 10/2/80, Washington, D.C. (phone).

Gonzalez, Henry B., interviews, 9/30/82, 10/1,9/82, Washington, D.C.

Gray, Robin, interview, 10/10/80, Washington, D.C.

Kawior, Philip, interview, 10/1/82, Washington, D.C.

Ludtke, Melissa, interview, 2/14/83, New York City.

Mankiewicz, Frank, interview, 6/22/83, Washington, D.C., (phone).

Meek, Kelsey, interview, 9/30/82, Washington, D.C.

Milas, Maris, interview, 10/13/80, Los Angeles (phone).

Mottl, Ronald L., letter to RD, 11/30/82.

Pickle, J. J., interview, Fall, 1981, Washington, D.C.

Public Broadcasting System, "A Conversation with Ronald Reagan," Bill Moyers' Journal, 7/10/80.

RR to Mrs. Barbara Trister, letter, 1/13/72.

Stetson, Bill, interview, 10/13/80, Los Angeles (phone).

Stevens, Robert S., and 5 GOP colleagues, letter for general release, 7/15/76.

Udall, Morris, letter to RD, 1/7/83.

Wilder, Steve, interview, 1/20/83, New York City.

Wright, Jim, interview, Fall, 1981, Washington, D.C.

Index

601

About the Author

Educated at the University of Texas and Oxford University, Ronnie Dugger is an investigative reporter and a scholar. He is the author of *The Politician,* a life and times of Lyndon Johnson, the first volume of which appeared in 1982; *Our Invaded Universities,* a book about the University of Texas as a case study of corporate incursions into academia, published in 1974; and *Dark Star,* a biography of Claude Eatherly, a crack pilot in the U.S. atomic squadron who later became disabled by his feelings of guilt because of his role in the dropping of the atomic bomb on Hiroshima. *Dark Star* was published in 1967. Dugger is the publisher of the *Texas Observer,* which he founded and, for about nine years, edited. His articles have appeared in *Atlantic, Harper's, The New York Times Magazine, Nation, New Republic, Progressive,* and other magazines. He has received Rockefeller and NEH fellowships and has been a visiting faculty member at various universities. In 1983–1984 he is a fellow at the Wilson Center for International Scholars in Washington, D.C.